# Brown's
# Town

# Brown's Town

### 20 Famous Browns Talk Amongst Themselves

*by* Alan Natali

ORANGE FRAZER *PRESS*
*Wilmington, Ohio*

ISBN 1-882203-61-5

Additional copies of *Brown's Town: 20 Famous Browns Talk Amongst Themselves* or other Orange Frazer
Press books may be ordered directly from:

Orange Frazer Press, Inc.
Box 214
37 ½ West Main Street
Wilmington, Ohio 45177

Telephone 1.800.852.9332 for price and shipping information
Web Site: www.orangefrazer.com


Library of Congress Cataloging-in-Publication Data

Natali, Alan, 1952-
    Brown's town : 20 famous Browns talk amongst themselves / by Alan Natali.
      p. cm.
    Includes index.
    ISBN 1-882203-61-5
      1. Brown, Paul, 1908---Friends and associates. 2. Football coaches--United
    States--Biography. 3. Cleveland Browns (Football team : 1946-1995)--Interviews. I.
    Title.

    GV939.B77 N38 2001
    796.332'092--dc21
    [B]
                                                          2001036204


Printed in Canada

For Miss Betsy
Who Always Knows

Thanks to Alison, ever Daddy's little girl; Ron Forsythe, the best pair of ears a writer can borrow; John Baskin and Marcy Hawley, endlessly loyal and patient; the Cleveland Browns, then and now; Dr. Bernard DeFilippo, for the use of his pens; Mom and Dad; the Friday Night Gluttony and Trash-Talking Society, Pennsylvania and Virginia branches; Joe and Mary Ann; Demo, Jimmy, Pete, and Ray; Mr. Pooh and His Ladies; Dr. Pratul Pathak, the English department, and the staff of Manderino Library, California University of Pennsylvania.

Portraits by *Greg Storer*
Photography research by *Chance Brockway*

# Contents

*Holding onto power is like holding a wolf by the ears.*
—ancient Roman proverb

# Brown's Town

# *The* Truth About
# Me *and* PB

I

WHY PAUL BROWN?

We were playing tackle football
in the snow-covered backyard of the
fraternity house in which we lived. A
month earlier, we had been seniors on
our college team—a middle guard,
two defensive tackles, and me, a
linebacker. Now, padded with sweat
clothes, practice jerseys, and wool
caps, we were rivals colliding in a
championship game. Faces scarlet, we
slammed into each other, wrestled
each other down. Our metal-tipped
Riddel cleats churned snow into icy
froth. Threats and curses drifted in
sparkling little clouds over the twelve-
foot hedge surrounding the yard.

A fraternity brother leaned from
a window and shouted that I had a

phone call. I caught my breath and said, "Tell them I'll call back."

"The guy says it's important," the brother said, pulling the window down.

I slogged through the ankle-deep snow and picked up the phone.

A unfamiliar voice, measured and somber, asked, "Is this Alan Natali?"

Perplexed, I said, "Yes."

"This is Paul Brown."

I almost dropped the phone. My pulse drummed in my throat.

I croaked, "Yessir."

"I just called to let you know that the Cleveland Browns are going to select you in this year's NFL draft," he said.

The glare of sunshine off fresh snow filled the room. My eyes blurred. Words clogged my throat. I felt like someone had taken a picture of me with a flash bulb.

Then I heard a cackle as dry as static electricity.

"I had you, didn't I?" the voice, thicker now and chafed by unfiltered cigarettes, asked. "Didn't I?" my girlfriend's father insisted.

"Yeah, you had me," I said quietly, trying to fake a chuckle.

I put the phone down. I felt like a fool. It was 1973. I knew Art Modell had fired Paul Brown a decade ago, knew Brown had been coaching the Cincinnati Bengals for five years. Besides, my college football career had actually ended in

the middle of my senior season. A hamstring snapped during the Homecoming game, tattooing my right leg with a swirling purple-and-yellow hematoma. I still ran as if I were dragging a ball and chain. Even if I had played at USC or Notre Dame, instead of at a small college, no pro team would've drafted me.

I shuffled to my room and slumped onto the bed. Snow melted from my cleats. Why had the man chosen this one time to demonstrate a sense of humor, and why, of all coaches, had he chosen Paul Brown as the hook for his joke?

My friends called for me to rejoin the game. I ignored them. The same old dream had hypnotized me again. Paul Brown: the name was like a family curse.

II
A VOW

I discovered Paul Brown when I was eight, on the same day I discovered my father. One afternoon, bored, I explored our attic. Pallid light from a bare bulb revealed a massive cedar chest covered by tattered blankets. The cedar chest smelled of mothballs and musty perfume. It contained photographs of people I didn't recognize, a silk-lined baby's blanket the color of a robin's egg, a curl of golden hair in a tiny box, brittle flowers pressed between pieces of waxed paper. I found a coarse gray sweater folded into a square. A large red block "C" had been sewn to the sweater's front, number 34 on each sleeve. The sweater covered a thick scrapbook, and in the yellowed newspaper clippings and football programs, I met a father I didn't know I had.

I knew in a vague way that my father was a football coach, but he had never talked about playing, and except for the scarred and bloated ball my friends and I played with in the yard, our house contained no evidence of the game. However, the swarthy, 5' 11", 195-pound fullback in the scrapbook had gained 1,035 yards, scored 14 touchdowns, and made All-American the year I was born. In one newspaper photo, my father knelt in his grass-stained uniform next to a pretty black-haired girl holding a baby wrapped in a blanket. The caption read: "Line Crusher and Future Line Crusher."

Two envelopes dropped from the scrapbook. The first—white—had been sent from "The Cleveland Browns, 405 Leader Building, Cleveland, Ohio" to, simply, "Elmo Natali, Sunnyside, Pennsylvania." I pulled from it a single sheet. A scowling elf carrying a football burst through the letterhead over five paragraphs typed in brown ink. The letter told my father that he had been drafted by the Cleveland Browns.

"You can expect to hear from us in the near future," the writer said, "to talk in a contractual way." It was signed, "Paul E. Brown, General Manager & Coach."

The second envelope was bigger, buff, and sent registered. Another letter told my father, "We are happy that you are going to be with us next season." It closed, "Looking forward to seeing you at that time and with the very best wishes, Paul E. Brown." A contract—one long blue sheet— had been signed by my father. I jammed everything back into the cedar chest and went downstairs to wait for my father to come home from work.

After dinner, I asked him, "What was it like playing for Cleveland?"

"I didn't play for them," he said.

"But I saw the letters from Paul Brown and the contract. He said he was looking forward to seeing you. Why didn't you play?"

"Because you came along, because they had a fullback named Marion Motley, and because of this." He held his left wrist against my ear and rotated his fist. His arm sounded like a dry branch snapping. I shivered but looked up at him and said, "Well, I'll sure play for the Browns some day, no matter what."

III

LOST IN THE DESERT

My childhood vow has influenced almost everything that has happened to me since the day I made it. It caused me, for example, to become lost several years ago somewhere on the edge of an Indian reservation near Scottsdale, Arizona. I had come to the Southwest to find Don Colo, former captain of the Cleveland Browns. Paul Brown died five years before I began researching his life and career, so in order to learn what I could about the man who had affected my life in so many odd ways, I criss-crossed the continent, seeking those who had played for him.

I live where I was brought up, in the Monongahela Valley of southwestern Pennsylvania, an area that has produced pro football stars from Deacon Dan Towler to Joe Montana. A friend and teammate of my younger brother, Joey—as everyone called him—was often around the house, a shy, slender boy. He looked up to me in the way an only child will look to a friend's older sibling, an admiration that, in retrospect, is pregnant with the kind of irony more entertaining in books than in one's life.

Many see the Mon Valley as a grimy collage of abandoned steel mills, played out coal seams, and crumbling small towns, but I leave it only out of necessity. Thus, I took the last flight possible from Pittsburgh to Phoenix, arriving late on a Saturday night. The corpulent parking lot attendant at the car rental agency was so drunk that when I asked her for directions, she could only mumble and shove a map at me. Neither the attendant nor the map indicated that the exit off I-10 to my hotel in Scottsdale had been closed. The car's domelight burning, I turned the map over and over in my lap, weaving through the weirdly empty streets of Tempe, Scottsdale, Phoenix, and Scottsdale again.

When I finally located the hotel, a prim desk clerk huffily assured me that I had no reservation. I read the confirmation number from my notebook. He poked around on a computer and said that I had to drive several dozen blocks to another motel in the chain.

There, a kid who looked like one of the Backstreet Boys informed me that the place was booked solid, and he had no record of my reservation. After a prolonged and increasingly loud argument with the Backstreet Boy, the night manager, and a stubby Mexican security guard who kept fingering a can of pepper spray, I was sent brusquely back into the alien dark with another map and a promise of a reservation at another hotel.

The map was indecipherable. The Backstreet Boy had faked

marking my route. Several wrong guesses later, I was creeping up a narrow road into the foothills of the Manatzal Mountains. I might as well have been driving across Jupiter. Shadowy hillocks rose around me. Silhouettes of cacti drifted against the dimming lights of Scottsdale like the black ghosts of hanged outlaws. Furious and exhausted, imagining rattlesnakes entwined in rocky dens and pebble-skinned gila monsters scenting the night with forked tongues, I was leery about turning around on the sandy shoulders of the road.

Just before dawn, I made it to the third hotel. The Backstreet Boy had booked me into a tony golf resort at $200 a night—a final act of passive aggressiveness against the surly aging jock who had threatened every employee in the chain with legal action and extreme bodily harm.

IV
FOOTBALL FAMILIES

Don Colo told me that he "didn't know a damn thing about football" when he enrolled at Brown University after World War II. Like many of the former players I talked to, he thought of himself as "athlete" rather than as "football player." Colo preferred basketball, as had Otto Graham, Lou Groza, and Dante Lavelli. Vince Costello, Galen Fiss,

Milt Plum, and Dick Schafrath had hoped to play professional baseball.

I grew up in a football family, one probably not unlike the family in which Mike Brown was reared. Like Paul Brown, my father was frequently away—at games, practices, meetings, on scouting trips. Also like Paul Brown, my father tried to steer his son away from football. But baseball was so tedious it gave me migraines, and basketball had too many restrictions on physical contact.

Once my father realized that I had made up my mind, I became, like Mike Brown, a waterboy and a partner with whom to watch film at night, the tiny scrimmages surging back and forth across a kitchen wall.

I was most content on practice fields and in locker rooms, amid the pinched and sweating faces of injured players, the sharp reek of Atomic Balm, fist-sized clumps of gauze and athletic tape lying on damp concrete floors.

V
PAUL BROWN, ERNIE DAVIS,
AND THE 300 SPARTANS

My father claimed to have no interest in professional football, but any time he heard "Browns," he stiffened and inclined toward the word. I felt as if I had contributed to a great disappointment in his life, and so I was relieved in the summer of 1962 when the Pittsburgh Steelers asked him to try out as a punter. When my father punted, the ball exploded from his foot in a reverberating ring like the sound of metal striking metal, arched high, and dropped like a mortar shell onto its nose. He tried to teach me the skill, but punting was too tame and mechanical for me.

After the Steelers called, I bragged to my friends that my father was going to play for them. They accused me of lying, a suspicion that seemed to be confirmed when Paul Brown wouldn't release my father from that old blue contract. I didn't know that Brown himself needed a punter, having traded Sam Baker to Dallas; all I knew was that he had made me out to be a liar and hurt my father.

I concocted a scenario in which Brown hated my father for having played at Monessen High School for John Reed, former coach at Canton-McKinley, arch enemy of Massillon, where Brown played and coached.

After football season ended that year, my father took a couple of my friends and me to the movies. As we were waiting for the movie to start, one boy asked me if I knew that Ernie Davis had died. I didn't believe him. Every time Syracuse played Pitt, the newspapers and radio made Davis seem immortal, more demigod than human.

"How'd he die?" I asked.

"He got bugs in his blood," my friend said.

My father interrupted. The light in the theater was coppery, the floor sticky with spilled soda and squashed candy, as he explained that leukemia could kill even a Heisman Trophy winner who had been the Browns' first draft choice.

The feature that day was *The 300 Spartans*. I still associate Ernie Davis with it, half-believing that he died at Thermopylae, defending Greece against Persian hordes. Only 10, I had no idea how Davis's death would affect Paul Brown; it was just another black mark against the man.

VI
THE AVENGER LOOKS BACK

Knowing Paul Brown had been fired, I watched happily as Cleveland upset Baltimore in the 1964 NFL championship game. Gary Collins became my avenger that day. His three touchdown catches shredded Paul Brown's reputation forever. That notion was silly, of course, but 35 years later, I spent hours with Collins as he tried himself to reach back, grasp that fleeting moment, and comprehend just what it really did mean.

"When I die, they'll say, 'Gary Collins, dead at whatever age,' and underneath they'll say, 'Caught three touchdown passes in the 1964 championship game, '" Collins said. "I had a lot of great seasons after that game, and to tell you the truth, I wasn't that good in 1964. But at least I'll be remembered for something."

## VII
## PROGRESSION OF DREAMS

Six years after I made it, I saw no reason my vow wouldn't come true. I often slipped back into the attic, opened the cedar chest, and like a monk studying an illuminated manuscript, reread the letters and the contract, always substituting my first name for my father's.

Ross Fichtner talked about "the progression of dreams" he had as a child, the series of grand feats he imagined himself accomplishing on the football field. A scrawny boy, Fichtner had to wait for his dreams to become reality. Mine came true immediately. Working with a set of weights my grandfather fashioned from cement-filled tin cans and lengths of pipe, I developed rapidly. When I went out for football in the eighth grade, I was by far the strongest player.

The day before my first game, our coach, a stocky former Marine drill instructor, passed out uniforms. He ordered me to wear number 44, instead of the 34 I had requested. I was hurt and angry, until I remem-

bered the picture sitting on a file cabinet in the coach's office. It was of him as a player. His hair was clipped and waxed. He didn't smile. He wore number 44. At practice that day, he made me captain.

After our last game, I was limping down the stairs on a swollen right ankle. I heard my father telling my mother, "He's aggressive and is really big for his age. He could be a real player some day."

He had finally realized what I had always known.

Jim Houston, who was cut from his junior high school squad, wondered, "Will I ever be one of those one percenters that will even get close to making it?" I had no such doubts.

## VIII
## BOUND FOR 'BAMA

The following summer, we moved from the coal and steel regions, where football was a series of brutal infantry charges, to Florida, land of the sleek, the swift, the sudden cavalry strike. I started for the ninth grade team and was one of several freshmen invited to spring practice with the varsity, which had made it to the state championship game the previous fall. In the big spring dress scrimmage, I sacked the quarterback three times.

As I was pulling my pads off in the locker room, the defensive coordinator called out to me. Paul Brown had looked so unlike a football coach that a security guard once refused to let him into Ohio Stadium. Our defensive coach was all football man: tall, lean, broad-shouldered, tan.

"Come on ovah heyah," his said. He pointed to a scale and said, "Git up on that." He moved weights and rulers around and said that I was 5' 11½" and 195 pounds.

"How ole are you?" he asked.

"Fourteen."

"You a whole lot biggah then I was at yer age, and Ahm 6' 4" and 225 pound. All you got to do is keep yer nose clean, and yer gonna play for the same man I played for—Bear Bryant, at 'Bama."

IX

THE BULGARIAN STUDIES
DYNAMIC TENSION

We moved back to the Mon Valley, though, and I played high school ball for a 300-pound Bulgar-ian, a former All-American center who wore sunglasses even at night and gleefully admitted to having bitten a chunk from a nose tackle's calf. Like most coaches of the time, the Bulgarian had been deeply influenced by Paul Brown. From backwater junior high schools to major market pro teams, ambitious young men believed that they could

win by imitating him, as if his "integrated system of football pedagogy" were one of those Charles Atlas Dynamic Tension regimens advertised in comic books: "You won the league championship! My hero!"

Like Brown, the Bulgarian was remote, humorless, without racial prejudice, thorough, obsessed with winning, determined to control every aspect of his players' lives, and acidly critical. However, the Bulgarian also drew on the other popular coaching model of that period: hot-tempered Vince Lombardi. The mixture was unpredictable and, at times, frighten-ing. I empathized with Jim Houston and Dick Schafrath, both of whom played at Ohio State for volatile Woody Hayes and in Cleveland for chilly Paul Brown. I had to make the same adjustment, only minute by minute.

X

BIRTHRIGHT DENIED

I made a bunch of all-star teams and prepared to accept my birthright: a scholarship to a major college football power. I visited Pitt, talked to recruiters from West Virginia and Duke, had a scheduled trip to Arizona State canceled by my father, who wouldn't hear of my playing for Frank Kush, the school's notoriously brutal coach. I ignored calls and letters from dozens of lesser schools, waiting for 'Bama, Notre Dame, USC. They must have lost my number or seen that the numbers I had given them—6' 2", 215 pounds—were bogus. In fact, I had grown a quarter inch and lost five pounds since junior high.

In the end, I became so dispirited that I made no decision, finally going to the local Division II school at which my father had played after stops at St. Boneventure and Virginia Tech and at which he had become a dean.

## XI
## A SOUTHERN GENTLEMAN SETS THE RECORD STRAIGHT

My college coach, a former all-conference end at Mississippi State, was a raw-boned, excitable, rugged throwback. K2 had used football as a way out of the Pennsylvania coal fields. Coaching at a school that gave little support to the program during an era that despised football as the embodiment of the military-industrial complex drove K2 to the verge of a nervous breakdown. He quit after my junior season.

The school about to drop football, my father volunteered to coach without pay. I played my last year for him. Mike Brown said that his father used more stick than carrot in handling his squads; my father did the opposite. He was the humanist

who believed in mankind's essential good. Graduate work in counseling had taught him to accentuate the positive, ignore the negative, and hope for the best. That view made him immensely popular among the players but didn't lend itself to winning—a shortcoming that didn't bother him at all.

Don Colo said that Brown would play "the worst son-of-a-bitch in the world" if that son-of-a-bitch could help Cleveland win. My father would do likewise, but because he thought he could turn the son-of-a-bitch into a productive citizen. I often thought his conciliatory attitude an excuse for weakness. However, courtly Dub Jones put matters in a different light when he said of Paul Brown, "He was aloof, and that's the safest way for a coach to be. You have to be a hell of a man if you're not going to be aloof."

## XII
## AN HONORABLE DISCHARGE

We started my senior year 3-1, but several other first-stringers were injured about the same time I was, and the season drained away. By then, I had renounced my childhood vow. I had never agreed with the guys who thought that they were only a couple of hot cycles of Dianabol away from the Pro Bowl, but I had gone the rest of the way: the agonizing running programs meant to reduce my time in the 40-yard dash, that arbitrary and implacable enemy that Paul Brown had created to devil mediocre athletes; the weight-lifting routines that left me rubbery with exhaustion; the useless dietary supplements hucstered in muscle magazines. I even strapped a 50-pound weight to my ankles and hung from a chinning bar until my hands bled, trying to stretch my spine and, at last, become 6' 2".

Nothing worked. I surrendered. With literature and writing, I purged my dream of playing for the Browns. I skipped rope and did push-ups to stay in shape, dropped to my natural 190 pounds, and accepted the ripped hamstring as an honorable discharge from the game that had dominated my life and ruined my faith.

I was named one of the top ten linebackers in all Pennsylvania colleges and universities that season, but I knew that the sports writers had voted for my last name, not my first.

## XIII
## OFF A CHRISTMAS CARD LIST

A dozen years later, I returned to the university as a teacher. I had coached in junior high school and high school, and so, like my father, I volunteered to help out at the school, which was trying to make its program respectable.

I suppose my approach to coaching fell somewhere between my father's and Paul Brown's. I wanted very much to win, but I also liked the players, a luxury Brown didn't permit himself until after they had retired.

One of my players spent several seasons in the NFL—giving me no feeling whatever of having made it by proxy; another became an undercover DEA agent given to calling me in the middle of the night to narrate the details of his latest bust; a third—a former high school star who maintained a lofty grade point average as a psychology major—once glumly informed me that he had been forced to remove my name from his Christmas card list because I yelled at him too much.

I saw football differently as a coach than I had as a player. "When I went into coaching myself, I really began to understand and appreciate what Paul Brown had to go through," Otto Graham told me. "As years went by, I found myself doing and saying the same things that he would do and say to me that I used to get so damned upset about."

## XIV
## "THE PAUSE THAT REFRESHES"

I left football to write books— and thus had to face men who had purloined my dreams. How is one to behave, sitting across a coffee table from Jim Houston, who played thirteen seasons in the NFL at outside linebacker—my position? The Browns made it easy for me, though. Houston, a pleasant and unpretentious former All-Pro, said that he planned to use football only to put together a grubstake. As a group, the Browns saw pro ball not as an end in itself—as I had—but as a means to coaching careers, investments, lucrative sales or management positions, or, in the case of Tony Adamle, medical school.

Besides, it's hard to remain envious or idolatrous after standing at a urinal in a scuzzy airport motel in Sarasota, Florida, and hearing the guy next to you—Otto Graham— say, "Ahh, the pause that refreshes."

## XV
## THE TIME OF HEROES

Occasionally when I was talking with the Browns, I felt like I needed a translator. Separated in age by up to three and a half decades, we shared neither a common core of experiences nor a similar view of the world. Many had survived childhood poverty, combat in World War II, or the Great Depression. They had rescued and helped to build a nation my generation tried to pull apart. Like their coach, many cherish stoicism and mistrust emotion.

Interviewing Otto Graham, Lou Groza, Tommy James, or Dante Lavelli was like talking with a survivor of the Titanic or an early explorer of the Antarctic. These Browns came from a time inconceivable now when professional athletes all appear to be pampered millionaires. These Browns lived next door and worked off-season jobs to support their families. My father said he couldn't have afforded to play pro football anyway, because players at that time were not paid for ten weeks during training camp. These Browns played when all pro football was a black-and-white  highlight reel of mud-splattered, bloodied titans, their ragged breath pluming over snowy fields, thrilling crowds who wore top coats, ties, and felt hats and who leaped to their feet, their faces torn open in rapture—when, for me, to watch a game on television was to race out into the neighborhood and pick one up among my pals. As Mike Brown said, "It was a time in my life when those players were still heroes."

Like so many of the Browns, I have little interest in pro football today. The hype and glitz and greed that Paul Brown loathed have turned the game tawdry, stripped it of dignity and romance. Or, perhaps, those beautiful, dark memories perched in a corner of my mind have turned me cynical. When I see an NFL game, I'm reminded of what George Orwell said upon returning to his hometown in middle-age: "How small everything has become, and how great the devastation within myself."

Now, those letters from Paul Brown to my father seem unsophisticated, primitive—odd relics of an older race.

## XVI
## SEARCHING FOR GUNNER

In some cases, I never did reach men I needed to talk to about Paul Brown. Marion Motley's health had deteriorated. Bill Willis sent a beautifully handwritten letter explaining that a stroke had robbed him of clear memory of his early days in Cleveland. Neither Art Modell nor Jim Brown would speak with me. Modell ignored advisers who suggested that he set forth his version of events in Cleveland. Brown agreed, backed out, vacillated, became embroiled in another in his long string of personal and legal troubles.

Some attempts to find the Browns turned bizarre. Through some kind of family association, a friend arranged a meeting with Frank Gatski, legendarily rugged Hall of Fame center for the original Browns. My friend even offered to drive me into the deep mountains of West Virginia, where Gatski lives. He pulled up in a sport utility vehicle as big as an armored personnel carrier.

He wore camouflage gear and an Australian bush hat. He looked like someone had given Crocodile Dundee an unlimited Mastercard and an L.L. Bean catalogue. In the SUV, he displayed both a 9 mm semiautomatic handgun and an entire frozen salmon that, even gutted, must've weighed 25 pounds.

As we wound through forests denuded by early January, my buddy regaled me with tales of "Gunner" Gatski's prowess as archer, angler, and marksman. Bearing gift of food and threat of firepower, we were like Lewis and Clark on our way to powwow with some great Indian sachem.

We were to meet Gatski at a diner near his home, but he wasn't there at the appointed time. My buddy phoned, but no one answered. He decided we should track Gatski down. He and I and the salmon, which had been basking in sunlight magnified by window glass, set out to find Gatski's lair.

Unable to read the sign, we wandered around for half an hour and returned to the diner. A grizzled codger sitting at the counter asked us what we wanted. My buddy explained, and the codger said that Gatski had been rushed to the hospital. As we headed off again, I pondered the health of my subject, the penalty for carrying a firearm into a hospital, and the condition of the fish. We pulled into a parking space. My friend adjusted the 9 mm in the waist of his camos, cocked his bush hat, slung the salmon over his shoulder, and strode up to the information desk.

I had expected to find Frank Gatski dressed in buckskin vest, leather breeches, and loin cloth, trotting down some mountainous trail like Simon Girty. Instead, he was in a cardiac care unit, sunken into starchy white linen, withered. My friend introduced us and presented the salmon—which had taken on a mushy, fretful pout—to Gatski's startled grandson.

Several of his former teammates told me that interviewing the laconic Gatski would be a waste of time, but if I hadn't begged off in deference to his health, I might still be sitting in the cardiac unit. Gatski invited me to see the Browns memorabilia that he keeps in a shed.

I went home and sent him a card but never went back to visit Gatski. I know that things change. Lou Groza and Tony Adamle died not long after I spoke with them. However, I was unnerved by seeing Gatski, a man of such storied vitality and toughness, rendered fragile. If that for Frank Gatski, what for me?

"Gunner" Gatski recovered. I don't know what became of the salmon.

XVII
WHAT PRICE VICTORY?

Looking at someone such as Galen Fiss, who is approximately my size, inevitably caused me to ask myself: "If you had been born twenty years sooner, could you have made it?" I did better Ross Fichtner by a couple strokes in a round of golf, but Fichtner was more concerned with my swing dynamics than with his score.

Paul Brown had three questions about a prospect: "Is he a contact man? Is he fast? Can he think?" I might've scored reasonably well in two categories, but I didn't inherit my father's 9.9 speed. I also confess to having lacked the respect, obedience, and team attitude that Brown demanded.

No, it wouldn't have worked out, and as I talked with the Browns, I wondered if my desire to be one of them hadn't been comically naïve from the beginning. The terrible physical toll football exacts is obvious in Fichtner, Tommy James, Walt Michaels, Dick Schafrath. As I write, a viscous liquid is seeping from an ulcerated surgical incision in my right knee, like cheap synthetic motor oil from a rusted crankcase. The operation was the third on that knee and the fifth I've had because of football. I shudder to think how ten more seasons would've ravaged my body.

Many former Browns also paid an emotional price for their careers. Gary Collins, Vince Costello, Fichtner, Fiss, James, Dub Jones, Milt Plum, John Wooten—even Lou Groza, who played 21 seasons—were all forced out of Cleveland before they wanted to leave.

I can't help thinking, however, that playing on such magnificent teams would've been worth any pain. Paul Brown said, "We used to call the last game of the season the world championship." On the succession of mediocre teams for which I played, we called it "deliverance."

During lunch with Costello, Groza, and Ed Modzelewski, I did, if only briefly, feel what it is like to be a famous former Brown. As word spread through the restaurant, waitresses swarmed, patrons gawked, and autograph seekers shyly approached.

In some way, my father and I both made it to the Cleveland Browns that afternoon. I gladly picked up the check.

## XVIII
## A RARE CREATURE

I am that rare creature: a Cleveland fan in Pittsburgh. I sat in my living room, barking at the television in some half-crazed attempt to stop John Elway from driving the Broncos to another playoff win. I've endured endless razzing over my Browns ballcaps and sweat shirts. I nearly incited a riot in Three Rivers Stadium by defending two gnomish fellows in Cleveland jackets from a drunken CPA. When Modell moved the team to Baltimore, I felt as if he had made off with part of my childhood.

## XIX
## OTHER LETTERS, OTHER ATTICS

To this day, my failing to play for the Browns seems like another bad joke, one far nastier than the prank my girlfriend's father played on me thirty years ago, one I've never really gotten over. However, I can't say that I wish I'd never played the game. The cliché that coaches haul up and wave like a battle flag any time someone challenges the value of football is true: I learned much from it that I have applied to the rest of my life. I also know exactly what Jim Ray Smith meant when he said that he wouldn't trade the friendships he made in football for anything. In the end, though, I played for the same reason so many of the Browns played: I liked football.

## XX
## REQUIEM FOR A DREAM

When I was young, Paul Brown was a mythic figure, both benefactor and tormentor. I have spent more than five years studying him, but he remains elusive. Of course, not even his own players—or his own son— claim to completely understand what made him tick. Whatever the secret to his true nature might be, it was typed decades ago in brown ink, placed into a buff envelope, and hidden deep in a cedar chest in the dark attic of a house whose address appears on no street map.

Like the Browns, I see him differently now than I did when I was younger. I have forgiven Paul Brown for his transgressions, real and imagined. After all, he is, as Jim Brown said, "the bridge from past to present"—football's, Ohio's, and mine.

## *The* Warrior Princes *of* Tigertown

BUD HOUGHTON saw the boy
playing in a pick-up game on a
vacant lot out in Genoa, a working-
class neighborhood between
Massillon and Canton. The boy was
small but fast and spirited, much as
Houghton's boss, Paul Brown, head
football coach at Massillon High
School, had been as a youth.

The boy—a redhead named
Tommy James—had never played
organized football. He also knew
nothing about Brown, even though
the coach's Massillon Tigers had won
twenty straight games and been state
champions in 1935 and 1936.

"I wasn't a fan of Massillon
football," James says. "My mother
had gone to Canton-McKinley, and
that's the story I heard all the time.
Massillon just happened."

After grammar school, students
who lived in James's area could attend
junior high in either Canton or

Massillon. James had enrolled at Canton-Lincoln Junior High, but Brown convinced the boy to come to Massillon.

When Tommy James drew his equipment at Longfellow Junior High School, he began an initiation into a secret society: "the warrior princes of Massillon," as one sportswriter put it. In Brown's carefully designed system, junior high was a trial meant to cull the inept, unmotivated, and timorous.

Brown approached his position with the fervor of an ambitious local boy determined to make good in front of his hometown. "The job at Massillon was as important to me as though I had been offered the Presidency," he said.

Born in Norwalk, Ohio, Brown moved with his family to Massillon when he was nine. He grew up on the city's West Side, "totally intrigued by anything that could be moved, caught, jumped over, or learned."

After the bladder of his first football burst, he stuffed the ball with leaves and rags and continued to play with it. Nonetheless, when the Tigers went to preseason camp when Brown was a sophomore, he was left behind. "I guess they didn't even know I was alive," he said. "I waited all morning with my bag packed, and then I realized they weren't coming for me. I couldn't eat or sleep for the next two days." His

father drove him to Turkeyfoot Lake, where the Tigers were practicing.

He earned his first monogram as a pole-vaulter and received the award wearing knickers. A 120-pound quarterback, he threw a touchdown pass on his first varsity play.

"Brownie" went on to captain the football and basketball teams. In his three seasons, the football team lost only five games, and Brown impressed the city. The local newspaper called him "a youngster with a keen mind, coolness under fire, and courage that would have done credit to a 200-pound giant."

After college, Brown began coaching at Severn, the Naval Academy's preparatory school near Annapolis, where he lost one game in two years. At 22, he was hired to teach English and history and coach football at Massillon. He came home to a city inflicted with, in his words, "sleeping sickness."

The Tigers had gone 2-6-2 in 1931. The athletic department was $3,700 in debt. The rocky, bare-dirt field had to be sprinkled to prevent dust from choking the few spectators sitting in dilapidated bleachers. The band wore shabby military surplus uniforms.

Brown lost four games in 1932 and two the next season. Six years later, in the opening game of 1939, Tommy James, now a 141-pound junior halfback, raced 39 yards for the first touchdown in brand new Tiger Stadium. By then "the Miracle Man of Scholastic Football," as a wire service dubbed Brown, had won four consecutive state titles and thirty-eight of his last forty games.

When Brown was a high school quarterback, his coach, Dave Stewart, sent a guard into a game with a play. Brown ordered the messenger to the bench. "What in hell's going on?" Stewart wondered. "He's taken over the world."

For nine years, Brown did take over Massillon. He became basketball coach his second year and, soon, was track coach, athletic director, and the city's recreation supervisor, giving him control over all sports.

He charmed the "downtown quarterbacks," an irritant to other coaches. Brown founded the Tiger Booster's Club in 1934, during the Depression, supposedly to help pay for one meal a day for each player. Only a hundred or so fans showed up for the first meeting. Eventually, 2,500 regularly turned out to watch game films narrated by the coach, and no hall in Stark County could accommodate the organization's yearly banquet.

Boosters enjoyed such privileges as a preseason invitation to the gym, where, the Massillon *Evening Independent* said, "Coach Brown will strip each member of the squad to the waist to give boosters an opportunity to see the muscles that will propel the boys around the field this fall." Members became a network of informants who helped Brown enforce his ban on dating, attending dances, or riding in cars.

Brown instituted a Spartan ritual in which every baby boy born in the local hospital received a tiny plastic football, a photo of the ceremony appearing in the local paper. Those fortunate enough to grow up and make the varsity practiced until 5:30 each afternoon and reported back to school at 7 a.m. for a "skull session." Brown placed blocking sleds around town and instructed players to hit each one fifty times before passing it.

Brown knew that to ensure devotion, he had to offer something in return. From his first game against arch-rival Canton-McKinley, for which he audaciously raised ticket prices from thirty-five cents to a dollar, Brown's teams made money. He used the profits to help pay for activities that had nothing to do with football. Thus, no one could attack the Tigers without hurting the school newspaper, the camera club, the debate team, and the a cappella choir.

If creating faith through finance seems calculating, Brown cared genuinely for Massillon.

"Everyone knows how disciplined he was, how organized, what he did for the game," said Lin Houston, who played for Brown in high school, college, and the pros. "People didn't know much about his heart. When I was in high school and times were tough for a lot of people, Coach Brown used to go out and buy groceries for the people who needed them and take them to their house. People didn't know that about him."

The slender, brilliant  hometown boy gave Massillon an autumn-long pipe dream, hiding ugliness behind glorious armies and the dazzling halftime productions of George "Red" Bird's Tiger Swing Band. Let bums ride the rails and soup kitchens ladle gruel; for ten weeks every year, the good times rolled in Massillon. Football became the city's fantastic Busby Berkeley/Cecil B. DeMille/Flo Ziegfeld sideshow. The *Evening Independent* summed it up in one headline: "Massillon Opens Its Colorful Football Show So City Forgets World's Woes."

On the night 21,450-seat Tiger Stadium opened, Tommy James ran 31 yards for a second touchdown, and Massillon defeated Cleveland Cathedral Latin, 40-13. For the fourth time in five seasons, the Tigers went unbeaten; for the fifth straight year, they were state champions.

In 1940, Massillon outscored its first nine opponents 446-0. Now a single-wing tailback, James scored 27 points in one quarter against Alliance. Hobbled by a cracked rib, he came off the bench at his coach's

request and ran and passed his lethargic team to a victory over Mansfield, Brown's thirtieth straight game without a loss.

The Tigers didn't yield a point until the first quarter against Canton McKinley. Behind 6-0, James tied the game with a 55-yard touchdown pass to Horace Gillom. The Tigers won, 34-6. James rushed for 119 yards and a touchdown, giving Brown his eightieth win in ninety games at Massillon and helping him to the head coach's position at Ohio State University, a job previously believed to be beyond the reach of any high school coach, particularly one only 32 years old.

James and three other Tigers made first team on the Associated Press All-Ohio squad, and United Press named every Massillon starter first-team All-State. He was only 5' 8", 155 pounds, but James, whom a Warren reporter called "the fastest being" he'd ever seen, embodied Brown's belief that speed would inevitably defeat size. The 140 points James scored in two seasons convinced Brown to take the little speedster with him to Columbus, along with six other Massillon players.

Brown's hiring began his second attempt to make a name for himself at Ohio State. In 1926, he had come to OSU as an undersized, unrecruited, overwhelmed 16-year-old who dreamed of playing for the Buckeyes. Too small to make the freshman team, homesick, he moped at the railroad depot, hoping someone from Massillon would step off a train. He quickly transferred to Miami of Ohio.

Considerably more fanfare greeted James in Columbus. Before the 1942 season, the *Saturday Evening Post* predicted that he would be one of the Big 10's top sophomores. The subhead to a Columbus *Dispatch* profile of James that year called James "A Real Brown-ized Buckeye."

"For three years of high school, Tommy helped his idol, Brown, to state championships and growing success," the story said.

James wasn't done helping his coach. A starting defensive back, he also became Brown's "climax runner," the man who carried the ball on plays designed to go for long touchdowns. James intercepted three passes in his first game at OSU. During a tight victory over Northwestern and star tailback Otto Graham, he sliced through four blockers on a screen pass and saved a touchdown.

He caught Wisconsin's Elroy "Crazy Legs" Hirsch—"the antelope that runs like a man"—from behind four times in one game, while averaging over eight yards a carry himself.

"James, at 160 pounds, is a package of swiftness and elusiveness hard to get a hand on, much less to bring down—and is a little guy with plenty of old grit, too," Brown said.

The Buckeyes played Illinois that season in Cleveland, the first time either Brown or James had been in Municipal Stadium. "Ohio State's sparkling will o' the wisp sophomore" carried three times in the first half. He gained 112 yards and scored two touchdowns, one on a 76-yard run, and Ohio State won, 44-20. James also separated a shoulder that day and missed the team's last two games, victories that sealed a national championship for the Buckeyes in Brown's second season.

The following spring, James shipped out for the Pacific Theater. By then, sportswriters were hailing his coach as "the next Knute Rockne" and "the Great God Brown."

James played only one more season at Ohio State, in 1946. Brown had joined the Navy in 1944, and Paul Bixler was now the Buckeye coach. Wes Fesler replaced Bixler, and Fesler demanded from James a promise that he would not leave Columbus for professional ball. James balked. Although he had been elected captain for the upcoming season, he played in the 1947 College All-Star Game and turned pro.

However, rather than contacting Brown, who had already won an All-American Football Conference title in Cleveland, James signed with the Detroit Lions, who owned his NFL draft rights. He calls choosing Detroit "a whim," but James was probably motivated in part by the same reason that drove him from Ohio State: "I had been three years in the service. 'You can do this. You can't do this.' One too many orders." Under Brown, James knew, he could expect nothing if not more orders.

On his second carry for Detroit, James badly broke his arm. During the off-season, he bumped into Brown in Massillon, and for the third time, the coach recruited him. James became a Brown and was immediately banned from the NFL, which had barred players who signed with the AAFC.

"I'm home again," James declared when he arrived in Cleveland. He was right. Gillom and Houston were outstanding players, as was Marion Motley, from Canton-McKinley. Assistant coach Fritz Heisler played at Massillon and coached there and at OSU with Brown. Another Massillonian, Howard Brinker, soon joined the staff. "Red" Bird, who had become Cleveland's entertainment director, even insisted that his "Musical Majorettes" march at the same three-steps-per-second beat as the Tiger Swing Band. The team wore uniforms similar to Massillon's, followed the same practice routine, grumbled under the same firm rule,

and enjoyed the same success.

Cleveland lost only one game in James's first two seasons. In the 1948 AAFC title game, he intercepted twice, setting up two of the team's first three touchdowns in a victory that capped an undefeated season. When the offense managed only a field goal against the New York Yankees early in 1949, he returned an interception for a touchdown to preserve the Browns' twenty-seven game winning streak.

The following season— Cleveland's first in the NFL—he picked off nine passes in twelve games, a team record that stood for twenty-eight years. His interception in the end zone saved an 8-3 playoff win over the New York Giants and propelled the Browns to another championship, the seventh in a row for Brown and James.

The streak finally ended when Tom Fears of the Los Angeles Rams caught a 73-yard touchdown pass late in the 1951 title game. The next day, a Cleveland writer blamed James for the 24-17 loss. Brown immediately called the paper, absolved the cornerback, and put the blame "on me, where it belonged."

The Massillon connection could hurt as well as help. One year, while strikes shut down steel mills across the country, James asked Brown for more money.

"Tom, you know it's tough,"

Brown said. "You are from a steel town. People aren't working. How do we know we're going to have anyone coming to the games? I can't give you a raise."

James set another team record with three interceptions in a game—a mark that has never been bettered—and made All-Pro, the Pro Bowl, and Cleveland's all-time team.

After an exhibition game in 1956, James heard the order that every Cleveland player dreaded: "Report to the office Monday to pick up a letter."

The command cast him back to high school, when prospective Tigers learned if they had been cut not from a coach but by anxiously reading a list posted outside the locker room.

In Cleveland, Brown would instruct players to see a secretary in the team's offices. Some of the letters she handed out warned players that they were in danger of being dropped; some offered congratulations for making the roster; some told players that they had been waived.

Risking Brown's wrath, Heisler, the former Tiger guard, offered to phone James and tell him what the letter said so that James would not have to drive from Massillon to Cleveland. But, says James, "I already knew, because it was in the paper, in the *Plain Dealer*, that James was released."

Brown claimed to have "always

had a special feeling for James," but he cut the player after thirteen seasons without a word. James felt betrayed.

Some former Browns say that the coach released them anonymously to avoid confronting angry men much larger than he. Others say Brown was so callous that he didn't want to be bothered another minute with players who were of no use to him.

However, years later, both James and Brown offered another explanation.

"He just didn't want to call me in and tell me that, after all the years I played for him in high school and college," James says. "I think that was the soft-hearted part of him."

"I know Tommy would have broken down and cried, and I would have cried right along with him," Brown wrote years later.

Brown would come to regret releasing James so coldly, as he would trading Motley and cutting Gillom without talking to either man. He tried in unusually public forums to make amends, apologizing to all three in his autobiography and to James at a reunion of Ohio State's 1942 national champions.

"He said he had to treat me like he did the other people," James says.

Neither Paul Brown nor Tommy James ever really left Massillon, and Brown's life is almost allegorical in the city. As the discoverer, patron saint, and guiding philosopher of Massillon's most important institution, he is an icon there. Massillonians display his photograph in their homes as people elsewhere do those of John F. Kennedy, Martin Luther King, Jr., and Franklin Delano Roosevelt. He looks down from the scoreboard at Paul Brown Tiger Stadium and from a wall on Lincoln Way. Small vials of "Sacred Soil" from the stadium sell for twenty dollars.

Brown often called coaching in Massillon "the happiest time of my life." He followed the team and donated more than $100,000 to a scholarship fund for Massillon students. Brown met his first wife, Katy Kesler, during a fire drill. When she died, in 1969, he had her buried in Rose Hill Memorial Gardens. Twenty-two years later, he was buried next to her. As he had for Brown's wife and mother, James served as a pallbearer at the coach's funeral.

After Brown released him, James played two games for Baltimore and then left football. A widower retired from his sales job, he lives alone in the comfortable brick home he built several blocks from the high school stadium. A 1940 Massillon Tiger football poster dominated one wall of the living room. A framed picture of a tiger sat on an end table.

The man Brown described as

having "perfect football legs" is now troubled by so much knee pain that he has quit golfing. James's arms and shoulder are still thick with muscle, but he is an improbable warrior prince. He looks less like the willow-hipped star of two national scholastic championship teams than like a friendly parsimonious wheat farmer. He wore a white T-shirt, gray slacks, and incongruously fancy Avia sneakers. As he talked, he sat in a rocking chair and twiddled his thumbs and picked shyly at his fingers, his eyes downcast.

James is the eldest of four brothers to play for Massillon. His three sons and a grandson were Tigers. James hasn't played there in more than sixty years, but Massillon preserves her heroes. People speak of him as if he were still in the locker room, showering after a tough win over McKinley. James returns the loyalty. He rarely misses a game.

He admits to having been so furious with Brown that he took satisfaction in hearing that Art Modell had fired the coach. Now, though, James sees Brown differently.

"I enjoyed all the years I was with Paul," he says, "but I'm sure there are times that you get mad at your father. That's about the way I felt with him at times, but then when it's done, it's done. I don't hold any kind of grudge."

# Tommy JAMES

“ I WAS OUT PLAYING SANDLOT FOOTBALL
one weekend, getting ready to go into the ninth grade. We didn't have
football in the grade schools. Bud Houghton, the coach at Longfellow Junior High School, came out and said that he would like for me to come into
the Massillon school system. I wasn't any fan of Massillon football. I got
recruited, and so I decided to come in and go to Longfellow

That was 1937. I was in the ninth grade. At that time, there was
Longfellow Junior High School and Lorin Andrews Junior High School
and Jones Junior High School. Paul Brown had his fingers on all of them.
He was overseeing everything. We had an intercity series between the three
junior high schools, plus other games that they could pick up.

It was all new and surprising to me, because I hadn't been in any organized football. All I had was the sandlot ball we played as kids out in the
country. The team aspect of it was you had to do the blocking, so when
they gave you the ball, you were able to run. I could do that.

Paul told the junior high school coaches what to run, and they all ran
the same plays. We all had the same system we were going to get into when
we went to the high school.

When I went to Longfellow, all I was interested in was making the
ninth grade team. Nothing was assured. When you went down to practice
in the spring, you had to check the squad list every day, because they were
cutting kids. In the fall, you had to do the same thing. In those days, he
only kept about thirty-five players.

Paul wanted it limited to just the kids he was going to use. He didn't want kids there just because they were out. It was the Depression years. You couldn't afford to keep them around. We were lucky to even have uniforms. Every day, we had to check the list to see that we had made the team for another day. You went down there with your fingers crossed, hoping that you didn't see your name on the list of kids who got cut.

Football led into being on the track team and the basketball team. He encouraged us to play other sports. He was the basketball coach and the track coach, too. We'd go right from spring football into track. He wanted us all on the track team because he figured he could keep us in shape. Two of the three years I was at the high school, we were in the state basketball finals in Columbus, in what they called 'the Sweet 16.'

During the summers, we met once a week and went through our plays. The coaches were two blocks away, watching us, which they weren't supposed to be doing. The kids just got together—with instructions, of course; they told us what to do—and we ran through our plays.

We were undefeated the three years I was in high school. We wanted to win, and we wanted to win bad. My senior year, 1940, in the first five games, our first team never played more than the first half. We were so far ahead at halftime that Paul started getting his next year's team groomed up. The seniors were getting a little bit worried. We thought that if we didn't get any playing time, the colleges wouldn't even get to see us.

PAUL WAS STRICT ABOUT EVERYTHING. I always looked in awe on him. You didn't want to do anything wrong, not that he yelled at you, but he let you know. You knew yourself when you did something wrong, but he had remarks to let you know he was watching you. He had his mind made up about who he wanted to play, and if you didn't do what he wanted you to do, he'd bench you. The players admired him, they feared him, they respected him—and they hated him.

One game, we were playing Mansfield, and I had a cracked rib. I didn't start the first half, and we went in at halftime, and we might've been behind by six points. He said, 'You think you can go, Tom?'

I said, 'I'll give it a try,' and we ended up beating Mansfield. I guess me being in the backfield with the regular team gave everyone a little inspiration, and we finally won the game.

They had big followings at the high school games. When Paul came into town, he got the booster's club formed. He got a bunch of people in town and businessmen who were interested in being backers. That's still going today. All the Massillon people came to the games.

I never had any trouble with Paul in high school or at Ohio State, but one year playing for him in Cleveland, I had a particularly tough time covering a receiver. The second time we were supposed to play them one year, Paul said, 'Tom, I got a telegram from this receiver, and he just wanted to be sure that you were well enough to be in the game.' He was giving me the needle, getting me ready to do a little better defensively. As it was, he had me stirred up enough that I had a good day.

I'll tell you, everybody knew who the boss was. In high school, if you were sick, he said, 'You'd better let a coach know, or you don't have to show back up, because we'll clean your locker out for you.'

He picked what the coaching staff thought were the best players in each position. I can remember—I must've been a sophomore—and he had the players and their parents and everybody else in a group meeting. He explained to them, 'Now, I'm going to play the best players I have, regardless if they're sophomores, juniors, or seniors. If a sophomore is better than a senior, he'll be playing. Just because your son is a senior doesn't mean that he'll be playing.'

He also said, 'I don't care what religion or what color. The best is going to play.' And that was it. There was no backstabbing or anything. He played his best players. And he stuck by it.

We didn't waste a lot of time out at practice. We'd have it all done in an hour and a half. Even in pro ball, it was the same. He always believed that if you can't get it done in a certain amount of time, then the guys are just going to get tired and quit paying attention. He stuck to the rule. If he told us we were going to do this and do that, and we did it, it was over with.

He knew how to get the best out of his players. He might be harsh with one guy and joke around with another guy. I don't remember anybody ever challenging him. He was strict, truthful, and successful.

In 1940, the Associated Press named the whole first starting lineup at Massillon All-Ohio. That's the year we beat Kent State University in a spring scrimmage. According to Paul Brown, that was his best team. In fact, here's something that was just in the *Independent*, our local paper, about that team. See: 'The fewest points (given up): 6.' And that was Paul Brown's last team. They put that in the paper every now and then just to get the boosters excited. That was the only time that year we were behind. McKinley scored on us first. We were behind 6-0. We ended up winning the game 34-6.

My parents, thank goodness, wanted me to go to college. I was the first one in the family to go to college. My dad said, 'We have to get you guys an education. They can't take that away from you.' I didn't know what I wanted to be. I just wanted to go off and get a degree. They really didn't care if we played ball, but scholarships meant an awful lot during the Depression.

When Paul Brown went down to Columbus, he had a lot of backing from the Ohio High School Coaches Association. They were one of his big pushers, because they wanted to get him out of high school. They always said, 'Get him down there where we can send him players and he can't beat us all the time.' He knew if he kept those coaches happy, they'd funnel players down to him. He gave them tickets to Ohio State games. Even when he went up with the Browns, he gave coaches free tickets to games.

Paul didn't actually have to put much effort into us going to Ohio State with him. He asked us if we'd go, and we followed him. Even the guys who hated him respected him. I said the word 'hate,' but it's more that in the flare of the moment, you'd say it—under your breath, of course. It was a hate in a way that you just didn't want him to get on you.

I didn't have a hard time making the adjustment to Ohio State. He was the same in college as he had been in high school, and that made it a lot easier for us guys from Massillon, because we knew what to expect. The other ones fell in line real quick.

I WAS FAMILIAR WITH THE SYSTEM he was teaching, because I'd had it in high school. The numbering of the plays was practically the same we had in high school. The blocking was the same. The only thing was the kids were a little bit bigger. I was fortunate enough to have four, five, or six teammates who went down there together as freshmen. It wasn't like you were stuck there on your own and everyone else was strange.

Paul kept pretty close tabs on you. He checked with professors to see that you weren't missing any classes. He got us off-campus jobs, either at the state offices or at one of the local businesses there. It was legal then. I don't think it is anymore. I'd have a job at one of the Ohio state offices, downtown. At one time, I was filing bills from the state liquor office. The bills would come in from all over the state, and we'd have to file them by county. After we'd get that done, we'd do some studying.

My freshman year was '41, then I was on the '42 national championship team. I played in the secondary, but Paul put me in on offense in certain situations.

I played in '41 and '42, and then I went into the army. We had to go to ROTC, and they just called a bunch of us in and told us we were going. It got so that I didn't even go to spring football in '43. I knew we were going to get called up.

We all went in at the same time: Dante Lavelli, Lou Groza, me. Lavelli got shipped off to Europe in the infantry, and Groza and I ended up in the medics, in the South Pacific. I went to New Caledonia. They sent me to the New Hebrides, to a station hospital. I was there for eighteen, nineteen months. Then we got called in on Okinawa the day that the southern half was announced secured. I was on Okinawa until the bomb was dropped, and then I went into Japan. I was in Japan about three months before I got all my points together to get sent home. I was in the South Pacific for thirty months. Where I was sure didn't look like the places you see where they have the dancing girls and all that.

If I'd have stayed at Ohio State and the war hadn't come along, I'd have graduated at 21. I was 22 when I was in the South Pacific. But there was a lot who had it rougher than I had it. When I went into Okinawa, there were still a few Japanese hiding around in the caves but the fighting was all up in the north end. I missed it, except when a stray plane would come over at night and drop a bomb or something. When we hit Japan, the bombs had already been dropped, and the war was over. Thank goodness, because our unit was all packed up and ready to go in and invade Japan, and that would've been a mess. After seeing what they did on Iwo and what they did on Okinawa, casualties would've been way up.

I was over there about three years, and I went back to Ohio State. Brown wanted me to come with his first team in Cleveland, in '46. I said, 'No, Paul, I'm going back and finish school.' He had emphasized going back and getting an education. I got married as soon as I came home from the service, and I went back to school that fall.

As it ended up, I played my junior year, then I was elected captain for my senior year. Then Wes Fesler came in as coach. So, if I would've stayed that year, I would've had three coaches at Ohio State: Paul Brown, Paul Bixler, and Wes Fesler.

But I didn't play my senior year. Wes Fesler called me in his office and said, 'Tom, we're losing so many players to pro ball that unless you tell me definitely you're not going to play ball, I'm not going to let you practice spring football with your teammates.'

I says, 'Wes, I could've gone with Paul Brown in '46. I decided I was going to finish school. I was going to come back here and play in '47.'

He says, 'Well, unless you tell me definitely...'

I said, 'I won't do that, Wes.'

I walked up to the fraternity house, and I called the Detroit Lions. I never even called Paul Brown. I don't know why. I just knew I was the property of the Lions and the property of the Browns. That night, the Lions flew down, and I signed a contract in downtown Columbus. I gave up my senior year of eligibility, just because of that ultimatum. I had been three years in the service: 'You can do this. You can do this. You can't do this.' It just hit me at the wrong time. One too many orders.

Maybe I should've stayed and played my captain year. I did finish my degree. I transferred everything up to Kent, and I finished there. Paul Brown knew I was close to graduating, but I kept putting it off, putting it off. In 1950, contract time coming up, he called me in and said, 'Tom, when're you going to finish and get your degree?'

I said, 'Oh, one of these years.'

He said, 'I'll tell you what: How much time do you have left?'

I said, 'I have one quarter to go.'

He said, 'All right, when we come in to summer practice, if you have your degree done then, I'll give you a $500 bonus.'

I said, 'Put it in the contract,' which he did.

He gave me that final nudge. He did that instead of giving me a raise for my play. He gave me a bonus to get my degree.

I PLAYED IN THE COLLEGE ALL-STAR GAME in '47, and then went right up to Alma, Michigan, where the Lions had their training camp. I got my arm broke the second game. We were playing the Chicago Cardinals. I was spelling Bill Dudley on offense. I ran a sweep, got tackled, and got my arm broke. That set me out for the year.

When I was with Detroit, I would see Paul Brown all the time. He always came back to Massillon. I had trouble with my arm and they did surgery on the fracture. There was a nerve in there, and they didn't know if it was severed or what. Paul says, 'Why don't you come with the Browns?'

I was in Paul Brown's office, in '48, ready to go with the Browns, and I got a call from Detroit. Bo McMillin was the coach up there then, and he wanted to know if I would come back with the Lions.

I said, 'Ah, I'm close to home here with the Browns, and I don't know if my arm is going to be good enough or not.'

So, they never got into a lawsuit over me jumping from the NFL over to the All-American Conference. Today, you'd be in a big lawsuit. I only had a one-year contract with the Lions. That's about all they gave in those days, but I was still under the Detroit Lions' doctor. I used to go back to Chicago about every six weeks after the surgery was done. So, legally, I was under the Detroit Lions' doctor's care.

THERE WAS A NIGHT AND DAY DIFFERENCE between the two clubs. With the Detroit Lions, it was like going through a mess line. You had your aluminum tray and you went through a chow line. When you were with the Browns, you ate off silverware. Paul moved football into a higher class thing than the old NFL was. He treated us first class.

I didn't see all that much difference between the two leagues, with the exception that I got to a program that was organized. At that time, pro coaches only coached during the season. They didn't have a full-time job. Brown gave the coaches a full-time, year-round job. That was a step up as far as the organization was concerned. It was run first-class, and a lot of clubs followed what Cleveland was doing. I had Paul Bixler for a year at Ohio State and Gus Dorais at Detroit for that one year. Paul was way better organized than they were.

I made less money in Cleveland than I did in Detroit. I went in one year and I thought I'd get an increase in my salary. That's when all the steel mills were going on strike.

He says, 'Tom, you know, it's tough. You come from a steel town. People aren't working. How do we know we're going to have anybody coming to the games? I can't give you a raise.'

When I left there, he had me thinking that I was lucky to be getting what I made the year before.

Did you ever hear the story about when Mac Speedie took his attorney in with him? They both went out, and Mac ended up playing ball in Canada. Brown was the boss. It's not like it is with this union they have now. Now, for hitting the quarterback they fine guys more than I made in a year.

My biggest contract was for $8,200. In '55, we won the championship out in LA, and for winning that championship, we got $3,500 and some dollars, before taxes. That was our share, and they had a full house—90,000. That was before television came in.

We didn't get anything in training camp, and we didn't get anything for exhibition games. We were playing five, six exhibition games, and we weren't getting paid for them. We didn't have anything like the laundry money they get in camp now. He fed us and gave us a place to stay. That was it. We didn't have any money for incidentals or tooth brushes or anything. Then we'd play twelve games in the season and if you made the championship game, that was another game.

He always said that a defensive halfback is harder to find than an offensive halfback. He said he could find offensive halfbacks with no problem. I probably lasted longer by playing in the secondary. Physically, you didn't get beat up that bad in the secondary. Mentally, you did. Thank goodness I didn't get that many touchdowns scored over me in my career. I think, one year, I had one touchdown pass scored on me.

Cornerback is tough. You sit out there all by yourself in that secondary. You have to be able to tackle. You have to be like a linebacker with speed so that you can go deep with the receivers. I got moved back to safety the last couple of years I played. You had a little bit more leeway there. At cornerback, you had to diagnose real quick: run or pass? The way they play now, you're not allowed to touch the receivers past five yards. When we played, we were allowed contact with the receiver until the ball was in the air. They changed the rule to score more points and be crowd-pleasers.

PRACTICE WAS ALWAYS THE SAME. We'd go through the fundamentals of tackling, the side-tackle, the head-on tackle. You wouldn't do it full tilt, but you'd go through the form of it. Side tackle, you drop your right knee and roll; head-on, you aim your head for his chest, then at the last minute shoot it to the side. Every day when you went out there, before practice started, you'd take a tackle from both sides and a head-on tackle. It was like a warm-up practice. I'd been with him since ninth grade. He'd have me show the whole group the tackling position, the form. He had a right way to do it.

At that time, you had the different kinds of blocks: the long-body, the reverse-body. Nowadays, they grab and hold. There's no blocking done anymore. Now, you can't cut below the knees, where when we played, you could come back in and blindside the defensive ends. Now, you catch them below the knees and they got you for manslaughter.

He did things the same way all the time, but he thought he had the team that could overcome those obstacles and still produce. My final year, in '54, supposedly, the offensive players got together and said that Otto Graham wasn't going to call all the plays that were sent in. If Otto didn't like a play, he was going to check it off and call another play at the line of scrimmage. That's what they always say.

For a long time, I led the Browns in interceptions. I think I had nine one year, but then Thom Darden got ten. People don't know that Tommy Colella got ten in the All-American Conference. That's overlooked, because they only gave credit for the ones in the NFL. People didn't throw the ball back in those days like they do now, and we were playing twelve-game seasons.

The championships we lost, we think we could have won. We lost in '51 to the Rams. We lost in '52 and '53 to Detroit. In '54, we beat Detroit. But we lost a couple there we thought we should have won.

As far as we were concerned, that first game with Philadelphia in 1950 was like a Super Bowl. Brown had us so high with his remarks and all that Greasy Neale said—'We're going to show them what a football looks like'—that we could've run through the end of the stadium. We had a good night that night. We were going into the NFL. We weren't supposed to stand a chance against the league champions. And we crushed Philly.

Then at the end of that year, we beat the Rams for the championship. That's when Lou Groza kicked a field goal right at the end. That's the game the wind caught a bad pass from center on an extra point. It pulled me off my spot, so I threw a pass to Dr. Tony Adamle. It was right in his hands, and he dropped it. That's why we were behind. If he would've caught that, I would've had a one-for-one, and he would have had a one-for-one.

I said, 'Tony, I could've been a quarterback with a thousand percent, and you could've been a receiver with a thousand percent.' We still kid each other all the time about that.

There wasn't much fooling around when you were around Paul during football season. He stayed pretty aloof. He didn't get too close to the players. He told them like it was, and if you didn't want to adhere to it, he'd find another place for you. Jim Daniell (tackle and team captain in 1946) had that little problem that time, and it hit the papers, and he fired him. And Jim Daniell played for him at Ohio State.

I saw Jim Daniell years later, about a year or two before he died. He was the head man of a company up here in Youngstown, something to do with steel. He'd come in from Pittsburgh. I pulled up to the guard gate that day and said, 'I'd like to see Jim Daniell.'

The guard said, 'I think you want to see the traffic manager.'

I says, 'No. Tell him Tommy James wants to see Jim.'

I think the guard thought I was going to get kicked out. He told Jim Daniell over the phone, 'Tommy James wants to see you.'

Jim said, 'Send him right in.'

That guard's jaw dropped. Those things carry over from athletics. Jim said that in the long run, he was thankful it happened. Look what it did for him. He was the head of that big steel mill that I was making sales calls on. He said, 'He (Brown) woke me up.' It showed him what he had to do with the rest of his life—work.

Brown shipped about five or six players to Green Bay that made Lombardi's teams up there. They were good enough, but not quite good enough to make the Browns. Of course, if he wanted to get rid of you, he'd ship you to some place where he wouldn't have to play against you.

He sent my buddy Doug Atkins to the Bears, but I think if the truth were known, Brown would admit he made a mistake with Doug. Doug Atkins was a hell of a football player. I know. I had to practice against him. He went to the University of Tennessee on a track scholarship. He was a high jumper, at 6' 8". He could jump right over the offensive tackle onto the quarterback.

Every now and then, when we're out with some of these old quarterbacks, they tell the story of how they'd say to their rookie linemen, 'Whatever you do, don't get Doug Atkins mad at you, because he'll take it out on me. Don't cut him low or anything like that.' He played sixteen, seventeen years at defensive end, back in the days when they could whack you from any direction.

I NEVER DID HAVE ANY PROBLEM WITH PAUL BROWN until right at the end, and that wasn't really a problem. He was the boss. In training camp, they always had this thing where when it came down to the last five or six cuts, you had to go in and get a letter that told you either you made the team or you didn't. We played the Rams late in the 1956 preseason. I was in the twilight of my career. We were coming back from that game, and I was told to report to get that letter. Fritz Heisler was one of the coaches. He said, 'Tom, you don't have to travel that fifty-five miles to Cleveland from Massillon to get that letter. You just call me, and I'll tell you.'

Well, I already knew, because it was in the papers, in the *Plain Dealer*, that James was on waivers. Later, we had a reunion of our '42 team, our Ohio State national championship team. He was there, of course, and he apologized to all of my teammates and their wives for how he let me go up at Cleveland, for not calling me in and talking to me. That might've been fifteen or twenty years later. We had been in high school and college together, but he said he had to treat me like he did the other people.

He just didn't want to face me and look me right square in the eye and tell me that he had to let me go, I think. I think that was one of the big things with him. He didn't want to have to come right down and tell someone, 'You didn't make the team. You're cut.' I think it hurt him. He just didn't want to call me in and tell me that after all the years I played for him, in high school and college, that he had to let me go. I think that was the softhearted part of him.

Yeah, I was mad. But I had a feeling. You can tell from the way the assistant coaches talk to you and treat you. You knew you were on the bubble. But I was still mad. You know that those things happen in professional sports, but you still hate to see it. I thought I could've played another year or so in that system, with the knowledge I had. But he put me on waivers. He thought it was time to start making his chess moves and start moving the older players out and bringing the younger players in.

I was making sales calls over in Pittsburgh, and I was coming back here to Massillon when the news broke that Modell had fired Paul Brown. And you know what my thing was? I thought, 'Boy, he finally found out what it is to get cut.' That was the first thing that crossed my mind, but then after a little while, I started feeling a little sorry.

He held me 'til midnight the day before the league started. We opened up with the Chicago Cardinals, of all people. He had to pay me for the first game even though I got cut, because he held me past the deadline.

I went to Baltimore and played two games. Then they decided that they wanted to go with a younger team, and I got my release in '56. I got credit for enough games in '56 to get another year of eligibility on my retirement. And that was the end of it.

The only plans I had for after football were I had my degree in phys ed, so I could've taught and coached, but I ended up in sales for a trucking company. I never used my degree, really. I could've gone to work down here at Republic Steel, in an office, but I thought, 'Geez, I've got to go in there every day and look at the same walls.' My ex-teammate at Ohio State and Detroit, Cy Souders, called me. He was terminal manager with a trucking company. He wanted to know if I wanted to go to work with him.

I said, 'Geez, I don't know anything about transportation or trucking.'

He said, 'Your name will get you in the door. If you need to know anything about rates or anything, all you have to do is call the office.'

I said, 'Fine,' and that's what I did all those years.

People knowing my name helped a lot, especially in the Ohio area. They remembered me for being a Browns player or Ohio State. They remembered the name.

Once I left, I got completely out of football. The way these players move around now, I can't get all enthused about it. One year, they'll be playing here, and the next year, they'll be playing someplace else. I just lost interest in it. I still like to watch football, but as for getting close to a team, I can't.

I'D SEE PAUL BROWN MAYBE ONCE OR TWICE A YEAR. If the Bengals came to Cleveland, I'd go down in the locker room, or if I was down around Wilmington during their training camp, I'd go in there.

He'd say, 'Hey, can you still hold that ball for extra points and field goals?'

I'd get down, and he'd have that center snap one back to me.

I think he wanted to come back into coaching to prove something. And he did. I went up to Pontiac, Michigan, and watched that Super Bowl when the 49ers beat him right at the end of the game. I wanted to see a Super Bowl. I had never been to one, and I haven't been to one since.

He told me after he went down to Cincinnati and the players union got in there, he said, 'Tom, I've got to give up coaching.' He couldn't take what was going on with the players. That's when he became a general manager and got out of the coaching end of it. It just wasn't like it used to be, where he could reprimand and keep his thumb over their heads. He wasn't the whole boss anymore. He couldn't take on all those new ideas about coaching and spread his authority around.

I enjoyed all the years I was with Paul, but I'm sure there are times that you get mad at your father. That's about the way I felt with him at times, but then when it was over, it was over. I didn't hold any kind of grudge against him. In fact, I ended up being a pallbearer for him. He was buried here in town. I think it was one of the boys who asked me. Of course, I knew Katy, his first wife, and Paul Brown's sister lives right up around the corner here, and when his second wife comes into town to visit, she'll call me.

I've been going up to Hiram the past couple of years. It's a nice affair, if you don't mind sitting around and signing autographs for hours and hours. I enjoy it. The older people still remember, but these younger people, they don't know who the hell you are.

The last couple times I went up, I saw guys I hadn't seen for years—teammates. I don't know these younger players from Adam. I'm like a spectator. They have their badge on, so I know them that way.

I felt like everybody else when the Browns pulled out of Cleveland. I thought it was a darned thing to do, especially the way the fans treated him and the Browns. Modell had some stinking seasons up there. The company had four season tickets and I had two the Browns gave me, and sometimes I couldn't give them away. People said, 'Well, if we watch it on television we can turn it off .' The fans still treated them good.

I'm 74 now. I retired when I hit 69. I told my wife, if we can't make it from now on, we'll just have to go on food stamps. She started laughing. I kept working because she was on oxygen for eight years, and I kept working so I could get medical help. The company was good enough to keep me on, because I would only work two or three days a week. I was making enough of the old calls I had that I could keep up business to pay for my salary. It wasn't even work to me. I'd go visit old friends, kept up the old accounts that I'd developed over years. It was something I liked to do.

I'm collecting my NFL pension. It's not much, but it's a token. Back when we played, we never thought we were going to get anything. This is something they (the NFL Players Association) went back and brought us into. The players now are getting something fabulous, but we pre-'59ers never thought we would get anything. I think we get $80 a month for every year. I played ten years, I get $800 a month. None of the trucking companies I worked for had retirement plans, so I was going to just wait for social security.

Paul always said it was better to win than to lose, and I'm not a very good loser. He didn't like to get beat in a hearts game. What was his saying? He said, 'When you lose a game, say little, and when you win a game, say less.' I always stuck by that. I never gloated over somebody if I beat them, and I hated for somebody to gloat over me.

I don't know if he was a great man. I'd say he was a great coach. Everything says he did good in life, all the records he set in the field he chose. I respected him right down the line. I don't know, but I'd think that the other guys think the same way. 🥍 🥍

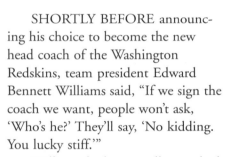

# PB Redux

SHORTLY BEFORE announcing his choice to become the new head coach of the Washington Redskins, team president Edward Bennett Williams said, "If we sign the coach we want, people won't ask, 'Who's he?' They'll say, 'No kidding. You lucky stiff.'"

Williams had personally searched for the man who could salvage a franchise that won only fifty-one games from 1954 through 1965, under three different coaches. A nationally prominent attorney with a flair for showmanship, Williams wanted a "big name." His clients included the glamorous and infamous, but when secret negotiations with his mysterious selection finally ended, Williams was dazzled.

"When you're looking for exactly the right man, these things take time," he said, introducing Otto Graham, Hall of Fame quarterback,

successful college coach, outspoken
television commentator, and celebrity
pitchman, as head coach and general
manager of the woeful Redskins.

Williams cajoled Graham into
taking the job. When he was still
quarterbacking the Cleveland
Browns, Graham repeatedly said he
would never coach. He had endured
enough pressure in ten seasons under
Paul Brown, coaching offered little
security, and the demand to win at
any cost would leech enjoyment
from the game and run counter
to his beliefs.

"I don't plan to keep any contact
at all with football," Graham said
when he retired in 1954.

Brown talked him into playing
another season, and Graham acquired
a taste for the profession several years
later as coach of the College All-Star
Team. In 1959, he accepted the head
coaching position at the Coast Guard
Academy, in part because expectations at the small school didn't go
beyond beating Kings Point or
Trinity once in a while. Graham
spurned offers from professional
teams and major colleges until
Williams doubled his salary and
promised him a free hand.

If Graham's fame were one reason
for his hiring, his reputation as a
disciplinarian was another. "I didn't
fire a fine fellow like Bill McPeak
simply to hire another pleasant man
in his place," Williams said. "We are

looking for a crackdown coach with a
winning background."

Graham appeared to be exactly
the hard master to vitalize a team of
scruffy underachievers. As the NFL's
most dynamic quarterback, he readily
chastised teammates who lacked his
passion. He benched renowned All-
Star players whom he thought slack.
He held the rank of captain in the
U.S. Coast Guard. Best, as every
article about his hiring pointed out,
Graham had studied under the
notoriously rigid Brown.

When Sonny Jurgensen, Redskin
quarterback and noted rascal, heard
who his new coach would be, he
asked, "Does this mean we'll have to
march to practice four abreast?"

Graham was as handsome as a
beefier Tyrone Power and exemplary.
Happily married father of three, he
helped to found the Fellowship of
Christian Athletes. He ate almost
every night at a cafeteria and touched
no drink stronger than a chocolate
milkshake. Writers called him "a great
big boy scout in the best sense of the
term" and "Otto Merriwell." He so
charmed the National Press Club
on a visit that a *Washington Post*
columnist rated Graham and Win-
ston Churchill equally entertaining
and witty.

Whatever their failings (one
newspaper called them "fringe players
and factory rejects"), the Redskins
were now directed by the most artful

and nervy quarterback in football history and one of the more storied athletes of all time. Graham had been a two-sport All-American at Northwestern University and played for both the National Basketball Association and All-American Football Conference champions in 1946. A pioneer of the T-formation, he virtually invented the modern quarterback position.

He was his league's most valuable player five times and its top quarterback nine times. Graham never missed a game. He accumulated the most passing yards and compiled the highest career quarterback rating in history. He retired as the game's preeminent player and the year before taking over the Redskins, became the youngest member ever inducted into the NFL Hall of Fame.

Brown called him "the most valuable player in the history of the game," and Jurgensen said Graham should have played in a "higher league."

Graham, though, had trouble explaining his own excellence. Pressed, he would pay lip service to hard work or the Browns' system or his teammates or, even, to the music lessons his father made him take. In the end, he turned mystical: "I just throw. Some days, I feel hot; other days, I can't hit a thing."

Unlike Brown, a middling athlete who slept at his college coach's home after late skull sessions, Graham played instinctively. Those marvelous instincts worked against him when he dealt with less gifted players. If he could put ten straight passes through a wire coat hanger bent into a diamond, why did the Redskins miss uncovered receivers? If he could take fifteen stitches in his mouth at halftime, without Novocain, then complete nine of ten passes in the second half, why did the Redskins limp off with pulled muscles?

"I never realized until I started coaching what a God-given talent I have. I was surprised that everyone couldn't do what I did," he said.

As the team staggered to a 12-13-3 record in his first two seasons, Graham often blamed—and alienated—players.

Expected to perform miracles, Graham became known as "Williams's personal mistake." Williams's real error had been mixing up Graham with the coach who could have solved the team's problems: Paul Brown. The image of Brown and Graham congratulating each other in a steamy, cramped locker room was indelible: the coach natty, sharp-featured as a fox, defiant; the quarterback beaming, hair sweat-plastered, his smashed face a fright mask painted with blood. Dismissed by Art Modell, Brown was idling away his exile in California when Williams went looking for a coach, but the Washington powerbroker wasn't about to relinquish the control Brown would have demanded. Williams hired the man most closely associated with Brown, the man he assumed had absorbed Brown's values, personality, and philosophy. Otto Graham, the theory went, really was a mechanism precision-tooled by Paul Brown. Williams didn't want PB; he wanted PB Redux.

Graham and Brown were similar in some ways. Both were reared in quintessentially middle-American homes by strict fathers who emphasized education. Each began his career as a puny high school quarterback. Neither was invited as a freshman to try out for his college team. Each was labeled a "genius." Each suffered the death of a son. Money lured both from jobs they claimed to prize.

Together, they forged one of sport's legendary franchises, but that collaboration strained the relationship between the two utterly independent men. Like Williams, some sports writers believed that the coach had created "Mechanical Otto." Others maintained the team should be renamed the Cleveland "Grahams."

At times, Graham said, he could have murdered Brown; at other times he "felt something like love" for his coach.

Estranged after Graham's

retirement, they grew closer over time. Each presented the other at his Hall of Fame induction, and Graham solicited Brown's advice after taking the Washington job.

"Not only was he the best football coach, I learned a lot of life from him," Graham said.

Those lessons seemed foremost in Graham's mind when he took over the Redskins. Like Brown, he surrounded himself with familiars, hiring former teammates as assistants. Repeating a move that Brown made, either by choice or by necessity, every time he began a new job, Graham quickly ran off two players. One, Johnny Sample, had led the team in interceptions, but Graham traded him because Sample turned in a blank playbook—one of the deadlier sins in Brown's personal canon.

Parroting the speech he had heard before every season, Graham warned that any player who embarrassed the team would be discharged. He changed the preseason workout schedule to include two daily practices in full gear, as the Browns had done, rather than one in pads and one in shorts, the Redskins' custom under McPeak.

His team foundering, Graham was accused of not understanding modern pro football and, peculiarly for such an audacious player, of being "unimaginative"—two charges made against Brown. Just as Brown had never found an adequate replacement for Graham, Graham could find no backup for the aging, battered Jurgensen; and just as Brown never figured out what to do with Bobby Mitchell before trading him to Washington, Graham also struggled with how to use the talented receiver/halfback.

Graham proved as insensitive as Brown to public relations. But where the inscrutable Brown became terse with reporters, Graham blurted out whatever he thought, to the happiness of sports editors.

So shy as a child that he didn't dare look people in the eye, he was now direct to a fault. He needed only one preseason game to offend both the President of the United States and the paying customers. Informed after a 35-0 loss to Baltimore that Lyndon Johnson had attended, Graham said, "He can stay at home in the future as far as I'm concerned."

Asked the next day how the shutout might affect fans, Graham answered that since the team had already sold its season tickets, he didn't care about the crowd's morale.

After each incident, Williams received calls from peeved NFL commissioner Pete Rozelle, as he would in seasons to come when the coach raged at officials.

Graham said that people took him too seriously. Williams said that his coach's humor was so subtle it

required a follow-up news conference to explicate the jokes.

At Graham's second appearance at the National Press Club, the master of ceremonies quipped, "Otto made one mistake—he did not get an immunization shot for foot-in-mouth disease before coming to Washington."

By not behaving like a martinet, Graham bewildered Washington. He once said that he wanted to coach where he "could be a sort of father to the boys," and paternalism colored his handling of the Redskins. He joshed players and even stopped practices for team soda breaks. Brown released players by means of a form letter. Graham cut them less ruthlessly: "with a pat on the back and some severance pay and advice to keep their courage." He said he could do little to deter loafing and saw no value in chewing out the same players every week. The mounting losses didn't visibly perturb him.

Graham was the antithesis of Brown. His exuberant style of play had depended upon emotion unchained. Brown's satisfaction came in cool analysis, logical strategy, proven tactics. For Graham, football was more intoxicating thrill than sacred calling. "I'm not the fanatic about football that Paul Brown is," he said.

He said he'd "rather risk losing some games by, say, 35-28, and have the fans up off their feet with excitement" than win every game 3-0; Brown said he preferred winning in an empty stadium to losing in front of 80,000. Graham understood the elemental pleasures of football in a way Paul Brown could not.

Edward Bennett Williams had confused Graham's fiery competitiveness, bursts of temper, and hardheadedness with Brown's total commitment to order—his own and his team's. What was for Graham a passing mood was the foundation of Paul Brown's existence.

Graham says now that he wasn't capable of imitating the dictator for whom he played, even though a little of Brown's caustic treatment of players would have helped in Washington. After a crucial loss to Dallas, he swore that he would learn to be hostile, but Graham never did. "It's been said that I lack the killer instinct," he said. "I suppose it's true." His good nature and high spirit led to claims that the team played "soft," a locker room in disarray, and anarchy.

Jurgensen recalled waiting for practice one sultry afternoon during training camp. Aching and tired, he dreaded another session. He glanced at a nearby set of tennis courts and, astounded, saw Graham and kicker Charlie Gogolak in a lively match. "I hope to tell you, we were none too happy," Jurgensen said.

Graham once wasted so much

time in locker room repartee that, he realized, he would be late for practice if he walked to the field as usual. He had to hitch a ride and listen to the squad's razzing. Saturday workouts became so casual that even in the midst of a losing streak, players brought along wives, girlfriends, and pets.

By the middle of 1967, team captain Sam Huff felt compelled to call a players-only meeting—a sure sign of turmoil. The following year, Graham met with the players to discuss their "respect gap" with the coaches. Questioned afterward, he uncharacteristically said, "No comment, no comment, no comment."

In the worst insults, Graham was paradoxically criticized for lacking leadership, and players convolved his first name into "Toots"—"Otto" turned inside out.

Graham also had the bad luck to work for one of the meddlesome "non-football people" Brown loathed. Graham almost refused the job when he learned that Williams had addressed the Redskins without Bill McPeak present—the ultimate affront to a coach. During the 1968 season, Williams did the same to Graham.

But Williams had already reneged on his promise of a free hand. He insisted that Graham draft huge fullback Ray McDonald, who turned out to be partially handicapped with a withered calf, gay, and unable to grasp the offense. Williams had Graham swap a number one pick for Heisman Trophy winner Gary Beban. Signed to a hefty contract the weak-armed, overwhelmed quarterback flopped. Graham stunned 1,300 people at a "welcome home" luncheon by announcing that Beban had been cut.

Graham tried to trade Jurgensen, but Williams vetoed the deal, as he did sending Mitchell to the Bears. By the end of Graham's third season, the team president had stopped taking the head coach's calls.

Graham had been insightful years earlier when he said of coaching in the NFL: "I know football fans. The first losing year, they'd give me the benefit of the doubt because of my success as a player. The second year they'd raise their eyebrows and say, 'I'm not so sure about this Graham.' The third year, they'd say, 'Send that bum back to the Coast Guard.'"

Which is just what happened.

In 1968, the Redskins had their worst record in six years, 5-9. In mid-season, the Washington *Daily News* ran a front-page editorial that "urgently recommended" firing Graham.

When he was hired, he had warned people not to waste money on paint to use in making "Good-bye Graham" banners, because he planned to coach the Redskins for

some time. The signs that speckled RFK Memorial Stadium like pustules in the late autumn of 1968 carried a different message: "SOS—Save Our Skins—Hire Lombardi."

Williams honored the request, and Graham became a bit player in his own demise. Two years left on his $60,000-a-season contract, he watched silently as Williams pursued Vince Lombardi, epitome of the taskmaster that every team coveted at the time. Amid much hubbub, Lombardi maneuvered out of his contract as Green Bay's general manager and came to Washington.

Graham returned to the Coast Guard Academy as athletic director. He later coached for two more seasons, leaving the game after an 8-2 record in 1975. He promised never to return to professional football, even if Paul Brown offered him a half-million dollars to coach the Cincinnati Bengals. No offer came, and Graham retired from the academy in 1984.

Graham reminisced in the unoccupied banquet room of a seedy, faux-tropical motel across a bustling thoroughfare from an airport tarmac in Sarasota, Florida. The frowzy room didn't befit a legend. Fluorescent lights cast metallic glare. Limp and scaled with dust, a pallid ficus slouched in a corner. Washed out prints of aquatic flowers hung crookedly from sagging pastel wallpaper. Two maintenance men preparing one side of the room for a high school class reunion chatted in Spanish as they tugged at a stuck partition as if at the reins of a stubborn horse.

Some of Graham's more familiar recollections could have sounded as weary as the setting looked, but he told each with relish, chuckling, eyes alert, voice rising and falling, punctuating important ideas by tapping the long unstable folding table at which he sat. His attire was Florida septuagenarian casual: thick-soled black walking shoes, knee-high surgical hose, black mid-calf polyester socks, olive cargo shorts that hung from his narrow hips, and a wrinkled golf shirt. A thin pale scar from the cheap shot that caused him to be sewn up in the dressing room 46 years earlier puckered a corner of his mouth.

Nearing 80, Graham retains the jaunty elan that made him such an exciting player. Like Brown, he is earthier in private than in public, eager for the next joke, not put off by the slightly coarse story. The backwardness of his youth and brazenness of his young manhood have given way to a deep strain of gentleness and solicitude: hints of the musician his family expected him to become. Married to his wife, Beverly, for 55 years, Graham makes charity appearances, speaks to youth groups, and

gardens. His skill rusted from lack of practice, his revulsion at doing anything poorly as strong as ever, he rarely golfs.

Graham laughs that his claim to fame isn't his playing career; it's that replacing him in Washington required Vince Lombardi. Though he looks back on his three years in the NFL without rancor, he would surely appreciate that one of Lombardi's first moves in Washington was to seize Williams's plush office—an act that strangely mirrors Art Modell's annexing Brown's office after buying the team in 1961.

In 1978, Graham had surgery for the same colo-rectal cancer that had killed Lombardi eight years earlier. The illness affected neither his courage nor his humor. He crossed the country, speaking about the importance of detecting the disease early and finding proper treatment. He said that the colostomy bag he had to wear was perfect for alleviating hemorrhoids and continued to play golf and tennis with it attached to his side.

Graham says that the two most painful events of his life—cancer and the death of his infant son—made him a better man.

"When you've been through what I've been through, winning a football game is not that important," he says.

# *Otto* GRAHAM

“ MY PARENTS WERE BOTH MUSIC TEACHERS. My father was head of the music department at Waukegan High School, and my mother taught at a little country school. In fact, she played the organ at Bob Feller's first wedding. He married a girl from my hometown. When you're born and raised in a family like that, you practice and you play. I started off on the piano, and I played the violin, the cornet, and ended up playing the French horn in high school and at Northwestern.

When I was young, I wanted to go out and play whatever game was going on. I didn't want to practice music. Most kids are that way. My name is Otto Everett Graham, Jr., so most everybody called me 'Junior.' It'd be, 'Junior, you don't go outside until you practice for half an hour.'

All of my brothers played sports, but I'm the only one who went as far as I did. My oldest brother played in the United States Marine Corps Band—the president's own band—for 40 years. The brother after me inherited my father's beautiful tenor voice. I've always been jealous of him. I would trade all of the trophies I have in the world if I could have had a voice like that.

Whenever I talk to kids, I very strongly tell them, 'Don't be an idiot. If you're playing an instrument, keep it up. If you don't, years later, you'll be like me and regret it very much.'

I can't play football at 80 years of age, but if I could sit down and play the piano, you'd love it, and I'd love it, too. Look at it selfishly: I can't play football now, but I could still be playing the violin or the piano, and people would still be coming to see me. Of course, we all look back and say, 'If I would've turned right instead of left, my life would've changed.'

I went to Northwestern on a basketball scholarship. I played guard and forward. I wasn't that big, but I even played in the pivot spot at times. I was a good ball-handler and passer, and I could shoot. Northwestern was only about 30 miles from Waukegan, so my parents could come and see me play, and I could get home whenever I wanted to. I often wonder what would've happened if I had gone to Dartmouth or somewhere, but it just made a lot more common sense to live just far enough away that my parents couldn't stick their nose into everything I did, but close enough that I could get home if an emergency happened.

When I got to Northwestern, I played intramural football on a fraternity team. It was six-man touch football, and of the six guys we had on our team, four of them were all-state high school players, including myself. I was a third-team all-state halfback. We won the intramural championship, and Pappy Waldorf, who was the coach at Northwestern, heard that I could throw the ball. He came out and watched us play and invited me to come out for spring football. I did real well that spring, and it got in my blood.

THAT SUMMER, I WAS RUNNING, getting in shape to go to football practice, and I heard cartilage in my knee pop. I stayed at college for that entire year, living at the fraternity house, never going to classes. I wasn't in school. I worked intramural softball and football games and was a very bad influence on my classmates. They'd have to study, and I'd be saying, 'Come one, let's go to a show.' I just had a ball.

The next year, I went out for football and from that point on, did very well. I was on a basketball scholarship, so I had to play basketball. Football was optional. I made All-American in football, but I made All-American in basketball, too.

I was a single-wing tailback, and it was much different from being a T-formation quarterback. But the footwork and the maneuvering in basketball are very similar to a T quarterback. You're pivoting and handing off right and handing off left, retreating, stopping, throwing, starting. I've always felt that basketball is the most demanding sport. The best athletes are basketball players. You have to shoot right-handed, shoot left-handed. They're the best coordinated athletes. I think Michael Jordan, for example, is the greatest athlete who ever lived. I would have loved to have had him as a receiver. You could just lob a ball out there to him, and he'd jump eight feet in the air and pick it off.

We played against Paul Brown's teams at Ohio State. Once, I ran to my left, stopped, and threw the ball way back to my right for a touchdown. He remembered that. I guess that impressed him, and that's why he contacted me when he was going to become a pro coach.

The war came along while I was in school. I always tell people, 'Show me some respect. My birthday is December 6, and the Japanese waited until December 7 to attack Pearl Harbor. They would not attack on my birthday.'

The whole damn country was shook up. You had to go out and fight for your country. There was just no choice. Nobody likes to go off to war. I thought if they did like it, they had to be insane. Who wants to go out and get killed?

Everybody else was getting called out to their units, but the mayor of Evanston, Illinois, was the head of the draft board for that area, and every time my name came to the top, I know he put it back on the bottom. It wasn't until January of my senior year that they called me up. I was a cadet in the Navy Air Corps, and my first training stop was Colgate University. This was in 1944. I was supposed to graduate in June. Northwestern just handed me my diploma. I didn't have to take any finals or anything.

I pulled into the train station at Colgate. They met me there and took me to the school. Some guy says to me, 'Okay, go back to the train station and get on the next train to Buffalo.'

I said, 'I just came through Buffalo three hours ago. Why?'

He said, 'You're playing on our basketball team tonight.'

I went back, got the train, walked into the gym, said 'hi' to everyone, and went out and played.


BASKETBALL ON THE EAST COAST was very different from basketball in the Midwest. In the Big 10, you're pounding on the boards, you're rough and tough. It was like pro basketball is today. At Colgate, all they did was pick and shoot two-handed. They never drove to the basket. I was dumbfounded. I'd be yelling, 'For god's sake, go to the basket! Go to the basket!'

I played four or five games with them, and the writers on the East Coast got a chance to see me play. They thought I was the greatest player in the history of basketball, because my style was so different. Back home, I was just another basketball player. If I hadn't played those four or five games on the East Coast, I would never have made All-American. There's no question about it in my mind.

Ninety-nine percent of the writers who pick All-Americans in any sport never get a chance to see the players play. They just read the papers and form an opinion. I wasn't going to say 'no,' but it was ridiculous the way they did it back then.

I played in one College All-Star Game before the war and one after the war. The first one, I played quarterback and safety. I intercepted one of Sammy Baugh's passes and ran it back for a touchdown. They put in the paper that it was 94 or 95 yards, and I said, 'No, 97!'

I had seen a receiver come downfield, but I didn't play him very tightly. I knew he thought that he was open. I watched him go back to the huddle and talk to Sammy Baugh. I knew they were going to come back and run the same damn play. I picked it off and ran it all the way back.

The first time I met Paul Brown, I was in awe. He was in the Navy himself at the time, at Great Lakes, which was right next to my hometown. I was at Glenview Naval Air Station, outside of Chicago, in Evanston. I was flying the 'yellow perils,' the two-wing training jobs. He came down to see me one night. We talked for quite a while, and he said that after the war was over, they were going to start a new league, and Cleveland was going to be one of the teams. He said he was going to be running the team, and he wanted me as his quarterback. I'm a cadet making $75 a month, free room and board, and the Navy's paying for my gasoline when I fly.

He said, 'If you'll sign a contract with me, right now, I'll give you a $1,000 bonus. Also, I'll give you a contract for two years for $7,500.'

Then came the final touch.

He said, 'Starting immediately and for as long as the war lasts, I'll send you a check every month for $250.'

My next question was, 'Where do I sign?'

It was purely selfishness, I guess. The money was so good that you couldn't turn it down. It was like finding a gold mine. Gosh almighty. My whole life, when it comes to finances, goes back to an incident when I was ten or twelve years old. My parents went into Chicago, and they left me a twenty-dollar bill to go pay some debts, and I lost it. They came back, and I had to tell them that I had lost it. That was a crisis. That hurt. Back in those days, twenty dollars was a lot of money. Since then, I'm not afraid to spend money, but I will not throw money away.

I MADE $7,500 MY FIRST YEAR, and Paul Brown upped it to $12,000 my second year, and I didn't even ask for it. I never had an argument with him about money; you didn't argue with him, anyway. He told you. That's the way it was. That's why I think that every athlete should have somebody negotiate for him. Then it doesn't get personal. You don't have Paul Brown saying, 'Look me in the eye when you talk to me.' The word 'agent' wasn't even heard back in those days.

I had been drafted by the Detroit Lions. I had not heard a word from them, because there was no competition, as far as they knew. There was no other league at the time. When the deal with the Browns was announced in the papers, I got a letter from the Lions saying, 'Send a copy of your contract. We'll give it to our lawyers and see if we can break it.'

I sent a letter back and said, 'What do you mean "send it to you and see if we can break it"? I signed a contract in good faith, and I'm going to honor it, period. It's as simple as that.'

These days, so many people don't honor contracts: owners, lawyers, coaches, players. I often wonder where I would be today if I had gone to Detroit. There's no doubt in my mind that I would never have reached the heights that I did, because the system would have been different and everything else. I made the right move, but at the time, it wasn't a brilliant decision. It was just plain luck.

My first year, I played both ways most of the time, and I was a pretty good safety. I could cover those guys. My second year, I played defense about half the time. After that, I didn't play any more defense. It's complicated as hell. Even on defense, you have to spend so much time learning what you're doing that it's impossible to play another position. You had all the keys to learn, all the changes. You couldn't absorb all that and absorb the offense. It was impossible.

It wasn't hard to adjust to playing quarterback in the pros, because I had played one year of quarterback at Chapel Hill Pre-Flight School, in the Navy Air Corps. We didn't have anyone there who had coached the T-formation, but we had an offensive lineman from the Chicago Bears. He brought a Bear playbook, so we used that for our plays. But I had to learn the position all by myself. The footwork was very similar to basketball, so that helped me immensely.

THE COACHING WAS SO MUCH BETTER in the pros. They paid so much more attention to detail. As you look back on it, you didn't learn the things in college that you did in the pros. Blanton Collier was the quarterback coach for the Browns. He was a very intelligent guy. The only criticism I had of Blanton Collier was that he was too nice a guy to be a head football coach. You have to be an SOB sometimes. Blanton was very meticulous: 'You put this foot here, and you put this foot here.' He practically put footprints down where you were supposed to put your feet. He expected everyone to do everything just perfect, and none of us is perfect. Blanton used to tell me that if I was half as meticulous as Paul Brown, I'd make a pretty fair quarterback.

Occasionally, Paul Brown might say something to me, but he didn't try to coach all of the positions. He let the assistants do the coaching, and if he didn't like the way it was done, he'd get rid of them.

Paul was a charmer, there's no question about it, but he was also very strict. He let you know that he ran the show. He wouldn't tolerate drunks or guys out chasing women every damn night. You had to be a decent person. Now, I found out later that if a guy was a great football player and did something wrong, he might overlook it.

What really impressed us was in our very first year of professional football, we won our division. We were in the championship game. Our captain was Jim Daniell. He was a tackle and a good one. He had played for Paul Brown at Ohio State. We had to wait an extra week for the championship game, because there was a playoff game in the other division. We had Saturday and Sunday off. Mac Speedie's wife was flying in from Utah on Saturday night. She was arriving around midnight.

Mac Speedie and Jim Daniell and Edgar Jones and Lou Rymkus were going out on the town killing time, going from this bar to that bar, having a few beers. They were right in downtown Cleveland, and a cop car was in the street, halfway in and halfway out of a parking space, blocking that lane. Edgar Jones told me exactly what happened. They had dropped him off about a half a block before that, and he saw the whole thing happen.

DANIELL WAS DRIVING, and instead of going around it, he got right up behind it and just leaned on the horn. The cops got irritated, came out of the car and hauled them down to the police station. When they got down there, Daniell demanded a sobriety test. He didn't just suggest it; he demanded it. They gave him one, and he had just enough beer in his system to be declared legally drunk.

Sunday morning, we get the paper, and headlines in the *Plain Dealer*: 'Cleveland Brown Captain Arrested for Drunken Driving.' I'm telling you, I almost died. It's our first year in professional football, we're in the championship game right off the bat, and our team captain gets arrested.

Our next meeting, we're supposed to be in our seats at nine o'clock in the morning. Usually, everyone gets there on time, but they're all talking and making a lot of noise, and then Paul gets there, and everyone quiets down. But this time, no one's saying a word. Everyone's just sitting there with their mouths closed. Paul Brown walks in and comes up to this little podium he had there. He turns to Jim Daniell and says, 'Jim, is what I read in the paper true?'

Jim said, 'Yes.'

Paul said, 'Okay, then you're through.'

Jim said, 'Do you want to hear my side of the story?'

He said, 'No, you're through. Get out of here.'

It was as simple as that. I'm telling you, all of us were just dumbfounded. He fired his captain before the championship game. You just don't do that.

I'm not very smart, though. I didn't realize it until years later, but Jim Daniell's backup was a good football player, too, so Jim wasn't really going to be missed in the game itself. Paul Brown saw the opportunity to get that team in the palm of his hand forever, and he took it. If Mac Speedie and Edgar Jones had been arrested, too, there's no way they would all have been kicked off. That would have hurt the team. This didn't hurt our team at all.

That incident set the tone. Everybody was scared to death of Paul Brown. Believe me, Paul Brown's word was law, and if you went against it, you were in trouble. We had good people, because Paul Brown wouldn't tolerate the bad people. We learned that very quickly.

HE REVOLUTIONIZED PRO FOOTBALL. There's no question about that. Within a few years, everybody was patterning themselves after the Browns. He started off each year by giving us these thick playbooks filled with blank sheets of paper. We had to write everything. For ten straight years, I had to do this. That's one of the reasons I quit. I got so sick and tired of doing this damn thing. By that time, I had it all memorized. I didn't enjoy it, but you had to go through it.

Every week, we had a test. We had several good quarterback prospects come in there, and they didn't do very well on the test. The next day, they were gone. If a guy wasn't going to work at it, he wasn't going to be there.

They traded for George Ratterman, who was a good quarterback, but a character. He was a fine piano player and tennis player and an excellent baseball player, but he was just a crazy nut. God, the things he used to do.

55

We'd be in the lobby of the hotel, and he'd run up and do a baseball hook slide and knock someone down. Once, we were staying on the fifth floor of this hotel, and there was a narrow ledge outside. Right around the corner, you could see this window. The blind was barely open, but you could see this man and woman in the room. Ratterman goes out of the window, crawls along the ledge, reaches in very quietly, raises the blind so everyone can see, and crawls back. If he had fallen off, he'd have been killed.

Ratterman was so intelligent that he bordered on insanity. We would have these meetings to go over these reports about the opposing team. You know, 'You can beat him to the outside but not to the inside.' Those kinds of tendencies. The assistant coaches would write up the report and then take it downtown and have it typed and pass it out to all the players. One time, the assistant coaches had something to do, so George said, 'I'm going downtown. I'll take the stuff.'

The next day, he comes back with the report, and it says thing like, 'Bill Jones, halfback, if you don't tackle him, he'll run for a touchdown.' He had doctored it all up. Crazy stuff like that is all through the damn report. Everybody's looking at it and laughing. Paul Brown raised hell, but I think, deep down inside, he was laughing, too.

One time, Joe Skibinski, a rookie guard from Purdue, comes into the huddle and gives George a play that Paul was sending in.

George says, 'I don't like that play. Go get another one.'

The guy turned around and started running back to the sideline. All of the players in the huddle are all laughing so hard that they had to call a time out. To my dying day I'll say that I would love to have been standing beside Paul Brown when Joe came out and asked for another play. That was Ratterman. You never knew what he was going to do.

I can only talk for myself, but Paul Brown was very businesslike with me. Now, if he wants something from you, he'll be nice to you, but if he's pissed off at you and you're playing for him, he doesn't show much mercy. Once, I was on the sideline, and he had substituted for me. I think Ratterman was in the ball game. I was close to Paul. He was talking to another coach. In his opinion, I had left the pocket too soon. It was breaking down, and I had run out of it.

He said to the other coach, 'At least now we have a quarterback in the game who has guts enough to stay in the pocket.'

He didn't say it to me. He said it to the coach. I wanted to get up and hit him. I couldn't do it, but I wanted to. A short time later, I was back in the game, and I said, 'I'm not leaving this pocket if they tear my damned head off.'

And, I have to admit, I played better.

HE COULD STICK THE KNIFE INTO YOU so bad that you didn't know it was in there until all of a sudden, your head was off. When I came back from the All-Star camp that first year, I missed the first week or so of training camp. Now, I come back to camp, and Paul Brown doesn't really know if I'm a prima donna or not. My first day, we're having practice, and I'm not wearing a red shirt. It was full block on the line of scrimmage, but when they got to me, they were supposed to ease up.

I'll never forget this. Mo Scarry was our center, a great guy who coached with me later. Big Bill Willis was playing opposite Mo, and he was giving Mo fits. He'd get down on all fours and just jump right over Mo. He'd go around the right, around the left, between his legs. Mo was getting sick and tired of this, so he snaps the ball and as he does it, he jumps backwards to get a better angle to block Bill. The quarterback, when he pushes off the one foot to drop back, the other foot is still there behind the center momentarily. So, as Mo jumped back, he came down on the instep of my left foot. I tripped and fell down.

Paul said, 'What happened?'

I very innocently said, 'He stepped on my foot.'

It's the very beginning of camp. We have 60 or 70 players there. He stops practice. He calls everybody, including the coaches, up into a big circle. I'm right in the middle. He says, 'From this point on, I don't ever want to see any of you again step on Graham's foot.'

I could've killed him. God almighty.

WE'RE PLAYING THE CHAMPIONSHIP GAME, against the Rams in '50. We're behind 28-27. It's in the closing minutes of the game, and we're in their territory, down close enough to where Groza can kick a field goal. I ran a quarterback draw, and I picked up 10 or 15 yards. I got hit from the blind side, and I fumbled the football.

I have been dejected in my life many times, but never more dejected than I was at that moment. Here I am carrying the football, and we have a chance to win the championship our first year in the NFL, and Graham blows it. I wanted to find a hole and crawl in it and hide. I headed back to the sideline, and I didn't even want to see Paul Brown. I could just hear one of those scathing comments coming out of him. I tried to avoid him, but I couldn't. I go up to him. He patted me on the back and said, 'Don't worry, Otts; we're still going to get 'em.'

Now, if he had chewed me out, that would have been the end of it. Our defense had to hold them. If they make one first down, we lose the ball game. But our defense held them, they punted, we got the ball back with about a minute and a half left and about 50 yards to go. By giving me a boost of encouragement, my voice, when we got in the huddle, sounded entirely different than it would have if he'd chewed me out. I know it was full of determination. I said, 'C'mon, dammit, we're gonna beat 'em! You guys block! Let's go!' We go down the field, Lou kicks the field goal with 20 seconds to go, and we win the game. There's no doubt in my mind that Paul Brown patting me on the back had more to do with us winning that ball game than me throwing the ball or someone catching the ball or whatever. If I didn't show optimism in my voice, it would never have happened.

I don't know if he calculated it all or not. I know comments like that were not the thing he would normally do. He was a very intelligent guy. He knew that it was not the time to chew me out. This was the time to give me a pat on the back.

'Irritating' is not strong enough a word for him. He could really get to you sometimes. He didn't give a damn if you were one of his coaches or one of his players. If he felt like a jab at you, with somebody else listening in, would help the team, he'd do it. I know he wasn't easier on me than he was on anyone else.

He was in control of himself all the time. He never showed much emotion—favorable emotion, anyway. He'd come out with those nasty comments, with the idea of giving you the needle, but he didn't throw too many compliments your way while you were playing for him.

That didn't bother us much. I think we probably made some comments about it occasionally, but as long as you're winning, and you know you're winning because of him, that's what really counts. We thought we were winning because of him, but at the same time, we thought we could win without him, too. As you get older, you realize that a tight ship is the only way to do it. When you're younger, you don't realize that. When we were younger, there were times we all could've killed him.

We had great players, too. When it comes to the passing game, quite frankly, Paul Brown doesn't get the credit. We, as players, had more to do with that than anyone else. After practice, we'd go down there and work at it. I got so I could tell where they were going to go just by the way they moved their fannies. Paul Brown had nothing to do with our passing game: the sideline pattern, the comeback, all of that. We did that on our own. He allowed us to do it, and Blanton Collier was involved in it, too, but we did most of it ourselves. We worked on it all the time.

It was just common sense: if I'm going to throw a pass to you, and you stop and come back, and the defender is going to be on your left hip, I'm going to throw the ball low and to the right, so he can't get to the ball. If you're going down to do a sideline pass, and you go straight to the sideline, the defender has the same distance to get to the ball that you do. If you come back a little bit, there's no way he can get there, if I throw the ball out away from him. That's what we did. If it's third down and 10, you go down 12 or 13 and fake and come back and just give yourself a little bit of leeway to make the first down.

WE HAD GUYS WHO COULD CATCH IT, TOO. You get to know personalities of people. Dub Jones was very intelligent. He would come back and say to me, 'I can beat him deep,' and you just knew it was there. It was good as gold.

Lavelli would come back and say, 'Throw me the damn thing!' His judgment was terrible. If he was an inch in front of the defensive back, he was wide open: 'Throw me the goddamn ball!'

It wasn't that he wanted to hog it; he just wanted to play. He had great hands. If I had to throw the ball to one individual and had to get a first down, it would be Lavelli, because of his hands. He'd go up and fight, bite, scratch, kick, anything to get the damn football.

Mac Speedie had better speed than Lavelli, but if the ball was thrown short, he wouldn't stop and come back with it: 'The hell with it.' He was a good receiver, but you had to throw the ball perfect for him. He was not a competitor like Lavelli was.

We're playing that very first NFL game, in Philadelphia, and they had a defensive back, Russ Craft. He was one of the top cornerbacks in the NFL. Dub came back one time and just simply said, 'He's ready.' That's all he said to me. Dub had gone down and faked and come back, faked and come back, faked and come back, and this guy kept getting closer and closer. Dub meant he could fake and go deep, so I called it. It was like taking candy from a baby. He was nowhere near Dub Jones when he caught the ball. He went about 60 yards for a touchdown.

If that had been Lavelli, it wouldn't have meant a damn thing to me. If Lavelli was supposed to go down 15 yards and run a post pattern, and he saw the corner was open, he'd just break off and go there. Lavelli would run down and hook the goal posts and change directions. You never knew where the hell he was going. He was something. We used to have this basketball team. In the off-season, we'd go around and play games. Now, I'm an All-American basketball player. I played pro basketball on a championship team. But Lavelli's doing all the coaching. He's a piece of work.

EARLY IN MY CAREER, I didn't feel like I could tell Paul Brown what I thought we should be doing. Once we'd been there for a while, though, I felt like I could. One year, we were playing the Rams (1955). That year, we went to the shotgun whenever we just had to move the football. I'd get back six or seven yards, and we had a whole shotgun offense. We felt that, against the Rams, the shotgun would be good. I talked to some of the players, and we went to Paul and the other coaches and said, 'If this offense is so good that we're going to use it when we have to move the football, why wait until those situations come up? Why not do it from the very beginning? It makes more sense.'

One-on-one, they just couldn't cover us. As an added factor, I could run the ball whenever I wanted to. Paul bought it. We went to the championship game, and went into the shotgun right from the beginning. They couldn't stop us.

If I weren't a mobile quarterback, then we couldn't have done some of those things. I was a good runner because I didn't like to get hit. They didn't pay me to get hit, dammit. That's why Doug Flutie did so well up at Buffalo this year. I had Doug Flutie in an all-star game, and he's a hell of an athlete. You get a guy with his ability, that presents a lot more problems for the defense. He can kill you anytime by running. It's tough to defense a guy like that. The negative side of it is that when you do it, you're taking a chance of getting knocked out for the whole year.

I never missed a game in ten years. I should have missed one, but I didn't. I got my face bashed in once, but they got me back in the game. That was against the 49ers one year. We weren't playing that well, and they could've beaten us. I ran, and right in front of our bench, they knocked me out of bounds, and the guy came in and, *boom*, hit me with a cheap shot right across my mouth. I was out cold. They draped my arms over the shoulders of a couple of guys, and they dragged me to the locker room.

When I woke up, I was lying on a table, and Dr. Ippolito, our team doctor, has got this big long hooked needle. He's sewing my mouth up. I think I got 11 stitches in there. You can still see the scar. I was in the insurance business in the off-seasons at the time, and I was lying there giving him the sales talk while he was stitching me. This thing is bleeding, and we're talking about moving money around. I figured I might's well give him a sales pitch. What the hell.

They found some kind of plastic thing, and, somehow, they molded it on my helmet. It was about two inches high and half an inch thick. It wasn't transparent, so my vision was obscured. It was hard to breathe with it on. It was terrible.

We came back in the second half, and we took it to them. They were ahead, but when they smashed me, they got our whole team riled up. I think I completed nine out of 10 passes. They made a mistake by knocking me out.

We didn't have to win that game, by the way. We had already clinched the championship. I don't know if Paul said anything to me after that game or not. He just expected you to play well and to try hard. Now, once I retired, he made some nice comments, but it just wasn't in him as a person to gush comments about how good you are. He wanted to be in control of everything, and if you say that kind of stuff to the average person, they're going to start thinking that they're better than they are. He wouldn't allow that to happen.

PAUL BROWN WILL NEVER BE A VINCE LOMBARDI when it comes to recognition. There's no way he's gotten his due. If you ask someone who's the greatest football coach in the history of the NFL, 'Lombardi' would be the first word out of their mouth. You have to admit that Vince Lombardi was far more apt at public relations than Paul Brown ever was. The headquarters of the press is really in New York City. Paul Brown would go into New York and not give the press the time of day. He'd say, 'Screw 'em.' Someone would come up to him and say, 'You don't remember me, but...' and he'd just say, 'No, I don't,' and walk away. He'd never bend over backwards for them; in fact, he'd give them the business at times. They didn't like it. It was wrong for him to do it, but he didn't give a shit about it, and it hurt him in the end.

I've always had mixed emotions about the press. For example, I remember reading big headlines 'Graham Could Be Traded.' No one ever bothered to call me and check on it to see if it was true or not. Many times they put things in the press that are either rumors or totally untrue. They don't try to verify it. All they're worried about is, 'Read it here for the first time!' If they would start off their columns with 'in my opinion,' then fine. But they write it as if it's the gospel truth, and that always irritated the hell out of me.

The All-American Conference was a good football conference. There were good football teams in that league. Of course, the NFL tried to make the point that we weren't as good as they were. What we did in 1950 seemed so amazing only because the average fan was so uninformed. They weren't told the truth. They were listening to the opinions of all these sportswriters who were NFL people all their lives. They got the free drinks and the free food and everything from the NFL, so they were not about to make derogatory comments about the NFL and build up the All-American Conference. I knew from my College All-Star days that the new league was getting just as good football players as the NFL. The fans and the press just didn't know.

THERE'S NEVER BEEN A TEAM—whether it's been college or professional in whatever sport—that's been more emotionally ready to play a game than we were against Philadelphia in 1950. We got to training camp that year, and we had a big bulletin board there. Every day, there'd be a column cut out from the Philadelphia papers. One paper sent a writer to our camp for the entire time we were there before the game. This guy would write articles that said, 'Hey, fans, this is a good football team. Don't let anyone tell you otherwise. The Eagles had better be ready, because this team is very capable of beating them. They have good football players and they are very well coached.'

It was all positive stuff, warning the guys back home, and no one wanted to hear it. It was like they thought someone was paying the writer off or some damn thing. We would've gone in and played that game for anything just to prove we were as good as they were. Some guys would've played for a keg of beer; I prefer a chocolate milkshake myself.

Paul never said a word about the Eagles. He just kept putting these columns on the bulletin board. Every day, for weeks, we read this damn stuff. If he did give us some kind of speech before the game, I've forgotten it. He didn't have to. When we walked into that stadium, we were ready, and he knew we were ready.

I'll never forget that week. Wives were not allowed to stay with their husbands before the game. Paul Brown had a rule: 'No sex after Wednesday. Save yourself for the game.' Paul Brown and his rules about sex are still a joke to the players. It was right there in our notebooks. We had to write it down. Cliff Lewis and I were neighbors out there in Bay Village, so our wives traveled together. Two nights before the game, we went out and had dinner. We escorted the girls back to the lobby of their hotel. We went back to the cab, and the driver said, 'What's the matter, couldn't you make out?'

We said, 'No, those are our wives.'

He said, 'Your what!'

He couldn't understand what was going on. I laughed about that ever since.

The highlight of my career would be that entire 1950 season. All of these people made all of these derogatory comments about us, and we start out by beating the Eagles and then win the championship game the way we did it.

THAT WAS THE GOOD OLD DAYS. Then, the fans got so used to winning that when we finally lost a few, they got madder than hell. Of course, we never lost that many. We won so much that it was one of the factors in the All-American Conference folding. No one wants to see a team run away with it. They want to see close games and excitement. That's true anyplace. We won 115, I think, lost 20, and tied four. We were in ten straight championship games and won seven of them. That'll never happen again. There's too many good teams now.

The first four or five years we played, I called most of the plays. Now, when I say, 'I called the plays,' I didn't call the plays; my teammates called the plays for me. The quarterback should not get the credit for calling a brilliant game. It's a team effort. Dub Jones would come back and say, 'I can beat this guy deep'; or, 'I can run the sideline pattern.' Someone would say, 'This guy can be trapped.' Most of the calls were made that way, especially in the passing game.

It was probably the year after we went in the NFL that Paul Brown started to call all the plays. Paul was the type of person who wanted to be involved in everything that had anything to do with the Browns: offense, defense, and everything else. I think he realized that as soon as I came off the field, I'd get on the phone and talk to Blanton Collier. Blanton had a brilliant mind, and he'd give me his thoughts on what was going on. Very frankly, I think Paul realized that he was being left out, to some degree, and that went against his nature. He doesn't want to be out of the loop on anything. Almost over night, he told me that never again was I to talk to Blanton Collier during a ball game. Period. Just like that. In my opinion, that's what caused the change.

When Paul switched over and began sending the plays in, I didn't agree with it at all, frankly. His theory was that you talk to the players when they come out of the game, you talk to Blanton Collier, who's up high, to get his ideas, then you coordinate all this information and send the plays in. That sounds good, but by the time you coordinate all the information, you're about two plays behind. It didn't make sense, but I couldn't say much. You had to use the plays. His guesses were as good as mine, but mine were better, I felt, because I'm getting them from the guys who are on the field.

Personally, it made no difference to me who called the plays. These old movies you see where the quarterback is in the huddle and looks over the defense and gets a brilliant idea and calls the play that goes for a touchdown are a bunch of bull. I had no idea what the damn defense was going to be in the first place. You know the tendencies for this hash mark and this yard line and all that, but if they change, I have to change, too.

The year Dub Jones scored six touchdowns against the Bears, I changed the play. We knew he needed one more touchdown to tie the record. We're out there, and in comes a play. Abe Gibron said, 'Fuck Paul Brown. Call your own goddamn play.' I called a deep pattern and hit Dub for the sixth touchdown. It was a touchdown, so Paul couldn't say anything. If I had missed that thing, I would probably have gotten chewed out pretty good. You didn't want to cross him too often, that's for sure.

WE DIDN'T HAVE ANY AUDIBLE SYSTEM at all. To a certain degree, I felt that not having one hurt us. Paul Brown's theory that the noise—people screaming and yelling—while you're up there on the line of scrimmage would stop everyone from getting the change, and the play would get all botched up, and he didn't want that to happen. I disagreed, and I told him so. If an end run to the right is called, and I look out there and see eight guys waiting for it, I think it would be smarter to go to the right. And our execution of the plays that were called, very frankly, was so good that we weren't hurt as much as we could have been. We might have the wrong play, but we had the right people running it. He got used to that, so he wasn't as concerned with an audible system as he might have been. I didn't agree with him then, and I don't agree with him now.

Abe and those guys were always telling me to run my own plays. Abe Gibron was a good football player. Back when the goal post was on the goal line, we had the ball down on the one yard line. The play was sent in to go off tackle. We get up to the line, and the goal post is right next to the center. Obviously, the defensive man can't get there. Abe is down in his stance, and he's whispering in this real funny high voice: 'Ot-to. Ot-to. Ot-to.' He wants me to run a sneak through that gap, but I started laughing. Finally, I just stepped across the line for the touchdown.

Those guys were great competitors, and the one thing about our team was that we didn't care who got the credit. We were a team. I try to emphasize that to kids when I talk to them: The most important thing is to be part of the team. You learn that very fast in sports. It doesn't matter if you're black or if you're white, Protestant, Catholic, Jewish. That's all very unimportant. What kind of job you're doing is what matters. I couldn't care less whether my teammates were blue or green or black, as long as they were doing a job. Jackie Robinson gets all the credit for being the first black to participate in professional sports, but it wasn't Jackie Robinson; it was Marion Motley and Bill Willis.

I played nine years. We won every year. I wanted to quit on top. I saw Joe Louis. He had been a great boxer. His name was tops. But they stole his money, and he had to go out and box when he was over the hill. His name diminished from what it had been. Businesswise, I thought it would be a good decision to quit when I was an outstanding football player instead of being just a half-assed football player.

My kids were getting older. Plus, I was tired of the playbooks and the routine. Every year, it became harder to do it. I didn't enjoy the feeling of getting up for games. I used to say, 'It doesn't bother me until Sunday morning when I wake up.'

My wife said, 'You might not think so, but it bothers you long before that.' She said that every day, I got a little bit worse. She could see it, and I couldn't.

I'd wake up Sunday mornings, and my stomach would be turning over and over and over. I'd be going to the bathroom every five minutes. The pregame meal was always steak with no ketchup, baked potato with no butter, salad with no dressing. I'd take two or three bites of it. I couldn't eat that dry stuff. My meal the day of the game was two or three oranges and two or three Hershey bars. That's all I needed. Then after the game, all I wanted was a big thick chocolate milk shake. That always tasted so good to me.

So I decided I was going to quit. I told him after the championship game in '54 that I was going to retire. We killed Detroit 56-14, and I played real well, and I thought that was enough.

But I said to him, 'Paul, if a quarterback breaks his leg, and you're in trouble, I'll come back. Otherwise, I'm not going to.'

He still wanted me to come back, but I wouldn't. The quarterback he had signed from Auburn (Bobby Franklin) had signed a contract in Canada and with the Browns. Well, the Canadian League took it to court, and they won out. That was just as good as a broken leg.

Just before he went out to the West Coast, he came to me, and I said, 'Paul, I want to quit when I'm on top. That's going to be a lot of hard work. I don't think I want to go through that any more.'

Later, I realized he went out to the West Coast and didn't really even try to find a quarterback. He comes back. He calls me in. Bev comes with me. We're talking to him, and he's asking questions. He asks Bev a question, and she puts her head down and is thinking before she answers.

He says, 'Beverly, when you talk to me, you look me directly in the eye.'

And he says it in a rough, tough voice. It's not, 'Beverly, would you please...' That's how he was

She starts shaking. She was scared to death. He's been dead how many years down, and she's still afraid of him.

So, I came back.

WHEN I CAME BACK, I decided to change my routine. Our first game is with the Washington Redskins, a team I later coached. We go down and stay at a hotel the night before the game, as always. I get up that morning and I think to myself, 'Why the hell should I get so excited? I'm doing these guys a favor. Why should I not enjoy myself?'

I went down to have the pregame meal. I bribe the waiter to bring me ketchup, butter, salad dressing, and I sat there and ate the whole damn thing. I just took my time, not nervous, stomach not jumping, didn't go to the bathroom every five seconds. I went down to the stadium, relaxed, and went out and played the worst damn football game of my life. I was terrible.

The press was very kind: 'Oh, Graham, you know, he just got back. He's not in shape yet.' They made all the excuses they could think of. I thought, 'Bullshit.' Down deep inside I knew there was one thing wrong and it was right up here in my head. My attitude was wrong. I couldn't play without the attitude I had. So, the next game, I'm back going to the bathroom every five seconds, I'm back with the Hershey bars and oranges. I'm ready to play.

It's like being a salesman. I don't care what you're selling, you walk into the office, and you have to have the knowledge about what you're selling and the confidence that you can do a good job. But at the same time, you have to have a little bit of fear that you might not be able to get the job done. If you walk in there with a hundred percent confidence that you're going to get the job before you even do it, you're not going to put out the effort. Football is a game of emotion. You lose that, you don't play as well.

I WAS A GOOD ATHLETE. I was born with coordination. It's a God-given gift, and God's not going to wave a magic wand and turn you from a bad passer into a good one. I could throw the ball hard if I wanted to, but it made more sense to throw it softer. If you see a guy 10 yards down the field, wide open, and you throw a bullet, it bounces off his hands and shoulders. You want to make it soft enough that the ball is catchable, and I always tried to place the ball away from the defender, so that the receiver's body blocked it off. I always tried to throw the deep ball long, so it dropped in to the receiver. If you throw it hard, the defender can still come back and pick it off.

I always threw the ball a little bit sidearm, too. Some coaches tell you, 'Throw the ball right past the ear.' Bull. When you throw the ball that way, the ball always comes in with the point down, so it's much harder to catch. When the ball comes in with the point up, it settles into your hands. It's much easier to catch. I can't tell you how I did it; I just knew that was what I wanted to do.

I wasn't a drunk, and I wasn't chasing women around all the time. I was a good leader, and the players had faith in me. I wasn't the type to say, 'C'mon, you bastards! You're playing lousy!' Norm Van Brocklin was a hell of a quarterback, but he was nasty, swearing at players and everything. I'd get in the huddle and say, 'I need just a little bit more time.' I never chewed anybody out.

Bobby Layne, if a receiver dropped a pass, might yell, 'Goddammit, what's wrong with you!' But after the game, he'd go out and buy you a beer. I think Van Brocklin chewed them out, and that was it. I never chewed anybody out because I knew damn well that they were trying as hard as I was.

Paul took me out of the championship game in '55, to let me get an ovation from the crowd, which was a nice thing to do. It shows he had a heart, too. After he did that, I told him, 'Thanks, but this year, there's no ifs, ands, or buts. I'm not coming back.'

He said, 'I respect that. Thank you, Otto.'

AFTER ME, PAUL HAD TOMMY O'CONNELL, who helped me coach the All-Star Game. We had playbooks, and Tommy left his lying on a chair in the locker room. It was turned over to me. We coaches got together and came up with his punishment. Before practice, we'd always have a meeting to tell them what we were going to do. We'd already established that when somebody did something wrong, we'd give them the whistle drill. Every time the whistle is blown, you had to run in place, or do grass drills or push ups or sit ups, all that kind of stuff.

I said, to the whole squad, 'I've got a problem, and I need my team to help me out with it and tell me exactly what I should do. We have a playbook here. When we handed these out to you, we told you to be very careful with them, because we didn't want Vince Lombardi and the Packers getting a hold of it. That'd be disastrous. This playbook was left out and turned over to me. The playbook belongs to Coach Tommy O'Connell. What should we do?'

They all yelled, 'Whistle drill! Whistle drill! Whistle drill!'

Everyone's screaming like crazy.

We go outside. Everyone's standing in a big circle. Tommy's right in the middle of it. I start giving Tommy the whistle drill, and I was giving it to him pretty good. I said, 'Okay,' but they're yelling, 'More! More!'

Then, I said, 'That's enough,' and Tommy said, 'No. Give me more.'

He went ahead and did twice as much stuff as I would have had him do. He almost killed himself. He wouldn't quit. He showed them what work is all about. I say there's no doubt in my mind that that team came together because of Tommy O'Connell, and we won that ball game.

We went out, and those guys hustled all the way, and we beat them. I still marvel at that.

About three years later, I went to the Coast Guard Academy. I had never planned to go into coaching. I had the insurance business, and I just wanted to make that go. My wife and I took the train to see what it was all about. We spent a couple of days there. I spent my time with the coaches, with the teachers, with the students. My wife spent her time riding around with the admiral's wife, looking at the countryside. She was not impressed. The area was kind of crowded, and the homes were not that beautiful. We get on the train to go back home, and her first words were, 'Thank god we'll never see this place again.'

I turned around and said, 'Bev, I liked it.'

She almost died.

After we went, of course, we were very happy.

When we first started playing, we didn't have television. I didn't even realize how many stations were carrying our games until I went up to the Coast Guard Academy as head coach and athletic director, and people told me they used to watch our games up there. They were all Browns fans. I had no idea.

Division III doesn't have the pressure you have in Division I. I was dealing with high-class kids. Those kids were all intelligent. They had to be, because the entrance exams were so tough. They didn't go there to be football players. They came there to be Coast Guard officers. You find out that your athletes make your best officers, anyway.

We didn't have scholarships at the Coast Guard Academy. We had some good athletes, a couple of guys who could throw the ball, but a lot of kids didn't have the coordination. If we got a lineman that weighed two hundred pounds, we'd go out and get drunk, and I don't even drink. They didn't know the first thing about pass patterns. After the first couple of weeks, I started to wonder if I'd made the right choice. God almighty, they were so bad.

I enjoyed teaching it from scratch, almost. You get so much personal satisfaction out of developing these kids who really are not that good. We had the only undefeated, untied season they ever had there. We learned how to play smart football. I thoroughly enjoyed my experience there.

MONEY GOT ME TO WASHINGTON, frankly. They offered me such a high amount of money that I couldn't turn it down. My wife said, 'You should go, because if you don't, you'll be asking yourself all you life, "Should I have gone down there or not." Do it and get it over with.'

I found out that you can't go around kissing people's butts all the time. Sometimes, you have to get tough with them. When I was coaching the Redskins, my assistant coaches told me, 'You're not really a good head coach, because you're not tough on these guys. You're too nice a guy to be a coach.'

Later on, after they fired me, I realized they were telling the truth. I was too nice a guy. In pro football, it's win or else. I was playing in a golf tournament in the off-season, and I read in the paper I was fired. I had a hunch it was coming. But I read it in the paper. That's how they told me. Pro sports is a rough business. That was the best thing that ever happened to me. I didn't think so at the time, obviously.

You have to be an SOB. There's no question about it. You have to be as tough as Paul Brown, if not tougher. That just wasn't my personality. The whole thing wasn't my cup of tea.

When I went into coaching, I really began to appreciate what Paul Brown had to go through. As years went by, I found myself doing and saying the same things that he would do and say that used to get me so damned upset. When I took over as the coach of the College All-Stars, I told them I would not do it unless they did away with the popularity contest they used to have to pick the team. I wanted it to be handpicked, by me, period, which is the way Paul Brown would have done it. I would talk to the scouts and find out who the best players were. In Division I, All-Americans are made by the publicity departments. Period. They start at the beginning of the year publicizing their heroes. Out of a hundred guys who are voting, maybe two or three have seen the guys they are voting on play. All they do is go by what they read in the papers. I refused to do it that way. The fans don't know who the good players are.

WHEN THEY ASKED ME to become the head coach of the College All-Stars, I had never coached. I said, 'I'll come and help out as an assistant coach, then after that year, I can tell you whether or not I want to coach.' I went as an assistant, and, quite honestly, I had never seen anything so terrible in my life. These were pro coaches, but after being with Paul Brown, there didn't seem to be any organization at all. We'd go to practice, and the assistant coaches had never met with the head coach to talk about what we were going to do that day. After that three weeks, I knew I could do better, and I knew why Paul Brown won. He was so much better organized. Organization was the key. He hired top-notch people, and they were loyal, or they were gone. It was a business with him.

If I had been like Paul Brown, and my personnel had been like his, I'd still be coaching. I was too immature. I didn't realize the kind of person you had to be. You have to be a dictator. You have to know when to be nice and when to be tough, and I didn't know that much about it at that time. I was too nice a guy. That's why coaching at the Coast Guard Academy was perfect for me. When you lose a game, you're not worried about getting fired.

The local press was tough. The sports editor of one of the local papers was always writing these columns like an expert, and in the three years I was there, I think he came to practice once. I got a lesson about sports writers from those guys. All those guys wanted was the headlines.

Professional football fans are not nearly as loyal as college football fans. There's a lot of good ones, of course, but I wouldn't give you two cents for the average professional fan these days. If I had my way, they would never sell liquor of any kind at any professional football game. Nice people get half drunk and turn into animals in the stands. That always bothered me.

It's like that Dawg Pound in the end zone. I think that's one of the sad things about it all. If I had been the top man, I would've given orders that said, 'Anyone who gets out of hand and is caught throwing things on the field, please escort them out, get their name and address, and they'll never be permitted to buy another ticket.' They were throwing flashlight batteries on the field. You could hit a guy in the eye and put his eye out. That was terrible.

There are good fans who sit in the Dawg Pound, too; don't get me wrong. It's just that in football, you get doctors and lawyers and otherwise outstanding people, and they get in those stands and maybe they have a few drinks because it's a little cold, and all of a sudden, they become animals.

Obviously, it's not going to happen, but I wouldn't go back into coaching professional football if they walked in and offered me $5 million. It ain't worth it.

After they fired me, I went back to the Coast Guard Academy as athletic director, then the coach quit, and I coached for a couple of years again.

I should be more active than I am. I play very little golf anymore. My golf game went south. I was a good golfer at one time, and I can't tolerate going out and shanking shots. I can't tolerate playing poorly. That's just my nature. When you get older, you're not competitive anymore.

My wife tells me, 'Go out and practice more.'

I say, 'Yeah, I know.'

I STILL DO SOME SPEAKING, but not too often. I'm living comfortably. I had cancer back umpteen years ago when I was at the Coast Guard. It was life-threatening, so I got a hundred percent disability.

All I know about the Browns anymore is what I read in the papers. Art Modell is like a Dr. Jekyll and Mr. Hyde. One side of him is really great, and the other side of him is just the opposite. If you'd meet him socially, you'd love the guy. It's a shame what he did to Cleveland. We're better of without guys like him.

I first didn't like Modell when I heard that he had fired Paul Brown. It surprised the hell out of me. The reason for it was obvious: only one guy can be the top man, and here's a case of both men wanting to run the show. With Modell being the owner, he was going to run the show, and Paul Brown was going to go.

There's nothing worse than someone who buys a new business and knows very little about it and all of sudden, he owns the business and now he knows something about it. It's a strange world we live in.

I won't have anything to do with the new franchise. To tell you the truth, I don't even think about it. I'm very happy they're going to have a team. I think they have the right people running it. You know it's not going to be run the way it was under Modell. Things are looking up. I don't want to sound like I'm callous, but whether they do or not won't affect me. I'm pulling for them, but when you've been out of town all these years, and you don't know the players, you don't have the same feeling.

I go to the Hall of Fame induction most every year. I'll go back this year for the first game the Browns play, and I might go to the first game at home. It's too bad they don't have a domed stadium. To me, when you're out there playing, and it's pouring down rain, and there's ice and snow on the field, it's not the same kind of football. Football wasn't meant to be played in bad weather and on frozen ground. It's no fun playing, and you can't play up to your ability.

The weather was so bad that Cleveland could be hard to play in. There shouldn't be a stadium up north anyplace that doesn't have a dome. This business of playing in the wide-open spaces is ridiculous. It's the same thing with instant replay; it's asinine not to have it.

It's all based on money. The owners don't want to spend the money. To do instant replay right, you need eight cameras: goal-line, 50-yard line, on both sides, and the end zones. The cameras alone would be expensive enough, and then you need the personnel to run them. The owners just won't do it.

Chuck Noll told me he was against it because they didn't want the referees to be embarrassed. If they are, then they won't make the calls. Mike McCormack, who played with me, said he was against it because the guys down on the field are friends with the guys up in the booth, so they don't want to call it. I say just fire them. Get somebody who will make the call. If I was still coaching, I'd be fined thousands of dollars every damn week, because if you miss a chance to go to the Super Bowl because of a bad call, that's terrible.

I DON'T PAY THAT MUCH ATTENTION to the NFL anymore, anyway. I'll glance at it occasionally, but I don't pay that much attention to it. I don't think that the top people are running it the best way it can be run.

Obviously, it's enjoyable, and you're glad you're part of it, but it took all those people to make a good team. How many times in this world do you find that many good people get together to accomplish something?

Even Morrie Kono was a very important factor to our team. His job was to take care of the equipment, but he kept us in stitches. He'd mimic the players, the things they'd do, their emotions, facial expressions, and then he'd put on a little show. He could mimic all of these guys on all of the teams over the years. He'd pretend he was this player and that player. He'd have you dying laughing.

One year, we got these Cleveland Brown tie clasps, for winning the championship. After I was done playing, I was jogging in Baltimore, and I went down some steps, and it flew out of my pocket. I never did find it. Years later, some guy claimed he had it, and he wanted to sell it to me for $1,000. I told him to go to hell. But Morrie Kono gave me his. So, I have one of those tie clasps, but it has Morrie Kono's name on it. That's the kind of guy he was. I didn't hear that he died until after the funeral, or I would have gone to the funeral.

I was at Paul Brown's funeral. I had to go to that one, and I wanted to go to that one. He was such an important man in my life. If it hadn't have been for Paul Brown, who knows what I would have been doing for a living?

I was born into a family of two wonderful people, and I've had a good life. I look back and I see that I could have played for so many other coaches and life would not have been the same. There's no doubt in my mind that if I had played for Detroit, no one would be interested in me today. I feel very fortunate that I played for Paul Brown. 〞

73

# Wargames

FOR SEVEN DAYS, "Hitler's weather" held. Snow clouds hung over the Ardennes like a dirty, wet canopy. As the German dictator had predicted, Allied aircraft could not stop the twenty-one divisions he had ordered to sweep through thin lines of exhausted troops.

When the blitzkrieg erupted, advanced squads of the 28th Infantry Division were shivering in foxholes only miles from the Siegfried Line, the wall of fortifications along Germany's western border. The soldiers had been anticipating Christmas packages from home and, maybe, a rare hot meal. Instead, behind the enemy emplacements, flashes of a thousand artillery pieces and Screaming Meemie rocket launchers bloomed in the dark like deadly, luminous flowers. For an hour and a half, explosions shattered the air and buried the living in debris and blew the dead apart from their souls.

"I didn't know what was going on," said Dante Lavelli, then a 21-year-old private. "I ran back to the company command post in a house, and a guy who was in the battle of St. Lo said, 'Lavelli, go back to your fox hole because they're going to burn this village down.' An hour later, it was burned to the ground. That guy saved my life."

The barrage ended before dawn. German searchlights bounced off the clouds and reflected from the snow. Outnumbered and surprised, the Americans crouched on hillocks, watching the Fifth Panzer Army stream past in the eerie false moon-light. The Nazi shock troops rode in armored half-tracks. They wore gleaming helmets and new green uniforms. Their pockets were stuffed with Norwegian salt cod. They looked as if they were on their way to some insane picnic, evil on holiday.

"They kept coming and coming," Lavelli said. "I said 'Our Father' over and over for three days."

Ordered to withdraw, Lavelli's squad walked backward at night and hid in the forest during the day. They passed the blasted remains of two regiments slaughtered before they could leave their transport trucks. They passed Malmedy, where the Germans shot scores of American prisoners. They fell back, straining to hear tank treads clinking on the frozen road behind them.

"We hadn't eaten for two or three days, and everybody got dysentery. Guys could hardly walk. It was unbelievable," Lavelli said.

On the seventh day, the clouds lifted, and the sky became a sheet of undulating steel, as if the torn and seared earth had grown a skin of armor. The P-47 Lightnings dove in shrieking waves, dropping napalm and fragmentation bombs, strafing. Storm troopers huddled in ditches. Hurled into the air, German tanks crashed onto their turrets, their treads still churning.

The counterattacked repulsed the Nazis, but not before nearly 200,000 men were killed, wounded, or captured. "My squad, in my platoon, was the only one that got out of the Battle of the Bulge intact. When I look back, I can't believe how lucky I was," Lavelli says.

Back home in Hudson, Ohio, Lavelli had two seasons of eligibility left on a scholarship at Ohio State University, but the year under fire had turned college football into a fading memory of a lost youth. "We'd all seen a lot. It matured us," he said.

Paul Brown had begun assembling his first team in the new All-American Football Conference. With a free hand to spend owner Arthur "Mickey" McBride's money, Brown had signed and paid monthly stipends to some players while they were still in the service. He had made no such attempt to woo Lavelli, but the former Ohio State coach remembered the promising sophomore end whose college experience had been limited by a knee injury to three games.

Brown dispatched an aide with an offer of a bonus. Broke, eager to gain a foothold in the society he had fought to save, Lavelli signed with the Browns. "The money at that time seemed like a million dollars," he says.

Lavelli arrived at his first training camp with little more than a duffel bag and a set of fatigues. The gear would prove appropriate. "Everybody that came out of the service was hungry," he said. "There were no jobs after the war. The toughest game I ever played in was the first intersquad scrimmage game. Nobody talked to each other for two days."

In the Browns, Lavelli found an organization that demanded as much discipline as the 28th Infantry. "We had to run on the field lined up in a certain way and hit the white line with the left foot. It was like the army," he says.

Slight and without combat experience, Brown commanded—and often intimidated—even veterans of savage fighting. The handpicked cadre of his first pro team included Jim Daniell, recipient of the Silver

Star for heroism; Lou Groza, who served with a frontline medical unit; and Lavelli, a member of the "Bloody Bucket Division," so-called by the Germans for the fury of its attacks.

Brown had come no nearer the horrors of war than learning that two of his former Massillon High School players had been killed in action. At Ohio State, he had argued on the grounds of providing entertainment for troops that college football should continue in spite of the manpower needs of the armed services.

The 1942 football season opened with the Buckeyes confronting their toughest schedule ever and the Wehrmacht besieging Stalingrad. It ended with American troops storming Guadalcanal and Ohio State winning the national championship with a team "great by all the chills down Hitler's spine," as a columnist put it.

At the squad's final practice that year, Brown told his seniors, "The game you're going into they play for keeps, with killing and dying, and risk to your very lives, but I want you to play it the same way you played football here—with courage, unafraid."

He added, "I never want to hear of any of you committing suicide because the going got too rough. I'd be ashamed of that."

After the call-up of ROTC students, including Lavelli, Brown spent one more season at OSU, warning fans that "the clear-cut precision of play will be missing." He joined the Navy, but unlike a future OSU coach, Woody Hayes, Brown didn't demand sea duty. In fact, athletic director Lynn St. John arranged to have him assigned to Great Lakes where he became "athletic officer" and a football coach.

Brown's lukewarm enthusiasm for the military seems not to have been a case of malingering or blindness to the threat against his country. Rather, he apparently considered the war—as he did so much that happened away from the football field— only in so far as it affected his "fierce desire to be the best in the business."

Accordingly, he used his time at Great Lakes to evaluate and recruit such future stars as Otto Graham, Marion Motley, and Mac Speedie.

Brown was praised for ordering his players not to slurp their soup at meals, not to smoke or drink in public, and not to have sex after Wednesdays during game weeks. He dominated the team without shouting or using what he called "mule-skinner language."

"He'd give you that beady-eyed look, and everyone knew you'd screwed up," Lavelli says.

Brown also kept his men in line through painstaking organization, knowledge of the game, and economic coercion. After beating out

four more experienced players, Lavelli caught all forty passes thrown to him in 1946. He tied for the AAFC receiving lead, scored the winning touchdown in the championship game, and earned the nickname "Gluefingers." By the following year, he and Speedie had formed the most productive receiving combination in football.

During the 1948 preseason, Lavelli fractured a tibia. A week later, his leg in a cast, he was taking calisthenics and jogging. He caught two touchdowns in the eighth game of the season and went on to help Brown to his first unbeaten record since Massillon High School.

"Amazing fellow that Lavelli," the coach said. "Amazing the way he catches passes. Amazing the way he recovered from that broken leg."

Expecting a raise for his courageous All-League performance, Lavelli had his salary cut for what Brown judged inadequate blocking.

Brown was zealously determined to prove "that the same ideals that won in high school and college could win in professional football." Early in his career, he had exactly the kind of player to demonstrate such a principle—one wholly committed to the mission. Lavelli, for example, simply resolved to become a better blocker.

"Everyone wanted to forget about being overseas," he says. "To us, pro football was fun.

There was no drudgery."

In 1950, "the most expensive war in sports history" ended when Cleveland and two other AAFC teams joined the NFL. In what amounted to the first Super Bowl, commissioner Bert Bell matched Cleveland, the only team to have won an AAFC title, and two-time NFL champion Philadelphia in the season opener. The Associated Press called the contest "the most talked-of game in the National Football League's history."

"The high school kids are coming to play in the pros," Eagle coach Earle "Greasy" Neale smirked.

"The last time I looked, we had ends who could catch and a guy who could throw," Brown said.

Neale planned to control the ball with his running game and throttle the Browns' offense with his "Suicide Seven" defensive front, which hadn't allowed a point in the last two title games. However, Neale was confronted with an offense that little resembled the hedgerow-to-hedgerow ground attack employed by NFL teams.

Sending halfbacks Rex Bumgardner and Dub Jones in motion, Brown attacked over a broad front, forcing the Eagles into single coverage. "No defensive back alive can cover Lavelli, Jones, or Speedie man for man," he said after all three players had caught touchdowns in

Cleveland's overwhelming victory.

"Jeez, they got a lotta guns, a lotta guns," Neale said.

"The Eagles have been noted for their pass defense, but even their fastest men were outrun, outmaneuvered and outreached by the Cleveland phenomenons," said a *New York Times*' writer. "Who will stop the Browns? I dunno. Their conqueror is yet in sight."

The supposedly higher level of competition affected neither the Browns nor Lavelli. Cleveland went 10-2 during the regular season, and Lavelli became one of the league's top pass-catchers.

"Lavelli wanted to win in the worst way," guard Lin Houston said. "The tougher it got, the tougher he got."

Fiery and impatient, Lavelli, who calls himself "the originator of the broken pass pattern," frequently ignored Brown's carefully designed routes and simply raced for any open space. Occasionally, he would hook a goal post with his arm, whirl around it, and appear uncovered in a corner of the end zone, waving and shouting in his high-pitched voice, "Otts! Otts! Otts!" to attract the attention of quarterback Otto Graham.

Such wild freelancing maddened Brown and drove Graham to the sideline, muttering, "Did you see what that crazy Spumoni did?" But Graham also said that if he had to complete one pass to any receiver in history, he would throw to Lavelli.

"He'd go up biting, scratching, doing anything to get the football," Graham said.

With uncharacteristic rhapsody, Brown described Lavelli's hands has having "an almost liquid softness which seemed to slurp the ball into them."

Lavelli also played with infinite confidence.

"He felt he could beat anyone anytime," said longtime Cleveland coach Blanton Collier.

On a frozen Christmas Eve in 1950, Lavelli did beat everyone. The Browns met the Los Angeles Rams, the franchise the Browns had driven out of Cleveland four years earlier, for the NFL championship. In his team's three-point victory, Lavelli set a championship game record with eleven catches and scored twice. After the win, fans pounded on the locker room door and chanted "We want the Browns!" and Brown was so thrilled that he couldn't remember the score.

In the next five seasons, Lavelli caught thirteen more passes in title games, establishing another league mark. He made All-Pro twice and played in three Pro Bowls.

The Browns, however, lost three consecutive championship games, including two straight to the Detroit Lions. As Cleveland prepared for the 1954 title game, Lion coach Buddy Parker had beaten Brown eight straight times.

"Every time we seemed to get a lead on Detroit by six or seven points in those days, Paul would put the clamps on us," Lavelli said. "He'd stop attacking and try to let the defense win for us."

The players of Lavelli's generation accepted authority, but they also believed in winning. Determined not to lose to Detroit again, the Browns' offense met early in the morning of the championship game to consider mutiny.

"It was about 2 a.m. We decided if we didn't think Paul's plays were right, we were going to call our own," Lavelli said.

No rebellion was necessary. The Browns annihilated the Lions, 56-10. Even so, for twenty-five years, no one dared tell Brown about the plot, Lavelli says.

When Cleveland defeated Los Angeles in the 1955 title game, Lavelli averaged over thirty yards a catch and scored. He followed Graham, who had thrown every one of Lavelli's 366 career receptions, into retirement.

Teammates convinced him to return for an eleventh season, but after catching twenty more balls in 1956, he quit for good when Cleveland drafted Jim Brown, a choice, Lavelli realized, that signaled the end of the team's emphasis on passing.

Disagreements over money and strategy aside, Lavelli and Paul Brown had enjoyed a productive association. At Ohio State, Brown transformed Lavelli from an uncertain, loose-limbed halfback into a receiver; later, he developed the post pattern specifically for Lavelli. Working after practice with Graham, Jones, and Speedie, Lavelli helped to create the modern passing attack for which Brown is often credited.

When Lavelli was inducted into the Hall of Fame in 1975, Brown paused from preparing the Cincinnati Bengals for the game that day to present him. "Dante was a handsome, unassuming man. I always said he was as good from within as he looked on the outside," Brown said.

"He was like a second father," Lavelli said.

As he talked, Lavelli fidgeted in a swivel chair behind a scarred metal desk in his cramped furniture store. Lavelli's Furniture occupies one corner of a small rundown strip mall along a bustling thoroughfare of fast food joints, glass and concrete banks, and gleaming steel office complexes in a Cleveland suburb.

A Browns helmet, the number "86," and "Dante" have been painted large on the outside of the building. The license plate on a Cadillac parked near the door read "Mr. Glue."

Invoices and bills of lading cluttered Lavelli's desk. Duct tape held plastic sheeting over windows and ceiling vents. Amid the easy chairs and love seats and vanities hung Cleveland Brown clocks and autographed photos of athletes, coaches, and politicians. On the wall behind the desk were a picture of Lavelli and Brown at the Hall of Fame and a framed, yellowed newspaper story headlined, "They Still Love the Legend of Lavelli."

He has operated the furniture business for more than forty years, through tries at coaching, scouting, sports casting, and real estate. Except for the two weeks he spends playing golf in Florida each winter, Lavelli works every day as "driver, delivery man, and window washer."

"Playing helps you a little bit with business," he says, "but when it comes down to dollars and cents, you can be Audie Murphy or Bing Crosby. It doesn't mean a thing."

Aside from his Ohio State national championship watch and NFL Hall of Fame ring, he looked like a pleasant New England shopkeeper. He wore a gray wool herringbone jacket, tan corduroy trousers, a plaid flannel shirt buttoned at the collar, suspenders, and ankle-high boots. Bifocals hung from a chain around his neck. His silver hair was thick. Still uncommonly handsome, he seemed as vigorous as a man twenty years younger. He can still break eighty, he says, still watches as many as four pro games on Sundays, still makes numerous public appearances.

When Lavelli becomes agitated—as he does about the scant pensions players of his era receive, the league's refusal to recognize Cleveland's accomplishments in the AAFC, or Speedie's absence from the Hall of Fame—he gestures. The hands he inherited from his father, an immigrant blacksmith, and which made him famous are large, the fingers long and manicured.

Although the war remains the defining moment of his life, nothing perturbs Lavelli more than Art Modell's decision to abandon Cleveland. For Lavelli, the move to Baltimore was a personal affront and an insult to tradition. He called the NFL and raged at an assistant in the commissioner's office. He attempted to organize fan boycotts. He ridiculed Modell to the media. Finally, to prevent a second heart attack and avoid legal action, he stopped even mentioning the owner's name.

"My feeling is he took the original Browns and promoted them to advance his own situation," he said. "He rode on Paul Brown's coattails for thirty years."

At times, Lavelli would suddenly stop talking and briefly stare at something only he could see, as if at some distant battlefield or long-ago ball game. At those moments, he seemed less robust, but after hours of reminiscing, answering phones, dealing with customers, and greeting fans, he leaped to his feet, pulled on a tweed slouch hat and heavy leather work gloves, and called for his assistant.

It was a chilly evening four days past Christmas, two months before Lavelli's 75th birthday, fifty-three years after the Battle of the Bulge. A truck had delivered a shipment of beanbag chairs for a New Year's sale.

Someone had to unload the merchandise. Someone had to clear the floor space. Someone had to set up the display.

If Dante Lavelli didn't do it, who would?

# *Dante* LAVELLI

**"** MY DAD WAS A BLACKSMITH. We lived in this little town of Hudson, Ohio, and he shod all the horses for the farmers there. That's how he started making his living in this country. After the horses went out, he fixed things for people and made ornamental ironworks—lamps, railings. There were only four other Italian kids in school, and there were only thirty-two kids in my graduating class. It was a very small town.

In high school, we had thirteen kids on the football team; basketball had ten; no size, nothing. I walked three miles to where a guy had a basketball rim on the outside of his garage. There were cinders on the driveway. During winter vacation, I put a brick in the window of the cafeteria to keep it open so I could get in the school and shoot baskets. I'd shoot eight hours a day. I played football, basketball, and baseball, and I caddied at the golf course in town.

I had a scholarship to Notre Dame, but what happened was in the wintertime, all the Ohio high school coaches pushed to get Paul Brown down in Columbus. When he signed to coach at Ohio State, everybody wanted to go play for him. They gave me a scholarship there, so I went.

What really made Brown was his high school teams. When we were freshmen, ten out of his eleven guys at Massillon made All-Ohio, and all ten of those guys went to Columbus. Going to see Massillon play was a big thing. They used to play Alliance and Canton McKinley in the Rubber Bowl, and there'd be 40,000 people. You could never get a ticket to the Canton-Massillon game.

I was very lucky at Ohio State. I was a quarterback in high school, but Brown never threw the ball. I was a halfback my freshman year. What happened was we were playing a touch-tackle game before practice in the middle of my freshman year, and I was catching everything. Those guys couldn't stop me. Horace Gillom had been a king in high school, and he couldn't come close to me. Brown saw it, and switched me to end. He still would never throw the ball, though.

Freshmen weren't eligible then, so I only played the one year, my sophomore year. We won a national championship. I have the watch on right now. Nineteen forty-two. We have a reunion every four years now. Fifty-five years ago, we won it, twenty-five guys still living.

I got hurt that year. I was going in to score just before the half against Southern Cal. I caught a shoestring catch I should never have caught. A guy grabbed my ankle, and he twisted one way while I was going the other way. The worst injury I ever got. It doesn't bother me, but I still have a bone out of whack. The guy just twisted me. Took me about three and a half weeks to get well again. I only played four games that year. I made my letter, though.

If you did what Paul Brown wanted you to do, you had no trouble with him. If you were never late to meetings, if you didn't make a mental error. A physical error, he didn't care, but if you made a mental error, that was it, because you should know your plays. He wanted you to be places five minutes ahead of time. You had to be dressed right. You hear a lot of things about Paul Brown, but he helped sixty-six guys get coaching jobs. That's how he was. He helped everybody. He got Don Shula the job, he got Chuck Noll the job, Weeb Ewbank, Walt Michaels.

A LOT OF US WERE IN ROTC, and at one time, if you were in ROTC, you thought you'd be able to stay in school. But they needed more recruits, and our whole team went someplace. Brown went to Great Lakes. We went to Texas. I tried to get in the ski troopers, but the battle for Italy had just got over, so they didn't need any more ski troopers. I ended up in the infantry. I was in the Pennsylvania Division, the 28th Infantry Division. I went in to Normandy by landing craft on D-Day plus 20. We went from a big boat, over the side on a rope ladder. From the rope ladder, you jumped into a landing craft. Then they pushed you up on the beach and dropped the gate down.

The front was inland about twenty-six miles by the time we got in there. The paratroops are the guys who really got cut up. They had no chance at all when they jumped onto Omaha Beach. Ninety percent of the 82nd and 101st Airborne were wiped out before D-Day, because they fell in behind the lines on electric wires and trees and things.

I was at Bastogne and the Battle of the Bulge. I was right in the middle of the Siegfried Line. They assembled us and put us in trucks. They drove you up to about two or three miles from the front, until you could hear the small arms fire. When you could hear the small arms fire, you got out of your truck and walked into your foxhole.

During the Bulge, they pushed us back to Bastogne. All we did was keep walking back, walking back. Nighttime, you walked back, and in the daytime, you stayed in the tree clusters so nobody would see you.

What happened was the Germans had Bastogne seventy-five per cent engulfed. We had to keep the main road open, for supplies. The Germans had this guy called 'Bed Check Charlie.' Every night at 10 o'clock, he'd come by and fire at you. That's how he got the name 'Bed Check Charlie.'

They pushed us back so fast that they were all the way back to the cooks and the medics, and we stayed in our holes. We could see them going past in halftracks, day and night. Brand new green uniforms. They had been in Norway, and they had dried fish to eat stuck in their pockets. When you fired an M-1 in cold weather, it left a muzzle blast, smoke, and the Germans would zero in on us. So our guys didn't shoot. We'd see them go by, go by.

I went back to the command post the first morning. We had captured about fourteen prisoners. They had all our Christmas cookies and stuff there. All the Christmas stuff was coming in. And I took the packages back and threw them to the next foxholes.

THE SHELLS HIT AND THE DIRT from the sides of the foxhole would come into the hole up to my neck. What happened was that the trajectory of the German artillery was over us. We were underneath. They couldn't get it up high enough to hit us. Our CP was in an old stone firehall, and the German fire leveled the whole town. Our staff sergeant had been in the Battle of St. Lo, where the Americans bombed the Americans on account of the wind blew the smoke signals away. This guy told us, 'You get back in your holes, because the Germans are going to come and burn this town down.' Three days later, the guy was right. I went back to my hole and stayed there for three days. The guy saved my life.

About 2 o'clock in the morning on the third day, a runner came down to my foxhole and said, 'We're leavin'.' I got the rest of our guys assembled, and we walked and walked. I don't even know how far we walked. We walked to the Hurtgen Forest and stayed there, and they reassigned us to another regiment.

They pushed us back to Nancy, France, and we reorganized. My squad in my platoon was the only one that got out of the Battle of the Bulge intact. The 106th Infantry was coming up to the front to relieve us. There are three regiments in a division, and two of the 106th Infantry regiments got killed right in the trucks. There was one regiment left. It was the worst defeat for the American army. We walked by them after they pushed us back. They were still in the trucks.

Some guy just brought me a great book. I think it's called *Bloody Aachen*. Aachen, Germany, was the first big city that the Americans captured. It was about the size of Akron, Ohio. They leveled it. I was walking up to the front, and there was no roadway or anything. They had to take a bulldozer down the main street to clear it out so that guys could walk. The street was filled with cement and junk. They just leveled all the buildings.

Boy, I'll tell you, when I look back and see how lucky I was: snow, wintertime, dark, no food. We were walking along the road and a lot of replacements came in. They had a chocolate candy bar that would take the place of a whole meal. They wouldn't give them to us, so we took them. We hadn't eaten for two or three days, and everybody got dysentery. Guys could hardly walk. It was unbelievable.

THE SKIES WERE ALL CLOUDY and they couldn't fly the bombers from the day of the Bulge (December 16) until December 23, and on December 23, it opened up like a big circle, and here comes 2,000 American planes, all shiny up there. We saw that silver, boy, we were all laughing and clapping and jumping. You could hear that drone—*ggggrrrrrr*. It went on for two hours. One hour would be 1,000 planes, two hours, 2,000 planes. And all silver, the sky was all silver. They were on their way in to bomb Germany. Guess what, Tom Landry was a pilot in one of those planes.

That's when they started to push the Germans back. You'd get 200 prisoners at one time. They had used up all their food supplies. The air corps took care of the German tanks. I saw German tanks on their backs, the tracks still going. They'd bomb them and flop them over on the road.

Paul Brown told us when we came back, 'Football's easy compared to what you guys have been through.'

I was in combat for a year. After that, we were in the army of occupa-tion for two or three months. I took care of the city of Mainz, on the Rhine River. After the Germans gave up, everyone had to be off the streets by 8 o'clock. If they were on the streets, we'd grab them and pull them up on the truck, take the truck down to the city jail, and throw the people in there.

I was in the service thirty-five months. I was overseas a year and a half. I was going to play professional baseball when I came back. Brown sent Fritz Heisler to my house to see if I wanted to play pro football. The money at that time—500 bucks—looked like a million dollars. That's what we got to sign, 500 bucks. Nobody had anything, except a green duffel bag. Our first training camp, guys went by bus, by train, and hitchhiked. That's how the players got there, to Bowling Green.

I really wasn't confident about making the team, but what made me confident that I could play was when I got off the boat in New York from overseas, if you had your uniform on, you could go to Giant or Yankee stadium for free. I went to a Giants and Green Bay game. They were play-ing in the Polo Grounds. And a guy who was behind me at Ohio State, guy named Sam Fox, he was on the third team at Ohio State. When I saw his name down there in the program, I said, 'Wow! Sam Fox.' That gave me confidence that I could play ball somewhere. So when Fritz Heisler came to see me in Hudson, I said, 'Yeah, I'm gonna take a chance.'

IF YOU SIGNED WITH THE CLEVELAND BROWNS, he wanted you to go back to Ohio State and finish your degree. I went back to school in January of '45. I got out of service in December and went to school in January. I went back, and they put me up for King of the Campus. The girl who married Howard Hughes, Jean Peters, was Queen of the Campus. I hated dancing, so I wasn't going to go to the dance. Finally, about 3 p.m. on the day of the dance, I called her and told her, 'I'll come over and pick you up.' I never got to see her after that.

We had about eight guys from Ohio State who had signed up with the Cleveland Browns, and so in the spring, we worked out down in Colum-bus. Man, we were in really good shape, because we knew what Brown was like. He used to send you a letter that said, 'You got to start running. You show up in shape, not out of shape.'

Everybody that came out of the service was hungry. There were no jobs after the war. If you didn't make the pro team, you usually went back to your hometown and ended up teaching. The toughest game I ever played was the first inter-squad scrimmage game. Nobody talked to each other for two days.

For three years, I never had a day off. I went to school, went to Bowling Green, went back to school in the wintertime. I finished in the springtime, and Lou Groza and I drove from Columbus, Ohio, to New York to watch his brother, Alex, play in the championship tournament for Kentucky in Madison Square Garden.

My first year, I played defense, too, but my second year, you could have unlimited substitution. My first year, you could only substitute one player at a time. After they changed, we went to thirty-three players. That opened the way for more jobs.

I never heard Paul Brown swear, and he never raised his voice. He'd just look at you with his beady eyes, and you knew you were in trouble. He'd never really insult you in front of the team, maybe just in the meetings, but he'd never let you get close to him. He always kept himself separated from you. Brown never took a shower with us in all the years I played for him. He always went to the hotel or home to take a shower. He had a phobia about that. All the assistant coaches took showers, but he didn't.

Even in practice, you couldn't make a mistake on your plays. 'Execution' was his main word—'execution,' 'execution,' all the time. You only need eight or ten plays. 'Execution with perfection'—that's all you need. The trap play, the off-tackle, the hook passes, the pass over the middle—just work on them until you get them right. We never used many trick plays.

We played in ten straight championships, and before every season, he'd say, 'We're not going to change anything we've been doing. We're going to do the same things.' Maybe that started to work against him after the fifth or sixth year. Then he started to improvise some things.

ONE YEAR, I CAUGHT FORTY FOR FORTY. They only threw me forty passes, and I caught every one of them. Otto was accurate, too. He never threw the ball hard. But with Mac Speedie and me and Dub Jones, they tried to spread the passes around. Everybody wanted to get the ball. It wasn't any fun when you just ran out there and didn't get the ball, especially in practice.

If we threw twenty-five passes, that was a lot of passes. In one game, we didn't throw any passes at all. What happened, that guy in Philadelphia

(Eagle coach Greasy Neale) called him a 'basketball coach,' and Brown got so mad he said, 'We're not going to throw any passes.' We beat the Eagles 14-10.

We wanted to play with the best teams. It was more fun playing the Yankees or the Lions than the Chicago Rockets or the Dallas Texans. Philadelphia was always tough, the New York Giants were always tough, the LA Rams, the 49ers. You really had to gear up to play against them. When you play a tough team, you just can't go to the game on Sunday and say, 'I'll go turn it on.' You have to start like Thursday and start gearing, thinking. I watched a game yesterday, and the Detroit Lions had no idea what it was about. They had no mental concentration.

The game against the Eagles in 1950 was a great game. Everybody was waiting for that. Before that game, we figured we could always throw the ball and get a touchdown. There were so many people that after the game, I walked to the hotel, and I beat the bus back.

I caught two touchdowns in the game. What happened was, that's when the flanker got started. We had to move away so the guys couldn't tackle us at the line of scrimmage, so you'd make the linebacker come out with you, two yards, three yards. We had too much speed. We had two other touchdowns called back in that game.

EVERYBODY RESPECTED PAUL BROWN. Some guys didn't like him while they were playing for him, but you liked him more after you got through playing for him. Most of the high-paid guys—me, Groza and Willis—we were pretty close to him. He sort of looked over us, and he really looked after the Massillon guys—Lin Houston, Tommy James, and Horace Gillom.

In the off-season, we didn't work out, but we played basketball all year around. Now, they pay the players $300-$400 a week to work out in the off-season. That's what it's come to. We'd leave 4 or 5 o'clock, drive from here to Pittsburgh, or Bradford, Pennsylvania, to a prison in Jamestown, New York, all over the place, play and drive back the same day. One year, I put 26,000 miles on my car. You had to work another job, too. I worked at Sears, here at the store. Now, all the quarterbacks have a foundation because it offsets their taxes. But that's the way it goes. You can't look back.

You never negotiated a contract with Paul Brown. It was Paul Brown's way or nothing. That's the way it was. Nobody had a choice. There weren't that many teams in those days. At that time, you didn't say anything.

You just tried to work hard as heck to try and make the least amount of mistakes.

Brown would call you in his office and give you a contract. Mac Speedie went to Canada. Speedie should be in the Hall of Fame, but he won't get in now, because he only played a few years in the NFL. That developed into quite a feud. Brown never liked Speedie after that. In Canada, he made twice what we were making. I almost went, but I decided not to.

Then, you were bound to the team that had your contract. You said, 'Yes sir, no sir.' It was hard to bargain with him, because he'd ship you to Green Bay. Green Bay was a hellhole. They had nothing. They were still playing single-wing football. I remember when I was getting married, I sent the contract back without signing it. I was mad as hell because he didn't give me any money. He called me and wanted to know why I didn't sign it.

I said, 'Why, I want more money.'

I called Speedie. I said, 'What'd he offer you?'

He told me.

I said, 'He offered me the same thing.'

We got him up $2,000. I went to his office and he gave me hell. That's when Otto was retired.

I told him, 'Listen, I can throw the damn football better than George Ratterman. Do what you want to do. Sign me, or I'm going home.'

Otto retired that one year, and I remember, we were in training camp, and Brown asked a couple of the old veterans what he should do. We said to go and ask Otto to come back, and he did. No one could replace Otto. There was such a difference in timing. Ratterman couldn't throw, couldn't run.

I'M REALLY LUCKY I DIDN'T GET HURT that first year. At that time, if you got hurt, they shipped you home. You didn't get a bonus, no money, nothing. You didn't get a chance to wait until you healed up to see if you could make the team. You had no spending money. You used your own money at training camp. In fact, I started the Players Association in my house right over here, in 1956. My last season, I went to the buses after exhibition games and got the players to sign a paper. The Bears wouldn't sign because they were getting $25 a week spending money during training camp. Nobody else was.

Elroy Hirsch (Los Angeles Hall of Fame receiver) worked with me. We'd pass a petition down through the bus, and guys would sign it. I'd get it and Paul Brown wouldn't see me. I'd run on our bus right away. I got the signatures and I got Creighton Miller to be the lawyer. That's why I played an extra year, really, to keep that thing going. I had to get somebody to carry over what I was doing.

We wrote up a charter. I still have a copy. I sent a copy to the Hall of Fame and a copy to the Players Association.

Bill McPeak, a Pittsburgh Steeler end, told Paul Brown that I was one of the guys that started it. He called a special meeting one day. He said, 'Lavelli, did you get the players in Pittsburgh to sign it?'

I said, 'Yeah.'

I thought he was going to can me. He didn't, though.

Finally, the Players Association got to where all the active players joined. It became a solidified group and had some muscle to it. Finally, we got a pension plan. That's why it was really started—to get the pension, not all the other stuff.

You were like a dog then. The Players Association changed everything. You have free agency, you have long-term contracts, you have a bargaining system, you have grievances, insurance. We had nothing. You had to watch so you didn't get hurt. You signed one-year contracts. That's the first thing Paul Brown told you every year, first day of practice: 'None of you guys have the team made, not even if you played last year.'

He hated the Players Association. Paul Brown was the guy who kept the salaries down. We were winning all the championships and never getting any money. But he never worried about money. We always stayed at the best hotels, ate the best food. He always said that he didn't care if there were ten people in the stands, you go out and play to your ability. He was just always very frugal. Brown wouldn't flash his money around. He had an ordinary car. His kids are like that today. I think that came from his upbringing in Massillon, a steel town.

WE HAD TO WRITE OUR PLAYS DOWN. They weren't mimeographed like they are now. We spent two hours every Sunday taking tests. You wrote your assignment out for a five-man line, a six-man line, and a seven-man line. The one year we didn't have substitution, I had to learn three defenses. Some guys got frustrated with it, but they put up with it. They didn't have any choice.

One time, a quarterback turned his book in blank, a guy named Stan

Heath, an All-American quarterback from Nevada-Las Vegas. He came to camp in one of those Chrysler station wagons that had wood on the side.

Paul Brown got so mad he ran up to the second floor, grabbed him, and said, 'Go on home!'

HE HAD NO QUARTERBACK there after Otto. He'd get ahead of Detroit or somebody by seven points, he'd get scared to throw the ball. He'd just sit there and let the defense play. As far as accuracy, Otto was like Terry Bradshaw, Montana, Steve Young, Staubach. I can only remember one time Otto went out of a game. He got cut on the face. But the blitzes weren't that prevalent at that time. I bet Otto wasn't sacked eight or ten times in the whole season.

At the end, our offense got very stereotyped. In fact, one year before we played the Detroit Lions in the championship game (1954), we had a meeting in Otto's room at 2 o'clock in the morning, in the Carter Hotel—all the offensive players. We made up our mind that if he sent in a play we didn't like, we wouldn't run it. We'd run our own play. We got so tired of him calling the wrong plays. *We* were playing. *We* knew what we could do. He got conservative. Paul Brown didn't know about that meeting until ten, fifteen years after we were done playing. We told him at a banquet in Dayton, Ohio, one time. He didn't say anything.

He'd listen to everybody. If you had a play to tell him about, he'd listen to it and try it. Some other guy'd tell him something, he'd listen and see how it would work. Guys would send him letters with plays in them, and he'd look them over and listen. One time we were at Syracuse for an exhibition game. We were on the two-yard line, and he always wanted to run the ball in. You can't always do it with all the big guys in there.

I said, 'Otto, you gotta throw me a little hook pass this time.'

He threw it and they intercepted it. Oh, I didn't hear the end of it. All year, Paul Brown kept saying, 'Lavelli, you remember up at Syracuse?'

I said, 'Yeah, but how many times did I catch the damn ball in the end zone?'

He didn't know anything about the passing game. We developed the passing game. Otto and Speedie and I developed the passing routes.

I used to break the pattern and get open all the time. I caught a touchdown against Los Angeles, out there, just before the half, to put us ahead by 14 points with two minutes in the half.

He said in front of the whole team, 'Lavelli, you broke the pattern.'

I said, 'Yeah, but I caught a touchdown, and we're 14 points ahead.'
He didn't say anything.

I did that against Emlen Tunnell a couple times, too. What happened was they'd look at the film so much and say, 'What're they gonna do? What're they gonna do?' As soon as you'd break the pattern the other way, man, you'd get wide open.

It took us a while to build up the fans, because none of us had played in college. We were all coming from the war. Nobody knew you. We drew well our first two or three years. We'd get 60-, 70,000. When I look back on it, we were just like a machine. That's where that word of his comes in—'execution, execution.' I played on eleven straight championship teams, counting my sophomore year at Ohio State. Otto and I are the only two guys that started all ten championship games in Cleveland.

The thing in Cleveland was that all the fans were actually Paul Brown backers. He's the one that really built the fans up, because he was the king at Ohio State and at Massillon, in the whole state of Ohio. He built the whole fan base himself, just by winning and winning. We'd be twenty points behind, he'd always figure we could come back and win, and we did.

MY LAST YEAR, A COUPLE GUYS GOT HURT, and what happened was Paul Brown wouldn't let the healthy second-team guys go in. John Sandusky got hurt, Don Colo got hurt, Lou Groza was hurt. He played them anyway, and guys ran through them. We ended up six and eight, or something (5-7). We could've won three or four games with the healthy guys, but he wouldn't do it. We could've gone to another championship game. A healthy second-team guy is always better than an injured number-one guy. We didn't have a good quarterback, either. Tommy O'Connell was no Otto Graham.

I would like to have kept playing, but he hired Jim Brown, and I knew he was going to go into the running attack, and he wouldn't throw. I knew it wouldn't be a lot of fun just running out there all the time and not getting the ball. He was going to make the running attack the whole offensive system.

When Tommy O'Connell was quarterbacking against the Rams, jeez, I was getting beat up all over, because the timing wasn't there. I was waiting for the ball, and guys were hitting me in the ribs and knocking me out of bounds. Boy, I was getting hit. When Otto was there, the timing was perfect. I never got beat up. I wanted to be part of the offense, and I just didn't feel like I was going to be. Jim Brown was the whole thing for seven or eight years.

After we left, the personnel wasn't there. Even when Jim Brown was there, they didn't win the championship, except in '64. And in '64, Jim Brown didn't score that many touchdowns. Gary Collins scored all the touchdowns.

After I was done, I watched the Browns pretty close, the personnel, the coaches. Paul Brown and I played in a lot of golf tournaments together. We played in the same tournament in Dayton for fifteen or twenty years. He was a lot more friendly then. He softened up.

I could've coached for him when he went to Cincinnati, but I just didn't feel right going. Coaching wasn't really that good a job at that time. Paul Brown's first contract was for $25,000, and his coaches were making $5,000. Twenty-five was very big money at the time, but five wasn't all that much. Now, there are guys probably making a million dollars.

Coaching today isn't like it was forty years ago. The assistant coaches at that time, that was their whole life. They didn't look for speaking engagements or radio shows or TV talk. It was football, football—summertime, springtime. That's how he was. Paul Brown never made any speeches. He gave them to the assistants so they could make the extra money. At that time, being a professional coach was a part-time job. They only worked two or three months. He worked twelve months. The Chicago Cardinals, the Bears, the Detroit Lions, they tried to work five or six months, but he was too far ahead of them.

I WAS IN FLORIDA WHEN MODELL LET BROWN GO. There were no Cleveland newspapers there. I flew up to Chicago for the furniture market, and there was a newspaper with a headline on it, and I couldn't believe it. He went right from here to the West Coast. I never got to see him.

What bothers me is that the league never writes about Paul Brown. They write about Lombardi. Hell, he didn't do anything compared to what Brown did. That's because television came in. Lombardi was in the television era.

I started my store about the last year I was playing, I think, but I had some guy running it for a couple of years. Then, when the Korean War came, I decided I better get busy and do something. That's when I decided to stay with business. I used to have a bigger store than this, but what happens is, when you have a bigger store and leave it all the time, you just can't watch it. Guys today, they don't even need off-season jobs.

Playing helps you a little bit with business, but when it comes down to it, it's still hard. I want to tell you something: When it comes down to dollars and cents, you can be Audie Murphy or Bing Crosby; it doesn't mean a thing.

I come in here every day, except that I take two weeks in the wintertime to go to Florida. I think I know the appliance and furniture business fairly well. As far as getting big, we see it every day: The big guys go by the wayside. You have to be either real big or real small. There's too much competition.

See this picture here? That's me and Groza and Lou Rymkus. This kid here was six years old. Last week, some lady brought this picture in to me. She found it in her house. He's 56 years old and married now, and his wife brought the picture in. We were selling clothes in this department store for outside income.

I see a lot of guys I played with. I play in twenty-five golf tournaments every year. I see them all over the country. I see a lot of them at the Super Bowl and the Hall of Fame Game.

The league doesn't do anything for the Hall of Famers. If you want to go to the Super Bowl, you pay your own way. They won't even pay for a hotel room. Maybe they'll change, maybe they won't, but I feel like that's a knock. If it weren't for the old guys coming back, they wouldn't have any program.

It's unbelievable down there at the Hall of Fame Game now. They get 300,000 people down there, for the parade and everything. Every guy who played for the Browns had Paul Brown as his presenter at the Hall of Fame induction ceremonies. Even though they hated him, they had him put them in. Well, I don't think Jim Brown had Paul Brown. I forget who Jim Brown had. There was a lot of friction there between Brown and Jim Brown, but it ironed out over the years. In fact, Jim praises him now, and Jim was as good as anyone who ever played. 〟〟

# One Great Scorer

LOU GROZA HAD NEVER seen so much money: $500 a month for the duration of the war and $7500 a year once he was discharged from the 96th Infantry—to play football for the professional team that his former college coach, Paul Brown, was starting in Cleveland. Groza had been born above the saloon his Hungarian immigrant parents owned in Martins Ferry, a gritty town on the Ohio River. He never dreamed anyone could make such a living.

Finding the contract in the company mail surprised Groza. He had been drafted after attending Ohio State for only two quarters and so barely knew Brown. He would sometimes see the coach silhouetted against a window high in Ohio Stadium, watching through binoculars as the freshmen practiced. Otherwise, Groza, who wasn't eligible for varsity ball, had little to do with the coach.

After he was shipped overseas, Groza began receiving letters from Brown. The coach sent footballs and cleats. The contract reached Groza on Okinawa, where the medical battalion in which he served as a surgical technician was preparing for a bloody invasion of the Japanese mainland. Groza signed and returned the contract immediately. "I figured I just might get killed over there, so I better take what I can get," he said.

Bankrolled by owner Arthur "Mickey" McBride, Brown was free to send retainers to soldiers in the field because the All-American Football Conference didn't hold a draft before its first season. He also signed players who had college eligibility remaining or who were under contract with National Football League teams. As he handpicked his squad, Brown stuck with the familiar. Nearly half the roster came from Ohio, and 90 percent had either played for or against Brown.

"We stayed close to our own people, Ohio people, the ones who believed in our system," he said. Signing local players guaranteed that the team would draw from throughout northeastern Ohio, as would Brown's reputation. He had become famous over 14 highly publicized seasons at Massillon High School, OSU, and Great Lakes Naval Station.

To name his team, McBride sponsored an essay contest with a $1000 war bond as prize. Soon, though, the winning entry—"Panthers"—was rejected. Lore has it that Brown refused to have his team associated with the Cleveland Panthers of the defunct American Football League, because the Panthers had been losers. However, the team finished 3-2 in 1926, its only season, and years later, Brown said that McBride had turned the name down. More likely, as some reports indicated, those who held the rights to the name asked a hefty sum for them.

McBride held a second contest, won by William E. Thompson, whose entry was chosen from among those of numerous people who had picked "Browns," supposedly in honor of the coach. The story goes that, at first, Brown was too embarrassed to allow his name to be used but was eventually talked into it. Yet in a history of the franchise published by the NFL, Jack Clary, who also collaborated on Brown's autobiography, quotes the coach as saying, "Joe Louis was the best known champion at that time, and we received a lot of entries suggesting we name the team the Brown Bombers. So we decided to shorten the name and call the team the Browns." Perhaps Brown was still being modest, but Clary's book came out in 1973, when Brown would be most likely to emphasize his connection to the franchise, if only to gall owner Art Modell, who had fired him 11 years earlier.

In a 1986 profile of Brown, the *Chicago Tribune* said that "the team was originally named the Brown Bombers after Joe Louis and was shortened to Browns because of owner Mickey McBride's affinity for both men."

Brown later denied any connection between Louis and the team. In fact, when he was at Ohio State, he insisted that writers not refer to his squads as "Brown's Bombers." That a franchise would be named for a black man when no pro team employed black players seems peculiar, but when he was hired, Brown said that he planned to build a dynasty to equal "the New York Yankees in baseball, Joe Louis in boxing, and Ben Hogan in golf."

Even Otto Graham, the first player signed by Brown, can't recall if the franchise was named for the coach, the fighter, or both. Whether or not the team name is eponymous, the AAFC and the Cleveland franchise built sophisticated promotional campaigns around Brown.

Groza, the second player Brown signed, was also well known in Ohio. He had led his high school football and basketball teams to state championships. As an 18-year-old freshman, he amazed reporters by making 49 of 50 field goals and driving a 70-yard

kickoff through the goal posts during a practice.

Groza carried his duffel bag into the sorority house at Bowling Green University that served as team headquarters during the Browns' first training camp, he hadn't played football in three years. Moments before his first game in Cleveland Stadium, he still wondered if he had made the right decision. "I was in awe coming out of those tunnels for the first time," he said. "I just felt so small."

He had survived worst. When his unit landed at Leyte two hours after the first wave, the beach was strewn with bodies and screaming wounded. Groza lived in foxholes, disinterred corpses to be sent home, helped doctors piece together broken and torn soldiers.

Before the largest crowd in the history of professional football, Groza kicked three field goals and seven extra points. The next day, a sportswriter called him "243 pounds of place-kicking magic."

He hit from 49, 50, and 51 yards that year. He set professional records for field goals and extra points in a season, led the AAFC in scoring, and caused Brown to stop ordering that all kickoffs be directed out of bounds to prevent long runbacks. Teammates began calling the territory inside the 20 "Groza Country." *Life* said Groza's kicking was "not mere brute force but meticulous science." *Newsweek* dubbed him "Brown's V-1 weapon." He was only 22 when a *Plain Dealer* writer first called Groza "The Toe."

"We always felt if we got within 40 or 50 yards of the goal post, he could make it, and 95 percent of the time he did," Graham said.

Graham exaggerated Groza's effectiveness, but Cleveland Browns were nearly perfect, losing only four games while winning all four AAFC championships. In 1948, Cleveland became only the second professional football team to finish undefeated. By that time, Groza had also become the starting left tackle, which he considered his true position. "I just kicked because I knew how," said Groza, a six-time All-Pro tackle.

In 1949, Cleveland lost only one game, its first defeat in more than two years. The team's 29-game unbeaten streak ended with a four-touchdown loss to San Francisco. Players expected to be consoled; instead, Brown warned them, "I'm telling you this, and it's cold turkey: If those of you who fell down on the job don't bounce back, I'll sell you."

"That got everyone fired up," Groza said, drolly.

The story leaked, and *Colliers* magazine, in an editorial entitled "Aw Come On, Coach, Relax," chastised Brown for his "win-at-any-cost attitude" and compared his behavior with Hitler's snubbing German athletes who failed to win medals at the 1936 Olympics.

"Winning is not an evil thing," Brown said, but what happened in Cleveland during the AAFC years contradicted him.

In just two games of their first season, the Browns drew almost 45,000 more fans than the Cleveland Rams had in all of 1945, when they won the NFL title. Already, though, a columnist speculated that the team was so good that the championship was a foregone conclusion and fans would become bored. The Browns did attract a record 82,769 to a game in 1948, but fewer than 23,000 watched them trample the Buffalo Bills in the title game.

With both a percentage of the profits and a fervent belief in winning, Brown grew increasingly perturbed as average attendance fell 26,000 in four seasons. He said, "We were too good, if that sounds possible. Even in Cleveland, the fans stopped coming because they just assumed we'd go out and dominate the opposition so strongly there would be no contest."

A *Plain Dealer* columnist wrote, "A chocolate sundae, topped by a gob of whipped cream with a cherry at the pinnacle would be infinitely exciting to one who had been marooned on a desert island for a protracted spell, but he might grow a little weary of chocolate sundaes after a four-year diet of the confection."

The helter-skelter manner in which some AAFC franchises were run violated Brown's need for order. The Miami Seahawks once skipped town without paying their lodging bill. McBride, who claimed to have lost $100,000 in the league's final three seasons, had to pick up the tab. Heavy snow fell before a game in Chicago in 1949, but the home team hadn't hired a grounds crew to pull up the tarpaulin. Asked to remove it, the Browns and Rockets ended up in a snowball fight. Had the two professional leagues not merged the day before Cleveland beat San Francisco 21-7 in the last AAFC title game, Brown might have returned to college coaching.

Cleveland, San Francisco, and Baltimore joined the new National-American Football League after four years of smear campaigns, player raids, lawsuits, and red ink. Bad blood remained. The NFL refused to acknowledge AAFC statistics. Groza's 259 points, Brown's 52-4-3 record, the perfect season, and the 29-game undefeated streak don't appear in NFL record books. The NFL also passed a regulation preventing Groza from using the length of adhesive tape he carried in his helmet to line up field goals.

Groza was injured early in Cleveland's first NFL game, a romp over defending league champion

Philadelphia. Nonetheless, 1950 would be a wonderful season for him. He set an NFL mark with 13 field goals, three of which won regular-season games. The Browns lost only twice, both times to the New York Giants, whom Cleveland tied for the American Conference title. In the Browns' 8-3 playoff victory, Groza kicked two field goals, including the winner with less than a minute left.

On Christmas Eve, Cleveland trailed the Los Angeles Rams 28-27 with 28 seconds remaining in the championship game. The Browns had the ball on the Los Angeles 16. As Groza prepared to try a field goal, teammates tossed their helmets, thumped each other's backs, and shook hands. "Made me bloomin' mad," Brown said of the premature celebration. "He made it, of course."

In the locker room, Brown, his face erupting in a rare smile, held Groza's toe as the player kissed his kicking shoe. "We had the greatest kicker in the world," Brown said. "It was that simple."

Groza, who called the most important field goal of his life "just another kick," spent the rest of the decade proving Brown right. His 52-yarder against the Rams in 1951 bettered the championship mark by 10 yards. He set a league record for field goals in 1952 and again in 1953, when he hit 23 of 26 attempts, all off grass. He was the league MVP in 1954, and by 1957, when he made five kicks longer than 50 yards, Groza had become the greatest scorer in NFL history. San Francisco coach Frankie Albert said that to make the league fair, Groza should have to change teams every year.

Groza closed out the 1950s by playing in his ninth Pro Bowl. The Fairview American Legion named him Cleveland's player of the year in 1959. The honor was a sort of lifetime achievement award. The entire city believed that Groza, 35 and hampered by back troubles, was about to quit. "The handwriting on the wall needs only a period to complete," a reporter said.

Brown confirmed that belief when he acquired kicker Sam Baker in 1960. During training camp, Brown told Groza, who had re-injured his back, that the team was going to go with Baker. The coach announced at the annual Touchdown Club luncheon that the last of the original Browns was retiring. Nearly a thousand fans stood and applauded. Teary-eyed, Groza said, "I guess you could say I've been playing on borrowed time." Later, Groza admitted he really hadn't been ready to quit, but said he "didn't want to put Paul in a difficult position by trying to squeeze out one more season."

Groza was working for the Browns as a college scout when Art Modell bought the club in 1961. Soon, he said, Modell asked him if he could still kick. The men met at Berea High School's field. Modell held. Groza kicked. Brown shortly traded Baker and told the press, "We have been thinking about this move for some time." The slight upset Modell.

"I guess one of their bones of contention was that Paul never gave him any credit for urging me to come back," said Groza, who led the team in scoring in 1961, missing only one attempt from inside the 40.

Over the next half-dozen seasons, the Browns brought in a series of kickers to challenge Groza: Fred Cox, Erroll Mann, Jim Martin, David Lee, Dick van Raaphorst. All failed. In 1964, Groza had his finest season. He kicked four field goals in each of two crucial games with St. Louis. He hit 22 of 32 tries and scored 115 points, most in his career. His second field goal in Cleveland's 27-0 defeat of Baltimore made Groza the top scorer in championship history. In 1965, he played in his 13th title game. Groza seemed to have been mistaken six years earlier when he said that "football wasn't going to be a lifelong thing."

He began the next season by hitting from 44 and 46 against Green Bay. Then, for reasons not even Groza, who had written a thirty-page treatise on kicking, understood, the toe that had been cast in bronze and displayed at the Cleveland Museum of Health failed. Four games later, he had missed six of nine attempts. Fans began calling him "The Stomach."

In a Thanksgiving Day loss to Dallas that eliminated Cleveland from playoff contention, Groza missed two field goals and had a third blocked. A *Plain Dealer* story asked "Should the Browns Retire Lou Groza?" Groza, the paper said, had become the scapegoat for the team's failure to win a third straight conference crown. Said Groza of the team that had employed him for the past twenty-one years, "From what I see and what I read, they've almost written me off. I hope that isn't true."

Several months later, the Browns drafted punter/place kicker Don Cockroft. The rookie was injured in an automobile accident, though, and Groza returned. Cleveland opened with a home loss to Dallas. Groza missed two short field goals, and the fans lashed out again. "Not since the Romans tossed Daniel to the lions has there been such a roar of 'thumbs down' as bounced off the ears of Lou Groza, Sunday," said the *Press*.

Owner of a prosperous insurance brokerage, Groza didn't have to endure abuse. He kept playing, he said, for the same reason he had begun playing for the Martins Ferry Purple Raiders three decades earlier, for the same reason the public wants

to believe that all athletes play: "I had fun."

He kicked two extra points in the team's playoff loss to the Cowboys but missed 12 of 23 field goals in 1967. Even the press beseeched him to retire, but Groza signed his 22nd one-year contract, hoping like any rookie free agent to make the club. He was released just before the 1968 season opened. Groza held 10 NFL and 24 team records. He still believed he was the team's best kicker and that he had been let go because Modell had never forgiven him for not renouncing Brown when the owner fired him.

Groza considered an offer from the 49ers but declined because of his family and because he didn't want to tarnish his sterling reputation in the city. "I thought I could still play," he said, "but I wasn't going to make a big scene."

Subsequent tributes seemed to make up for Groza's ignominious departure. The team retired his number. A stretch of State Route 7, which runs through Martins Ferry, became Lou Groza Highway. Every year the best collegiate kicker receives the Lou Groza Award, as does the best player in the Cleveland area. Groza's son Judd, one of his four children, won the honor in 1979. *The Sporting News* named Groza one of the 100 top players in NFL history. The Smithsonian Institution displays one of his size 12 high-topped black kicking shoes.

When Modell moved the franchise to Baltimore in 1995, Groza became a symbol of Cleveland's anguish. Asked by the mayor to speak during a press conference, he wept. "It's like a fire has just burned out, and all you have left is ashes," he said.

Groza was late for an appointment at his home in Berea. He had stopped on his way home from the office to pick up a prescription and forgotten the time. Parkinson's disease caused his hands to shake slightly. He took mincing steps as he led a visitor to the den to see his Hall of Fame bust and the bronzed shoe with which he kicked the field goal against the Rams in 1950. He dropped a packing slip; two hip surgeries made picking it up laborious.

Groza's crooked nose, paunch, and slender legs were still iconographic. He wore a navy blazer, beltless gray slacks, a crisp powder blue shirt, a "76" pin on a red-and-blue-striped tie, and a Hall of Fame ring. He was ponderous, affable, dignified, witty, and a bit backward.

Groza settled into a sofa. A prayer hanging behind him asked, "What is a home without love?" Slowed by the disease, his voice had the almost toneless stoicism of someone who while he was still a boy,

had seen the worst life has to offer. He bore no resentment over how he was treated at the end of his career. "I'm no different from the fans who rooted for me for all those years," he said.

"All of the good things that happened to me in sports were a result of our relationship," he said of Brown. "Where would I have been if he hadn't seen me playing basketball in Martins Ferry and Columbus?"

When his visitor drove off, Groza stood in the doorway, a bit unsteady, waving and smiling faintly.

Twenty five years earlier, almost to the day, Groza was inducted into the Hall of Fame. Brown left the Cincinnati Bengals training camp to present him. "He embodies everything that I value in a football player, husband, father and son," said Brown.

"It's a nice feeling," Groza said of entering the Hall, "almost like going to football heaven."

Groza died late in 2000, after having supper with his wife of 50 years, Jackie. The Browns lowered the flags in front of their training Center at 76 Lou Groza Boulevard in Berea and began wearing Groza's number on their helmets. Said former Cleveland tackle Doug Dieken, "I don't know if he was the greatest Brown, but he was *the* Brown."

# Lou GROZA

"MY PARENTS WERE HUNGARIAN IMMIGRANTS. My mother came over as a baby in her mother's arms, and my father came over as a young man to find an older brother who was a coal miner in a little town near Martins Ferry, Ohio. Eventually, he opened a pool hall and turned it into a tavern, Groza's Tavern. We lived upstairs. Athletics was important socially in Martins Ferry. My parents bought my older brother, John, a coronet. They wanted him to be in the band. He got hit in football practice one time and came home with a black eye, and they found out he wasn't playing in the band.

John went to West Virginia University to play football. He tore up a knee, and I guess in those days, if you didn't play ball, you didn't get your scholarship. He couldn't afford to pay for college, so he quit school, started working in the mill, and got married.

My brother Frank was playing professional baseball for the Johnstown Johnnys, a minor league team. He was sliding into third and hurt his ankle. He came home, and they had the draft on. He played some ball over in Hawaii, but when he got out of the service, he had gotten married and thought he was too old to play any more. He ended up owning a tavern, too. Frank is the one who go me started on kicking. When he was in high school, we'd go down to the baseball diamond, Mill Field, and I chased his kicks. He had learned to kick from my uncle, Andy Koteles.

There wasn't much kids could do outside of play ball. I was big for my age, so I always played with older kids. We played basketball, the backboards up on railroad ties, and I used to run into them all the time. We played tackle football without any pads on the nicest lawn we could find, and the owners would chase us off. We played touch football in the streets, but it really wasn't touch football. When you got 'touched,' you really got belted. I used to kick the ball over the telephone wires to see how far I could make it go. We played down by the river, then jumped in and washed off.

I just played because I wanted to play, period. I never paid much attention to what people thought about sports, except that you'd be pleased to win some particular award—All-Valley or something like that. I was the most valuable player in the state basketball tournament my junior year. We were playing Lima Central, I think it was. The score was tied, and they were coming up the court with the ball. Time was running out. I intercepted a pass, threw it to one of our forwards, and broke down the court. He threw it back to me and as I was shooting a lay-up, a guy fouled me from the rear. I didn't make the shot, but I had two fouls after the game was over, and I was the worst foul shooter on the team. I looked at the coach. He was pale. He said, 'Go ahead and shoot.'

I shot the first basket, and it went in, so I just shot the second basket, and it went in, too. When we got home, they had the fire engine waiting for us at the city limits, and they rode us around town on this big hook-and-ladder truck. What an experience that was.

I was an All-Ohio center in basketball, and an All-Ohio tackle in football. We were co-champs in football, state champs in basketball. I was most valuable player. I was just doing what came naturally.

I HAD HOPES of being able to go to college, and as it ended up, I could've gone anywhere in the country. The last two schools I looked at were Notre Dame and Ohio State. A fellow drove me out to Notre Dame to see Frank Leahy. This fellow owned a pool hall, where they sold punchboards and things like that. He was a subway alumnus of Notre Dame. He had a great big Buick and he let me drive it over to Notre Dame.

I was very impressed with Notre Dame. I was thinking, 'Oh boy, I don't know what to do.' But I knew the military was beckoning, and I didn't want to go too far from home, and, of course, Paul Brown was at Ohio State. I went to Ohio State, finished two quarters of my freshman year, and I was in the army.

I knew of Paul Brown from Massillon. He had all of those great teams there, and he had been successful at Ohio State. The first time I met him, he had his assistants there, and the guy who owned the newspaper in my hometown was there, Gomer Jones, my high school coach, was there. Gomer had been an All-American center at OSU. They had me surrounded. Paul Brown said, 'What we can do is give you one of our varsity jobs.'

They really didn't pay much, but I had a job with a meat-packing company. I'd go to school, go down and load some meat trucks, then come home. My roommate was sleeping, and I'd be studying.

You couldn't play varsity football as a freshman then. We only played three freshman games. We didn't have much contact with Paul Brown, but when we kicked after practice, I used to look up at the windows of the locker room in Ohio Stadium, and I'd see him sitting there, watching us.

After two quarters, I went to the induction center in Columbus, and a colonel called me in and wanted to talk to me. I thought, 'Boy, I'm going to get one of those football deals!'

I thought I'd go to one of these places where you play football for the military. I ended up on a train with all of these other Ohio State guys. I was a freshmen; they were all upperclassmen. We all thought we were going to go someplace and play football.

WE STOPPED IN CHICAGO, they cut Dante Lavelli's car off our train, and he ended up in Camp Walters, Texas, in the infantry. I ended up going to Camp Barkley in Abeliene, Texas, in a medical replacement training center. Basic training then was three months. They pulled me out after two months and sent me to Briggs General Hospital in San Antonio to become a surgical technician.

I ended up in Hawaii for general training. We came in and saw all those bombed-out ships. They put us on a train. We were all standing up in coal cars. We carry our bags into the dormitory where we were staying, and the first sergeant says, 'Report downstairs. You're going out for jungle training.'

I thought, 'Geez, jungle training! What's that?'

After we left Hawaii, we went first to Leyte. I ended up with an infantry division, and we were the first medical installation they brought the wounded back to. We were about five miles from the front lines, but if we were overrun, we couldn't leave. We had to stay and take care of our wounded.

We got into Leyte, and for as far as you could see, there were ships. There were Russians, British ships. They were unloading. Guys were falling off the rope ladders right into the boats. They never even made it to the shore. They had to get us in there to take care of the wounded.

The landing craft would circle around until they got the signal to go in.

All the fumes were just hanging there. Then they'd get in a line to hit the beaches. The first two guys I saw got hit in the face. Their faces were blown off. Someone would go into his wallet and take his identification and just leave him laying there.

We went up into the jungle, and we got separated from our outfit. Here comes this big Filipino carrying a machete. We thought he was Japanese, but he ended up climbing a tree and getting coconuts for us.

We finally found our outfit. We had fox holes as our domiciles while we were there. It was tough at first, but, actually, you get so used to death that you don't see it. A guy would come in wounded. We'd clean out his wounds and put the needle in for the intravenous bottles. The doctors would operate, and we'd clean up. It was tough duty, but that was just the way it was. You just had to accept it. It was like: 'What else can happen now?'

When it was over in the Philippines, there were some Japanese nurses who got caught behind our lines, and they killed themselves. They used hand grenades. They were only a little distance from where we were, and some of the guys went over to see them. I wasn't interested in seeing that.

From the Philippines, we went to Okinawa, from there, we went back to the Philippines to get ready to hit Japan. We were en route when they dropped the atomic bomb and the war ended. We were on an LST, and everyone was running around hollering and jumping. There was a first sergeant sleeping there. I shook him and said, 'Joe, wake up! The war is over!'

I saw him later, and he said, 'You son-of-a-gun. I thought you said the ship was sinking.'

PAUL CONTACTED ME WHILE I WAS IN THE SERVICE. He had decided to go professional, and I got a contract in the mail. Someone said that Otto Graham and I were the first two guys he signed. I was surprised to hear from him. I wasn't paying much attention to anything like that, and I never thought about it until I got the contract.

I was going to go back to school at Ohio State and play football. I wanted to get my education. I knew football wasn't going to be a lifelong thing. I guess I was almost wrong about that, though.

I was just a kid. I had never signed a contract before, but I started getting money while I was in the service. That's what really attracted my attention. That was more money than I had ever seen. I had grown up across the street from a steel mill, so that money was quite attractive to me. I figured I just might get killed over there, so I better take what I can get.

I don't know how many guys got the paychecks in the service. I know I did and Otto did. Lavelli didn't. I didn't want to break his heart, so I never told him that I got money in the service.

Everybody needed the paycheck, but, of course, the paychecks weren't as big then as they are now. I was getting $500 a month while I was in the service, then my first contract was for $7,500. That wasn't bad then.

When I was discharged, I went back to school and finished my freshman year and I reported to my first training camp. I got there and said, 'Oh, boy, what did I do?'

They had Jim Daniell, an All-American from Ohio State, Ernie Blandin, an All-American from Tulane, Lou Rymkus from Notre Dame, Len Simonetti, Chet Adams. And then there was me. Some of them had played four years of college and professional football. In that first camp, they didn't have a draft. They signed players who had played before. Paul only signed players that he knew something about. I was only 22 years old.

When I showed up, I said, 'These guys are all great talents.' I knew who most of them were, and what they had accomplished. I was wondering if I hadn't made a mistake.

MY FIRST YEAR, I tackled Marion Motley head-on, and I thought a truck had run over me. He was tough and he was big. He had those big thighs and that big butt. I tackled him, and it was just like a load of something fell on me. From that point on, I tackled him from the side.

That year, all I did was kick, but the next year, Jim Daniell was gone. By the end of the season, I started to get some playing time. By my third year, I took over the left tackle spot. I played my position and kicked. They didn't carry enough players to have someone just kick. In those days, I wanted to play my position and play on the special teams. Today, with the kind of money they're making, a kicker would try to avoid playing.

I was a real rookie. We didn't wear masks, and a guy named Lee Artoe hit me right in the nose. He skinned my nose good. The next play went to the right. I'm the left tackle. I'm releasing to go across the field. He wore one of those small masks. I unloaded on that mask just as hard as I could. The thing cut his chin. I kept on running. Our guy got tackled, and I turned around and saw Lee Artoe coming. He was going to blindside me. I just ducked, and he went ass over teacups. That was a learning experience.

Paul was a very intense type of guy. He was hard to get close to. The only time you could get close to him was when it was all over, when you had finished your career. He didn't want to get too close to any particular player, because it would be to hard to cut him. You really couldn't get close to the guy.

We had a priest named Father Connelly. He was from Martins Ferry, where I'm from. We were at the Bowling Green training camp, and Father Connelly was on his way to Detroit. He stopped because he wanted to see me. He goes in the dormitory, and the first guy he runs into is Paul. At that time, we were having some trouble because we had signed some guys off the Rams. Father Connelly went into the dorm without his collar on.

He said, 'Mr. Brown, where can I find Lou Groza?'

Paul said, 'Who the hell are you?'

From that point on, they got along pretty good, though, and Father Connelly became our chaplain.

HE USED TO CALL ME 'LOUIE.' People say I was one of his favorites, and I guess I was. I left Ohio State to go with him, and there's no telling what would have happened if I had stayed at Ohio State.

He worked you hard, but he used the time efficiently. You didn't have a long time on the practice field, but when you were there, you worked. There was no lost time. You had one day dedicated to offense, one day dedicated to defense, and one day for both offense and defense to brush up on all the details, and on Saturday, you had special teams. You'd stay at a hotel in town the night before the game, which was unusual for pro teams in those days, and then you were ready to go.

I never got into much conversation with Paul about what he was doing. I just appreciated doing what I was doing. I accepted the things he pointed out to try to make me better. I didn't want do deal with him when he was unhappy.

The only time I saw him really angry was one time he was writing on the blackboard, and he turned around, and this guy was nodding. He had a wet towel there to wipe the board. He saw that guy nodding, and he took that towel, and, *pow*, he hit him right in the face with it.

I accepted the note-taking and the writing for what it was worth. In those days, you didn't have the mechanical equipment to project the plays on a board. Actually, he wanted to keep you busy so you weren't going to get into any mischief. If you were doing anything wrong, people would call him and tell him. They'd call and say, 'I saw one of your football players and he was doing so and so.'

You'd be watching the movies, and he'd say, 'Look at yourself.'

That sort of thing didn't bother me, but, one time, I got a contract from him. I didn't think it was enough money, so I sent it back unsigned. I didn't sign it, and I didn't put a note or anything in with it. I had to go to Cleveland for something, and he told someone to tell me that he wanted to see me while I was in town. He and I were in his office together. He said, 'Are you planning to play this year?'

I said, 'Well, yeah.'

He said, 'But you sent your contract back unsigned.'

I said, 'Well, I didn't think there was enough money in it.'

We went back and forth. Eventually, he jacked it up a little bit, but not a hell of a lot.

He didn't like to spend money, but he liked to make it. Of course, in those days we didn't have agents. I never had one. It just wasn't in vogue at that time. In those days, as just a kicker, you didn't have much negotiating power. Now, the agents have a lot of power. They represent not just one guy but a lot of guys. They have a better bargaining position than one guy does.

I ONLY SIGNED ONE-YEAR CONTRACTS. They had multi-year deals, but I didn't want one. If you had a bad year, you were going to get cut anyway. If you had a good year, you wanted to be able to negotiate.

It was great to play in Cleveland. In the AAFC, it got to the point where it wasn't a contest any more. He kept us motivated by watching the movies. When you watched the movies, and you did something wrong, he'd let you know about it. I never caught much hell from him, but I think the reason for that is I didn't want to catch much hell from him.

About the time you got your name mentioned too often, you weren't going to be around very long. Jim Daniell was his team captain at Ohio State, and he was captain for us, and Paul let him go.

Paul said, 'As far as drinking goes, you get caught drinking, and you're off the team. If you have to smoke, smoke in your room.' Paul liked to be in control, and I'm sure McBride didn't mind that, because we were winning. There was only one boss. That's where Paul and Art Modell became separated.

McBride got rid of the club after having it for only a short time. As time went by, I'm sure he wished he would've held onto it longer. He would've made a hell of a lot more money.

We were just glad we had survived the other league. There was just the

San Francisco 49ers, the Baltimore Colts, and us. We had some players come in from Buffalo and join us.

I thought the football in the All-American Conference was better than it was in the National Football League. When that league folded, all the good players came out of that league and were distributed throughout the NFL, and those teams were all improved by those players. They were quality football players.

We were confident that we could play in the NFL. That's the only way Paul Brown ever trained his teams: If you don't think you're going to win, you shouldn't be there. When we first went into the NFL, teams were passing around information on us. In those days, you weren't supposed to pass the movies around, but they were passing them around to our opponents because we were winning.

We beat the champions of the NFL in our first game in the league, by a big score. Paul was very quiet before that game. He knew psychology. They had said some things about us, and he'd post those sayings up around the locker room. He never did do much to pep you up, but the guys knew that Paul wanted the game real bad, and they went after it. We had had a long time to think about it.

I STARTED THE FIRST GAME IN THE NFL, but I got hurt. I was on the punt-return team, and just as I was blocking a guy, another guy came up and caught him from behind and knocked him into me. I caught the whole load on my left shoulder. I think I missed a couple games, and when I started playing again, I always had to have my arm taped up.

That year, it went down to the closing minutes of the last game, and I kicked the winning field goal. At that particular time, when I was kicking it, all I was thinking about was the fundamentals of kicking—just watch the spot.

Paul Brown exploited the passing game to a greater extent than anyone did before. He had players who could catch the ball and players who could block. That really created the big difference in professional football. The defenses adjusted to what the offenses were doing. Otto just repeated what the guard said to him. Some time later, it came out that he really wanted to be calling some of his own plays. He didn't say anything at the time, but as long as we were winning, there was no reason to say anything.

I never thought of myself as anything but a tackle. I was just a tackle, and I just kicked because I knew how. Of course, the more we used it, the more teams emulated us. Horace Gillom was the punter, and I was the place-kicker, and they used to talk about field position all the time. We were always trying to kick the ball as far as we could so that we started out in a more advantageous position. We tried to shorten the playing field up.

Our playbooks had all the special teams assignments in them. We had our special teams day on the Saturday before the game. We'd go over all the assignments then. We kicked after practice all the time. The guys would have to chase my kicks, and it was invariably the offensive and defensive tackles who had to do it. They'd complain about it. He made them catch the ball and run with it so that they got a little more running in.

I played against Doug Atkins, Ernie Stautner, Andy Robustelli. I only weighed about 235 in those days. I was 6' 3". Doug Atkins was 6' 8". We couldn't extend our arms then. I had to try to get close to him, so he didn't have a two-way go on me. You only wanted to give him one way to go. If you tried to cut him, he'd jump right over you. You had to stay upright. You wanted to say inside and move him out, so that when he ran by you, he'd run by the passer, too.

GETTING BEAT UP just went with the territory. Someone—I can't remember who it was—came up under my mask one time and knocked these two teeth out. You had to play when you were hurt. A guy who was hurt all the time couldn't be counted on. A guy who could play when he was hurt was part of the machine.

He was always looking for people to fit his idea of the position. When he made a trade, he was always weighing the capabilities of the guy he was trading against the capabilities of the guy he was trading for. It was like when he traded Bobby Mitchell because he wanted to get Ernie Davis. Of course, Ernie Davis never did play. He died.

I missed the '60 or '61 season with a bad back. I even had trouble walking. We were scrimmaging during training camp. I felt someone behind me, and I didn't want to step on him, so I stopped. The guy in front of me didn't know I was going to stop. I went over backwards and injured my back. I missed the one season and when I came back, I just kicked.

I was so used to doing everything. I really thought I was done, but the kicking let me stay part of the game. They expanded the size of the squads then.

When I was hurt, I was a scout, and I did some work in training camp with the tackles. I was in the South one time, scouting, and these Klansmen with their hoods on stopped me. There were about twelve of them.

They said, 'What're you doing down here?'

I said, 'I'm scouting for the Cleveland Browns.'

They said, 'Let me see your credentials.'

I showed them my wallet and everything.

They said, 'Well, what're you doing down here now?'

I said, 'I'm going to see a game. I'm trying to find some football play-ers.'

They let me go.

I think Art prevailed in bringing me back. He asked me if I could still kick.

I said, 'Yeah, I can still kick.'

He said, 'I'll meet you at Berea High School.'

We went over there. I was kicking field goals 40, 50 yards. I went to the hash marks and kicked some. He saw I could still do it, and he went to Paul. I guess one of their bones of contention was that Paul never gave him any credit for urging me to come back.

Whether Paul was right all the time or not depends on who you're talking to. If you're talking to him, it was all right. He was a kind of a proud individual. He didn't want anyone messing around with his football team. Art bought the club originally because of Paul Brown's capabilities. Paul was very protective of his team. He didn't want anyone interfering with his team, so he and Art weren't going to get along.

Art wanted to get involved more, and you could tell there was tension. I never felt comfortable around Art. I always thought he felt I was carrying things back to Paul, which wasn't true. Art was always talking to different guys. Paul couldn't tell you not to talk to him, because Art was the owner of the club. Art would come and sit in on meetings. Paul was kind of looking over his shoulder all the time, which may have interfered with his coaching ability.

I WAS SURPRISED WHEN HE FIRED PAUL, but there were a lot of rumors going around that he was going to do that. I was surprised when it happened, because when Art bought the club, he did it because of Paul Brown's winning record.

Naturally, some guys were glad to see Paul go. You're never going to have a hundred percent agreement. I thought they made a hell of a mistake, though, because Cleveland Browns football was Paul Brown. Paul just disappeared when he was let go. I found out later that he was staying with a friend of mine, and then he went out to California.

I think it was '64 when I was named the MVP by the *Sporting News*. We beat Baltimore bad that year in the championship, and I had two field goals. I had a 45-yard field goal, I think, to start the scoring, and the second one was from up close.

I decided to get out when Blanton Collier said that I could go to San Francisco if I wanted. I'm sure it was because of Modell, because I didn't get involved in the situation when they got rid of Paul. I don't know for sure, but I always had that feeling. I couldn't get involved either way. I wasn't mad at Paul Brown, and I wasn't about to start saying things about him, because I had nothing to accomplish as a player by doing that. And that just wasn't my nature. I didn't have anything against Art Modell either, but I think he had something against me, because I wouldn't say anything.

My last year, I was going down under a kickoff. A guy tries to block me. I sidestepped him and kept on going. He gets up. The ball carrier broke upfield, and just as I turned to try to make the tackle, he hit me from the blindside. My feet went out from under me, and I went right down on my back. *Pow!*

He says, 'Oh, excuse me, Mr. Groza.'

I said, 'What the hell are you talking about? That was a hell of a block.'

I WASN'T READY TO RETIRE, but I didn't want to go to San Francisco. I had played my whole career here, I had a business here, my family had a home here.

I thought I could still play, but I wasn't going to make any big scene. I was fortunate to play as long as I did. It was a good relationship, and I didn't want to taint it in any way.

Any time you end an association that's been such a big part of your life, it's not easy to do. You play 21 years, and it's like working somewhere for 21 years. You lose that relationship, and it's hard. You're used to going to practice and playing, getting ready for the season, the excitement of a game.

I still went to games after that, but I didn't go to watch practice. You have friends who like to go to practice, and I'd go with them once in a while. It wasn't much fun, though, because you're not part of it.

The one year I was hurt and doing some scouting, that was kind of fun, but that's a tough thing to do when you have kids at home. You're traveling all the time. So I just went with my business. The thing is, the older you get, when you get let go, you really have it tough. It's tough to see some of these old guys struggling.

In my first four years of pro ball, I went back to Ohio State to get my degree. I majored in marketing, and I worked for a couple of off-seasons as a purchase expediter at the Cadillac plant up here, where they were making tanks for the Korean war. I could buy Cadillacs at a discount, but I could see that when the war was over, there wasn't going to be much of a future in that job.

If I was going to improve myself in that job, I'd have to go to Detroit. I didn't want to do that. I wanted to stay in Cleveland. I don't know what I'd do if I'd retire. I don't play golf. I can't sit around and do nothing. Now, we sell property, casualty and life insurance. We're brokers for various companies.

THE BIGGEST CHANGE IN THE GAME, of course, was financially. Lou Rymkus used to say, 'You can't beat the hours and the pay,' but it's a hell of a lot different now than it was then. These guys now make so much money that when they retire, they can quit working altogether.

I made more money as I went along, but when you compare it to anything else, it wasn't that much more. I had fun. I enjoyed it. That's one reason I got into the insurance business. I could do that and still play. During the season, if I did any business, it would be during the week. After the season was over, I could work a full day.

We didn't have a great pension plan. We had to get ready for the game of life. We had to get something else going. I was always getting ready for the day I was going to retire, and it finally came. I had gone back to school to get my degree, I had all of my kids educated.

Now, I have my grandchildren, and I'm part of their activities. I like to go out and watch them play baseball and swim. My wife is from Martins Ferry, too. She and my brother Alex went to high school together. I was going to Ohio State at the time, Alex was playing basketball at Kentucky, and they were playing in Madison Square Garden. Between quarters, we had a week or ten days off, so I went up to see him play. He had a date, but he was sick, so I went and met her. We struck up a relationship, and it's worked out all right. We've been married forty-eight years and have nine grandchildren. My family is all in this area. The one who's farthest away is in Columbus.

Any time you're part of a team, you have relationships. You have guys who think like you and have the same background as you. You maintain those relationships. Lavelli and I are as good a friends as you can be. I was a freshman at Ohio State when he was a sophomore. He had played one year of varsity football there. I never got to know him until after the war was over. We were going back to school, and we roomed together.

I go every year to the Hall of Fame induction ceremonies. I go to some Brown reunions. Being recognized by people is one of the nice things that happens as a result of having played. Paul Brown presented me at the Hall of Fame. All of the good things that happened to me in sports were a result of our relationship. He opened up a whole new world to me. I appreciated what had happened to me as a result of our relationship. He was a tough guy, but I never had any problems with him.

He changed over the years, but it was a natural thing. It wasn't abrupt. He changed because he had to work with people. For so many years, he ran the whole show, with no one looking over his shoulder. After Art bought the club, that all changed. The change in him wasn't that evident, but you could see all the whispering that was going on was wearing on him. He was in control, and he didn't want anyone else to run his football team, but it just didn't happen that way.

When I retired, he was in Cincinnati, and I didn't have any contact with him. I'd see them play here, but I wouldn't go down to the locker room. The only thing was they had 'Lou Groza Day' here once when we were playing the Bengals. Paul waved at me, and I waved back. That was something, now that I look back at it.

Where would I have been if he hadn't have seen me playing basketball in Martins Ferry and Columbus? That's where I first got the idea that I could be something.

It's hard to believe I've been retired so long. It's been a great life. I've been lucky. I look back, and I feel fortunate to have survived a war and all the things that can happen to you when you play ball. I look back and ask, How lucky can a guy get? To play his whole career in one city for a winner and enjoy the success we had. It makes for a very happy existence. **〞**

# Dead-End Kid

"BROWNMANIA" GRIPPED Ohio late in the autumn of 1941. Paul Brown was finishing his first season as head football coach at Ohio State University. He had inherited a downtrodden squad that ended the previous season by losing 40-0 to Michigan in Ohio Stadium, costing coach Francis Schmidt his job.

Only thirteen lettermen returned. The "High Street Quarterbacks"—influential alumni, faculty, and townspeople—meddled in the program. The state's high school coaches sent their most talented prospects to Michigan, Notre Dame, and Pittsburgh. Ohio waited to see how "the Massillon Miracle Man" would take losing. Even athletic director Lynn St. John said he expected the Bukeyes to lose as many as four games.

Brown was the youngest head coach in Big 10 history and had

never coached in college, but he declared, "We play to win them all." And they nearly did. Ohio State came within eight points of the conference title. After the Buckeyes tied powerful Michigan in Ann Arbor, Brown raced onto the field, hugging them and slapping their backs, and Wolverine coach Fritz Crisler proclaimed him the league's "coach of the year."

Brown was the most popular man in a state giddy over its new "football dynasty," and scholastic stars flocked to Columbus. Among the dozen All-State players in Brown's first full recruiting class was a brawny "can't-miss" fullback named Tony Adamle, from Cleveland's tough Collinwood section. Adamle attracted numerous scholarships, some sweetened with crooked inducements tempting to a boy who once had to share a single pair of shoes with his father and brother. But from the time he watched Massillon beat Alliance before 27,000 at the Akron Rubber Bowl, Adamle longed to play for Brown.

Part of "the greatest yearling crop ever harvested" at Ohio State, Adamle grudgingly became a center and endured a practice regimen that forbade kneeling, removing helmets, or drinking. Eligible only for freshman games, he looked on as the varsity swept to a national title. The Buckeyes defeated Michigan on

Homecoming and carried Brown from the field while Ohio Stadium shook with the chant "O-U-R man is C-O-A-C-H Brown!" In the locker room, Brown gasped, "We waited a long time for this." He had been in Columbus for less than two years.

"When we look back in the future at Paul Brown, we will say: 'He was a fruitful vine in the garden whose branches ran over the wall,'" said university president Howard L. Bevis.

"I was 18 years old, and I was completely, completely in awe of the guy," Adamle says.

He would have to wait five more years to play for his hero. As a radio operator on a B-25 based in Cairo, he next played in the "Pyramid League" of service teams in the eastern Mediterranean. By the time Adamle mustered out in 1945, Brown had left Ohio State amid controversy that would wrack the school for years.

After a disastrous 1943 season with a squad of inexperienced players and 4F military rejects, Brown joined the Navy. With St. John's help, he was assigned to "special duty" as an assistant football coach at Great Lakes Naval Station. Brown chose as caretaker for his program Carroll Widdoes, an aide who had also coached with him in Massillon.

Three weeks before the season, Great Lakes head coach Tony Hinkle received sea duty. Brown took over, knowing that on October 21, his new team would face Ohio State in a game the *Cleveland Press* called "an embarrassing and unwelcome job for Brown."

Columbus buzzed over the return of "Friend Paul" and the meeting between the 3-0 Buckeyes and one of the nation's top service teams. By Friday, fans jammed every hotel, night club, and restaurant in the city. That evening, Brown spoke to 1,500 members of the Quarterback Club, who stood and applauded for five minutes.

Widdoes followed Brown on the program, telling the club that Brown had warned him of "a rugged, man-to-man go with no quarter given."

Members presented Brown a new shotgun. One joked, "You may have to use this tomorrow if you win."

Brown didn't need the weapon, at least not for self-defense. His sailors treated the game as liberty, and Ohio State won 26-6 in front of 73,447 fans, three radio networks, five newsreel services, and writers from around the country. During the game, he paced, his expression frozen, but when he met Widdoes at midfield, Brown said, "You've made a reputation. You're big stuff."

After the game, Widdoes and Brown ate dinner with their wives. According to a reporter, "It was all in the family." But the family was about to be torn apart.

Widdoes's only other experience as a head coach had been at Longfellow Junior High in Massillon, but he led Ohio State to its first perfect season in twenty-eight years. Tailback Les Horvath won the Heisman Trophy, and Widdoes was the national coach of the year—the first time both honors had gone to the same school.

"The Paul Brown bombshell" dropped on February 9, 1945. Brown signed with Cleveland businessman Mickey McBride to coach a team in the All-American Conference, a new professional league.

Brown said his decision wasn't based on money, but the press and public made much of his contract. McBride had first tried to hire Notre Dame's Frank Leahy. Rebuffed, he said he would make Brown "the highest paid coach in America" and gave him a $25,000 salary and a percentage of the team's profits.

Decades later, Brown called leaving Ohio State the toughest decision of his life. At the time, McBride said, "Paul was the easiest person I ever hired. I could've signed him for $15,000, but I wanted to make a big splash."

St. John also claimed to have offered Brown $15,000—a fifty percent increase over the coach's prewar salary—to come back; Brown said St. John made no such offer.

Ohioans were resigned, incredulous, outraged: A man with three small children was obliged to better himself financially; the military had tainted the very personification of the college spirit; Brown was a mercenary who sold out his student body, the alumni, and college sports followers everywhere.

Fans worried that Brown might also lure Widdoes to Cleveland, a fear that was soon allayed. Within months, Widdoes was accusing "the most celebrated and revered Buck since Chic Harley" of undermining Ohio State by signing veterans who still had college eligibility, even though the Browns wouldn't play for more than a year.

"When he was here, I heard him in all of his speeches advise boys to get their college education first and then sign professional contracts. Now that he's in the pro game, he's doing an about-face," Widdoes charged.

Brown responded that his contracts included bonuses for players who finished their degrees.

Saying he didn't like the pressures of running a major-college program, Widdoes abruptly resigned after the 1945 season. He traded jobs with assistant Paul Bixler, who had also been hired by Brown.

Adamle returned to Ohio State in 1946, the dispute growing more spiteful. Criticized for making a halfhearted attempt to rehire Brown, St. John stated in a letter to the alumni magazine that the university was well rid of a man "who has, by his false statements, definitely unfitted himself for all time to come for holding any position in a reputable institution."

Brown said that the athletic director's attack must be camouflage for problems in his own department. "Maybe these recent events give some insight as to why I really left Ohio State," he remarked.

Brown had never been St. John's choice. After Schmidt was fired, the state clamored for Brown's appointment, but the aging athletic director continued, in his own expression, to "window-shop." Rumor had St. John hiring everyone from Marty Karow, varsity captain when Brown failed to make the OSU freshman team in 1926, to a mysterious "experienced coach who knows 'big-time' football."

"Remarkable as has been his success with school boys, I doubt much if he is sufficiently experienced to handle more mature adults," St. John said of Brown.

"College boys are just high school boys two years older," Brown said. "I'm not in the least fearful of the difference."

Brown was so confident that when he finally realized his "ultimate dream," he took three of his Massillon assistants with him to Ohio State and hired a fourth high school coach. He was called arrogant, foolhardy, paranoid, blinded by loyalty. Actually, Brown was paying a debt.

The Ohio High School Coaches Association had pressured St. John into hiring one of its own, hoping to set a precedent for future college openings. The association sent St. John a letter extolling Brown's virtues and implying that if he weren't hired, its members would direct their players anywhere except Ohio State. St. John capitulated.

Adamle had been a part of the bargain, but in 1946, the program was again in chaos. The Buckeyes began the season by forgetting to take a football on a trip to USC and ended it by losing to Michigan, 58-6—"one of the darkest days in school history," the *Columbus Dispatch* said.

Adamle, however, excelled as "6 feet, 205 pounds of bone-shattering linebacker." Against Northwestern, he intercepted two passes, returning the second 38 yards, then ripping off his helmet and bowing three times.

"He loves contact, he's gaining the experience he needs, he has good speed, and he's a good holler guy in there. His linebacking has been terrific," Bixler said.

During halftime of the Michigan game, St. John, who was to retire the next summer, received a new Chrysler in appreciation for 35 years of service. As "Mr. Saint" accepted the automobile, the crowd "booed to a fare thee well," according to *Sport* magazine.

Shortly thereafter, Brown also received a new car—a gift from McBride for winning the first AAFC title—and Bixler quit.

The "Bring Back Brown" contingent mobilized even as Adamle considered jumping to the pros. In February of 1947, the Ohio House of Representatives voted 66-21 to direct the Ohio State athletic board to hire Brown, who refused to talk about the job. St. John circumvented the High Street Quarterbacks by quickly hiring former Buckeye star Wes Fesler and arranging to have Dick Larkins become the next athletic director.

Meanwhile, Brown had heard that the Chicago Bears were interested in Adamle. Saying he liked the former Air Force heavyweight boxing champion's "viciousness," Brown signed the junior. When Adamle announced he was leaving school to join former Buckeyes Lou Groza, Tommy James, and Dante Lavelli in Cleveland, one paper ran the news above its masthead, and some in Columbus began calling Brown "public nuisance number one."

The coach said that he was merely keeping a good player away from a rival league. "We're going to run our business aggressively—that means to win," he said.

Columbus remained split over

Brown, the factions growing more vociferous as Fesler staggered. He resigned after the 1950 season, and early in 1951, Brown finally returned to campus to interview for his old job. Fifteen hundred students and a drum corps greeted him. A riot nearly erupted when a Browns' fan plowed through the crowd in a car decorated with a sign reading "There's No Place Like Home! Cleveland Wants You Back!" Demonstrators ripped the sign off and burned it.

Despite the enthusiasm of Brown's devotees, Woody Hayes, a compromise candidate, was named to the post. Brown said that he had interviewed for the job only to "have some fun" and generate publicity for his professional team.

Even as late as 1967, when Brown founded the Cincinnati Bengals, Ohio State fans were still angry. Some held that the Bengals were sure to draw large crowds because of the Buckeye faithful who would turn out to watch Brown lose. Still, in 1989, the National Football Foundation Hall of Fame gave Brown its gold medal for his contributions to college football.

Attempting to make the Cleveland Browns after only one year of college play, Adamle ignored the conflict. Between fist fights in practice, he told reporters that he planned to start at his old position,

fullback, Marion Motley notwithstanding. The brash rookie didn't beat out Motley, but he moved Brown to say, "I would be a pretty sick fellow today, knowing what I do about Tony, if George Halas had gotten him."

Adamle did replace Motley at outside linebacker, allowing the future Hall of Famer to concentrate on offense. But playing for Brown was not as blissful as he had imagined. He became one of the coach's more outspoken critics as well as ringleader of the "Filthy Five," a rugged crew who wore the same practice togs all season without washing them—a custom their fastidious coach couldn't have appreciated. Yet, in 1950, Brown made Adamle team captain.

That season, the Browns allowed the fewest points in team history and won the NFL title, and Adamle was named to the league's first Pro Bowl. Brown called him "one of pro football's greats," adding, "He smacks 'em so hard the opposition must think he's a sadist."

A year later, neither Adamle nor Brown would think much of each other. In an opening loss to San Francisco, Adamle badly injured an ankle. A doctor said he would be out at least a month; he kept the ankle loose by hobbling the corridors of the team's hotel in slippers, took a shot of Novocain, and played the following week. Cleveland trailed Los Angeles at halftime, but Adamle intercepted a pass to set up a touchdown and exhorted his teammates to victory.

"The whole team caught that flaming spirit when they saw what their leader had done," Brown said. "If we hadn't won that one, well, maybe we wouldn't have won a few others."

Two weeks later, after Cleveland had beaten New York 14-13, Adamle lay on a training table in a nearly-empty locker room. A deep cut under his swollen left eye had been stitched. His left hand was twice its normal size. He had been bashed across the nose and kicked in the shins and the ribs and had the wind knocked out of him.

"You've got to hand it to Adamle," Brown said. "He gives this team its attitude. He's a fighter all the way."

Cleveland won eleven straight games. The defense was again the league's best. Adamle made All-Pro and the Pro Bowl.

In the championship game, the Browns held the Rams to 81 yards rushing, intercepted three passes, and limited Los Angeles to a field goal on seven straight plays from the one yard line. But the Rams scored on a long touchdown pass midway through the fourth quarter to win, 24-17.

Otto Graham had thrown three interceptions in the second half and

been sacked five times. Also, according to the *Cleveland Plain Dealer*, Brown had become panicky after the last Ram touchdown and abandoned the short passes that had worked all day. Earlier in the week, in fact, Brown had predicted that his team would eventually lose a title game, perhaps on a long pass near the end. Nevertheless, he blamed the defense for the loss.

Adamle was infuriated. During practices for the Pro Bowl, hostility festered. Adamle decided to pursue his own dream, an odd one for a man who described himself as a dead-end kid who had been "a hell of a thief," one that would require him to use his hands as skillfully as he did glomming items off shopkeepers' shelves or brawling on streetcorners: country doctor.

Encouraged by Brown, Adamle, the first in his family to graduate high school, had completed his bachelor's and master's degrees. He thought, "The hell with it. I'm gonna shoot the works," and quit at 27 to attend medical school. Before Adamle could announce his retirement, though, Brown traded him to Green Bay, his penal colony for those in disfavor. Calling the trade "not worth a comment," Adamle never reported.

By the fall of 1954, Adamle was in his last year at Western Reserve Medical School and almost bankrupt. Likewise, Brown was in a bind.

Cleveland opened by surrendering 90 points in three games, two of them losses. Brown, who had reacquired his rights, asked Adamle to come back. At that moment, Adamle said, the vindictive dictator with whom he had been so angry "seemed like the Lord standing on the mountain."

Adamle practiced only on Thursdays but helped solidify the defense. "He's working as hard as a rookie," Brown said. "He's like a kid with a new toy. His spirit is wonderful and infectious."

The Browns allowed only 72 points the rest of the season and routed Detroit for the championship. Adamle missed the title game because of a broken leg, but the $2,478 winner's share erased his debts and allowed him to retire.

"I was 30. I was an intern. I was a real doctor. I didn't need to play football anymore," he said.

He became a general practitioner, team physician at Kent State University, and an early specialist in sports medicine. "The football doctor," as he came to be known, had six children, including former NFL running back Mike. He retired at 70, took up the accordion, and joined a Polka band. Before his death in 2001, arthritis caused him to limp badly and he had had colon cancer, but he still golfed and skied.

Emotion sometimes overcame him as he talked in the small restaurant of a Kent motel. His voice thickened. Tears welled. But he also laughed frequently, a playful glint brightening his intelligent eyes.

Patrons and employees greeted "Doc" often. He smiled and waved and called back to them. He wore a thick gold chain over a baggy dun crewneck sweater, creased gray dress slacks, white athletic socks under OP sandals, and a 1950 NFL championship ring. He was bandy-legged and burly, his short gray hair combed forward. He spoke rapidly, lisping slightly, his language salty. He was like the roguish old sawbones in a Humphrey Bogart picture.

"I came up from the mud," he said. "I owe everything I've got to football."

Like Brown, Adamle survived his first wife. The loss made him feel a kinship with Brown, who, Adamle now says, was the greatest coach ever, despite his faults.

"Anybody who ever played for him, when it comes down to it, they have to say really good things about him," Adamle said. "Maybe he screwed them up a little bit, or maybe he got too conservative and all that shit, but deep down, every one of them would play for him again in a damn minute if they could. I would."

# *Tony* ADAMLE

**"** I SAID, 'PAL, WE GOTTA GET
the hell out of here.' I was two and a half months old, and had just been
born in Fairmont, West Virginia. That's when I knew I was smart.

My dad worked in the coal mines, and when we came up to Cleveland,
his cousin got him a job at Fisher Body. He never got off the boat, really,
poor guy. He was an immigrant—Slovenian. I think there used to be a 'j' in
the name somewhere. My father went home to Slovenia for the first time in
fifty years, was there ten days, and died in the house he was born in.

When I was in elementary school, I was always in the high IQ classes,
but I remember one year, we only had one pair of shoes between my brother,
my old man, and me. I couldn't go to school. When I came back, the school
gave me some clothes, but they took me out of the classes I had been in and
put me back with the low IQ kids. You know how it is; when you get
thrown in with the apes, you become worse than the apes are. From then
on, I was really bad, until I went to the service.

When I was in the ninth grade, the principal gave me a suit. I never had
a suit in my life. It was a used suit. I was watching the shot putters at track
practice one day. The track coach came up to me and said, 'That's a nice
suit there.'

I said, 'Yeah.'

He said, 'I gave that to the principal.'

I'll never forgive that guy. Sometimes, little things like that make people
different.

I got started in sports because all the people I looked up to were athletes. They were either good players or they were in jail. I came from a really bad neighborhood in Cleveland, in Collinwood, right by the railroad tracks. You were either on one side of the tracks or the other side. I went to Collinwood High School and majored in machine shop. I was voted 'least likely to succeed.' The only thing I did was play football. The thing that changed me was, my last year in high school I made All-Ohio. All of sudden, I'm somebody.

When I got to be a senior, people are coming to look me up to go to school here and there. People I'd never heard of were coming to my house. That's when I started waking up a little bit.

IN '42, PAUL BROWN RECRUITED ME to Ohio State. Everybody knew about Paul Brown. Our high school coach took us down to see Massillon play, and I was amazed the whole time. The star of that game was Tommy James. He ran for about four touchdowns. He was a gazelle.

People recruited me for different places. They were going to give me everything, clothes, this and that. I was going to go to Georgetown. But all Paul Brown had to do was talk to me one time, and, *boom*, I threw everything out the window and went to Ohio State.

He got me a job in Columbus. I worked at the state capitol building, pulling the flag down on Saturday and Sunday nights. A fraternity recruited me, and I got my room and board at the fraternity house. It was like getting a scholarship, but they didn't have scholarships like they do now.

Brown was the varsity coach that year, but I was on the freshman team. I was so enamored with this guy, about how smart he was, that he could've talked me into anything. I was 18 years old, and I didn't have any experience with anybody like that.

I only spent about two months at Ohio State. I played on the freshman team, then I went into the service. I enlisted in the Air Force because all my buddies were gone and everybody from the fraternity was gone. This was in fall. Football season was over. The war was going on. Buddies of yours were getting killed, so we all went. I had just turned 18.

"The hell with it," I said.

The service really changed me around. I probably would've been in jail, otherwise. I was a heck of a thief. I could steal anything. I did everything you're not supposed to do. Three years in the service really woke me up.

I went to Egypt and, son-of-a-gun, somehow I ended up on the football team. I played in the overseas bowl game. The called it the Wienie

Bowl. We had all these all-stars from the Mediterranean, and we played the all-stars from Italy. We had a bunch of Arabs in the stands selling hot dogs. I played service ball a couple of years, and then I went back to Ohio State.

I originally went to Ohio State to play for Paul Brown, but he left before I came back from the service. I had three years eligibility left, but I was really unhappy at Ohio State. We lost a lot of games, and I was sitting on the bench. We got beat by Michigan something like 50-6.

Dante Lavelli was my roommate, and I said, 'Dante, I'm not going through this crap again.'

I WAS GOING TO SIGN WITH THE BEARS. I had a letter from George Halas and one from Arch Ward (the sports editor of the *Chicago Tribune* and principal organizer of both the College All-Star Game and the All-American Football Conference), inviting me to play in the College All-Star Game. I was only a sophomore in college, but I could play in the All-Star Game because my original class had graduated.

Groza and Lavelli and those guys had turned pro already. I saw that letter from Arch Ward, and I said, 'Shoot, I'm gonna turn pro.'

Lavelli called up Brown and said, 'Hey, Paul, George Halas is going to sign up Adamle tomorrow morning. You better send somebody down here to sign him.'

So Brown sent Bill Edwards down, and they signed me that morning. I was going to sign with George Halas that afternoon. I was still a first-quarter freshman when I quit Ohio State and went to the Browns.

I played in the All-Star Game, and we beat the hell out of the Bears in front of the biggest crowd in history, 103,000 people.

That first year in Cleveland, I made $5,000 and got a $750 bonus. That was a lot of money then. There was no messing around about contracts. He just told me what the contract was and I said, 'Okay,' or I told him what I wanted, and that was that. He didn't try to finagle you down, but he paid you what he thought you were worth, period.

Every training camp was a rat race, because you wanted to make the team. It was terrible. You never knew whether you were going to make anything or not. That's why Brown could have such great teams.

He found out that you learn everything in the first hour of practice. After that first hour, it becomes diminishing returns. The more time you put in, the less you learn. So by the time two hours are up, you've forgotten everything that you learned in that first hour. Our practices were an hour and a half, and that was it, *boom*. Not because he was a good guy; because he knew you didn't get anything after that. He planned everything right down the line, *boom, boom, boom, boom*. I wish I still had my notebook. It'd be worth about $100,000 now, at some of these shows.

He remembered things, boy. If he had it in for you, he could be one tough guy. I remember the time he threw Jim Daniell off the team. Three of the guys went out and got drunk. I think it was Daniell and Mac Speedie and Lou Rymkus. Daniell was trying to keep them from being arrested. Brown kicked him out in a team meeting.

He said, 'Daniell, you're through. Speedie and Rymkus, I'll take care of you later.'

Daniell just got up and left. I heard that after that happened, Daniell's one ambition in life was to make so much money that he could buy Paul Brown out.

ONE OF THE FUNNIEST THINGS that ever happened is we were playing Green Bay down in Akron, and a bunch of guys got drunk the night before the game. We got on the elevator afterwards, and Paul Brown gets on. I'm shoving guys in the corner to keep them away from him. I wasn't even drinking, but the next morning, I was sicker than hell. I was throwing up, and I had to play both ways because Marion Motley was hurt. When we got there, I gave this big speech before the game about what good shape we were in, and I was the first one to conk out. I said, 'I'm gonna start drinking like those guys.'

Brown would make allowances if he thought you could play. If he caught you doing something, you were in trouble—if he didn't need you. If he needed you, he would overlook some of that stuff. It's like old Motley. Motley was not a great football player at the end. He did all his playing in the first few years. He had only one good year in the NFL. That was in '50.

Jimmy Aiken was the coach at Nevada (University of Nevada-Reno). He'd been at Canton-McKinley, where Motley went to high school. When Motley got out of the service, he went to Nevada, and there was a professor there who prided himself on the fact that he had never put a student to sleep in thirty years of teaching.

Two minutes, and Marion's head went down. After two weeks, this guy couldn't stand it anymore. He finally stopped the class and said, 'Marion, what is there about my voice that puts you to sleep after five minutes of me talking?'

Motley said, 'I don't know. It must be this high attitude.'

There were a lot of funny stories about Marion.

Paul Brown made me his captain in Cleveland, and I don't know why he ever did that. The team didn't choose captains. He made guys captains. That was probably the greatest day of my life, when he did that. I guess part of the reason he did it is because I always told him the damn truth. I didn't feel like I had any kind of special relationship with him. He didn't want that. If he wanted to get some points across, he'd just throw them to me. I didn't pull any punches; no matter what I thought. I talked back to him, and I could get along with the guys. That was the big thing.

The guys would say, 'If you want to get something done, just tell Tony.'

I'd get guys raises, because the guy would listen to me. When he used to come down to the final cut, he always brought somebody in from the team to see what *we* thought about who should be playing. One year, it came down between Don Shula and another guy. The other guy was a real flashy guy who could run like hell, and Shula was a guy who just trudged along. He wasn't a real special athlete or anything, but he always got the job done.

I said, 'I think when the going's tough, we should have Shula. Shula puts out to the end.'

He traded the other guy. We kept Shula. If he had been put on waivers, he'd be teaching down at Mentor High School now. Life is funny, the little tiny breaks that make things happen.

Here's a 1950 championship ring. Look at that son-of-a-gun. That's the year Groza kicked the field goal to win it at the end of the game.

We played the Eagles that year in the first game. The Eagles had Chuck Bednarik, they had Steve Van Buren, they had Tommy Thompson. We had Otto Graham, we had Motley, we had the guy I think was the greatest end who ever lived, Mac Speedie. George Young was probably the best defensive end I ever saw. We beat the hell out of them.

I SAID THIS MANY TIMES: they don't talk about us defensively in the '50s. Almost all of the guys who are in the Hall of Fame were on offense, because they wrote about those guys then. George Young, John Kissell, Tommy James, I include myself, too—we had some guys on defense who could really play. But we were all so closeknit that one guy wasn't always outstanding.

On our team, it was Graham, Speedie, Lavelli, Motley; Graham, Speedie, Lavelli, Motley. We didn't get any publicity on defense. There wasn't the media hype like there is now. But we were a great damned football team because we won defensively. We tied New York in 1947 (28-28), and I made four tackles on the goal line. Brown doubled my salary for that game.

Tommy James was one of the great defensive backs, but nobody wrote about him. The year the Rams beat us for the championship (24-17 in 1951), Tom Fears caught two long touchdown passes. Tommy James got blamed for that, and it was damned Cliff Lewis's fault. The pictures showed Tommy James chasing Tom Fears, and it wasn't even his man.

James was a great runner, but something happened to him in the service so he was never the great runner again. He was a heck of a defensive back, though. He's one of those guys that people overlooked all the time, but that guy belongs in the Hall of Fame.

The only reason I had any publicity at all is because I was the captain and played in the Pro Bowls, and I got to know the sportswriters. The only other guys who got written about were Bill Willis and Len Ford, Ford because he was so big. George Young was ten times the football player Len Ford was. One time, we were practicing, and all this snow was on the ground. Lenny came to practice, and the snow was all over the ground, except around him. He had so much booze in him that the snow all melted.

Our team had good guys and guys who weren't very nice. Maybe we should've been more like Otto Graham. He was a good guy. But the guys who weren't very nice people were good football players. We had 'The Filthy Five,' they used to call us: me and Tommy James, Abe Gibron, John Kissell, Frank Gatski. They make up stories now about why they called us 'The Filthy Five.' You know, we didn't wash our equipment and all of that. As you grow older, the stories get better.

IN '48, WE PLAYED THREE GAMES in eight days, and one of those games, I played with a broken ankle. I played the whole game. I got shot with novocaine, and I was walking in the hallways of the hotel to keep my ankle loose. I played that whole year by getting shot with novocaine before every game. I didn't practice at all, just played in the games.

One thing Paul Brown really liked was people who had some brains. He always wanted to get rid of this image of football players being dumb as hell. When he heard that I was going to go to medical school, the guy almost went crazy.

See, I had always had it in the back of my mind that I was going to go to medical school, but I never thought it could happen. It was one of my fantasies, you might say, because I looked up to doctors.

Brown encouraged me, so the winter quarter and the spring quarter and half the summer, I went back to school, to Kent State, because it was closer than Ohio State. On the side, I was taking all these anatomy courses, and I was doing good in them. I got my degree in phys ed, then I got my master's degree in phys ed and then I looked at the degree and I said, 'What the hell do I know?'

I didn't know anything. It was just a piece of paper. It was just a bunch of b.s., and I can b.s. with anybody. I had a minor in physiology and physics, so I had all of my premed work done.

I said, 'I got two kids. The hell with it. I'm gonna shoot the works,' so I went to med school when I was 27 years old.

I probably quit a couple of years too early when I quit the first time. I played the first five years, then I said, 'After this is over, what the hell is there?' I wanted to make something out of myself.

I only applied to one school—Western Reserve. That was the only place I could go so that I could practice and go to school at the same time.

I went in and said, 'Paul, I'm gonna go to med school.'

He really wanted me to do that, but he was a smart son-of-gun. When I told him that I was going to go to med school, before I could announce my retirement, he traded me to Green Bay.

I said, 'That son-of-gun.'

SO, I GOT A JOB RIGHT AWAY, scouting for Joe Stydahar (head coach of the Chicago Cardinals) and George Halas. I said, 'Shoot, I'll just be a scout on the side.'

When Brown heard about me scouting, he went crazy. He sent Fritz Heisler over to my house, then he sent somebody else over to my house.

I said, 'The heck with 'em. I'm not going back. I'm going to med school and that's it.'

So, before I could sign with Green Bay or anybody, he trades me back. He got my rights back.

He told me, 'If you're going to scout, you're going to scout for me. We own your rights again.'

When I came back to the Browns in 1954, I called Stydahar up. I said, 'Joe, I can sign with the Browns if I want to.'

He said, 'Go ahead. I don't even know if I'm going to be here next week.'

That's the kind of guy Stydahar was.

When Brown got me back, Tommy Thompson broke his leg, so he asked me to come back. I was about broke, but he didn't know that, or else he would've got me for nothing. I made more money that year than I did any other year I played for the Browns. I was in my third-year of med school. I played and went to school at the same time.

When I started school, the dean of the medical school told me, 'Tony, I don't want you coming in here and telling me that you're going to take off a little bit to go back and play pro football.'

I told him 'okay,' then Brown asked me to come back. In med school, we had one day off a week to do whatever we wanted to do. That was my defensive day. We had our defensive day on Thursday. I practiced on Thursday, played on Sunday, went back to school on Monday.

I had the two kids, the wife, and I didn't let her work, either. I said, 'Why should she have to pay a price for something I want to do?'

I HAD SAVED UP ENOUGH that I could get through three years, and when Paul called me back, he gave me enough money so that I could finish school.

The guy who got me to come back the second time was Abe Gibron. When Tommy Thompson broke his leg, Abe told Brown to call me. Abe got into Brown the same way I did. He listened to Abe even though he didn't like him sometimes, because the son-of-a-gun could play.

We lost our middle linebacker when Tommy Thompson got hurt, and Abe told Brown, 'Damned Adamle is over there. We got a guy already there. Get him.'

I hadn't played for two and a half years. I had two days of practice and then I played against the Cardinals. The first play of the game, Ollie Matson ran a reverse, and I caught him from behind. My first play. I knew everything about them.

I played that whole year, and I finally got in shape, and I broke my leg the last game. Pittsburgh beat us. Some guy hit me on a kickoff.

I said, 'It's about time to quit,' and then I graduated from med school.

I retired for the last time when I was 30. I was an intern. I was a real doctor. I didn't need to play football anymore.

I started practicing medicine in Akron. I had my own practice in Kent, and I got to be the team doctor for Kent State. I was the team doctor for thirty-eight years. I started out as a general practitioner, but I gravitated toward sports medicine. I was in the practice before there was even such a thing as 'sports medicine.' They used to call me 'that football doctor in Kent.' Everybody came to me because I had played for the Browns, and they figured I must know something about football. I worked on more players than you can imagine.

I had a great relationship among the players I played with. I had a great relationship with my patients. I don't miss the medicine so much, but I miss the people.

People say, 'Doc, why'd you retire? We need you.'

I say, 'I'd rather quit two years too soon than two years too late.'

Let's face it, once you reach 70, there's little things you forget, and you've got to recognize that.

I HAVE SIX KIDS, every one of them graduated from college, and I'm the only one in my family who graduated from high school. Mike was my firstborn. He's 42 now. I was at a football game every Friday and every Saturday. On Saturday, I was Kent State's doctor, and on Friday, I was the high school doctor. I had him with me on the sidelines every game. All my kids were, and they all got scholarships, too. Mike played at Northwestern and with the Chicago Bears; Mark played at Purdue; Vic, my baby boy, is coaching at the University of Minnesota with Glen Mason.

I didn't see Brown much after I retired. Right after I was done, I didn't go to games. By that time, I was tired of football. When Mike played for the Bears, I had a motorhome. Vic was playing high school ball. Some weeks, we'd get in the motorhome, watch Vic play, then go watch Mark play for Purdue, and then the next day, we'd go to Chicago and watch Mike play. One Friday, one Saturday, one Sunday. Come Monday, I had enough football. On Sundays, of course, you saw all the players who got hurt on the weekend. Sunday was one of my busiest days.

I saw Brown years later, after he remarried. I remarried, too. My first wife died, too. They had this big thing, 'Bogey Busters,' for Paul Brown. My wife bought me this red sport coat, and I got on the elevator with him and his wife. He looked at me and said, 'Tony, I never thought I'd see you wearing a pink coat.'

That's all he said, but there was like a message that long to it. He was so terse. He'd come right down to the point, and that was it.

I don't think Paul Brown lost too much at all, because he just went from one phase of football to the other, from the coaching to the management. Don't forget that Paul Brown was 70 years old and he still had the Bengals. This guy was about twenty years ahead of everybody else. Take a look at some of the offenses now, the split backs, the wideouts. They're using the same damn offense that he had then.

He was a very smart person, except that his smartness got him in trouble there at the end. Brown did make the Browns what they were, but he didn't understand how things were. That's when mercenary things became the most important things in this country. It was the money that counted.

What I hear is that when he sold the team to Modell, Brown had ten or fifteen per cent of the Browns, and he made like 300 per cent profit on it. I heard he turned about $75,000 into $600,000 or something like that. But he thought that he could still run the whole thing. Modell paid all this money for the team, and Brown didn't have a word to say about it. He made all this money by selling the team to Modell, and he thought he could sell it and own it at the same time.

Everybody started making a lot of money then. Mickey McBride had all the money in the world, but he didn't give a damn. When owning the franchise got to be too much, he just said, 'The hell with it. I don't need the headache.'

Money doesn't mean anything when you come right down to it. I had this cancer of the colon. What's money do? It doesn't do a damn thing.

Modell had the money, but he didn't know the football. He wanted to be involved, but you have to know the football to be involved. He was something like this Jerry Jones is over in Dallas.

It was a terrible time here when Modell fired Brown. The only thing that saved Modell then was that they had a big newspaper strike, and they couldn't put all the stuff in the paper. For about seven or eight or nine weeks, they couldn't write about it.

I'm sure different guys have different opinions of Brown. A lot of guys hated the son-of-a-gun. I could never say I hated him. I could stand up to him, although I knew deep down inside, he could do anything he wanted to me. I think he treated me the way he did because he knew I didn't give him any bull. That's the way it was.

Players said a lot of b.s. about him. When Brown didn't need them anymore, then they all thought he was no good. I was mad at him at times, and when he traded me to Green Bay, that's when I really got pissed off at him. But I said, 'The hell with him. I'll just do my thing.'

I could've been mad at him a million times, but I knew what kind of guy he was. I could see the real guy. That's one reason I really looked up to him. I could see through all his faults.

Anybody who ever played for him, when it comes down to it, they have to say good things about him. Maybe he screwed them up a little bit or maybe he got too conservative, but down deep, every one of them would play for him again in one damned minute if they could. I would, if I could do that.

It will never be the way it was again, though. There's just so much money involved in the thing that it's incomprehensible. I got $15,000 my last year. That was big money.

IT'S HARD FOR ME TO EVEN TALK ABOUT THE GUY, because even now, to this day, he's such a big idol to me. If the guy had wanted to be a doctor, he would probably have been the greatest doctor who ever lived. He was so precise in everything he did, even in the way he talked. In my life, there's nobody like him. Tom Landry and all the rest, they learned from him. There's one guy I can compare him to, but I never met him: Jesus Christ.

Do I ever think about the part I played in the history of the NFL? I think about it all the time. It's been a big part of my life. I have another part, though. I came into another life.

Football is a big part of your life, but life does go on. That was a good part of my life. I had some bad parts in my life, but that was a good part, and the good parts were certainly better than the bad ones ever thought of being.

I had this life as a football player, and it was a great life. But it wasn't the whole thing. I had this other part, as a doctor. You've got to be able to go from one part to another. I think about football, but it wasn't the only thing. 🙶🙶

# Dub's Day

"HARD BLOCKING and tackling still are the things that win football games, and that's the way we expect to play against the Browns Sunday," Hunk Anderson warned.

Anderson, line coach of the Chicago Bears, was delivering a pep talk to the team's alumni association, a large and boisterous group of fans and former players whose president was the legendary Red Grange. The Bears and their supporters were eager to trounce Cleveland, a team Chicago viewed as impudent upstarts.

The Browns had won all four titles in the defunct All-American Football Conference, but the NFL had dismissed them as straw champions of a minor league. The Browns also romped through their first two seasons in the NFL, bewildering opponents with a sophisticated offense based on timing, speed, and deception. As Anderson whipped up the crowd in the midst of the 1951 season, Cleveland had won twenty of its twenty-three games in the NFL and was the league's defending champion.

That Sunday's game would be the first regular-season meeting between the NFL's new glamour team and its most storied franchise, and the first between football's two most famous coaches—George Halas and Paul Brown.

Anderson had a simple and ominous plan for whipping the Browns. Chicago would forget about matching wits, unleash infamous tough guys such as Ed "Hatchet Man" Sprinkle, and bludgeon Cleveland. The Bears would give the Browns a lesson in vintage Monsters-of-the-Midway football, which, as one writer put it, consisted of "the science of the right cross, the left hook, the cleated foot in the teeth, and the armored knee in the kidney."

Anderson sneered of the Browns' complex offense, "I don't get all this calculus stuff." He then revealed the fail-safe for his strategy: "If the boys hit with a little more enthusiasm than usual and get fined, we have a jackpot ready to take care of that for them. Trouble with our boys is that they've been too worried about fines. They don't need to worry Sunday."

The Bears should have worried. Anderson's game plan worked for only a little more than a quarter. It

was undone not by a massive fullback gouging out yards or by powerful ends ripping down passes but by a spindly halfback who was so thin he looked frail. In the most sensational individual performance in team history, Dub Jones scored six touchdowns as Cleveland humbled Chicago, 42-21.

Early in the second quarter, Jones ran two yards for the game's first score, and he added a 24-yard touchdown catch before halftime. His 12-yard sweep put Cleveland ahead, 21-0. After the Bears finally scored, Jones raced 27 yards for a touchdown on what one newspaper called "an almost supernatural sprint." His 42-yard dash gave Cleveland a 37-7 lead, and he caught a 43-yard touchdown in the fourth quarter. Jones handled the ball only twelve times but gained 196 yards.

"They spent all their time trying to beat us up, and they weren't watching Dub," linebacker Tony Adamle said.

Jones's feat tied a record set by Ernie Nevers twenty-two years earlier, when the league included such questionable competition as the Staten Island Stapletons. It would not be equaled until Gale Sayers did it in 1965, and it has never been bettered.

The game was also the triumph of Paul Brown's "scientific football" over its brutal forebear and the high-water mark of the Cleveland franchise.

"There's nothing left to do—except win a second straight championship," a Cleveland sports editor smugly opined after the Bears had been vanquished.

There would be no title for Cleveland in 1951. With three minutes left in the championship game, the Browns had the ball on the Los Angeles Rams' 42, trailing 24-17. On fourth and two, Brown called for a pitchout to Jones. The Rams threw him for a loss, and for the first time ever, Cleveland did not win the title of its league.

A year later, Jones badly injured a knee and missed the loss to Detroit in the championship game. He never recovered.

He gained only 28 yards rushing and did not score in 1953. He retired, but teammates talked him into coming back. After two more seasons, Jones finally agreed with Brown's carping assessment of his older players as "over the hill" and went home to northern Louisiana to tend his construction firm and his growing family.

Soon, though, Brown phoned to offer him a job as an assistant coach. He admired Brown's ability to organize and his attention to detail and says the coach had such a special regard for him that, at times, Jones served as an intermediary between Brown and other players.

"You might say I was the teacher's pet," he says, "but I ran with the rat gang—Abe Gibron, Frank Gatski, and those guys. I was out with Tony Adamle's Mafia friends and the whole deal. But Otto and anyone else who was really involved with the football world knew that Paul had respect for me and what I thought."

However, the pragmatic country boy in Jones recognized Brown's flaws: his inconsistent discipline; the way he hid behind a curtain of aloofness, a composure so unwavering it became unearthly; his minor hypocrisies—"I never saw him in church, although he made it comfortable for *us* to be there."

He had also watched Brown freely tongue-lash his assistants—"the poor devils," Jones calls them—and knew he could expect no different treatment and would probably have little freedom. He decided to stay in Ruston, his hometown.

It was not the first time Jones had refused Paul Brown.

Jones was brought up in the Deep South of the early part of the century, a place where matters of honor quickly turned violent. His father had spent time in jail for killing a man and was himself shot to death. His mother moved her four sons from the family farm to town, where she kept a boarding house.

They survived on rent, odd jobs, and public works.

"People looking in on it would say it was tough, I guess, but I wouldn't take anything for those days and that experience. We had a cow and a garden and what have you, and we made it okay," Jones says.

Despite his gangly frame, he followed his brothers into sports, playing on Ruston High School's first state championship football team and making All-Louisiana in 1941.

Jones won a scholarship to LSU, but when war broke out, he enlisted in the submarine service and was sent for training to Tulane University, where he also played running back.

At the time, Brown was assembling a powerhouse at Great Lakes Naval Station, and he attempted to call Jones to recruit him. Jones never responded. Six years later, at lunch the day before a game in New York, Brown, who was sitting at the head table, suddenly demanded to know why.

From across the dining room, Jones said that he had wanted sea duty, not to play football.

"I know that," Brown snapped. "They told me of your ambitions, but that still doesn't explain why you ignored my call. How come?"

"I didn't want you to talk me into playing," Jones said. "It would have been easy for you to persuade me, and I took no chances."

"How do you like that? A fightin' man," Brown said.

Asked why he had broached the subject, Brown said, "Just been thinking," and quickly added that he was trying to inspire Jones for the game.

The war ended before Jones went to sea, and he was drafted by both the Chicago Cardinals of the NFL and the Miami Seahawks of the AAFC. He signed with Miami, a team so poorly financed that other franchises had to help pay its bills. The Seahawks lost their first three games on the road by 111 points and came home to paltry crowds. Jones pulled a hamstring, and the coach who drafted him was ousted in a coup led by an assistant who despised the highly-paid rookie.

Traded to Brooklyn, where he was expected to play tailback, Jones broke a hand and was relegated to the secondary. After two seasons, the teams he had played for had won six games. Jones had handled the ball fewer than a hundred times and had scored only four touchdowns.

"You play with losing ball clubs, and you start to wonder how much a part of that losing you are," he says.

Brown frequently claimed to have traded the rights to a number one draft pick for Jones because he recognized his potential as a receiver. However, Jones had caught only twenty-one passes as a pro, and

Brown first used him on defense. Actually, Jones says, Blanton Collier, then an assistant, urged Brown to make the deal.

Jones welcomed the change, but he didn't immediately impress his new coach. At one point, Brown removed him from the starting lineup and insisted that Jones's hands were not good enough for him to play receiver. Even after assistant Dick Gallagher lobbied successfully to move him to halfback, Jones was overshadowed by Cleveland's offensive stars. Brown seems to have been unsure just how to use a 6' 4" sprinter in a scheme that featured neither outside runs nor passes to halfbacks.

Jones's four-yard touchdown run—Cleveland's last in the league—capped the 1949 AAFC championship game, but he remained unappreciated.

"The Browns have great ends, a peerless quarterback, a fine fullback and a superb line, but they never had that halfback who could go all the way. Never a (Cliff) Battles, a (George) McAfee, a (Steve) Van Buren," a reporter wrote as the Browns were preparing to enter the NFL.

That perception soon changed.

In their first NFL game, the Browns faced defending champion Philadelphia and its vaunted "Eagle Defense." Philadelphia coach Earle

"Greasy" Neale sent Russ Craft, a veteran defensive back with a solid reputation, to watch Jones when he ran pass routes from the backfield.

Jones burned Craft for the Browns' first score, on a 59-yard reception, caught four more balls, and set up Cleveland's last touchdown with a 57-yard run. The Browns crushed Philadelphia, 35-10, rolling up 346 yards and four touchdowns through the air and causing the *New York Times* to gush, "The Browns have another (Don) Hutson in Mac Speedie. They also have another one in Dante Lavelli and they have a third in Dub Jones."

Jones was, in Brown's words, "the third dimension in our passing game." Cleveland's attack became the prototype of modern professional offenses.

Jones ran sweeps and flips, went into motion and darted into the secondary, split wide as one of the game's early true flankers, and was adept at turning screen passes into long touchdowns. In 1951, when Motley and Speedie were hurt, he led Cleveland in rushing, gained over a thousand total yards, and scored twelve touchdowns.

The same reporter who had so recently lamented Cleveland's lack of an outstanding halfback now wrote, "The skinny speedster from the Cajun country each week cements more tightly his claim to the title the best ball carrier in American football. Add to that his recognized position as one of the greatest pass-catchers in American football and you've got yourself a pretty fair country halfback."

Shortly after Jones stunned the Bears, Brown called him "the best halfback in the NFL" and one of his favorite players. Jones was the first Cleveland halfback to make All-Pro. Over ten seasons, he averaged nearly eight yards every time he touched the ball. Brown later said that Jones should be in the Hall of Fame.

Seven years after he retired, Jones received another entreaty from Cleveland. Collier, who had taken over after Art Modell fired Brown, wanted him as an assistant, even though Jones had little to do with football except to watch his sons play. Reluctantly, Jones agreed to help out for six months. That season as a "consultant" turned into five years as offensive coordinator, as Collier, who was partially deaf and unable to hear all that was happening on the sidelines, turned much of the responsibility for the offense over to Jones.

The Browns' attack flourished. In 1963, Jones's first year, Cleveland set a league rushing record. The team rode its offense to the NFL title the following season, averaging nearly thirty points a game and scoring more points than Cleveland had in any year since 1946. The defense gave

up almost twenty-four points a game in 1965, but the Browns still made it to the championship. In 1966, the Browns set team records for total touchdowns, touchdown passes, first downs, passing yards, and total yards.

As the *Cleveland Press* put it, "Jones has a warmth, a contagious enthusiasm, and a personal magnetism that had an effect on the team."

Jones, unlike Brown, based his coaching on personal relationships with his players, an approach that would, in an odd way, cost him his job.

Quarterback Frank Ryan, receiver Gary Collins, and tight end Milt Morin were injured in 1967. The offense faltered, and Jones took the blame.

He was summoned from a hunting trip to a meeting with Modell, Collier, and general manager Harold Sauerbrei, a former sportswriter who had once sung Jones's praises. Jones says that he immediately quit when Modell suggested that Jones needed help with the offense. The team claimed in a news release to have fired him because, among other reasons, he refused to move to Cleveland and coach full-time.

He said, "I thought I had resigned until I read that release from the Browns' office. Man, that was rough. I can't say it was inaccurate, but I still believe the way it was written was an unnecessarily low blow."

The media suggested that Jones and Ryan were in conflict, but Ryan was the first to defend the coach. The truth was uglier. Although Cleveland won the Century Division title, Modell took Collier to task about the team's 9-5 record and 52-14 loss to Dallas in the first round of the playoffs. The head coach claimed to have lost control of the offense to Jones, who was the only coach Ryan or Jim Brown would listen to, Collier said.

"Collier convinced Art Modell that the poor season was Dub's fault. Modell had pecked Collier, so Collier pecked Dub. Dub could've pecked Ryan, but he didn't," according to cornerback Bernie Parrish. "He was asked to step down to a lesser position on the team and instead he quit and went back to Ruston, Louisiana—Dub is one of the few coaches I've known with that kind of integrity and backbone."

In the game of front-office intrigue to which Jones was so ill-suited, he was replaced by Nick Skorich, who also replaced Collier five years later.

In 1966, Jones's wife said that he had come to love coaching so much that he could never quit, and he made one more attempt to stay in the game, seeking to become the first head coach of the New Orleans

Saints. But Jones had learned from the sad example of Fritz Heisler, the long-time Cleveland assistant who never found the head job for which he yearned. When Jones didn't receive so much as an interview in New Orleans, he left football.

"I'm real proud of my coaching experience," he says. "I think the best thing about it was my second-string quarterback was as good a friend of mine as my first-string quarterback. He was second team, and he knew why he was second team, and I took that as a great compliment."

Jones reminisced in the attractive low-slung, white-brick home he built nearly fifty years ago on a pine-covered knoll on the outskirts of Ruston. Periodically, one or another of his grandsons would burst in, asking to shoot some pool or to borrow the car. Jones's home sits just off I-20. Motels and fast food joints are growing up around it, pocking the pine forest with neon and concrete. For now, though, the little patch of woods, in which he also built a home for his mother, is idyllic. Jays and cardinals flashed through columns of sunlight, humming birds floated around feeders like colorful toys suspended from branches, and small red squirrels skittered between tree trunks.

Jones has turned the operation of the construction company over to his eldest son. He drops by the office or job sites frequently and closely follows the Ruston High Bearcats, the team for which he and his five boys all played. Bert, a former Baltimore Colt quarterback and NFL MVP, made All-Pro in 1976 and the Pro Bowl in 1977, a quarter century after his father was similarly honored.

Beneath a shock of white hair, Jones's blue eyes are set wide in his unlined, tan face. His nose is long and hooked, and although Jones no longer looks gaunt, one can immediately see why teammates nicknamed him "Six O'Clock." He resembles Gary Cooper, but his manner is that of a courtly squire out of Faulkner.

Jones will say what he thinks but only after he ponders his words— sucking his teeth, extending his long fingers and patting their tips together, the drawn-out silences awkward.

He still feels the sting of betrayal, but his natural reserve won't allow him to denounce either Collier or Modell. In fact, one jarring contradiction about Jones is that so decent a man had his finest day in the most savage game in NFL history.

The Bears did everything they could that afternoon to make Hunk Anderson's game plan work, but the Browns were not intimidated.

The Browns—not the Bears—set an NFL record with 209 yards in penalties. The teams amassed 374 yards on thirty-seven penalties—both league records that still stand.

Four Bears were carried off the field. "Hatchet Man" Sprinkle broke Graham's nose. During one melee, Adamle told Halas to "get the hell out of here." Cleveland halfback Dopey Phelps was ordered from the sidelines even though he was hurt and not even in uniform. The Browns' defense was hit with personal fouls on three straight plays, two of which had been interceptions.

"That was one of the roughest games I ever saw," an official said when the carnage was over. "We had to call 'em. There was nothing else we could do. There could have been a regular riot out there."

"It's a shame a performance like Dub's had to come in a game like this," Brown said.

Jones crossed his long legs and leaned back in a wicker chair on his glass-enclosed gallery. In a drawl redolent of crepe myrtle and wisteria, he recalled his big day, not as an heroic achievement but as a curiosity from which he has taken his own kind of satisfaction.

"I'm proud of the fact that my friends were as happy, or happier, about it than I was," he says. "I had that moment of glory, and they were happier than I was."

# *Dub* JONES

" I LOST MY FATHER
when I was three years old. He was killed. It's a hard thing to imagine now, but that was in 1928. He was a farmer, and one of his hired hands was put in jail for doing I don't know what. My father went up and bailed him out. He told them in no uncertain terms to leave his hired hand alone or else. He was driving in his automobile to town, and he was ambushed by his neighbors and shot. They just riddled his little A Model Ford.

The grand jury came back with a no-bill. The defense was my father had threatened them, and he had a gun in his glove compartment, but all of my people tell me he never touched the gun. He was a tough man, though. My mother thought he was a good man, but in his youth he had killed a man and served a prison term. That probably worked in the defense of the people who killed him.

I was the youngest of four boys; my oldest brother was maybe 12. We moved into town, and my mother kept boarders. We didn't have electricity because we couldn't pay our electric bill. We burned coal oil lamps. My mother sewed and made mattresses for the WPA, and my brothers and I delivered papers.

When my oldest brother finished high school, the best he could do was go to a CCC camp. They're the ones who planted all this country in pine seedlings. The Depression came, and there wasn't any way to make a living, and people just abandoned their cotton farms and went north. The government paid landowners $10 an acre to plant pine seedlings. I thought it was silly at the time, but it turned out to be a great thing, because what it did was put us in the timber business. I don't know how many plywood plants and sawmills we have in Louisiana now, but it's the biggest industry we have here in Ruston, and we should thank the CCC program.

There were probably four or five hundred students at Ruston High. At first, we didn't have basketball in our school; we didn't have a gym, to begin with, and our play-yard was sand. You couldn't dribble a basketball on it. But we had great football teams. I played on the first state championship team that Coach Hoss Garrett had. He was just a young coach, and he stayed here for over 40 years. I don't how many state championships he had. I was always sort of jealous when I would come back and he'd be there with another team on another championship march. I'd think, 'Now, that's just not right for him to do that with another team. He's just supposed to do that with *our* team.'

I thought that about Paul Brown, too. I just knew that he could never have another team like we were. How could you have a bunch of boys that fit as well as we did?

MY MOTHER WAS FROM A FAMILY OF 12 CHILDREN, and all of my aunts and uncles stressed how important it was to go to college. All of my older brothers went to college. My one brother went to LSU on a football work scholarship. He milked thirty cows a day, twice a day, in order to go to school.

I really didn't think about getting a scholarship. I thought about making whatever team I was playing on that day. Even if I thought about it, I would be ashamed to tell people that I was expecting to play football in college. I hoped and wished I could, but my junior year in high school, I weighed maybe 140 pounds and was over six feet tall. When I weighed in at LSU my freshman year, I was 6' 2½" and weighed 158 pounds. A year later, I was 6'4" and weighed probably 185.

When I laced up my shoes for the first time at practice at LSU, I was so nervous I could barely tie my shoestrings. At that time, a scholarship was a big thing. I looked on it that I was one fortunate guy. My first year at LSU was 1942, and in the spring of '43, we all went to the service. I ended up at Tulane, in the Navy. I played two years at Tulane in the service. It was what you called the V-12 program. When I got there, you lined up according to what department you were in. There was a big line in front of a sign that said 'Supply.' I didn't know what 'Supply' was, but I didn't want to be there. They had a line for 'Deck' and a line for 'Medicine.' The nearest line that fit me was 'Engineering,' so I got in that one. It turned out that the people who were in 'Supply' and 'Deck' were there for only three semesters, but I was there for five, and the war ended before I got shipped out.

I'm in the hall of fame for Tulane, but I started out at LSU and eventually graduated from Louisiana Tech. There was a big rivalry at that time between LSU and Tulane, and I have the distinction of playing for LSU against Tulane and for Tulane against LSU.

In 1946, I was drafted by Miami in the All-American Conference and by the Chicago Cardinals in the NFL. I was still in the service. The Cardinals acted as though they really wanted me, but I had never thought about playing professional football. I had school to finish and eligibility left in college, and I thought that's what I would do.

I had a teammate who had recently signed with the Cardinals, and he told me what (fullback) Pat Harder, from Wisconsin, had signed for. Pat got $10,000, and that was just powerful money to us. So I said, 'I really don't want to play pro football right now. I want to go back to college, but I'll play for $12,000.'

Jimmy Conzelman, the coach, hit the sky. He said, 'That's unheard of. We have Pat Harder, and we have Charley Trippi, and they signed for less money than that.'

I said, 'Well, that's what I want.'

HE SAID IF I CHANGED MY MIND, I should let him know. In the interim, the Miami Seahawks, from the All-American Conference, contacted me. Jack Meagher was the coach. I told Jack Meagher what I told Jimmy Conzelman—that I wanted $12,000—and he said he would pay that. I told Jack I was committed to let Conzelman know what I was going to do. I really preferred to play with the Cardinals because I knew the league was established and they had a great team, but I told Meagher I would sign with him after I contacted Conzelman.

I called Jimmy Conzelman, and he didn't believe me at first, or he pretended not to. I guess he found out it was true, because he came back to me and said, 'We'll pay you the $12,000.'

I said, 'But I already told Jack Meagher I would sign.'

He said, 'We'll pay you a $2,000 bonus.'

I said, 'I'm sorry. I told Jack Meagher I would sign with him, and that's that.'

I thought a contract was a contract both ways, but it wasn't. I found out when I got to training camp that the contract was a one-way contract. It was good if you were man enough to make the team, but they could cut you at any moment. There was no guarantee. If I had realized they could cut me, I would've felt a little bit different about my commitment to Jack Meagher.

The Miami Seahawks were a terrible team. They didn't have the resources to fulfill their contract obligations throughout the year, and the league had to pick up the tab for the salaries. We opened with the Cleveland Browns, lost 44-0, then went over to San Francisco and lost big out there. After about the fourth game, they fired Meagher. He was a great man and a great coach, but the team just wasn't there. They had drafted a lot of prewar ballplayers who were once fine ballplayers, but they had finished college and been to war and hadn't played a down in three or four years.

We were playing San Francisco in Miami. It was hot as Hades, and I was covering Alyn Beals, a great receiver. He perfected the slant pattern. He'd go down and break in, and Frankie Albert would hit him on that slant pattern. You didn't have a lot of linebacker help, and just about the time you got aggressive on your coverage, why, he'd fake the slant and break out on a deep out. Oh, man, it was tough.

I'm playing single coverage, and I go in to clamp him, and he breaks out. I plant my foot, it slips, and I pull a hamstring muscle. That's a tough injury, because nobody knows how bad it hurts except you. So I'm traded to the Brooklyn Dodgers before the last game of the season.

In Brooklyn, I'm supposed to be a single-wing tailback, one of those triple-threat, pass-run-punt guys. Glenn Dobbs was sort of a superstar there, and management was having its problems with him, which is why they wanted me. He and I were alternating, and then they traded Dobbs to the Rams, and I ended up as the tailback.

WE OPENED THE SEASON AGAINST CLEVELAND again, and I got killed. Bill Willis was back there before the ball could get centered to me. I wrenched my knee, separated my clavicle, and got a hip pointer. I couldn't even walk after that game. I was out for a few weeks. In fact, I came home to heal. On my first game back, I was tackled on a punt return and broke my hand. They put it in a cast, and from that time on, I didn't play anything but defense. I couldn't play tailback with a cast on my hand.

The situation at Brooklyn wasn't any better than Miami. It was still a flimsy situation. After those two years, I thought, 'What am I doing?'

I thought I'd had it with pro football. You start to think, 'Maybe I'm part of this losing act.'

We played Cleveland, and I intercepted a couple of passes, and that's what got Paul Brown's attention. The Cleveland Browns traded their number one draft choice, Bob Chappuis, to Brooklyn for me as a defensive back. Paul Brown used to tell this story at every occasion he could. He'd always say, 'The best trade I ever made was for Dub Jones.'

I felt like I was really something. It wasn't until years later, when he wrote his book, that I found out the full details of the trade. They traded Chappuis to Brooklyn for me and $20,000. I don't know what that $20,000 would be worth today. I didn't know anything about the $20,000. I thought it was me for Chappuis. So not only did Paul Brown get me, he got $20,000. He might've made the trade for just the $20,000.

I was ecstatic when I found out I was getting traded to Cleveland. Paul Brown already had a reputation as a top coach who ran a tight ship. I had always been in chaos, but everything in Cleveland was orderly, even the little things. It wasn't uncommon in the Brooklyn dressing room to see everyone fired up with a cigar or a cigarette. Paul Brown was well-groomed, very businesslike, and the Browns reflected Paul Brown's demeanor. His demeanor worked all the way through to the equipment manager.

I STARTED THE SEASON AS A DEFENSIVE BACK. They were pleased with my play, but we had Tommy James, who had played with Paul at Massillon High and at Ohio State and was a fine ballplayer. He was playing behind me. We play Baltimore, and they have a young quarterback, Y.A. Tittle. No one knew anything about him. We played them in Toledo. They also had Lamar Davis, who had been with me in Miami, and who had been a sprint champion at Georgia. He was about a 9.4 man.

Two minutes before the half, they run a play. The flow is coming my way, and I saw they had the coverage on the outside man. Lamar goes for a post pattern. He really was not my assignment, but I could see it developing, and I make the pursuit. The safety, Cliff Lewis, came up and played the ball. Tittle threw the ball about 60 yards, Lamar caught it, and all Paul could see was me chasing Lamar Davis into the end zone.

Boy, he pulls me out of that game: 'What happened? What happened?'

I said, 'The flow was here, and it wasn't really my assignment.'

He didn't put me back in after the half. Blanton Collier was off scouting. There wasn't anybody to say that it wasn't my responsibility.

Paul Brown takes me off the defensive team. Finally, Blanton comes back, and we get the movies, and they establish the fact that it was *not* my assignment. It was Lewis's, and Paul's reasoning wasn't right. He must've figured that since he jerked me off the team, he had to jerk Lewis off, too. He reinstated me as a cornerback, and he put Otto Graham in at free safety.

We're playing the Los Angeles Rams, against Glenn Dobbs and Lenny Ford. They'd send this man in motion. I would pick him up. Lenny Ford would come down and hook, and Otto would make the tackle, after the fact. Paul pulled me out of the game two or three times: 'What's happening? Go over and talk to Blanton!'

After that, he benched me and put Tommy James in as the cornerback. That was a low moment in my career. I sat on the bench for one game. Dick Gallagher, who was the backfield coach, insisted on playing me on offense. We laughed about the story many times. Paul said, 'Well, he's a good runner, but I don't think he can catch the ball.'

Paul didn't do anything that he didn't want to do, but Dick did go to battle for me. So, I made the transition, and the first game I played on offense, I caught a touchdown pass, and from that day on, Paul didn't have to worry about that phase of the game.

You get different versions of this story, but, actually, Paul Brown was not an innovator. He didn't even pretend to be. But he did innovate one thing, and I give him credit for it: the Browns were the forerunner of the three-receiver pro offense which you've seen so many years. Maybe the credit should go to Clark Shaughnessy and the Bears, but the Browns are the ones who really perfected it and utilized three receivers.

YOU HAVE TO REALIZE THAT AT THIS TIME, Mac Speedie and Dante Lavelli were established receivers, and halfbacks were no factor in the passing offense. It was tough for me to get that many opportunities to catch the ball. They'd throw a touchdown pass to Speedie, a touchdown pass to Lavelli. I could do that, too, but I didn't get near the opportunities that I would like to have had, and what was I going to complain about?

Pass-wise, our offense evolved more from Otto Graham and the receivers than it did from Paul Brown. But Paul did create the atmosphere for us to do that. Other teams saw what we were doing passing, and then they started to do it. We taught a lot of people how to play pass offense. I know when I went to the Pro Bowl as a coach, I said, 'Boy, I sure hate to go out there and let these guys know just how simple this game is.'

Otto Graham was a big factor in the development of that offense. It wouldn't have happened without an exceptional quarterback. When you have a quarterback like Otto Graham, you know that at some point in time, he's going to make that play to get you back in that game. You know you have that resource, and you don't break. Another team might get behind by a few points, and they're broken. That seldom happened to us.

Otto was great in the huddle. He gave you confidence. We always had a little something besides the call of the play. Otto would say, 'If so and so doesn't work, we'll look for this.'

Shoot, he would just get the job done. He was a ballplayer; that's all. He didn't act like a prima donna, and in his era, he was way up there, and everyone else was down here. He was head and shoulders above everybody. A lot of times, what he did didn't look pretty, but somehow he got the ball out there to you, particularly long passes. He was just super on long passes. Of course, it was easier throwing when I was playing than it is now. Defenses weren't what they are now.

I USED TO THINK THAT PAUL could see everything about you. He gave you the feeling that he could. That's how he did with the IQ tests. You took it, and then you knew, 'That son-of-a-gun knows how smart or how dumb I am. He knows everything.' That was the main asset to the IQ test. Seeing how smart you were wasn't the value of it. He knew who was smart and who was dumb without taking that IQ test, but after he took the test, the individual *knew* that Paul knew.

He was persistent about breaking the film down after the game. Oh, man, you dreaded to go in there for that Tuesday session, because the first thing you'd do is turn that movie on. He had his little criticisms ready. He did it right out in front of the whole squad. It wasn't any business of a coach coming in and saying, 'Oh, come here. I want to have a little private conversation with you.' Today, you hear people say that all the time: 'Oh, you shouldn't reprimand in public.' Look, you're a player, and this guy's a player, and he lays an egg, damn it, *say* it. The worst thing that could happen was the coach not saying anything about it. Then, you're wondering, 'Why didn't he say anything to this guy?' You never had that with Brown.

Now, if he had been wrong, that's one thing, but a large percentage of the time, he was right. You've got to be right. That's the secret to coaching. The personality doesn't have anything to do with it—whether he talks rough, whether he cusses, whether he doesn't cuss, whether he's soft-spoken or loud and boisterous. That doesn't have anything to do with it. What counts is the decisions that are made day after day. If you're going to have the respect of the players, you have to be right a good percentage of the time. What made Lombardi is the same thing that made Paul Brown: He was right a large percentage of the time. They went about it in entirely different ways, but they were right. You can mark that down.

LISTEN, I FELT MISTREATED A LOT OF THE TIME. He had a very cutting tongue, and you were fearful of your job. It was a different world. I fractured my cheekbone in a game and stayed in the hospital overnight. They decided not to do anything about it and let it heal, but the doctor told me to wear this facemask for six weeks. This was before facemasks were put into use, and they designed this facemask for me. Paul Brown was responsible for putting facemasks on helmets, but this was before that. Mine was the first one. I had this facemask on, and we play San Francisco. I'm out in the open for a pass, Otto pitched it right in my hands, I dropped it, and Frisco beat us. There's not much you can say about a dropped pass. He ran it back and forth a few times.

We go to L.A. and play this next game, and before the game I'm sitting there in the dressing room, and he's trying to be nice about this thing, but he says, 'When do you think you'll take this mask off.'

I said, 'Vic (Ippolito, the team physician) said six weeks, and it's been three weeks now. It should be another two weeks or so.'

This is a typical cutting remark that he would make. He said, 'This facemask is killing our team' and kicked the ground and walked away.

Then, I was determined that I wouldn't take the damn mask off. We went out and played the game, and I wore the facemask. Of course, I was pretty tight after that session. Otto threw me a pass right on the sidelines, and I could've caught it, but I didn't.

As I came off the field, he said, 'Could you have caught that ball?'

I said, 'Yes, sir, I should've caught it.'

He said, 'Well, you're paid to catch the football.'

That was true, but it hurt. His remarks wouldn't have hurt nearly as bad if you didn't have respect for him. You respected his criticism. That's the reason it hurt so bad.

I went back out on the field, and I caught a touchdown pass. I made a special effort to walk right by him. You know what he said? Nothing.

The game when he told me he was sick of that facemask is the game we lost to San Francisco after we had won 29 straight. He told us we were all over the hill. He threatened to fire us all. We were mad as hell at him, but that's what he wanted.

We usually played two games out on the West Coast back then. We went down to L.A., and they had it all rigged up for us to go out to a Hollywood set. We all loaded up on the bus, and Paul comes out to the bus and starts to get on, and he says, 'I can't go. You all go out and have a good time—if you can,' and turned and walked off the bus. We kidded about that for years after: 'Have a good time—if you can.'

Well, we did. We went out and just had a ball and then we came back and beat the hell out of the Rams. We came back and won the rest of our games.

He was aloof, and that's the safest way for a coach to be. You have be one hell of a man if you're not going to be aloof. I was not aloof; I was friends with my players. I was a different coach from Paul, but I certainly respect Paul's good traits, even though I didn't incorporate all of his traits into my coaching. It wasn't my personality.

I RESPECTED PAUL. I wanted to like him, but a lot of times I questioned if I got to know him, would I like him or not. For example, he insisted on us going to church, but I never did see *him* in church. I would've felt a little more comfortable if I had seen him in church. I had the feeling he was a devout man, but I never saw him in church. I had to surmise certain things in his personality. None of us was ever in his home or ever really knew him, other than the few hours of the day we were with him.

You remember him as being distant more than anything. One of his pet peeves was a man coming up to greet him and saying, 'You don't remember me, do you, Paul?'

He'd say, 'No, I don't remember you.'

He really disliked that, for some reason.

He didn't mind using fear to run the ship, he wasn't always fair in his discipline, and, probably, if you pinned him down to it, he'd tell you that he didn't even pretend to be fair. He had a sliding scale for discipline, but what you never knew was where you fit on that scale. It's like the time Speedie and Rymkus and Daniell got put in jail. Oh, my goodness, here we've got the best offensive tackle, the best offensive end, and the best defensive tackle. What does he do? Well, what he did was he cut Daniell. That's not fair, but he's not looking for fairness; he's looking for discipline.

He's looking for what's best for the team, and what's best for the team is to cut one guy and keep the other two. He cut the one he could replace the easiest, and he didn't make any pretenses.

Probably the most awful position I've seen Paul in was with Lenny Ford. Lenny was a great pass rusher. He was the first big defensive end to really rush the passer. He was 6' 5", 260, and Paul took him and made a pass rusher out of him. Lenny was an offensive end with the Rams. Paul had the best defensive end in the league, and he didn't want to press the discipline issue. He backed off, and the players recognized that he backed off. I guess he felt that was the best thing he could do at the time.

Paul was never one to celebrate, and that wasn't a bad thing. I wouldn't have expected him to be at any of our parties. Nobody would want Paul there when we're enjoying ourselves and drinking and having a good time. What do we care what Paul is doing? We didn't want Paul there, and he knows that. That's why he's not there. He doesn't want to be there. He knows you're going to be smoking a big cigar, and he stays out of your way. He never kibitzed with the boys.

He was terrible to his assistant coaches. He criticized them just like you would a ballplayer, and we always wanted to defend the poor devils. They were just as intimidated as the ballplayers were, more so. Paul could show his anger real easy—in his eyes, in his facial expressions. You could tell that he was angry, but I never heard him cuss or throw a fit. I also never saw him really happy.


PAUL DID LISTEN. I don't mean that he listened to 33 ball players. You've got to know who you're listening to, and I guarantee you he listened to the ones he had respect for. They used to kid me when I was playing; they said I was the only person Paul Brown would listen to. Even the assistant coaches would come to me if they wanted to implement something in our offense. They'd say, 'Would you talk to Paul about this?'

Paul went strictly by results. So many coaches would try to develop a ballplayer. They'll look at a guy and say, 'You look like you have the proper height and the speed and the proper attitude. I'm going to try to make a ballplayer out of you.' Not Paul Brown. He didn't give a damn what you looked like or anything else. He looked to see whether you did it. That was his strength. Paul recognized talent. He knew ballplayers. He made a lot of good trades.

He made some obvious errors with players. Some of them he knew were ballplayers, but he just didn't want them around; some of them, he just had too many players. The two most obvious are Henry Jordan and Doug Atkins. Later on, he gave Vince Lombardi Willie Davis and Bill Quinlan. Paul and Vince Lombardi were friends. Vince was with the New York Giants; he learned his football from us. We taught him how to play ball when he was looking at us.

Paul Brown probably had as much to do with our offensive football team as anybody, but I can't remember him doing any coaching of techniques. He taught mostly from athletes' demonstrations. The athletes themselves would develop techniques, and he would recognize them and incorporate them. He would say, 'Do this like Speedie,' or something like that.

Do you think that Paul Brown coached Otto Graham? Blanton would say, 'Now, you do this and you do that. You take two steps here and two steps there and square those shoulders.' Paul's attitude was, 'Look, all I want is the ball out there in the receiver's hands.' He went by results.

THIS IS MY NOTEBOOK. This entry is for November 14, 1948. We're sitting there, writing, as he writes on the board and talks. This is one of the great strengths of Paul Brown. This was written on a Thursday, which was the defensive day. He would come in and write on the board, and you would have to write it. We were playing the 49ers. 'One: This is a big one. San Francisco has terrific scoring power. We will rise or fall with our defensive team. Two: They are the fastest team we have played. Their strength lies is passing, outside running, trapping, and power.' I don't know what else is left. 'Three: A controlled and terrific line charge. A fundamentally sound blow as per our team defense every time will determine our chance to win. Four: Gang tackling, including the secondary, is the only thing that can cope with their speed. The tackling must be vicious and sure. Five: Albert can be licked by rushing the ends from the outside in. Secondary must never relax and think that Albert is caught. Six: Know your adjustments perfectly for men-in-motion who become flankers to the open side. Double flankers: It can mean ball game.' I don't know exactly what he was talking about there. I hope I did then. 'Seven: The way to lick a great offensive team is to maintain possession of the football. Eight: Never lose your poise. If they get ahead of us, just play the best football game you can play.'

Now, that's Paul Brown.

It's a funny thing, but this is a great strength of his coaching. There you are, on Thursday, probably in the morning, and he's got you thinking about a Sunday game. If you wait until Sunday to think about that ball game, you're in trouble. He claimed that he checked the notebooks to see what we wrote, but we don't know if he ever did or not.

Morrie Kono was a dear friend of all of us. He was raised in a Jewish orphanage. He was with the Browns from day one. He was like Sid Caesar: a great mimic and comic and entertainer. The team was always seated and in place for meetings well before Paul Brown came in. You were waiting with your pencil in hand and your notebook open on the table. Morrie would come in and entertain us by mimicking Paul Brown. He'd go through all the little mannerisms. Paul always pretended that someone was getting information from us, so he was always whispering, and Morrie would whisper like Paul. I don't think Paul ever really believed that people were spying on him, anyway. He was just going for the dramatic effect.

COMING INTO THE NATIONAL FOOTBALL LEAGUE was the most exciting thing you could imagine. We had dominated the other league for a long time. The Philadelphia game that year was bigger than any game we had ever been involved in, bigger than the world championships. Paul had a great strategy for that game. It showed how good an offensive mind he had. The Eagles had dominated the league for a couple of years. Greasy Neale was really a fine coach. I always give him the credit for that 'Umbrella Defense' that everyone says the Giants developed for us. We had won all of our exhibition games before that decisively, and we crushed Philadelphia. That was a great year. It ended up with Groza kicking that field goal for us to win the championship.

The Browns always had a plan. I don't know how many times we started a game and we'd be like clockwork going into that end zone. We had an audible system, but we never used it. An audible system is not what it's cracked up to be anyway, I don't think. I'm more interested in adjusting a play to a defense. I don't mean to say that there's not a place for audibles, but you can't read defenses that good. If you spend a lot of time going from this play to that play, instead of concentrating on the execution of the play, I think you lose a little something.

It caused some discontent among us. We lost two championship games to Detroit, and the third time we played them (1954), we were going to rebel. We had listened to him talk long enough about how over the hill we were, which he said in the paper after we had lost the second game to Detroit. Otto and I and a number of others said that this was going to be our last game. We decided that if we were going to lose, we would lose our way. We went into this game, and we just wiped them off the field. It was the first time we were going to rebel, and we never got the opportunity.

I don't think Otto had a lot of resentment about the play-calling, but I have my own feeling about how an offense should be run, and Paul Brown didn't do it exactly how I would have. Paul Brown did the right thing in controlling the game and calling the signals. He was the forerunner of what everyone does now, and there's no question that it's better than having the general on the field call the plays. The quarterback is out on the field getting knocked down. He can't call the play nearly as well as a coach in a pressbox communicating with a coach on the ground. They are not disturbed. They are right with the game.

There's a step beyond the coach calling the plays, though. You've got to have a combination of the two. Paul did some of this, but not nearly enough. You need all the input you can get from your quarterback, and you call the plays jointly. It's only when you get to a critical situation, and you want to change something, that you need to send in a play. It needs to be coordinated between the coach and the player.

Our big rivals, up until Detroit, were New York and Frisco. Detroit was completely different from us. They had Bobby Layne running that show, and Buddy Parker was a player's coach. He was an innovator, too. I think the 4-3 defense originated with him and his coaches. They threw that in our face in '52, and it was tough for us to cope with, having not played it.

The game was not a dirty game at that time. The main difference is the headgear. Back then, a head shot was considered a cheap shot, and not many people took them. Now, they glamorize these head shots on television. One thing about Paul Brown is that he never encouraged dirty shots. Dirty play wasn't part of our game.

The game I scored six touchdowns in, against the Bears, set a record for the most penalties. They were what you would consider dirty. They had Ed Sprinkle, and he was one of those guys who thrived on cheap shots. He was publicized as the meanest man in football, and I guess he was.

I scored six touchdowns that day and 12 that year, and I think I might've scored 12 the year before (actually 11). I don't know what happened that day. The last five times I touched the ball, I scored a touchdown. I've seen so many versions of that last touchdown that I'm sometimes confused myself. My version is that it wasn't a check-off. No record had every been mentioned until after my fifth touchdown. Then, they got word down from the pressbox that I was one touchdown from tying the record. On the side-lines, Paul and Otto talked, and I didn't hear exactly what they said, but whatever was done was done for me.

DEALING WITH PAUL BROWN OVER MONEY was awful. I'll tell you what kind of negotiator he was: You took a cut in salary and felt happy about it. He'd convince you that he was doing you a favor by keeping you around. That happened to players numerous times. We were hungry ballplayers. That was one of the clichés about Paul Brown: 'He likes his players lean and hungry,' and, I guarantee you, we were lean and hungry.

I don't even remember anything about a union then. It came in years later, after the money. No one had ever thought about a union, because we believed what the owners told us, and they told us they were not making any money.

The owners back then, like Mickey McBride, who was a great owner, were doing it just for the fun of it. He and Art Rooney went to the races, and they had fun with their teams. They didn't make money. I think a lot of teams were losing money. They loved the game and wanted to be associated with it. When it got to where it wasn't any fun for Mickey, he sold the team.

To illustrate how things were, I played in the Pro Bowl game in the early '50s, and then I coached in the Pro Bowl game in the mid-'60s. Glenn Davis was putting that second game on. He worked with the *Los Angeles Times*. He kept saying, 'You remember, Dub, we didn't know whether we would get paid for the game?'

I said, 'Oh, yeah, I remember.'

They couldn't sell the television rights then. They couldn't even give them away. And they could barely pay us to play. About ten years later, Davis said, 'Oh, man, this is a lucrative deal (for the players).'

When I started playing pro football, people in Ruston, Louisiana, didn't know anything about it. They didn't hardly know who the Cleveland Browns were. It took about ten years to educate the public what this game was all about. It took television, which came along about 1952, and *Sports Illustrated*, and NFL Films. Then, it changed overnight, almost, and the money was out on the table. You think about it: Art Modell bought the Browns for $4.5 million, and, I guarantee you, four or five years later, that team was worth $90 million. When the money got on the table, the union came into being. It's hindsight, but if the owners had shared some of that money earlier, they would have saved a lot of headaches later.

We had no leverage to bargain with. There weren't but 12 teams or so. The money wasn't there, and if they would've tried to bargain, they would've destroyed the league, probably.

PAUL CALLED ME THREE TIMES after I left the Browns and tried to persuade me to coach with him. He said, 'You can have the offense. I have talked to my owners, and if I had my choice of a person to succeed me, it would be you.' That always made me feel good. But I had played under Paul, and I knew it wouldn't work. I coached with Blanton by accident. I read in the paper that Paul Brown was fired, and the next day or so, Blanton Collier calls me and tells me he wants me to come and work with him. I guess he must've liked my football mind when I was playing.

I was in the retail building business, the same thing I'm in now. I'd been out of football for seven years. When I left the Browns, I could've gone many, many places to coach, but the money wasn't there, and I had played ten years, which is a long time, and I was sort of tired. I had my family here, and I wanted to be home.

I said, 'Blanton, no, I can't. I'm not about to move to Cleveland.'

He said, 'Would you just come and work for six months?'

Finally, that's what I went to do—work six months; and I ended up staying there for five years. I was the offensive coordinator up there during the season, and I was down here in Ruston, Louisiana, after the season. It just wasn't a good situation. Art Modell would hug my neck after the game and say, 'Please move to Cleveland.'

Blanton was handicapped. He couldn't hear, and he delegated authority to me that nobody else would have, so I had an experience with coaching that was delightful. I had a great time with Frank Ryan and Gary Collins and Paul Warfield and Jim Brown. I just knew it wouldn't have been delightful with Paul. I wouldn't have had that type of freedom.

I came in with Blanton in '63 to work with the receivers, but, really, I was offensive coordinator from day one. I evolved into the quarterback coach, too. We lost the first exhibition game in '63, and we lost to Detroit. We started Ninowski at quarterback, and we lost that game something awful. Then we go out to San Francisco, and we change quarterbacks. We go with Ryan. We had groomed Jim Ninowski for six or eight weeks of training camp, but mainly because of Blanton, we change. I'm in the pressbox, and somehow, inadvertently, I start calling the plays. Accidentally, I started to communicate with the quarterbacks, and, boy, we start moving the football. Blanton realizes what had happened, and from that moment on, that's the way it went—I controlled the game through the quarterback.

I sure as hell didn't control it like Paul Brown did. Frank Ryan knew he could change a play any time, but he had better have a damn good reason, and he'd better hope that he did well with it. I told him, 'There's nothing I like more than for you to change it. Boy, when it's third and three, you're out there in a world by yourself. You'll find out what you need to do.'

I think that we started defensive play-calling. When I was coaching, I would communicate with Blanton as much as I could, because he didn't hear very well. But it worked so well that I suggested to him, 'Why don't you have the defensive coaches call the defensive plays?' That's what we did, and now, everybody does it.

MY BIG PLAY WHEN I PLAYED was what we called a 'flip.' It went right or left, with a tackle pulling, which was unusual for then, but we had fast tackles—Groza and Rymkus. It wasn't an innovative play; we picked it up from Frisco, I think. But I would say that we perfected it. The halfback would just sprint out, and Otto would turn and pitch it to the halfback. The tackle pulled and blocked the cornerback, the flanker blocked down on the safety, the tight end took the man in front of him and walled him off, the weakside guard tried to get the middle linebacker.

I was so amused. When I was coaching, I said, 'We got to get back to using this flip right and left more. I always thought that was a great play.'

Jim Brown said, 'What?'

I said, 'Oh, I always liked that play.'

He said, 'You mean you ran that play back when you played?'

I said, 'Oh, yeah. We did.'

That was a surprise to him, but one year, he averaged 15 yards a carry on that play.

All of the coaches were afraid of Jim Brown as they were a snake. They were afraid for their jobs. They didn't want to cross him in any way. In '63, during the season, I made a criticism of a pass route he had run. It offended him, and he came back to the huddle and said, 'I'm not paid to catch the football. I'm paid to run the football.'

I said, 'Jim, how about you meeting me after practice right over here, and we'll talk about this.'

He met me after practice under the goal posts, and Blanton Collier and Modell are sitting over there just scared to death. Their fair-haired coach and their fair-haired super ballplayer are having a confrontation. We talked a long time, and I told Jim that I felt he was dead wrong. I said, 'As long as I'm here, I'm going to criticize your play just like I would anybody's.' Then I said, 'I want to tell you one other thing: We will never win a world championship if you're not a factor in the pass offense.'

He went on to win I don't know how many games for us by catching passes. The year before that, they weren't worth a hoot, but in '63 we won game after game and the next year, we won the world championship.

I HAD ONE OTHER INCIDENT WITH JIM BROWN. Frank was always having problems with him in the huddle about whether they were going to run or throw. I met with Jim and Frank after a game. I set up the meeting, but I called Blanton into it. Poor Blanton doesn't know about the confrontation they had during the game. He can't hear. He doesn't know what is taking place. But it was about to come to a fist fight during the game. I told Jim that, without any question, he was wrong. I told him that whatever is done is done, but he has no business second-guessing us out there in the huddle. I finally got them halfway pacified, and we went on.

I know Jim has respect for me. In fact, Jim is the one who went to Blanton during that first training camp I was there and said, 'I want Dub Jones coaching me.' I had been there primarily for the receivers. Blanton never told anyone what had happened, but he put Paul Bixler in personnel, and I went with the backs, too.

We won in '63. We won the world championship in '64 and we sure did have a good offensive football team. We played in the world championship in '65 and should've won that, too. We had a fantastic year in '66 with a quarterback who was hurt and without Jim Brown. In '67, Frank couldn't even throw the ball, and we ended up bad (9-5, with a 52-14 first-round playoff loss to Dallas).

I was hunting with Frank in South Texas, and they called me to the Super Bowl in Miami to visit with Art and Blanton. They said they had to make a shakeup in the coaching staff. They wanted to put Nick Skorich in to do what I was doing. I said, 'Man, that's the greatest thing that could happen to me. I been meaning to quit anyway. I'm out of here.' I left Blanton crying. I never did see any Cleveland papers, but I imagine they looked at this as getting rid of me, which it was. Later, I found out from some friends that Blanton told Modell that the reason we lost was 'the quarterback wouldn't listen to anybody but Dub Jones.'

When you lose, people start pointing fingers. That was a real blow, but it was true: The quarterback *wouldn't* listen to anybody besides me. When he was there, Jim Brown wouldn't listen to anybody but me. But I didn't usurp any boundaries; that's just the power Blanton had delegated to me.

In Blanton's defense, he had his job to protect, too. His defense was, 'I just don't have the same control that I did. They only listen to Dub Jones.'

We were faltering. We were in a hell of a situation. I was a friend of Collier, but Collier had a dislike of Howard Brinker, the defensive coach of the Browns, and I liked Howard Brinker. I found myself in all kinds of positions. It was that way with Modell. Modell knew I was a Paul Brown man. That didn't help, even though Art and I were good friends. He loved me for a long time, right up until the last two years, when Frank was hurt. First, he hurt his shoulder; then he hurt his elbow and had to have an operation. His arm was his strength. We were in tough shape.

I never really thought I would stay in coaching. In '63, '64, '65, I was all fired up about it, but then I was about ready to get out. When the New Orleans Saints came into being, I wrote for an interview. I was at a crossroads. My family was here in Louisiana, and I knew I wasn't going to continue on like I was in Cleveland. I thought I might's well move on, but they didn't even interview me. That was sort of a disappointment to me.

IT WAS STRANGE WHEN MODELL FIRED Paul Brown. I had been away for seven years. I had been back for a reunion in '60, so I got a little feel for the situation. I could understand where he could fall out with Paul. Paul had been spoiled, because the owners had always left everything to him. Of course, Modell had signed a contract to make him head coach and general manager in charge of every frazzling thing. He shouldn't have signed a contract with him. But I guess it was Art's prerogative to fire him, too, and that's what he did. If I had known Art the way I know him now, I would've told you for sure that they weren't going to get along. Art wanted to be down there throwing footballs with the boys, like Jerry Jones. That was all right, but I knew that wouldn't fit with Paul Brown.

When I came back, I had to get bits and pieces to fit the puzzle together. The plain fact was that Paul Brown didn't like Art and didn't show him any respect at all. As far as his contract went, he was in the right to do what he wanted to do. He traded Bobby Mitchell to Washington. That was his business. He didn't have to talk to Art. But he should have.

The first time I saw Paul afterward was when Baltimore (for whom

Jones's son Bert was the quarterback) played Cincinnati. He came off the bus, and we had a short visit. I saw him once at one of those Bogie Busters golf tournaments in Dayton and once in Cleveland. One year, I had a re-union for the Jones and Lahr families. Warren was dead, but I had his widow and all her children here. I wrote to Paul and invited him down. He wrote a great letter back saying that he couldn't come. He was too sick, so that was in his later years.

AFTER I GOT OUT OF COACHING, I went back to my business full-time. My youngest son is my boss now. We do mainly commercial construction. Now, I see all this fantastic money these coaches make. The coaches never knew they could make that kind of money. The same time the players made their play, the coaches should've made theirs. They didn't recognize the position they were in. The money was out there.

Playing and coaching in Cleveland were terrific. We had fans year-in and year-out who seldom ever relinquished their season tickets. They were blue-collar fans, and they were really true fans. Sometimes when we prac-ticed we'd have thousands of people watching us. They looked inside the team and got to know personalities. They lived and breathed with that team.

I just can't describe what football meant to my life, but the main thing was the friends that I made, people like Warren Lahr, Otto Graham, Lou Groza, Dante Lavelli, Bill Willis, Horace Gillom, Mac Speedie, Tommy James, Frank Gatski, John Kissell—there's no stopping. They say a person only has a handful of friends in a lifetime. Believe me, I've had a whole lot more than that, because there's 33 men on a roster. Even a guy like Ed Susteric, who played with us for only one year, I still recall him as a dear friend. That was the real value of it.

I have received so much notoriety from the six touchdowns that I scored, and I'm proud of the fact that my friends were as happy, or happier, about it than I was. I had that moment of glory, and they were happier than I was. That's a good feeling.

Most of what I remember about Paul Brown is positive. Looking back, you only remember the strong points. Of course, there were negative points—a lot of painful moments that players had, a lot of criticism they made of him, some of it warranted, some not. But most of the decisions Paul made were the right decisions. That's what gave him the strength and the discipline that he had. That's what made him a fine coach. **"**

## Class Action

FOR THIRTY-TWO seasons, Walt Michaels had played and coached professional football. A longshot draft pick, he became one of the National Football League's top linebackers. He played on two championship teams. He helped establish the American Football League. He fashioned the New York Jet defense that smothered overwhelming favorite Baltimore in the most celebrated Super Bowl. In five years, he revived a decrepit franchise.

Nevertheless, seventeen days after his team lost in the AFC title game, an astounding *New York Times* headline declared, "Jets' Michaels Retires."

Michaels had been rugged enough to miss only three games in eleven seasons as a player and persistent enough to labor fifteen years while waiting to become a head coach. He had always professed that hard work could solve any problem, but according to the newspaper, he had quit without explanation at the height of his career and when he was only 53. Even his close friends were bewildered—and for good reason. The headline was wrong.

In fact, even though Michaels had taken the Jets to consecutive playoffs, the club had issued him an ultimatum: quit or be fired.

He told a reporter, "It's a cold game on every level. It's always been like that."

Paul Brown had tried to teach Michaels that harsh lesson decades earlier. Throughout his coaching career, Michaels invoked Brown's name. He said his former coach had schooled him in everything from planning practices to meting out discipline.

"You have to be fundamentally sound. You can't beat yourself," he said. "I tell my players that just like Paul Brown used to tell the Browns players when I was there, and that philosophy is as true today as it was then."

Some Jets described Michaels as caustic, intimidating, aloof, and demanding, as well as consistent, thorough, and straightforward—all adjectives Cleveland players applied to Brown.

But although he was bright enough to gain admission to an Ivy League school and to earn a degree in psychology, Michaels hadn't fully understood one of Brown's more important teachings. Once, when coach and player were negotiating over five hundred dollars, Brown told Michaels, "Walter, you have to understand, this is a business."

Brown knew that professional teams exist to turn profit, and that football, like any business in America, consists of those who do the work and those who pay to have it done.

"When I came out of college, it was in the depth of the Depression, and any job you could get was a miracle," Brown said of being hired in 1931 to coach at Massillon High School.

Son of a railroad dispatcher, Brown was no doubt grateful to have work while hordes of vagrants shuffled outside soup kitchens. However, reared on the success ethic, Brown was aware of class distinctions and fiercely upwardly mobile. Never flashy, he seemed to have an innate knowledge of what money really buys: control.

That concept was made clear to him when his agreed-upon salary of $2,500 was reduced by a third before he ever held a team meeting in Massillon. Soon, Brown began fielding the best high school squads in the nation and drawing overflow crowds to Tiger Stadium. His salary rose to $4,500, an amount said to have been augmented by local businessmen.

Brown was almost not hired at Ohio State University in 1941 because some questioned whether a high school coach was qualified to serve as chief executive officer of "a business with 200,000 potential customers and 50,000 stockholders," as the *Columbus Dispatch* put it. The city viewed Buckeye football "as a $2 million investment, no differently than they would a glass factory or a cast-iron foundry."

Brown's introduction to true wealth came in the person of Mickey McBride, newspaper circulation manager, real estate magnate, taxi cab entrepreneur, betting-wire operator, and first owner of the Cleveland Browns. Brown left Ohio State during World War II to coach and supervise physical training at Great Lakes Naval Station. When the university offered Brown $9,000 to return, McBride responded with an incredible yearly salary of $25,000, a percentage of the profits, and a monthly stipend for as long as Brown was in the Navy.

"The time had come for me to decide whether I was to continue as a professor or a businessman," Brown said.

He chose business.

When McBride sold the franchise in 1953 and again when Art Modell purchased it in 1961, Brown benefited handsomely. He reportedly made as much as a half-million dollars on the latter deal, but the transaction also reinforced how expensive security can be. Lacking control over a sufficient chunk of the team, Brown was fired in 1963.

He wouldn't make the same mistake again. Later, he became coach, general manager, and part owner of the Cincinnati Bengals, and Brown repeated his advice to Michaels, then an assistant with the Jets. Perhaps Michaels was just too inexperienced to comprehend what Brown meant, but he had also come from a much different background than his mentor. Michaels's parents were Polish immigrants who came to the coal fields of eastern Pennsylvania to gouge a living from the ground and raise a brood that would eventually include seven boys and a girl. He was born Wladek Majka in Swoyersville, near Wilkes-Barre.

They newcomers followed as best they could the traditions of their forefathers, but the old ways wouldn't graft onto the New World. Even ancient family names disappeared, as when a tone-deaf schoolmarm misheard "Majka" and entered "Michael" in her attendance ledger.

The mines paid poorly. Strikes turned violent. The work was dirty, exhausting, and dangerous.

"They weren't looking for

streets of gold," Michaels says of the immigrants. "They were looking to make a living."

Webbed with veins of pure anthracite, the Susquehanna Valley of Michaels's youth was a blue-collar patchwork of Polish miners, Italian block layers, and Welsh pit bosses. The immigrants stayed in their closeknit ethnic neighborhoods, clung to their churches, and hoped their children would have better lives.

Black lung killed his father when Michaels was still in high school, two of his brothers afterward, the men slowly suffocating as fibrous tissue as thick and dry as insulation filled their chests.

To avoid the mines, Michaels began playing sports and studying. He attracted twenty scholarship offers, selecting Washington and Lee because of its academic reputation and an alumnus who sweetened the bargain with some new suits.

A powerful fullback, Michaels propelled the Generals to the 1951 Gator Bowl. Torn between teaching and law school, he was surprised when Cleveland drafted him in the seventh round.

He says, "I thought, 'If I can just make it to the All-Star Game, I'll get a half-game's salary.'"

Michaels earned his paycheck; however, Brown traded him to lowly Green Bay. Michaels started at both linebacker and guard, but the Packers won only three games.

"We had to go all out every week or face the possibility of losing our jobs," he said. "We were on a week-to-week basis."

Needing a linebacker to replace Tony Adamle, who had entered medical school, Brown brought Michaels back. Never fast, he earned the job with savvy and what one writer called "his particular brand of bone-breaking tackle."

The Browns opened 1954 with two losses in three gamesand appeared to be a faded power. But the defense, led by Michaels and end Len Ford, allowed only nine touchdowns over the rest of the season. The Browns surged into the championship game against the Detroit Lions, who had beaten Cleveland for the title in 1952 and 1953. The underdog Browns intercepted six of Bobby Layne's passes in a 56-10 victory, after which Brown said his team was "a fine bunch of workmen."

With Michaels calling signals, Cleveland gave up the fewest points in the league for seven straight years. Nicknamed "The Phantom," Michaels also became an enthusiastic member of the so-called "Filthy Five," the hard-nosed, rowdy core of the team and the antithesis of the choirboy image of his players Brown fostered. Regardless, the coach called Michaels "one of the most intelligent players we ever had and a no-nonsense player."

Michaels played in four consecutive Pro Bowls and made All-Pro. When the Browns visited Philadelphia in 1961, 1,700 people from Swoyersville traveled 250 miles to present him with a new automobile.

Knowing Brown's penchant for hastening veterans into retirement, Michaels accepted an offer of $10,000 to become defense coordinator of the Oakland Raiders in the newfledged AFL. A franchise in turmoil, the Raiders lost thirteen games and fired two head coaches in 1962. Michaels was out of a job and, he thought, out of football.

On a hunch, he called former Cleveland assistant Weeb Ewbank, who had taken over the New York Jets. Ewbank needed help, and Michaels began crafting an opportunistic defense that would become the complement to Joe Namath and the Jets' potent offense.

The defense held Oakland to fifty yards rushing in the 1968 AFL championship game and caused five turnovers as the Jets defeated Baltimore, 16-7, in Super Bowl III. "We had the city after that," Michaels says.

What Michaels didn't have was the head coaching job he wanted.

Ewbank retired in 1973 and designated his son-in-law, Charlie Winner, as his successor.

"I don't think it's ever going to happen," Michaels said glumly as he went off to work in Philadelphia for former Cleveland tackle Mike McCormack.

The Jets fired Winner after less than two seasons, but bypassed Michaels again in favor of fast-talking Lou Holtz. Persuaded to return to New York, Michaels assembled a defense that led the league in turnovers. Holtz bolted after thirteen games, and Michaels became the Jets' fifth coach in fifteen months. The job would prove a mixed blessing.

In 1977, the Jets won only three games for the third straight year, but they finished 8-8 the next season, and Michaels was named AFC coach of the year. By 1981, however, he had the worst record among active NFL coaches.

Fans wanted him fired. One of the wealthy troika who owned the Jets recommended his dismissal. Players claimed Michaels intimidated and demoralized them.

The rapacious New York media asked how Michaels could lose with the league's best talent. They credited players and assistants with wins and blamed Michaels for losses. They treated Michaels like a typecast *lumpenprole*, a Bohunk good mostly for brawling and heavy lifting: steer-thick body, face as bulbous and coarse as an upturned bucket of concrete, stubby fingers tipped with scallops of grime.

Michaels never developed Brown's knack for handling reporters. Brown sometimes referred to himself—not without irony—as "the farmer boy," but his lofty manner and precise speech seemed to elevate him over the hired press.

Michaels cultivated the role of noble immigrant workingman. He displayed in his office a picture of his father wearing a miner's helmet and stained coveralls; the photo was inscribed, "Glad he made the boat." Michaels wore a "Polish Power" button and sprinkled press conferences with "sayings of the wise old men," delivered in Polish. He said he saw himself as a foreman and the players as laborers.

After the Jets opened 1981 with three embarrassing defeats, Michaels dumbfounded all of New York by saying, "We're right on schedule to being a championship team." The work was about to pay off.

The Jets won ten of their next thirteen games and made the playoffs for the first time since 1969. They returned to the post-season in 1982. After New York upset Cincinnati in the first round, All-Pro tackle Marvin Powell said of Michaels, "He's a fine man. Today, he has been vindicated."

The Jets surprised Oakland the following week, setting up an AFC championship clash with the Miami Dolphins and their coach, Don

Shula, Michaels's *bete noir*. Michaels now says that he created the illusion of conflict with Shula to spark interest in the Miami/New York rivalry, a trick he had watched Brown pull years before. At the time, though, Michaels and Shula traded accusations, insults, and threats that sounded genuine.

Michaels, the *New York Times* wrote, "saw demons behind those of his adversaries who had achieved greater eminence, men like Don Shula and Al Davis." Peculiarly, Michaels had consistently bettered his adversary, dating back to the Super Bowl victory over the Colts, whom Shula had coached.

The Jets arrived in Miami to find that the Orange Bowl's grass had not been covered, as league rules required, during torrential rains. In the muck, New York managed only 139 yards, threw five interceptions, and lost 14-0.

Michaels complained bitterly after the game that Shula had been allowed to flaunt NFL regulations. During the flight home, team president Jim Kensil, a former aide to commissioner Pete Rozelle, ordered Michaels to drop the subject. They argued.

All night, Michaels paced the halls of the team's training center, muttering. The next morning, he didn't attend a team meeting he had called.

Michaels had always approached football as if he were one loss away from shoveling coal behind a half-blind mule 500 feet deep in the core of blackness itself. At the press conference announcing his hiring, he had said in Polish, "As you work so it will become." Now, that adage seemed to mock him.

Michaels met with Kensil and Leon Hess, the millionaire oilman who had purchased the Jets. Afterward, he said little, the club less. Reporters guessed that the team had delivered Michaels from his own grim intensity or that he had quit out of grief over his mother's recent death. They alluded darkly to unconfirmed rumors about his drinking or suggested that his not infrequent tantrums had alienated management. Yet through the team's bleakest days, Kensil and Hess had supported Michaels, Hess even claiming to "love him like a younger brother."

According to Michaels, he was actually dismissed for criticizing Rozelle, the NFL, and one of the league's glamorous coaches. Wladek Majka had forgotten his place.

"I got tired," he said. "I got tired in the mud."

Michaels had finally—and painfully—learned that a coach without a substantial share of the franchise and ironclad legal protection is merely an employee at the mercy of bosses "who had never put a jockstrap on straight."

Michaels spent ten months listening to Polka bands and helping out in a buddy's appliance store until a second chance came from the strangest of sources. Donald Trump, flamboyant real estate developer, had bought the New Jersey Generals of the United States Football League. Trump saw the Jets stagger to seven and nine. He heard fans chant, "We want Walt!" and hired Michaels.

After the Generals' first game, Michaels joked that the owner "didn't send any plays down to the bench." The team won fourteen games and made the playoffs, but Trump wanted to become a "playing owner," as Modell had once described himself. As if he were ordering from room service, Trump called coaches and demanded specific numbers of rushing and passing yards. Without telling Michaels, he dealt away quarterback Brian Sipe and signed rookie Doug Flutie to an $8.3 million contract.

The Generals returned to the playoffs, but before the USFL folded in 1986, Trump had already decided to fire his coach. Michaels had learned another lesson: A man with enough money doesn't have to know anything about the business.

"I had the Forbes (400), all right. No one can say they had as many Forbes as I did," he says.

Whether it was because of his association with the despised USFL, the unwillingness of insecure head coaches to hire him, or, as he claims, unnamed Jet officials mounted a smear campaign to justify firing him, Michaels couldn't get so much as a returned phone call from anyone in the NFL.

Michaels is now paying for his toughness. Operations on his spine and inner ear have divided his life into what he calls "BC and AC"—before and after he needed a cane to walk. He filed a disability claim over his neck injury, but the NFL denied it. In small, determined, torturous, corkscrewing steps, he navigated his sprawling, overgrown farm in the hills not far from Swoyersville.

In a cluttered garage, Michaels came across an original LeRoy Neiman of himself and his brother Lou, who played for the Colts in Super Bowl III. The painting had been wrapped in bubble plastic and shoved into a dusty nook. Michaels seemed uninterested.

Back in his living room, surrounded by football memorabilia, he rocked jerkily in a chair. Volumes on politics, history, human behavior, the Holy Grail, and the Bible stuffed bookcases and formed mounds on the floor and furniture. Michaels lives comfortably on investments he manages himself, holds season tickets

to both the Browns and the Jets, attends team functions, oversees the on-going forty-five year remolding of the farm, and doggedly pumps an exercise bike for rehabilitation.

He once admitted to suffering panic attacks, and a vulnerability sometimes appears through hairline cracks in Michaels's stoic countenance. Although resentful over being forced from the game, he is serene and philosophical.

"My father died when he was 54, and he only knew two things about football," he said. "If you hit, you win, and if you win, you're successful."

He might not always have been successful, but in the end, Michaels did win one for the men who wear the helmets. In New Jersey, he hired an ambitious young coach named Chris Palmer. When Palmer became head coach of the new Browns, he brought in Michaels's son Mark as an assistant.

Walt Michaels's favorite Polish parable is about a sea captain who returns to port after a stormy voyage. Encountering the ship's owner, the captain begins complaining about the passage.

"Don't tell me the sea was rough," the owner says. "Did you bring the ship home?"

# *Walt* MICHAELS

"I'M FIRST-GENERATION IMMIGRANT Polish. 'Majka' is the actual spelling of the name. I was the seventh in a family of eight. Lou (Baltimore Colt tackle and kicker) was the eighth. My dad was born near Krakow, Poland, which was split then, before World War I, between Austria-Hungary and Germany. My dad said, 'When they got us marching, we knew we had to get out of there, because we were going to war.'

They didn't want to get shot. They knew there was a better way to live than what they had. Take the 'e' off 'slave,' and what do you have? 'Slav,' and that's what they were—Slavic people. Who were your first slaves? The eastern Europeans. That's nothing to be proud of.

They hiked their way across Eastern Europe to get here. Eastern Europe is a long way from the boats that came here. Ask my dad a hundred questions about how he got across Europe, and he'd just say, 'Oh, I stopped and worked here and there.'

When they got to the boats, all they could afford was to get into the hold for someplace to sleep. 'Oh, yeah,' he said, 'I remember the Fancy Dans up on deck celebrating. After we were at sea three days, they were all throwing up over the side. Eighteen days later, we saw daylight for the first time. We were in the New York Harbor.'

The change in the name came when we went to school. My oldest brother went to the first grade, and the teacher says, 'What's your name?'

'Stanley Majka,' he says. The teachers were mostly Irish or English. To her, 'Majka' sounded like 'Michael,' so that's how she spelled it out: Stanley

Michael. Eventually, they stuck an 'S' on it: 'Those are the Michaels guys.'

I was the seventh, and when I went to school, everybody was playing football, so I was going to play football. Everybody was playing basketball, so I was going to play basketball. Then, you played sports so you could shower every day. You didn't have showers in the house so you could wash and keep clean.

Our teams were always a mixture of Polish, Slovaks, Lithuanians, Italians—mostly Eastern Europeans who settled on the same side of the railroad track. Our two coaches were Italians. One year, we had five Polish, five Italians, and one half-Italian, half-Polish playing on the varsity team.

We all had good grades. Then, you didn't come home and say, 'Dad, the teacher this and the teacher that.'

He'd say, 'Hey, you don't like it, go to work. I can always get you a job in the coal mines.' He'd say, 'Oh, you want to play football? Good. You still have to come home and do the chores and study.'

Today, some people would say, 'Oh, your father was overly tough on you.' He wasn't. Paul Brown was as tough as my father. My father just said you were going to do it, and when he said it, he meant it. That was those first-generation people.

WE HAD TO PICK COAL TO HEAT THE HOUSE. We picked coal and cracked it by hand. This isn't the bituminous coal—the soft coal. The anthracite had to be cracked, but it burned cleaner. The bituminous smokes. This coal burns clean, with a blue flame. You could actually charcoal over this, if you get the good deep-mine stuff.

Coming up here, when you hit Shickshinny, you can see the coal. It's what they call 'culm' or 'culm banks.' That's the material the miners had to work with until they got down about five hundred feet to the good stuff. They pulled it out and stacked it all over. Now, they reprocess it, and they can burn a lot of it. If you go up the river another twenty-five miles, to Scranton, everything was anthracite coal. It supplied New York City, Washington, and Baltimore.

When my daughter was about 13 or 14 years old, I had the place here, and we were driving up. She said, 'Hey, Dad, what're those black rocks?'

I never thought in all my life I would have to explain to my own children what coal is. When I bring up picking coal, they say, 'Oh, Dad, we all know how tough it was.'

I say, 'If you didn't live through it, you don't know.'

We picked the coal in the summer time, and in the fall, we cracked it and put it in the basement. We would have five, maybe seven tons of coal sitting down there. We didn't have central heat. We burned it in the kitchen stove. It was designed to use coal to bake and everything else. The hottest part was over the coal fire, and as you moved away on the burners, you had medium heat and low heat and warm. The rooms were right above it, so it would heat them, too. We had a pot-bellied stove in the living room, which heated the other end of the house.

Was it tough? Yeah. Could it have been easier? Yeah. But when you look at it, if it would've been easier, would we have come out of it the way we did?

I think my dad died of a broken heart. I had a brother killed at Guadalcanal, and there were three others in action. He'd sit down and ask you in Polish, 'Where are they now?'

He couldn't understand what they were doing. He understood Europe, but he didn't understand the Pacific.

'What do you mean?' he'd ask. 'What's the matter with those people?'

I'll never forget when the telegram came: 'Killed in action.'

My dad said, 'Where is this place?'

You can't even see Guadalcanal on a map.

Then come the neighbors. They know about the telegram. Then some guys who were in the service with him come, and they want they to talk about him.

Now, there's another son in Europe, in the engineers. He has to cross the Rhine River. My dad knows about that. He knows how those people are going to fight. The other one—the youngest one—has just finished training and is going the other way, to the Pacific.

The war ended. The guys were coming home. One of my brothers had just come home from a year and a half in Europe. I was out somewhere, and my dad had dinner one night and went over to have a couple of drinks with his friends. For coal miners, a shot and a beer was standard procedure. He came home that night, and that was it.

THERE'S NO QUESTION FOOTBALL was going to be a way out for me. I was sixth in a class of one hundred and thirty, and I had all the pre-college courses, but I dreamed of playing football. Of those of us on that football team, I think there were six scholarships passed out. That was quite a bit for one football team then. From the little high school I went to—Swoyersville, which is between Wilkes Barre and Scranton—there were five of us in pro football at one time.

We weren't worried about mom or dad having a job so they could send us to college. If we weren't going to get a scholarship to play, we were going to get it for school. It was that simple.

I had about twenty scholarships. I was matriculated at Cornell. But I decided to go to Washington and Lee. I looked at both schools, the schedules and everything, and I decided, 'What's the difference? I'm going to Washington and Lee.' Besides, some alumnus bought me a couple of suits.

I went there to play football, and I started four years, fullback and linebacker. We played in the Southern Conference. My freshman year we played Army at West Point. We played Georgia Tech. West Virginia was always on our schedule. My senior year, we were going to the Gator Bowl game. We were leaving from Richmond to go to Jacksonville, and the championship game was on television, the one where Groza kicked the field goal to beat Los Angeles (in 1950). I'll never forget seeing it. If someone had told me after seeing it that I would be drafted by the Browns, I'd tell them, 'You're crazy!'

I was a seventh-round draft choice. Today, that's equivalent to about a three. That's big money today. My contract was $5,000.

They didn't even contact me after the draft. I read about it in the paper, and then my coach said, 'Hey, Walt, you know you're the property of the Browns?'

I said, 'Good.' What was I going to say? You just went to class. You didn't think about that.

THE WAY THE TEAMS SCOUTED YOU in those days was with these penny postcards. You'd get this penny postcard in the mail. The post card said, 'Would you be interested in playing professional football?'

There was no bonus. A coach came in from the Browns. We sat down and had dinner, I signed a contract for $5,000, and that was the end of it. Just before camp opened, I got a letter to report. I had to have my own money to get to camp. They reimbursed me, but I had to have my own money. I took a train from Wilkes-Barre to Buffalo, then down through Cleveland to Toledo. I got off the train at Toledo and took the bus to Bowling Green. It took a day and a half.

Paul drafted me, and then he traded me up to Green Bay. I was at the All-Star Game in '51 when he traded me. After the game was over, he got to looking around, and he said, 'We're going to go with our veteran guys. There's no doubt that you can play pro football, but we don't know where it's going to be.'

Coming from him, I had to believe it. I thought, 'What am I going to do? I'm single. I've got no problems. I'm going to go.'

I said, 'Fine, if I can play, I'll go.'

I was just glad he sent me to Green Bay. Cleveland had won the championship that year. That was the time of Otto Graham and all those guys. There were thirty-one guys coming back out of thirty-three. You'd go to camp in those days, and you'd play six preseason games. If you went to camp and were the last one cut, you'd be there for eight weeks, and you didn't get a penny for it except room and board. You'd be broke.

There must have been some kind of deal going, because Blanton Collier came up to me when I was leaving, and he was telling me, 'I don't want to let you go. You're going to make pro football. If I can ever get you back, I will.'

At that time, the Browns' training camp was in Bowling Green. From Bowling Green, I went up to Toledo, caught a plane to Detroit, from Detroit over to the Green Bay training camp, and I was on with Green Bay.

The next thing you know, the season's over, and I'm back in Cleveland. Paul traded to get me back. I got a big raise— $800. I think Chubby Grigg and two other guys went up to Green Bay. I felt pretty good. I said, 'Wow! Three guys.' But these were guys who weren't going to make the Browns' team anyway.

THE BROWNS WERE THE FIRST ONES to time the 40-yard dash. People tell you Dallas was the first. They're full of crap. Dallas copied Paul Brown. Paul Brown and this guy Eddie Finnegan, from Western Reserve, who coached the Olympic track team, were looking for some kind of barometer of speed. For whatever reason, the distance that approximated how far you had to run in football was 40 yards. It started there, then Dallas copied it and publicized it, so they think they did it.

Pass protection as it's taught today started with Lou Rymkus. The Brown coaches worked all off-season one year to find out why Lou was able to block so well. They said, 'Why in the world is Lou able to keep these guys off of the quarterback?'

They attacked the problem scientifically. They spent the whole off-season looking at his footwork, his stance, how he lined up. They found out that pass-blocking has to be done like you're catching a ball. The first requirement is that you better have good feet. You can't pop out at people. Now, the Browns have got the book on how to pass protect.

Otto Graham isn't getting hit, but the people coaching on that other team aren't dumb. Their pass protection techniques aren't what they should be, so they're going to the Browns. They said, 'Why spend the whole off-season doing this? We'll watch their film or find someone they trained, see if he has his playbook copied.' I saw Paul copy some plays out of other teams' books, but they copied a lot more of his. Paul would think we didn't know what he did. Everyone just laughed about it.

I knew I was going to make it, but I'll tell you, in those days, you better not open your mouth, because there would be someone waiting. If you don't watch yourself, you're in trouble. In the first scrimmage with the Browns, I tackled Motley. I made some good hits. The veterans invited me to come out and drink some beer at the quarry near Bowling Green on the weekend. When the veterans invited you to drink with them, it meant they accepted you.

That stuff about no one drinking beer is a bunch of baloney. We just sat in the back of the plane. If anything was out of hand, Paul handled it. If it was done within reason, it was no problem. Mac Speedie would drink six, eight bottles of beer on a Saturday night, so he could sleep. If Dante Lavelli drank two, he couldn't play, so he didn't. Dub Jones would maybe have one bottle of beer and look around him and say, 'You guys get out of here. I can't hang around with you guys.'

PAUL COULD USE YOUR RULE-BREAKING as a reason to get rid of you. That was an opportunity for him to say, 'I got rid of him because of his behavior.' But if you were good enough, Paul wasn't going to do that.

Paul would say, 'You've got to be in these meetings, and you've got to take everything down, and you're going to do it, and we'll have no dozing or sleeping. Now, there's Marion here. Marion has a little bit of a problem. He has a kind of disease. We don't know exactly what it is, but he'll doze off, and we understand that.'

That was Marion's excuse to fall asleep. Paul was something else. He knew how to get around things.

There's an old saying: Would the guy sit back-to-back with you in a foxhole, or would he shoot you in the back and throw his gun out? Those guys would sit in a foxhole with you. I'll never forget Lavelli and Kissell talking. They were both in the Battle of the Bulge. Lavelli is really excitable. He said, 'These 40-yard dashes. I ran better than a 4.6 in the Battle of the Bulge with a full field-pack. When those German Tiger tanks started coming, I outran them all.'

Kissell is laughing and hollering: 'Yeah, you tell them, Dante. We had those Germans beat.'

THERE WAS NO MONKEY BUSINESS with Paul Brown. There was just business. He was very disciplined, very organized. When he said we were going to do something, that's what we did. A lot of guys couldn't stand him, until they realized what he was trying to do.

It didn't bother me, because discipline was part of my life. He was like my father. He told you, and he expected you to do it. Now, he wasn't like my father in the way that my father might end up swinging and catch you wherever he caught you, if you did it the wrong way. But the basics of being orderly—yes.

Discipline was part of everyone's life then. This was the World War II generation. There were quite a few World War II veterans on the team: Groza, Lavelli, Speedie, Gatski, Otto Graham, George Young, Don Colo. Of the thirty-three guys on the team, about twenty of them were veterans. These were disciplined guys. These guys just laughed about Paul.

As time went on, Paul said, 'The guys I first had, when I said, "We're going over the top," they said, "What time?" When I got the next generation in, and I said, "We're going over the top," they said, "Coach, let's talk about it for a while."'

Everything was a discussion. The guys who were there when I came up were disciplined players. They said, 'You know what you want us to do, we'll do it.'

I don't know if it was blind allegiance. We sat down many times and said, 'Well, Coach was right again.'

Paul wasn't a big guy. He was always looking up to everybody. But he would cut you up verbally. One year, we lost the championship in Cleveland. After the game, he's giving us the business. He says, 'And, furthermore, merry Christmas and happy New Year, if you can. We'll find out who belongs here next year.'

Guys who did it wrong, you looked around, and they were gone.

Paul told me himself. At the end, when he was in Cincinnati, I was coaching, and we sat down and talked a couple of times. I thought he was a tough guy, but we sat down and talked like two coaches.

He said, 'Walter, now you understand the business.'

I said, 'Paul, it's different now.'

He said, 'Yes, but I enjoyed having you. You were one of my better players.'

AT FIRST, I WANTED TO SAY I didn't know any better, but it wasn't that you didn't know any better. You knew that if you did it his way, you were going to win. If you did it some other way, you weren't going to win. Paul was on top of the world, and you were going to do it that way.

Can you say that everybody liked him? No. I was sitting there, trying to get a $500 raise, and he's not going to give it to me. I get to $250, and he looks at me and says, 'Walter, you've got to understand one thing: This is a business.'

My eleventh year, I'm All-Pro four years, Pro Bowl games off and on, and I have my highest contract: $13,000. Now, you go to the Pro Bowl, you're All-Pro, you're calling for a million and a half. Golly, would I have a house here. 'Course, then they would've just raised my taxes.

Paul was hard to deal with over money because he got a piece of the action. No matter how they kept the books, he got a piece of Mickey McBride, the owner then. Mickey McBride and Dan Sherby, a Washington and Lee man, were the owners. When Mickey left, when he was being investigated by the Kefauver Committee, Paul just got more of it.

They were investigating Mickey because of his horses and stuff. He was supposedly a piece of organized crime. Where does Mickey McBride fit into organized crime? I don't know. He's the wrong nationality. Kefauver was investigating anybody.

I remember Mickey coming in. He'd walk around: 'Saw you in church this morning. Hi, how you doin'?'

Paul would look over there and see him. He'd want to talk to Paul. Paul would say, 'It's time for you to leave. We can't have you in here. We have team meetings now.'

And Mickey, like the good little owner, would leave.

After that came the guys from Nationwide Insurance, Dave Jones and those guys. Mickey sold because he had no choice, but Mickey's heart was always in it.

In 1954, Detroit beat us in the last game of the season, 12-10 or something (14-10). Boy, the championship game (also against Detroit) was supposed to be a nightmare. We beat them 56-10. The next year, Paul got Otto Graham back for his tenth year, and we win out in Los Angeles, 38-14.

When you look at all these passing records, you have to keep something in mind. With Paul Brown calling the plays, there is no way Otto Graham could have a passing record like Dan Fouts, Johnny Unitas, Joe Namath, and how many others. The minute we were ahead, Paul's concern was, 'How do we win the game without getting anybody hurt?' He wasn't going to let Otto Graham sit back there and throw, throw, throw for a record. Paul's attitude was, 'Win the game, and let's go home.'

Art Modell wanted to open it up more. Art wanted control. Art wanted to be a Jerry Jones kind of owner. Art was a young guy, 37, 38 years old, at the time. Whatever broke out between them, I don't know, because I was gone, but you could see those personalities were going to clash right away, and they clashed within a year.

Paul was an old football man who was there from 1946. Art Modell came to the Browns in 1961 and wanted to get involved. How much can you learn between Madison Avenue and professional football in one year that the other guy hasn't forgot between '46 and '62?

IN '58, WE HAD JIM BROWN and Bobby Mitchell, Jim Ray Smith, Mike McCormack. We still had the top defense in the league. That was the year of that famous Pat Summerall kick in the wind (giving the New York Giants a 13-10 win and a tie for the Eastern Conference title). They should not ever have had an opportunity, because Gifford fumbled the ball, and I had it.

There comes Charley Berry, an official, running from the other side, waving. The Giant defense was coming on the field. They said, 'What in the world?' Charley Berry never officiated another game, but we lost. That was the year of the famous Baltimore-Giants game. *We* would've been in that game.

There was no question that Jimmy Brown was going to be special. Ask Mike Brown. Mike was still at Dartmouth at the time. It was Jim's first game. I think we were in Philadelphia. Mike was sitting at the end of the bench where I used to sit when I came out. I told Mike, 'That guy is the most unreal running back that you've ever seen.'

Years later, Mike said, 'Walter, I hope you remember the day I was sitting on the bench, and you told me how good Jim Brown was going to be.'

Jim Brown's first play from scrimmage was just a couple days after he came back from the All-Star Game. They handed him a draw on about the 35-yard line going in. It was: 'There he is. There he's gone.' Nobody touched him. Nobody got close. He just took off, and everybody thought, 'Where is this guy coming from?' He just outran everybody right to the corner.

It was even more impressive than when Ollie Matson came back from the Olympics. We're playing against Ollie for the first time. George Young goes to make the tackle, I go to make the tackle, and Warren Lahr goes to make the tackle. All of us miss. We didn't do the right pursuit angle.

I thought, 'This guy can outrun all of us at once.' That's the way Jim Brown was. You just better take a different pursuit angle, or you're not going to touch him. And at 230 pounds, Jim was bigger than Ollie Matson.

IN PRO FOOTBALL, I missed two games in eleven years. I missed one game in '52 in Cleveland, and I never missed another game in Cleveland until '59. I don't think I missed ten practices in all that time.

How rough the game is depends on who hits you and what position you're in when you get hit. If you're prepared, if you're in shape, it's not a problem. Sometimes, they catch you the wrong way, and you say, 'Oh, that hurt!'

The old trainer for the Browns, Leo Murphy, said, 'You were here ten years. I can count on one hand the number of times you were in here to see me.'

I said, 'You're right, Leo, because if Paul walked into that training room and saw you sitting there too often, you were cut.'

When we went to camp with the Browns, Paul Brown wouldn't even give us a physical. He'd say, 'You're grown men. You're responsible for your own bodies.' And he got by without a lawsuit. It's unreal.

There was a guy in training camp who was overweight. What does Paul see him do? He went right to the dessert and got about three scoops of ice cream. Paul cut him the next day. He said, 'The man can't control his weight.'

He cut rookie quarterback Stan Heath over a test. He gave a test on all the pass routes and everything. I got a higher score than Stan Heath. He was gone. You didn't score, you didn't stay on the team.

We had a guy from Tennessee State named Willie Carter. He was one of the fastest guys I ever saw. He was outrunning everybody. They had him at a 4.3 time. He lasted a long time with a low test score. That 4.3 made him brilliant.

Willie couldn't learn the plays. Somebody said, 'How in the world is Willie still here?'

Someone else said, 'What do you mean, why is he still here? He *has* to be here. Did you see his time in the forty? Paul will never cut him. He'll let him cut himself.'

He was there to the last release, and Paul still tried to find a way to keep him, because he could run that fast.

In the early years, if you were released after a while, you figured you were going to get picked up by somebody. If you were with the Browns, unless you were hurt, they picked you up.

Cleveland was a great city to play in, a very blue-collar town. They've got all those ethnic groups, and they mesh well together. Some of my best friends were Lebanese. This Lebanese guy had a place where Johnny Rae got started, the Four Aces, Louie Prima. Gatski and I would go up to Frankie Yankovic's. He was Slovenian. There was a little place on 105th and Euclid where this black guy had a band. We'd go in there, and we were like kings. Of course, we were winning. I never knew what Cleveland would be like any other way.

One night, Abe Gibron decides we're going to sprint. We're walking down the street, and he says, 'I can still outrun you, Michaels.'

I said, 'You can't outrun me, Abe.'

A guys starts us out, and here come the cops: 'Hey, what did you guys steal?'

Then they saw who we were. They said, 'You won, Michaels.'

Abe was overweight, but he could really run.

THE LAST YEAR, THE SMARTEST THING I ever did was retire. I was already in my eleventh year, and I was making a tackle. I felt a stinger go through my shoulder. Then, I thought I felt it in my head. I was 33 years old. It's the same as in life. You hit 50, 55, the things you used to do, you don't do anymore.

I wasn't sure what I was going to do when I got done with football. Paul Brown wanted me to come back for a twelfth year. The American Football League was just coming in. Paul Wiggin was playing in front of me. Suddenly, I got a call from Marty Feldman, the head coach of the Oakland Raiders. Marty said, 'I was talking with Paul (Wiggin), and he said that you were considering retiring, and you might want to coach professional football.'

I said, 'I'm not sure. Let me think about it. What can I make?'

He said, 'An assistant makes $10,000.'

I was making $13,000 at the time. That $10,000 sounded pretty good. They said they'd give two grand or so for moving. So, away I go to Oakland. I coached there one year. I coached the whole defense all by myself, and we had a good year. It was wild out there. They fired Marty Feldman after the fifth game. Red Conkright finished the season, but they were going to go with a guy with experience, and when Al Davis interviewed, Al was their guy. There are some people, when they interview, they get the job. It doesn't matter if they have the credentials; they get the job. One thing led to another, and I put whatever I had into a trailer and pulled it back East. It was a combination of things. He wasn't going to hire me, and I wasn't going to work for him.

I thought, 'Well, I'm out of it now.'

Weeb Ewbank got the job with the Jets, and I thought, 'Let me give it a shot.' I called. Weeb called the Browns. Fritzie Heisler recommended me, and I'm with the Jets.

I played one game with the Jets. That makes me an alumnus. We were sitting around on a Wednesday. We had two linebackers hurt from the last preseason game. We only had two healthy. Weeb's looking around for what to do. Chuck Knox is kidding around. He said, 'Walt, you played linebacker. You know the plays.'

Weeb says, 'Will you consider it, Walt?'

I PLAYED THE WHOLE GAME with two or three days' practice. We were playing Boston, which is now New England. Babe Parilli, the former Cleveland quarterback, was still playing with Boston. It was hot that day. I held up, but I didn't do any good at all. I got $350. I said, 'For $350, I can't do this any more.' I was smart enough to quit right then.

There were only four assistants—two on offense, two on defense—and Weeb. Five years later, when we won the Super Bowl, Buddy Ryan had the defensive line, and I had the secondary and the linebackers and was defensive coordinator. And Buddy was doubling up as special teams coach. Joe Spencer was with the offensive line. Clive Rush had the receivers and the running backs. Weeb was with the quarterbacks and handled the money. All those guys they have today, what do you need them for?

The AFL was kind of free and easy. Everyone threw like crazy. It was wide open. Of course, Weeb was always wide open. Weeb always wanted to pass. No matter what was going on, Weeb said, 'Throw the ball! Throw the ball!'

I said, 'Weeb, in Baltimore, you had Johnny Unitas to throw the ball.'

Before Namath came in, we had Dick Wood. Dick was a good, smart guy, but he wasn't a Johnny Unitas or a Joe Namath.

When Namath came in, Weeb wasn't even going to start him. I was on defense, so I couldn't say anything, but I thought, 'This's crazy.' Chuck Knox is going nuts and so is Clive Rush. But we were out-gunned. Weeb was the general manager and head coach, and he wanted Mike Taliaferro. Mike blows right up in the air, and Namath comes in and goes crazy. That solved the problem of who starts at quarterback.

Namath's contract his first year was about $380,000. Just the year before that, Matt Snell (New York fullback) had about a $50,000 package, and Weeb said the league couldn't survive the big contracts.

WE WERE INVOLVED IN STASHING PLAYERS, although the NFL was doing more of that than we were. They had guys with Emerson Boozer (New York fullback). I went down to see him at Maryland State after the Steelers drafted him, and I said, 'Emerson, what the hell's wrong with you? *Pittsburgh*? You belong in New York City.'

I signed Emerson in the rathskeller of the president's house at Maryland State. The biggest problem is that I don't have any money to sign him. I had a personal check, though, so I wrote out a personal check for $17,000. I didn't have enough to cover it. 'Hey, don't worry about it,' I told him. 'This's the way we do it on the road when things come up. Just don't cash it until I get back to New York.'

I can't get away from there to get back to New York to get the money. I rented a car and drove all the way. When I got there, I told (Jet owner) Sonny Werblin, 'You better get that money in the bank, or I'm done.'

He's laughing. He says, 'Ah, don't worry about it.'

I take Emerson out of Maryland State with halfback Earl Christy. It wasn't two years later, I'm down there trying my darndest to get tackle Artie Shell.

Weeb says, 'What are we going to do with all these guys from Maryland State.'

I said, 'We're going to play them. This guy's a good one.'

Weeb let Shell go to the Raiders, and he ends up in the Hall of Fame. The guy who really belongs in the Hall of Fame is Sonny Werblin.

Sonny Werblin was responsible for the TV contract between NBC and the AFL, and without a TV contract, there wouldn't have been a league.

I was there at the 21 Club with Chuck Knox, Weeb, and Hank Stram. Sonny Werblin was in the back room with NBC. They're talking. We're out there eating smoked sturgeon for sixteen bucks a pound. Here comes Sonny, smiling. He convinced NBC that with Namath, we got a marketable product. We got Namath and NBC, and the NFL just went right out the back door.

They said, 'We've got to get together with the AFL.' They didn't want any more bidding. They knew with the kind of money that was in the TV contract with NBC, it was all over. They didn't want to fight anymore. The NFL owners were not that wealthy. Pound for pound, financially, the AFL had money.

Kansas City was in the first Super Bowl, the Raiders were in the second, and we were in the third. We won it, and that broke it lose. I had some good players on defense. We all stayed healthy in '68, and we went into the Super Bowl and intercepted four passes.

WE HAD THE CITY AFTER THAT. Of course, Namath fit perfect. Namath was just like he was written about. Sonny Weblin wanted him flamboyant. But the thing about the guy was he was gifted. He couldn't run, of course. He had the bad wheels right away.

Of course, with Joe, two years after the Super Bowl, who were his receivers and his running backs? Weeb wasn't going to pay any money. Weeb was a farmer from Richmond, Indiana. He was very frugal. Weeb had the same thing as Paul Brown on his contract: a piece of the action. Anything under the budget, Weeb got a piece of it.

As a head coach, I know you have to be like Paul. These guys who say, 'I'm going to go in there and treat them like men, and I'm going to be their buddy,' forget it. It doesn't work. No matter what you think, you better discipline them. You can be their friend and still be their boss and have the respect, but you can't be their buddy on the golf course, because they're going to take advantage of you. They're young. They'll look back on it years later, and nine out of ten times, they'll say, 'He wasn't tough enough on me.'

I was just in New York with a couple of guys I coached. I said, 'Maybe you just didn't understand.'

They said, 'You're right. It was different then.'

Even Joe Namath says that now. It's a whole different ball game. Now, he says, 'I didn't understand.'

One time, Namath was out. I grabbed him. I said, 'You know, Joe, you can stay out after hours for anybody but me. I'm over the barrel to turn you in. Weeb's over the barrel to turn you in to Sonny Werblin, and Sonny Werblin isn't going to accept it. So, why don't you come in and then go out *after* we check you? That way, nobody will be on the hook.'

Nobody ever paid pro football players to become role models. Do you want to know the living habits of some of these Forbes 400 people? I'm not so sure I do. Are they role models for everybody? Don't bet on it. If a player had five illegitimate children, I wouldn't want him as a role model for my kids, but I wouldn't criticize him in the paper. Role models for kids ought to be their parents. Don't equate a guy's brain power or his personality with his ability to perform as an athlete.

I WAS A GOOD GUY, but being a good guy isn't enough. I made too much noise. I was loud. I had an incident with the president of the team. I hollered about the field after a playoff game with Miami in 1982. The field wasn't covered, and we lost. That was my last year with the Jets, in the conference playoff game. The next game's the Super Bowl. We beat Cincinnati, we beat the Raiders, and we come to play Miami. It rained since Wednesday, and they didn't cover the field, and they never turned the pumps on. I jumped all over Shula. I jumped all over the league office. My president, instead of defending me, defended Shula and the league office. When he does that, I'm dead.

I made the mistake of saying, 'I wonder what would have happened if Al Davis had been my boss instead of Jim Kensil.' Al Davis would have gone crazy.

When this happened down in Miami, who was going to defend me from the Jet organization? Nobody. If they would've defended me, it would've been a closed issue. When you're by yourself, you lose.

Let's put it this way: I didn't expect to get fired. But I argued with someone above me. You've seen corporate trees. Who do you fire? I knew enough about corporate structure to know who that was.

I jumped on the NFL for not having the field covered. I jumped on Shula for not having the field covered. So what? Everybody loved it. It was good stuff.

It could very well have been different for me if I hadn't been in New

York. I was very vocal about the NFL, and you're not supposed to be vocal about the NFL. The NFL has been wrong a lot of times. Everybody knows it. Now, here's a guy sitting in an NFL office who never put a jockstrap on straight, and nobody can criticize him? Come on. Why do I have to be the sacrificial lamb. I'm Abraham's son. I don't want to be. All I want is, if I'm wrong, I say it. If you're wrong, *you* say it.

I can't change what happened, so I try to forget that stuff. I'm sure there are things I aggravated some people over, but I think there were some things I had a right to be aggravated about. And it's very easy to get real aggravated when you think you know more about the situation than someone who won't let you do what you think is right. They say, 'You can't do this'; or, 'You don't dare criticize Joe, even if Joe happened to be wrong.' Well, I'm sorry. If Joe happened to have been in the NFL office, I couldn't care less, and if Jim happened to be Don Shula, I couldn't care less, because this is Walt Michaels talking. I've also got credentials I have to live with.

One of the worst ones for interfering was Donald Trump (owner of the New Jersey Generals in the USFL) . He didn't know what he was doing. I go for my interview. I go to the Trump Tower, up to the fifty-seventh floor. It was like going out to Hawaii, to see the *Arizona* in Pearl Harbor. You have to watch this indoctrination film, and then they take you out to the *Arizona*. It's very eerie, and that's what Donald Trump does. You go up there, and you have to watch this film about the Trump Tower and everything, before you can talk to the man. He's something else.

THE USFL ONLY SURVIVED TWO YEARS. The first coach of the Generals was Chuck Fairbanks. The first owner was a guy from Texas, Walter Duncan, an oilman. He's the one who signed Herschel Walker (Heisman Trophy running back from Georgia). He sold to Donald Trump, who hired me, because we had a good record in New York.

For the first couple of months, I don't have time to scratch my rear end. I can't even get a staff together. I get guys who are head coaches in college, coordinators in the NFL. He doesn't say anything. Then, about two or three months into the season, he starts coming in with all of these suggestions: What I should do, how much I should do it, who I should play.

I said, 'Donald, for two, three months, you're the best guy in the world. What did you do, talk to the guy who shines your shoes in the morning or the limousine driver?'

I was the smartest guy in the world for three months. How can a guy know so much and suddenly become so dumb? And we won fourteen games that year, with Brian Sipe at quarterback.

I warned my coaches when I came with Trump. You're dealing with a different kind of guy in Trump. So I warned the assistants. He just hires a guy, and he's on the phone before one season is over making sure he lines up someone else, in case something happens. A guy like Donald Trump wouldn't think twice about firing his staff, paying it off, and getting another one.

It's not unusual for the owner to become brilliant. Look at Jerry Jones down there. You don't know how many of the owners are going to get involved. They wouldn't do that if they were dealing with their life and I was a doctor.

I HAD DOUG FLUTIE AS A ROOKIE. He was something else. He was always good enough to do what he's doing now. Doug has a problem when you get to the real good teams, and the last two, three games you have to win. His stature won't let him do the things he needs to do. He's limited to doing certain things. He's a smart guy. He knows what to do. But he can't stand in there and do certain things. When you get him closer to the goal line, you're shrinking up the size of the field you have to work with. It creates a problem for Doug, but he knows exactly what he wants to do, he knows how, and a lot of times, he'll do it.

I had Doug at the beginning of his career and Sipe at the end of his. With Sipe, if you threw any more than twenty passes in practice, you better look out. You had to save his arm for the game. So you had a practice problem with Brian. In baseball, if a pitcher's arm gets tired after three innings, you take him out. You can't do that in football. 'Go ahead and pitch two quarters, and we'll take you out.' Who does that?

The United States Football League had a good shot to make it. That would've been another American Football League/National Football League merger. There was enough money. If Trump doesn't hurry it up, that league is going to make it. We were averaging 40,000 in New Jersey. If Donald doesn't go to court, the league survived. He sued (for antitrust violations) the NFL and won three bucks. Donald Trump killed that league by pushing that law suit. He flaunted that ruling around the courtroom, and the judge, for whatever reason, gave it to the jury to decide the reward. The jury said, 'This guy's too rich. Give him a dollar.' He won the suit, and he got three times the award, so he got three dollars.

I think there were some shenanigans there between Trump and Pete Rozelle. Someone was promising Trump something. I could never prove that today. It would have to be one of those surmise deals: 'According to an informed source....'

We won twenty-five games in two years, and I couldn't get an interview for a job in the NFL. I guess I shook up too many people. I can't get a word out of the NFL office. The man who could maybe have answered all of that—my boss with the Jets (Phil Islen)—was dead. Either him or Leon Hess, and Hess isn't going to say anything. You're not going to have a guy from the Forbes 400 group ever make a mistake. I had the Forbes, all right. No one else can say that they had as many Forbes as I did.

So I never got another interview in the NFL. I made the mistake of not waiting for Paul to do something. Paul would've done something. But Paul was different from your other owners. Paul Brown would do what he wanted to do. Al Davis might've done something like that, but Al and I weren't going to get along. But I'd rather be respected by somebody like that, who knows football, than be respected by a Leon Hess. Maybe if I were in the oil business, I'd think differently, but not in the football business.

Paul Brown used to say, 'We'll tolerate you until we can get rid of you.' When you're in your eighth year, and he's telling you that, you start to wonder how long you can last. But when you got out of football, it was different. When the baloney hit the fan in New York who's a letter come from but Paul Brown: 'Walter, I suspect a lot of things could have happened, but if I can ever help you in any way, you let me know. You belong back in football.'

I called him one time. His secretary said, 'He's in a meeting, but he said if any of his boys ever call, be sure and get him.' He stopped the meeting and took my call.

Sure, it was hard to get out of the game. What do you do when you're 54 or 55, and your highest earning capacity is between the ages of 55 and 60 years old? When they drop the bomb on you, it's rough. But I got all my kids educated. I sit down retired and not have to kiss any rear ends, and I can go to the games and root for whoever I want to.

AFTER I WAS OUT OF IT A WHILE, I called a good friend of mine about being an assistant. He said he'd get back to me. I didn't hear anything, didn't hear anything. Finally, I talked to him. He said, 'Gee, Walt, it'd be great, but...'

I said, 'What are you talking about "but"?'

He said, 'The first time anything went wrong, you'd have my job.'

I said, 'What do you mean?'

He said, 'You didn't leave as a losing coach. You left as a winning coach. Writers pick that up, and we have a bad time, you're the new head coach.'

I said, 'But that's not *me* cutting your throat.'

He said, 'I know that. That'd be the media forcing the issue on management.'

I said, 'In other words, you're playing not to lose instead of playing to win.'

That's the last I went shopping for a job. You know other coaches are thinking the same thing.

I went over to Europe about five years after the Generals. It was the International League of American Football. I had the team in Finland. There was Finland, two teams in Germany, two in England, a team in Holland, a couple in Italy. They had $25 million to start it out, which would've been enough to do it over there, but suddenly, for some reason, they pulled the money away.

I had a good team going in Finland. Finland was one of the most advanced countries in American football. They have about sixty teams playing American football. We would've done well. My son was coaching with me, and he stayed with a Finnish team and won the championship.

Over here, if a father and son are coaching together, it's nepotism. Over there, they thought it was the greatest thing in the world that I had my son with me and I was teaching him.


I'M ON A CANE NOW because of surgery for a football injury. It was in the neck, from banging. The surgery created an imbalance. I use the cane for balance. I ride that bike over there for rehab.

I still think they messed up a little bit, but who are you going to argue with? If I ever have to go to surgery again, I'll need a *fifth* opinion. It was bad.

The NFL tells you, 'Oh, they're non-football injuries. They came on after you were out ten years.' They said, 'It can't be football-related. You could've had that in an automobile accident.'

How do you prove anything? They have lawyers sitting on retainer. You're dead.

My surgery was seven years ago. I was born with a slightly narrow canal that carries the spinal cord. The doctors looked at it and said, 'If we had had these pictures, we wouldn't have let you play.'

I said, 'That's good. I already played nineteen years and only missed two games. What happened?'

'Well, I don't know, Walt. You were lucky, I guess.'

I'm part of a professional spring league that we'd put together if we only had a couple of more dollars. I just had a meeting with people from Turner and NBC, but I don't know how dedicated they are to doing it. I told them they have to decide if they want to do it in the spring or do it in the fall. 'If you think it's practical to buck the NFL in the fall, with their seventeen billion dollars, go ahead,' I said.

The only thing you have going for you is the other networks, but what good are they without ratings? Who's going to watch you? You go in with a nice little spring league, and you have a player here or a player there. A lot of players develop in three or four years that you're not sure are going to be good players. You get enough of those, and you're fortunate enough to sign one or two big ones away, then you can apologetically move into that seventeen-billion-dollar corner. But if you think you're going to buck them, I don't care how much money you have. They have more.

You think the NFL isn't a monopoly? They have money in Canada, so nobody else can go up there. They got money in Europe so that nobody can bother them there. They're putting money into Arena Football. They want control of it all. If they're not a monopoly, tell me what is. I know. I've been there.

To go back to the NFL? Maybe, if I didn't have a cane. It hasn't changed that much. I know in two years I could make more money than in any ten I ever coached. They say Chris Palmer's got a five-year contract for five million dollars, and I'm happy for him, because I know I barely got $35,000 for him when he was my coordinator with the Generals. I hired Chris out of Colgate, and he had one year in Canada. Chris was younger than Brian Sipe, but I hired him. What a bright young guy. He's gone from $35,000 in '85 to a million dollars a year, if the newspapers are accurate.

I'M HAPPY. I've got the kids and the grandkids. One of my sons is on the Browns staff. He's the only one involved in football. After the incident in New York (his being fired), the boys were kind of down on it. My son who's in New Jersey could've stayed in coaching, but he got out. 'Ahh,' he said, 'there might be a problem.' You never know. Some people are crazy.

You add it up. There are thirty teams, three hundred coaches. They say, 'Hey, we can get three hundred coaches anywhere. Why should we worry?' They see the name, and they push it aside.

Al Davis called me when Weeb died. If someone would've told me that Al Davis would call me, I'd say they were crazy. I'm up with my son in Massachusetts. I said, 'Al, what in the world are you doing trying to chase me down? It's good to hear your voice, but this is crazy.'

He said, 'Nothing special. I was reading your quotes about Weeb and all the things that happened. I just wanted to tell you it was good to build the American Football League with you and Weeb.'

I felt good about that.

I talked to Paul just before he died and sent him a letter, wishing he would get well. We played Cincinnati the year we won the Super Bowl. It was the last game of the season. We're practicing before the game. Paul's walking around with his team. We shook hands. You know: 'Paul, how you doing?'

We talk a little bit.

He's watching Namath. He says, 'Walter, I watched him in the films, and now I watched him up close. You guys can win it all with that guy throwing the football.'

I said, 'Paul, we think so, too.'

I said, 'Can he throw as good as Otto?'

He said, 'Yeah.'

Namath wasn't the first one to guarantee the win. Paul Brown said we could win it, too.

I had a lot of fun in Cleveland. We won, but it wasn't just winning. First of all, we had good coaches who made history. You can't say you played with anyone better than Otto Graham. You can't be around more Hall of Fame people. I have a picture of the '54 team, and I think there were something like thirteen guys there that were Hall of Famers. I'm not sure about role models, but if you wanted to pick a team of role models, you'd find more in Cleveland at that time. And you had Weeb, the first coach to win everything in two leagues. Where did it all start? Cleveland. I was part of Cleveland, and I'm proud of that. **" "**

# This Football Business

UNLIKE ALMOST EVERY
other football coach of his era, Paul
Brown believed that the true location
of the game was neither the adrenal
glands nor the testes. "Football," he
said, "is a state of mind and heart as
well as a physical experience."

By the time he began coaching
professional football in 1946, Brown
had devised a method for dealing with
his players' minds, one that was a
logical extension of his own personality.
"Aloof, unemotional, made of iron, he
seemed to have all the warmth of a data
bank. He produced football teams that
were like him—meticulous, methodi-
cal, and impersonal," one West Coast
columnist wrote.

A magazine editor is said to have
dispatched a writer to research a
human interest piece on the coach.
The exasperated journalist wired his
boss "Brown ain't human" and
abandoned the assignment. "Preci-

sion Paul" ate his breakfast—half a banana, cereal, and orange juice—in a prescribed sequence.

His first wife, Katie, said she had never seen him so upset that he neglected to hang up his shirt and tie. Brown said that he never lost sleep over a football game, composure that came from his ability to "shut off" his feelings. "It's just a natural thing with me," he said. Indeed, in his autobiography—a book almost weirdly terse about personal relationships—Brown's only comment about the death of his eldest son, Robin, of cancer in 1978, is, "Burying him was the hardest thing I have ever done."

Sportswriters compared him with "a trim intelligent attorney," "an alert school teacher," "a homicide detective viewing the body," Edison, Jefferson, an undertaker. He was, in the words of the *New York Times*, "the man who built a better mousetrap."

Brown wasn't, like Woody Hayes, another William Tecumseh Sherman, or, like Vince Lombardi, another George S. Patton. His counterparts are the Henry Fords, the John D. Rockefellers, the men who found a better way to do something and worked tirelessly to perfect their ideas.

Brown's revolutionary concept was to apply modern corporate practices—attention to the bottom line, efficient management of resources, application of new technol-

ogy, division of labor—to what he called "this football business." Says former team captain Don Colo, "Playing for Paul was just like being in industry. Paul and I had a very businesslike relationship."

An adage holds that George Halas founded the NFL, George Preston Marshall made people notice it, and Paul Brown gave it dignity and direction. The frequently repeated list of Brown's innovations includes: full-time, year-round coaching staffs, timing players in the forty-yard dash, detailed playbooks, classroom instruction, careful evaluation of college talent prior to the draft, scripted workouts, scouting opponents long before games, and splitting the squad into small groups during practices.

He put a radio receiver in a quarterback's helmet forty years before the rest of the league adopted the device. He invented the single-bar facemask and was among the first to experiment with faxing information from coaches boxes to locker rooms. The "pass and trap offense" he employed from the beginning in Cleveland is the forerunner of the modern "West Coast" attack.

What he didn't originate he purloined. "He was a great copier and implementer," Colo says. "I always said that no matter what business he went into, he'd be a sonofabitch of a competitor, because he'd do what you're doing better than you do it."

Brown said that he "worked harder at every phase of the 'people business' than at anything else," and he seems to have clearly understood one aspect of human nature: "It's the heart that's the tricky part." He avoided appeals to his players' emotions, calling pep talks "false and dishonest." In the most inspired bit of oratory anyone can remember, Brown advised players that their financial futures depended on that day's game. "Football is not a shouting match or a contest of bullies. It's a scientific game," he said.

Enamored of data and gadgets, Brown made unprecedented use of film, scrutinizing "the moving pictures" for every nuance. Says former quarterback Otto Graham, "He would break down the film in the off-season, and then, if we had a run to the right, he'd come out to the next training camp and say, 'Okay, we ran this one hundred times, and it averaged four yards a try. We fouled it up once because the guard pulled the wrong way and three times because of fumbles.' Then we'd work on the plays that worked and throw out the ones that didn't."

Believing "repetition is the first law of learning," he required even the most experienced veterans to fill notebooks with his verbatim instructions on "How to Run" and "Proper Backfield and Line Stance." To determine if players were suited to his "integrated system of football pedagogy," he began administering a lengthy "football aptitude test" while he was still coaching high school ball. During practices, Brown urged his team to "Think! Think! Think!" rather than, *a la* Lombardi, to "Hit! Hit! Hit!"

As a Cleveland *Plain Dealer* reporter wrote, "Few players understand him, because they are built for the hot world of combat, and his is the icy world of theory." Brown often spoke of players as if they were interchangeable components in some intricate contraption. "It's like building a Cadillac," he said. "You machine the parts to perfection, put them together, tune them, and the engine runs."

He called Lou Groza "the most valuable tackle chattel in football," Graham "one of the finest pieces of mechanism in the game," and his Cincinnati Bengals "franchise assets." Fullback Jim Brown said he felt like "little more than a spoke in the wheel." After Graham retired, a newspaper cartoon depicted Brown at a workbench, assembling a replacement from spare parts.

Throughout his career, Brown—and others—described his teams as machines. The Massillon *Evening Independent* praised his Tigers for "their precision attack and their machinelike maneuvering." Brown called one of his Ohio State squads "a beautiful mechanism." Quarterback Tommy O'Connell referred to the 1957 Browns as "the eleven mechanics." Fifteen years later, writers said the Bengals were "computer programmed."

Don Colo wasn't thinking in metaphors when he came to Cleveland in a 1953 trade. "All I was interested in was making a living, providing," he says. "You just came through a war. Everyone came from poverty or near poverty." Brought up by his widowed mother, Colo played basketball, rather than football, in high school. In World War II, he earned nine battle stars as a radioman aboard a destroyer escort. He saw action in campaigns from the Marshall Islands to Okinawa, where a kamikaze hit his ship.

He grew two inches and gained sixty pounds in the service, attended Brown University on the G.I. Bill, made All-Ivy League as a senior, and became a third-round pick of the Baltimore Colts. In Colo's first three seasons, he played for three teams, each of which won one game, all of which folded. "The teams I played for were so bad that the first time I met Paul Brown, I told him, 'I don't want to say anything, but if you brought me in here, you might get jinxed,'" he says.

Brown said he obtained Colo from the reconstituted Colts not because of the player's workaday competence but because he was "a rough, almost brutal type of defensive tackle who punished offensive blockers."

The coach said, "I knew our guys did not like to play against him. That made him the kind of player I wanted for our team." At 260 pounds, Colo stopped the run and rushed the passer with equal ferocity. In his six seasons, Cleveland gave up the fewest points in the league five times and played in four championship games. Colo made All-Pro twice and the Pro Bowl three times.

Colo says Brown was dictatorial and remote but also impartial, organized, and consistent. Happy in Cleveland, he also understood why some teammates resented the coach. "Everybody can't work in a totalitarian organization," he says. "It frustrates them." In fact, Brown's clinical approach to the game was about to shake professional football.

Brown fretted about profits and losses as only a self-made social climber with a share of the business can. He studied those same "moving pictures" to compile the exhaustive data he used against players who asked for raises. "He has reduced money to an exact science," said quarterback George Ratterman.

Brown customarily mailed contracts to players, whom he expected to sign and return the documents without discussion. He ordered the team not to discuss salaries, and the Browns apparently obeyed, because a number of them claim to have been the first to send back an unsigned contract—and to have received both a small raise and a tongue-lashing for their audacity. "You never negotiated a contract with Paul Brown," says receiver Dante Lavelli. "It was Paul Brown's way or nothing."

Colo says he was unbothered by the coach's frugality: "If you were single, it was good. It was tough if you were married, because you had to move back and forth a lot and probably never ended up too far ahead when you were done. A lot of guys did it and then took five years or so to get out of the hole. Wife had to work, they had to live with their in-laws, whatever."

Brown frequently warned players, "You don't have to be here tomorrow." Star receiver Mac Speedie infuriated the coach by bringing an attorney to a bargaining session—and finished his career in Canada. When a first-round pick in 1954 insisted on a no-cut deal, Brown promptly traded him to Green Bay. Such high-handed tactics were common in the NFL at the time, but that the players union began in Cleveland was not a coincidence.

According to Mike Brown, the coach's son, Paul Brown learned by accident that his players were plan-ning to organize. Riding the rapid transit from his home in Shaker Heights to the team's offices one morning in 1956, Brown found on the seat next to him a misplaced letter outlining the first demands of an incipient "players association." He was stunned but shouldn't have been. Major League Baseball players had been organized for ten years, and in 1949, the San Francisco 49ers threatened to strike unless they received $500 a man for an All-American Football Conference playoff game.

Professional football players had no pension or hospitalization plan, were not paid during training camp, bought some of their own equip-ment, signed one-year contracts that could be voided at the franchise's whim, could not move from team to team, and made so little money that even the most celebrated stars worked off-seasons as haberdashers, insurance salesmen, or construction laborers. Hurt, they were bound by the decisions of team physicians, one of whom was said to have actually been a dentist. The Washington Redskins once shipped an injured player home in a freight car. "You were like a dog then," Lavelli says.

In November of 1956, Lavelli, Ratterman, and guard Abe Gibron met in Lavelli's basement with attorney Creighton Miller. Miller had been an outstanding halfback at

Notre Dame, where he roomed with a son of Mickey McBride, the Browns' first owner. Also a nephew of Ray Miller, mayor of Cleveland when the franchise was founded, he helped to introduce McBride and Brown and was listed as an assistant coach for the 1946 club. The day after meeting with the players, Miller announced the association and asked for more meal money on road trips, a pension, and pay for exhibition games. The Browns voted unanimously to join.

Brown's reaction to the organization—which he called "a conspiracy between marginal players and the government"—was predictable. In 1956, Brown blamed union organizing, rather than Otto Graham's departure, for his only losing season in Cleveland. Says former safety Ken Konz, "He'd say, 'Let me tell you something: I see anybody messing around at all with this players union, you're gone today, not tomorrow.'"

Like many contemporary American businessmen, Brown identified unions with communism and the Mafia. He was particularly sensitive to the latter connection because of still-fresh allegations that McBride, who sold the team in 1953, had been associated with gangsters.

In the cold light of history, the notion that Bolshevik agitators were preparing to lob Molotov cocktails into rigged games officiated by made members of La Cosa Nostra seems preposterous; however, at the time, the House Un-American Activities Committee was combing the nation for Reds, and President Eisenhower was calling for the government to "fumigate" unions that had been infested with hoodlums.

Because no one else dared to face Brown, Colo became the team's first player representative. Soon after, Colo says, "He called me down to his room and said, 'I want to talk about this players association.'

"I said, 'Well, Paul, I did it because I think there was a need for it, and it was the right thing to do.'

"He said, 'You know you're never going to reap any of the benefits of this.'

"I said, 'Well, you're probably right, but I still want to do it anyway.'"

Brown dropped the matter, and rather than retaliating, lobbied for Colo's selection to the Pro Bowl.

Brown worried needlessly about the organization's leanings. A *Plain Dealer* headline declared "Pro Gridders Form Union," but the players, sensitive about their image, insisted they had created an "association." If the term "union" didn't exactly link them with the Wobblies, players seemed to think, it at least brought them uncomfortably close to the working stiffs who idolized professional athletes.

Nevertheless, the NFL refused to recognize the association as the official bargaining unit for the players. To dodge antitrust laws, owners claimed not to be running businesses but pursuing a mutual hobby. By the time Brown was fired in 1963, the NFLPA had gained only insurance, a small pension, and $50 a player for exhibition games.

Cleveland remained a hot cell of union agitation mainly because of defensive back Bernie Parrish, who believed that all pro athletes should belong to one big union. In 1965, Parrish, vice-president of the association, called for NFL commissioner Pete Rozelle to be fired and replaced by, of all people, Paul Brown. "He treated me well, and I never even had to ask for a raise," said Parrish, who later claimed not to have been entirely serious about his demand.

When Brown did return to professional football in 1968, as coach, general manager, and part-owner of the Bengals, labor unrest greeted him. Pressured by Parrish's efforts to affiliate players with the Teamsters, the NFLPA reluctantly registered with the National Labor Relations Board as a "de facto union." Some players were appalled. "A member of a players association is one thing, but a member of a union—even if it's unaffiliated—is something else again," said New York Giant quarterback Fran Tarkenton.

The association also fired Miller—for being too conservative. Miller's union activities had made him persona non grata before, though not for the same reason. On a visit to the Cleveland offices after Brown's firing, Miller noticed that he had been painted out of the 1946 team photo. Brown, Miller said, remained cordial but never failed to remind the lawyer that he had started "that thing."

On July 6, 1968, the NFLPA, demanding that a larger share of television revenue go toward the pension fund, mounted the first strike by professional athletes since 1890. Veterans who tried to enter training camps were locked out. "We have created a monster. I'm scared to death," said new counsel Dan Shulman.

The American League Players Association, including the Bengals, had signed a new agreement, but the two leagues—and the two bargaining units—had already planned to merge. The stalemate lasted eight days, during which Brown, whom the *New York Times* dubbed "the conservative advocate of free enterprise," revealed that he was considering doing away with no-cut contracts. "They're like the guy who goes out with his secretary," he said. "Pretty soon, he's working for her." (Oddly, Brown's second wife, Mary, whom he married in 1973, had once been his secretary.)

The league averted another walkout in 1970, Cincinnati's first season in the NFL, but four years later, the NFLPA became the first American athletes to man picket lines. In a demand for unrestricted free agency—which the owners refused to consider—players carried signs emblazoned "No Freedom, No Football." The College All-Star Game was canceled. Squads of rookies and castoffs met in the Hall of Fame Game under security measures straight from *Black Sunday*, while, outside the stadium, members of a United Auto Workers local picketed with the players union.

During the 45-day strike, players counsel Ed Garvey called Brown "intellectually bankrupt." Rugged Kansas City running back Ed Podolak said the slender 67-year-old coach was "intimidating." One picketing Bengal confessed to being frightened by Brown's eyes; other players charged that, looking for handwriting samples, he dug their anonymous ballots from trash cans. Player representative Pat Matson said afterward that Brown traded him to Green Bay out of revenge. "He's a very vindictive person," Matson said.

Bengal captain Bob Johnson, though, saw his coach differently: "Paul Brown is a man of the true American spirit. He believes that if you do your job, you will be paid accordingly. There's no touch of

communism in his outlook."

The dispute ended without an agreement but with the stirring of public anger against the players, and a year later, what Brown called "this tiresome and demoralizing issue" began anew. The New England Patriots boycotted an exhibition game, and only the union's promise to pursue lawsuits against the league's labor practices preserved the season. That year was Brown's last as a coach, even though his team finished 11-3 and made the playoffs.

The union, he said, had finally helped to drive him from coaching after more than thirty years. "The old way was better," Brown said. "Pay the players who are carrying the load. Pay them based on their performance. But we'll probably never see those days again, thanks to the agents and the union."

"He was against the union because it was outside his control," says Colo. "As an entrepreneur he was against it." As head of his Bengals, his "small business enterprise," Brown in Cincinnati continued to oppose the union—through two more strikes, scab games, the NFLPA's voluntary decertification as the players' bargaining group, limited free agency, and ever more lavish contracts that eventually turned NFL players into fabulously wealthy migrant workers whose lives little resemble those of their predecessors, such as Don Colo.

Brown's prediction that the union would turn its back on its own founders came true, Colo says. Those who played before 1959, when the plan was adopted, receive far smaller pensions than those who played later. "I'm not altruistic," Colo says, "but there was a need there, and we were trying to fill the need. And he was so right, because they screwed us; they screwed the pre-59ers. He was prophetic. He was smart enough to know not only football. He had a pretty good handle on life in general."

His nose long and hooked, his blue-gray eyes hooded, Colo was lunching on peppery Southwestern cuisine at a swanky resort near his home in Scottsdale. Outside a picture window that made up an entire wall of the terraced restaurant, Camelback Mountain hunched into a powder-blue sky that spread like a huge filmy mantilla over sun-baked saguaro and cholla cactus, desert palms, mesquite bushes, and sprawling stucco and tile estates.

Somewhere in Colo's swarthy countenance and supremely confident manner lurks what caused Jim Brown to call him one of the last of Cleveland's "genuine thugs," but Colo's speech, broadened by a New England accent, mixes street-tough bluntness with Ivy League diction.

He retired at only 34 and worked in transportation, eventually owning trucking companies and warehouses in Nevada and Arizona. Well-to-do, he now views unions much as his coach had. "All the companies I've owned have been nonunion," he says. "We don't do it for the wages. We pay them more money than the union. We just hate to have someone come in and say, 'You gotta do this, you gotta do that, you gotta do this.' It's a third party telling you how to run your business."

Colo also says that the impersonal relationship he had with Brown never changed. After retiring, he saw the coach only once. He says, "There wasn't a lot of sentimentality there, and I didn't promote it, either. I was in California every year, and Paul was at La Jolla, and it never entered my mind to call him and say, 'Let's have lunch.'"

# *Don* COLO

**"** I CAME FROM A SMALL TOWN
in Massachusetts. My father died when I was two years old. I never knew
him. He died when there wasn't any Social Security. There wasn't anything.
My mother worked all her life, washed clothes, did housework. She raised
me and my two older sisters. We survived, if you know what I mean.

I went in the Navy when I was 18 years old. I was 6' 2", and weighed
about 190 pounds. I was in the Pacific for two and a half years. When I
came out I was about 6' 4" and 275. The service was good for me. I had a
lot to eat and a clean place to sleep. We got around the world. I enjoyed it,
except for dodging bullets now and then, but when you're young, you don't
worry about things like that.

I didn't have much on my mind when I got out of the service. I kind of
thought I'd like to go to college, because we all had the GI Bill. I wanted to
go to Boston College, but the coach who was supposed to come by missed
the road, and I didn't get to see him. A gentleman came by and took me in
to Brown. Another fellow took me in to Harvard. I didn't like the atmosphere at Harvard, though. Coming from a poor family and suddenly going to Harvard didn't make much sense.

I went to Brown, and I liked it, but little did I know that Brown was
just as highfalutin as Harvard. Of course, the greatest shock to you when
you go to a good college is how many more smart people there actually are.
All of a sudden, you're one of the poorer ones. But school had always been
pretty easy for me, and I got by.

Brown took me on the basis of size. I weighed like fifty pounds more than the average guy. That was before weight training and nutrition and steroids. There were very few natural 250-pound guys. I didn't know a damn thing about football. They were patient, and the caliber of the league was easy, so each year I improved a little bit. I didn't become a very good football player until my senior year, which was good for me in a way, because I didn't go to the pros with a lot of physical baggage. The body hadn't been beaten up too much.

After Brown, I intended to go into coaching, but I got drafted and ended up in Baltimore. So I reported to Baltimore, never thinking I was going to make it, right? The first pro game I ever saw, I played in. We went to camp, they didn't have much materiel, and I got to play a lot.

My first year with the Colts, we went 1-18, including the exhibition games. Baltimore didn't have any money, and at the end of the season, they disbanded the team and spread the players with a special draft. Anybody who wanted any of the Colt players could draft them. I went to New York with Artie Donovan. Y.A. Tittle went to the 49ers. Adrian Burke went with the Eagles. Everyone was spread throughout the league.

Then the New York franchise was sold to Dallas. Dallas went bankrupt in midseason, and we went on the road to play every game. Then they started another franchise in Baltimore. The good part of playing for Baltimore, the Yanks, and Dallas was that I got more playing time in three years than the average guy would get in ten years. We only had four tackles, two offense and two defense, and you stayed in until the other team got the ball. I was single, so I really didn't give a shit. You played, you made a couple of bucks, and you had a good time.

It was chaotic from a management standpoint, though. Jimmy Phelan was the coach in Dallas. He was a wonderful guy, but he used to come up to the rooms and want to bullshit all night. Finally, you'd have to throw him out so you could go to bed—the coach.

The difference between playing in Baltimore and playing in New York was, in Baltimore, you went in a bar, and someone would say, 'Hey, you play for the Colts. Get him a beer.' Nice people. I go to New York the next year, and someone says, 'He plays for the Yanks,' and someone else would say, 'Hey, buy me a beer, you sonofabitch. You have more money than me.'

BALTIMORE WAS A GREAT CITY. I'd be there today if I hadn't have had to leave. In fact, when I got traded to the Browns, that was bullshit. That's when Cleveland and Baltimore traded ten for five, and Mike

McCormack and Tom Catlin and I went to the Browns. Shula and Carl Taseff and all those fellows went down to Baltimore. It was a good trade for both, but I didn't want to leave Baltimore. I loved it there.

The biggest cultural shock I had when I went to the Browns was that Cleveland was dry on Sundays. You'd go into a restaurant after a game and couldn't even get a drink.

The teams I played for were so bad that the first time I met Paul Brown, I told him, 'If you brought me in here, you might get jinxed.'

We played three preseason games with the Browns in '53, and I already won as many games as I had in three years. The game was the same, but everything else was more organized. The thing that impressed me about Paul Brown was every coach I had played for before had his favorites. Brown treated Otto Graham and Dante Lavelli just the same as everybody else. If he wanted to get on their ass, he got on their ass. Brown would cut somebody from Massillon or Ohio State just as fast as anyone else. You didn't have to worry about anyone's good uncle. You were judged on what you did. That impressed me.

PAUL BROWN HIMSELF was not a brilliant football strategist. He was not a guy who came up with an idea and saw it through to fruition. He was a great copier and an implementer. I always said that no matter what business he went into, he'd be one sonofabitch of a competitor, because he'd do what you're doing better than you do it.

We always practiced at one o'clock in the afternoon. Why did we practice at one o'clock in the afternoon? Because you play ball games at one o'clock in the afternoon. He wanted your body rhythms to be used to one o'clock. Those were the kinds of things he did.

One time we had a field goal blocked. In practice the next week, we must've spent thirty minutes on detail: how many inches this guy would move here, just the little, minutest detail. But there was a problem, and that's the way he would solve the problem. It was a clinical approach, I guess. There's few real geniuses in the world. Empiricism is the best thing in the world, take the best of something and do it better than somebody else. Paul was a master of this.

For example, if the quarterback is going to throw a screen pass, he acts differently. Today, they're probably better at it, but then, the fake was almost a deliberate fake, and you knew it was a screen. The minute I'd see the guy fake, I'd slow up a little bit and go out on the back and either make the tackle or knock the thing down. The first year I was with the Browns, I did that in practice.

Paul said, 'How come you did that?'

I said, 'The quarterback's eyes just weren't right. I suspected it and ran out there.'

We came in the next year, and it was in the book: 'Defensive linemen, when rushing the passer, pay attention to the quarterback's eyes to determine if he's throwing a screen pass.'

Then, two years later, I missed one and got hell for it.

He said, 'Hey, how come you didn't read the quarterback's eyes?'

And two years ago, I'm the one who told *him* about it.

He was a little bit paranoid, too. We were playing the Eagles one year. I forget who the coach was there, but they put in an unusual play. You don't see much of it anymore. It was like a halfback trap. All the linemen would pull one way, and the up-back to that side would come down and block on the tackle. It was a finesse play, because, obviously, a 200-pound halfback was blocking a tackle. They ran it against us and make some yardage. That's the first time we'd ever seen it.

The next week, the play's in our playbook. We have numbers attached to it and everything. We played a team two or three weeks later, and they ran the thing, and Paul Brown said, 'Look at that. They stole our play.' And he believed it. Yeah, 'They stole our play.'

Paul did originate a lot of things. He tried using the quarterback head-set in the '50s. We were playing a preseason game down in Akron in '53 or '54. It worked, but George Ratterman was the quarterback, and he was so flaky that you'd never know the truth, and he never would admit it. Paul sent in a play, and Ratterman called something else. Paul pulled him off and said, 'What happened?'

Ratterman said, 'I heard jazz music.'

So Paul pulled it out, but it may have been functional as early as the mid-'50s.

BASICALLY, PAUL BROWN STARTED OUT as a schoolteacher, and he really embellished teaching principles all through his career. When I joined him, in '53, he had been successful in the All-America Conference, he'd been successful in the NFL, and the Browns were way the hell ahead of everyone else in organization, and in detail. He used basic teaching principles: you see something, you write it, you do it.

You know how most coaches are: 'You got to do more, you got to do more.' You know how paranoid they are: 'If we're only on the field an hour and fifteen minutes, and he's on the field an hour and a half, then they're going to beat us.' Not what you accomplish, but how long you're on the field. One of the greatest changes was how Paul organized practices. Most coaches sit around until they get tired of practicing. Paul was programmed. You hit the field and kept moving the whole time. Even if you hadn't accomplished what he wanted, when it was time, you were done. That was the schoolteacher in him. It was like going to work. You knew what your workload was.

Most coaches do everything that someone else did before. The classic example of coaching stupidity is the duckwalk. It's the worst exercise in the world. It ruined more guys than anything, but every team did duckwalks. Why'd they do it? Because everyone before them did duckwalks. That's where Paul Brown probably made the greatest contribution to the NFL— the organization.

It would've been strange to think what Paul Brown would've done without football. I propose the question, but I have no idea. He would've been competitive. I know that. He wouldn't have been a school teacher. That's too low key for him.

PAUL BROWN'S NEED TO CONTROL everything never bothered me personally. I'm the type of guy who could play for anybody. It never made any difference to me who I played for. When the whistle blows, you do the job. Some guys, though, were different. We had Vito Parilli. He came down from Green Bay, and he went on to a good career. But Paul Brown got on him so bad. He'd say things like, 'We thought we traded for a quarterback, but we got you.'

Paul Brown got on him so hard that he'd come in and take a shower, and from his nerves, he'd have shingles from his waist all the way up his body. I'm sure he gave guys ulcers.

After Otto Graham retired, Paul never did find a quarterback he was happy with. Parilli didn't make it. Tommy O'Connell was pretty good, but he was too small. Milt Plum didn't really make it.

Part of it was that Paul had been a quarterback. How good a quarterback nobody knows. He always said: 'I know exactly how to do it, because I was a quarterback.' With a good quarterback, you go someplace; without a good quarterback, you don't go too far.

We'd be in a meeting, watching films, and Paul Brown would say to Weeb Ewbank, who was my tackle coach, 'Hey, Colo didn't block that guy out. Why?'

He'd get on me a little bit, and after a while, it started to get to me. I said, 'The hell with this shit. I've got three years in. I know what the hell I'm doing.'

It was all part of the pattern. He was sort of testing you to see if you had the guts to take it. Pretty soon, I just quit paying attention and went out and did my thing. But if you let it get to you, pretty soon you'd be wondering, 'Am I good enough to play here? Should I be here?' It's a little mind game, and I think he did a lot of it just to see if the guy had any balls or not.

He was tough. The first year I was there, we had a number one draft choice from Illinois or someplace, and Paul Brown had a fetish about getting hurt. You weren't supposed to get hurt; you better not get hurt. If you get hurt, you'd better get well fast. He walked into the training room, and this kid's in there getting taped up.

Paul Brown said to him, 'Hey, do you get hurt a lot?'

The kid said, 'Yeah, I'm hurt most of the time.'

I don't think he ate dinner that night. He was gone.

It was part of the test. He figured if he could get to you verbally, down on the field, an opponent would beat the shit out of you physically. You either accepted it and did it, or Brown would drive you out. Some guys quit when they still had some good ball in them. They just couldn't take it any more.

HE WAS ALWAYS VERY QUIET and unemotional about what he said. He say things like, 'Maybe you should be in another profession,' or, 'What do you plan to do next year?' I don't think I ever heard him yell at anybody. He wasn't a screamer; he was a needler.

After a week or so of that, I didn't pay any attention. I said, 'I'm going to be here, and I'm going to play, and I'm not going to change how I play.' And he left me alone after that.

I knew where he was coming from, and he knew where I was coming from. Two things happened that were interesting, though. We were playing the College All-Star Game up in Chicago, and I was playing opposite of (future Hall of Fame linebacker) Sam Huff. He was playing offensive guard at the time. This is before most guys had facemasks, but he had one. I belted him, and I broke two or three bones in my hand. I didn't know they were broken. I got them taped up and went back out. I couldn't get down in position, but I kept playing. The next day, I still didn't know they were broken. We didn't have X-ray machines or anything. I get up and read the paper. Paul Brown is pissed off. He says, 'I knew we were going to get beat when our captain, Don Colo, was getting pushed all over the field.'

I said, 'Well, shit, I guess I'm in the doghouse now.'

I go to the hospital and find out I have two or three broken bones in my hand. Paul never said a word about it. I never said a word about it. It was just one of those things that you don't say. I understood it. He wasn't going to come and apologize, and I didn't expect him to come and apologize. It didn't make any difference.

PAUL RULED BY FEAR. I had nothing to fear, so we got along fine. The most he could do was fire you, and if you have confidence in your ability to do a job, what do you have to fear? That's the way I looked at it. If he fires me, that doesn't diminish my ability at all. If I'm good enough to play here, I can play somewhere else.

When the league changed, unfortunately, the players changed, and Paul became an anachronism. He couldn't change. He couldn't adapt.

It's almost tied into society in general. Stop and think about the foul balls we have running this country now. When did they start? The '60s. Guys from the '50s were different. When I went to college, all I was interested in was making a living, providing. You just came through a war. Everyone came from poverty or near-poverty.

There's a correlation between the hippies, the flower children, the rat pack we have in control now and what happened with athletes and sports. I think Paul was incapable of dealing with that. I think when he was out of football, in California, for that time, he had a chance to, quote, smarten up, but when he came back to Cincinnati, he didn't know how to implement his old philosophy into the new way of doing things.

Paul wanted a certain kind of player—if the guy was productive. He would keep the worst sonofabitch in the world—morally, ethically and everything else—as long as he was playing well. The only difference is that as soon as he slipped one inch, instead of keeping him around another couple of years, he was gone. Paul wanted winners. I always felt like if I performed at a decent level, he'd leave me alone. But if you weren't producing—*wooo!*

Take a guy like defensive end Lenny Ford. Lenny Ford went into the Hall of Fame, and I wrote a thing to the paper. I called it a well-deserved tribute to a great athlete who had no peers on the field but was a lousy person off the field. Paul would keep anybody as long as he was productive, but as soon as he wasn't productive, there was no sentimentality involved at all. He never got rid of anybody he needed.

Lenny Ford was a great athlete but a miserable bastard. He was drunk all the time. We were playing in the Pro Bowl one year, and he was playing beside me, and he was messing around and messing around and messing around. I said, 'Lenny, what the shit is the matter with you?'

He said, 'I got a dose of the clap. I got a hundred thousand cc's of penicillin this morning.'

I said, 'Get the hell out of here and sit down.'

YOU HAVE TO UNDERSTAND—Paul made a lot of mistakes. He got rid of a lot of good guys, too. Like Bobby Mitchell. I see Bobby every once in a while. I still say, 'Why'd Paul get rid of you?'

He says, 'Oh, I don't know,' and chuckles.

Doug Atkins came in, a real shitkicker from Tennessee, but a good kid. Big fellow, 6' 8". He played right beside me. I remember the first game he played in, a little back went to block him. He jumped right over him and got the quarterback. Well, shit, I never saw anybody do that before. He got hurt the first year, and I don't know if Paul thought he was going to be injury-prone or what.

Paul had a prototype in his mind of what people should be physically, and I'm not sure he understood a 6' 8" end, I really don't. I think he understood 6' 5", 270, but I'm not too sure he really understood Doug. Doug was a hellraiser, but he wasn't worse than the rest of us at the time. I think it was that Paul really didn't know what to do with a 6' 8" kid.

I don't think there was ever a case where he got rid of someone he really needed. With Doug, he had someone to replace him, obviously. I'll give you a better example than that. You had to fit the mold. We traditionally had a good defense. My last couple of years, we had (defensive end) Willie Davis. He tried out with us as a guard and went to the service and gained about fifty pounds and came back. We had defensive tackle Henry Jordan, and we had Bill Quinlin, who was a tough Irishman from Massachusetts. He traded all of those guys to Green Bay, because he had somebody he thought could play better. What happened was Lombardi took those guys, and instead of making them  conform to the system, he built the system around them.

You had to do certain things on the defensive line. You had to protect your spot, you had to rush the passer. You had to do everything. Willie Davis was an excellent pass-rusher, but he wasn't really strong against the run. In our system, you didn't compensate. In other words, even if you were an exceptional pass rusher, you didn't compensate. The same with Henry Jordan. Henry was a good, active guy who could run around the field and make tackles on the sidelines. He could rush the passer. He wasn't worth a shit in the line. What Lombardi did was let someone cover for Willie on the run and let Willie rush the passer. He had Bill Quinlin to play the run. He let Henry Jordan run around. He adapted to the players, whereas with Paul, you adapted to the system. You had to be fundamentally sound in every area. Henry and Willie were not fundamentally sound.

It brings up the point: should a guy like Henry Jordan, who wasn't good against the run, go in the Hall of Fame? That's why I maintain that someone like (former Los Angeles Rams defensive tackle) Merlin Olsen should be in the Hall of Fame, not because he was a great player, but he played 14 years at a consistent level, solid in all phases. Alan Page (former Minnesota defensive end) is probably the worst example of anyone going into the Hall of Fame. He wasn't worth a shit at anything except running around. He was quick and fast, but he wasn't worth a shit otherwise.

PAUL DID STRANGE THINGS. He used to intimidate his coaches as bad as his players. You know what he told Weeb Ewbank? Weeb wanted to leave to go to the Colts, and Paul told him, 'You can go, Weeb, but you'll never make it.' The guy won championships in both leagues.

Paul and I had a very businesslike relationship. I was amazed the second year I was there when he made me captain of the team. I had only been there for one year. Here's Otto Graham who's been here for ten years. There was Groza, Motley, Lavelli and all these other guys who had been with him eight, ten, twelve years. Why would he make me captain? I'll tell you why. First of all, I'm not bragging, but he wanted a tough sonofabitch. He wanted somebody who was durable. And the way he said it was, 'I want someone the players look up to and who plays their position well.'

I think it was the toughness that was more part of it than anything else. You played well for him or you didn't play for him. Whether the guys liked the sonofabitch or not, anybody who played well got respect. It boiled down to whether guys were physically and emotionally tough.

As a captain, you did very little. To give you an example—and this was probably the role of the captain—if we had a guy who was suddenly becoming too big for the team, we had ways of bringing him down to size. I don't mean in a really vindictive manner. You might have someone who says something like, 'Oh, if you guys were playin' as good as me, we'd be winnin' more games.'

We could ostracize him, we could belt him on the side. Very few guys can take that overall pressure. If some guy was getting out of line, we'd stay on him, needling him 24 hours a day, in and out of the game. I know no one who has ever stood up to that. It came mostly on rookies, guys coming in from other teams, guys who didn't know what we were trying to accomplish. Everybody had a job to do. You can make an excuse to your wife and to your coach and to everybody else, but you can't make an excuse to a guy playing beside you.

Today, when the guy is a rebel, he's exalted. There's no peer pressure to perform to the ultimate. It's going back to the '60s bullshit. It isn't the team concept. It's the individual. We played to win because winning is good, winning put us in a better financial situation, and winning was the right thing to do. Today, these guys aren't worried about winning.

The biggest single thing lacking today on all sports teams is the rapport, and that starts with the captain or some other guy who's a leader. A lot of times we didn't have to say anything. We just let it be known: 'Hey, knock it off.' Nobody ever said, 'Fuck you.' If they did, they'd be in deep trouble. There isn't anybody to say 'knock it off' anymore.

The athlete today is pampered from junior high school on. Some of them are social misfits. They have no idea what goes on in the world. They start out in grammar school. Someone says, 'Oh, you don't belong in this school. We're going to get a waiver so you can go to this better school.' Then they start to get them out of trouble. By the time they get to college, they're done. You can't change them anymore. By the time they get to the pros, the coach has to kiss their ass, pure and simple.

PLAYING THEN WAS TOUGH, but there was a lot of good about it. I think it was the NEA (National Education Association) doing a survey one time, and we were asked to summarize in a brief statement how we viewed pro football. I answered the question by saying it was a delightful interlude between college and one's life work. Obviously, that'd be out the window now, but that's how it was then.

After the first year, I enjoyed it. We didn't make a lot of money. I think my first contract was for $5,000, but we lived on it. It was a good lifestyle. We truly played for the fun of it. There were guys who didn't go to camp because they couldn't afford to go ten weeks without a paycheck. We'd be in camp for ten weeks and not get paid for that time. We were staying in the Shamrock Hotel in Houston on the road one time, and here we were in a $200-a-day room, washing underwear in the sink because we didn't have money to pay for laundry.

If you were single, it was good. It was tough if you were married, because you had to move back and forth a lot and probably never ended up too far ahead when you were done. A lot of guys did it and then took five years or so to get out of the hole. Wife had to work, they had to live with their in-laws, whatever.

In fairness to the owners then, they were not making a lot of money, either. A lot of those franchises were not real stable. By the same token, we were not asking for a lot, so it wasn't a case of all of a sudden, costs were going to go sky high. In 1953, we played a championship game in Detroit, and we were coming back on the train, and the business manager had the check right there. The total team check was something like $63,000. That was the whole team's share of the pool.

I STILL THINK THE OWNERS ARE STUPID, but there wasn't a lot of dollars to throw around in those old days. If you look at the genesis of the league, you see most of the original owners were gamblers or promoters. Who else was going to bet on a new league? They weren't really the affluent old rich people.

Back then, we needed a Players Association. We had about three things we needed to do. First of all, we needed the teams to buy our shoes, which was a big deal. We bought our own shoes. They wouldn't buy us shoes. Second, if we got hurt, we wanted to be paid and have the hospitalization paid. We didn't actually pay our hospital bills, but the teams had a remarkable facility for if a guy got hurt, they'd send him to their doctor, and the doctor would conveniently say, 'You're all well.' You'd go to your own doctor, and he'd want to put you in the hospital. And, third, we hoped that somewhere down the road, we would get a pension. Those are the three things we wanted.

We had a meeting in 1956 at the Waldorf Astoria. I can't remember who all was there: (Detroit linebacker) Joe Schmidt, (New York receiver) Kyle Rote, (Redskin fullback) Chuck Drazenovich, (San Francisco kicker/

end) Gordie Soltau, myself. The reason I went to the meeting is that no one else from the Browns dared to go. I was the captain, so it was, 'Hey, you better go.'

They all chipped in and gave me money to go, but they didn't want to go, because they knew they'd get fired the next day. I figured, 'If I get fired, I get fired. I'm not gonna worry about it.' That was the start of the Players Association.

It was pretty tough. It took years before the league even let us in on a meeting. They fought it pretty hard for a very long time. We came in one day, and Paul Brown said he had heard about the, quote, union. He never said much to me about it. I think it was my last year or next to last year, he called me down to his room and said, 'I want to talk about the Players Association.'

I said, 'Well, Paul, I did it because I think there was a need for it, and it was the right thing to do.'

He said, 'You know, you're never going to reap any of the benefits of this.'

I said, 'Well, you're probably right, but I still want to do it anyhow.'

I'm not altruistic, but there was a need, and we were trying to fill the need. And he was so right, because they screwed us, they screwed the pre-'59ers. He was prophetic. He was smart enough to know not only football. He had a pretty good handle on life in general. That's the only time he and I ever talked about it. Otherwise, we never said a word.

HE WAS AGAINST THE UNION because it was outside his control. As an entrepreneur, he was against it. All the companies I've had—I've got two or three companies—were always nonunion. We don't do it for wages. We pay them more money than the union. We just hate to have someone come in and tell us, 'You gotta do this, you gotta do that.' It's a third party telling you how to run your business. He viewed it the same way, except he probably used a little more discretion. He couldn't fire guys as quickly.

In fact, we had a case. (Longtime Brown center) Frank Gatski, I think it was my last year, got into some kind of contract dispute with Paul. I never did find out the details, but Frank never came to training camp. The first week of the season, he came up to League Park, where we trained in Cleveland, and he told Paul Brown he wanted to come back.

Paul Brown said, 'No, I'm not taking you back. You're all done.'

We told him, 'You just go down and see (lawyer and one of the organizers of the NFL Players Association) Creighton Miller.'

He went to see Creighton Miller, and he got traded the next day to the Detroit Lions and played his last year with the Lions.

Creighton Miller was the genesis behind the Players Association. After a couple of years, they threw him out, which tells you how much loyalty there is in the Players Association.

When I left, the Players Association was barely recognized. My last year was 1958. They had been recognized, but they had no real power, no real contract, hadn't really gained anything at all.

WHEN IT CAME TIME TO RETIRE, I was 34, and I just figured it was time to go. You play that many years, and you're not going to get any better. First week of the season, I went and told him, 'Paul, at the end of this season, I'm going to retire. This will give you time to work with your draft or whatever you want to do.'

He said, 'That's fine.' He appreciated that.

I think as a bonus for being legitimate with him about that, I went to the Pro Bowl the last year I played. I don't know exactly how they did it in those days, but I'm sure he helped me get to the Pro Bowl, which was a nice way to go. That was a good way to end a career.

I always believed in getting out while I was ahead. When I retired at 34, no one said to me, 'Get out.' I probably could've played a couple more years and probably should have, financially, but it meant something that no one said, 'You should've retired.'

We played a lot of preseason games. We'd start about the first week in July, and we'd play five or six preseason games. The owners needed the money then. We didn't get paid anything. We were usually done by Christmas, even with the playoffs, then the Pro Bowl would be the first week in January. I don't think the human body is able to play three or four pre-season games, 16 regular-season games, and the playoffs. I don't give a shit. You can have all the off-season training in the world.

If I were a coach, I'd tell every player to take three months off and enjoy life. Don't lift a weight, don't run, don't do a goddamned thing, just don't gain twenty or thirty pounds while you're doing it. Mentally and physically, cleanse yourself. They say the players are bigger, they're faster, they're stronger, they're tougher. Bullshit. A lot of these injuries are because people are tired and overtrained.

I'll tell you a funny story about Art Modell. Modell is a nice, sleek-looking Jewish boy from New York. For a few years after I quit, when the Browns played the Colts in Baltimore, my wife and I would drive down for the weekend. My wife is a great gal. She goes along with most everything I want to do. So, we're down there one night. We go out and have a nice dinner on Saturday night, and I said, 'Let's go down to East Baltimore Street. I'll take you to the 408 Club.'

It was a pretty raunchy area, but she's game. The 408 Club was owned by the stripper Blaze Starr. I didn't know her, but I knew who she was. We go in there. We sit down. We're watching the show. I look over, and there's Art Modell on the other side of the bar. I said to my wife, 'Hey, there's Art. Let's go over and see him.'

The next thing I know, Blaze Starr comes up, and she's hugging him and kissing him.

I said, 'Arthur, Don Colo. How are you?'

He almost choked. I said, 'What the hell you doing in here, Arthur?'

She's hugging him up.

He said, 'Oh, I was just walking by.'

I said, 'That's good, Arthur.'

He never did introduce us to Blaze Starr.

Modell, in his own way, is fine. He bought the club, and he didn't want it as a toy. He wanted to help run it. The only problem is that he wanted to be an autocrat, and you can't have two autocrats.

WHEN I GOT OUT OF FOOTBALL I knew what I was going to do, because two or three years previous to my retirement from the Browns, I started to work part-time in motor freight sales. The company I went to work for, the owner was from Columbus, Ohio. He had been a rabid football fan. He had guys from Ohio State working at various terminals in the Midwest. They bought a company in Cleveland, and when they came up there, they interviewed Tommy James, who had been a great player at Ohio State. Tommy helped me get the job in Cleveland, and he was the salesman down in Canton-Massillon.

A company called Leaseway Transportation bought a company in Phoenix, and a friend of mine who was the group head asked me if I would run it. I came down in '75, and it's been my home for twenty-three years. My son has a small warehouse operation here, and I help him on a daily basis. My daughter is a staff assistant for the mayor of the city of Phoenix. My wife has an antique shop here.

You know, there's only one game in nine years of pro ball that I can tell you the score of. To me, once the game was over, it was done. It was history. The only game I can remember is we played out in California in 1955. We beat the Rams 35-13 (38-14). There were 100,000 people in the Coliseum (paid attendance was 85,693) at five bucks a head, the payoff to us, the winners, was $3,300 ($3,508), and it was Otto Graham's last game. So, there were about four things that made the game memorable. Other than that, I can't tell you about any one game.

It's not that I'm blasé about it. I still go back to Brown, and guys say, 'Oh, you remember that Dartmouth game?' It's just that I never had any interest in being a coach, so as a result, I never categorized or tried to figure it all out.

HAS PAUL EVER RECEIVED THE FULL CREDIT for his accomplishments? I don't think he has. A lot of what you hear about Vince Lombardi getting much more credit than Paul is true. Vince was on television more, and the Super Bowl came in while he was in Green Bay. Remember, Vince came from New York, the media capitol of the world. He'd gone to Fordham, had coached with the Giants. Paul used to hate going into New York. He detested it.

Now, Blanton Collier, who coached with him, was somewhat of a genius in strategy and devising things, and Otto Graham was one of the best quarterbacks of his time, but Paul Brown would've been successful without Blanton Collier and Otto Graham, though. He became successful quicker and probably better because he had them, but he would've been successful regardless of who he had. He later went on to have some success with the Bengals, but that's another story.

You had the same thing with Chuck Noll that you did with Paul Brown. I think Chuck accomplished more than Paul or Vince Lombardi. Chuck Noll has never gotten the credit. You know why? First of all, he never sought it. He never tried to promote himself or his legend. He didn't need that to make his life. I don't think Paul Brown ever promoted himself. I think he was satisfied knowing what he could do. That's a sign of a strong man.

Chuck Noll came out of the University of Dayton. He was from Cleveland, working class family, a nice kid. Here's a case where Paul was more understanding. For whatever reason, the average person would've been gone, but I think Paul liked Chuck and respected him. Chuck was clean-cut, did his job. He was the kind of guy Paul wanted.

I don't think I saw Paul once after I was done playing. No, I take that back. I did see him once. I ran a small trucking operation for a company in Akron after I was retired. My son was about six or seven years old, and I asked him if he wanted to go to training camp. I went to training camp, and Paul said, 'Come on in the locker room if you want,' and I introduced Dennis to him. That was around 1958. I think that's the last time I saw him.

There wasn't a lot of sentimentality there, and I didn't promote it either. I was over in California every year, and Paul was in La Jolla, and it never entered my mind to call him and say, 'Let's go to lunch.'

I'm sure he felt the same way, but I'm also sure that if I had seen him, he'd be polite and social. Even Joe Paterno told me, 'Paul always had nice things to say about you.'

I said, 'Well, that's fine. I appreciate that.'

I never asked him what those things were. It didn't mean anything.

From the time I quit football, I've never been back to a locker room, other than to take Dennis. When I quit football, I quit it emotionally and every other way. I've never been back since 1958. I make a clear dichotomy. It was an era of life I enjoyed. I had a good time. I'm delighted I did it. I still enjoy some of the people I met and played with, but it never became a particularly strong factor in my life.

Twenty years later, people would say, 'Hey, the Browns have a good team.'

I'd say, 'Oh, yeah.'

I felt like saying, 'I don't give a shit. I don't know anybody there. I don't know the owners. Why should I root for them?' I'd root for the Steelers or somebody where there was someone I know.

You'll find in talking to these older players who maybe for years were violently critical of Paul, all of a sudden, at age 65 or 70, are starting to understand why he did a lot of the things he did. The things he did were true at the time, and they're valid and proper today. As you get older, you either get smarter or dumber. You hope you start to understand some of the things that people were trying to tell you fifty years ago. You'll find guys who called Paul everything they could think of when they played for him. Today, they respect him. 〞

# Nightmare *in* New York

AT ITS WORST, the "Nightmare in New York," as one newspaper called it, was frightening, a wild spectacle that looked like a grotesque collaboration between Leroy Neiman and Hieronymous Bosch. With 1:53 remaining in the 1959 season and the New York Giants beating the Cleveland Browns by 41 points, thousands of spectators surged through the chilly dusk onto the field at Yankee Stadium. Drunk on whiskey and the nearness of violence, they ripped down goal posts, barged into huddles, howled for more touchdowns, brawled.

Someone turned off the arc lights. In the gloaming, the Giants withdrew into a clutch. Fans surrounded the Cleveland bench, hooting, shoving, punching. A slender man wearing a brown felt hat and a brown overcoat bolted. His left hand jammed into a pocket, the hem of his coat fluttering around his knees, Paul Brown wove through the rioters, who brayed insults and grabbed at him. In a ragged uncertain line, the Browns followed their coach.

"I decided it was the best thing to get out of there," Brown said later. "Life's too short to get mixed up in something like that."

Brown took refuge in a tunnel beneath Yankee Stadium. Giant management called in the 70 baton-wielding New York City cops who were on duty outside the stadium, and the public address announcer warned that the great victory was about to be forfeited to Cleveland.

After 20 minutes, the fist fights ended, but many people refused to leave the field, and referees told Brown that his team had to finish the game. His felt hat somehow still straight, Brown told Milt Plum the three plays he wanted called and sent the quarterback onto the field to run out the clock. The coach did not leave the tunnel.

"This was a blood vendetta," the *New York Times* wrote. "So intense has been the rivalry between the Giants and Paul Brown's Cleveland Browns that the humiliation of the visiting team sent the spectators into raptures of delight."

Among the Browns, there was no joy.

"The only thing I'm sorry about in my career is the time we played New York in New York," says Ken Konz, a Cleveland defensive back for seven seasons. "Paul left the field, and he was going to leave everyone out there. It was 'fend for yourself,' so to speak."

Konz had to come a long way to witness the Nightmare in New York. He had been reared in tiny Weimar, Texas, by his grandparents and mother, a sometimes sickly woman who feared her son was too small for football. But Konz was as swift and shifty as a hare, once scoring 50 points in a game for Weimar High's six-man team.

At Louisiana State University, he played six positions, on offense and defense, place-kicked, punted, and returned kicks. The Associated Press called him the best all-around player in the Southeastern Conference in 1950, but he was only 5'10", 180 pounds and unknown in the North. Everyone was surprised when on the first round of the draft, Brown chose Konz, rather than a quarterback who could eventually replace Otto Graham.

The decision was not so strange. Brown probably saw in Konz something of himself as a player. A writer once described Brown, a quarterback and safety, as "a little fellow with a lot of speed and elusiveness who was light and fast but hard to keep down" and who "did some of his most effective running on returning punts." Brown and Konz had both been outstanding students; both were smart players, both competitive.

Konz served two years in the Air Force and joined the club. He says that Brown, who had cut two of his three most recent first-round selections, seemed as omnipotent as a pasha. "Scared to death," Konz made the team because of defensive backfield coach Blanton Collier's patience, advice from veterans, and the characteristic that Brown treasured most—speed.

When Konz came into the NFL, Detroit was Paul Brown's nemesis. The Lions were an unruly bunch who answered not to eccentric head coach Buddy Parker but to quarterback Bobby Layne, a legendary tippler. Brown disliked Parker, a feeling no doubt aggravated by Cleveland's losing to Detroit four of five times while Parker coached the Lions. Detroit beat Cleveland in both the 1952 and 1953 NFL championship games. Brown's only victory over Parker came in the 1954 title game, 56-10. Konz had two of Cleveland's six interceptions that day.

The Browns faced the Lions for the league crown again in 1957. Layne was injured and did not play. During a "Meet the Lions" dinner in August, Parker had abruptly stood, told the crowd that he could no longer control the team, and quit. Nonetheless, Detroit routed Cleveland for the title, 59-14. Says Konz, "We'd be playing Detroit, and we could be 28 points ahead in the third quarter, and for some reason, we just knew we were going to get beat."

That Eastern Conference title was Brown's last. Cleveland was replaced at the top of the conference by the Giants, a team that represented a city Brown detested. The very idea of New York City seemed to offend Brown's small-town Midwestern sensibility and threaten his ego, yet there was always something cosmopolitan about his dress, about his speech, about his manner. He fondly recalled catching bluegills in the Vermillion River as a boy, but Brown said that he wanted to make his team "the New York Yankees of football."

Early in his career, Brown dominated New York clubs. After losing to Cleveland in the 1946 All-American Football Conference regular season, New York Yankee coach Ray Flaherty, who had won two NFL titles as head coach of the Washington Redskins, complained that his team had been beaten by "a bunch of podunks coached by a high school coach."

Thereafter, Brown called his rival "Ray Flattery." When Cleveland beat New York for the third time that year—in the championship game—

players carried Brown from the field.

The following season, Cleveland was losing 28-0 at halftime to New York. The Browns' rally for a 28-28 tie was so stirring that the crowd in Yankee Stadium stood and cheered for the visitors.

In 1950, Cleveland's first season in the NFL, the team's only two losses were to the Giants. After the second defeat, Brown told New York coach Steve Owen, "I'm glad I don't have to play you again." However, the teams tied for the Eastern Conference title. In the fourth quarter of the playoff, Giant halfback Choo Choo Roberts broke into the open and raced toward the game-winning touchdown, but middle guard Bill Willis somehow caught him at the four yard-line, saving an 8-3 win and sending the Browns to their first NFL championship.

Cleveland won six of the next seven Eastern Conference titles; despite that success, facing the Giants came to shake Brown. "Brown acts petulant and angry when we start workouts for the Giant games each season," a former player said in 1962. "Nothing pleases him. During the week, he gets more and more wound up until, by game time, he has reached a state where he can't possibly help the team much."

The 1958 season contributed to the coach's agitation. Cleveland came into its first game against the Giants

with a 5-0 record and a stranglehold on the conference. The Browns led at the half 17-7; they lost 21-17. The defeat not only pulled the Giants within a game of the Browns but also opened wounds that festered as long as Brown coached in Cleveland.

Before the Giant game, Jim Brown and Bobby Mitchell had been the league's two top rushers. Mitchell fumbled three times against New York. The fumbles were Mitchell's first of the season, but Brown never again started the speedy halfback. The demotion angered Jim Brown and puzzled other players. Three years later, Brown traded Mitchell to Washington, where he became a Hall of Fame flanker.

Konz fared only slightly better against the Giants that day. He intercepted two passes, preventing one touchdown and setting up another, but with 2:50 left, he was called for pass interference at the Cleveland five. He subsequently missed a tackle on halfback Alex Webster, who scored the final touchdown for New York. Konz would not easily forget the penalty, which by all accounts was questionable.

He says, "The next day, it came out in the sports pages. Someone had made a good block. There were two pictures. One was the block, and one was me with my hand on the guy's shoulder. It said, 'This is the way to do it. This is the way not to do it.'"

To win the Eastern Conference that year, the Browns needed only a tie with New York in the final game. Jim Brown stunned the crowd in Yankee Stadium with a 65-yard touchdown run on the first play. Lou Groza kicked a field goal, and Brown, as had always been his way, sat on the lead. In the third period, though, he acted on a hunch for perhaps the only time in his forty years of coaching.

On fourth and eight from the New York 13, he called for a field goal. As holder Bobby Freeman ran onto the field, Brown stopped him and whispered an order for a fake. Freeman was smothered far short of the first down.

With 2:07 left and the score tied 10-10, the Giants lined up to try a field goal of their own—one of 49 yards, even though their kicker had missed two shorter attempts and was hampered by a pulled charley horse. "The weather was horrible. I mean it was snowing. You couldn't see the lines on the field," Konz says. "The wind was blowing in their face. Pat Summerall kicked it, and I stood there and watched it go through the goal posts. I don't even see how he got the ball that far."

The Giants and Browns had tied for the conference title again. In the dressing room, some Cleveland players wept, and Brown said, "If we would have made a touchdown then, they never could have climbed out of the hole."

The *Plain Dealer* politely noted that the fake "was an unusual call." Brown, somber, told the Cleveland Touchdown Club, "I lost my genius rating for the second time against the same team." He compared the Giants and Browns to "fighters who toured the tank towns, battling each other every week or so, until each one knew every move of the other."

Brown promised "a few new wrinkles" for the playoff in New York, but the Giants scored the only touchdown on a lateral off a double reverse, defeated Cleveland for the third time that year, and went on to play Baltimore in the most significant championship game in NFL history.

Three days after the playoff, Brown signed a ten-year contract extension. "We believe he is the best coach in the business," said club president Dave Jones. Not everyone agreed. Fans, the press, and Brown's own players questioned the fake field goal.

"It's rather interesting to be on the end of the second guess," Brown said. "You know, I don't recall that happening to us in Cleveland before." But Brown himself said he probably should have called for more passes against the Giants.

New York reveled in the victory. The city liked Brown as little as he liked it. Brown heightened the ill feeling by engaging in a cold war with New York reporters, whom he blamed for manufacturing his image as an emotionless autocrat. At first, Brown sneered at them.

"Paul Brown would go into New York and not give the press the time of day," says Otto Graham. "In fact, he'd give them the business at times. They didn't like it. It was wrong for him to do it, but he didn't give a shit about it, and it hurt him in the end."

Later, Brown became hypersensitive to the New York press, imploring his team before one Giant game to play well because of all the reporters who would be on hand.

After the debacle in 1959, New York writers downplayed the chaos. They implied that Brown was somehow responsible and barely suppressed their glee in seeing "the moody genius of the lakefront," as the *Times* once called him, driven from the field by a besotted mob.

The Nightmare in New York was Cleveland's worst loss in 11 seasons and fifth straight to New York, and it had far-reaching consequences. "During and after that terrible licking in New York, I could tell by their eyes and expressions that some fellows don't belong. When a player quits on me, he goes," Brown said. Sixteen of the 35 men who played in that game were not Cleveland Browns in 1960.

By 1961, Brown had to endure

more than one trip a season to New York; the city had come to him—in the person of Art Modell, a Madison Avenue advertising executive who had made it big hawking products to housewives during daytime television shows, and Modell's financial backer, Rudy Schaefer, a beer baron from Brooklyn who was looking to open up new markets.

Modell came to town declaring that purchasing the Browns was "like having a chance to buy the New York Yankees dynasty." Now, an embodiment of the glitz and hype that Brown loathed about New York was right down the hall, sitting in what had once been Brown's own office: an ostentatious promoter who squired around actresses, drove Cadillacs, smoked several packs of cigarettes a day, traveled with a retinue of go-fers, and decorated his apartment with a pair of brass gladiator helmets.

New York and Cleveland were tied 7-7 in Yankee Stadium as time ran out on the final game of 1961. The Browns, eliminated from the conference race, had a first down on their own seven. Brown called three runs and a punt, shunning the long pass, he explained, because the field was icy and the day misty. "It was an utterly useless kick and utterly senseless," wrote the *Times*.

"Frankly, we were flabbergasted," said Giant defensive end Andy Robustelli. In the locker room,

Modell didn't hide his displeasure.

By then, questioning Brown's decisions had become a ritual in Cleveland, the old story being that the crowd sat in Municipal Stadium every Sunday announcing each play before the Browns even broke their huddle. Claimed New York safety Dick Lynch, "I would not say we could anticipate every play, but we had it narrowed down pretty well." Plum says that when he wound up in New York at the end of his career, some older Giants still chuckled about how predictable Brown had been.

"Brown's offense depends on superior execution rather than new stuff," Robustelli said in 1962. Of course, Brown's first—and best—players had long since retired, and his string of championships had deprived him of the high draft choices he needed to restock the squad.

Brown opened 1962 by calling for a triple-reverse pass that went for a touchdown in Cleveland's victory over New York. Afterward, Modell embraced Brown and told him, "You are the architect. I'm just the ticket seller." The team, though, lost five of its next ten games.

Before the second meeting with the Giants, Modell, who had promised to win the NFL title that season, said of the coach, "If we could win this thing, I'd carry him down Euclid Avenue on my shoulders."

No such effort was necessary. The Giants beat the Browns for the eighth time in eleven games and won their fourth Eastern Conference title in five seasons. The next week, Brown coached Cleveland for the last time, winning 13-10 in San Francisco. Early in January, Modell fired him.

New York had been so successful against Cleveland that both the Giants' offensive coordinator, Vince Lombardi, and defensive coordinator, Tom Landry, found head-coaching positions. In time, their reputations rivaled Brown's.

Under new coach Blanton Collier, the Browns opened 1963 with six straight wins. Brown must have found some solace when the Giants, on their way to yet another conference title, ended the streak in Cleveland Stadium, 33-7.

When the Browns did win the NFL title in 1964, much of the credit went to Dick Modzelewski, a defensive tackle Cleveland acquired in a trade with New York. "He taught us how to act like winners," said linebacker Galen Fiss of Modzelewski, who had come to prominence against the Browns in 1958 and who, for one game in 1977, was Cleveland's head coach.

Ken Konz was one of the players whose last game in Cleveland was the Nightmare in New York; but, he says, he left not because Brown purged him after the Giants threw for 401 yards but because his in-laws convinced him that football was neither a profitable nor respectable profession. "I didn't really quit when I wanted to quit," he says. "I did what other people wanted me to do."

Konz worked in sales and marketing and as a sports agent. Ohio winters and a divorce eventually drove him back to Louisiana. As Konz sank into a soft club chair in a hotel room near Mandeville, his drawl was mossy and slightly nasal. He wore an NFL Alumni windbreaker and his ruddy face was as unlined as a child's.

Brown said that he never regretted using a first-round pick on Konz, who during his career also punted, place-kicked, and held for Groza. Konz calls Brown "a great teacher" and "a much better coach than Lombardi," but he says the coach was a driven man who became increasingly obsessed with winning.

In 1955, Cleveland beat Los Angeles 38-10 for the NFL title. Konz killed two Ram drives with interceptions and set up a touchdown with a long punt return. The game was also Otto Graham's last. The hotel in which the team was staying had arranged a party for the victors. According to Konz, without having a single drink or saying a single word, Brown went to his room. During the evening, an assistant coach went to

Brown and said, "Come on, Paul. This is your team. They won the championship for you."

Says Konz, "He came down and said, 'Okay, I want to thank you guys,' took a sip and walked out."

Brown was also tight-fisted, Konz says. In 1956—the coach's only losing season in Cleveland—Konz made All-Pro and Brown called him one of the year's "pleasant surprises."

Konz, who had intercepted more passes than any other Brown over the past four seasons, met with the coach to discuss his contract. He said, "Paul, I just led the whole National Football league in punt returns. That's worth a few bucks, isn't it?"

Arching an eyebrow, Brown replied, "What do you think I'm paying you to do?"

Such incidents not withstanding, Konz was upset when Modell fired the coach. "I probably felt as hurt as Brown did, because this guy did so much for football, and you bring in this guy from New York who is strictly a money man," he says. "Paul Brown was such an astute businessman and had everything so organized that I can't believe they shot him out of the water like that."

# Ken KONZ

" ALL OF THE PEOPLE who originally settled Weimar, Texas, came from Weimar, Germany. When I was young, the population of the town was between 1,200 and 1,700, and it's still that today. I had a paper route, and I swept out both banks in town. After football practice, I worked at the cleaning and pressing shop, delivering clothes. The people were mostly farmers. They raised livestock, and they planted cotton. Chopping cotton, picking cotton. I went to work on a cotton platform one summer, and soon I could throw around a bale of cotton like it was a feather pillow.

For two years, I rode a combine from 4:30 in the morning until ten o'clock at night. That was about 45 cents an hour, but when you made over a quarter an hour, you thought you were getting rich. It was so hot that I sunburned through my shirt. As soon as I got of age, which was 14, I drove an 18-wheeler from Weimar to New Orleans and then from New Orleans to Baton Rouge, hauling chickens and eggs. That was another one of my summertime jobs.

I liked the thrill of sports. I had speed. I ran a 9.8 hundred. When I was in high school, no matter where I went or what time I came home, I'd change my clothes, go to the track, and run three miles. Every night. Then I'd go back home and take a shower. I didn't care if I got home at four o'clock in the morning. I still did it.

When my brother first went out for football, my mother didn't say anything to him, because he's so much larger than I am. He was 220 in high school, and here I am, a 175-pound weakling.

She said to me, 'You can run track and play baseball. I don't want you to play football. It's too rough.'

I said, 'I'm going to play everything.'

I had a good game the first game or two. About the second week, she came out and watched me play, and she never missed another game.

Six-man football is a wide-open game. I was a quarterback and a half-back. I scored a lot of points, but it's like when I went to a reunion at LSU one time. These guys who were freshmen when I was a freshman were talking, and I heard on guy say about me, 'Yeah, well, he was so goddamned fast nobody could catch him.'

Every night after I was through playing sports and working, I went home and I studied. No one at home ever mentioned college, and I never thought about going to college until I was a senior in high school. Even before then, someone would say to me, 'You planning to go to college somewhere?'

I'd say, 'Well, I don't know.'

I HAD AN ARTICLE FROM SOMEWHERE that said I was the most sought-after back in the state of Texas. A guy used to come over from Baton Rouge to go deer hunting every year. He'd come over on Friday night, and he'd go to the football game. He told LSU people, and they invited me over. He kept trying to get me to come over to Baton Rouge.

We had a truck going from Weimar all the time with eggs and chickens from another guy. I rode with him. I was supposed to stay for two days, and I stayed two weeks. I said, 'This's where I'm going to school.'

I had this competitive spirit about me. It was either the first or second practice I was at LSU, and they said, 'Okay, we're going to have punting drills against the first defensive unit.'

Bernie Moore (head coach at the time) says, 'Okay, boy, you go back there, and let's see how you can do.'

They punted the ball, and I ran the first one back all the way. I did that three times. He said, 'Okay, you proved yourself. You don't have to run any more back.'

They put me on the varsity right then. I was the only one out of 31 freshmen who made the varsity, and I had never played 11-man football.

Even going from a little high school that had two, three hundred people to a stadium with 80,000 didn't bother me. I wasn't intimidated at all. I guess it was because of my speed. I always felt like I could run away from them. Once I got to college I learned that when you're on the field, you tune everything out. You concentrate on every play. You don't hear any noise. You don't think about anybody hollering or anything. You just think about what you have to do.

I was just a little kid who didn't know anything except how to run and how to dodge. We were playing Ole Miss one night in Baton Rouge, they punted to us, and I took it back about 80 yards for a touchdown. They called it back on a penalty. They kicked it again, and I took it back again for a touchdown.

When I was a junior at LSU, they knew I had good hands and could throw the ball, so they decided they were going to make a quarterback out of me. They said, 'We're going to let you play some quarterback, in case someone gets hurt.'

I went up to SMU and watched Doak Walker play. All the teams around us played 11-man football, but I had never played it. When I first got up to the line, I was supposed to call out the defensive formation. I would say just anything. I didn't know defenses.

About the second practice, the backfield coach said to me, 'Do you know what you're doing when you call a defense?'

I said, 'No.'

He said, 'You mean you don't know the difference between a 4-3 and a 5-4?'

I said, 'No.'

He said, 'I'm surprised the team even worked for you.'

He had to sit down and explain it to me. Evidently, those linemen knew what they were blocking.

WE HAD A GOOD TEAM THAT YEAR. In '48 we had a terrible losing season. In '49, we had a great season, and '50 was just mediocre. But you don't have to have a great team for LSU fans. You just have to show up on Saturday night. Even when they have losing seasons, you can't buy a ticket.

If you've never been in Tiger Stadium on a Saturday night, you need to do it. It's different down here than it is anywhere else. The stadium is so large and there's so much racket and commotion that you wouldn't believe it. The first time I went out there to warm up, I looked up and thought, 'What *is* this?'

In '49, we were in the Sugar Bowl. We beat three conference champions that year. The thing I will never understand about that year is that we had probably the best defensive ball club in the United States. Then, we're getting ready to play Oklahoma in the Sugar Bowl, and the coaches changed everything we did (LSU lost, 35-0). Oklahoma wasn't that strong offensively, but we were stupid defensively.

That's the year we were 21-point underdogs to Tulane and we beat them by 21 points at Tulane. That's one of the greatest memories from college, because we had such a bad year in '48, I mean a *bad* year. Tulane beat us 63-7, or something like that, in Baton Rouge.

There's a big rivalry between LSU and Tulane. A couple of years ago, someone stole the tiger, I mean a big Bengal tiger and its cage. That year, we were warming up before the game, and we noticed this big green area on the field. It said, '21-0 LSU' in the grass. Someone had painted it in the middle of the field at Tulane Stadium with green paint. No one to this day knows who did it. What's ironic about the whole thing is that we beat them 21-0.

We were out practicing on Friday afternoon before the game, and I was punting the ball. The coach came over, and I said, 'Boy, I sure hope we can win this ball game.'

He said, 'Kenny, if you wanted to, you could beat them yourself.'

The next day, we kicked off to Tulane. They got a couple of first downs and then they punted. I took the first punt of the game 92 yards for a touchdown. I also had three interceptions.

I DON'T KNOW IF I WAS A CELEBRITY, but I could go anywhere, and if someone said my name, someone else would say, 'Oh, you're the guy who plays for LSU.'

One of the things I enjoyed doing after I was out of school and playing for the Browns was going down to Pat O'Brien's. There was this guy who stood in the doorway to kind of keep track of things. Every time I'd walk in, he'd stop and say, 'I want you to meet Kenny Konz, one of the finest football players in the history of LSU, and now he's in pro ball.' It embarrassed me, but I enjoyed it.

I had no idea whatsoever what I was going to do in life. I got a bachelor's degree and 33 hours toward my master's degree in geology. I never worked in geology in my life. I've been a salesman and marketing man ever since I can remember. I like talking to people. I could b.s. about anything, and I always kept up on everything, so that when anyone started to talk about something, I could sort of fill in a little bit. It was fun. Heck, life was fun.

I played in the Blue-Grey Game in 1950, and in 1951, I played in the Senior Bowl. After the Blue-Grey Game, someone came up to me, handed me a trophy, and said, 'Congratulations, you're the most valuable player.'

I said, 'What did you say?'

He said, 'You're the most valuable player in the Blue-Grey Game, and you're supposed to report to Mobile in four days.'

I said, 'For what?'

He said, 'The Senior Bowl.'

I said, 'Oh, Lordy.'

In those days, they didn't pay anything but expenses. They didn't start to pay the players until later.

I was out doing something one day at LSU, and I came back, and someone said, 'Oh, you were drafted number one by the Browns.'

I didn't know what he meant. I didn't know anything about pro football.

I said, 'What's drafted?'

They said, 'You were the number one draft pick by the Cleveland Browns.'

I said, 'Oh, that's great, but I wanted to be All-SEC and I wanted to be All-American.'

I DIDN'T KNOW MUCH ABOUT PRO FOOTBALL. After I was drafted, I started listening to the games, but it was seldom that you could pick them up. The little television they did have was black and white and not very good. What's amazing is that everybody used to get the Browns down here. When they just started television, no matter where you went, someone said, 'Hey, I saw the Browns the other day.' So I did know who the Browns were.

Fritz Heisler and someone else came down to talk to me after they drafted me. I met them in the hotel in downtown Baton Rouge where they were staying, and they offered me a contract.

I said, 'Let me think about it. I'll be back tomorrow.'

They said, 'Fine. No problem. We figured you'd want to think about.'

So I went back and talked to (LSU coach) Gus Tinsley about it. Gus played pro ball, and he and Buddy Parker were real good friends. I told Tinsley what they offered me, and he said, 'Don't take it. I can get twice, three times, that from Buddy Parker.'

I said, 'Okay.'

I went back the next day, and they were sitting there. They said, 'Well, what do you think?'

I said, 'Coach Heisler, I talked to Coach Tinsley, and he said he can get me two or three times more from Detroit than what you're offering me.'

He said, 'Let me tell you something, boy. You play for Cleveland, or you don't play anywhere.'

I said, 'Where do I sign?'

There was no way to get out of it. I didn't even know they had a league in Canada. I was telling someone the other day, if I was a first-round draft choice today, I'd get $2 million for just signing my name.

TO ME, ONE OF THE GREATEST HONORS I ever had was being asked to play in the College All-Star Game. That was the cream of the crop out of all of the colleges. They had some high-powered people there. I thought, 'Wow, this's really something.'

Herman Hickman was the coach of the College All-Stars. We were playing Cleveland. Come game night, he named the starting offensive team, he named the starting defensive team, he named the punt return team, and I wasn't on any of them. I didn't say anything. It was about two minutes before the game was over. We were behind 33-0 or something like that.

He said, 'Go on in, just so you can say you played.'

I never did know why he didn't play me. I even asked him.

He said, 'You'll find out some day.'

I got in for the last minute and didn't do much of anything except stand around, because the Browns were just running out the clock. Two years later when I got out of the service and went to the Browns' training camp, I mentioned that game to somebody.

They said, 'You know what happened, don't you?'

I said, 'No. What?'

He said, 'Somebody from the All-Star camp was sending all of their plays, all the defenses and everything, to Coach Brown. They blamed you.'

I said, 'It wasn't me.'

It was an end from Vanderbilt named Bucky Curtis, who was in camp with us for a while. He sent everything to Paul Brown, and Herman Hickman blamed me. Why would Herman Hickman choose me at random and say I was the one doing it? That really broke my heart.

I wasn't scared when I went to LSU, but when I reported to the Browns in 1953, *Whew*! I had never been north before. I had my own car, so I drove up to Hiram. Paul was sitting in his office like King Farouk. He wasn't smiling when I went in there. He rarely smiled. He just said, 'Today, you get your room. Tomorrow, you'll draw your equipment.'

He gave me my itinerary and said, 'Don't get out of line.'

The first thing he'd say in meetings was, 'If you get in any trouble, especially with another woman, your wife is going to be the first one to know. I'm going to see to it personally.' And he would. 'If you're going to play around, do it in the off-season,' he said. 'When you're here, you're going to do it like I tell you to.'

One training camp, one of the colored players supposedly got involved with a white woman. Nobody knew anything about it. One Sunday afternoon about five o'clock, we were either finishing eating or getting ready to eat, and this guy comes in the front door of the dining hall. He walked down the hall to Paul's office. He knocks on the door. Paul says, 'Come in.'

The guy is carrying a shotgun over his shoulder. He says, 'Either you keep that guy away from my wife, or I'm going to kill him and you.'

He turned around and walked away. That's the first time I ever saw Paul stunned. He got that corrected pretty quickly, I think.

YOU FEEL LIKE IF A TEAM DRAFTS YOU and brings you into camp and lets a good player go to make room for you, they're going to keep you. I figured, 'Hey, I'm going to give it my best shot. If I make it, fine. If I don't, I'll go back to work.'

We were in a scrimmage, and Marion Motley ran that draw. I hit him just a little bit too high, and I thought my shoulders were knocked down to my butt. I said, 'Oh oh, you know where to go from here.' I haven't hit anybody above the knees since then. He was powerful. There used to be a sign in the stadium that said, 'The World's Greatest Fullback,' and I tell you, he was. You see old pictures of him running, and he looks like Jim Brown.

We got good training because of the receivers we had—Dub Jones, Ray Renfro, Dante Lavelli, Pete Brewster. Thank God, Mac Speedie was gone. They used to have what they called the 'Speedie Test.' They would put him on a defensive back, and Mac Speedie had more moves than anybody, from what I understand. For one whole session, you would have Mac Speedie on you, and if you could cover him, you made the ball club. He was that good.

After Speedie was gone, they tested the players with Lavelli and Ray

Renfro. Ray Renfro was a 9.5 hundred man. He could fly. You just had to play a little farther back. If he caught the ball in front of you, you had a chance to tackle him. If he caught it behind you, you ain't got nothin', and he's got six points.

I didn't hear that much about Dub Jones, but I thought he was one of the greatest ballplayers I'd ever seen. He held the record with six touchdowns until Walter Payton tied it. He never got the recognition he deserved. My rookie year, I roomed with Dub Jones and Ray Renfro. We had the upstairs of a house. Dub and Ray would sit down every night and draw pass routes. A lot of the stuff the Browns put in was what Dub and Ray drew up every night. Ray made Paul Warfield. Ray showed Paul everything.

WHEN I GOT TO THE NFL, everybody was bigger and faster. In college, I was first in all the sprints. When I got to Cleveland, I was second or third. Ray Renfro was there, some guy who was a world-class sprinter, and Milt Campbell, the Olympic decathlon guy. Campbell wasn't that fast straight ahead, but he had a lot of talent. He could never make the ball club, though. He couldn't hold on to the ball. Paul brought a football into the classroom. He'd say, 'You put the nose of the ball *here*. You hold it *here*. A lot of people say you should move the ball around while you're running, but if you hold it properly, there's no way they can knock it lose.'

He did it year after year, and you wrote it down. We'd start: how to run; why to run; anything and everything you could do. You heard him say it, you wrote it down, and then you went out and did it. You took an exam every Sunday. They'd give you a list of plays, and you'd have to draw up every formation and every play, from the right side and the left side, both offensively and defensively. Everybody knew what they had to do plus what everybody else had to do. You could go in and play almost every position.

We didn't have that many guys. Even if you played defense, you worked on the offense once every two weeks or so, and you worked on offense when we ran the opposing team's plays against the other defensive guys. Defense wasn't all that different then. How's it different now, except that the offense has more wide receivers?

All the writing stuff down drove you crazy, but you had to do it, and you did it. It got to the point where you could write it down before he even said it. He would not only say it; he would write it on the board, and you would copy it.

There was a right way, a wrong way, and the Paul Brown way. If you did it his way, you never got in trouble. He was the boss, I guarantee you.

Brown said, 'Nobody smokes. Nobody drinks.'

Hell, Groza would sit up in his room and smoke cigars until smoke came out the windows, and no one ever said a word.

I admired the guy, though. I'd never been around anybody who ran an organization like that. I don't think he even let reporters in after the game. They had to stay outside and wait. If they weren't careful, he wouldn't let them in to watch practices.

Paul surrounded himself with good assistants. Fritz Heisler was a good coach; Ed Ulinski was a good coach. When they had a meeting, Brown would listen to them about this guy should play or that guy should play. Blanton Collier was my defensive backfield coach, and he knew what your weaknesses were and what your strengths were and how to help you to improve both.

When I started, they had me as a right side cornerback or safety. Blanton immediately said, 'You'd do better on the left side.' They moved me there, and I did better. Don't ask me why. I asked him, and he said, 'You react from the left side better than you do from the right side. I can tell without even watching you on the left side that you were going to be better over there.'

I admired Blanton, but every night, we'd have a meeting of all the defensive backs and linebackers. We'd go in there at 6:30. At 8 o'clock, we're supposed to be through. We're supposed to go study our playbooks and go to bed. Blanton would look around the room and say, 'Do you understand all of this?'

Someone raise their hand and ask about some little thing, and he'd go through the whole thing again. He'd be back up on that chalkboard, drawing X's and O's and pass routes. We kept telling everybody, 'If you don't understand something, ask us. *We'll* teach it to you.'

I ALWAYS HEARD THE COACHES had Sunday nights off after the game, but I often heard them say they got the pictures right after the game and started on them. They'd work on them all day Monday and all day Tuesday. Come in Wednesday, Paul would go over the list of things you did wrong, and then they'd split you up into groups to watch it.

I don't care who you were. You came back on Wednesday morning, and everybody went in this room. There would be a long sheet of paper there, both sides. He'd take you individually: 'Konz.'

'Yes, sir.'

'What are you supposed to do on such and such a play?'

You'd tell him.

He'd say, 'Do you know what you did?'

'No, what did I do?'

And, boy, he'd go down through it. He didn't care who you were, star or not. Otto Graham, Marion Motley, Jim Brown—it didn't matter to him.

My first exhibition game, we played San Francisco in San Francisco. I was playing defense and running back punts. I returned six punts anywhere from 30 to 60 yards. I came off the field, and I heard Brown tell somebody, 'Man, look what we found here.' That made me feel good.

You had to be crazy to run back punts. You've got to do two things: keep an eye on the ball, and know where the players are. Once you see the ball, you adjust to it, then look down to find the players. It takes the ball four to four and a half seconds to get there, so you have time. I don't ever remember fumbling a punt.

I never got knocked out, even though we had the single-bar helmet and no mouthpiece in those days. But I do remember we were playing San Francisco one year, and we were staying up at Sonoma Mission. We were practicing the day before the game, in full pads, and Billy Reynolds, one of the halfbacks, took a hand-off and, *boom*, ran right into the other halfback. The next day, he goes and has one of his best ball games and never even remembered playing.

One new experience for me was that I went all the way through high school and college without ever playing with a colored person. The SEC wasn't integrated at the time. The Browns had Marion Motley and Lenny Ford and Sherman Howard and Horace Gillom. Paul was just looking for the best football players. It was different for me, but they treated me like I was good people, and I treated them like they were good people. They took me right in.

I was with Jim Brown in '57, '58, and '59. He was the greatest running back I've ever seen, including Walter Payton and Barry Sanders. He was phenomenal, and you see Jim now, he looks like he could still play. He's sort of quiet and goes his own way. Jim and I always got along, and we still do.

WE USED TO GO TO THE MEETINGS on Wednesday mornings, and we had a saying: 'If you went in there on Wednesday morning, and

Paul couldn't say anything bad to you, you had hurt him.' There weren't many weeks like that, but every once in a while, he couldn't say a word to you. It might not be that you played a great game, but you didn't make any mistakes. You'd sit there and go, '*Whew*! Made it through another one.'

He got to me a couple of times. He called me down when they had the last cut one year. I'd had my best season the year before. He said, 'Bring your book and come on down here.' He said the same to three or four other guys. I had to take my book and go down to the office. There was a rumor I was being traded to San Francisco. I guess I wouldn't have minded. I had been stationed out there in the service. I knew some people. He said, 'Well, I was going to let you go, but too many other teams want you, so I'm going to keep you.'

He benched me one game. He said, 'Kenny, you're not hitting enough.'

I said, 'Paul, you told me and the defensive coach told me, "You're the safety. You're supposed to catch the last man. If you think you're going to miss the tackle, grab him and drag him, let him drag you, do whatever you have to do, but do it." That's the way I was playing the game, the way you told me to play it.'

He said, 'Well, we're going to let you rest a little bit.'

He held me out. I think that was the third year I was there. That's the first game I didn't start, but by the fourth quarter, I was back in there. He still had me running back punts and all that.

He didn't always do it right. He made some bad trades. He traded Willie Davis and Jim Marshall, and both of them are in the Hall of Fame. He traded Bill Quinlan. He got rid of Doug Atkins.

Doug Atkins came there my second year. He weighed like 250, 260 pounds as a defensive end. He could high jump like seven feet. By the second game of the season, he lost maybe sixty pounds. Paul got under his skin, and he couldn't take it. Paul just kept sticking that needle in, and he had a needle, I'll guarantee you.

WE'D BE PLAYING DETROIT, and we could be 28 points ahead in the third quarter, and for some reason, we just knew we were going to get beat, and nine-tenths of the time, we *would* get beat. With New York, we never had that problem. We never lost to New York much when I was there. Ray Renfro used to own Dick Nolan. He could catch anything he wanted on him all day long.

One game I'll never forget was against the New York Giants in New

York. If we won, we won the Eastern Division title; if they won, we had to have a playoff. The weather was horrible. It was snowing, and you couldn't see the lines on the field. We were tied, 10-10, I think. It was in the last two or three minutes of the ball game. The Giants lined up for a field goal. The wind was blowing into their faces, and Pat Summerall kicked a 35- or 40-yard field goal. I stood there and watched it go through the goal posts. I don't see how he got the ball that far.

In 1957, we were playing Detroit for the championship. They lined up for a field goal, and they faked it. A guy did an out pattern on me. I reached up, and I barely felt the laces as the ball went by my hand, and he caught it for a touchdown. And it was Tobin Rote who threw the ball; it wasn't even Bobby Layne. I can feel those laces on my hand right now.

Bobby Layne was tough, boy. We were playing Detroit one time in the preseason. I was playing left cornerback. The Lions had the ball. They were in the huddle, and Buddy Parker sent in a play. Layne calls time out. I'm not but from here to the door from their sideline. He walked up to Buddy Parker and said, 'Look, you run this ball club, or I run this ball club.'

Parker didn't say anything.

Layne says, 'If *I* run this ball club, I'll call the plays. If *you* want to run the ball club, you call the plays and send somebody else in there to do 'em.'

He turned around and walked back to the huddle. If Otto would've said that to Paul Brown, Paul would probably have sent him to the dressing room and told him not to come back.

When I played, we had the only losing season the Browns had ever had up until that time. That was in 1956. We had a lot of injuries that year. Paul understood, but then again, he didn't understand. We didn't hardly have enough men to field a team the last game of the season. We had defensive players on offense, offensive players on defense.

I PLAYED ON FOUR CHAMPIONSHIP TEAMS, and his obsession to win got worse. To my knowledge, Paul didn't mellow. He might've gotten that way later, but even the last two or three years I was there, he was very intense. He did not like to lose.

Every year we played in the next championship, he got more intense than the one before. We won the game in Los Angeles in 1955. We were staying at the Hotel Green in Los Angeles, where we always stayed because it only had one entrance and one fire escape exit. One coach would sit at the fire escape exit, and one would sit at the front door.

We won the championship, and we went from the Coliseum back to the hotel, and the hotel put out cocktails and beer and sandwiches for us. He wouldn't even come downstairs and have a drink. Finally, one of the assistant coaches went up and got him. You know, 'Come on, Paul. This's your team. They won the championship for you.'

He came down and said, 'Okay, I want to thank you guys,' took a sip, and walked out. About an hour later, we had to go catch a plane, and he didn't say anything to anybody on the plane, either, not, 'Thanks, guys, for winning,' or anything. I guess he was thinking about next year already: 'Who am I going to cut? Who am I going to draft?'

I ALWAYS GOT ALONG WITH PAUL. I never had a disagreement with him. I still think he was the greatest organizer I've ever seen in my life. You did this, this, this, and this, and, tomorrow, you did the same thing. He was a great teacher. I think Paul was a much better coach than Lombardi was. But he never wanted to be associated with the players. He wanted you to know that he was boss, and you were working for him.

After Otto left, we had Milt Plum, Jim Ninowski, Tommy O'Connell, Babe Parilli. We had Len Dawson, and the reason he couldn't make the ball club was because of the ball we used then. It was rounder than it was long. Now, it's longer that it is round. Len couldn't hold it. He went to Kansas City and took them to the Super Bowl with that ball they used in the American League.

George Ratterman could've been a hell of a quarterback. He was the best ball handler I ever saw in my life. He could hide that ball so you could not find it. Of course, Ratterman was as crazy as they come. You'd go into these big theaters in Washington or someplace, and he'd be hooksliding around people. He'd walk on the railings on bridges. He'd be in the huddle, and Paul would send a play in by the guard, and he'd say, 'I don't like that one. Go get me another one.' Guy would turn around and start away, he'd yell, 'No, no, no.' He'd actually sit there and draw up plays in the infield, and they'd work.

In training camp, Brown would make you work both offense and defense. I went down and ran a little hook pattern. Otto threw it to me. I had been watching him throw it, and it didn't look that hard. Shit, that ball hit me, and I thought it was going to go through me. It was like a bullet. It stung my hands.

Paul was tough about money. I got a $500 raise two years in a row, and the next year, I led the National Football League in punt returns. Contract time, I went in and said, 'Paul, I just led the whole National Football League in punt returns. That's worth a few extra bucks, isn't it?'

He said, 'What do you think I'm paying you to do?'

Now, what're you going to say?

Paul's attitude was: 'You've got a job to do. Go do it. That's what I'm paying you for.' You were playing for your contract.

He made more money than you can shake a stick at. He got a salary, he owned a piece of the franchise, and he got paid something like $10-, $15,000 a year just for them to be able to use the name 'Browns.'

In all, they had eleven teams—punting team, punt-return team, kick-off team, goal-line defense, and all that—and I was on nine of them. You think he didn't work my butt off? I didn't need to run any halfback. I worked hard enough on nine of the eleven teams they had.

I even held for Lou for a couple of years. Lou was a great guy, but any time he missed a field goal, it was the holder's fault. He'd go tell Paul that, and I'd come off the field, and Paul would say, 'Can't you hold the damn ball right?'

I took the ball, put it on the spot, laces to the front. What else could I have done except kick it?

PAUL THREATENED TO FIRE ANYBODY who had anything to do with the union. Creighton Miller had something to do with that. He came to Hiram several times when we were there. We used to be in the damned toilets signing petitions to get things done. He'd hear something about it. He'd say, 'Let me tell you something, I see anybody messing around at all with this players' union, you're gone today, not tomorrow. You're gone today.'

Nobody said a word, of course.

We were looking for some way to help control the pay a little bit. We wanted a pension plan, a hospitalization plan. Now, if you're not under 60, you can't get the NFL health insurance. Even if you can get it, you can't get it for your family. They don't provide a policy for your family; it's just for the players. If you get sick, they take care of it, but if your wife has a baby, the maternity fees are yours.

They didn't even start giving us shoes until my second year. Paul wouldn't give you a T-shirt with 'Cleveland Browns' on it. He'd rather throw it in the garbage than give it to you. We had warm-up jackets, but the only way you could get one is if you won the championship. You don't win, you don't get a jacket. Most teams gave them away. Every year, you'd get your warm-up jacket with your number on it. Then, you didn't win, you didn't get it. And ask for a football? They cost $24.95. You'd think you were asking for Fort Knox. It broke his heart to give the game ball away.

I think we got $10 a day in camp plus meals and lodging, but that was only after the exhibition season started. Until the exhibition games, you didn't get anything. Then, it was $10 a day. You went for at least a month before you got paid. League Park had four showers, two on each side, and one toilet. They had little bitty things for dressing areas and a meeting room across the hall.

I NEVER KNEW PAUL TO HAVE MUCH OF A SENSE of humor, but other people who played golf with him say he was completely different. I saw him once after I got done playing. I stopped by his training camp in Cincinnati and got him to sign his book for me. He was very nice. He said, 'Please come back whenever you can. If you want to stay overnight for a few days, feel free to give me a call.'

The only talk about Paul when I was there was like the typical talk about your boss. You'd get aggravated with him, and you'd say I wish he would do this, that, or the other thing.

The problems with Paul and Art Modell didn't come until a year or so after I was gone, but I knew Art. I thought it was terrible when Art let him go. I probably felt as hurt as Brown did, because this guy had done so much for football, and you bring this guy in from New York who is strictly a money man.

I don't know how the Browns' owners could let him do it. I guess he made them an offer they couldn't refuse. Paul Brown was such an astute businessman and he had everything so organized that I can't believe they shot him out of the water like that.

I didn't really quit when I wanted to quit. I did what other people wanted me to do. I had been getting a lot of flack from my brothers-in-law. They were saying, 'You're almost 30 years old. What're you going to do when you quit playing football? You don't have any experience. You're not going to be able to get a decent job.'

Coming from a small town, I listened to all of that crap. My father-in-law was a big sports fan. He watched the games with my wife at the time, but my two brothers-in-law put all this stuff in my wife's head. She'd pass it along to me. I was a kid from a small town. I said, 'I have a good opportunity. I better go ahead and take it.'

You look today and you see this guy is 38 years old, and he's still playing; this guy is 40 years old, and he's still playing. You wonder how many licks you can take, but if you've never been hurt, who knows? I smoked a cigar now and then and had a couple of beers every now and then, but I was in perfect physical shape. When we played the championship game against the Rams out there in 1955, I was playing cornerback. They sent Elroy Hirsch, then Glenn Davis, and then somebody else. They just ran down the field, and I had to chase them. They were trying to get me worn out, but they couldn't do it. I always stayed in shape. When I was in high school, I wouldn't even drink Coke. I had stamina.

I didn't even pull a muscle the whole time I played football. I quit in 1959, and I pulled a muscle playing tennis in 1976. That was the first time I had ever pulled a muscle. I never missed a game and never missed a practice, except for that one time I hurt my neck.

WHEN I QUIT PLAYING FOOTBALL, I was in Cleveland as vice-president of marketing and sales for a company in the nut and bolt industry, then I went to work for International Management Group, Mark McCormack's organization there in Cleveland. McCormack had Arnold Palmer, Gary Player, Jack Nicklaus. He had all the big tennis players. It was a great job. In every city McCormack was involved in, I would check with the agent who was there to see if there was anything I could do to help them.

Then I got a divorce, and I said, 'If I never see another snowflake, I could care less.' So I came back down here and went to work in sales. From '75 to '90, I had my own business. Now we just got a little raise in our NFL pension, but we still make about a third of the baseball pension. This's the first time we had a raise in about twenty years.

The league didn't want to give me credit for two years after I was drafted—'51 and '52, when I was in the armed services. They had a deal where if you were in the armed services but you had signed the contract and were unable to report to camp, you got credit for those years. When I first started getting my pension, they gave me those two years, then they came back and said, 'You're not eligible for those years because you didn't sign a contract.' They took that money back away from me.

They said I had to show them proof that I had signed the contract.

I said, 'You're the National Football League. You should know when I signed a contract.'

They said, 'We can't find one.'

All I had was a little clipping about the Cleveland Browns drafting me number one. I went to Cleveland to go to the Browns' archives. They said, 'Oh, we lost all of those records. We don't know what happened to them.'

A few years ago, at the Hiram reunion, a guy came in from New York who had a bunch of original contracts. He bought and sold them. I asked him, 'Could you possibly have my old contract?'

He said, 'Yes, I do have it.'

I said, 'What will you take for it?'

He said, 'If you take it upstairs and have it Xeroxed, I'll give you the Xerox copy.'

That did it.

I STILL WORK. I do a lot of funny jobs. I deliver flowers on Valentine's Day and Mother's Day. I deliver phone books every year. For two years, I worked for the Census Bureau. I'm always looking for something to do to keep busy. I play golf, but I even get tired of doing that.

I talked to the Browns about becoming a scout for them, but they said I was too old. I would love to do something like that, but whatever comes, comes. If it doesn't, it doesn't.

A couple of years ago, a guy intercepted two passes in a Super Bowl and was the most valuable player. Hell, I did that three times, but then again, that's what Paul was paying me to do.

I like seeing the old guys and meeting all the new ones. It's fun even seeing guys you didn't play with, like Paul Warfield, Ernie Kellerman, Frank Minnifield. They're still nice to you and know that you played before them. Some guys have died. I lost track of some other guys. There's a lot of guys I'd just like to see again. Hell, it might be the last time for me, too.

My athletic career was a wonderful part of my life. It was something I would never have dreamed about, even when I was a little kid. I'm glad I got to be part of history. **" "**

# On *One* Given Day

"I THOUGHT you were bigger," Paul Brown said, eyeing the nervous rookie who had just stepped off a bus at the Cleveland Browns' training camp.

*Man*, Galen Fiss thought, *I'm going home tomorrow.*

Actually, Fiss had decided long before that Brown had forgotten about him. After assistant coach Blanton Collier scouted him at the University of Kansas, the Browns chose Fiss on the thirteenth round of the 1953 NFL draft. But Fiss, an All-Big Seven fullback, heard nothing else from the team: no contract offer, nothing about training camp, and no suggestion that he enroll in a college near Cleveland, put off fulfilling the military duty he owed as an ROTC cadet, and play for the Browns that year.

Also drafted by the Cleveland Indians, Fiss spent a summer as a catcher in Fargo, North Dakota, and then began a two-year hitch in the Air Force.

Planning to give baseball another try when he mustered out, Fiss was surprised in the fall of 1955 to receive a contract from the Browns.

"Obviously, they were keeping track of my service commitment, which I wasn't aware of," Fiss says.

He signed the contract but went to spring training with the Indians anyway, figuring that if he made the major league club or one in the upper minors, he would stay in baseball. Knowing that Fiss had signed with the Browns, the Indians wouldn't place him on a team. When he insisted on being assigned or released, the Indians let him go.

He was a 25-year-old late-round draft pick who hadn't played football in nearly four years and who had never even been to a professional game.

Now, he was about to try out for the team that had won the last two NFL championships.

To make matters worse, Brown implied that Fiss might be too small to even bother drawing practice gear. In fact, he was not small. At six feet and more than 225 pounds, he had large, powerful thighs and calves. He had never lifted weights, but years of farm work had left Fiss country strong.

But in 1956, no one had reason to doubt anything Paul Brown said about football. Cleveland had played in ten straight league championship games—four in the AAFC, six in the NFL—and had won seven titles. Football's "licensed genius" had won more than eighty percent of his professional games. Fiss believed that if Brown found him wanting in any way, he might as well head back to the family wheat farm in Johnson, Kansas. Cleveland tackle Mike McCormack, his college teammate, convinced Fiss to stay.

He got lucky. Outside linebacker Chuck Noll was injured in the preseason, giving Fiss a chance to demonstrate his aggressiveness and athletic ability.

In the third game of the season, Fiss set up a touchdown with a 55-yard interception return against the New York Giants, solidifying his grip on the position he held for the next ten years.

The team did not fare as well. By 1956, Otto Graham and Dub Jones had retired, Marion Motley had been traded, and Dante Lavelli was in his final season. Twenty-five years after he began coaching, Paul Brown finally faced what he once called "the worst thing, the very worst thing": losing.

"I've never gone into a season without feeling we could win, and this one is no different," Brown said after his team had lost five exhibition games. "But there is no question that we're in for an ordeal week after week."

The season was more trying than Brown anticipated. Cleveland averaged fewer than fourteen points a game, went 5-7, and for the first time, didn't win its conference. After opening with a 9-7 loss to the Chicago Cardinals, Brown warned that unless the team improved quickly, he would restock it with free agents.

Midway through the season, he said the Browns would "stay in there like bulldogs and play every game to the hilt."

After another loss to the Cardinals—by seventeen points on the season's last day—Brown threatened to hit players where he believed he could hurt them worst: "They've been paid as champions in the past, but they aren't champions this time."

"There was a lot of turmoil," Fiss says. "We had a lot of turnover. We had people coming and going, it seemed like every week, people who had been prominent players some-place else. Most of them didn't make it. Some of them never suited out for a game."

One unit on the team did not disappoint Brown, though. Before the season, he said that Cleveland would have to rely on its defense, and the Browns allowed fewer points than any other team in the league. Brown

singled out Fiss, praising him for making a smooth transition into professional ball.

The coach brought in seventeen new players in 1957, but Cleveland was expected to continue its descent through the Eastern Conference.

However, the defense was again the league's stingiest, and rookie fullback Jimmy Brown gave new life to the offense. Cleveland finished atop the division, and UPI named Brown Coach of the Year.

"This must be considered the finest coaching job of the brilliant Brown career," the *New York Times* declared.

Even a blowout loss to Detroit in the title game was passed off as a fluke, because quarterbacks Tommy O'Connell and Milt Plum were both injured.

By the last game of 1958, Cleveland was 9-2. To win the conference title, the Browns needed only to tie the Giants, who were a game behind in the standings.

With a little more than two minutes left and the score tied 10-10, New York had the ball on the Cleve-land 44. On third and eight, quarter-back Charley Conerly hit Frank Gifford over the middle for an apparent first down.

Fiss slammed into Gifford and knocked the ball loose. Walt Michaels grabbed it and raced toward the New York end zone. The crowd in Yankee

Stadium groaned. The dejected New York offense trudged toward the sideline. Only then did a referee rule the play an incomplete pass. Cleveland lost, 13-10, and the next week, dropped a playoff for the conference championship.

Dethroned at last, the league's most stable franchise entered four years of ever-increasing upheaval.

Cleveland slid to 7-5 in 1959, ending the season with a humiliating 48-7 loss to New York. The Browns went 8-3-1 in 1960, but Philadelphia won the conference. Writers and fans began to question Brown.

Early in 1961, what had been unsettled turned volatile. A syndicate headed by young advertising executive Art Modell purchased the team. Modell installed himself as president and soon began to covet what Brown cherished most: control.

"Modell came in, and you could see that they weren't like personalities at all," Fiss says. "Modell wanted to be very much out front, and Paul wanted to stay behind the scenes. He knew he was it, and he had the control to back it up."

Apparently star-struck, Modell hobnobbed with players, buying beers and slapping backs. All the while, Fiss believes, the owner was gathering information he could use against Brown.

"I don't think Art wanted to be one of the boys," Fiss says. "I think

he wanted to be in control, but he felt to do that, he had to circumvent Paul's power."

Cleveland fell to third in the conference in 1961, yet the following year, Modell mounted a public relations campaign that guaranteed an NFL title.

The team began the season as if it meant to make good on its owner's promise. Fiss intercepted, and the defense gave up only seven points, as Cleveland upset the Giants. In the locker room after the game, Modell kissed Brown.

The opener was the high point of the season. Cleveland lost three of its next four and reeled to 7-6-1.

A mob of detractors assailed Brown. He was called a puritanical dictator who alienated players. His offense, in the view of a New York defensive tackle, consisted of "the brutal crash of the same old plays." *Sport* ran a caustic story entitled "Has Football Passed By Paul Brown?"

*Sports Illustrated* called him "one of the most controversial men in the world of football." Critics said Brown was obsessed with his image and shackled by his memories.

Fiss disagrees: "I don't think the game started to pass Paul by when he was in Cleveland. I knew we were floundering a little bit and we weren't doing some things, but I don't think he was inept or anything like that. As long as he won, he was right, and that is the case with anybody."

At one point, Brown told the squad, "If you think things hang heavy over you, you've got company in me."

He couldn't have known how many of the men to whom he made that uncharacteristic confession were contributing to his downfall.

In addition to being an impediment to Modell, Fiss says, Brown had become a convenient excuse for lackluster play: "Part of the reason he lost has to be put at the feet of the players. Maybe not all the players. Maybe some of them were good enough to win. But I think a lot of that was the players trying to find someone to blame besides themselves. I'm including myself in that category. I was never a big critic of Paul. There were times I wasn't happy with some of the things he did, but I just think the players were trying to deflect the cause of our own shortcomings, and Paul was a very good target at that time, and Modell loved to have that brought out."

As the intensely private coach endured the glare of a nationally-publicized soap opera, Fiss became recognized as one of the league's fine outside linebackers. The media often overlooked Fiss, who was low-key and workmanlike, but the *Cleveland Press* said of him in 1962, "It's high time he was given a rating—and anything below an A-plus

would be an injustice."

Fiss throve not least because his coach liked him. Brown once remarked that he enjoyed coaching players from Kansas, but Fiss and McCormack were the only two Jayhawks to play for him. When Michaels retired, Brown charged Fiss with calling defensive signals and made him a co-captain, along with McCormack.

"I think he just took a shine to the two guys from Kansas," Fiss says.

Brown felt a kinship with small-town Midwesterners, men, like himself, from a world of grain silos, swimming holes, and ice cream parlor courtships. He likely saw in Fiss the type of player he always sought: "lean, hungry, and clean to the bone."

"Fiss has been a steady player right along," Brown said-high praise from a man who regarded steadfastness as a cardinal virtue.

As he was preparing to play in the 1963 Pro Bowl, Fiss learned that Modell had fired Brown and replaced him with Collier.

"I was dismayed when Art Modell fired Paul Brown, but Blanton was a good replacement. Blanton was like your favorite uncle. Paul was more regimented, like a general," Fiss says.

If Brown's firing had been the public humiliation of a proud man, the 1963 season seemed to be a testament to Modell's courage and 1964 a repudiation of Brown's entire career.

Though Collier changed almost nothing about the team, Cleveland began its first year under him with six straight wins. The Browns faltered but remained in contention for the conference title until the next-to-last week.

Throughout the 1964 season, Cleveland clung to first place in the East. To win the title, they had to beat New York, Paul Brown's antagonist, in the final game. The Browns smashed the Giants 52-20 for their first championship in seven years.

The victory seemed hollow, because, with it, came the unpleasant task of facing powerful Baltimore for the NFL title. The names of future Hall-of-Famers peppered the Colts' roster. Quarterback Johnny Unitas, the league MVP, had directed his team to a record fifty-four touchdowns. Elusive halfback Lenny Moore had scored twenty. The Cleveland defense, by contrast, had surrendered the most yards in the league.

Nevertheless, on a frigid, wind-raked afternoon in Municipal Stadium, the Browns humbled Baltimore 27-0. To smother the explosive Colts, Cleveland made some minor defensive adjustments — and followed the example of Fiss, a 33-year-old off-season insurance

salesman whose left arm was in a cast nearly to his elbow and who had taken to wearing carpet slippers in the locker room.

Flanker Gary Collins was named the game's outstanding player, but many who were there say the day belonged to Fiss.

"If there was ever a perfect football game, it was played by Galen Fiss that day," says former Brown defensive end Paul Wiggin. "Galen would never say it, but everything he did was right. Fiss was the best player on the field. Being a coach, you appreciate the greatness of the performance of that one guy on one given day. It was amazing."

Years later, Unitas still vividly recalled Fiss's hitting him on a blitz. Fiss tipped a pass that middle linebacker Vince Costello intercepted, and his relentless pursuit helped to hold Baltimore to 187 total yards and cause four turnovers.

"The captain and linebacker from Kansas made tackles that rattled teeth in Row Z," the *Plain Dealer* said.

Fiss that day also made one of the renowned plays in Cleveland history. In the middle of the second quarter, Moore caught a screen pass and turned upfield with two blockers and an open field in front of him. The swift halfback seemed certain to break the scoreless tie. Somehow, though, Fiss evaded the blockers and as Ross Fichtner, the Browns' strong safety at the time, puts it, "hit Lenny Moore and just upended him like he did a flip."

"That kind of thing determines how the defense will play," linebacker Jim Houston said. "It was a spark. You see someone hitting a guy, and all of a sudden, 'Hey, I want to make sure I get my share.' Then your offense sees it, and they want to be part of it, too."

During the heady days after the game, the media proclaimed that a new dynasty had arisen. *Sports Illustrated* called the game "a day when the Browns' good, gray coach, Blanton Collier, eliminated the last traces of any yearning for Cleveland's good, volcanic ex-coach, Paul Brown." It was as if a string of titles would soon exorcise Brown's specter from the franchise.

One Cleveland writer speculated that during the game, Brown had probably been "resentful, bitter and indifferent."

Brown had actually watched the game at the home of one of his sons.

"The Browns looked very good, too," he said.

He didn't mention that three of the four head coaches in the NFL and AFL championship games that year—Collier, Baltimore's Don Shula, and the Buffalo Bills' Lou Saban—had been his protégés.

There would be no second

Cleveland dynasty. The Browns lost to Green Bay in the next championship game and failed to make the playoffs in 1966.

That season left Fiss dejected. Cleveland's first-round draft pick in 1966 was gifted tight end Milt Morin, but the team already had veteran Johnny Brewer at the position. An undistinguished pass-catcher, Brewer was nonetheless an imposing athlete the Browns did not want to lose. Fiss says that to keep Brewer happy, the team moved him to linebacker and guaranteed him he would start—in place of Fiss.

Fiss says he met with Modell and Collier before the season, and they assured him he would compete for the position. When training camp began, however, he found himself not only on the bench for the first time since high school, but also switched to the other outside linebacker, behind All-Pro Jim Houston.

In the kind of irony that seems inappropriate to the life of so straightforward a man, Fiss became a captain toiling on special teams, a recent All-Pro reduced to security measure, a reserve who had been offered a no-cut contract as a sop.

"I was getting older. They had to start thinking about replacing me," he says. "I can see that. I just didn't like the way they did it. I wish we would've leveled with each other, had an understanding, and gone on from there."

The quiet team player didn't hide his anger.

"I was a little bit of a pill for a while, I'll tell you for sure," he says. "I let them know I wasn't happy, but it didn't matter."

Though he wasn't prepared to quit, Fiss retired after the season.

"I got out when they told me it was time to get out," he says.

In a story about his retiring, the *Plain Dealer* called Fiss "one of the finest persons ever to grace a Browns' uniform," and he remains open and pleasant. Fiss has a subtle sense of humor, a pragmatic intelligence, and a lurking hardness—the suggestion of a levelheaded man who is better left unriled. Unusually expansive for one reared on a farm, he seems incapable of evading a question, as if he were bound to forthrightness by some ancient agrarian code.

Obviously well-off after his insurance career, he wore a creased sport shirt and slacks, an NFL championship ring, and a gold University of Kansas watch. Nearing 70, he looks far younger, his nose bent, his forearms as thick as squashes, his gypsum-block body powerful.

The business turned over to his son, Fiss is an avid follower of Kansas sports teams. He remains fond of the Cleveland fans and immensely proud of having been the team captain on the day the Browns won their most recent NFL title.

At that same time Fiss grudgingly left football, Paul Brown was preparing to start his second professional team, the Cincinnati Bengals. One Sunday a half-dozen years after he retired, Fiss watched the Bengals play Kansas City in Arrowhead Stadium. He had always thought Brown humorless, aloof, and intimidating, but after the game, Fiss felt compelled to see the coach.

"I didn't know whether to go down in the locker room to visit with him or not," he says. "I didn't feel that close to him. But I thought, 'Hell, I'm going to go down there and see him. I played with the guy seven, eight years, and if he's too busy to see me, he's too busy to see me.'"

He went to the visitor's locker room but, reticent as always, hesitated in the doorway, not wanting to interrupt a press conference that was going on inside. Brown glanced at the door, spotted Fiss, called excitedly to him, and told reporters their questions would have to wait while he talked to his old Cleveland Brown captain.

Still touched, Fiss says, "I think he was a very caring person under that veneer of cool."

## *Galen* FISS

" I GREW UP IN A LITTLE TOWN
in southwestern Kansas—Johnson, about 500 people. My parents were farmers. We grew wheat, primarily. The farm wasn't that huge, not by the standards out there. We lived in town, but my brother and I and my cousins went out and worked in the fields every day with my grandfather. There wasn't much to do there but work on the farm and play sports.

On the night of the basketball game, that's the only thing there was to do in town, so you went to the basketball game. There was a movie part of the time, but most of the time there wasn't. It finally closed down. If you go back there now and you want to see a movie, you have to drive twenty-five to forty miles one direction or the other. There were no taverns, no beer store in our town. There probably weren't any kids in the high school who'd ever drunk anything. There were no smokers. We only had fifteen people in my graduating class.

We played some kind of sport every day. When the season changed, we changed sports. We had a basket out on the wall of the pumphouse, and we had a game going on out there all the time, sometimes up to midnight. My dad put up lights.

My family was close, and my dad encouraged me to play. In fact, he almost commanded me to play. I don't mean to make him a domineering guy. He was just interested. He was a little guy, but he was competitive. Growing up, he had been a pretty good wrestler. He'd watch my brother play high school football and then get in the car the next day and drive to Dallas or Salt Lake City or wherever it was and see the Kansas game. He

257

and my mother came to Cleveland every year for games, and that was no small feat.

Watching my brother and me play was a big part of my dad's life. I retired from the Browns in 1966, and my dad died in 1967. I blamed myself to a degree, wondering if my retirement had anything to do with it. He was wrapped up in our sports. I know it's foolish, but I really had a feeling in the back of my mind that I might've had something to do with his premature death because I quit playing football.

I PLAYED TWO YEARS of high school football, because the school had given up football during the war. We had a new coach come in and he reinstituted football my junior year. I liked football because I had an advantage over all the kids on my high school team. There were some good athletes, but I had more size, and I could run well enough. I was physical, and I liked to hit people.

There were eighty-seven kids, total, in the four grades of my high school, and we probably had twenty or twenty-two out for football. We played the single-wing, and I was the tailback. I threw the ball some, but mostly we ran the ball. We had a good football team for being brand new, but the competition wasn't great out there. Nobody had a really good football team. We liked it because we won. We only lost one game my junior year and then we went undefeated my senior year. We had little kids playing on the line, but they were determined.

There weren't many people out of that high school who went to college. My cousin, who was three years older than me, went to KU. She was on campus for three weeks and still couldn't find one of her classes, so she came home. I had a lot of doubts about whether or not I could play in college. I just knew it was what I wanted to do, and I was willing to try. I had nothing to lose.

We'd never had anybody recruited out of my hometown. So suddenly, I heard from KU. A coach down in Hugoton, who was also an official, had reported Ollie Spencer and me to KU. Ollie played for Ulysses, Kansas, which was twenty miles away from us. We both had size. I weighed about 200, 210 pounds then, and Ollie was closer to about 230.

I can remember to this day my dad and my grandfather in the living room of our house, sitting by one of those big old console radios. One of them sat over here, facing this way, and one of them sat over there, facing that way. They'd have their hands up to their ears, trying to listen to the KU basketball games. They'd sit like that three or four nights a week, if KU played that many times.

Ollie Spencer ended up going to KU with me. We'd been there one time, on a recruiting visit. Neither of us had ever seen a major college football game. There was no television then. We're going to KU, driving up there by ourselves. We were scared to death. We didn't know what we were getting into: 'What're we doing? Why'd we do this?' We were excited but apprehensive. Back then, you had to come up Highway 59. There's a place when you get about eight miles from Lawrence, you come around a big hill. You come around that corner and, suddenly, there's the campus, looming up there on Mt. Oread, just about the only hilly country in Kansas. It's pretty impressive.

It shocked us both so bad that neither one of us could talk. When we finally got into Lawrence, we didn't know where we were supposed to go. We looked in the phone book and got the address for Coach J.V. Sykes's house. We walked up and rang the doorbell and said, 'We're here, Mrs. Sykes.' She sent us up on campus where the coaches' offices were and called and told them to watch for us because we'd be lost.

Talk about country bumpkins. There were a couple of them there. When we came around that hill, if either one of us had said 'Let's go home,' I don't think we'd've ever have seen the University of Kansas. And Ollie went on and played pro football for Detroit and coached for the Raiders.

I played fullback on the freshman team, but I was kind of a backup fullback after that. I was a linebacker. After football was over, there was nothing to do, so I went out for basketball. Freshmen weren't eligible then, but they let me play a couple of junior varsity games.

I didn't have much trouble with the school part of it. I was the salutatorian of my high school senior class. Of course, I already told you how many people were in my senior class. Don Fambrough, one of the legendary coaches at Kansas, always laughed about that. He'd say, 'He was the salutatorian of his class, and he had five whole people in his class.'

BETWEEN MY SOPHOMORE and junior years of college, the Korean War was going on, and they had enrolled all the scholarship athletes in ROTC so they didn't lose them to the draft. We had to go to the regular ROTC course of study, and then we had a two-year commitment to the military. So I knew that I would be going. It was just a matter of when.

When I got out of school in May, I was going to play semipro baseball in Nebraska. It was a pretty good league, but I only played one game. The Cleveland Indians signed me and sent me up to Fargo, North Dakota. I wanted to play in the major leagues, but it wasn't a life-consuming goal. I hadn't even thought about it, to be honest. I was always just going on to the next season. This stuff all just more or less happened to me. It wasn't any great and glorious plan.

I enjoyed the minor leagues, but I hated the bus trips. We traveled all over the country that summer, and we won the division. We had Roger Maris. He was just out of high school, 6' 1," probably 200 pounds, and could run like a deer. At the end of that summer, I went back to Kansas, because all of the teams knew that the Browns had drafted me and no one wanted a catcher who was going to be leaving to play football.

Ollie Spencer and George Mrkonic and I were all three in the same boat as far as the service commitment. Ollie and George went ahead and played in 1953. They enrolled in small schools in Detroit and Philadelphia and took some hours toward their degree. As long as they were making normal progress toward their degree, the ROTC people wouldn't take away their commission. I hadn't made any arrangement to go to school in Cleveland, and the Browns hadn't contacted me about doing so. Of course, I might not've been able to make the ball club at that time. They were pretty dominant then, more so than the year I came.

I had been drafted by the Browns, but I had no contact with the team until I was in the service. I got out in April of 1956. They contacted me in the fall of 1955, trying to sign me to a contract. Obviously, they were keeping track of my service commitment, which I wasn't aware of.

There was an officer on our air base who had played some professional baseball. I went to him and talked to him about the contract. I didn't know what to look for or agree to or anything. He advised me, we settled it, and the Browns told me to report after I was out of the service.

I DIDN'T KNOW MUCH about the Cleveland Browns at all. The only thing that was comforting to me was that I had a friend there, Mike McCormack, but he was the only soul I knew. I was scared to death. I didn't have any idea what I was getting into. I had never seen a professional game.

I didn't know anything about Paul Brown, either, other than he was a dominant coach in the league. My period was just prior to the grand exposure on television. For the most part, we didn't even know who the coaches were.

I asked Mike a lot of questions, but he wasn't answering the questions I wanted answered. He just said, 'Oh, you can make this ball club.'

I lost my first roommate before we ever put on pads. We had to ride a shuttle bus from Cleveland out to Hiram College, where they had training camp then. I got on the bus, and there was a guy on it who was so big he couldn't have been anything but a football player. I don't remember his name, but his face was all beat up. He must've been in a terrible fight. He was so beat up his face looked like raw meat. It turns out that he's my roommate.

The first night, he goes out and brings in a whole lot of beer. He carries in all these cans and wants to put them in the drawers. I'm nervous about it, because I know if someone finds those cans, I won't be around long. The next morning, the first thing we do is go down and take an IQ test. In the afternoon, they called him in and sent him home.

The first time I met Paul Brown, I got off the bus with that big guy who was beat all to hell, and they took us in and introduced us to him. Paul looked at me and said, 'I thought you were bigger.'

I thought, 'Man, I'm going home tomorrow.'

Later on, they had their annual football luncheon, where Paul introduced all the players and said something about every one. When it was my turn, he said, 'This's Galen Fiss, rookie linebacker out of Kansas. He weighs 210, but you won't believe that until you see his legs.'

Then after our daughter Leslie was born, which was our first child, he said, 'We can't cut Galen, because that little baby is so sweet Mrs. Brown won't let us cut him.'

I've thanked my daughter for that ever since.

OUR TRAINING CAMPS WERE NOT BRUTAL at all. We went through the drills and repeated things and got them hammered down. Paul Brown would have been a success in anything he did, because he had that organizational aptitude. He saw the full game, and knew what to do with it. Because of his drive and his organizational capabilities, he would have been a good writer or a good banker or anything outside of coaching.

In camp, you just went out and did your job every day. It was like every other sport I was ever involved in, except the odds were a little greater and the stakes were a little higher. You just did your thing and went on.

I played for all those years, and I bet I tackled Jim Brown maybe once. We didn't have scrimmages. I hear people go on about how brutal their training camp was, how they hit every day. We didn't do that. Paul Brown didn't believe in it. He wanted to teach you the fundamentals. To him, repetition was learning, and if you weren't a hitter, he'd know that before he ever signed you.

The thing I remember is the second year I was there, Mike McCormack had made friends with this guy named Gordon Cooper, out of Port Clinton, Ohio. He was an auto dealer up there and a big Browns booster. He'd come to training camp, and one day he said that after one of the games during the season, he wanted us to come up to Port Clinton.

I said, 'I will, if I'm still here.'

He said, 'What are you talking about?'

I wasn't that confident. I knew there was definitely a chance I wouldn't be there. I was never much of a positive thinker. I'd give it a go, but I really didn't ever feel that I was a lock to do anything.

Gordon always laughed about that. Bernie Parrish, on the other hand, hell, he knew the team couldn't exist without him.

Chuck Noll was playing linebacker, and he got hurt, so I got a little bit of playing time. Maybe that's what allowed me to make the ball club. Chuck and Walt Michaels were the two outside linebackers at the time, and they were in the prime of their career.

The pro game was a lot more open. They threw the ball more than they did in college, everyone was bigger and faster, and there was a lot more balance between the people. You weren't going to go out and dominate a given team. You could be better than a given team, but you weren't going to dominate them like you could in college.

MY MEMORY OF PAUL BROWN is of him being very serious. I've seen him smile, I know, but the first image I have is of him coming in with a very serious look on his face. He was hard to get close to.

When he was going to cut somebody, he'd make you go to the office and get a letter. He might call six or eight guys in when he had to cut three or four. They'd hand you a letter that either said, 'Congratulations, you made the cut,' or gave you the details about being released. He was just trying to make you know that you don't sit back on your haunches.

One year in a preseason game against Detroit, I blew a play pretty badly. He hated to lose to Detroit, and I missed a coverage. It was just a mistake, but it turned out to be the winning touchdown. We were in Detroit, and he was reading off the names of the people he wanted to come in on Monday, and he read my name. Then I really think he felt bad about it, because as a second thought, he called Walt Michaels in, too. I think he wanted to tell me that, by God, I better play better than that, but I think he also wanted to tell me that he wasn't going to cut me, because he had no reason to call Walt Michaels in.

I thought the thing with the letters was a little bit different, but Paul had his own style, and it was hard to find fault with his style. At that time, he was it; he was the number one guy. They had won the championship in '55, and '56 was the first losing year they ever had. I tell people that's because Otto Graham departed, not because I came in.

Having Mike McCormack there as my buddy probably helped me with my relationship with Paul. He had a lot of regard for Mike, and I think he related me with Mike. He once said something about how he liked to coach Kansas people, and Mike and I were the only two Kansas people who ever played for him. In fact, we were the co-captains, appointed by him.

Being a captain meant something to Paul, but I don't think it meant much to the team, at least not as much as when you're elected by your peers. I was really surprised when he chose me. I was a starter and calling the defensive signals, which was really just being a relay man, because they called the signals. I think he just took a shine to the two guys from Kansas. Then, when Blanton Collier came on the scene, he named me the team captain, without an offensive captain, until '65, when he named Dick Schafrath co-captain.

PAUL BROWN WAS A DOMINEERING PERSONALITY. There's no question about it, and the owners before Art Modell had allowed him to do that. Most of us accepted the fact that he was in control. If you were going to play for him, that was just part of the deal. It might've been better that way, because you always had that supreme power there. He was going to have the final say. Things weren't left hanging.

Paul was outspoken and critical of people. He wouldn't come out and praise you when you won, and he was a different person after a loss than after a win, like we all were. But he wasn't a bully. There was no question he was the boss, but he didn't try to bully us.

A lot of people, in moments of despair or anger, might say something about him. I never saw anybody confront him, player or otherwise. All you had to do was have someone confront him, and you'd have a move coming. He wasn't physically intimidating. He was a little guy, maybe 5' 11". He always had a hat on. And even in old League Park, you never saw him in the shower. A lot of people laughed about that. When we went out to California to play, and we'd all be in the same locker room and have the same shower, he wouldn't take a shower. A lot of people used to make a lot out of that, behind his back.

I don't think I ever saw him lose his temper. I've seen him get irate on the sidelines with an official, or this or that, but it was very brief and out of character for him. He wasn't the kind who lost it easily. He was in control most of the time.

He was very blunt about not wanting bums around. Paul would almost boast about the people he got rid of because of their character. Paul would tell people, 'We recruit people who have character, and the others are not going to make it—*if* they get here.' Mike McCormack had that kind character. Paul Wiggin was in the same class, and, of course, Bill Glass, the minister, was.

One guy he never did run off was Abe Gibron. He and Abe drove each other nuts. One day, Abe was sitting in the locker room in old League Park. They had torn down the old stadium, and they just left one wing. We only had one section of locker room and one meeting room. The coaches had a room in there, and to get to the bathroom or whatever, they had to come through the locker room. Abe would sit there on his bench, and Paul would come walking through. You'd see Abe's face, watching him. Next thing you know, he'd say, 'See, he's trying to catch us doing something. He's sneaking around.'

IN LEAGUE PARK, we had one shower room, about five showers and one stool, for thirty-six guys. That was the extent of our locker room. Bob Gain (a defensive tackle) would come in and start a conversation with you. Unbeknownst to you, he's peeing on your leg the whole time. Some guys would really resent it. Bob just thought that was the greatest joke.

The one bad year, there—1956—was a lot of turmoil. We had a lot of turnover. We had people coming and going, it seemed like every week, people who had been prominent players someplace else. Most of them didn't make it. Some of them never suited out for a game. But that was my first year, and I didn't know any better.

We had about four quarterbacks. Tommy O'Connell was there. John Borton was there. Bobby Garrett was there. He'd get in the huddle and get so nervous he'd start stuttering. We had a big left-hander who had a hell of an arm. He could throw the ball through the wall, but he couldn't do the other things very well, make the reads and all. Babe Parilli came in from Green Bay. Babe had no confidence and Paul really took off on him, because he expected a lot from him. Babe just became a ghost of himself.

There wasn't another quarterback like Otto Graham at the time, and Paul grew a little spoiled. There was Bobby Layne and that was about it. Otto was the leader of that ball club, spiritually and every other way. The players all looked up to him, and as a result they performed for him.

Otto Graham was gone, and Paul had the same problem a lot of coaches had. He maybe hurt himself by putting too much pressure on the quarterbacks, Milt Plum and Jim Ninowski and Bobby Garrett. He expected a lot from them because he had a guy before who could do those things. He would be a little short with them because they weren't performing up to his standards, and his standards were Otto's standards. They might not have been doing it, but probably no other quarterback in the league was either.

About the only time you had anything to do with Paul on a one-on-one basis was if you had done something poorly or played poorly. The only other time was when you agreed to a contract with him over the telephone. Of the eleven years I was there, I went to Cleveland only one year to sign a contract. The rest were all done over the telephone. He had us intimidated. No one was going to argue with him very much. You just hoped that he was going to give you something that you could stomach.

THERE WAS VERY LITTLE 'NEGOTIATION,' at least as far as I was concerned. Some of the players were probably a little more aggressive than I was. I just kind of sat and listened and hoped that things would come. He'd always give you a little resume about what your year was, your strengths and weaknesses and so forth. He'd recite his evaluation of your entire year, over the phone, then he'd tell you what he was going to pay you. I just took it and went on.

I suppose we were paid about as well as any ball club, maybe with a couple of exceptions. My understanding was that the biggest contract was Jim Brown's for $75,000, and he was the greatest player in football. That's a sign of the times, because no one was making five million playing then.

Paul Brown had another secret that was very, very advantageous to him: the first and last thing he'd tell you was, 'I don't want you to talk to anyone else about this contract, nor will we.'

Believe it or not, most guys didn't talk about it. In the early years, I had no idea what anybody made, and no one knew what I made, not even my roommate, a good guy like Mike McCormack. Now, you'd get guys, like Bernie, who were different. One time, when he was dealing with Art Modell, Bernie went in, threw a tantrum, and tore up his contract. He said he told them, by God, he wasn't going to play any more for that amount of money. He swears up and down that he got a big raise. He might have, I don't know, but he was happy to tell the story.

There's a good story about that. Don Paul, who was really a character, was a great defensive back. He said at the end of the negotiations one year, Paul told him, 'Now, Don, we expect you to keep this between yourself and the ball club.'

And Don said, 'Don't worry, Paul. I'm as ashamed of it as you are. I won't tell anyone if you won't.'

I don't know if Don actually did that or not, but he's told that story a million times, and he's the kind of character who could get away with it. Paul Brown loved Don Paul. He once said about Don, 'You know, we have to keep him around because he looks good sitting in the hotel lobby.' Don was just off-the-cuff enough that he could make Paul laugh, and he's the only one I ever saw who could do that.

One year, Mike McCormack decided he was going to retire. He came home to Kansas City and was offered a job by an insurance agency, so he called Paul and told him he was going to retire. This was just shortly before the NFL draft. We all knew that Paul didn't receive the lack of notice very well. What happens is the guy who hired Mike died. Now, Mike's job is up in the air, so he ends up going back and getting the big contract.

I told him, 'You know, McCormack, you're the luckiest Irishman I've ever seen in my life. Here you are, you get this big contract increase over these chance events you had nothing at all to do with.'

In the off-season, I always had a job. I worked for a construction machinery company. I worked for a life insurance company. We weren't making enough money to live six or seven months a year without any income. Everybody worked. It was a given that you had to have another career. The bank account dictated that.

Dealing with Art wasn't much different from dealing with Paul. Art was trying to sign us for as little as he could get by with. I had a little more courage with Art than I did with Paul, because I was intimidated by Paul. In negotiations, he was in charge. He was very businesslike and very firm. Usually, you didn't talk about many figures. You talked about the one he wanted to talk about, and that was it. He put a number out there, and I can only remember one or two times that we even messed with the number. I accepted the fact that he was in charge, and I didn't consider myself a good negotiator anyway. With Art, I thought I was in a position to at least have a say about things. I might not accomplish anything, but I could have a say. My last year, my contract was for $25,000. It's certainly not true that all of who played are millionaires now, but pro football helps open some doors for you. It gets you entrée.

I DON'T THINK THE GAME started to pass Paul by while he was in Cleveland. We were floundering a little bit, but I didn't think he was inept. As long as he won, he was right, and that's the case with anybody. Part of the reason he lost has to be put at the feet of the players. We weren't doing the job on the field, so we were looking for someone to blame besides ourselves. I'm including myself in that category.

I was never a big critic of Paul. There were times I wasn't happy with some of the things he did, but I think that the players were trying to deflect the cause of our shortcomings. Paul was a very good target at that time, and Modell loved to have that brought out. Maybe I was more loyal to Paul than some of the other people were, but I just never bought the rebellion-against-Paul that people like to say there was. I think the biggest part of that whole thing was that they were just trying to make Paul a scapegoat. Had Paul Brown come back the next year, I don't think a single one of them would've walked away voluntarily. You couldn't walk away in those days. You could quit or you could coerce the club into trading you, and you might not be successful at that.

We were kind of struggling along then, and, of course, Modell was a very aggressive owner. He wasn't but about four or five years older than some of us, and he came in and wanted to be a players' owner. We'd go on train trips, and he'd get guys in his club car and listen to their complaints about Paul. He'd get four or five veterans in there, and he'd try to pull bad stuff out about Paul. Paul was in a lot of disfavor, and Modell was milking it. He loved to hear that kind of stuff.

And the complaints about Paul were coming because we weren't doing that well. We were struggling, and there was a struggle between Paul and Modell. You could sense it. Modell came in and undermined him. He worked at it. If I heard Art Modell say this once, I heard him say it ten times. He said, 'It's too bad you didn't play your whole career for me, because you would've been wealthy. You would've been set.' Here's this big television guy out of New York telling you this, and all he's trying to do is undermine Paul. In my mind, he was always trying to build his own image. I don't think Art wanted to be one of the boys. I think he wanted to be in control, but he felt to do that, he had to circumvent Paul's power.

UNTIL A DISAGREEMENT we had at the end of my career, I never had any problems with Art. I just resented him for the way I felt he went about trying to unite the players on his side to undermine Paul. He didn't know any football. That was no contest. Paul had that hands down. Art knew about some business aspects of it, the big television contracts and all. He was a New York television guy coming in there and trying to capitalize on the situation, and he did pretty well.

When Modell fired Paul, I couldn't believe it. Paul was an institution, and I just didn't think that could happen. Paul allowed it to happen to himself. Now, maybe I'm overestimating his control of the stock, but he had control over those guys for everything he wanted to do. I know that. There were two or three major stockholders in Cleveland and several minor stockholders. Paul was a minor stockholder, but he had control over those other guys. They would do whatever he wanted to do, but, somehow, Modell was able to get that control.

Most of us were comforted when Modell moved fast and named Blanton Collier the new coach. He was somebody we all knew, so we weren't going to be starting over. You have to give Art some credit. He handled it pretty well and got the most out of it.

I hated to see Paul go, even though it might've been a positive for our success. That's not to say that because of Paul, we couldn't have won, but the fresh idea of a new guy running it at least shut a lot of mouths.

If someone would've asked me to vote on whether Paul should stay or go, I wouldn't have voted for him to go, because I don't like change. I would've thought, 'Who's going to replace him?' I never even thought of Blanton, because he'd only been there a couple of years.

Jim Brown was quite vocal about it after the deal (fire Brown and hire Collier) was made, about how we needed a change, and this would be good for the team. Jim was smart enough to know the guy was in control. Supposedly, Jim had threatened to retire if Paul Brown came back. If that's true, it would mean that Jim was on the inside and knew there was a possibility he (Modell) was going to do it. He might've been, but I don't know that.

The transition wasn't that hard because of Blanton's personality. He's the favorite uncle. He was easy to work with. He was a likeable guy. We came together a little with Blanton, because Blanton was the perfect guy for that situation at the time. The atmosphere was more relaxed, and that was for the better, provided we could handle it properly. For the most part, we could and we did. He knew football. He knew football better than Paul did. Paul was an organization guy. Blanton was an X and O guy. That's why he'd always been a coordinator up to that point. Paul didn't let anything go without his approval, but he was not a guy who came up with new ideas. He had time-proven, tested systems, and he went with them. He had stayed with those things an awful long time. Maybe a change was in order.

Blanton was just a real nice down-to-earth guy. You never heard him raise his voice. We all accepted him because he was a known quantity. We'd all played for him. We were all impressed that when he came back and took over the offensive coordinator's job, the offense had some rhythm to it and some flow.

We also got Dick Modzelewski at that time. Mo's attitude was very good for our ball club. He had come off a winner in New York, and people respected him.

NINETEEN SIXTY-FOUR WAS JUST FANTASTIC. We knew which games the big ones were, but we didn't think we could just go in and beat anybody, and that was true of the championship game itself. Baltimore was a pretty heavy favorite. We didn't like to admit it, but the oddsmakers had us as big underdogs. We didn't accept that. We thought we could play with them, and as it turns out, we could.

Everyone was confident before the game. We didn't think they could come in and dominate us, but there was no one who believed that we were going to shut them out like we did. We'd given up quite a few points that year, and they had a tremendous offense. A lot of people were pounding their chests about that shutout, but no one thought that we would be able to shut that offense out. As the game wore on, we kept looking at the scoreboard and saying, 'Geez, you know, they haven't scored yet.'

Shutouts were a goal, because you didn't have many. Any time you got one, it was important. In Paul's regime, there was a little resentment between the offense and the defense. He always favored the offense and always worked with the offense during practice. And he'd be vocal about it. We always felt that Paul preferred the offensive unit over us.

We didn't get a lot of recognition as a defense, but when you have guys like Jim Brown and Gary Collins, Frank Ryan, Ernie Green, you're not going to get a lot of recognition. There was no dominant player on our defense. We didn't have a Jim Brown

Playing with Jim Brown was funny in a way. Jim was kind of aloof. He kind of stood to the side. He had a few good friends among the black guys and never did much with the rest of us.

AFTER EVERY HOME GAME, we had a party in the Hotel Cleveland, downtown. We got a deal set up with the hotel. They'd put it on, and we'd invite guests. There'd be a band. They'd make liquor available, even though you couldn't buy it in Cleveland on Sunday night. We used to have some great parties.

We'd have those parties after the games, and the black guys never came. They were 'team' parties. We were disappointed that they didn't come. We thought it was part of the unity. Whether it be a big celebration or a big letdown, we wanted to get together. It's hard to do without your main guy and his followers there.

Other than Jim's influence on the black players in not going to our postgame parties, we were pretty much together. Jim tried to keep them aside in some ways. The parties weren't mandatory. We just wanted to get everybody there because we had fun. A lot of times, we had players from other teams come to our parties. It would have been fun to sit down with them and shoot the breeze.

Jim was a great player, and we all got along okay. The era was such that the racial thing wasn't quite as well defined as it is today. He came in, and one of the first things he did was buy a house in Cleveland Heights, which was one of the better areas of Cleveland. He was not welcome there, and he understandably resented it.

There was no better player, though. He went for nine years and never missed a game. I can remember so many games, coming back into the locker room, and the first thing you'd hear is, 'How many yards did Jimmy get today?' We were always concerned about that, because he was always in the race for the rushing title.

Jim's a lot friendlier now than he seemed to be then. He was in town recently, and we had dinner with him.

Schafrath and Jim were pretty close to the Browns' organization there at the very end of the franchise. They were on the sidelines practically every game. That meant Jim was doing a lot of traveling. I was surprised to see him do that kind of thing with Modell still in charge. Brown and Modell, supposedly, fell out and didn't have a lot to do with each other. Modell had said something in the paper about Jim calling and telling him he would be late coming to camp from making that movie (*The Dirty Dozen*). Art told him not to bother, and Jim and Art had some real words. I guess Art tried to pacify Jim by bringing him back to be a liaison or something.

I WAS REALLY FORTUNATE. I never got hurt bad. I've never had surgery in my life. One time, I fractured my cheekbone. I tackled Preston Carpenter in a scrimmage at Hiram. When I tackled him, he lifted his knees real high, and his shoe got through the bar of my helmet and hit my cheekbone. They made a small incision right beside my eye and went in and reduced the fracture, set it back in place. I missed the rest of training camp and the first two or three exhibition games. All the years I played football, and it's my wife, Nancy, who has the artificial knee. She covered too many kickoffs, I guess.

One time when Bernie Parrish and I were rooming together, we were in New York, and I had pulled a calf muscle. Bernie was telling me, 'If you'll just take some Benzedrine, you can play.'

I said, 'You think I can, really?' Because I had never taken them.

He said, 'I know you can.'

I took some that game. I played, but I might've been able to play without them. The only think I could see that happened to me was that I got cottonmouth real bad. I never had any other reason to take them again.

They were available. They didn't give them to you, but people knew where they were and would go get them. There were guys on our ball club—on all ball clubs, I'm sure—who didn't think that they could go into a ball game without Benzedrine. They did not keep them away from you in Cleveland. The guys who needed them and wanted them knew where they were. They were not being coerced by anybody to take them. It was just one of those crutches they thought they had to have. Now, you hear guys saying that football made them become drug addicts.

Bernie was one of the guys who really instigated the union. It kind of floated along in Cleveland for a long time and nothing happened, then Bernie gets there, and Bernie's kind of a rabble-rouser anyway. He went to work for the Teamsters in St. Louis. He wanted us to become Teamsters. At one point, Bernie was going to be the president-elect of the Players' Association. He never made it, because the hierarchy got concerned about Bernie's attitude. He was still radical after that, and he knew that's why he lost. He was still doing everything he could to organize the players, because he thought that was the best thing for them, and I'm sure there was some good that came of it. His union activities might be part of the reason he was waived out of the league.

Basically, the only thing the union did for us in that era—and I think that's about the only thing now—is the pension plan. For playing eleven years, I get about $1,200 a month. I get two different pensions. I get one from '59 on and one for the three years I played before then. You can't live on that. But I didn't feel like a union was necessary. Remember, though, I came from country roots. I had never been around organized labor. I didn't know what the values were. I was just thrilled to death that the team would give me a job.

That's the problem with football today. You don't ever get to the point that you relate to anybody. You don't know who's going to play for who next year. When I played, we were their property until they released us or traded us, and I'm not sure but what it wasn't a good deal. If the right guy would've refused to sign with his team then and become a free agent, you would've seen teams standing in line to sign him. The way it was added to the stability of the whole thing.

I realize that it would limit, to some degree, some of those people's earning capacity, but they're going to make big money anyway with the kind of television proceeds that are coming. They don't have to jump from club to club to do it. That's one of the reasons I haven't bought any professional sports tickets for the last however many years. I guess I feel like they don't make 'em like they used to.

I GOT OUT WHEN THEY TOLD ME it was time to get out. They moved John Brewer, who was a tight end, to outside linebacker. They didn't shoot straight with me, because I told them I heard that was what they'd done, and they told me, 'No, we're not going to do that. That's not happening.' Then the first week I go to training camp in '66, they've not only put Brewer ahead of me, they've moved me to the other side, behind Jim Houston, who's just coming into his own as a linebacker. That just didn't set well with me. John Brewer was a good athlete, but he wasn't a linebacker. He'd never played linebacker.

I think they were trying to keep him happy. They were worried about moving him from tight end, a glamour position, to linebacker. Of course, tight end, as he played it, wasn't a glamour position. He was a good football player but not a great receiver. He would've been a good defensive end. They wanted to keep him happy and encourage him to make this change, so they just guaranteed him that he would start. They wanted me as a security blanket. In the event their move didn't work, I could step in and play.

At a party at the end of the year, John told me that himself. Some guys had a party for the ones of us who were leaving. At the end of the night, John came over and told me that in his contract they had guaranteed him that he would be the starter.

I tried to level with them. I told them, 'Look, I know you're concerned about my age. I think I can play another year, and I'll be willing to come back and compete with anybody you've got for my spot, but I don't want you to give the job away. If you do that, I'll retire.'

I said, 'I know how you guys are. You try to say the right things to the right people.'

About that time, Blanton Collier spoke up, which was a little bit unusual for him, and said, 'Galen, are you calling me a liar?'

I said, 'I'm not calling you a liar. I'm just telling you that I know you pretty well, and you have a tendency to tell people things they want to hear. What you're telling me now is not what you believe. It's what you think I want to hear.'

After all that conversation, I went back to training camp, and I was a little bit of a pill for a while. I jumped the linebacker coach, Eddie Ulinski, who had nothing at all to do with it. I let them know I wasn't happy, but it didn't matter. I didn't play that year.

I JUST FELT LIKE I WAS A BETTER LINEBACKER at that point, even though my skills weren't as good as Brewer's. I couldn't run as fast and this and that, but I'd played the game for eleven years and had some experience at it he didn't have. But that was my thinking, not theirs. There was no question I was past my prime. I was 35, 36 years old, but I thought I could still play. I think they were looking at the numbers more than anything else. And I can see the Browns' position. I was getting older. They had to start thinking about replacing me. I can see that. I just didn't like the way they did it.

When I left, I had ten great years and one bitter disappointment. It still weighs heavily with me. I think that a guy should be allowed to compete, and I didn't have a chance to compete. Maybe he would've beat me out, but I don't think so.

Art wanted to give me a no-cut contract that year. They were taking the job away and offering me a no-cut contract. I said, 'Art, I don't want a no-cut contract. If I can't make this ball club, I don't want to be here.'

I think he was just trying to entice me to buy the situation. He kept insisting on it. I came home, and sure enough, when he sent it out, he sent out a no-cut contract. By that time, I figured, 'It's out of my hands. I'm going to sign it.'

I didn't want it to end, I guarantee that. But you knew that the combination of age and lessening abilities was going to take care of that. I just didn't want to see it.

It wasn't hard for me to leave football then, although my wife would disagree. I missed it, I'm sure, because it was an exciting time of my life. But I didn't miss the Cleveland thing, because I was so disappointed. I go to most of the KU games, and I still get excited about them, even though I'm just watching.

I had a couple of chances to coach, but I didn't want to coach. I had a couple of buddies who coached, and I saw them moving around from place to place. I was lucky. I played eleven years in one place. For the last seven years, we lived in the same house. My whole career was in Cleveland, which helped my family situation a lot. We didn't have to move around every year, and we were a contending team every year. My first year, '56, was the only losing year we had. A lot of that speaks for the organization, and the organization is what Paul Brown bred.

AFTER I LEFT, I was still interested in the players and what happened. I went to Cleveland every chance I got. I stayed in contact with some of the players. We still have an awful lot of good friends from that time. When it's the only club you played for, you can't cut that out of your life. I've always had a feeling for Cleveland, not for the management, but for the fans.

The town really adopted the club. It wasn't a matter of winning or losing. It was, 'They're our team.' They're having a problem here in Kansas City with the baseball team. They're not doing very well, and as a result, people stopped going. That never happened in Cleveland. They supported that club with 70-80,000 people a game right up to the very end.

I think the move to Baltimore was the worst deal that ever happened.

As if Art wasn't making any money. I was totally shocked. Had they been dwindling in attendance, it wouldn't have surprised me as much. Baltimore just put together a package that they knew couldn't be resisted. I hate to say it, but there are a lot of prostitutes in the business. That's the name of the game today. It's money, money, money.

I ONLY SAW PAUL BROWN a couple of times after he left Cleveland. I remember one time Cincinnati was playing the Chiefs out here, and I didn't know whether to go down in the locker room to visit with him or not. I didn't feel that close to him. But I thought, 'Hell, I'm going to go down there and see him. I played with the guy seven, eight years, and if he's too busy to see me, he's too busy to see me.'

So I went down, and he was very gracious. He was talking to some interviewers, and a guy let me in the door when I told him who I was and why I was there. He looked up and saw me and said, 'Galen! Galen! Just a minute! Just a minute!' And he started to tell these guys who were interviewing him, 'Hey, can we do this later?' That made me feel awful good.

The only other time I saw him was we went to a deal in Columbus— 'Paul's Guys.' It was a golf tournament, the last one that Paul had in relationship to the Cleveland organization.

I don't know how old Paul was the last time I saw him, but he sure hadn't slipped any. I think he had it by the throat right up to the very end.

I've often thought about what my life would be had I not had a chance to play at KU. I would probably have wound up being a farmer in western Kansas.

When I played, we were close together, like a military experience. It was more family than it is today. It's such a spectacle now. Then we were going to live and die together. Today, because of the unionization and the money and agents involved, everybody could care less about one another. They'd walk out on you the night before the Super Bowl if it served their purpose.

Yeah, I feel fortunate to have played for Paul. He was stern but fair. He ran a good organization. Playing for him was a break for me that a lot of other players didn't get. I could have played for eleven years in a lot of other places for a lot of other coaches and not played for anybody who was notable. But I played for Paul Brown, and he was a legend. 〞

.

# Our Type
## *of* Man

FIVE MASSILLON High
School reserves suspended midway
through Paul Brown's first season as
head football coach for not attending
to their school work.

Charley Anderson, All-American
candidate at Ohio State University,
dismissed during Brown's first season
"for the benefit of the squad and the
future of our football team," because
Anderson cut classes, frequented
night clubs, and came tardy to
practice.

Jim Daniell, team captain,
released on the eve of the Cleveland
Browns' first All-American Football
Conference championship game,
after being arrested.

Rookie quarterback Stan Heath,
the nation's top passer as a college
senior, waived for missing every
question on a quiz at the end of his
first week of training camp.

Ten Browns traded to lowly

Baltimore because "a festering mood of selfishness had infected our team."

Defensive end Doug Atkins, a number one draft pick and future Hall of Famer, shipped to the Bears because "his lifestyle became incompatible with our philosophy."

"The forgotten men," as he called them, littered Paul Brown's coaching career. They were the players he banished for not living up to his ideal of athletic ability, intelligence, obedience, and virtue—for failing in some way to be "our type of man."

"Puritan Paul," as fullback Jim Brown once referred to him, said that "discipline pervaded everything" in his life; he insisted, for good or ill, on dealing with players as strictly as his father had treated him. "The greatest compliment Paul Brown could give anybody was, 'He's our kind,'" says five-time Pro Bowl guard Jim Ray Smith. "When he said that, you knew you were okay."

Little in Smith's early life suggested that he would become the kind of "high-grade" player Brown favored. Brought up poor by his diabetic mother, Smith spent his childhood "just surviving" in a house built from scavenged lumber and without electricity or plumbing. He played ball, worked the southeast Texas oil rigs, and pulled pranks borrowed from a Larry McMurtry novel: leaping from the hood of a

souped-up Model A careening across a pasture, snatching jackrabbits by their ears, and depositing them at night in the classroom of a despised teacher.

He had few ambitions beyond working as an oil field roughneck, but hardship, manual labor, and four years of Baptist influence at Baylor University, where he made All-American in 1953 and 1954, prepared him for Brown's demands, if not for some of the coach's methods.

"I have no list of do's and don'ts," Brown once said. "These players are grown men. They know what's good for them and what isn't. I suppose you've heard that I'm a whip-cracking so and so. Maybe I am, but I don't think so."

The coach must have momentarily forgotten his annual indoctrination speech. Wearing half-glasses, he rehearsed the speech at length, illuminating its margins with notes. The speech advised players about their attire, language, and acquaintances and warned them of the dangers-and consequences of strong drink, tobacco, and loose women. "If you've been drinking, I'll ask you in front of the squad. If you have, you're through. If you have and you deny it, you've branded yourself a liar in front of the team," he declared.

During flights, Brown tested players on game plans. He flung a wet towel at fullback Marion Motley, who had fallen asleep in a meeting. He vowed to call the wife of anyone caught with another woman. Scuttlebutt held that he hired former FBI agents to tail players. For several years, a priest traveled with the team. *Time* once called Cleveland "the praying professionals."

"I ask nothing of my players that I wouldn't ask of my sons," the coach said. During football season, Brown himself abstained from golf, gin rummy, and dry martinis, of which he never drank more than two. He believed that "young men want to work in an atmosphere of reasoned discipline" and reacted with scathing ridicule to transgressions, on or off the field. "I'm realistic enough to know that the boss has to be tough at times, but you think about it later, and you think, 'Grade school, high school, college, I never have been talked to that way," Smith says.

Smith nonetheless easily accepted Brown's supremacy. "You have more respect for people like that—the authority he had, the sternness he had with the players— than you would with someone who's loose," he says. "Those are the worst kind of people to be around, because you don't know what they're thinking. You don't know where you stand with them. With Paul, it was definitely clear."

That Smith was both an unusual athlete and a young man of flawless

character soon became clear to Cleveland. At 6' 3", 245 pounds, he ran 40 yards only two-tenths of a second slower than 190-pound scatback Bobby Mitchell, the fastest Brown. Smith was the prototype of the league's big, swift, agile offensive linemen and a key to one of the more potent running attacks in NFL history. "When I'm carrying the ball, I love to see that cat ahead of me," Mitchell said.

Later voted to Cleveland's all-time, all-star squad, Smith made All-Pro three times and was named a captain. "He's a natural leader, by deeds more than words, and helps set a high standard for his teammates, on and off the field," a reporter wrote.

A decade earlier, Brown made his reputation as a disciplinarian by summarily firing a player he had appointed Cleveland's first captain and praised for having "very intensive spirit and desire to win." A 230-pound tackle, Jim Daniell had starred under Paul Brown at Ohio State. His blocked punt for a safety against Purdue in 1941 gave the coach his first Big 10 victory. As a gunnery officer in World War II, Daniell survived the sinking of two destroyers and won a Silver Star for bravery. He made second-team All-NFL for the Chicago Bears in 1945 and then jumped to the AAFC to play for his old college coach.

At 3:15 on the morning of

December 14, 1946, Daniell, tackle Lou Rymkus, and receiver Mac Speedie were arrested in Cleveland, Daniell for public intoxication, Rymkus and Speedie for creating a disturbance. Brown awoke to a newspaper story headlined "3 Browns Penalized—offside on Euclid Ave." At a team meeting later that day, Brown asked Daniell if the story were true. Daniell admitted it was, and Brown ordered him out of the room and off the team—just as he had Anderson, one of his former Massillon players, five years earlier at Ohio State.

"Daniell's not being made an example of. He's simply getting what's coming to him," Brown said. Regardless, the squad saw their captain as an object lesson. "That incident set the tone," said Otto Graham, quarterback at the time. "Everybody was scared to death of Paul Brown. Believe me, Paul Brown's word was law, and if you went against it, you were in trouble."

Over the years, Brown acted with similar inflexibility in numerous less publicized cases. He protected the franchise from scandal but, some believe, so sanitized the Browns that they lacked the brute ferocity needed to win championships in a violent game. "I always thought Paul lost his biggest asset when he found he couldn't handle certain types of players, fellows who liked to stay up

late and have a good time," said receiver Ray Renfro after Brown was fired in 1963. "Just look around the league. There's an awful lot of horses that used to belong to us. So they weren't Paul's kind of people? But they could play football."

Some players also questioned Brown's objectivity, holding that necessity, performance, and, perhaps, bias influenced his decisions. "He didn't mind using fear to run the ship, and he wasn't always fair in his discipline. Probably, if you pinned him down, he'd tell you that he didn't even pretend to be fair," says former halfback Dub Jones, a Brown favorite. "He's not looking for fairness. He's looking for discipline."

Thus, Daniell was released, and Rymkus and Speedie went unpunished. Brown claimed he handled the cases differently because Rymkus and Speedie had been trying to extricate Daniell from an argument with a policeman; however, Daniell had also recently been demoted to second string, while the other players were outstanding starters. "Paul Brown saw the opportunity to get that team in the palm of his hand, and he took it," Graham says.

The day after Cleveland beat the New York Yankees for the crown, Daniell, acting as his own attorney and brandishing a Presidential Citation for heroism, won acquittal on all charges. In an odd and perhaps unrelated twist, when Brown was vying for the head coach's position at Ohio State, the Buckeye who spoke most publicly against hiring a high school coach was Jim Daniell.

Brown tolerated Len Ford's drinking as long as the huge defensive end's pass rushing outweighed his disruptiveness. "The Filthy Five"—a boisterous crew whose ranks changed over time—celebrated as vigorously as they played, but the coach overlooked their shenanigans as he did the sometimes dubious business affairs of the team's first owner, Mickey McBride.

A self-made ruffian with shady associates, McBride seems an unlikely partner for Brown. Reared in a rough Irish neighborhood in Chicago, McBride came to Cleveland in 1913 as circulation manager of the *News* and eventually owned taxi cabs, radio stations, and real estate in Ohio and Florida, where he was involved with Alfred Polizzi, allegedly the retired head of Cleveland's Mayfield Road Mob. McBride also owned Continental Press, a telegraph service that, authorities asserted, wired horse racing information to bookies and was controlled by the Al Capone gang.

Subpoenaed in 1951 by the Senate Special Committee to Investigate Organized Crime in Interstate Commerce, McBride swore that he had no dealings with mobsters. He testified that he bought into the wire service to create a job for his brother in law and purchased it outright in 1947 for his 23-year-old son. He said he sold information only to legitimate horse racing publications and had never committed a crime.

Unconvinced, the committee's chairman, Estes Kefauver, insisted that Chicago gangsters did indeed own Continental Press, which Kefauver called "Public Enemy Number One." Kefauver charged, "The wire service keeps alive the illegal gambling empire which in turn bankrolls a variety of criminal activities in America." Soon after, Congress outlawed the wire service. Perhaps Kefauver had been grandstanding, because McBride was not indicted for any offense, but some lawmakers found the owner so repellent that the Ohio House of Representatives refused to pass a resolution praising the Browns for winning the 1950 NFL title until his name had been removed.

Brown apparently saw no contradiction in his association with McBride. Yet after McBride sold the club in 1953, Brown reported to the NFL that he suspected one of the new owners, Saul Silberman, of pumping him for information to use in betting on games. Of course, while McBride had been so mindful of Brown's autonomy that he paid for his own bleacher seats, Silberman asked Brown to step aside as general manager in 1955 in a dispute over which brewery should sponsor broadcasts of Cleveland's games. Shortly thereafter, Silberman sold his interest in the club.

The relationship that most obviously vexed—and damaged— Paul Brown was with gifted fullback Jim Brown. The harbinger of a new kind of professional athlete, Jim Brown was intelligent, outspoken, independent, strong-willed, and fully aware of his value to the team —not unlike Paul Brown had been as a quarterback at Massillon High School and Miami University, where he rejected his coach's conservative plays, once tried to catch a punt behind his back, married against school rules, and thought football should be fun.

Though each acknowledged the other's talent, the Browns, at best, worked uneasily together. "The two simply disliked each other, and the feeling is understandable," said one writer. "Jim and Paul have some things in common. Both are proud, somewhat arrogant men with small regard for the feelings of others."

Jim Brown once remarked that the coach's "aloofness put him beyond approach." He said, "I've always wanted to play for a coach I feel like dying for. Paul Brown is not that coach."

JB sought "freedom of expres-sion." PB demanded "acquiescence." Social changes that were transforming the country and new owner Art Modell complicated matters. "Art was on the scene, and my father felt that, in some way, his power had been affected. And Jim, for his part, came into pro football just as at the time the civil rights movement was starting, and he had thoughts about his role in that movement," says Mike Brown. "And there was the element that Jim was difficult to control sometimes, off the field. Some of the things Jim did there bothered my father."

Former captain Mike McCormack called the coach's inability to dominate Jim Brown "the first chink in Paul's armor." McCormack said the "double standard" Paul Brown made for his star "all of a sudden lessened Paul a little bit—it was the first crack, and then everything went bad."

In more subtle ways, players had challenged the coach before. After Brown cut him, the squad voted Daniell a full share of playoff money and presented him with a pen and pencil set. Speedie, who finally bolted to Canada, said he kept at training camp a pet skunk named "Paul." Atkins bedeviled Brown, who hated country music, by repeatedly playing the same hillbilly song on a juke box in the dining room at Hiram College. Guard Abe Gibron needled the coach at every opportunity. Substitute quarterback George Ratterman was a storied prankster. With Jim Brown, though, the problem became far more serious. Saying "six years with Paul was as much as I could stomach," Jim Brown, according to his 1964 magazine article "My Case Against Paul Brown," told Modell "that if Paul Brown remained as coach, I wanted out." Already anxious about whispers of Paul Brown's plan to trade the fullback for Johnny Unitas and driven by his own desire for more power, Modell fired the coach.

Jim Brown said that he wasn't the only player who threatened to quit if Paul Brown weren't fired, but Jim Ray Smith has no memory of what the *New York Times* called "the palace coup that ousted the moody genius." Smith says, "It comes back to the way I was raised. He's the boss man. What he says goes. He answers to a higher power, but I'm not it."

In 1958, Cleveland lost a playoff to New York for the Eastern Conference title, but the defeat allowed Smith to make it home to Texas two hours before his father died of tuberculosis. "Paul, I don't know how to say this, but I think the Good Lord has done this," Smith wrote the coach afterward. "I just want you to know my daddy has passed away, and I got to see him."

Smith had also planned to retire

after the 1962 season, not to escape Brown, but to work full-time brokering real estate in Dallas. Traded to the Cowboys, he was talked into playing two more injury-shortened seasons.

For years, writers have drawn easy comparisons between Paul Brown and Tom Landry, the equally terse and natty coach of the Cowboys. According to Smith, the similarities go no deeper. Smith admired Landry's essential decency but says the transition between orderly Cleveland and chaotic Dallas was frustrating: "I'm in training camp seeing one of the backup quarterbacks see if he can roll a ball down one arm, over the back of his neck, and catch it with the other arm while Tom is trying to explain a new play. You got another one of the back-up quarterbacks out there seeing how far he can drop-kick a football. That drove me up a wall."

In 1986, Smith was inducted into the College Football Hall of Fame. To Smith's surprise, Brown attended the ceremony. "I said, 'Paul, what are you doing here?'" he recalls. "He said, 'Any time my boys are getting honored, I'm going to be there.'"

As early as 1949, Brown, the aloof dictator, remarked that the most gratifying aspect of winning the AAFC championship game was the number of former Browns who showed up in the locker room that day.

Likewise, the players came to view their coach differently. Even Jim Brown wrote fondly in his 1989 book about playing with Brown in a "Paul's Guys" charity golf tournament. "Paul was still the General, deciding how to play the holes, and I was still the guy coming through for him. Christ, what a day," he said. "I flew home on this lovely high."

"Paul Brown might have been a tyrant, but he was my tyrant," Brown said.

Paul Brown contended that class would eventually tell, and in the case of Jim Ray Smith, he was right. Smith still calls himself "a little old nobody from West Columbia," but he had the easy grace of old money as he talked at a linen-covered table near the sumptuous luncheon buffet at elegant Bentwood Country Club, near Dallas. Well off from his real estate business, Smith is a member of corporate boards of directors, important civic organizations, and prestigious clubs.

Tall, blue-eyed, deeply tan, his face unlined, he looked like a younger, bigger Richard Crenna, the physique he developed hefting 85-pound drill bits on oil derricks still fit. Starched creases razored his yellow and blue checked shirt and khaki slacks.

"Football's been good for me," he said. "It's been good for a lot of people, if they use it right."

As a boy, Smith borrowed a neighbor's .22 to shoot squirrels that his mother would pan fry and serve with cream gravy and mashed potatoes. Now, he nodded toward a spotless picture window. Outside, away from the glittering chandeliers, rich woodwork, muffled conversations, and clatter of heavy silverware, gray squirrels as big as plump house cats reared on their haunches and looked saucily over velvet greens and shaded tee boxes.

"Life's just like that golf," Jim Ray Smith said. "If you're not in the middle of the fairway, you're in the rough."

# Jim Ray SMITH

" WHEN I WAS A KID IN WEST COLUMBIA, Texas, all the roads were dirt and people still had wagons. When we got paved roads, we couldn't believe they were actually putting all that pavement down. We didn't have electricity, no running water, and no indoor plumbing. Mother cooked on a wood stove. When she got a kerosene stove, boy, she was really uptown. Mother and Dad divorced, and we didn't have any money. We'd get one pancake for breakfast in the morning. It'd be just as big as the frying pan. We'd take that and put butter and peanut butter and jelly on it.

When I was nine years old, I would borrow the neighbor's .22, because I could afford five of those little bitty shells. They cost about a penny apiece. I'd go squirrel hunting, and mother cleaned and cooked them. If they were older squirrels, we'd make squirrel with dumplings. If they were young in the springtime, we'd have fried squirrel with cream gravy and mashed potatoes.

One of the big things when we were kids was: 'Can you clean a squirrel without getting hair on it?' You really had to know how to do it. Now, I have squirrels running all over the house. When I was a kid, I would have them all eaten.

I really don't know why I started playing sports. A lot of it was peer pressure. My graduating class was 48. I played my first organized football when I was in the fifth grade, and the seniors on the high school team coached us. When I was in eighth grade, the varsity didn't have enough players to scrimmage against. They got about five of us eighth graders, and we'd go out and line up against them. They'd just rock us all over the place.

What helped me as much as anything with football was playing basketball and running track. I threw the shot and the discus, ran on the sprint relays, and went to the state in the high jump and the shot put. Speed, of course, is all Paul Brown wanted. If you were big and fast, then it was a double plus.

I was going through my scrapbook a couple of years ago, and I came across an article that Chuck Heaton had written on timing the Browns. Bobby Mitchell ran a 4.6 the first time he was timed, in full uniform on a grassy field, which was pretty good. He'd run a 4.3 in track clothes on a cinder track. The next fastest was Jim Brown. He was 4.7. The third one was Jim Ray Smith, along with Ray Renfro and some other wide receivers. And I weighed 245. Jim was about 218 or so, and Bobby was probably around 180.

GOING THROUGH HIGH SCHOOL, I never thought about playing ball in college. The only time I thought about college was at a service station one day, and I heard a guy inside talking to the guy who owned the station. He said, 'You know, that Jim Ray can go to any school he wants to.'

I thought, 'That guy talking about me?'

I figured I'd dig ditches or work in the oil fields. All through high school, and two years of college, I worked on the drilling rigs. I started when I was 15. When I first started, I think I got fifty cents an hour; by the time I was in college, I was getting a dollar fifteen or a dollar twenty-five.

I worked on the floor, throwing chain over pipes, and stacking it over on the floor. That sort of thing. Then this fellow wanted me to work derrick, ninety feet up. Well, it was a lot cleaner. All that mud didn't get on you, your shoes didn't eat out so fast from the acid in the mud, and, besides, we got fifteen cents more an hour. Between oil rigs and playing football, I've had seven broken hands. My dad lost two of his toes working in the oil fields. Dropped a pipe on them.

I never lifted weights, but I worked with a guy on the drilling rig who was pretty muscular. He was about three or four years older than I was. We'd get the used drilling bits on their way back to get repaired; they weighed maybe eighty-five pounds, and we'd shot-put them around. Then we'd get a drill collar, which was probably a couple of feet long, and see who could press that the most times with either arm. That's how we lifted weights.

I was a guard my freshman and sophomore years in high school. My junior year, they were going to make me a center, but I was pretty fast and so they made an end out of me. My senior year, I went to fullback. I got offers from quite a few schools: Rice, Texas, Baylor, Tulane. Rice was close to the house, only about forty or fifty miles away. I went up there to work for the summer, because I had committed to them, but I hated Houston. It was too big. I spent the night and came back home the next morning.

I ended up at Baylor. Waco was just a big old country town. There was probably only about four or five cars on campus. I played one day as a fullback at Baylor, and they put me at end. The day before the spring training game of my sophomore year, it came out in the Waco paper that 'Smith is moved to tackle.' Nobody told me anything about it. They called me in and said, 'Oh, we forgot to tell you, you're a tackle now.'

So I played the spring game at tackle. That was in '52. They didn't change from two-platoon to one-platoon until the next year, and I came back playing offensive and defensive tackle and made All-American. We played California the first or second game of the season out there. They were number three in the nation, and we beat them 25-0.

On the plane coming back, this sports writer from the *Dallas Morning News* told me, 'You're my All-American selection at tackle after what you did today.'

The next year, I was hurt, but I still made a lot of the All-American teams.

I MET MY WIFE, PAULA, my senior year at Baylor. It was kind of an unusual situation. You read about these guys with this 'turf toe'; well, I had that my senior year. I told her, 'I may not play this week against Arkansas.'

She said, 'Why?'

I said, 'I'm not going to tell you. You'll laugh.'

She said, 'I won't laugh. Tell me about it. I want to know.'

I said, 'I hurt my big toe.'

She just burst out laughing.

I fiddled around with it for about a week, and there was this guy we called 'Uncle Jim.' He went down to a metal refinery and said, 'I need a solid steel innersole for a shoe.'

The guy said, 'No problem.'

You pack it in your shoe, you can't get up on your toes, but you still have your quickness and your speed.

I was drafted seventh, I think, by Cleveland. I'm saying seventh, but it might've been fifth. Charley Smith, on our team, was an end, and he was drafted before me, by Baltimore, because they thought Charley Smith was me.

Paula and I got out of school and got married in April of '55. I was in the Army in North Carolina. We didn't have any money. I bought a car, $200 down, and we went to North Carolina. We found a little garage apartment out back of a house, on a dirt road in Fayetteville. Saturday night, we'd go down to the appliance store. They had a TV in the window and speakers outside. We'd sit on the fenders of the car and watch *Gunsmoke,* then we'd go home.

Finally, we met some people in church who invited us to come over on Saturday night and have Coca-Cola and we got to watch *Gunsmoke* inside.

I didn't know a thing about the Cleveland Browns, except that I watched them on TV. They were on TV even down in Texas. They were the only pro team you could get. They were such great winners, they were like the Yankees of football. When the Browns came to sign me, I was about to play in the College All-Star Game. Dick Gallagher came down and wanted to sign me for $4,500. I had my coach with me. He had played ten years in Canada. He said, 'No, no. Jim Ray, you go out. Let me talk to Dick.' I went out, came back, and I had an $8,000 contract with a $500 bonus.

When you graduated from college then, the best job you could get was probably $450 a month with a car, if you got with a drilling firm. That was a good job. So, if you got $8,000 your first year, that was a pretty good salary.

I know when I got my first house, they asked me what I did for a living. I said, 'I play pro ball.'

They said, 'Well, how long are you going to be there?'

I said, 'I don't know. How long is this note?'

When I was at the College All-Star Game, we played the Browns, and I played guard. Don Colo was in front of me and Lenny Ford was out on the end. I didn't weigh but 218 pounds right out of college. Don Colo, I don't know what he weighed—260, 265. Lenny was about the same.

I had a decent day against Lenny. The first play, though, he ate my lunch. I wasn't going to let him do that again, and we won the game, 30-27, or something like that.

My first training camp, during the preseason, I got my ankle tore up. I was still in the Army. The Browns said, 'You can't play for a couple weeks. Why don't you just go on back to the Army?'

I go back to the Army. I'm rehabilitating my ankle. It's about three weeks. I write the Browns a letter and say, 'I'm ready to come back. Tell me what to do.'

I didn't hear from them. I thought maybe they didn't want me. Then, one day, they called and said to get there as soon as I could. I took a leave, they had twelve games that year, and I think I played in the last seven of them.

PAUL BROWN IS ONE of the greatest organizers I've ever seen. You've got your Landrys, your Lombardis, who were great coaches, but Paul is the one who let everyone know how to organize. Bill Walsh had a book signing here one day, and he was giving his philosophy of football. I said, 'Man, you sound just like Paul Brown.'

He said, 'Where do you think I got it from?'

I don't know if this is true or not, but I heard that during the season, he hired ex-FBI guys to check on guys. Paul said things to me that indicated they did. He said to me once, 'Jim Ray, we've never had to check on you. We know what kind of person you are.' Now, whether they followed me or knew where I went after practice during the week, I don't know.

The greatest compliment Paul Brown could give anybody was, 'He's our kind. He's our kind.' When he said that, you knew you were okay.

He always wanted to make sure that the team was a family. He said, 'We travel first class,' and we stayed at some pretty classy places. You always wore a coat and tie in the lobby of any hotel. You never talked to strangers—that stranger could be connected to the Mafia and gambling. You always had to wear a hat in cold weather. You always had to get a flu shot.

Paul Brown hated the union. He thought if we were with the union, we'd be with the Mafia and they'd take control of his business. My first year was the first losing season he had ever had, and he blamed it on our union organizing. It was tradition to give the players their warm-up jackets after the last game. He was so mad that year that he didn't give anybody a warm-up jacket after the game. But then he sent them to everybody a couple of weeks later.

When I went to Cleveland, I learned more football in two weeks than I did in all the previous time I played. I didn't know anything when I got to Cleveland. The only thing I knew is that if I hit a guy and stuck with him, he wasn't going to get on the passer. If you could hold him for three seconds, then the pass should be off. You learn to set up like a boxer. If that guy comes around with a head slap, all you do is get that arm up. You've got your arms up all the time, knocking those slaps away.

The core of any football team is the offensive line. The offensive line controls the game. You need a good defense to get the ball back, but the offensive line controls the ball. The line has to communicate with the running backs and the quarterbacks about what's going on. If you're leading the running back on an end sweep, or if you're flaring out the tackle, you've got to tell the back what the guy's going to do: 'You've got to set him up for me. Fake outside so he'll go out, and then you can cut back behind me'; 'On the dive play, I'm going to stand him straight up. You can go inside or outside, because he won't see you, but don't go straight'; 'Look back to the inside.' If you've got one bad link, the line is going to come apart.

I had to learn what I called 'gathering myself' before I hit somebody. Fritz Heisler taught the technique. He called it 'a genuflect.' When you're blocking or tackling, you gather yourself to go through the guy. Fritz taught that when you're leading the plays—trapping or whatever—you want to get an inside-out block. You go straight down the line. If the defensive man isn't coming across the line, you have to adjust to get an inside-out block. If they're coming across the line, you already have inside-out, and they're going to be easy to block. You did the same thing on sweeps. You go out and get around that end, so you can come upfield and get an inside-out block. On pass plays, you hit the guy with your head right in his throat, looking at him all the time, and as soon as you set him up, then you cut him to get his hands down so that the quarterback could throw the ball. Or you hit him, cut off his charge, neutralize him, and just hang with him. Whatever way he wants to go, you just let him go. Stay with him and keep pushing him.

I had a little technique on a cutoff block that Fritz just loved. If they were in a four-three, and we were running a dive play to the right, I'd tell Jim Brown, 'Look back to the middle, because it's going to be open.'

The center was on the linebacker. The right guard was going after the tackle. They're trying to flow to the play to stop it on the right side, because the quarterback is turning that way, and Jim is running that way. I had to cut off the tackle, and if I could do that, it was going to make a huge opening over the center. And Jim made you look good, whether you were good or not.

Jim had tremendous balance. You'd watch Jim running, and I don't think his feet ever got more than two or three inches off the ground. When he got hit, he neutralized the tackler. When I blocked the tackle over me, I had to neutralize his charge. Jim did the same thing when he was running. He'd lower that arm and shoulder and hit the guy almost as hard as they hit him, and then he holds his balance and glides out and leaves the guy lying. Against Pittsburgh one year, five guys hit him: linebackers, halfbacks, safeties. They never got him down, and he ran about 40 yards for a touchdown.

Jim's second year, they had a television program in Cleveland. They compared him to Marion Motley. It showed Marion Motley—245, 250—just running over those little old defensive backs. It was like a cartoon. I got to know Marion a little bit over the years. What was sad was we were at workouts, and he was delivering mail there. The story goes that he had given his brother money to open a bar, and the brother spent all the money, but I don't know whether that's true or not.

IN MY SECOND YEAR, I HURT MY SHOULDER, and I couldn't lift my arm up. They had X-rayed it, done everything with it. They couldn't find out what it was. Vic Ippolito, the doctor, said it was all in my head.

I said, 'No, it's in my shoulder.'

He said, 'Ah, we can't find anything. There's nothing wrong.'

I said, 'Then why can't I reach my arm all the way up?'

He said 'We'll shoot it with some Novocain.'

That didn't help. Nothing helped.

We got over to Pittsburgh, either the first or second game of the season, and this guy was eating my lunch. I just couldn't get to him, because of my shoulder.

They're giving me a bad time about it.

Paul said, 'It is that bad?'

I said, 'Well, it's pretty bad.'

We're on the bus on the way back to Cleveland, and Fritz comes back and says, 'Paul thinks we ought to let you lay off this week. You're going to play this weekend, but you won't hit anybody in practice for two weeks.'

That sounded great. So I went out in shorts and shoulder pads. We're running our plays, and I pulled my hamstring. I came back limping, and Fritz said, 'What's wrong? What's wrong? What's wrong?'

I told, 'I think I pulled my hamstring.'

He said, 'Get over there and don't do anything.'

I'm over there on the sidelines. At the end of practice, we run down under punts.

Brown comes over and says, 'Why aren't you out there?'

I said, 'I think I pulled a hamstring.'

He ate me up. He chewed me up one side of me and down the other: 'You got hurt in practice? Don't you know any better than that? You get hurt in a *game*! You don't *ever* get hurt in practice!'

I was so mad at him I wanted to kill him.

I COULDN'T SAY A WORD. I was going home. That was it for pro football. I go back to the hotel and pack all of my bags. I said, 'Lord, this is it. I know you don't want me playing with all these injuries.' I keep saying this while I pack all my bags. I grab ahold of that door to leave the hotel, and the Good Lord hits me between the eyes: 'Why don't we talk about it?'

I take my bags back and put them in the closet, don't unpack them. I get on my knees, and I just pray about it, and it was kind of like a deep fog that just went away.  He said: 'Why don't you go try it one more time.'

The next morning, I left my bags packed, but I went back out to League Park. I got there about an hour early, so they could work on my shoulder and my leg. Fritz is there waiting for me. He's all excited. He says, 'Jim Ray, we got it. We got it. We're going to change you to the messenger guard. That way, when you pull and block, you'll be blocking with the other shoulder, and you'll play only half the time.'

He was really excited about it. By the time he got through, Paul walked in. He's just all bright eyes and laughing: 'Fritz tell you everything that's happened? Isn't that the greatest thing that ever happened?'

I said, 'Thank you, Lord.'

Answered prayers.

I played that week as the messenger guard and played the rest of the season and made some of the All-Pro teams. I had a real good year.

I'm realistic enough to know that the boss has to be tough at times, but you think about it later, and you think, 'Grade school, high school, college, I never have been treated that way. I have never been talked to like that before.'

That hurts a lot of kids. That runs a lot of kids off. Some guys couldn't play for Paul. Babe Parilli came in there, and he just broke out in hives all over. Ray Renfro did, too, the last several years. He'd go home, and they'd go away. He was hard on Ray. Here'd go Ray down the sidelines. He'd put on a move. Paul would say, 'Ray, you've got to make those cuts sharp! Sharp! You're not running the route right!' But Ray was one of the great Cleveland receivers.

You never knew if he was really angry, or if you were seeing his management philosophy in action. I never saw him out of control, though. It was like he had you write in your playbook: 'How do we run? We run thusly, with our hands like this, and we always, always run under control.'

He'd say, 'You can't block, you can't tackle, you can't cut running full speed. The only time I want you running full speed is if you're running for a touchdown or trying to catch someone to stop *him* from running for a touchdown.'

I HAD HAD A DIFFERENT ROOMMATE every year when I came to Cleveland. Ray and I were both from Texas. Finally, about the fourth year, they put us together. After the first night in training camp, I asked him how he slept. He said he didn't sleep too well. I thought, 'What in the world is that all about?' I couldn't understand why he didn't sleep. *I* slept. That next night, he came in with a bunch of books and magazines. The next morning, I woke up, and those books were all over my bed, all over me, all over everything else. I finally figured it out: I was snoring so loud that he was throwing them at me to wake me up.

Then I started to think, 'Now, why am I with Renfro? He's had all these other roommates, too.'

We broke training camp, and we had our first game in Cleveland. We go down to the hotel. We have our meal that night. We go to the movies, we come back, go to bed. Something happened that next morning that scared the living daylights out of me. I came out of that bed; I almost hit the ceiling. He was in the bathroom at six o'clock in the morning with dry heaves. He was going *Eeeeyackk! Eeeeyackk!* Then I figured out why they put the two of us together.

Before games, things would get real quiet, and you'd hear old Ray in there in the head: *Eeeeyackk! Eeeeyackk!* You could hear it all over the dressing room.

Brown would say, 'That's one guy who's ready.'

Paul's motivation to the players was money. That's the ax he held over everybody's head. He'd say, 'I'm the head coach. I'm the general manager. I negotiate all the contracts. You have to go through me. Just so you know.'

The first time I negotiated with him, I think: Who am I to be negotiating a contract, anyway? It was all one-year contracts. After that first year, he calls up and says, 'Okay, Jim Ray, you had a good year. We're going to give you a $2,000 raise,' which I thought was pretty good, 'and if you keep this up, you'll probably get that, or somewhere in that neighborhood, every year.'

He calls up this one day and says, 'Well, you know, Jim Ray, we signed Bobby Mitchell. We had to give him a little increase, and we need those good running backs, so we just don't have the budget to give you a raise this year.'

I said, 'Paul, now you said $2,000 a year, and I'm not going to take anything less. I might take more, but I'm not going to take less.'

He said, 'I'm not going to do it. We just don't have the money.'

I said, 'Paul, it would sure make me happy if you would do that.'

He said, 'What do you mean "make you happy"?'

I said, 'It'd make me happy. Don't you want me to be happy?'

He said, 'Well, okay,' and gave it to me.

WE WERE OUT AT THE PRO BOWL ONE YEAR, and I asked Renfro, I said, 'Ray, you know, I don't know what kind of salary I should be getting. I've played in the Pro Bowl several years. I don't now what's a good salary for a lineman.'

He thought for a minute. He said, 'I don't know, but you ought to at least be getting $12,000.'

I was making a lot more than that, so I kept my mouth shut. I said, 'Man, I don't know what he's making, but he doesn't know what he's talking about, either.'

Nobody every told anybody what they made. Everybody knew what Bobby Layne made. He was the highest-paid player. He got $22,000 playing for Detroit.

We played in a couple of Pro Bowls together. He always had a 'guard around' play. He say, 'Guard around, to Smith,' and I'd pull, and he'd hand it off to me.

Most of the stories about Bobby that you think can't be true are true. I think he's the first one who said, 'If I'd have known I was going to live this long, I would've taken better care of my body.'

He always gambled a lot in the afternoons, and he used to tell those guys, 'Man, if you can't make a living by noon every day, you're in the wrong business.'

We'd be riding out to practice, and he'd get to telling stories about when he was with the New York Bulldogs. He said, 'Boy, we had a lot of people in the stands, just our families. Our wives were the cheerleaders.

The greatest yell they could do was: "Bulldogs! Bulldogs! Bulldogs! Bow and wow and wow."'

He was a big-hearted guy. We were at the Pro Bowl one year, and we went over to see Dinah Washington, Night Train Lane's wife, sing one night. There were about three or four tables of us there, and she got up and started singing this real jazzy number, and Bobby's clapping and hollering, and then she started singing this love ballad. It wasn't two seconds, and his head was on the table. He was fast asleep.

PEOPLE TALK ABOUT 300-POUNDERS TODAY. We had Big Daddy Lipscomb. We beat Baltimore in 1959, in Baltimore, by something like a touchdown (38-31). Big Daddy caught me on a draw play. He weighed about 310, and I was about 245.

Bobby Mitchell got tackled and fell on the back of my legs. Big Daddy was in front of me, and he just kept pushing me over until he buckled me, trying to break my legs. I was screaming bloody murder. The refs were trying to pull him back. His eyes were about that big. His teammates got him off me. I went off the field for about three plays and then came back in, and I was bound and determined to get back at him. I tried to blindside him or whatever, and I never could get him. But we did make three touchdowns over him, and he was traded to Pittsburgh in the off-season.

The next time we had a game against him, I told John Morrow, who was the center, 'This's the play. I'm going to hit him just as hard as I can, but if I miss him, he's going to kill the quarterback, so be ready to back me up.'

I come out, I'm right there, and just as I was getting ready to hit him, he took this big old hand, and, *wham*, right upside my head, and the film shows my knees buckle, and he kills Milt Plum.

John Morrow was nowhere around.

I said, 'John, where were you? Where were you?'

Now it's the second quarter. I said, to John, 'You going to back me?'

John's always blowing air out of his nose and spitting, and all this nasty stuff is hanging in his facemask. He says, 'Yeah. Yeah.'

I said, 'Okay, this's the play we're going to do it on.'

I come out, I get just right there, and, *wham*, upside my head, and my knees buckle again. Paul liked to show that back and forth on the movies on Wednesday mornings. I come off the field, and he's chewing me out: 'What're you doing? You're killing us!'

I said, 'It'll never happen again, Paul, never again.'

Meanwhile, I'm chewing Morrow out about not backing me up. He's saying, 'Oh, I thought you had him. I thought you had him.'

About halftime, we're winning, and we're trying to run the clock out. We run a sweep. I pull and knock the outside linebacker down. I'm down on the ground, about to get up, and Big Daddy comes along and kicks me in the side. Man, I come up after him. The ref gets in front of us. We're yelling back and forth.

The next play, we run a pitch to that side. I pull and go inside and curl back out and get the linebacker. Then I hear *boom, boom, boom* behind me. The ground is shaking.

'Oh, no,' I said. 'Big Daddy.'

I bulled my neck up, 'cause I know he's going to hit me. He comes up, puts his arm around me, and he says, 'Jim Ray, you're my buddy. Let's not do this. Let's stop all this fighting. You don't hold me. You don't whip-block me. You're the best there is. I want to be friends with you.'

And we were friends from then on.

THAT SEASON I SPENT AT MESSENGER GUARD, I called at least half of the plays. When I say 'I called them,' I asked the receivers and the running backs: 'What do you want run this next play? I'll get it called for you.'

I'd get the other linemen: 'What's good on your side?'

I used the power of suggestion. Paul always carried his little paper in his back pocket, and he'd pull it out and look at it. I'd say, 'Paul, we need a twenty-five.'

'Okay, twenty-five on two! Let's go!'

He'd pull that paper out and look at it. He'd say, 'Well, let's see.'

I'd say, 'We need a Z and deep.'

He'd say, 'Okay, okay, on two now, on two!'

And we won the division that year. That was a fun year.

The happiest I ever saw him was when he'd make a good call, and the play went for a touchdown. Boy, he was happy. When I called one that went for a touchdown, it was his play. You don't say, 'I did it.' *He* did it.

If you wanted a play sent in, you'd get behind him or to the side of him, where he could hear you, and say, 'Boy, if we had this play, it would be great.' Next thing you know, we had it in there.

One of the happiest times I had was in 1957. We were in our lockers, getting ready to go out to practice, and Paul was coming around and giving out letters. There were five of us who went out. He gave one to Jim Brown. I don't remember who the other guys all were. He had one envelope left in his hand.

He said, 'Well, Jim Ray, congratulations.'

I said, 'What about, Paul?'

He said, 'You're going to the Pro Bowl.'

That was one of the biggest surprises I ever had.

I was selected for five Pro Bowls, but I didn't play in five. We were out there practicing for the game in '61, and Norm Van Brocklin and I got the Asian flu. That was something else. I'm dying, and they wanted us out in our uniforms. This one doctor came in and said, 'Ah, you look great. You ought to see Norm. He looks horrible. Can't you just put on your uniform and go out there and stand on the sideline?'

I can hardly talk. My head is about to burst.

Another doctor came in and checked me over. He said, 'Don't you dare go out there on that field. It'll take ten years off your life.'

I said, 'I'm not planning on getting out of this bed.'

Then the other doctor came around: 'Well, what do you think? You going to make it out there on Sunday afternoon?'

I said, 'No.'

He said, 'But you look great. You ought to see Norm. He looks horrible.'

Later, I saw Norm, and he said they were doing the same thing to him: 'You look great. You ought to see Jim Ray. He really looks bad.'

THERE'S NOT ANOTHER TEAM I played on that had more team spirit, more enthusiasm than the teams I played on in Cleveland. If you have to have someone motivate you, then you're probably not a very good pro. Motivation has to come from yourself. All great players—and I'm not saying I'm one of them—start playing the game two or three days ahead of time. You play it over in your mind. You watch film. You see what you're going to do on different plays. If I have to start getting up for the game when I'm running out on the field to be introduced, then I'm late.

My first home game in Cleveland, my rookie year, we got on our knees and said the Lord's Prayer, and as soon as we got through, someone—I think it was Bob Gain—jumped up and said, 'Let's kill the sons of bitches!'

They fired Paul in January of '63, which was a month after I had left

Cleveland. When I heard he was fired, I thought about another one of Paul Brown's sayings: 'This is my livelihood. If you're not performing, you're messing with my livelihood. I will not allow that.'

He used to tell us that the mark of a champion was when you win you say nothing, and when you lose, you say less, and when he was fired, he didn't say one word, until he wrote that book. Of course, he was still under contract for five years, for a lot of money.

Art got friendly with all the players, which I think was a mistake. In my business, you need a broker between the two principals. You need somebody between the principal owner and the players. If you want to get that close to everybody, you can do it in the off-season. From what I understand, Paul was very upset about players going to Art. He told Art that, and Art said something to the effect that, 'Paul, you don't need to worry about that, because you're not going to be here.'

Paul said, 'Don't say one more word. I'll be here in the morning with my attorney,' and got up and left.

I knew he had to be hurt deep, because every year, he used to say, 'I'm the one who makes the decisions. I'll be here when you're gone.' When you say that every year, and then *you're* gone, it's a slam to your ego, your pride.

I wasn't aware of any tension between Paul and Art until afterward. I think the biggest problem was Jim Brown. That's hearsay. I don't know. But I understand that Jim went to Art and said, 'If Paul Brown is here, I'm not going to play.' Now, I never heard Jim Brown say that myself.

If there were players trying to get rid of Paul Brown, I wasn't aware of it, and I didn't listen to it. I was too naïve to even think about it. It comes back to the way I was raised. He's the boss man, and whatever he says goes.


EVERYTHING WAS DIFFERENT IN DALLAS, and I had a different attitude, too. But if I was going to play, I was going to play to the best of my ability. They tried to make a tackle out of me. After you've played guard all those years, on the left side, playing right tackle is very hard. I didn't like it at all.

You go to training camp in Cleveland, you're on the field sixty-five minutes in the morning, and in the afternoon, sixty minutes, and you're working every minute. Then you come to Dallas, and you're on the field two hours in the morning and two and a half, in the afternoon. You're standing around, and you got those old cleats on. Your feet are dying.

In Cleveland, you had Paul Brown demanding perfection, and in Dallas I'm watching one of the backup quarterbacks see if he can roll a football down one arm, over the back of his neck, and catch it with the other arm, while Tom Landry is trying to explain a new play. You got another one of the backup quarterbacks seeing how far he can dropkick a football. That drove me up a wall.

The other thing that was different about Dallas is that, in Cleveland, usually, you pretty much knew everything you wanted to do by Wednesday, and you start running your plays in Wednesday afternoon practice. Everybody said that the Cowboys' system was so hard to learn. The system wasn't hard to learn. The problem they had when I was there was that you'd go out on Tuesday, and they'd give you your game plan, and then they'd change it on Wednesday. On Friday, you'd go back to the way you did it on Tuesday.

I PLAYED TWO SEASONS IN DALLAS. I had knee operations in the middle of both of them. That doesn't leave you with a real good attitude. You're not contributing to the team. If you're not contributing, why are you here?

Once you're done, you miss the fellowship, but having two knee operations made it a lot easier to quit. Man, they hurt. The last one is a big U-shape. They opened it up, went in there with a chisel, and cleaned it up. Then they sewed it back up. You wake up, and it feels like someone pulled your leg off—not cut it off, *pulled* it off. It hurt tremendously. For two years, I couldn't step up on a curb without it killing me.

I went a year ago and told them, 'My knee sounds like a cement mixer. I want to get it cleaned.'

The doctor said, 'I don't know if we want to do that or not. Let's X-ray it.'

He looked at it and said, 'We're not going to do that.'

I said, 'Why not?'

He said, 'You're probably going to hurt it more. Now, everything in there is pretty stabilized. You go in there and clean it out, and it might become unstable and start deteriorating more.'

I said, 'When would you recommend doing that?'

He said, 'Oh, in about fifteen years.'

I said, 'Then what?'

He said, 'We'll wait another ten years and replace the knee.'

I said, 'I'll be six feet under by then.'

He said, 'That's what I'm trying to tell you. We're not going to do anything.'

My first thought, when I heard that the Browns were moving out, was that the city told Art they weren't going to build him a stadium, when they built a basketball arena and the Rock 'n' Roll Hall of Fame, the aquarium, the new baseball stadium.

Art said, 'What about me?'

They said, 'Nope.'

He said, 'Well, okay.'

It was a financial deal for him. I don't think he really wanted to move. Everyone says, 'Why?' Fifty million dollars. I guess you'd move about anywhere for $50 million. They gave the rest of them what they wanted, and he was wanting his share, too. They tell him no, and then they end up building a new stadium anyway to get another team. I don't know what that says about the leadership in the city. You'd have to come to your own conclusions as to the burden they put on the fans and the taxpayers.

I'M IN THE REAL ESTATE BUSINESS NOW, mostly raw land. When I started, I built up to about six or seven sales people, and after a year or so, I said, 'These guys are not working for me. *I'm* working for *them*.' They had deal problems, family problems, every kind of problem, and they came to me with them all, and it wasn't business. I finally got rid of everybody and said I was just going to do my own deals.

I've been involved with Bill Glass Ministries, an evangelical mission to prisons across the country, almost since Bill Glass (former Browns All-Pro defensive end) started. It took him three years to get me into it. I didn't want anything to do with it. To me, the prisoners were just like a dead cow on top of a hill in a hundred and ten degrees. I didn't want anything to do with it. But he has counselors from all over the United States who pay their own way to go into prisons and witness to the prisoners. They aren't called 'counselors'; they're called 'teammates' or 'friends of Bill,' because with a prisoner, a 'counselor' is sort of a no-no. A counselor is a shrink.

The first prison I went into was Soledad, in California. Tommy John was there. He brought a little duffle bag in with him with three brand new balls, a bat, and a glove. He was going to do a demonstration of the curveball and all that. He gets to talking a little bit. He's been there an hour or so. He gets ready to do his demonstration. He goes to get the bag. He opens the bag, and those three brand new balls are gone. There's three old beat-up balls, all dog-eared, with broken strings, in there. He gets up anyway and starts throwing. He's letting the guys hit them. When he gets through, everyone's wanting his autograph. They're handing him bits of paper and every little thing and, he said, here comes that brand new ball through, then here comes another one, here comes another one.

I've been in about fifty prisons. A guy put it in a nutshell in McAlester, Oklahoma, a real tough prison. We had dinner together on Friday, and he said, 'We cannot change the prisoners' lives. The only way you're going to change the prisoner's life is to change his heart, and the only way you're going to change his heart is through Christ.'

I DIDN'T SEE PAUL UNTIL YEARS AFTER he was let go in Cleveland. I would call up to Cincinnati to talk to him occasionally and once I had trouble getting him for a couple of weeks. This was long after he was done coaching. I said to the secretary, 'What's the best time to get him?'

He said, 'The afternoons.'

I said, 'Well, what in he world is he doing in the mornings.'

He said, 'He's going over the game film.'

I said, 'He's what?'

He said, 'He goes over the game films and writes out suggestions to the head coach and sends them to him.'

He did that every morning.

I was inducted into the College Football Hall of Fame when it was still in Cincinnati, before they moved it up to South Bend. Paul came over for the induction. He was just as happy to see me as could be.

I said, 'Paul, what're you doing here?'

He said, 'Any time my boys are getting honored, I'm going to be there.'

He died about three years after that. He was a good one. I wish he was still around. I remember when he was 50 years old. We won the game on his birthday.

I look back on those days and look at today and think about the background I came from. The Good Lord got me out of West Columbia, I guess, where I should be digging ditches. God looked down on me and said, 'I don't know what we're going to do with him, but until we find out, we're going to make him a football player.' **"**

# Coach Brown
## *and* Paul Brown

PRUDE WHO USED no
word stronger than "divil." Teaser
who liked off-color stories. Tyrant
grasping power. Family man caring
for his ill wife and doting on his
three sons. Innovator unbound by
convention. Bureaucrat undone by
archaic beliefs.

He saw himself as a freewheeling
"fire and fall back" leader but was
criticized for being cautious. Praised
for bringing organization to an
unruly game, he was also condemned
as a prisoner of his own rigid system.
He accepted no excuses but attributed losses to officials, weather,
fumbles, incompetent bus drivers,
and tainted water. He was educated
in literature and history but rarely
referred to either. He cherished
victory but won so much that he

created expectations that he couldn't live up to.

Some who knew him well said he was egoless; others claimed he cared more about his image than about his team. In the same article, a magazine called him "comical," said he behaved like "a town lunatic," and proclaimed him "a genius." Quarterback Otto Graham wanted to murder him and "felt something like love" for him. A columnist who followed him in his heyday maintained that he was actually two men: "Coach Brown and Paul Brown."

Says Vince Costello, who played for Brown in Cleveland and coached for him in Cincinnati, "When you get older and you're done playing, everyone likes him, but when you're playing for him, he's a horse's ass because he gets on you."

Costello came to the Browns as a free agent linebacker in 1956. He weighed only 215 pounds and hadn't played football in over two years. He was 24 and nursing a hamstring he had pulled in minor league baseball. His résumé included quarterbacking a six-man high school team and a basketball scholarship to Ohio University, where he tried out for football as an afterthought.

Brown released him, but the heartless coach who cut top draft picks for as little as missing questions on quizzes not only invited Costello back to camp the following year but

also found him a job coaching high school ball while his leg healed.

Although most went unacknowledged, such thoughtful acts weren't rare for Brown. When he coached at Massillon High School, he bought groceries for needy families; later, he donated more than $100,000 to the school's Paul Brown Scholarship Fund. After he won the national championship at Ohio State in 1942, the American Football Coaches Association voted Brown its coach of the year, but he declined the award so that Bill Alexander of Georgia Tech, who was gravely ill, could receive it.

In a 1949 letter to the *Plain Dealer*, Myles Hay, Jr. said that he had written to Brown, requesting an old program or a couple autographs for his eight-year-old son, Tommy, who had been in a body cast for 17 months because of a bone disease. Instead, Brown sent a football signed by the entire team. "This incident I have just told you about probably seems insignificant to you," Hay wrote, "but words can never tell what it meant to my son."

Brown was eager to help former players—"my guys"—find coaching jobs and loath to fire his assistants. He knew that he was the butt of equipment man Morrie Kono's hilarious impersonations and secretly chuckled about them. In Cincinnati, he carried candy to pass out to children during his nightly walks.

When Brown was living in LaJolla, California after being fired by Art Modell in 1963, the public imagined him an embittered recluse, but acquaintances said he was a sparkling conversationalist over a martini, a delightful golf or gin rummy partner, and a lover of zoos who was particularly fond of aard-varks. "He had great affection for his friends," a neighbor said. "You don't run into many people like Paul Brown. The people who knew him loved him."

Still, Brown's harsh reputation preceded him when he became head coach in Cincinnati in 1968. After losing their first game by twenty-four points, the Bengals cowered in the locker room. Said center Bob Johnson, "I expected him to come in screaming, but he was always in control. He came in and said, 'Wasn't bad. Could have been worse.' That was it. He knew we needed the encouragement."

The American Football League had granted Cincinnati a franchise two years earlier, and Brown spend that time evaluating hundreds of résumés from coaches. Costello, who had been traded to the New York Giants, hadn't considered applying, but he was among the first men Brown offered a job. He played two more seasons and then joined the Bengal staff.

Costello learned that "you could never work for a better guy." He says that Brown was not a great "X and O guy" but hired outstanding tacticians, and his discipline and organization made coaching easy.

Coaching for Brown was much like playing for him, Costello says. "I don't think I felt like I had a real great relationship with him when I played for him, but he really enjoyed seeing his old players come back," he says. "I think that meant a lot to him. I was the only coach he had on the staff who was an ex-player, and I think he liked that."

Under Brown, Costello had developed into one of the league's better middle linebackers. Aggressive, intelligent, athletic, he played in the shadows of some of the top middle linebackers in NFL history: Dick Butkus, Sam Huff, Ray Nitschke, Tommy Nobis, and Joe Schmidt.

"He has the speed for the job and is an extremely sure tackler. Vince has the right attitude, too. We're very pleased with him." Brown said in 1957. That year, *Newsweek* called Costello "Cleveland's defensive discovery of the year," and the Browns returned to the NFL title game after a year's absence. Costello was the team's starting middle linebacker for a decade.

In 1963, the team's first year without Brown, Costello intercepted more passes—seven—than any other linebacker in the league, and as the

Browns won the Eastern Conference in 1965, he saved three games with interceptions.

Before Cleveland met favored Baltimore for the championship in 1964, *Sports Illustrated* predicted that an important aspect of the game would be how well Baltimore's line handled Costello on running plays. The Colts gained only 92 yards rushing, and Costello picked off a pass in the 27-0 win. "We had a tough, undersized linebacker named Vince Costello," Jim Brown said, "and Vince kicked some ass."

Two years later, Costello was shipped to New York in a contract dispute with Modell. He started for the Giants in 1967, but missed most of the next season with a knee injury.

Surprised when Brown invited him to Cincinnati, he couldn't believe the freedom Brown gave a first-year assistant coach. "He said, 'We have some young linebackers here. Let's see what you can do with them,'" Costello says. He molded Bill Bergey, Al Beauchamp, and Jim LeClair into important contributors to AFC Central Division title teams in 1969 and 1973.

When Costello resigned in 1974 to become defensive coordinator of the Super Bowl champion Miami Dolphins, he saw a different side of Brown. Brown was miffed at Costello, as he had been in the past with assistants who left for new jobs.

"I lost a little glitter with Paul," he says, "but it was a chance for me to get a coordinator's job and to work with Don Shula, who had coached for Paul Brown."

Over the next several years, an even less flattering portrait of Brown emerged. Former tight end Bob Trumpy said that year after year, Brown, who had worn a stylish leather jacket to practice at OSU, dressed for workouts in the same rumpled slacks and T-shirt.

Reprising old allegations, writers said that he had lost touch with his players, and a Bengal executive complained, "In this organization, there is only one vote, and Paul Brown has it." He was accused of diagramming 12-man formations and talking about plays that Cincinnati didn't run.

In 1974, Brown charged Houston Oiler head coach Sid Gillman with violating league rules by failing to send game films to Cincinnati before the teams played. The 63-year-old Gillman snapped to a reporter, "Tell him to keep his mouth shut. He's getting senile."

During the game, the crowd in the Astrodome chanted "senile old man." According to a writer who covered the Bengals at the time, Brown cried.

As they had throughout his career, some in the media searched for cracks in Brown's glacial facade.

"A newspaperman's delight" as a young head coach at Ohio State, where a writer called him "easy to meet, wholesome in his opinions, direct in his statements," Brown seemed to grow more wary of the press in professional football. As long as he was successful, the media treated him gingerly.

"People said about Paul Brown that you played out of fear and that he was too negative," Costello says. "I guess when you won, he wasn't too negative, and when you lost, he was too negative."

Brown's longtime friend Paul Hornung, former sports editor of the *Columbus Dispatch*, once called the coach "a private man in a public profession." If Hornung was right, Brown's reticence sometimes showed itself in smugness. He tolerated local writers as long as they acted as cheerleaders but shunned any unfamiliar reporter because "I've been nipped too many times."

Brown repeatedly advised his players, "When you win say little, but when you lose, say still less." He said reporters didn't know much about the game, and he didn't have time to explain the details to them.

He could be dryly condescending, as when one writer dutifully printed Brown's assertion that he "liked to maintain an approximate fifty-three to forty-seven percent ratio between runs and passes."

Brown could also be hostile. In 1971, he expelled from the Bengals training camp a magazine writer who had once published a "hatchet job" profile of Vince Lombardi, whom Brown counted among his close friends. Before a roomful of journalists, he led the writer to a door, lecturing him that the recently-deceased Lombardi had been "a credit to the game" and had "literally died for pro football." Brown said, "You are not welcome in our football camp. I will ask you to leave."

Ironically, Brown was much less adroit than Lombardi with the press. Whereas Brown dismissed them, Lombardi alternately charmed and intimidated reporters. By the early 1960s, Lombardi's reputation had surpassed Brown's.

Brown wasn't the firebrand who exhorted others to great deeds or the hard and ready defender of the old days and the old ways; he advocated no world view other than the Darwinian capitalism he trotted out whenever it suited him. To an audience who paid to see elemental passion, Brown symbolized dispassion.

Brown was the theorist in the game whose primary attraction has always been physical, a figure of icy resolve in a culture that, more and more, celebrated the emotions, the joyless suit who saw that the remittance notice was in the mail box and the payment duly recorded. He was the first wizard of the game's modern age, and when he faltered, he was renounced as only a man who has once been called a genius can be.

Consciously or unconsciously, Brown helped create his own bloodless persona. "I sure don't want to lose the image of being the cool, deadly, brutal, calculating Brown," he said. "You know that would be bad." At the height of the coach's fame, a *Plain Dealer* columnist called him "the least artificial human I have ever seen in my twenty years of sports writing," but Brown's own players frequently couldn't tell where the genuine man ended and the shrewdly fabricated coach began.

Said former Bengal head coach Bruce Coslet, who both played and coached under Brown, "He wanted to be portrayed, deep down in his heart, as a stingy, cantankerous old guy. He really enjoyed playing that role, but he wasn't like that at all."

A celebrity for more than fifty years, Brown gave the public ample time to judge him. Lombardi's unexpected death—seventeen days before he was to open his second season as head coach of the Redskins—fixed his legend. Brown lived long enough to be seen as both mastermind and crank. In fact, Brown said, he came to be discriminated against. "If we won, it was in spite of how old I was," he said. "If

we lost, it was because I was too old."

He said, "I got so damn engrossed that all of a sudden, I pinched myself and woke up, and I was getting along in years. It goes so fast when you're so wrapped up in it."

Brown, 67, retired as head coach on New Year's Day 1976. Still the team's general manager and part-owner, he named Bill "Tiger" Johnson rather than Bill Walsh to succeed him. Together, Brown and Walsh had modernized the old Cleveland Brown offense into the moving pocket and controlled passing that pro teams still use.

Walsh had even begun calling many of the Bengals' plays, a privilege Brown had always jealously guarded. Brown never explained bypassing Walsh, but some close to the team said he recognized in the younger coach someone as imperious as himself.

As he had said to Weeb Ewbank when the assistant coach left Cleveland in 1954 to become head coach of the Colts, Brown told Walsh that he would never be a successful head coach in the NFL. Walsh became offensive coordinator in San Diego, but not before angrily saying that Brown was "filled with poison" and had an almost "warlike nature." He eventually won three Super Bowls, two of them over the Bengals, as head coach of the San Francisco 49ers.

Brown was soon accused of

meddling with Johnson, much as Modell had meddled with Brown himself. He denied the charges but said that he reviewed game films with Johnson every Monday morning. "We'll talk over the things we see," Brown said. "The ultimate decision comes back to me. Nobody is cut unless I say something. Nobody is kept without my say." Five games into his third season, Johnson resigned, despite having an overall winning record.

Costello, however, says that Brown never once interfered with how he handled the Bengal linebackers. Long criticized for ignoring any idea that wasn't his own, Brown held the staff accountable for its views, Costello says, but listened carefully to everything his assistants said.

"When I started coaching, Paul set up the format. I just followed the format. He turned me loose on the coaching part," Costello says. "I respected him, and he knew I respected him. He knew I was an outspoken, candid guy, and I think he respected that in me. I had a good relationship with Paul."

Drawing invisible football formations with a forefinger on the interior of the gleaming white Mercedes-Benz in which he was being chauffeured around northeastern Ohio, Costello was animated. Occasionally, he smacked the dashboard to underscore a point about

taking on a block or reading the quarterback draw or choosing between covering the swing or hook route on short passes. He was like an intense high school teacher, a job he held every off-season while he played in Cleveland. In contrast to his vehemence, Costello's face is jovial. Blue-eyed, his nose squashed, he looked like Robert DeNiro playing Jack LaMotta at the end of *Raging Bull*.

The jolly hustler planned to market action figures of Hall of Fame players. He was on his way to show the prototype to Lou Groza. Eating breakfast with a gang of his hometown cronies at a Rax near Magnolia, winding through traffic on I-77, over lunch with Groza and Ed Modzelewski at an upscale restaurant in Rocky River, in Dante Lavelli's furniture store, at the Browns' headquarters, at the home of his father-in-law, who played quarterback on Paul Brown's first undefeated Massillon team, Costello talked about his old coach.

Costello left Miami after a year to work with his closest friend, former Cleveland teammate Paul Wiggin, who had been named head coach in Kansas City. When the Chiefs failed to win, the relationship between the two men fell apart. Costello quit and for twenty years, ran a popular restaurant, Costello's Greenhouse, in Kansas City.

Costello says that he has never stopped being "a Paul Brown guy." He says he liked Brown and "kind of understood him," but to Costello, as to many others, much about the coach remains enigmatic.

As well it might.

He was the suave, austere Coach Brown who frightened his players, the cruel chief executive who discarded honored veterans the first time they displeased him, the hypocrite who seized credit and assigned blame, the tiresome codger who lived among ghosts from his long-ago salad days.

He was the brilliant, compassionate Paul Brown who was devastated when his first wife died, who loved music, children, and the cornfields around the Bengals training camp in Wilmington, who amused his staff with yarns about his illustrious career, who once did the "Ickey Shuffle" in the locker room, who revolutionized his profession and his game.

"He had most people fooled about what he was really like," said Walsh, who recovered from his disappointment to acknowledge that he built his San Francisco teams on the model Brown created in Cleveland.

The reasons for Brown's contradictions seem obvious. He was the little fellow forced to control giants. He was the son imbued with his father's need for order. He was the *nouveau riche* commoner trying to fit in with old money. He was the manchild frightened by the unknown. He was the perfectionist, as someone once remarked, caught in an imperfect world, worried that others might find out that he wasn't perfect.

Such psychobabble leads nowhere, though. Vince Costello spent eleven seasons with Brown and holds a master's degree in counseling, but he can't so much as compare the coach with anyone. "Paul Brown was unique," he says. "I can't think of anybody like him. Nobody. I would say he had the charisma of a college president, but he was definitely a football coach, and I don't know many people like that."

In the end, only Paul Brown knew what he was seeking or why he was seeking it.

# Vince COSTELLO

**"** MY MOM AND DAD CAME OVER from the Old Country, through Ellis Island. My mother was 16 years old, and she had a sister who was living in Canton. My dad worked in the coal mines when miners got paid by the car, for every car they loaded with coal. He couldn't read or write his name. He spoke English, though. He said if you live in this country for ten years, learn to speak English or get the hell out.

I was the youngest of seven kids. My mother sent me to school when I was five. We had a coal stove, and I used to hide behind it and fall asleep all the time. She said, 'You're big enough to go to school.' So I went to school. They never kicked me out, so I stayed.

Everyone I played against was older than me. I started as a centerfielder and leadoff hitter on the high school baseball team when I was 13 years old. Other guys were playing Little League, and I was playing high school baseball. I graduated when I was 16. In the long run, it helped me. I went to college, played professional baseball, got called to the service, and I was still young enough to play football.

I got in this discussion the other night with my niece. Her kids were not good athletes, but she got involved and got on the coaches' butts all the time. I told her, 'You don't know anything. You don't even know what you don't know.' My mom and dad, when they came to the games, they just sat up there and enjoyed them. When I came home, they didn't ask me how many points I had, they didn't ask me how many hits I got, and I enjoyed every minute of it.

311

I got my master's degree in counseling, and I've thought a lot about what a parent's job is. A parent's job is to find out what your kid is good at and help him progress. That's what started that conversation with my niece. She said, 'My boy is not going to play football. I said he can't play, and I'm the boss. I'm not going to let him get out there and get killed.'

I said, 'What if my parents had said that? What would have happened to me?'

I was never embarrassed by my parents coming to the games and yelling and screaming, so I was able to enjoy everything I did in sports. I loved playing, and no one was going to keep me from playing, and so I went as far as I could go.

I was an athletic guy from day one. I played basketball, baseball or football every morning and swam every afternoon. We played tackle football in the fields, and my brother and I played 'bunt' in the streets. We'd get a bunch of guys together and argue and scrap. You'd be pitching to some little guy and not letting him hit the ball, and someone would yell, 'Who do you think you are, Bob Feller? Let him hit the ball.' You'd pitch easier. We'd play all morning, and the score would end up like 35-24. We batted twenty times in one day.

We'd put a bushel basket up in the rafter of a barn and play. There was so much dust you'd be all black when you came out, your mouth full of dust. We sneaked into school by sliding down the coal chute and played basketball until the janitor came and kicked us out.

I DIDN'T PLAY FOOTBALL until I was a junior in high school. We had to threaten a strike for them to give us football. There was no reason we shouldn't have had football. Everybody else around here had it. We just wanted to play. We told the principal, 'We're not going to come to school until you get us football,' so they got us six-man football.

We ended up with fifteen or twenty guys on the team. My junior year we weren't very good, but my senior year, we beat everybody bad. We played Lafferty, Scio, Jewett, all those little Ohio towns. You had a center, two ends, a quarterback, and two backs. I was a quarterback. Two men had to handle the ball on every play, and anyone was eligible for a pass or could carry the ball, including the center.

We had a play where the center would give me the ball, and I'd give it right back to him. We'd do a lot of the basic T-formation type things: little passes over the middle, straight hand-offs to the backs, passes to the ends.

There weren't a whole lot of things you could do. We weren't bad for a wee little school. There were only twenty-two kids in my graduating class.

I never had any plans for after high school. I just played and loved it, and after I was done playing, a coach I had played against took me down to Ohio U. I went there to play basketball. I had a scholarship, one where you work for your room and board. I really didn't know what I wanted to be, so I majored in physical education. When I got down there I decided to go out for football. My freshman year, I played football, basketball, and baseball. I practiced every day of the year except Thanksgiving.

There were a hundred guys out for football. I was one of the monkeys. I had my little helmet with my name taped on the back, and no one knew who the hell I was. The first freshman game was at Bowling Green, and I didn't make the trip. The second freshman game was at Pitt, and I didn't make the trip. Now, we're going to play the third freshman game at Miami of Ohio. In practice I was cannon fodder, playing Miami's defense. There was a kid from Powhatan Point playing fullback, a big slow guy. I was about 195 pounds then, and I was pretty quick. There was nothing they could do to block me. I could get away from the guards, and I could hit the fullback any time. I nailed him a bunch of times and had a really good scrimmage. From that one scrimmage, the coaches were giving me respect. I went from not making the trip to Miami to starting the game as a linebacker.

THERE WAS A GUY NAMED BOXCAR BAILEY, who went to Hamilton High School. He wasn't a very good player, but he had a big reputation. He played for Miami, and that day, I had two of those real nice tackles on him, where you just pick the guy up in the air and put him down. I was just lucky, but the coaches were impressed, because they thought the guy was a really good player, and he wasn't. He stopped just before you hit him. He came to the Browns, and he got cut right away. But he had the reputation. After that, I had the coaches' attention, and I started at linebacker as a sophomore.

We were never a bad team, but we were always a 6-3 kind of team. My junior year we lost to Miami, our big rival, in the last six seconds. Ara Parseghian was the head coach. Carmen Cozza, who became the coach at Yale, caught a long pass to about our six-yard line, and on fourth down, John Pont, who coached at Indiana and Northwestern, took it in. They beat us 6-0. If we would've won that game, we would've won the championship.

When I got out of college, my coach took me down to Cincinnati. I hit and ran and fielded, and after I got done, I signed a contract with the Reds. They sent me to Burlington, Iowa. Johnny Vander Meer was my manager. Then I got called into the service. I spent two years in the service, and that's when I decided I was going to try football. Howard Brinker had been my defensive coach in college. He had gone with the Browns. I contacted him, because I knew he had liked me as a player and thought I was a pretty good athlete. And he signed me when I was coming out of the service. I signed for $6,000.

I KNEW THEY WERE A GOOD TEAM, but I didn't follow the Browns that close. I was more into baseball. I signed with the Browns because I could find out in two or three weeks whether or not I was going to make it. You go to training camp, and you either make it or you don't. I could have played baseball for five years and maybe never made it to the big leagues. I didn't want to waste all that time in baseball if I wasn't going to make it.

I was a long shot to make it with the Browns. I got out of the service, and I used leave I had accumulated to go play baseball. I had signed a contract with the Reds and a contract with the Browns. I had sixty days' leave coming. I called the Reds and told them I had leave coming and that I'd really like to play baseball. I didn't tell them that I had signed a football contract. They sent me to Wausau, Wisconsin. I went to Wausau and played baseball for May and June. I was getting out of the service June 30, and the Browns went to camp in August.

We're playing in Wausau, and I walked. It was a rainy, chilly night. Guy behind me got a single, and I rounded second, and I felt a little twinge. Next time up, I walked again, and the guy behind me got a single. This time, when I rounded second and went into third, my hamstring snapped. Now, I can't play baseball anymore. I'm on the bench.

I go back and get discharged. That's when I told the Reds I was going to go with the Browns. I'm going to try to play football with that hamstring pull. I was solid black and blue from my ankle to my ass.

Paul Brown called me in and said, 'There's no way you're going to make this football team. I'll get you a coaching job. Why don't you go and coach and get better and come back next year?'

That's what I did.

I didn't know much about Paul Brown when I signed with them. I knew he was from Massillon and Ohio State. I knew that. I liked his style. I was impressed with his practices and I was impressed that everybody was afraid to death of him. Now, when you get older and you're done playing, everybody likes him. But when you're playing, he's a horse's ass because he chews you out. I've always been a Paul Brown guy.

He was never a yeller or a screamer, but he was sharp and curt: 'Just so you know. We won't tolerate that here.'

One time, he got on Bill Quinlan's butt. He said, 'They didn't want you at Michigan State, they didn't want you in the military, and we're sure as hell not going to put up with you here.'

But he would also turn his head to a lot of off-field things. Paul weighed the bullshit against how much a guy hurt or helped the team. As good as Jim Brown was, he could've done about anything and gotten away with it.

They took my picture the year I reported to the Browns. I still have it. I'm wearing number 68 (instead of 50, which he wore throughout his career). They thought I was just going through the motions. Here I was, rookie, free agent, new position. I had been out of football for four years.

They put me right in there to see if I could be a middle linebacker or not, before all these guys who were drafted and everything. They put me in, and I never came out. When I reported to the Browns, it was the beginning of the 4-3 defense, and I was the perfect guy for it. I was 225 pounds. I was athletic. I had good footwork. I could open my hips and run and cover.

I played the first exhibition game against the Detroit Lions. They're running all those crossing patterns. Guys are going everywhere. I thought I was in the middle of a freeway.

ONCE YOU GET IT DOWN, though, you got it. You can see the outside flare, the inside flare. You know you have the inside flare. You have help on the outside flare. I used to have these hundred percent rules. Nobody else knew them. The coaches didn't even know them. If I had a weakside drop in a zone, there's a back and a wide receiver to that side. If the back does an outside flare, and I'm dropping to that zone in the middle, I know the only route that affects me is a turn-in.

I always had the rule: 'If the quarterback throws a turn-in with an outside flare, it's like throwing the ball to me.' I'd go back with the intention of getting that ball just like we're playing catch. I'm going to get that ball. Just like the receiver thinks he's going to get it, I think I'm going to get it. If he doesn't throw it to the receiver, there ain't nothing I can do about it anyway except come up and help out on the flare they throw to the back. That was a hundred percent rule.

Another thing that was a hundred percent rule was when the quarterback takes those first two steps back, you can look, turn your head, because he's never throwing anything quicker than a two-step drop for a quick out. Now, if they flare both backs out of the backfield, and the center blocks back, trap blocks, you know damn well it's not a pass. They're not going to send two backs out of the backfield with the center blocking aggressive and still throw the ball, because they need help to pick up the blitz. The center's got to be the one to pick up the blitz.

At first, when those two backs flared, I would fly out of there. The way I learned that was my first year, we played Detroit in the championship game. Bobby Layne got hurt, and Tobin Rote played. They knew what I would do when the backs flared. They just flared those two backs out of there, and they'd block the center on our tackle, send their tackle down on me, and Tobin Rote would run that quarterback draw.

Six years later, I remember that shit. I remember: 'They run two backs out of the backfield, you see an aggressive block from the center, you get your ass up in there, because there ain't no way it's a pass.' Bobby Layne runs that same play on about the 20-yard line. I tackle him for a three- or four-yard loss. He jumps up and yells at me, 'What the hell are you guys doing?'

They didn't have a chance. I had all of those rules, and I called on them. I knew the X's and O's real well. I understood the game.

I KNEW I WAS GOING TO MAKE THAT TEAM. Galen Fiss was there, a good player and a good guy, could very well have been the most valuable player in the 1964 championship game. Walt Michaels was there, and Chuck Noll was there. Those were the three linebackers. There were some other guys there, but I felt like I did when I was in college: I was a better athlete than those guys. I could run good. They saw I had good footwork and flexibility. In those days, I could get down in a three-point stance on the line and cover the closest guy out of the backfield all the way down the field. I thought I could do that as good as anybody. I'd get down in that three-point stance, off-set the center. I'd play it soft. If they wedged me out, I had Don Colo and Bob Gain on either side of me

I felt very confident, but nobody else thought I had a chance. I didn't know until the last minute if I was going to make it. They only carried thirty-five players in those days. Everybody said that the Browns never kept any rookies. But the year before, '56, they had a bad year, and I was fortunate to come in right after that. There was another guy, named Roger Zatkoff, who the Browns had traded for. So they had four veteran linebackers. I'm the one who's playing middle linebacker all the time.

We were playing the San Francisco 49ers, ahead by two touchdowns with two minutes to go. They score a touchdown. We fumble the damn kickoff. Now, they come out, and they have Hugh McElhenney. They run a screen. I played it perfect. I read it, I went to make the tackle, and I missed him. He goes 57 yards for a touchdown and we lose the game.

In those days, we used to take a trip to LA and San Francisco. We'd play Frisco, then we'd fly down to LA and stay in a hotel all week, practice, play the Rams, come home, and that's the end of training camp.

San Francisco is a Sunday game. We have Monday off. We're staying at this real nice Hyatt in Palo Alto. We go in there, and I say, 'I'm gone,' because they all said, 'You make one mistake, and you're gone.'

Paul Wiggin said, 'Nah, you're not gone.'

I JUST THOUGHT I COULDN'T MAKE A MISTAKE. We had to chart every play. They'd have an overhead projector. They'd put the play up on a screen. We'd draw the play, then draw the coverage in. Defensive back Warren Lahr and those guys would go in there, and it would take them ten minutes. I used to think, 'How do they do that? They can't be doing it. How the heck do those guys know that? How am I supposed to keep up with them?' It used to take me a long time. I didn't even know pro formations then. It took me a long time to get it all. Now, I can do it in a second, but not then.

So we go in the meeting room that Tuesday morning after we played Frisco, about 9 o'clock. Paul Brown said, 'We traded Roger Zatkoff this morning to the Detroit Lions. We're going to go with the four linebackers we've got.' I about passed out. The other three guys are veterans. Galen was in his second year. Walt Michaels was in his sixth or seventh year. Chuck Noll was probably in his fourth or fifth year. They didn't think anything of it. Me, I went from the outhouse to the penthouse.

O yeah, Paul Brown flipped me off. Yeah, he put the needle to me. One time, he said to me, 'Either you slipped a lot in one year, or your ankle's really bothering you.' I had played against the Bears on a bad ankle. I had Novocain in it. I didn't have a good game, and we got our butts kicked. The

Bears kicked the shit out of us. Another time, when I was coaching for him in Cincinnati, we had a guy named Boobie Clark, and we got into a big discussion about why we weren't protecting the passer. On a blitz, Boobie Clark just didn't pick up the block. That was it. He just didn't pick up the blitz. Paul Brown liked Boobie Clark, and when he's got a guy he likes, sometimes he protects him a little bit.

It's a staff meeting. All the coaches are looking at this game film. He's going on and on about this. Finally, I said, 'There's no question about it. The guy misses the blitzer. That's all it is. Boobie Clark missed his assignment. He does his job, and we're okay.'

I wasn't even an offensive coach. It was just the way he was protecting Boobie and making a big issue for everyone else.

He said, 'And just what the hell would you like me to do about it?'

I said, 'I'd like to see you give Boobie Clark an ass-chewing just like you would any other player who missed that play.'

He said, 'Well, if you don't like it, you know what you can do.'

I said, 'Yeah, I can leave,' and I started to get up and leave, and he said, 'Sit your butt down.'

I just kind of understood him. I really liked him. As a coach, you could never work for a better guy.

I had absolutely no problem with Paul Brown over my contracts. He almost always gave me exactly what I asked for, but in those days, we weren't asking for millions. After my first year, they gave me a $3,000 or $3,300 raise. Everyone said, 'Vince, no one ever gets a $3,000 raise.'

Five figures was the big thing then. If you got five figures, that was big money. I never had a hard time with Paul Brown over money. I did with Modell. I started off bad with Modell right from the start, because I knew he gave some guys increases in salary for talking against Brown. I just wanted to make sure I got what they got. That's something that Bernie Parrish put in his book, that I was against Brown, and I wasn't. I didn't like Modell.

PEOPLE ACCUSED PAUL OF BEING PREDICTABLE. In my opinion, he was falsely accused. 'We knew what you were going to do' is probably the oldest cliché in football. They say the same thing in every city. First of all, ninety percent of the fans don't know anything about it. We used to run that fullback slant with Jim Brown, and Jim Brown averaged 5.1 per carry. Everyone in the league knew he was going to get the football. The thing is, you work on it until you can do it perfectly. Jim Brown could come down the line of scrimmage and read where the blocks were going and cut up into that hole. Everyone is going one way, and he cuts back the other. He's going to make some yards. How many times did Lombardi run that same sweep to Paul Hornung? Nobody said he ran it too many times, because he was *winning*.

The way the plays are run today, you run to daylight. The linemen block out, hit somebody, take them where they want to go, and the back runs off the blocks. He reads the blocks, and with footwork and acceleration, he comes off the blocks.

People keep saying, 'We knew what you were going to do.' Hell, the *players* don't even know where they're going. How do the fans know? You never know until the blocking scheme develops. I mean, there's one back back there now, and if they're going to run it, *he's* going to carry it. That's no great revelation. But don't say you know *where* he's going to run it. He *himself* doesn't know.

That's all press stupidity. They make stories up. They want to criticize, and they don't know what they don't know. Anybody who makes that statement, that's the first indication they don't know a lot about football.

DUB JONES USED TO HAVE THIS PHILOSOPHY. A receiver has three moves. You've got a take-off, one where you go to the right, and one where you go to the left. You come down, you freeze that defensive back, and you've got three ways to go. If you do it good, make your cuts sharp, he doesn't know which way you're going.

Football isn't out-fooling somebody. It's out-executing them. The game is a game of angles. If the defensive halfback is *there*, and the receiver comes down and makes a direct ninety-degree cut, the defensive back backs up and then comes across *here*, and we meet at the crossroads. But if the receiver comes back a little bit when he makes his cut, he has about a yard and a half head start on a three-yard sprint. They said Fred Biletnikoff (Hall of Fame Raider receiver) didn't have any athletic ability. But Biletnikoff had the ability to make that move, make that guy give up that yard and a half, and accelerate back to the football. And the defensive back has to come over his shoulder every time to get at the football.

In retrospect—and I never thought about this when I was playing—we had Jimmy Brown, Bobby Mitchell, and Ed Modzelewski all at the same time. He should've put Bobby Mitchell at wide receiver with Ray Renfro and put Ed Modzelewski at fullback. Mo could block and catch and run the ball. I'd rather let Jim Brown carry the ball thirty times than let him carry it fifteen and Bobby Mitchell carry it fifteen. Jim was a horse. He could carry it thirty times. You didn't need a second guy to carry the ball with Jim Brown, and if you did, Mo could get good hard yards. Bobby Mitchell would've been great at wide receiver.

We always had a lot of good players, but we could never find a quarterback. Milt Plum wasn't quite good enough. Somehow, he didn't have the confidence. He wasn't strong in the huddle. We had a guy named Jim Ninowski. We traded him to Detroit, and then we traded Plum to Detroit and got Ninowski back again. Milt was a rookie with me. We had Tommy O'Connell that year. He was one of those cocky guys, threw the ball real accurate. We won the division championship with him. Well, what happened was Tommy O'Connell broke his leg. This is what really bothered Paul Brown. It was either Thursday or Friday night before the championship game, after practice, and Milt has someone throw him a long pass. He's running after it, and he pulls a hamstring. We ended up playing that game with a guy named John Borton, a smart guy and a good guy but not so hot as a quarterback. I think he was a linebacker one year at Ohio State. We got our butts kicked by Detroit.

IT DIDN'T SHOCK ME when Paul Brown got fired. We had heard all the rumors. I knew that Modell was looking for an excuse to fire him. The papers were on strike. It was a perfect time to fire him.

Modell's got some balls. I don't know where his balls come from, stupidity or what. Let me tell you something, and it was Paul who told me this. Modell said he was a big TV guy. He got Carling Black Label beer to back him, and he had the option to buy, so as he got money, he was able to buy that stock. He didn't know much. He didn't have money. He was just the right guy in the right spot. All those guys who wanted to sell their stock were older guys. Paul said he couldn't stop them from selling. He didn't own enough of the Browns to stop the sale.

I always said that the guy who fired Paul Brown was Art Modell. That's what got me in trouble. As a matter of fact, Art Modell called me in the office and said, 'That's libel if you continue to say things like that.' What happened was there was this sports writer for the *Canton Repository* who called me, and I said, 'Hey, I'm not making any statements. Don't print this, but Art's the guy who fired Paul Brown.' It got back to Art through Hal Lebowitz, who was Art's crony and a sportswriter. The Canton sportswriter must've said something to Hal Lebowitz at a baseball game.

See, the newspaper was on strike at the time, and the Cleveland management came out and made it look like it was a player revolt. There was no player revolt. I was there. There was always talk about Brown, but there was no revolt. Nobody threatened to quit. What I think Art Modell did was give those guys—Bernie Parrish and them—a little bit more in their contracts to make it look like they were conspiring. That's my interpretation. He did it to take the heat off him. Jim Brown didn't get Paul Brown fired. Bernie Parrish didn't get Paul Brown fired. Art Modell fired him, that's who fired him. He made it look like the players did it. That was the easy way of getting it out, and it made the players' egos feel good: 'Oh, I got Paul Brown fired.'

Now, there were a lot of players upset with Paul Brown. I got upset with Paul Brown at times. Guys say the wrong thing when they're not winning. Players are always looking for someone to blame, including me. You don't want to take the blame; nobody wants the blame for anything.

People said about Paul Brown that you played out of fear and that he was too negative. There's a certain amount of negativity when you coach. When you win, it's a good idea; when you lose, it's a bad idea.

You put those players together on a train to New York, and they're going to talk about a lot of things. It's the end of the season. You know you're out of it. When I was with the Browns, we never played in many games where we were out of it, but this one year, when Paul got fired, we were out of contention before the end of the year, and that's the worst time. That's when the dogs start barking.

THOSE GUYS ALL HAVE EGOS. Lombardi had an ego. Paul Brown had an ego, but Paul managed his ego pretty well. When Modell fired him, that ruined Paul's whole life. Here's a guy who's been climbing, climbing, climbing all of his life, then all of a sudden, he's got nowhere else to go.

The transition between Brown and Blanton Collier was bad. I don't want to say too much about it, but I'm not a Blanton guy. Blanton didn't particularly like me, and he did some things that I didn't think were right.

We're playing against Green Bay. Blanton starts shooting off about Ray Nitschke: 'We've got to stop Nitschke. We've got to do this. We've got to do that.' I'm getting a little teed off because he's blowing up the middle linebacker for the other team. You don't normally do that. You don't go and tell your team how great everybody else is, make your players feel lesser. After he got done, I yelled, 'Hey, the guy we've got to worry about is Lombardi. That guy is one smart son-of-a-gun. His game plan is what we've got to worry about.'

I know he heard that, and I know his assistants heard that. We didn't get into any shouting matches or anything. Nothing like that. But we never hit it off.

The easy part of the transition is that we didn't change anything. The assistant coaches were the same. The defenses were the same. I had never had that much of a football relationship with Paul, as far as game plan or anything, and neither did I have it with Blanton. I don't know how anybody could say that if Paul had still been the coach, we wouldn't have won the championship. Four guys on that team made the Hall of Fame. Paul Warfield was a rookie, and he's in the Hall of Fame. We had him at wide receiver with Gary Collins, two great wide receivers.

Gary Collins was tall and could run. He had quick feet and accelerated good and had great hands and was a great competitor. He had that little bit of arrogance, but he was good and knew he was good. He thought he could catch it better than any of them, and I think he's right.

There's three guys who came into the Browns' training camp while I was there that nobody ever doubted that they were going to be great: Jim Brown, Leroy Kelly, and Paul Warfield. Paul Warfield had the great moves, and he wasn't even an end at Ohio State. There was no great revelation that these guys were going to be tremendous. You could see it right away. They'd make that little toss to Jim Brown, and you'd see that big body moving, the acceleration.

Jim Brown was the greatest running back in the history of the game, not *one* of the best—*the* best. His average per carry was 5.1 yards. He got a first down every two times he carried the ball, and he could catch it, too. You can take O.J. Simpson, Franco Harris, and all of those guys and put them in one, and he wouldn't be as good as Jim Brown, and then they say he didn't block. He carried the ball thirty times a game. Why would you *want* him to block? Why would you waste him blocking? Why would you want anybody else to carry the ball *but* Jim Brown?

We were confident that we could beat Baltimore in the '64 title game. We never thought for a minute that we were going to get blown out. When you've got a player like Jim Brown, how can you even begin to think that? We had Groza, who was a better kicker than they had. We had better receivers than they had. We had a better team than they had. We beat them the last time we played them (34-16 in 1962). They had Unitas and John Mackey and Jimmy Orr and Lenny Moore, but we had Jim Brown and Ernie Green and Paul Warfield and Gary Collins, and Frank Ryan was a good quarterback.

We were better than Green Bay, too. We lost to Green Bay the next year in the finals, and I still think we were better than them. Our backs were better than theirs. Paul Hornung and Jim Taylor couldn't carry Jim Brown's jockstrap. We had really good offensive linemen. Gene Hickerson and John Wooten and Monte Clark and Dick Schafrath were all good. And we had a good, smart defense. It snows, it's muddy, one guy slips and falls, which costs us a touchdown. They come out the second half and had a drive for a touchdown. They beat us something like 24-10 (23-12), and we could've won that game. We just had some little things go wrong.

WE WERE A GOOD TEAM. We could beat anybody. I'm not saying we weren't capable of losing, too, because shit happens, but there's nobody we played that didn't think they had their hands full. I don't think there were a half dozen games in my whole career that we weren't in contention to win, but almost all my career in Cleveland was played with Jim Brown.

The chemistry on that team was excellent. I'm sure there were little things that happened, but we had about as good a relationship as you can have. When you're winning, you always do.

Bernie Parrish said that he put in the game plan for the championship game. The guy who put in the game plan was Howard Brinker. I'll tell you what Howard did. He drew every pattern that they had against every defense we had and then gave us a test on what those patterns were. Howard Brinker had a hard time expressing himself. He wasn't a real aggressive guy. But he knew football.

The way I got traded from the Browns in 1967 is, I think, they were looking for a reason to trade me. I was older. I was at the end of my line. We played the Minnesota Vikings, and I hadn't signed my contract yet. I played pretty good that game. They had Bob Matheson and a guy named Dale Lindsey. We won, and Art Modell comes in the locker room drunk. He says, 'When're you going to sign your contract?' We're arguing over $500.

I said, 'When are you going to put the $500 in the contract?'

He said, 'I throw $500 over the bar in one night.'

I said, 'Then why don't you take that $500 and jam it up your ass.'

First of all, he should never have come in the locker room and talked to me about my contract after a game. He could've caught me on the plane or wherever. It was right in the locker room, in front of all the players. You can ask Groza and those guys about it. They'll tell you.

I had a boys camp then, and the next Monday, I'm down at the boys camp doing some work. I got home, and my wife said, 'The Browns have been calling you all day.'

I called. They said, 'Vince, we traded you to the Giants.'

I said, 'Okay.'

I didn't ask anything else. I was playing pretty good. They were much better off with me than they were with Matheson or Lindsey. I played on know-how. I had it down to a science. I knew the blockers, the patterns, and the quarterbacks. I knew all the tendencies. There's no way they were going to get more out of Bob Matheson or Dale Lindsey than they were out of me. But they probably figured, 'Hey, down the road, we're going to have to make this move anyhow.' Obviously, if I wouldn't have said what I said, they wouldn't have traded me.

I called Earl Morrall, the Giants quarterback, asked him where they practiced, and went up there. I got there on a Wednesday. I walked into the middle of practice. They dressed me, I practiced, and on Saturday I started at middle linebacker and called the defenses. I had an interception against St. Louis, and we won the game. I had a pretty good year.

I went back the next year and in the third game I hurt my knee. We were playing Philadelphia. They ran a draw to the fullback. I had him, but he cut, and I chased him parallel to the line of scrimmage. We got to the sideline, and a defensive back went to cut him with the shoulder, and he hit me. It was a weak little pop. I didn't think I hurt it. I stayed in, went to make the next play, and it just gave out. I had an operation, and that was the end of my career. I still wanted to play. I just didn't want to sit around and watch. My knee was hurting, and I was hanging around, and I was getting to be a pain in the ass. I couldn't stand not playing.

I NEVER TALKED TO PAUL BROWN after he got fired, until he called me and said, 'Vince, I got the franchise for Cincinnati, and I'd like for you to be a coach.' I don't think I felt like I had a real great relationship with him when I played for him, but he really enjoyed seeing his old players come back. I was the only coach he had on his staff who was an ex-player, and I think he liked that.

Paul wanted the right situation to come back into football. He got the right situation, and he did a heck of a job. He owned twenty percent of the franchise, but he had total control. All the decisions were his. We were in contention right away. My first year there, '69, we won the first six games, including beating the Kansas City Chiefs the year they won the Super Bowl. We beat all good teams, too. Then Greg Cook, our quarterback, got hurt, and we were in trouble.

A big thing with Paul was you better be right about things. He didn't say it like that but you knew it was, 'Okay, you believe in this? You like this guy? Well, okay, let's go with him, but you better be right.' He'd come back some times and say, 'Hmm, that guy wasn't what we thought he was, was he?' He'd put his dig in. He'd make a comment like, 'Funny, we thought that guy was faster.' You knew he was just ripping your ass.

He knew I knew those X's and O's. Paul Brown's real strength wasn't as an X's and O's guy. There are a lot of great coaches who aren't X and O guys. But he knew who knew the X's and O's, and he knew how to organize a practice so that all you had to do was coach. I knew those X's and O's like nobody in the country. There might be some other things wrong with me, but I knew my X's and O's. When I was in Cincinnati coaching with him, he had Bill Walsh there. He knew that Bill Walsh knew those X's and O's.

THERE'S AN OLD SAYING: 'He that knows not and knows not that he knows not is a fool. Get away from him. He that knows not and knows that he knows not is ignorant. You can teach him. He who knows and knows not that he knows is asleep. Wake him. He who knows and knows that he knows is wise. Follow him.' I can give you examples of all of those guys. Don Shula is a guy who is wise. You follow him. A guy who didn't know and knew that he didn't know was Jim Lee Howell; he won a championship with the Giants in 1956. He had Landry as his defensive coach and Lombardi as his offensive coach. Jim Lee Howell didn't do any coaching. He just kept things in order. Modell—he doesn't know it, and he doesn't know he doesn't know it. He hires a coach. He doesn't know what he's hiring. He never hired a good coach. The only good coach he had, he fired, and that was Paul Brown.

Most of those big money guys think they know what it takes to be a good coach. They think they can hire anybody who's a good guy. You know, 'Oh, I like this guy.' They think it's like hiring somebody for business. It's not. A good coach has all of these certain qualities. Tone of voice is important; discipline is important; the way he organizes practice is important; his ego is important. Some of these coaches develop big egos after a while. Well, they shouldn't have ever been there. The quality of horseshitness was already there. It just doesn't come out until they get in that position.

PAUL BROWN'S STRENGTH might not've been in X's and O's, but he was strong in everything else. He was strong in organization. He had disciplined practices. They ran by the clock. With Paul, you went to practice, and everything was scheduled. You were going to be out there just so long. You knew when you were coaching that you had this much time to get this in. *Boom, boom, boom, boom, boom.* Everything was organized: 'We'll go on the field at 9 o'clock. Nine to 9:10 will be calisthenics, then we're going to have this, this, and this.' We'd practice about an hour and a half, an hour and forty minutes and be off the field.

Season's over, he comes in and says, 'I'm going to do this. I'm going to be here. I want you guys to have this done by this time. I'll be back here on this date. We'll have a meeting on this day. I want the notebooks ready to go this day. You have a month's vacation beginning on this day. We'll start training camp on this day, and we'll have our first meeting at this time.' He'd have the whole off-season planned. All you had to do was follow the schedule.

When I was coaching with him, he would sit and take notes on the films. The coaches weren't allowed to look at the film before he did, which was a really good idea, because I've been on staffs where the coaches look at the film first, and they have all their excuses ready. With Paul, we looked at the film together, in the coaches' meetings. You see it for the first time just like everybody else. That's the kind of little thing that people don't have any idea about. Guys like Modell wouldn't know anything about that.

We're playing, and we have Bob Trumpy and Kenny Anderson. Trumpy runs a crossing pattern, Anderson drops back, and someone just nails his ass. But he hangs right in there, just tough as hell, throws the ball to Trumpy. Trumpy short-arms it. Guy was coming to hit him. He could have reached out, pulled the ball in, took the lick, and we have a 12-yard first down. He short arms it, and the ball goes flying in the air, and he kind of bumps off a guy and slides away from a guy and doesn't get touched. I'm looking at the film, and I say, 'Run that back. Look at this. Look at the shot that Kenny Anderson took. He took one hell of a lick, and look what Trumpy does on the other end. Kenny Anderson might's well have thrown the ball away and not taken the hit.'

Paul said, 'Run it back again.' That's all he said.

We got into the team meeting on Tuesday, and he has this whole list of things he wants to bring up. He got them from the coaches' meetings, but it looks like he really knows all these little details. He said, 'Bob, on that 82 X-in, you did that crossing pattern. Take a look at yourself, just take a look, then take a look at what Ken Anderson went through to get you the ball, and look what you did on your end to receive it.'

Now, you know what he's referring to: the guy's chickenshit. They're going to run it again, and there's Trumpy pulling his hands in while Kenny Anderson is taking this lick. If that doesn't cure you, then you're not getting cured. That's what I'm saying about what makes a good coach. He knew just how to do it. Trumpy's sitting back there just squirming around. No other coach might look at it that way or manipulate it that way.

OOO, HE HAD AN UNBELIEVABLE GRASP of human nature. He had a great sense of people, boy. He knew who to get rid of. We made one of the best trades we ever made in Cincinnati. We traded a guy named Paul Robinson, who was Rookie of the Year but really wasn't that good a ballplayer, and a guy named Fred Willis, from Boston College, for Ron Pritchard and Charley Joiner. Fred Willis wasn't a bad player. He was tough, good blocker, but one time, we played the Pittsburgh Steelers, and Fred Willis didn't carry the ball much. We win. Everybody's in the locker room happy, but Fred Willis is over there pouting because he didn't carry the ball much. I looked at that, and I just thought, 'That's it for Fred Willis.' That's the worst thing that can happen.

You can't be selfish. Don't get me wrong. There's competitive juices that'll piss you off and make things happen, but when you win, that's the ultimate goal. Everything else is secondary to that.

Paul wasn't much different to work for than he was to play for. I respected him, and he knew I respected him. He knew I was an outspoken guy, and I think he respected that in me. I had a good relationship with Paul, and I had a good relationship with Mike Brown.

When I started coaching, Paul set up the format. I just followed the format. He turned me loose on the coaching part. He said, 'Let's see what you can do. We have some young linebackers here. Let's see what you can do with them. I think you can bring some of these guys along pretty good.'

Let me tell you something about playing linebacker. If the defense makes penetration and the back is running parallel to the line of scrimmage, it's easy to come up and knock the shit out of him. Your daughter can make that tackle. It's like knocking down a bowling pin. Everybody goes, 'Ooo, did you see that?' When the back is coming right at you, and you're coming off a block, you want to accelerate into him, stick your shoulder in there and knock him down. Now it's second and eight or second and seven. You might take a shot from a knee in the pit of your neck. You might take the guy's helmet sideways. If you want to make it easy on yourself, you just put this arm out in front of him and this arm behind him, drag him down from behind. But instead of second and eight, it's second and five. That's the difference between getting a plus or a minus on the defense. Less than three yards, the defense gets a plus; more than three yards, the defense gets a minus. They're both tackles, but there's a difference.

Another thing is, you play a zone defense, and you go back into the zone. Some guys will drag ass back into the zone. You go back into the zone, you take your feet back with you, you turn, open up and flex those knees and get ready to explode up. If the ball is thrown to a back in front of you, your job is to get up there, not necessarily to make the tackle. If the guy cuts back, you make the tackle. If he doesn't, you help out with the tackle on the outside. You get guys who will never turn and flex their knees. They never come up to give the help and never want to. You have to do all the little things right to help the defense.

Most people don't even realize that the game of football is played on one foot. When you walk, you've always got one foot in the air. When you run, you've always got one foot in the air. Now, if you're the guard in a three-point stance, you come out after me with that first foot. That foot's in the air. Me, as a linebacker, I've got to get you right there. *Boom!* Because if you get that next foot into me, you leverage off of me and push off. Those are the kinds of things you have to work on.

You have to beat the fold block by the guard before he gets that foot planted and gets into you. If you're into him and you push up on him, you have a chance to make a play, but if he gets that foot planted and leans into you, then he's going to move you out of there.

Jim Brown asked me one time why I thought he was so good, and I gave him this whole theory. He listened and said, 'Hmm, I've got to think about that.' I'll tell you one thing about Jim Brown: Jim Brown was a shuffler. God blessed him with the ability to move those feet real quick. His feet were never far off the ground, so he always had a chance to get that good leverage into you. That's how he could hit that forearm into you, knock you back, bounce off you. He could accelerate from a standing position quicker than anyone ever could. One step, he's full blast. He was always going full speed, and you only had a tiny bit of room to catch him with his foot off the ground.

And what do coaches say: 'Get those knees up high! Get those knees up high!' That's bullshit. All the great runners are stand-up runners: O.J., Gale Sayers, Jim Brown. Coaches say, 'Get low! Hit that line of scrimmage!' That's left over from the old single-wing offense.

IN CINCINNATI, I helped draft Jim LeClair. Bill Bergey came the first year I was there. He was one of the best linebackers I ever coached. When I left there, we had good linebackers and a really good defensive team. We lost to Miami in the playoffs the year after they went undefeated. We had real good players. We had Mike Reid and Sherman White. We had Ron Carpenter and Royce Berry, two journeymen with good speed. Ron Pritchard was a great player. Al Beauchamp was a good cover guy. We had great cornerbacks: Lemar Parrish and Ken Riley. Tommy Casanova was the free safety and Neal Craig was the strong safety. A very good defensive team.

I don't think Paul Brown had any trouble adjusting to the players when he was in Cincinnati. In fact, I would say that the players in Cincinnati probably gave him less trouble than his players in Cleveland. And he didn't change much. He handled things pretty much the same way as he always had.

I don't think there's been all that big a change in the players in the National Football League. People like to say that. Obviously, they're a lot bigger now, but they play in the National Football League because of their quickness. An offensive tackle can be 350 pounds, and if he doesn't have quick feet, he's not going to play. You have to have the right ability for your position. A running back has to be able to accelerate, a linebacker has to have quick arms and hands to attack somebody blocking him, a defensive lineman has to have quick hands and acceleration out of a three-point stance.

Mass times acceleration equals thrust. You take a 200-pounder and put him on a quickness scale at a four, *pow*, you have 800 pounds of thrust at the point of impact. If you beef that guy up to 250, but you drop one notch on the quickness scale, that's 750 pounds of thrust. Strength comes from quickness, and players play in the National Football League because they're quick. Now, if they're big *and* quick, that's another thing.

The attitudes of the players are certainly different, with all the show-boating and everything. That probably bothers me more than anything. Paul always said, 'Act like you've been here before.'

The equipment manager in Cincinnati was Tom Gray. In Cleveland, the equipment manager was Morrie Kono. Paul sort of broke in Morrie Kono, and Tom Gray worked for Morrie Kono. Morrie had this very organized system. When Tom Gray applied for the equipment manager's job in Cincinnati, he wrote to Paul Brown and said, 'I can do it just like Morrie. In fact, I even know where you keep your rubber galoshes.' And Paul hired him.

I PLAYED TWELVE YEARS OF FOOTBALL, and there's no guarantee I would even have made it in baseball. I see these first basemen in the Major Leagues today, and I can't see myself competing with them. But I can picture myself playing middle linebacker in the National Football League even today.

I enjoyed all the time I played in Cleveland. I'm not so sure Cleveland was a special place to play, but I think it was as good as any other place. I thought the people in Cleveland were great fans. They were loyal. They supported you on the field and off.

Those old NFL teams had the blue-collar fans. The AFL teams and all of these teams that came in later, like Cincinnati, had a completely different fan. Pittsburgh, Cleveland, Baltimore before they went to Indianapolis—those were the blue-collar fans. Those were the steel mill guys who went to the games, but when the AFL came in, they sold to the husband and the wife and the family. They'd buy tickets and go to the games and the cocktail party afterward. Cincinnati was that type of crowd, with the suites and all that stuff. Now, they're all getting like that, except Cleveland, the New York Giants, the Pittsburgh Steelers. The Pittsburgh Steeler fan is the hard-core steelworker type. When we played the Steelers, it was always a battle.

I have no bitterness against the Browns. I said what I said. I'm glad I said it. They traded me, and so be it. That's the way I feel about it. The end was going to come some time. I don't regret anything. I wish I could've made more money, but I'm not bitter about not making it.

I'd see Art Modell once in a while after I left. When I coached in Cincinnati, we played the Browns twice a year. I'd see him at Hall of Fame functions or parties or whatever. I didn't hold a grudge against him, because

I really wasn't sorry I left, but I didn't particularly like him. He was not one of my favorite people. I'm certainly not envious of Art Modell. There's nothing about Art Modell that I would want to be. He can have all the money in the world. He can have the Baltimore Colts and the New York Giants, the whole damn league, and I wouldn't want to be Art Modell. I would love to have coached the Browns, but that wasn't going to be.

When I heard he was pulling the franchise out, I felt sorry for the people like Lou Groza and Dante Lavelli, who really liked the Browns. That's who I felt for. Now, I feel good about it, because I think they're going to be better off without him, and people are going to enjoy it. I didn't care for myself. It didn't matter to me. I don't have a favorite team. I like to judge the players and then judge my judgment. I don't want my judgment to be clouded by whether or not I like the team.

THERE WERE GUYS WHO NEVER made a move without Paul Brown. They changed jobs, they called Paul Brown first. Rick Forzano, who coached the Lions, was like that. Rick was with the Bengals the first year, and he never did anything without talking to Paul. I never called Paul for any kind of advice. The only thing I did was when I left Cincinnati, I was still very close with Howard Brinker. I said to Paul, 'If you want me to, I'll call Howard and tell him the atmosphere is very receptive to him calling you for the job.' And Paul hired Howard Brinker to take my place.

I didn't go to Paul's funeral. I was in Kansas City. I went to his wife's funeral. But, you know, Paul was sort of a private guy. I didn't feel right about flying in for a funeral and seeing a bunch of guys that I'd be really glad to see. I thought Mike Brown and the family would just as soon bury him with nobody there.

Paul Brown was a unique guy. If I had to tell you who he was like, I can't think of anybody. Nobody. I would say he had the charisma of a college president, but he was definitely a football coach, and I don't know many people like that.

I always thought I was lucky that I played for him, and I told Jim Brown this. One time, Jim Brown said that we would've been better off without Brown. I said to Jim Brown, 'Jim, let me ask you something: You gained this many yards, you did this and this and this. You had a great year. How can you blame Paul Brown for anything? How much more could you have done?'

'Well,' he said, 'you never know.' 〟

331

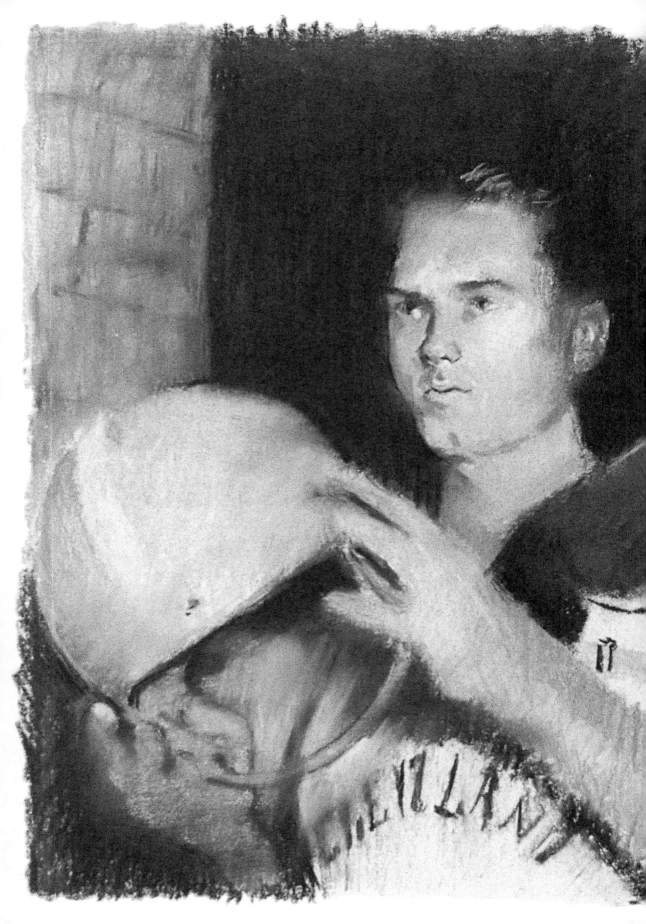

# *Not* Automatically Otto

MILT PLUM KNEW he was in trouble. The headline that February morning in 1962 was startling and incriminating: "Browns 'in Rut,' Says Plum; Hits Checkoff System."

"I thought, 'Holy Shit!'" Plum recalls.

There in the *Plain Dealer* was a catalogue of complaints about celebrated head coach Paul Brown, every gripe attributed to Plum, Cleveland's outstanding young quarterback. A photograph of Plum nestled like a serpent's egg in the stark lines of type. He seemed to be grinning, as mischievous as an English boarding-school lad amused at the spectacular audacity of publicly criticizing his stern headmaster.

According to the story, Brown had made numerous mistakes over recent seasons. His dictatorial control ruined players' spirit. He didn't inspire the team for important games. He clung to a "stereotyped" offense. He insisted on calling every play through linemen who shuttled in and out of games. He refused to allow quarterbacks to change ill-advised plays at the line. It was "time to straighten things out," Plum said.

He retreated a bit in follow-up stories, saying his comments were "not an indictment of Paul," but Plum knew that Brown, severe and unforgiving, wouldn't overlook his transgressions.

"I hope that Paul doesn't take it the wrong way," he said, "and that nothing serious comes of it for me, but I'll take my chances."

Milt Plum's chances weren't good.

Sounding like Sam Colt, Brown once referred to the forward pass as "the great equalizer." For years, he had sought a player who could wield that weapon with the skill and boldness of Otto Graham. Exquisite thrower, courageous runner, dashing leader, Graham directed the Browns to ten straight championship games. He retired after throwing two touchdown passes and running for two more touchdowns in the 1955 NFL championship as Cleveland won its second consecutive title.

"Cleveland will have a new quarterback—George Ratterman or Babe Parilli—and no flipflop in the success string is anticipated," the *Plain Dealer* assured fans.

But in 1956, the team had its first losing season, and Brown declared, "Our limitations stemmed from the pass offense."

The deeds of "Automatic Otto" fixed in his mind, Brown proved fussy. Ratterman was too slow. Parilli grew so jittery under the coach's demands that he broke out in a rash and became virtually catatonic during games. Bobby Garrett, a number one draft pick, stuttered so badly that he couldn't call cadence.

Brown rejected even two future Hall of Famers. Len Dawson's arm wasn't strong enough. When Johnny Unitas asked for a tryout, Brown put him off until the following training camp, and Unitas signed with Baltimore.

"I guess I was looking for Superman," the coach admitted.

In the 1956 college draft, Brown lost out on All-American John Brodie, Dawson, for whom he later traded, and Paul Hornung, a quarterback at Notre Dame. On a lost coin toss, Cleveland settled for a running back: Jim Brown.

Scouting Brown, an assistant noticed another intriguing player—a 6' 2" quarterback/defensive back/place-kicker/punter by the unlikely name of Milton Plum. Though Plum had thrown only 75 passes as a senior at Penn State, the Browns chose him in the second round, mainly, Plum says now, to hand off to Jim Brown and throw the occasional short pass.

Desperate, Brown invited six players to a "quarterback school" before training camp in 1957. That undistinguished group included Plum, who had played mostly safety in the East-West Shrine Game; Tommy O'Connell, who had filled in for the last half of 1956 in Cleveland; Garrett, whom Brown had already traded once; and John Borton, a former Ohio State linebacker. In all, thirteen quarterbacks took snaps for Cleveland that preseason.

O'Connell remained the starter but fractured a leg late in the year. Plum came on to run and pass for nearly 300 yards in a season-ending victory at New York. Afterward, the *Cleveland Press* proclaimed him "a sprightly reincarnation of Otto Graham."

Cleveland reached the championship game, but several days before, Plum badly pulled a hamstring while playing catch—"a careless action," Brown said. The Browns gained but 112 yards passing, threw five interceptions, and lost to Detroit 59-14.

A "Milt or Tommy?" controversy had barely begun when O'Connell, despite leading the league in passing, abruptly quit. Brown said shortly thereafter that the stocky quarterback "didn't have the physical potential with which we could build over a long period."

Unsatisfied with Plum, Brown drafted Jim Ninowski and tried to give him the position. Plum held on. He finished behind only Eddie Lebaron among NFL passers in 1958, and the team went 9-3.

For the next three years, the Browns fielded not only the league's finest runner—Jim Brown—but also one of its top passers. In 1960, Plum compiled the highest quarterback efficiency rating in league history, 110.4, a mark that stood for nearly 30 years. He led the NFL in passing in both 1960 and 1961. He threw at least one touchdown in 18 consecutive games and 208 straight passes without an interception, another league record.

Brown said that Plum had earned the coach's admiration. He added, "Once we get receivers set up with the ability of Dante Lavelli and Mac Speedie, Plum could show us a few things Otto Graham once did."

Yet all wasn't well. Cleveland possessed one of the league's more productive offenses but couldn't win a title—the only measure of success Brown acknowledged. Fans, and more important, new owner Art Modell began to question Brown, and as coach drew fire, so did quarterback. With each disappointment, the relationship between Plum and Brown soured more.

Cleveland entered the tenth game

of 1961 needing a win over the Giants to tie for the conference lead. New York intercepted Plum's first pass—Brown said the ball was underthrown; Plum said the Giants knew the play was coming—and after the quarterback missed a wide-open Ray Renfro later in the game, Brown benched him. He sent in Dawson, whose first pass was picked off and returned for a touchdown. For the fourth year in a row, Cleveland failed to reach the championship game.

Nonetheless, when some of Plum's teammates groused about him, Brown said, "Milt is in the upper echelon of quarterbacks in the National Football League."

A local American Legion post named Plum its "Pro of the Year" in 1961, but a team already splitting into factions over Brown's regime had developed another fault line, one between those who backed Plum and those who found him wanting. Plum's supporters—main among them Jim Brown—said the coach had browbeaten and made a scapegoat of the quarterback. His detractors accused Plum of shortcomings ranging from indecisiveness to throwing a "heavy" ball that was hard to catch.

The disagreement became irrelevant when Brown saw the lead paragraph of the *Plain Dealer* story: "Milt Plum doesn't believe things will get better for the Browns until the quarterback becomes something more than a mechanical man."

At first, Brown appeared to shrug off Plum's accusations. He said idle players have too much time to brood during the off season and he wasn't going to be drawn into a public debate. Edwin Anderson, general manager of the Lions, also read the piece, however, and Anderson guessed that Brown, always composed on the surface, was seething. In fact, Anderson said later, Brown was so furious that he was willing to ship Plum to Detroit for Ninowski, whom Brown had discarded two years earlier.

In the final deal, Plum, linebacker Dave Lloyd, and running back Tommy Watkins went to the Lions for Ninowski, defensive end Bill Glass, and aging halfback Hopalong Cassady.

The quarterback heard about the trade from a neighbor. He didn't receive confirmation from the club until days later and then only by telegram. The Cleveland Browns, the message explained, didn't have Milt Plum's telephone number.

In his most famous barb, Plum joked, "Last season, I called almost a dozen plays for Cleveland," leaving unsaid that the Browns ran 849 plays that year. Plum said he asked Brown to open up the passing game and to install more plays that allowed the quarterback to move in the pocket.

Brown said that Plum was either unwilling or unable to throw deep and not mobile enough to execute the rollouts, quarterback draws, and waggles that Graham had perfected.

"Right from my rookie year, I was told I ran when I should have passed and I passed when I should have run. Finally, I just laughed it off," Plum said.

Simply, he was good enough to tantalize his coach, but Milt Plum couldn't automatically become Otto Graham, and neither Brown nor Cleveland would be satisfied by any less a player.

Graham's ghost hovered ever near in the collective subconscious, a doppelganger in white leather helmet, facemaskless, wearing basketball shoes for traction on frozen turf, darting past befuddled defenders, unleashing prodigious throws that bolted from his hand like startled gamebirds and arched into smoky winter skies as chilly as gray aspic, then folded their necks and hunched their shoulders and fell feathery onto fingertips. Always.

Milt Plum also had to cope with Brown having played quarterback in high school and college. "The quarterback, invariably, has always sort of been my pet project," Brown once wildly understated. He frequently referred to his playing days, called every play—by messenger or, briefly, by radio transmitter—and

compulsively governed every move of his quarterback. The Cleveland Touchdown Club, only half-kidding, one suspects, presented Brown a plaque naming him "All Pro Quarterback of 1955," and a letter to the *Plain Dealer* once suggested "we might as well put pads on Brown and send him down on the field to call the plays."

Brown went beyond the usual uneasy symbiosis between professional coach and professional quarterback. He synthesized himself with the man calling the signals. A quarterback's failures were personal betrayals.

Milt Plum, like it or not, had become the player who defied Paul Brown. Plum was an unlikely mutineer: certainly less likely than the brash Graham, who for years needled Brown over calling plays. Brown himself described Plum as having "a worrying, conscientious personality." Reserved, handsome in an Ivy League dining club way, hoping to please, he seemed out of place in the violent, out-sized, adrenaline-spiked world of professional football. He was the reluctant quarterback whose practicality caused him to trade for a football scholarship his dreams of professional baseball.

Cleveland sports writers warned that Brown had taken the most serious risk of his career. "If Plum succeeds at Detroit and Ninowski fails in Cleveland, the effigy hanging mobs will assemble in our public square," one wrote.

Detroit, meanwhile, hailed its savior. In his first three games as a Lion, Plum threw nine touchdown passes and hit sixty-three percent of his throws. A national magazine rated him Bart Starr's equal, and Detroit coach George Wilson said Plum would become the team's greatest leader since Bobby Layne.

In his next four starts, Plum had only one touchdown pass, and lost his job to Earl Morrall. When Plum's interception late in a game with Green Bay cost the Lions the conference championship, defensive tackle Alex Karras accosted him in the locker room.

After a 31-10 loss to the Packers early in 1963, Plum was last in the league's quarterback ratings. Fans and players clamored for Wilson to call plays. Over the next four seasons, Plum battled Morrall and Karl Sweetan for the position—losing, regaining, sharing it, and putting up respectable, if unspectacular, numbers. He was traded to Los Angeles in 1968 and finished his career in New York the next season.

Plum competed with the image of Graham in Cleveland, the image of Layne in Detroit. In Cleveland, he was belittled for not throwing deep, in Detroit for forcing long passes. He wanted to make his own calls in Cleveland but was deemed a lackluster playcaller in Detroit. The Lions said he was too passive; when he asserted himself in Cleveland, he was banished. He chafed under Brown's iron fist but was unsuited for life among the freewheeling Lions. Forbidden to use audibles in Cleveland, he was given license to change any play in Detroit but hesitated to do so, because he feared someone on the undisciplined offense would miss the call. Twenty years after being traded, he said Paul Brown was fine as long as you were honest with him, but the time he was most honest with the coach cost him his job. In the end, Milt Plum went against his own creed, "When you get your chance, don't muff up."

As Jim Brown put it, "The Cleveland Browns were the ideal team for Milt to handle, if only Paul Brown had given him a pinch of freedom."

The coach fared worse. Ninowski balked at returning to Cleveland, then injured his shoulder. Ironically, Brown was forced to use the player who turned out to be the tough, brainy, driven quarterback the coach had wanted for so long. Frank Ryan finished fourth among league passers in 1962, but Modell fired Brown shortly after the season ended.

Brown finally reincarnated Graham in 1971 when as coach of

the Cincinnati Bengals, he drafted Kenny Anderson. A willing alter-ego, Anderson prospered under the coach's scrutiny; still, Brown never won another playoff game.

Apparently, he also never forgave Plum. Some of the nastier recollections in Brown's autobiography concern the quarterback who seems to have exasperated him most.

Plum is not without his accomplishments, however. He threw for more touchdowns than Frankie Albert and more yards than Don Meredith and completed a higher percentage of his passes than Roman Gabriel or Norm van Brocklin. He has a better career quarterback rating than Sammy Baugh, Zeke Bratkowski, Terry Bradshaw, George Blanda, John Brodie, Charlie Conerly, John Hadl, Jim Hart, Bill Kilmer, Layne, and Eddie Lebaron. He threw for more yards and a higher completion rate and attempted and completed more passes than Ryan. Although former Browns still disagree over Plum's ability, he is the winningest quarterback other than Graham in Cleveland history.

Plum remains perplexed by Brown, to whom he never spoke after the trade. He now claims not to have made the damning statements, and even if he had, he asks, why would Brown summarily fire him without talking to him about the story?

Plum looks like the Jimmy Stewart of *Harvey* or *The Far Country*. He has clear blue eyes, long porcelain-white fingers, and groomed salt-and-pepper hair. He wore a pristine sweatshirt and pressed corduroy slacks to lunch at a restaurant near his home in Raleigh, North Carolina. Though pleasant and direct, he also seemed solemn and a little distant, like a calculus professor working out an equation in his head while talking to a garrulous neighbor.

Retired after a long career in sales, Plum had heart surgery in 1996 but still plays in charity golf tournaments and, to keep busy, works part time for a friend who sells promotional items to schools. Divorced, he has dated the same woman for nearly twenty years. He watches a game now and then but has little to do with the NFL except to point out how meager pensions are for players of his era.

In 1989, Joe Montana broke Plum's long-standing record for quarterback efficiency. As Montana was about to do so, Plum expressed his unconcern. He said he remembered little about the 1960 season and was satisfied to be just another former professional player.

"I don't know how many people remember me now, anyway," he said. "I know my kids always will."

# *Milt* PLUM

 " MY DAD WAS A MILKMAN
in Westville, New Jersey, which is just across the river from Philadelphia.
Every Thursday after school, I jumped on my bike and collected milk bills,
which hurt me tremendously, because I didn't get to play ball that day. We
got out of school at three. We ran home, grabbed something to eat, and ran
to the field to play. There wasn't any little league football back then. There
wasn't any organized ball of any type until I got into high school.

In high school, I played for the baseball team, and in the summer league.
Sometimes, they overlapped. Before school was out, we'd start the summer
league. The school gave permission so that I might be playing a high school
game in Pennsville, and the summer league team would pick me up there,
and I'd change uniforms and play another game thirty miles away.

One year, I played for three teams. If one hardball team wasn't playing,
I'd call the other one and say, 'Hey, Westville doesn't have a game tonight.
You have a game?' If they did, I'd go there. If neither one of those teams was
playing, I'd go play softball for the church.

I was a catcher. My freshman year, I played varsity baseball as a short-
stop, and the football coach was the baseball coach. One day he had me
catch batting practice, and I found out that's the only place to be. You're in
the middle of the action. I don't know how outfielders do it.

We went to school in Westville until eighth grade, and then we went to
Woodbury High. I went out for football there and made the JV team as a
freshman. I was a single-wing tailback. My sophomore year, the head coach
brought in a T-formation coach, and I went to quarterback.

My senior year, we walked over everybody. Our closest score was 19-7. I'd run the option to the right, flip it to the left halfback, and he'd run 35 yards for a touchdown. I'd run the option to the left, flip it to the right halfback, and he'd run 22 yards for a touchdown. We just went up and down the field. I think we could have done it without a coach.

I DID NOT PARTICULARLY want to go to college. I just felt my life would be to go in the minors and play baseball, but I was recruited by Notre Dame, Miami, Florida. Maryland made a big push. Auburn made a big push. The fellow at Auburn told me, 'Every girl in our school is some kind of high school queen—Apple Queen, Peach Queen, Cherry Queen, something or other. We'll send you a yearbook.' He did. He was right. But I wasn't interested in the Southern schools.

The coach took four or five of us up to Yale, and one by one, the dean of men, or whoever it was, called us in the office. I went in, and he opened my folder up and said, 'Do you want to come here?'

I said, 'Not really.'

He said, 'Good,' and slapped the folder shut.

We went over to the University of Pennsylvania. They ran the single-wing. I thought, 'What am I doing here? I don't want to be a blocking back.' And I didn't want to go close to home. I could be from my house to the University of Pennsylvania in twenty minutes. I knew there would be a lot of distractions. I think I heard from one or two California schools, but I didn't want to go all the way across the country, either.

I'll tell you, it's confusing—thirty schools. If you're good, you're going to hear from at least a couple dozen schools. You're going to weed half of them out in a hurry. Then, even if you're down to six, it's a tough choice. Are you going to be happy?

Penn State was four and a half to five hours away, so if I had to get home, I could drive all night and make it. Finally, I called them and told them I wanted to come up, and I think they were surprised.

Rip Engle, the Penn State coach, said he wanted me to come out for football that freshman spring. He said, after that, I could play baseball. My sophomore year, there were only three quarterbacks, and after spring training they pretty well knew who was going to do what. They don't have time in September to find out who's going to play where. I thought I'd better go out and fight for my position, and then I'd play baseball for two years. My junior year, though, we changed systems, and I was behind the eight ball.

I didn't know whether to go out my senior year or not. I ran into this scout I knew from the old St. Louis Browns, in the hallway at Penn State.

He said, 'Milt, how you doing? You remember me?'

I said, 'Yeah, sure.'

And he went down the hall and told the baseball coach, 'Why isn't Plum out for baseball? He's a pretty good baseball player.'

And the baseball coach never spoke to me again after that. Boy, I was lucky. I had just finished a class from him. Who knows, I might've been a big failure in baseball, anyway.

WHEN I FINISHED PLAYING COLLEGE FOOTBALL, pro football still didn't register. I had only seen one pro football game. When I was in high school, my dentist had taken me and one of the halfbacks over to an Eagles game. I got out of school in June, and my thinking was that I would try football in September, and if it doesn't work, I'll try to do something with baseball.

My favorite team was always the Cleveland Indians, and I got drafted by the Browns. When I was drafted, the Browns were playing the Giants, and I met Paul Brown in New York. He asked me to come up and watch them play and to talk contract. They played on Sunday, and there were a couple of bald-headed guys out there practicing on Saturday.

I didn't know anything about Paul Brown. He was kind of small in stature, no kidding around, all business. The thing I remember most is that he asked me to get up and walk away from the table and pull up my pants leg. He wanted to see how big my legs were. That's the first time anything like that had ever happened to me—at least with another man in the room.

I met him in a hotel someplace. I didn't know anything. I'm 19 or 20. I'm naïve. I did not sign right away. Paul Brown was not pleased. I went back to Penn State and talked it over with them, and they thought it was all right, so I signed it and sent it back in the mail.

People say, 'Well, what did your agent think about it?'

'Agent' was not in the dictionary at that time. You walked in, and Paul Brown said, 'This's it.'

I made $11,000, with a $2,000 bonus. That sounded good to me. It was that deal or I could've gone to the Vancouver Lions (of the Canadian League) for $2,000 more.

Brown said to me, 'I'm going to give you a $2,000 signing bonus. Is that all right? Do you need any more?'

I said, 'No.'

Of course, he might've made it a $3,000 signing bonus and $10,000 salary, so it still came out to $13,000 total.

When I was a kid, I was a miser. My dad paid me seventy-five cents on Thursday and Saturday. I cut my aunt's yard. I helped my neighbor with Christmas tree sales in the wintertime. If I wanted to go to the movies, I had the money. I didn't go to my mother and ask for the money. My brother borrowed off me, and I charged him interest.

The first thing Brown told me about the contract was, 'Don't tell any-body.' They didn't want you comparing. If you came in and said, 'I think I'm worth more than that,' they would come back and say, 'What's your father do for a living? How much does he make?'

They knew if he wasn't a doctor or a lawyer, he wasn't making 10,11, 12, $15,000. That's what they usually hit you with.

My first year, when I went to camp, everything was hunky dory. I show up, and there are six quarterbacks there. Bobby Garrett from UCLA. He stuttered. You believe that, a quarterback that stuttered. A real nice guy. Tommy O'Connell, John Borton, Joe Clark, and Bob Freeman.

O'Connell had been with the Bears for one season. He came to the Bears in midseason of '56, when George Ratterman and Babe Parilli got hurt. O'Connell was the starting quarterback in '57, and they kept John Borton and me around.

I HAD JUST GOTTEN MARRIED IN JUNE. I went to camp in July. Everyone's asking me what's going on, and I'm saying, 'I don't know. Nothing's been said.'

Paul Brown was telling guys, 'We want you to make plans. Bring your family out here.' But he never said anything to me, and I still had baseball in the back of my head.

We always went out to the West Coast for two exhibitions. We'd go out on a Thursday, play the Rams on a Friday or Saturday, then go up to Frisco and play, or vice versa.

I played that week against the Rams. I played all right. Nothing exceptional, because we didn't throw the ball that much, and he still didn't say anything.

We came back, and I went to Paul Brown. He never did tell me to bring my family out. He just said, 'Hold tight.'

I went back to New Jersey. He finally called and said, 'Get a U-Haul and throw in everything you've got.' So we came to Cleveland.

With Paul it was all one-year contracts. My second year, I sent the contract back unsigned, no letter, no nothing. Brown called me and said, 'No one ever did that to me.'

That was an insult to him. I was the first one to ever do that.

I didn't know. You're not happy, what do you do, just sign it because he sent it to you? Somewhere, I got the idea that I deserved more, or at least wanted more. Maybe I just wanted more. I don't know what I deserved. Looking back now, I probably should've put a letter in there that said, 'Paul, I'm not satisfied with this. Can we talk at training camp?' But I didn't. I just stuck it in an envelope and sent it back. I was doing it all on my own. I didn't have anyone to say, 'Milt, do this. Milt, do that.'

Knowing him, he didn't want to negotiate. When I got to Detroit (after a trade in 1962), if you wanted fifty, they started at thirty-five and you started at sixty-five, and then you argued your way down to what they were going to give you and what you wanted anyhow. Paul Brown was probably the other way: 'This guy deserves twelve. I'm going to offer him twelve.'

I went to that early training camp in July and we sat down and worked it out in the matter of half an hour. I think I got an extra $500 or something.

In those days, you really didn't have the option of becoming a free agent. We had a situation in Detroit. I went to the Lion coaches and told them, 'So-and-so is unhappy in Cleveland. He really wants to get out of there.'

He said, 'Tell him to hang in there, because there's an unwritten law that no one will pick up players who play out their option.'

Then about two or three years later, R.C. Owens plays out his option in Frisco, and Baltimore picks him up. That broke the ice, but for years, that was an unwritten law: 'Someone plays our their option, let him go. Nobody touches him, that'll stop that.' Then Ron Kramer did it—went from Green Bay to Detroit—and after that there was no more allegiance.

CAMP MY FIRST YEAR IN CLEVELAND was probably the easiest of any I'd ever had. Apparently, Paul Brown had taken a lot of psychology courses. His belief was that after about an hour and a half, your learning period begins to go down, and that's when injuries start to happen. A guard pulls the wrong way and two guards hit each other.

At the end of the third week, on Saturday, was a scrimmage. We'd practice in the morning, scrimmage in the afternoon. Then those who lived in the area could go home. We'd run into town for a few hours and run back.

The next day, Paul would always say, 'That was probably the best steak we ever had last night.'

They always had steak on Saturday night, because a lot of people weren't there. As sure as could be, steak on Saturday night.

For five years, it was instant replay. Nothing ever changed. I can't think of one time that he said, 'This year, we're going to do this' or 'This year, we're going to do this.' It was always the same.

I WAS DRAFTED TO HAND THE BALL OFF to Jim Brown and to throw a couple of short ones every once in a while. I'm not bragging, but I probably threw more balls on third down than all the other quarterbacks combined. It was first down, Jim Brown; second down, Jim Brown; and if we had more than five to go, we threw it. If we had four and a half, we ran it. And he was a hell of a runner.

Back in those days, you didn't throw the football, even in the pros. Now, my arm gets tired just watching some of these guys throw the football. One year, we played Pittsburgh and I threw eleven or twelve times. Jim Brown had 300 and some yards on the ground; that was part of the reason. But that's unheard of—twelve passes in one game.

Everything was the running game. The Browns traded Bobby Mitchell because they wanted to get Ernie Davis, from Syracuse. They wanted Davis and Brown to be another Hornung and Taylor. You ran the ball, and you ran the ball, and you threw it when you had to. That's it.

I think it was in the off-season of Bobby Mitchell's rookie year. I told Howard Brinker, 'We ought to put Mitchell out at receiver.' We had basically one receiver—Ray Renfro—that was it. When we had to throw, Renfro got doubled all the time. I thought we should move Mitchell to the other side and move Preston Carpenter back into the backfield again. He had a great rookie year in '56 in the backfield, and then they moved him to tight end. Preston was the kind of guy, you tell him to run through a wall, he'd do it for you. I said to put Preston in the backfield again, put Mitchell at the flanker, and now you have two speedsters out there. You have the best running back in the league, and you have Preston, who can run the ball and would block a train for you.

No, that's when they went with the deal with Mitchell to Washington and getting Ernie Davis. That's the kind of football Paul Brown wanted:

first down, second down, then throw that little short pass. A lot of our passes were just little flares over the middle and stuff.

The joke was that Paul Brown had a sheet of paper with all the plays on it. The running plays were all on the front, and the passing plays were on the back, and he never turned it over.

One year, we started to bitch and moan: 'We never throw the ball on first down,' so about three games in a row, we threw on first down. That was it. We played the Giants; they knew what we were doing. We'd throw a hitch, and on a hitch, you don't set up and look, you just throw. We had done that three or four games in a row. Giants were in a zone defense. Guy picked it off.

Paul Brown says, 'Yeah, there, we throw on first down,' and that was it. Throw it, get it done with, and let Jim Brown run it the rest of the time.

For a man of his stature, he did some things that made you wonder what he was thinking about. For example, he would say, 'You're better off if you don't read the papers. I don't read them.' Five minutes later, he'd quote something out of the paper.

That's when Unitas was coming into his own. He'd say, 'Baltimore has that guy Ukneekas,' as if he had never heard of him.

HE HAD SO MANY IDIOSYNCRASIES. He liked ice cream as hard as a brick. In the cafeteria, we had young girls working. They couldn't even dip it. Players would eventually have to do it. He always had somebody there for dinner, maybe his secretary from the office. She would come out about once a week with things for him to sign. Maybe a newspaper person and his wife. I think it was just to make sure that everyone was acting like a gentleman.

The Browns always wore coats and ties on the road. Other teams didn't. Saturday night before a game, we all went to the movies together. It looked funny, all these big guys crossing the street in Cleveland in a line, going to the movies, like ducks in a row.

He was the little guy who wanted to make good. He wasn't a big man, but he could sure look through you. He had piercing eyes. I was never injured, except for my rookie year, I pulled a hamstring. One day, I had turned my ankle, and I was in the training room. He comes in and says, 'You're always in here.'

I hadn't been in there in about three years. I don't know if it was just something to say instead of 'Hi, how ya doin'?' or what.

Leo Murphy, the trainer, said, 'Just forget it. It gives him something to say.'

He had three boys, and if anyone had a girl, he would come around and go, 'Ha, ha, ha, ha, ha. Too bad you had a girl.' But I found out later he really wanted a girl, but he never had one. That was his way of shaking it off.

We played a crucial game once, and I threw a ball and hit a guy right in the belly button. He dropped it. Paul Brown told me on Tuesday that if the ball had been a little higher, it would've been easier to catch. In the five years I was there, he never said, 'Nice game. Nice throw.'

They tell stories about when they used to practice at Baldwin-Wallace. A car stopped at the end of the field once. He sent the equipment manager down there to check on it. It was a salesman. He was tired and just taking a nap.

After Labor Day and the kids started back to school at Hiram, we moved into Cleveland, to the old League Park, the original Cleveland Indians park. It was used as a playground by the city. It was very old, and could be a rough neighborhood. We had to park our cars inside the fence, and we had to pack a sandwich because there was no place to eat lunch. There was a three-story house behind the field. Only the first level was lived in. They say that the Colts paid some money to whoever lived there and went upstairs with a camera.

Airplane flew over, we didn't run a play until it passed. One time, again in League Park, there was a telephone repairman up a telephone pole, and he sent an equipment manager out and asked him to leave.

THE FUNNIEST ONE WAS, we were playing an exhibition game in Akron, at the old Rubber Bowl. The College All-Star Game was Friday night, the night before. They tried to get all of the guys who'd played in the College All-Star Game into camp as soon as possible. They'd pack a uniform in the trunk for them, and they'd dress for the game even though they couldn't play in it, because they didn't know the plays. Jim Ninowski, the quarterback from Michigan State, came in that year. We're in the locker room, and Paul Brown says, 'We want to throw the ball this many times,' and he uses his fingers to signal, doesn't say the number.

Ninowski says, 'What's the matter, he lose his voice?'

He'd write on the board. 'All right, we're gonna do this. Everybody got it?' He'd erase it off real quick.

The last game of the season, we're playing at Philadelphia. I'm half asleep. Jim Ninowski is my roommate. Comes a knock at the door. I know who it is. It's (assistant coach Ed) Ulinski. He does the bed check. He says, 'Milt, get up.'

I wonder why I have to get up. I'm in bed. He can see that.

'What for?'

'You gotta get weighed.'

He's carrying a scale around with him.

I guess they wanted to see if anyone put on a lot of weight during the season. Did some lineman start at 250 and end up at 265?

When someone's going for a record, does everyone else talk about it all week? Hell, yes. Jim Brown was going for the touchdown record. We get down at the two-yard line, one-yard line, and Paul Brown calls a sneak. So I snuck it in. Jim Brown misses the record that week, and Paul says he didn't know about it. But he was not going to give Jim Brown the ball to break the record or tie the record or whatever. He's in control.

MY FIRST YEAR IN CLEVELAND, I went back to school to get my degree. The next year, I moved to Cleveland. Paul Brown didn't like that either. Don't ask me why. Very few players lived there. I lived there. Lou Groza lived there. Bob Gain lived on the East Side. Lavelli lived there. For some reason, I was told, he didn't like players living there. I guess he figured if you did something wrong, he didn't want it hitting the papers. It was just a pain in the neck looking for a place to live every year. You only wanted it for four months, at the most, and if you could get one for six months, you were lucky. It's a pain in the neck to bring your family in, find a place to live, get the kids in school.

I found it odd that when he cut people, he never did it face-to-face. After an exhibition game, he would announce that four, five, six, seven people were to report to the office on Monday morning, the team office, not his office at training camp. The secretary would give each one an envelope, and if yours had the pink slip, that meant that you were cut. If you didn't have a slip, it meant to get your fanny out to training camp, but you knew you were on the bubble. He never faced anybody.

Another funny thing is that in training camp, the coaches would vote. 'What about so-and-so?' Instead of five coaches talking about it—'I think he can be great on special teams'; 'I think he can be our third guard'—a couple guys walked past his room one night and saw how they did it. The coaches were standing there with their backs to Paul Brown, with fingers fanned behind them. He'd say, 'If you want so-and-so, put down one finger. If you don't, put down two.' So this way, if he didn't want you—even if everybody else voted for you—you were gone.

I don't think there was a coach who would stand up to him. I don't think any of them would go in and say, 'Paul, I think we have to do this,' or anything like that. He threw out the plan, and they followed it. Whether he changed in Cincinnati, I don't know. He stayed out of the game for five years. Things had changed in those five years.

SOMETIMES, YOU'RE ALMOST AFRAID to walk in the locker room. You feel stiff, tight. He controlled things. It was his deal. He got Cincinnati, and he had the guy who used to shake in the end zone, Ickey Woods. Can you imagine Ickey Woods in my day? Paul Brown would've had him out of there in two seconds. I'll bet that made him lose more hair when he saw Ickey do that.

He gave up coaching in the Pro Bowl, because in the Pro Bowl, they don't do anything but sit around and prop their feet up and smoke cigars. That would've driven him into the insane asylum.

Art Modell came in, and that was a bad relationship from the first second. Back in those days, the coach was everything. We saw the owner maybe twice a year. They came to one of the scrimmages and ate in the same chow hall. Someone would say, 'That's so-and-so, and that's so-and-so.' That's it. Now, Jerry Jones and Al Davis and those guys are in the meetings, on the field.

We'd be in practice, and Modell would come out on the field, and Paul Brown would walk over, and they'd talk a few minutes, and Brown would walk away, and he'd have this look on his fact that something wasn't right.

I could not audible off at all. If a run was called, and all the defensive backs went into the men's room, we still ran it. I'll never forget, we played Pittsburgh, and, boy, guys are in the huddle and everybody wants to audible back to the weak side. We didn't have any way of doing it. The word 'audible' was not in the dictionary. Along about my third or fourth year, the blitzing started. It seemed like every down, someone was coming. Teams knew we could not audible.

Paul Brown had the messenger system, and everyone criticized him for it. Now, everyone's doing it. You'd be surprised, though, how many times a guard came in and just blank, nothing, or called the wrong play. But I knew from the game plan what Brown wanted on third down and so many yards. The guard might come in and get the play right but the formation wrong. No problem. I'd just clean it up.

Once in a while, we'd be watching films and he'd say, 'What'd you call that play for?'

Well, the guard came in and said '16 left,' when we didn't have a 16 left out of that formation.

For the first couple of years, it was better to let him call them and take the blame. After that, though, you want to call some of your own. I can't say that I wanted to call all of the plays on my own. I just wanted a little leeway. One time, against Pittsburgh, we lined up at the one-yard line, and they were a defensive back short. I look, and there's Ray Renfro standing out there with no one on him. I hurried up and called that cadence and, quick, threw it out there. Touchdown. Brown didn't say anything.

IT WAS A SHAME we couldn't have audibled. Guys would say, 'Change it, Milt. You want to change it, change it.'

I'd say, 'Yeah, are you going to stick up for me?'

Are you going to argue with Paul Brown? He had bad teams? In '56, they were last (actually, tied for fourth in the six-team NFL East); in '57, we were in the championship. How many teams go from last to the championship?

I hung on in Cleveland for five years. We finished first my rookie year, second two times and tied for second the other time (actually, first in the NFL East in 1957, second in '58, tied for second in '59, second in '60, and third in '61).

A newspaper guy, Chuck Heaton, got me traded. He wouldn't even say hello to me at Hiram at the reunion. I saw him out of the corner of my eye. He never came over. Anyway, I don't know what was behind it. He called me up and said, 'Milt, I'd like to do a story about what players do in the off-season.'

We agreed to meet at the Browns' office in the old stadium.

Chuck asked about my family, this, that, and the other. Next thing I know, the headline says, 'Plum Says If We Had An Audible System, We Would Have Won the Championship.'

I thought, 'Holy shit.'

Nothing was even said about an audible system, not even close to it. I don't know what inspired him to do that. I don't know if his editor said,

'Let's get something controversial going.' I had no idea.

Paul's ritual was to go to Florida for the month of January. Of course, the story got back to him in Florida, and I was traded. I got traded to Detroit on a Wednesday. My neighbor hears it on the radio and about dinnertime, he comes over and says, 'Mr. Plum, I heard you got traded.'

I said, 'Huh?'

I went in and told Modell, 'I'm going to throw a lawsuit against the reporter.'

He said, 'It won't work. It's your word against his.'

I said, 'What proof does he have that I said that?'

He said, 'What proof do you have that you didn't?'

Friday, I get a telegram from the Browns' office: 'Sorry could not reach you. Did not have your number. Wish you good luck with the Lions.'

My number wasn't unlisted. I was in the white pages. Paul Brown couldn't face people. I don't know if he was afraid if someone was going to smack him or shoot him or what.

I said, 'That son-of-a-gun. I'm gone.'

I WASN'T ANGRY AT BROWN. The weird thing is I was very surprised he didn't call me from Florida or have somebody contact me and ask, 'Milt, did you say these things?' Or call Heaton and me in face-to-face. I was shocked that he didn't contact me himself: 'Milt, what is this?' Or have an assistant coach do it. That would've made more sense than him doing it himself. I was gone, no ifs, no buts, no nuts. That was it.

In Detroit, I started out playing for George Wilson, then Harry Gilmer, then Joe Schmidt. After Paul Brown, Detroit was loose. We would go down the locker room in the afternoon before practice and say, 'What kind of equipment are we wearing today, shorts or pads?' And no one would know.

'Let me call the office and see.'

'No one's up there.'

We had a lot of crazy guys up there. Joe Don Looney (gifted halfback and legendary eccentric) had so much natural ability, but he had his own way of doing things. Joe Don had eyes like Paul Newman and spoke real softly. Girls fell in love with him walking down the street. Health nut. His whole dresser was filled with bottles of pills. Wore ankle weights to meals. He could throw. He could punt. In the first exhibition game he ripped off about a 70-yard run. He came to camp with one of his University of Oklahoma University buddies, Don Fleming, a linebacker. I think they came to camp with two pair of pants and three shirts between them.

We'd do skeleton passing drills, against the linebackers and defensive backs. Don Fleming just stood there. Backs are going out for passes, and he's just standing there. So they cut him. Joe Don didn't think they had given Fleming a chance, so he boycotted practice.

Joe Schmidt (Detroit's Hall of Fame linebacker) was an assistant coach that year, so Gilmer thought he'd send Joe down to talk to him, player-to-player, about how important practice is. Joe Schmidt goes down and says, 'Joe Don, you really can't afford to miss practice. We just thought that Don Fleming wasn't doing the job and didn't have the enthusiasm. Practice in training camp is vital. Thirteen years, I never missed a practice in training camp unless I was hurt.'

Joe Don, in his Texas drawl, says, 'Joe, it's about time you took a day off.'

He got caught running guns over the Texas border, I read somewhere. Then he was killed in a motorcycle accident.

WE HAD SOME WEIRDOES in Cleveland, too. In early camp, we had a guy who claimed to be a right- and left-footed kicker. He was a bartender somewhere. I think the first three kicks, he kicked the center right in the butt. We had a mountain climber. He wanted everyone to stack up in a pile and then he'd wear sneakers and go up over the top. One guy wanted to pipe in marching music during practice.

In Detroit, I could audible off the whole book, which is not necessary. You need about four to six plays. But in Detroit, you were scared to audible off, because someone would miss it. That might've been my fault for not going into training camp and doing it consistently in practice, and maybe the coach would've gotten on the ball and said, 'We've got to get this down.'

They audible all the time now. You can see the quarterbacks do it. I was scared to. Somebody was either going to miss the count or miss the play.

One year (1965), it came down to an exhibition game, and they were making the decision about who they were going to trade to New York, me or Earl Morrall. I was thinking, 'Hey, that wouldn't be such a bad place to go.' I knew what they were doing. Word gets around. Now, do I go and throw three or four interceptions on purpose?

Of course, I didn't, but I didn't have a great game. Earl didn't have a great game. I came in the locker room, and I'll never forget this: there was this little equipment manager's room there, and William Clay Ford (Detroit owner) called me in there and said, 'Congratulations, you're going to be our number one quarterback.'

I remember thinking, 'Am I happy or am I not happy?'

What would've happened if I had gone to New York? Who knows?

MY LAST TWO YEARS THERE, I was ready to leave. If they would've said, 'Fine, go,' I would've gone. We started to negotiate in January. Training camp started on a Sunday in July, and I signed Saturday night for what I asked for in January.

Russ Thomas kept saying, 'You're making more than Bart Starr.'

I said, 'How do you know this?'

He said, 'That's what Lombardi tells me.'

He said, 'That's an awful big raise, Milt.'

I said, 'Russ, I know that, but that's where I feel I belong, in that range. I don't care if I had been making ten the year before, I'd still be asking for the same raise. You tell me you wouldn't trade me for Starr, then put me in that ballpark.'

In Detroit, they gave out bonuses. Catch so many passes, you get a bonus. Gain so many yards, you get a bonus. So where's that leave me with two more games to go? Word gets back that so-and-so needs two more catches; so-and-so needs 75 yards. If I don't give them the ball or throw them the ball, I'm a whatever. That was lousy.

I knew a middle linebacker who had played in a couple of championship games. He told me, 'Milt, I make $150, $200, $300 a game extra. If the game was in the bag, I'd call blitz every time.'

Get the quarterback, $25; throw the runner for a loss, $25.

I told Russ, 'All you have to do is set up a point system: interception, fifteen points. No money. End of the year, you can give a set of golf clubs, a golf bag, golf shoes, small TV.'

'We can't do that. It's illegal.'

'I know it's illegal, but everyone's doing it. They all have incentives.'

Players are funny. They can make $2 million, but they like these little gifts. Everyone does.

I WAS NOT A 'RAH-RAH' KIND OF PLAYER, but in those days, nobody was. I couldn't play now, the way those guys are leaping and jumping on each other, slapping hands and everything. I always felt that if I performed well, that's what I was getting paid for. It blows my mind to see these guys getting $2 million a year, and if they score a touchdown, they're prancing around like they did something great.

I had one compliment I really appreciated. I was still with the Browns, and we played down in Baltimore. I have this friend, and he's one of these guys who can get into any sporting even, ticket or no ticket, and he went into the Baltimore locker room. He got a hold of Unitas and said, 'What did you think of Milt's performance?'

Unitas said, 'They finally realized what he can do.'

When we had the reunion in Cleveland a couple of years ago, I saw Jim Brown, and the first thing he said was, 'Remember the Baltimore game? You completed nine in a row. That's the only thing we had going for us.'

I had 208 passes without an interception. You know who broke it? Starr. I happened to be home watching a Saturday game, after the colleges were over. The Packers were playing the Bears, and they were talking about the record: 206, 207. The 208th is intercepted. Penalty. It didn't count. So Starr went on and broke it.

IN MY DAY, THE PLAYERS WEREN'T THAT BIG. Chuck Noll was the right guard and the center for all of the kicking game. He weighed 210 pounds. Now, running backs are 240. We never lifted weights in my career. They start in high school now. A lot of injuries now are caused by mass. Instead of a 210-pound guard blocking a 240-pound defensive end, it's a 260-pound guard trying to block a 350-pound man. And they all can run.

In those days, kids were more enthused about football because they could follow a team. Players weren't leaving. I wish they could put in some rule where a player had to stay three years minimum with the same team.

The money? I don't know. No one seems to say anything when Seinfeld gets $5 million an episode, but a player gets $2 million a season, and it's terrible. Seinfeld can act for what, fifty years? An athlete can make some money, particularly in a sport where they can get hurt, like football or hockey, and people can't accept that. I don't think players should be making $4 million a year, but how many are making that much?

In some cases, it's out of hand. The agents and the players are too independent. I know of one player where the agent was negotiating a contract, and he said to the player, 'We're going to go for this much money. What do you figure you need to live on?' And the guy told him, 'Two hundred thousand.' That's not to build a house or anything; that's just to live on for a year. Can you imagine that?

I worked every year in the off-season. I had to. I always worked some kind of sales. After I got out in '69, I went into a training program with a company and moved to Raleigh. I've been here ever since. I have three kids and five grandkids, and to make me feel old, I have one grandchild out of high school.

IT WAS A DIFFERENT GAME. I was drafted thirty-one years ago. The coach ran the team. There was very little disgruntlement. We went from twelve games to thirteen to fourteen, but they didn't want to pay us any more money. They say that Namath was the first $100,000 player, but I understand that was a lot of other stuff: an insurance policy, a car, that sort of thing.

Fans frustrate me more than anything. They don't know. A couple of weeks ago, O.J. was on CNN, and the next day everyone was calling the local sports radio show. They said on CNN that he didn't have any money, and people were calling in and saying, 'What's he worried about money for? He's getting $50,000 a month from his pension.'

Where in the hell did they come up with $50,000? I have my book at home. I can tell you exactly how much he gets. Now, another called in and said he'd heard on another show that O.J. was getting $50,000 a year. That would be closer to the truth.

I get it every once in a while: 'Boy, why're you still working, all the money you made in football?' They think if you played professional football, you're a millionaire. No, no. My thirteen years don't add up to one year for half the guys who play today.

When I was in Detroit, I think it was around '65, I went into the accountant and said, 'I'd like to have some money held back, so after I play football, I have something.' I wasn't making that much. I think around 40. I wanted five or ten held back.

They said, 'Oh, no, can't do that.'

I said, 'But you're gonna be getting the interest.'

They wouldn't do it. Now, you need a mathematician to figure out some of these contracts.

When we were fighting for a pension, Edwin G. Anderson, the general manager of the Lions, and I were walking down the hall to the office, and he said, 'Milt, what do you need a pension from football for? You'll get that with the company you go with after your playing days.' I was speechless.

The pension is terrible. We don't have an alumni association to go in and fight for it. For years, the Alumni Association was a farce.

A good friend of mine pitched from '57 to '70. I played from '57-'69. He took his retirement early, but I asked him, 'If you would've waited to 65 to take your pension, how much would you have gotten?'

He said about $100,000. I'm looking at $33,000. Baseball's pension is three times better than ours.

The thing is, the money's there. There's $400 million in the bank. They give maybe $200,000 a year to hardship cases, and then you have to pull teeth to get it. I have a friend, Eddie Sutton (former Ram defensive back), a doctor on the West Coast now, and he had Dick Christy, the running back, as a patient. He had cancer. Sutton told me, 'You can't believe what I went through trying to get some money to pay his bills.'

Roman Gabriel told me about this defensive back who played with the Rams, Clancy Williams. He had like seven kids, no insurance. He died early. Roman said, 'We had a hell of a time trying to get money to pay for his burial.'

When we started the union, Unitas said Baltimore had three sets of books. He just caught them lying. The big mistake was made in the '50s. The choice then was between hiring legal help and the players doing it themselves. Baseball hired legal; football tried to do it themselves.

I think some day—and I might not be on this earth to see it—something will be done. I can understand if you have two dollars and I say I want three, but when they say the money's not there, that's malarkey. The press party at the Super Bowl, you know how many they invited, casually? A hundred thousand.

SHOULD I HAVE PLAYED BASEBALL?
Hell, yeah.
People say to me, 'Would you do it again?'
Yeah, sure, I'd do it again.
'Would you have done things differently?'
Probably, yes.

I never talked to Brown after the trade, not by e-mail or by phone or by letter or by any means. I go to Detroit, and he was out of football.

He was living around San Diego. We went out and played an exhibition game. Before the game, one of the Lions' executives says, 'We had dinner with your old boss last night.'

I thought, 'My old boss? Who?'

He said, 'Paul Brown.'

I didn't know he was living in San Diego.

He said, 'He wants to stop and see you after the game.'

I thought, 'This's going to be interesting,' but he never showed up.

I don't know how to describe Paul Brown. The Browns, when he ran them, were a good show. He had some quirks. But everybody has some quirks. Gosh, the guy was successful, no question about it. He was an innovator in many, many ways. And he got rid of me. Maybe he was going to get rid of me anyway. Who knows?

I had never had any argument with the man, never showed any disgruntlement about what we were doing, never moaned to people so that it would get back to him. People didn't go around saying things in those days. It was pretty tight there. It was his way and only his way. **" "**

# Command
# Factor

EYES NARROWED INTO icy slits, thin arm aimed like a rifle barrel, long bony finger wagging—Paul Wiggin hadn't played for Paul Brown in over a decade, but he remembered "The Look," and it still chilled him.

In 1957, Wiggin had been an eager sixth-round draft pick scrambling to make the Cleveland Browns. Covering a punt in a preseason game, he chased a player who had faked catching the ball. The actual receiver raced through Wiggin's abandoned lane to set up the winning touchdown. Wiggin saw Brown glaring at him and knew he "wasn't long for the Cleveland Browns world."

He made the team, but the next season, Cleveland was undefeated and beating New York by ten points in the third period of an important Eastern Conference game. The Browns had stopped the Giants near midfield, but Wiggin roughed the punter, preserving a 72- yard touchdown drive that led to defeat. On the sideline, Brown called him "dumbhead," and at a film session that week, the coach turned off the projector, fixed The Look on Wiggin, and announced, "Gentlemen, if we are not in the championship game on the twenty-eighth of December, we'll know who to thank."

Sixteen years later, Wiggin, defensive coordinator of the San Franciso 49ers, was on his way to the locker room after a loss to the Cincinnati Bengals. He heard the familiar, imperious voice, the sharp sound of his name like a screen door slapping shut on a winter morning. He turned, saw The Look and froze, players eddying around him.

"You're ready," declared Brown, head coach of the Bengals. "When the opportunity comes, don't hesitate!"

That Paul Brown would pronounce him capable of being a head coach in the National Football League seemed to fulfill Wiggin's lifelong ambition. Even as a two-time All-American defensive tackle at Stanford, he had planned not to play pro football but to coach and teach.

Brown was leery of drafting players from California, because, he said, they often asked to be traded to West Coast teams. Wiggin, however, had the sort of background Brown

sought: he was a modest farmboy from "a hard-working, high-ethic, good family"; and although he had to attend junior college before Stanford would admit him, he became Phi Beta Kappa.

Undersized at 230 pounds and tentative, Wiggin hung on because the NFL had increased rosters from thirty-three to thirty-five and because seventeen players from the 1956 team, which had finished five and seven, had either retired or been released by Brown. Thrilled when Brown told him he had made the squad, Wiggin seethed when the coach humiliated him in front of teammates. "I really thought I hated him," he says.

Wiggin found Brown Machiavellian, a sharp-tongued dictator who ruled by fear. Once Brown scolded an injured player who wasn't even in uniform for yawning during halftime of a loss. He cut rookies for slovenly attire, cast out veterans for infractions as minor as sneaking a drag on a cigarette in the training room, publicly chastised stars.

"Paul was heavy on players," Wiggin says, "and, finally, when it was over, he didn't say, 'Let's go out and have a drink and let me tell you why I was the way I was.' That was for you to figure out."

However, Wiggin says, Brown was also a "very, very natural" teacher. Two weeks after the Giant fiasco, Brown surprised Wiggin, who had been backing up Willie Davis, by starting him. After Wiggin's three sacks helped Cleveland stop a two-game slide, Brown placed his hands on the player's shoulders and thanked him.

Over the next several seasons, Brown kept Wiggin and traded Davis, who is now in the Hall of Fame; Henry Jordan, a five-time All-Pro in Green Bay; Jim Marshall, a Pro-Bowler for Minnesota; and aging Len Ford, also a Hall of Famer. Later, Brown called Wiggin "a very special person to me" and, along with John Yonaker and Ford, one of "the three greatest defensive ends in my time with the Browns."

Wiggin says that Brown "did what he had to do to get people to do the things they had to do," but in spite of years of reflection, he is unable to explain the coach's "command factor"—Brown's extraordinary ability to inspire respect as well as fear.

He says, "I had a German shepherd mentality. I loved the master, and I think I would almost have killed for him when I had my costume on."

After Art Modell fired Brown early in 1963, Wiggin continued to excel under easygoing Blanton Collier. Teammates voted him the Browns' best defensive player that season, and he became captain in

1967. He made two Pro Bowls and was named the team's outstanding player in 1966 and the city's top professional athlete the following year. He played in 146 consecutive games, including three NFL championships.

Preparing for his twelfth season, Wiggin unexpectedly received an offer to become an assistant coach in San Francisco. He had dreamed of the chance, but when it came, Wiggin didn't welcome it. "No player ever loved the Browns more than I did. It was the hardest thing I ever did to put down that Brown uniform," he says.

When he pointed at Wiggin that afternoon in 1974, Brown might have been responding to a spunky effort by the 49ers young defense or just exercising his need for control. More likely, though, he was designating a successor in the lineage of coaches he deemed worthy of leading the NFL. A relentless competitor, Wiggin was also intelligent, well-educated, and disciplined; however, he had not considered becoming a head coach. He was living back home in northern California, and in his five seasons there, San Francisco had won three division championships and played in two NFL title games.

Soon after, Jack Steadman, president of the Kansas City Chiefs, talked with Wiggin about replacing Hank Stram, who had been fired after fifteen years as head coach. The Chiefs claimed to have conducted the most thorough search ever for a coach, contacting seventy candidates and interviewing fourteen. "One person stood out, as far as we were concerned, and that was Paul Wiggin," owner Lamar Hunt said.

At 11 o'clock at night, a press conference scheduled for the next morning to announce his hiring, Wiggin turned the job down. He soon changed his mind, mainly because he didn't want to disappoint Brown. He became one of fifty of Brown's former players to coach an NFL team.

"I didn't know Kansas City was even interested in me," he says. "They called me. I didn't call them. And (Brown) inspired that somehow. I didn't ask Paul Brown to call; they called him. A year or so later, I asked the people who hired me what possessed them to pick me, because I wasn't a perfect match for what they wanted to get done. They said, 'You need to know that the one person who made a difference was Paul Brown.'"

Brown himself spent only one more year on the sidelines. He had won seventy-three percent of his games over forty seasons. He had produced championship teams at every level from high school to the NFL. He had founded two professional franchises. He had given

credibility to three leagues. He had been recognized as the game's foremost innovator. He looked around and wasn't pleased with what he had helped to create.

"I had seen the sport change drastically since I returned to football in 1968, and not much of the change was good. Society had become different, and with it, some of the fun I had always found in my profession had begun to wane," he said.

Brown's notion of a peaceable kingdom was "high-class, deadly, smart, hard-hitting and hard-running players" under the thumb of an omnipotent coach. Before collective bargaining, no-cut contracts, and high-powered agents, such a world was possible. The benign coach/ father-figure/counselor didn't exist when Paul Wiggin entered the NFL and was rare when he left.

"Things were different in those days," he says. "There were an awful lot of people on the street that were awful close to your abilities, and so you better make a difference in some other ways. If he wants class, you better be class."

In 1975, the year Wiggin became a head coach, pro football was a newer and not necessarily braver world than it had been in the days of the All-American Conference, when Cleveland players held their own pep rallies. "You had drugs and you had steroids, and the money was beginning to accelerate a little bit. All of those factors were coming together, so you were dealing with a completely different player," Wiggin says.

Greed and disloyalty—forces that were beginning to drive the NFL—repulsed Brown. He detested unions, agents, and rich dabblers "willing to risk a lot of money to have the fame and glory of getting in the Super Bowl." Having been "catechized" about college by his father, he was appalled by players who "had been exposed to education but not actually educated."

Brown had always been sensitive to the accusation, made against him since the early 1960s, that the game had passed him by. When he came back into football in 1967, he seems to have tried to adapt. He talked about having fun and allowing his "kids" to do likewise. He said long hair and beards didn't bother him because "I judge people by more than just their hair length."

However, he also said, "There is no new Paul Brown," and he saw no reason there should be. He lived by the words of Elizabeth Hamilong, a dean at Miami University when Brown was a student there: "The eternal verities will always prevail. Such things as truth, honesty, and good character will never change, no matter how people and times change."

From his earliest days, Brown

gave to players a long preseason speech that addressed their mental, moral, social, and athletic lives. He even invited reporters to sit in, as if the force of his beliefs would surely convert them to his world view. The Bengals heard essentially the same address as had Otto Graham and Lou Groza three decades earlier. In it, Brown said, "I don't want to think or act like a hard man. I would like to earn the thought from you that I am just and understanding—but you must know from the beginning that there is no way to circumvent the principals in which I believe."

Thus, he made center Bob Johnson, an outstanding student and member of the Fellowship of Christian Athletes, his first draft choice for the Bengals. He referred to players as "grand boys." He called quarterback Ken Anderson's parents' spending their vacations at training camp every year "Americana." He arranged screenings of "decent movies" for his team on nights before games.

Brown was, as he had always been, the visionary whose feet were planted in the past.

Apparently, though, he realized that the age of the "divine right monarch," as Wiggin calls him, had ended in professional football—that a new kind of coach would replace autocrats like himself and Lombardi. He seems to have recognized in Wiggin a forbearance he thought would be necessary in the new NFL. Certainly, Wiggin was hired in reaction to the authoritarian Stram, much as the gentle Collier had been appointed to offset Brown's despotism.

Although reluctant to accept the Kansas City position, Wiggin saw in it the opportunity to employ his "people first" approach to coaching. "I could never treat someone other than the way I wanted to be treated," he says. "It was hard for me not to be understanding."

Wiggin and his staff of "good people who thought of people first" took over a team made up of battered veterans of Kansas City's 1970 Super Bowl victory and young players of a sort Brown couldn't have anticipated when he became a professional coach in 1946. Wiggin quickly imposed some Brownian regimentation, requiring players, for example, to wear coats and ties on trips.

"They bought into it, but I probably should have been more ferocious in some other areas," he says. "But it was hard times, and they had a hard time adjusting to some of the older things I wanted."

During one training camp, he saved the life of John Matuszak. The gargantuan defense end and notorious carouser overdosed on Valium and vodka after Wiggin, exasperated, ordered him out of a meeting. Awakened in the middle of the night by the player's hysterical girlfriend, Wiggin rushed Matuszak to an emergency room. "I can't imagine Paul Brown dealing with anything like that," he says.

Injuries multiplied; losses mounted; discipline deteriorated. However, despite winning only ten of twenty-eight games in his first two seasons, Wiggin, popular with players and fans, received a three-year contract extension. In the seventh game of 1977, the Browns beat Kansas City 44-7 in Cleveland Stadium. It was the Chiefs' sixth loss of the year. The next day—Halloween—Wiggin was fired. "We felt Paul was no longer a positive force," Hunt said.

Wiggin admits to having been naive when he became a head coach. "I don't think that I had that command factor, either," he says. "Jack Steadman looked me right in the eye at one point and said, 'Paul, you're not enough of an asshole.'"

He believed that caring for players would pay off, and in a way, he was right. The day he was fired, his team issued a statement unique in the history of professional sports. They said, "We are shocked and saddened with what has happened today. Every man on this football team feels a deep sense of guilt for the actions that were taken. It is our fault that we lost a fine man and a great individual—Paul Wiggin."

That confession contrasts starkly with the statements of Cleveland players who lined up to renounce Brown after his firing.

The Chiefs also vowed to rededicate themselves. They won their next game under an interim coach, and then lost six in a row to finish two and twelve.

Wiggin didn't leave Kansas City without paying a personal price. The first coach he hired was Vince Costello, former Cleveland linebacker and Wiggin's closest friend. As rookies, the two spent hours speculating about roster cuts, devising ways they could both stick with the Browns. Each planned to coach and promised to hire the other should the opportunity arise. Pressured by the meddlesome Kansas City front office, Wiggin demoted Costello from defensive coordinator. Costello quit. They have never completely patched up their friendship.

"That happened in Kansas City," Wiggin says, "and a lot of things happened there."

In 1980, Paul Brown went looking for a coach to replace Homer Rice. He opted not for solicitous Wiggin, who had become defensive coordinator in New Orleans, but for stern Forrest Gregg. In that his record as head coach of the Browns was eighteen and twenty-three when he resigned shortly after the game that cost Wiggin his job, Gregg's principal

qualification to coach the Bengals seems to have been his reputation as a disciplinarian.

That same year, Stanford asked Wiggin to become its head coach. His three largely unpleasant seasons at his alma mater are memorable mostly for the bizarre, last-second, game-winning kickoff return by California that included five laterals and dozens of unintentional blocks by the Stanford band and cost the Cardinals a bowl invitation. That loss, a one and ten record in 1982, and a strained relationship with administrators resulted in his firing.

"Perhaps I have cared too much," Wiggin said. "Maybe I shared too many ups and downs with players, but I truly care for the young men that play for me."

He promised to never again be a head coach.

"I love to teach, and I got away from teaching, and I think that's what the administration of the game is all about. You don't teach anymore," he said. When he was with Cleveland, Wiggin taught high school or junior college every spring; like Brown, he had a master's degree in education and thought of himself primarily as a teacher.

Hired as an assistant to Brown disciple Bud Grant in Minnesota, Wiggin fashioned some of the league's better defensive lines until he became an assistant general manager in 1992. *Pro Football Weekly* voted him one of the NFL's most underrated front office personnel in 1998, but Wiggin says he still suffers "withdrawal" from coaching and so privately tutors some Vikings.

In the comfortable study of his home in a wooded subdivision overlooking a lake near the Vikings' offices and the homes of his three daughters, Wiggin said, "If you check my background, you'd probably find there are not a lot of people that dislike me." He is likable, although he says he would trade some affection for "a little more respect."

He still wears his hair in a stiff brushcut and is still fit, his posture ramrod straight, a few liverspots the only signs of age on his unlined face. He wore a cardinal sweater vest over a starched white long-sleeved shirt, khakis, polished penny loafers, and an expensive looking silver and gold bracelet. He looked like a NATO general on leave, but the shyness that caused some college fraternities to reject him belied his stately bearing. Eloquent and serious, he sometimes teared up, as he had before reporters in Kansas City and at Stanford.

The tall bookcases around Wiggin's shimmering desk held a biography of Hemingway, novels by Len Deighton, John Grisham, and Larry McMurtry, and Bible studies. Wiggin calls upsetting Baltimore for the 1964 NFL title "the greatest

moment of my life," but the only football memento in the room was a cheerless photograph of the Browns' front four—mud-spattered, weary, determined—lining up in the muck against the Packers during the 1965 championship game, which Cleveland lost.

His disappointments as a head coach still hurt, but Wiggin says he left both jobs with his belief in himself and in the essential decency of people intact. "There are a lot worse things than losing a job," he said. "I could have lost my faith."

He had copied Brown's playbook but couldn't mimic his "demeanor," which, Wiggin holds, "made the difference of the Browns being special."

Those in charge of the new incarnation of the Cleveland Browns must have agreed with that assessment. When the team hired Chris Palmer as its first head coach, management and reporters made much of the similarities between the two balding, bespectacled coaches, calling Palmer "quiet, cerebral, tough."

According to Wiggin, those same qualities created conflicting responses to Brown: slavish loyalty, anxiety, resentment, admiration. But, he says, "with a complex man like Paul Brown, there are bound to be complex emotions."

# *Paul* WIGGIN

" YOU COULD TAKE MY HOMETOWN—
Lathrop, California—and put it on an airplane and fly it someplace. It was
very small. I remember going back home after being at Stanford for a quarter or so, and everybody wanted to talk about what college was like and
what you did there and how you acted. I remember guys sitting around in
their bib overalls on fruit boxes out back, and I just talked to them about
college. To them, college was just something completely different.

It was a wonderful little town in a lot of ways. After my junior year,
when I made All-American, they had a dinner at Rosie's, which was a restaurant down the highway, and everybody in town contributed. Some of
them contributed a dime. And they bought me a watch. They had it en-
graved and it ran for about a month, but it was a wonderful gesture. One
time, they had a party for a guy who went to Europe. They all got together
and bought him a suitcase, because nobody in my hometown ever did anything like that. It seemed like such an exciting thing for somebody to do.

My mother's side was the athletic side of the family. When I came down
the assembly line, I got more of my grandfather's genes.  He was quite an
athlete, and my mother was, too. I got my size from them. My dad was
about 5' 11", 180 pounds. My mother was a big, strong woman. I think she
still holds a couple of track records at Modesto Junior College, primarily
because they don't do the events anymore.

I was one of seven children, one of four brothers in the row, and my
youngest sister is 21 years younger than my older brother. In the summers,
my father put us in the brickyards. One of my brothers and I each handled

20,000 bricks a day. That doesn't sound like much, but you ought to try handling 20,000 wet bricks a day. Because we twisted a lot, we were really muscular, and we were very strong when football began in the fall.

When I was in my first or second year of high school, one of the farmers next door gave me a set of weights, and I sent away a coupon on the back of a funny book and got a Charles Atlas program. I started lifting weights, and no one lifted weights then. I made a squat rack out of two-by-eights. I didn't know what I was doing, but I lifted all through high school, college, and the pros, and not many others did in those days.

I played four years in high school, actually five years in college, including the one year I was a redshirt, and eleven years of pro and never once left the field with an injury. A lot of it's luck, I'm sure, but some of it was that my body was put together really well.

In junior high, I was lost for a while, because I was kind of a fat, dumpy-looking kid. I didn't look athletic, but I was athletic, and I was a tough kid. I kind of wandered around the school for about two or three months, and all of a sudden, in PE, they realized that I could outrun people, and I could play basketball. I was explosive. My brothers and I used to talk about jumping up and touching a 10-foot ceiling. None of them had ever done it, but I could go up and hit it with the flat part of my hand. Pretty soon, I went from nobody to somebody.

SPORTS WAS MY VEHICLE FOR BEING ACCEPTED. I wasn't going to do it on anything else. I was a good basketball player. I was a good football player. I broke the record in the shot-put. I had strength and explosiveness. The vehicle for Paul Wiggin was going to be athletics.

I was a big fish in a small pond, and I didn't know the size of the pond. I didn't know until I was a senior that I was going to be a scholarship athlete. I didn't understand that sports could get me anywhere. I played sports because I loved sports.

I remember my coach said, 'There's a scout from Santa Clara here tonight to watch you play.'

That was the first sign of somebody being interested in me.

I was recruited by Stanford University in my junior year of high school, probably through the influence of my Uncle Ray, who knew the freshman coach at Stanford. Uncle Ray thought my older brother and I should meet the coach. We went up there, and now that I look back on it, they kind of rolled their eyes and pretended like they were recruiting us. But I was very impressed with Stanford. It looked like a farm community, with a lot of pastures around. It wasn't so formal, and the environment fit my shy personality.

My grandfather had actually been hired and paid to play for Stanford back in 1897. He was a great rugby player and baseball pitcher. He wasn't a student at Stanford, but he played for Stanford. I know that sounds strange, but that really did happen then.

The summer after my senior year, I played in the first annual High School Shrine All-Star Game in Los Angeles. I was still an unknown. Stanford recruited me, but they said, 'We just can't get you in,' and maybe they were saying, 'We don't want you.' So I played in this game, and typical of me, I trained hard. Most of the kids in the summer weren't in great shape, but I was. I lifted those weights, and I ran. I was ready to go, and in the game, I played both offensive and defensive tackle. I was a dominant player.

Now all of a sudden, the summer prior to going into college, I'm recruited by Notre Dame and USC and everybody in the country. I'm recruited by places I don't even know are on the map. I got really confused. My dad said, 'You know, Paul, why don't we talk to (Stanford coach) Chuck Taylor?'

I'm sure Chuck was far more interested in me then than he was prior to this all-star game. Chuck said, 'I'll tell you what you ought to do. Why don't you go to junior college for one year. We'll monitor your grades. You've got to hit it hard now.'

SO I WENT TO MODESTO JUNIOR COLLEGE for one year. I was not a real strong student. I was bright enough, but I was not a good student in the sense of discipline. I wasn't a horrible student, but I was not a *Stanford* student. So I played football at Modesto, and what really helped me was that I was good. I was very much a dominant player. That whole year, I was recruited by everybody, but in my heart I wanted to go to Stanford. And I did well enough that I got into Stanford on probation.

That transition, from a cultural point of view, was very difficult, because basically I was so challenged at Stanford. I barely made it the first quarter. Stanford was hard for me, because Stanford is so verbal. I was so shy there was no way I was going to try and compete, especially with those bright young people. I wasn't a very conversational kid. The prep school kids were so much further along. I was embarrassed to open my mouth. I may have come off as aloof, but I was just a shy country kid.

I was a sophomore when I got to Stanford, so I was thrown right in there on the field, and I was a lost soul in football, too. But I'm sure they saw some things, because they probably would not have redshirted me had they not. They pretended like it was an injury redshirt, but it wasn't. They had players that were established in the tackle position. As a sophomore in '54, my first year on the team, I was sixth in time played. As a junior, I was second in time played, and as a senior, I played all but ten minutes of the entire season.

They didn't have a kick-off guy, and I'd never kicked off in my life. But I said, 'I think I can kick off. What's complicated about kicking off?' And I could kick off to the end zone. So I kicked off my whole collegiate career. I wasn't as consistent as a guy who did it for a living. And every once in a while, I'd hit a line drive or get under one, but I was probably as good as there was in the Pacific Coast Conference at that time.

We had a terrible team when I was a sophomore. We got beat 72-0 by UCLA. We had a really good team when I was a junior. Our senior year, we had an even better team but played bad. We should have challenged for the Rose Bowl, but we didn't. We lost four games by a total of about five points.

We beat Ohio State 6-0 when they had Hopalong Cassady (1955). That was a great win for Stanford, a great day for me, because I got so much national recognition and was eventually named an All-American. I really didn't deserve to be, but I was. It was based on that and one other game.

When I played in college, I never had any idea that I would ever play pro football. I majored in physical education and history, and I thought I would be a high school coach. I thought only special people coached in college. When I played pro football, I taught high school in the off-seasons, back in California. If I had my life to live over again, I would probably have done more of it. I loved it, and I was good at it.


I WAS IN BED when one of my fraternity brothers walked upstairs and said, 'You were just drafted by the Cleveland Browns.'

I don't remember whether I had gone to class and come back and gotten into bed or what, but I was in bed. Can you imagine that compared to the draft today?

I just said, 'Great.'

I knew I could be drafted, but I never gave it much thought or I wouldn't have been in bed on the day of the draft. I didn't know the draft was going on; that's where I was. Certainly, the draft was a big deal for some people then, but it wasn't for me. I was happy to be at Stanford. I just thought life was going to unfold for me, I guess. I say that not out of intelligence, but out of ignorance, out of not knowing.

I can say this sincerely: I think Stanford had more influence in my life than it had for anybody that ever went there. It introduced me to a whole new level of thinking. I was this shy kind of a kid, and I crossed paths with incredible people. When I graduated, I took a look at myself, and I couldn't believe who I was versus who I had been. That just doesn't happen. I saw people in my hometown who were 55 or 60 and had been like that since they were nine years old—country bumpkins who just never changed at all. That's what they knew, that's what life was, and they were content with it.

When it was all said and done, it was the most exciting time of my life. I tell my wife, 'I love you, and I love our marriage, but the happiest I've ever been in my life was when I lived at Stanford University.' It was the greatest experience that anybody in the world could ever have.

I WENT TO THE COLLEGE ALL-STAR GAME in Chicago after my senior year and didn't play very well. They decided to play a nose-guard defense. I was going to be a wide tackle and defensive end in pro ball, in a four-three. No one wanted to play nose tackle. I said, 'Hell, I'm not going to start. They're going to start Lamar Lundy (of Purdue, a future Los Angeles Ram All-Pro). I'll play nose tackle.' It was a childlike mentality, but I wanted to start. So I started at nose tackle, and, man, I got chewed up. I played against Ray Wietecha, the offensive center for the New York Giants, the Giants were the defending NFL champions, and Wietecha just turned me every way but loose. It was partially skill, but it was partially just not knowing what I was doing. I was married by then, and I called Carolynn at home in California and told her, 'I'm going to go to camp tomorrow morning with the Browns.' I said, 'You know, Carolynn, get ready, because I may be coming home early. This is a different level.'

When I played in the All-Star Game, Otto Graham was one of the coaches, so I sat and talked to Otto, and I learned more about Paul Brown in that little short time than I had ever known. I said, 'Do you call him Coach Brown? Do you call him Paul? What do you call him?'

He said, 'Well, if you're screwing up, you better call him Coach Brown.'

When I got to camp, I felt lost. We always had these meetings. Paul Brown would start with running: why we run, how we run. You go through this whole day of just writing. Your playbook was blank paper, and you wrote everything in the Paul Brown playbook. To him, it was all part of the learning procedure. Four of us came from the College All-Star Game: Henry Jordan, Jim Brown, a guy named Joe Amstutz, and me. When we got there, Paul Brown put us in one group. In these meetings, he'd tell the players what they were going to do, and then he'd say, 'And for the All-Stars, we're going to meet tomorrow morning to go over that before practice.'

I'm in the back of the room and, finally, on about the 20th 'All-Star' thing, I'm shaking my head and saying to myself, 'Why does he have to call us "All-Stars"?' I felt like we were separated and people were kind of making fun of us.

He saw me shaking my head, and he looked at me and said, 'Paul.'

I looked up, and he said, 'You know, Paul, we're doing this for you. Now, if you're uncomfortable with it, do you think we should do it some other way?'

I wanted to say, 'Paul, what I'm saying is, it's just a little bit uncomfortable to be singled out,' but other players had told me that if Paul challenges you, your best answer is, 'Paul, I don't know why I did that.' They said, 'Don't give him some magic to work with.' So I just kind of backed off and sat there, and to this day, I think he felt like I was upset because I was going have to do something a little bit more than the other players because I got there late.

Paul Brown wanted you to have the same training grounds that every player had. We were going to get the Paul Brown foundation, and he was going to meet with us the next morning before breakfast, and we were going to be brought up to speed by the basics of what Paul Brown believed in. That was his way of doing it. You were going to write in the playbook exactly the same thing that everybody else had.

VINCE COSTELLO AND I were rookies together. We used to make the team cuts ourselves. We had a little place in Garrettsville, right out of Hiram. We were not the beer crowd, so we would sit there and drink coffee and cut the team, trying to find ways that we would still be there.

Then it was about our third or fourth preseason game, and we were at the Green Hotel in Pasadena, at a meal. I was still thinking I was going to get cut. I was leaving the table, and Paul called me up and told me to find a place to live in Cleveland. I was so excited I don't think I touched the floor going out of there.

I think the thing that saved me was the fact that pro football went from

33 to 35 on the roster that year, and there were two more bodies that could be on the football team—that, and Paul liked me. The second game against the Giants in 1958, we had to win or we would have a playoff with them for the championship. In the fourth quarter, we went ahead. We held them, and they went back to punt. I was on all the special teams, and I rushed in. I guess I tried to do something extra, and I roughed the kicker. I gave them the first down, and they went on to score and win the game. That was one of the most devastating things that happened to me in athletics.

In those days, we didn't go in to practice until Wednesday. That was horrible, because we didn't have money to do anything, so I had two days to relive that play. I couldn't sleep; I couldn't do anything. The guilt and letting the team down were the hardest things I probably ever went through in my life.

We lived in a residential hotel on Euclid Avenue, which was right in Little Italy. There was a little shoe store across the way. It was getting to be cold weather, and Carolynn had a bunch of shoes, and she wanted rubber tips on all the heels. I said, 'This is such a miserable day for me anyway, just give me all those shoes and I'll take them over there and get them done.'

She loaded them in my arms, and I go out of the hotel to this huge, four-way intersection. I see the light's okay so I decide to go diagonally across the intersection to the other corner. I take off in a dead run, and as I get to the middle of the intersection, I hook my foot or something, and I go spread-eagle. I've got shoes all over this intersection. I'm laying there in the middle of the intersection, and I'm saying to myself, 'How can it be any worse than this?'

I'm just taking shoes and throwing them over to the curb. That was the crowning moment. I'll never forget how low I felt.

I GO IN ON WEDNESDAY, I get to work, and I realize I left my playbook at home. With Paul Brown, each guy has his name on his chair, kind of a pecking order, and the lowest form of humanity sits in the front row. My chair is in the front of the room, with my name on it. I'm going crazy. I'm saying to myself, again, 'How in the hell could anything be any worse than this?'

Then, I have a thought. I go to Lou Groza and I say, 'Lou, what does the Old Man do to guys that have forgotten their playbook?'

'You know, Paul,' Lou says, 'I don't know that anybody has ever forgotten their playbook.'

I said, 'Lou, do me a favor. Can I carry your playbook? Let me carry your playbook in and sit it on my desk. You're in the back of the room. He's not going to see you. I promise you I'll back you up if anything goes wrong. I'm in so much trouble anyway that I'm going to stand up and say, "Look, my playbook's at home and I asked Lou if I could use his because I didn't want to make it any worse than it was." I promise you won't get in trouble.' Lou let me have it, and I went and sat in my chair.

Paul came in and said, 'Gentlemen, if we're not in the championship game on the 28th of this month, then we will know who to thank.'

I'm sitting in my chair, and I'm thinking, 'It's over.'

When it was time to break, I got out of my chair, and I'm walking down the row, and he's standing there. He jumps right in front of me, and he looks me in the eye and says, 'Paul, why, why?'

I said, 'Paul, I don't know. I really don't know why.'

He just shook his head at me, and I went on.


I REALLY THOUGHT THAT I HATED HIM. I thought I hated the man. I had been starting, but I had hurt my hand and was floundering. Willie Davis was starting some of the time ahead of me, but I started the next week against the Washington Redskins. In fact, during this time, I was recreating his playbook by hand, because I was going to go coach. I knew that the way things were going for me, I wasn't long for the Cleveland Brown world.

Then I had a great game against the Redskins. I had three sacks in a row. I think maybe I got a game ball. It was like, 'Here's your last chance. What're you going to do with it?'

After the game, I was sitting in the locker room. I was usually not the last one out, but there were actually some people from the press visiting with me about this, and that wasn't normal for me. I wasn't a hot item with the press, believe me, but they were talking about the game and me playing so well. After that was over, I was getting my shoes on. Paul Brown walked up to me. He put his hand on my shoulder and said, 'Wig, thanks,' and he walked out the door.

I still get kind of emotional when I think about that. The feeling I had was exactly the opposite of what I had thought before. I would have done anything for him. It was amazing how he knew when to strip you down pretty raw and then pick you back up. I thought that was a measure of a great man.

I used to go to California to talk to John Brodie (Stanford All-American quarterback and future All-Pro), my former teammate, and some of the guys in the off-season. I'd tell them about the control that this man had over people's lives, the things he would do, the clever things he would say to people. Brodie would say, 'He couldn't coach for the 49ers. We wouldn't take that crap.'

I'd say, 'You would. There isn't a person in the world that wouldn't take what he gives you. There's a certain something about him that's different from anybody you've ever been around in your life.'

People were afraid. Someone said he saw (defensive back) Junior Wren someplace, smoking a cigar, and everyone was nervous about it. They said, 'Oh, my God!' You did not want Paul Brown to think anything other than the right things about you. He had an unbelievable control of people.

WHEN HE SAID, 'What made you do that?' The answer was, 'I don't know.' You learned that the first week. We had a guy named Rich Kreitling, a receiver. Rich was a good guy, but if there was only one case of flu in Cleveland, Rich Kreitling was going to get it. He just had no luck at all.

We were playing a preseason game against the Detroit Lions, and Paul didn't like the head coach, Buddy Parker. Rich Kreitling had beat his man. The guy had fallen down, actually. Rich was in the end zone, and they threw the ball to him. He was facing the ball, and it hit him in the hands. It's one of those things that happen in sports: He dropped the ball and we ended up losing the ball game. We didn't lose totally because of that, but that was part of it.

Paul said, in that way he had, 'Rich, how could you drop the football?'

Instead of saying, 'I don't know,' Rich says, 'Well, I had my contacts on, and I was looking up, and when I looked up, you know, the lights got in my eyes, and when I put my hands up the ball hit me on the wrist instead of my hands.'

We all went, 'Oh, oh.'

Paul says, 'Let me get this straight, Rich—the ball hit you on your wrists, instead of your hands? Well, Rich, where on your wrists?'

Rich knew he was dead now. He said, 'Well, about two inches below my hands.'

Paul turns to Milt Plum, who threw the ball, and says, 'Milton, next time throw the football two inches higher.'

He loved to work with stuff like that. He loved for you to give him some ammunition to play with, because he was so much smarter than you were. Paul was heavy on players, and, finally, when it was over, he didn't say, 'Let's go out and have a drink together, and let me tell you why I was the way I was.' It was for you to figure out in your life.

But when (former Brown defensive back) Jim Shofner, who was a good guy and a classy guy and a good player, was trying to get a job with the 49ers as a defensive backfield coach, Jim called me and said, 'Paul, do you think Paul Brown would recommend me?'

Paul was magical. If Paul put a word in for him, he had a chance to get the job, but Jim was so nervous about calling Paul Brown that he didn't know how to go about it.

I said, 'Jim, you know you represent class. Paul Brown believes in class. I can't imagine that he wouldn't at least talk to you about it. If he didn't believe that you belonged there, he would probably tell you that, but what do you lose by asking him?'

When Jim called him, he got hold of his secretary and said, 'This is Jim Shofner. I'd like to talk to Paul Brown.'

Paul Brown got on the phone and said, 'Jim, my Jim,' like Jim Shofner was the most important person in the world, and he got Jim the job.

I took a course one time at Stanford, called 'The Age of Louis XIV.' Louis XIV regarded himself as a divine-right monarch, and I think there was a feeling of that with Paul. I say that respectfully, but Paul felt very strong about his word being the last word.

THERE WAS A PLAYER NAMED LEROY BOLDEN, a good little player, a good little guy. He had done something in a Detroit game that had cost us the game. He was so distraught that he wouldn't even get on the team train, to go back to Cleveland. He showed up the next meeting, and Paul stood up in front of him and said, 'There's only one person in this organization who will decide whether you do or don't ride back on the team transportation and that person is Brown.'

He always wore a big tee-shirt that said, 'B-R-O-W-N-S.' He looked at it and went with his finger, 'B-R-O-W-N,' and it was like law. He was making a point for everybody.

You couldn't challenge him. He always said, 'We wait for nobody. If you're not there when the plane leaves, it leaves without you.' And we never did wait for anybody. It was a mind thing. I guess you call it mentally programming, that this guy was the divine-right monarch.

People did get into trouble. They did things that Paul didn't like. Jim Brown got in some trouble, but Jim Brown was a model player. He dressed like a champion and played like a champion. When it was time to play football, Jim Brown played football. There were some things that went on behind the scenes that I am sure Paul wasn't thrilled about. Paul wasn't stupid, and he knew that the world wasn't perfect. He also knew if you're going to be bad off the field, you'd better be damn good on it, and, at some point, he wasn't going to compromise.

Paul sold class hard. He would talk about us being 'the Yankees of football.' He used to have the Yankees stop in. I vividly remember saying, 'That's Moose Skowron. How can they call a guy *Moose* when he weighs 185 pounds?' We were at old League Park with all the rats, and Paul was talking about 'class.' Yet because he said it was the truth, you actually believed it.

It had nothing to do with size; it had to do with command. He only weighed 145 pounds and was maybe 5' 10", but he was clearly in a class all by himself. To some degree, it was fear-related—fear of losing your job. Things were different in those days. There were an awful lot of people on the street that were close to your abilities, and so you better make a difference in some other ways. When he spoke, you better damn well listen. If he wants class, you better *be* class. The element of fear was always there, and every once in a while he had a way of showing you that fear.

There was some resentment there, but I don't know that you would have traded your position with the Cleveland Browns for anything. His demeanor made the Browns special. You could have gone to any other industrial city and played on a Pittsburgh Steelers team or a Detroit Lions team, and I don't think you would have felt anywhere near the same. If you looked at the staff he had, it had to be him. Howard Brinker was a shy guy who kind of stuttered. When I first got there, I thought Fritz Heisler was Doctor Zorak from Mars. He had these things on his glasses, and I thought, 'Who's this guy,' but he was one of the most brilliant technicians that ever walked the face of the earth. Paul was the focal point, however, and, boy, I tell you what: He did it his way.

You would like to be the rebel and stand up and say, 'Not me, baby,' but, man, I was right there with the rest of them, and there were some pretty heavy-duty guys there, hard-nosed, street-type guys, and when he spoke, they listened every bit as intently as I did. I don't know that I am proud of going along with it, either, but I sure wouldn't trade it for anything.

The heavy-duty criticism of Paul during that era was his play-calling. I think the offensive players in general had a sense that we weren't maximizing the creative game as it was at the time. It's hard to remember whether that's true, but I'm not so sure—in fairness to the offensive guys—that the game hadn't passed him by a little bit. On the other hand, he went to Cincinnati and was successful there in a hurry, so something was right. Maybe he updated his thinking with regard to offense.

Paul always ran the offense. He didn't know what was going on with the defense. It was my second or third year with the Browns, and we were playing a preseason game out in San Francisco. Jim Pace was playing running back for the 49ers, and he makes about 30 yards around my end. All of a sudden, here comes a substitute for me. I come to the sideline. Paul always thought that if you were the end, then you stopped the end run, but there's forces and all kinds of stunts involved.

So I got to the sidelines, and he was just chewing me out about this run. I had a stunt on and was coming down to the inside. I couldn't be farther away from an end run on what I was asked to do. Somebody was supposed to be scraping to the outside and taking care of that. Finally, I looked at him and said, 'Paul, you don't know the defense.'

And he looked me right in the eye and said, 'I may not know the defense, but I know who's on it, and you're not. Now, go sit down.'

Talk about defusing somebody in a hurry. He just needed a little ammunition, and he'd eat you alive.

He never lost his composure very much. His volatility range wasn't as wide as some people's. I remember Floyd Peters coming to the sidelines, and Floyd was so mad that he had his fists up around his face. Paul looked Floyd right in the eye and he almost whispered to him, 'Floyd, put your hands down. Now, go sit down, Floyd.' He wasn't a ranter and raver. He would eat you alive with the little comment.

MY FIRST CONTRACT, I signed with Dick Gallagher. From then on, I signed with Paul. After the first contract, the negotiating was done on the phone, and it was over in a hurry. It seemed to me if you didn't do it in three minutes, he'd be mad, because you were trying to rob his cornfield or something. He told you what you were going to get, and that was it. You could negotiate to some degree, but it had to be reasonable, at least in his estimation.

I got an $8,000 contract and a $500 bonus when I signed, and $500 was the most money I'd ever seen in my life. By my fourth or fifth year, I was making $10,000 or somewhere in there. If he went up $500, that was a heck of a good deal.

He intimidated people a little bit in that area, but at least we challenged him at one point. Floyd Peters, one time, I don't know exactly what he was making; I'd say $7,000. It wasn't a lot, because he was a free agent guy.

I said, 'You know, Floyd, I don't think that is really fair. You've got three boys now, and you have to think in terms of your family. Let's you and I sit down, and I'm going to write him a letter, and you look at it and see what you think.'

We put this thing together—I think we asked for another $500 or $1,000—and I said, 'What do you think?'

He said, 'Yeah, that sounds reasonable. It's not pushy. It's logical.'

I said, 'Okay, then sign it and we'll mail it.'

We put that in the mailbox, and Floyd called me and said, 'Is there any way we can get that out of the mailbox?'

After he thought about it, he was panicked that Paul Brown was going to be mad. But Paul read it and called him back, and he said, 'You know, those were good points.' Floyd ended up getting the raise. So Paul was pretty fair about it.

MONEY WAS DIFFERENT in those days, though. The only way you could save money in those days was to have a job in the off-season. I went into the army for six months after my first year with the Browns. The next year, '59, I went to Stanford and took 21 units in one quarter and completed my masters and worked a construction job. In those days, you worked in the off-seasons. I taught school from then on. Even in my last year with the Browns, which was 1967, I was captain and a starting player in the Pro Bowl, and I made only $27,500. Still, we were probably making more money than a lot of people I went to school with.

When I went to Cleveland, League Park had one meeting room and a locker room. The meeting room had wooden floors and a chair with your name on it. Wednesday was offensive day, and everybody listened to offense, and we wrote it all down in our playbooks. Thursday was defensive day, and everybody listened to defense and wrote it down. Friday we kind of tied everything together. And we won.

Paul was a great teacher. Certainly, he must have understood teaching, in his own way. I don't know that Paul ever manipulated his thinking to be what he was; I think it just came very, very natural to him: 'This is who we are, this is how we get it done, and this is how I'm going to do it.' I'm sure that's what he felt.

WE HAD AN INKLING OF WHAT WAS GOING TO HAPPEN between Paul and Art Modell. In fact, Modell indicated to me that it might happen. I don't know really what Modell was doing when he told me that. We were surprised, but you could feel it coming. We knew something was going to happen; we didn't know what. There was a lot of friction there. It was Modell's deal, and he was going to do it the way he wanted to, so he replaced Paul with Blanton Collier, and the world was stunned.

Our last game of the 1962 season was out in San Francisco. Coming back on the plane, we were talking about it. It was: 'Wonder when this is going to end. This is a mess.' It was just kind of general talk. I can't say that the problems really affected the atmosphere. We still won, but it was not one of our better years, as I recall (7-6-1).

I found out about the firing in the training room at Stanford University. The trainer told me.

I said, 'Really.'

He said, 'Here it is, right here in the paper.'

I'm not sure how I felt, because it wasn't the happiest of marriages for any of us. I don't know that I took a toll of my feelings at the time. There was relief and there was frustration, there was anxiety, there was concern, there was a sense of loss. There were all those emotions. With a complex man like Paul Brown, there are bound to be complex emotions.

After everything, Modell asked me if I was comfortable with Blanton being the head coach, because I think they saw me as not a leader, but one of the people that made some sense if you talked to him. You couldn't help but like Blanton Collier. I wasn't pushing his cause, but I liked him. We all liked him, but I don't think there was anything done behind the scenes to push Blanton into the job.

Blanton was an absolute detailist. He took football to the finest point. He could tell you exactly what to do. He'd say, 'Paul, you might want to look at putting your heel down, because I think, fractionally, it will get you off better on the pass rush.'

It didn't, but he said he'd read somewhere in biomechanics or kinesiology that it would. He knew every little thing about everything. That wasn't Paul's deal; Paul wasn't like that. They were two separate coaches. Paul Brown was cold-blooded in dealing with people. One time I played bad, below my lowest standard of play. Blanton came into the locker room and said to me, 'Today, Paul, I'm going to get down on you hard. I want you to know it in advance so be prepared for it.' Paul would have never done that. Paul would just eat you up.

AFTER PAUL WAS LET GO, he almost went into seclusion. During that seclusion is when Jim Shofner called him about the job in San Francisco, and in that conversation, Jim said to him, 'You know, Paul, I was really sorry about what happened in Cleveland.'

And Paul said to him, 'Jim, it just ruined a life. That's all.'

I don't think it was true that I was anti-Paul Brown at the end. I was probably just like everybody else. We complained a lot about him. Everybody did, because that's the way it is with that kind of a command situation. That didn't mean that when you were in the fox hole, he wasn't the guy you wanted in there with you.

I don't know that I actually made the decision to retire. I had made a commitment to Carolynn that when our oldest daughter, Kymberly, was starting school, we would either move to Cleveland, or I would retire. We had already moved her in and out of school once, and she had gone to school in Cleveland and had to come back, and she was enrolling in school back in Northern California. After Jack Christiansen was let go (as head coach) in San Francisco, Jim Shofner was retained by (new 49er head coach) Dick Nolan. When I came home after the Pro Bowl, Jim said, 'You ought to interview with the 49ers. Your home's here.'

I said, 'Well, you think I have a chance? I mean I have not coached, and I don't know Dick Nolan.'

Jim said, 'I know, but I'm gonna talk to him and see if he'd consider interviewing you.'

I said, 'Well, it's worth a try.'

I had to fly back to Cleveland because I was the Cleveland Pro of the Year. It sounds more impressive than it was. I go back for this thing, and I go into the office, and I tell Blanton Collier that I've got a chance to interview with the 49ers for the defensive line job.

Blanton said, 'Paul, I think you'd probably get the job. Go ahead and go for it.'

This started one of the problems I eventually had with Blanton.

I go back and I interview. I talk to Dick Nolan, and Dick Nolan takes me down to an industrial psychologist, who gives me a battery of tests. Dick tells me, 'Okay, I'm going to let you know next week.'

I'm almost relieved, because I'm thinking he's putting me off, and I'm not going to get the job. I'm almost not wanting to have to make that decision, because I really wanted to play. I loved playing football. The next night, he calls me at home and offers me the job. I just sat there. I wasn't ready for that. So I said, 'Can I just talk to my wife? Can I set the phone down? Just a minute.'

I told Carolynn, and she went, 'What did you say?'

I said, 'I'll take it.'

I was making $27,500 and it paid $18,000, which meant we could make it work. We had just bought a house a couple of years before that in Los Altos Hills.

WHEN I HUNG THAT PHONE UP, it was like a cannon ball hit me in the stomach. My teammates were all so important to me. Fortunately, I had to make a decision right there, because if I'd had to wear it for a while, I think I would have gone back and played, and I was at a point where I was playing really good. But I was 33 years old, and I was probably not far away from playing *not* really good.

What ended up happening was that Art Modell called and just ripped me. He said, 'You can't take that job, because you're still under contract. You didn't even ask for permission.'

'Art,' I said, 'I did ask for permission. I asked Blanton.'

He said, 'I checked with Blanton. He has no recollection of it.'

And then Art tried to get a draft choice from the 49ers for tampering, which even made me look worse. At the time, it was really a bad thing. That was painful for me, because I loved Blanton Collier. I never thought he would do that to me. I couldn't believe it. Paul Brown would have never done that. My feelings were painful. I've never had a divorce or the emotions that go with something like that, but I've heard how devastating it could be to you, and it was that kind of emotion, believe it or not.

And, oh, did I miss the game. I missed it the next day. It's amazing what I missed. I even missed the hard times. Whenever things went bad, we used to get the defensive linemen together before the next practice and say, 'Now, look, you guys are down. We lost. We've got to get together. If we work hard and set the tempo, we'll make a difference.' It was a wonderful thing to be part of, and I've been blessed.

It was probably easier to become a coach than go cold turkey and become an insurance salesmen. But, then, coaching was so intense under Dick Nolan that I just didn't have time to think about it. I think the players and I did okay, except that they saw me as one of the guys, and I had to overcome that.

Then I finally got a little bit creative and did some things that helped me grow in the off-season. I got film of all the great NFL defensive linemen and made a reel of the common positive denominators and why they were successful at what they did and how they did it. It included Deacon Jones, Ordell Braase, Willie Davis, Gino Marchetti, and Merlin Olsen, just to name a few. I bet that reel was copied a hundred times by coaches because it's such a great film. I wish I had it now.

I was the defensive line coach for the next six years, and then I got to edge up to defensive coordinator. I probably should have prepared a little more before I became a coordinator, but I did it. I don't know that I was a great coordinator because I think the great coordinators have a little better understanding of the intricacies of secondary play than I had, but we did okay.

WHEN I TOOK THE KANSAS CITY JOB in 1975 as head coach, I was a little immature in some ways. I'd like to blame the personnel, but I think I could have done a better job, and I've got to finger myself first. We didn't have a good football team. To be honest with you, one of the reasons we went there was we would be in the same city with a great guy named Galen Fiss. Isn't that interesting? I mean it seemed like he was the clincher, because Carolynn just broke down and cried. We were talking about the team and how hard it was going to be. She said, 'We don't want to do this.'

I didn't know Kansas City was even interested in me. I didn't call them. They called me. And Paul Brown had inspired that somehow. I didn't ask him to call; they called Paul Brown. A year or so later, I asked the people who hired me what possessed them to pick me, because I wasn't a perfect match for what they wanted to get done. They said, 'You need to know that the one person who made a difference was Paul Brown.'

I just didn't match up with Lamar Hunt, the owner, or Jack Steadman, the general manager, very well. I think what happened to me was I got away from teaching. I love to teach, and I got away from teaching, and I think that is what the administration of the game is all about: You don't teach much anymore.

I don't know that I had that command factor, either. Jack Steadman looked me right in the eye at one point and said, 'Paul, you're not enough of an asshole.' He was probably right. I could never treat someone other than the way *I* wanted to be treated.

I REALLY PUT MY HEART into Kansas City. I really did. I don't know that I sold my soul to it, but I came awful close. And it's amazing how you feel with the team. About two days after I had been fired, I was home alone. I tend to show emotion during good times; rarely do I show emotion during hard times. I just broke down and cried, and I've never done that before. I felt like I gave it everything I had. The feeling was that it was my team and they took away from me. It was very painful.

After Kansas City, I was a defensive coordinator with the New Orleans Saints. Dick Nolan (New Orleans head coach) did that Magnificent Seven thing. He got the job and then went out and rounded up his whole gang. We were a good football team, the best they'd ever been. I was there two years and then I went to Stanford as the head coach.

I was a pretty good player at Stanford and pretty well thought of. I kind of came in as a hero. Mighty Mouse was going to save the day. We had John Elway, and we had some magical things happen along the way, but not enough of them happened.

Stanford's an awfully hard place to recruit for, particularly on the defensive side of the ball. The characteristics that make a great defensive player are not necessarily the things that inspire someone to go to the library. I guarantee you, the defensive player is a different breed. I could take you to our locker room today and show you the difference between offense and defense, just by comparing the neatness of the lockers.

I think it would have been a lot better had I not been a Stanfordite and not gone back to where I had been a popular person. They voted for their players of the century, and Jim Plunkett was the offensive player, and I was the defensive player. That probably tells you how bad the defense at Stanford has been over the years, but that's the kind of status I had when I went in there.

After a year with the Olympic Committee in Los Angeles, I came to the Vikings. I was always happiest as a position coach, teaching. I spent the next seven seasons as their defensive line coach. When a head coaching change took place, I was offered a different position with the organization. My wife and I talked it out and I chose to go to this administrative level that I'm in now. But I really missed coaching my group; the withdrawal that I felt after coaching was the same withdrawal I felt after playing.

It's incredible how things have changed. I was looking at a book from when I was head coach at Kansas City, which wasn't that long ago. We had seven coaches, and I had to fight to get the seventh. Now, we've got fourteen or fifteen coaches. We can do technical things that we never imagined before. We can sit in a room, and if we want every draw play on third down from a one-back formation, we can push a button and, *boom*, the video is on the screen. This new digital system is so advanced I can't even explain it.

WHEN I PLAYED WITH THE BROWNS my first year, Paul Bixler was the end coach, so after we warmed up, I was with Paul Warfield because he was an end and I was an end. Except I was a defensive end, and he was an offensive end. I would go stand and be a defensive back, and Paul Bixler would show Paul where to cut and other than that, that was what I did. Even as bright as Paul Brown was, that didn't make an ounce of sense, but that's what we did.

We used to go to League Park and pick up glass so we could practice. It was like picking up cigarette butts in the army. We didn't do it every time, but you'd come in, and they'd say, 'Somebody threw some bottles in there. Let's go and pick up glass 'cause we don't want anybody to get hurt.'

The game is just a different game. The size of the players is incredible. At the NFL scouting combine last year in Indianapolis, there were fifty-nine offensive linemen; forty-three of them weighed over 300 pounds, and the rest of them were knocking at the 300-pound door. The average weight was about 313 for the lineman.

I read somewhere that Paul Brown said that Lenny Ford, John Yonaker, and I were the best defensive ends he'd ever coached. I wasn't a great player. I was a smart player. I was a guy who could tell you that if they were in split backs and I was on the weak side, whether or not they would run a play back at me. I made plays sometimes out of intelligence and not of skill, and from the standpoint of a being a great player, no, I really wasn't. I was smarter than most players. I was a good competitor, and I had a German shepherd mentality. I loved the master, and when I had my costume on, I think I would have killed for him.

If I had my life to live over, and you'd say, 'Paul, you can go anyplace in the United States to play football,' I'd say, 'I'm going to Cleveland, Ohio, to play with the Browns.' It was a great time. 〟〟

# The
# 62-Mile Run

HE OVERSLEPT and was late for the 62-mile run. He wore a WWI aviator's cap, thick pilot's goggles, and coveralls, and he jumped into a phone booth and burst out seconds later in adidas running shoes, sweat pants scissored off at the thigh, and a Superman T-shirt stretched across his broad chest. Reporters, cameramen, and tipsy chums swirled around him outside the Cleveland Browns' offices at Municipal Stadium until a race-track herald wearing a red frock coat blew a long trumpet, the blast sharp in the June dusk, and he began running briskly across the Detroit High Level Bridge.

Dome lights flashing, a police cruiser led the way, and one of his brothers ran next to him, and another drove a camper that carried his wife, son, daughter, and a young teammate who hoped to replace him some day.

The little knot of his friends didn't make it past the first tavern, and so he ran with just his brother down West 25th Street, heading thirty-five miles south on Route 42 to Medina and then twenty-nine miles slightly southwest on Route 3 to Wooster, his hometown.

For hours, autograph seekers shoved paper and pens at him, uninvited fans jogged behind him for a few miles and quit, and supporters offered him towels and cold drinks. He ran thirty-five miles in under seven hours, but at three o'clock in the morning, his hamstrings tightened into piano wire, and his knees would no longer bend, as if they had rusted, and he lurched along, his adidas slapping flatly against the dark highway. He wound elastic bandages around his knees and feet and propped himself up with a five-foot tree branch.

As the sun rose the next day, he resisted riding in the camper or staying on his back in dappled shade when his brief rest periods ended. He forced himself on, incoherent at times, and with a dozen miles left, he could barely walk and was in more agony than he'd ever imagined and nearly gave up. He had drunk twenty-five gallons of ice water and soda and Quick Kick and still lost twelve pounds. He said that when he made it to Wooster, he would need new legs and feet and a week in solitary confinement.

Eighteen hours and twenty-five minutes after it began, the 62-mile run ended when he limped through the gates of his old high school stadium, weeping with joy and relief. A friend picked him up in a fancy antique convertible and chauffeured him to the showroom of a car dealership, where a band played and a crowd cheered, and he collapsed and had to be carried—all 265 pounds—to his car.

"What I proved I don't know," Dick Schafrath told a reporter.

Schafrath had often driven between Wooster and Cleveland; during those trips, he had to have marveled at the unlikely events that took him from village to city. He had been brought up on a farm by a father who wanted only to be known as the hardest worker in the county. He learned to use only one utensil— the spoon—and in barnyard, school, and church, wore the same clothes.

Every weekend, he went with his mother into town, where a grocery store kept a television set playing, and she would dawdle while her son watched a few minutes of an Indians' or a Browns' game.

He played baseball in the fields with his brothers, using cowflop bases and balls his mother knitted. He went out for school teams partly because he could use the showers to scrub the pump-water rust from his skin. A veterinarian gave Schafrath his first physical, and he did his chores, walked five miles to and from school, and took whippings when his father caught him sneaking to practices and games.

Schafrath's father finally accepted the inevitable, telling his son, "Kid, if you're going to get into them (sports), work as hard as you can, and you won't get hurt."

He captained Wooster High School's baseball, basketball, and football teams and was drafted by the Cincinnati Reds. Schafrath was preparing for professional baseball when Woody Hayes, football coach at Ohio State University, showed up at the farm. Hayes ignored him but charmed Schafrath's parents. When the coach left, Schafrath said that playing football at Ohio State was out of the question.

"I'll tell you what, son," his mother replied, "you are going to Ohio State."

Unhappy in college, Schafrath sloughed off his studies. Poor grades earned him not a bus ticket to Wooster but residence in the Hayes home, where Anne Hayes, the coach's wife, became advisor, tutor, and surrogate mother.

In Schafrath's three seasons, Ohio State went 21-4-2, winning a Big Ten championship, the Rose Bowl, and the UPI national title in 1957. The Browns picked him in the second round of the NFL draft although he hadn't made any all-star team and was so light—under 215 pounds—that Schafrath had no idea what position he could play in the pros.

Schafrath had never been able to gain weight, despite a voracious appetite. As a boy, he could eat a hundred pancakes at a sitting and was perennial champion of the eating contests at the county fair. "My motto was, 'Eat just enough to win,'" he says.

Sundays, the family went to the Smithfield Chicken Inn, where adults could eat all they wanted for a dollar, children for fifty cents. "They brought out so much chicken that by the time they were through, I couldn't see my dad across the table because of all the chicken bones," Schafrath said.

He once ate nine dozen hamburgers. He ate $130 worth of food at a $10 all-you-can-eat clambake before being asked to leave. At small restaurants, he ordered the entire menu; at larger ones, he had four entrees: chicken, fish, meat, and pasta.

He began as a 220-pound defensive end, but Brown, for reasons he never explained, moved him to offensive tackle and ordered him to report the next season at 250. Schafrath spent the summer digging holes for a construction company and eating the two dozen sandwiches his mother packed each day in a peck basket. Nevertheless, he was so far under his prescribed weight that some coworkers fashioned an iron jockstrap for him to wear beneath his shorts to weigh in. Brown quickly discovered the ruse, but was impressed by Schafrath's resolve.

"I had to make a quick decision after that first year, and I really got committed. I could never have played for him if I wasn't really committed. I was going to get my weight up and make it," he said.

A weight-lifting regimen with Mr. America aspirants added forty pounds, but Schafrath was unprepared for his new position.

Groza, whose back problems forced him to give up left tackle, tutored him, but pass blocking confounded Schafrath. He won the job through hustle and Brown's unexpected patience.

After years with the volatile Hayes, Schafrath, as a rookie, had been so put off by Brown's austere and cerebral approach that he didn't believe he could last long in Cleveland.

"First, Paul gave us a mental exam," he said. "And right away, I figured I was in trouble. Lou Groza was sitting next to me, and he had ten cards full of cheat notes. He had taken the same test for fifteen years. He left the room in ten minutes. I was there for two and a half hours."

Missing most of training camp because of Air Force duty for his first several seasons didn't help Schafrath make the transition to tackle, but Brown remained understanding.

"Paul hung with me," he says. "Eddie Ulinski, the tackle coach, would call me the night before practice and say, 'I just want to warn you. Paul's going to be singling you out (in films). You didn't look too good on some plays.' That's the only way you learn, but he saw some good things I was doing."

He says Brown's lack of emotion perplexed younger players and hurt the squad, but after Schafrath was depicted by the media as backing owner Art Modell's firing of the coach in 1963, he sent an apology to Brown.

"If I had killed my own son, I could not feel worse as I saw my name totally supporting Art's actions," he wrote. "I know that Art used me then, and I tried to blame him for what I had done, but I can only say that I am not much of a man for not standing on my own two feet and keeping my mouth shut. I feel pretty cheap, and I am sorry."

By the time Blanton Collier replaced Brown, Schafrath had become a star on what he called "a proud, confident line." He was Cleveland's most valuable player in 1963, when the Browns broke a team record with 2,639 yards rushing, and

Jim Brown set an NFL mark with 1,863 yards. The Browns led the NFL in rushing from 1965 through 1967 and had its top ground gainer seven of nine seasons. Schafrath, a team captain, played in six Pro Bowls and was named the league's best left tackle three straight years.

Jim Brown has long insisted that Schafrath deserves to be in the Hall of Fame. "How in the world can you have three Hall of Fame runners (Brown, Leroy Kelly, and Bobby Mitchell) and not have anybody from the line?" Brown asked.

"We had the best downfield blocking in history," he said. "As I look at the game, there's no doubt in my mind I'd take Gene Hickerson and Schafrath on my all-time team."

Injuries kept Schafrath, who was among the league's smaller tackles, from only two games in thirteen seasons, but he paid for that resilience. Rules forbade blockers from extending their arms or using their hands, and with every block, pinched nerves numbed his shoulders. Pass rushers were allowed to club and slap. Schafrath could never master Groza's technique of slipping blows, surreptitiously clutching his man's jersey, and hanging on. Schafrath led with his helmet—turning his head into a punching bag for much larger men—and played with numerous concussions.

After winning a vicious battle against 6' 8", 275-pound Doug Atkins in Tulane Stadium one broiling afternoon, Schafrath began to vomit and cramp. He blacked out and convulsed; teammates carried him to the training room. Trainers searched for ice, but it had all melted. Doctors cut away Schafrath's uniform and saved him with injections of muscle relaxants and an intravenous drip of saline solution. He regained consciousness after ninety minutes and asked, "How did Atkins do?"

He said the only other time he'd come close to passing out was while working in a cornfield with his father.

In 1969, Schafrath intervened in a fight between Cleveland center Fred Hoaglin and Detroit linebacker Mike Lucci. He missed with a punch, and his elbow stuck in Lucci's facemask. Infection grotesquely swelled his right arm. Schafrath had to eat and shave left-handed and sleep sitting in a chair. Incapable of pushing off with his right hand, he labored to come out of his stance and attempted to block while protecting the elbow. He tore the triceps in the same arm. A virus left him unable to eat or sleep. He had an allergic reaction to flu shots. A rash covered his body, and his eyes became so bloodshot that his vision blurred. To fight inflammation, infection, and blood poisoning, he took ten pills a day. His weight dropped to 228 pounds, and after Cleveland lost the championship game to Minnesota, Schafrath was rushed to Shaker Medical Center.

Schafrath claimed that without hypnotism, he couldn't have played the last several games of that season. He first tried hypnotism, which he called his "edge," in 1963 to achieve "total concentration." By the Minnesota game, he was using it as painkiller.

"I needed an edge because I always felt handicapped," he said. I wasn't a natural athlete. I wasn't big, and I wasn't fast. I didn't have natural ability."

A columnist wrote, "He had to carve out a place for himself through sweat and physical torture. Fortunately, he was built for the job."

Eighteen months later, when Schafrath made the 62-mile run, he had been an acclaimed player for over a decade. Nineteen seventy-one would be his last season, however, not only because of a salary dispute with Modell, but also because his legs didn't recover until well into autumn from the hours of pounding.

The 62-mile run had been quintessential Schafrath: equally sentimental journey, publicity stunt, labor of Hercules, business venture, and whim. The Cleveland media covered it as if it were a moonshot; Schafrath, always popular with reporters, became their darling and received, as a bonus, free use of an automobile for a year.

"Next time," he said when it was over, "I'll try something easy, like swimming from California to Hawaii."

Schafrath's difficulties hadn't begun. Over the next decade and a half, he worked as a sports agent, line coach of the Washington Redskins, television commentator for high school sports, farmer, supervisor for a temporary agency, director of a fitness club, and owner of a boys' camp and two canoe liveries. He fell nearly two million dollars in debt and was sued by a former business partner. He went through his second divorce, was diagnosed with cancer, and developed heart trouble.

In 1985, as he was about to begin managing a ranch in Wyoming, Schafrath's life took yet another peculiar turn. The Ohio senate's Republican caucus asked him to replace a senator who had resigned to become a divinity student at Harvard. At President Ronald Reagan's request, Schafrath had been chairman of Athletes for Reagan-Bush '84, but his only other brush with politics was at a 1972 White House dinner, at which he ate the mint sprig and drank the water from a finger bowl.

Schafrath was well known and had always been community minded. He flew directly from the 1969 Pro Bowl to Vietnam, touring bases for two weeks and coming home to deliver messages and photos to soldiers' families. He visited schools in low-income areas, spoke to civic groups, and was a member of the Fellowship of Christian Athletes. At one Big Brothers of Greater Cleveland Christmas Party, he and teammate John Wooten had pictures taken with all 145 kids and signed every photo.

Schafrath accepted the senate appointment, and the following year, waged a campaign for the permanent seat that became so nasty that a senate aide said of it, "This makes the Seven-Day War in Israel look like a picnic."

Schafrath opposed an old friend, Thomas Van Meter, in the election. Their clash rived the Ohio Republican Party. Van Meter, a career politician who had left the senate to run for governor, called Schafrath "a liar"; Schafrath countered that Van Meter was "a loser."

"I've got Jim Brown's cleat marks on my back," Schafrath said at the bitterest moment of the campaign. "I'm not going to quit because of all these negative things. He's trying to clip me now, knock me out by not getting in the issues but by personally attacking me."

His father, Hayes, and Paul Brown chaired his election committee, and Schafrath won by a hundred votes. He had little trouble in subsequent races, serving thirteen

years before term limits ended his tenure.

One January morning when 20-below temperatures stalled his car and prevented cabs from running, Schafrath walked almost an hour and a half to attend a committee session. He could barely breathe, his feet nearly froze, and his glasses iced over so thoroughly that he couldn't tell when he was crossing a street. He arrived at the State House to find the meeting canceled.

Schafrath called that walk "crazy," as he did his paddling a canoe across Lake Erie at its widest point seven months after having a malignant section of his small intestine removed. With a buddy nicknamed "Wolfman," Schafrath, who was fifty-one at the time, made the fifty-five mile crossing in seventeen and a half hours.

He said of the voyage, "There is just so much depression in so many people who may have had a setback in their lives—heart problems, cancer problems, divorce. All I'm trying to say is, 'Accept that challenge and go for it.'"

Schafrath was anything but depressed as he sat in his office in the Browns' new training center and looked out over the practice fields, vibrant green in the robust late-spring sunlight. Injuries, financial setbacks, personal travails, and dire illnesses seem not to have tainted his natural cheeriness. Schafrath had just moved into the office, which he uses as president of the Browns' alumni association. Boxes jammed with memorabilia and files were strewn amid sparse furnishings and bare walls.

Three cancer surgeries and a faulty heart have left Schafrath so thin as to appear pop-eyed behind spectacles that jut from his face. His cropped gray hair was tousled, his complexion sallow, the stalk of his spindly neck lost in his collar. He was clad in the mishmash of hayseed, ex-jock, and senior citizen that drives his daughter, who also is also his secretary, to distraction: lined Ohio State windbreaker, rugby shirt, thermal longjohn top, faded black jeans tucked into cowboy boots.

As he talked, Schafrath frequently cleared his throat and referred to a pile of notebooks he has filled over the years. The notebooks were in his car when it was stolen and driven into a creek; their cardboard covers were bowed and faded, their pages swollen. Thumbing the smeared notes, he was by turns wistful, contemplative, and giddy.

As a younger man, Schafrath had a reputation as a rogue with a talent for fun and an astute view of his own image. He had, some said, an eye on Hollywood, and with his chiseled physique and small-town insouciance, he could probably have made a

living as a character actor in Westerns. At times, he is so earnestly homey and self-effacing that one has to wonder if he isn't a sly country boy shucking the world. However, just when he begins to appear the opportunist, Schafrath laughs. It begins in a feather-duster tickle fluttering far down in his chest, catches and builds into a naughty adolescent chuckle, and bursts into an ebullient peal of abandon that is genuine and infectious.

He says now that he has succeeded only by virtue of the work ethic his parents instilled in him, the grace of God, and the lessons he took from Hayes and Brown, and although he still wishes he had played baseball, he is without regret.

Thirty years ago, as Schafrath stumbled into Wooster near the end of the 62-mile run, he was in so much distress that people lining the streets begged him to stop. He brushed them aside and staggered toward the high school stadium, still a mile away.

The next morning, he was back in the Browns' weight room, lifting and blithely telling reporters, "My body feels great. I feel real good, except behind the knees. I can't straighten up. I have to walk bent over, like an old man."

# *Dick* SCHAFRATH

" MY DAD HATED SPORTS.
He thought they were a waste of time. He was a hard-working German who grew up with eleven children in the family. He worked two jobs until he was 22 and gave every penny to his dad. I learned my hard work ethic through my dad, and I'm very grateful for that, but it drove him crazy when I was hounding him about playing sports. I never played organized sports until I got to high school. We played softball in a cow pasture. We had manure piles as bases, and Mom knitted us softballs out of yarn. We'd take an old potato basket, cut a hole in the bottom of it, and hang it up in the barn. Sometimes, Mom would get these hard rubber balls at a salvage place, and I threw them up against the barn and pretended I was catching Dale Mitchell or Kenny Keltner with the '48 Indians.

When I was a freshman, I finally talked him into letting me play. The veterinarian was at the barn, and my dad asked him if he would give me a physical. We didn't have doctors. 'Line him up,' the vet said. 'We just finished the pigs. We have to do the calves next. We'll do him in between.' He gave me a little slip of paper, and that was my physical.

I hate to even think about playing high school ball. My kids don't like to hear about it, either. They're like, 'Yeah, Dad, you ran uphill ten miles both ways.' I read a book one time about Jim Thorpe beating the bus into town, so I liked to do that. The bus would go by, and once in a while, I'd run into town. It was about five miles into Wooster.

As I went through school we got some electric, and by the time I was graduating from high school we got a toilet and a shower in the house. We didn't even have vehicles. The only time I ever dated is when some kid from town came out and got me. All through school, I helped my dad do chores. After sports, I had to walk five miles home again, then do my chores. After every game, after every practice, I had to walk home and do my chores.

I didn't even know how to shower. My first shower was in a football uniform. I didn't know you had to take it off. I'm in the shower, in high school, very puzzled by how you do it. We didn't even have a bathtub at home. We had an actual tub that each kid got in. By the time it got to me, it was pretty dirty water. Going into a friend's house who had a bathroom was very confusing to me. We had outhouses.

When I was in high school, we got a one-party phone line. There were twelve people on the line, and even if you could get on the party line, you couldn't call a girl for a date because everybody was listening. I gave my dad a personal phone when he was 80 years old, and he was mad as hell because I took away his party line. He used to just sit and listen to everybody.

A LOT OF GREAT COACHES CAME TO THE FARM. Blanton Collier tried to recruit me at Kentucky. Frank Leahy came out from Notre Dame. I really wanted to play baseball, and I was drafted by the Cincinnati Reds, but Woody Hayes entered the picture. It became a battle of whether I was going to Ohio State or play for the Reds.

One day, Woody stopped by the farm and went to church with us and helped Mom cook lunch and was out at the barn with Dad. Of course, it was the typical story: He never said a word to me and left. I told Mom an hour later I certainly wasn't impressed with Woody Hayes and wasn't going to Ohio State.

She said, 'I'll tell you what, son, you *are* going to Ohio State.'

I couldn't see four years at Ohio State. I wanted to get right into playing baseball or go right to the Browns. But for Mom and Dad, Ohio was the United States, Wooster was the capital, and Woody Hayes was the second god. I just couldn't get out of the grasp of Woody Hayes.

Every other quarter, I'd fail a course to get out of there, and then he'd make me come back and live with him. Woody knew I wasn't going to be there if I didn't live with him. So, I lived with him for two years, off and on. Anne spent more time with me than Woody. We'd go over my classes, then she'd take me to my tutor.

Sometimes Woody would get Anne riled and she would throw plates at him. She stood up to him all the time. Phone calls would come. They'd call

Woody every name in the book, and she'd agree with them.

My second quarter at Ohio State, Woody had me go to an Emily Post etiquette class, so I would know how to eat properly. I didn't even know how to pass things. At home, we just helped ourselves. I had never eaten soup with a spoon. Woody saw that right away. He said, 'I think you need to go to Emily Post.'

President Nixon invited us to the White House one time, and I ate the plants in the finger bowl. A lot of that etiquette people learn today just wasn't there when I grew up. It wasn't because Mom and Dad didn't care; we always said grace before a meal and always went to church on Sundays. It's just that a lot of the finer things weren't that important.

MY BACKGROUND WITH MY PARENTS made me willing to out-work anybody. It really took work ethic to mesh in with Woody. My father pushed me hard, and I liked that. I liked to be pushed. That's the only way my father knew how to have fun. We'd be out chopping wheat, and it would be who can chop the most shocks of wheat. If we were pitching manure, it was who can pitch it the fastest. If we were throwing bales, it would be who could unload the wagon fastest. So when I was with Woody, I responded very quickly to him. I loved the emotional part of Woody. That was the reason I stayed there and didn't go into baseball.

That first fall, I failed two courses. I knew I was leaving. There's eleven strings of ballplayers, and I was eleventh string. I couldn't even get on the camouflage and go against the varsity on Mondays. It's the last game of the season, against Michigan, and I knew I was leaving, so I wasn't going to school. So what the hell. I called Mom to tell her that I was coming home.

I started to tell her, and she said, 'Hey, Dick, glad you called. Two bus loads of people are coming down to watch practice tomorrow.'

It was Sunday before the Monday of Michigan week. I'm thinking, 'Oh, my God, two bus loads of people coming to practice.'

So I run back to Woody. I said, 'I know I haven't been too good for you. I know I've been a problem child.'

He said, 'Well, Dick, what do you want?'

I said, 'Somehow, you have to let me practice against the varsity. Mom's bringing down about 500 people to watch.'

He just said, 'All right.'

When they got there, I was apologizing to everyone: 'Oh, I have a bad leg. You might not see me play much.'

I didn't know if he was going to put me in or not, but right away, I was in there, right over Jim Parker, perhaps the greatest offensive lineman in the history of the game, and Bill Cummings. Both of them went about 260. And Woody ran ten straight off-tackle plays over me. I'm bleeding from the nose, my pants are ripped, mud all over me. He never let up. We went for almost two hours, and, God, I was limping, I was bleeding. But I wouldn't give up.

Mom was so proud. And Woody never said a word about it.

WOODY ALWAYS STRESSED he didn't care about All-Americans. He wanted team players. If you became an All-American, fine, but he wanted team players. I liked what he said, so I would play any position. I played all the line positions, and learned the positions so well that even though I wasn't gifted, I had knowledge and good footwork. He said that hurt me for being selected one of his All-Americans.

My senior year, Woody said, 'Now, if nothing happens, you're going to be an All-American.'

Rusty Bowermaster, a starting end, broke his ankle a week before the first game, and I volunteered to be an end. Woody always apologized because that cost me being an All-American. It never bothered me, though, because it helped me become a professional athlete.

He even had me out as a lonesome end for one game. I told him the hell with that because he never threw the ball, so I never went out anymore. But I caught probably six or seven passes that year.

Woody wouldn't let me play baseball at OSU, but I kept nursing the idea and talking with the Reds. After I got out of college, I was going to be a baseball player. But after the last game, against Michigan, I went to Fort Lauderdale with three guys, and on Monday I was drafted. Then, they had the draft on the Monday after your last game of the season. I was picked by the Browns in the second round, and I didn't know about it until I came back from Florida six days later.

I was still thinking about baseball. In the summer, I played in the Senior Bowl, the North-South Game, and the College All-Star Game. By then, I was stuck. I was a Cleveland Brown, and baseball was over with.

It was difficult for me to make the adjustment from Woody to Paul Brown. I reacted to emotion and was used to it. I came to the Browns, and everything was so unemotional. Everything was so individual it was just hard for me to understand how I would enjoy playing there. I wasn't really happy for the first couple of years. My first year, I played some on both offensive and defensive line, as backup. I learned every position on both offensive and defensive line. Woody and Paul Brown both believed you won with fundamentals. They'd say, 'Never give a poor team a chance. Don't ever let up. Work your fundamentals, and keep pounding away.' Yeah, Paul was predictable. Woody was predictable. Most generals were predictable, but they beat you because they had good people. They were fundamentally sound and had great team attitude. No one was selfish.

WHEN I CAME UP TO CLEVELAND, I was going to be a defensive end, but Paul Brown thought I should be an offensive tackle or a center. He said, 'You pick center or left tackle or right tackle,' because they weren't sure how long Mike McCormack was going to play.

I said, 'Well, tell me, which one is the toughest?'

He said, 'Left tackle, because you're on the quarterback's blind side and you don't get much help.'

I said, 'I think I'll try that.'

So I took the toughest position. That kind of tells you my mentality. You have to be crazy to play left tackle. I don't know why I chose tackle; I should've been a center. That would've been a little easier place to play. Tackle was a tough position because you were always left one-on-one. At that time, defense was all 4-3, and nobody was ever over the center, so I liked that idea. When you got out there at tackle, there was the fastest guy on the defense and he used the famous headslap.

I thought center was what it was going to be, because Willie Davis was still at tackle. They drafted Fran O'Brien. There was Groza, McCormack, and myself. They also drafted two Buckeyes, Jim Houston, and Jim Marshall (later a star defensive end with the Vikings). Can you imagine all of those people fighting for three tackle positions? The center, John Morrow, wasn't there yet. Art Hunter was having problems there. So I'm thinking: I'm going to be a center.

But we all kept going at it, and the first thing you know, Fran O'Brien was traded, then Jim Marshall was out the door. Houston, they put at middle linebacker. Groza had a sore back. When Willie Davis left, that was it. That all happened my second year.

When I started playing tackle, my mentor, Lou Groza said, 'Be like a boxer, Dick. Duck the first blow. When they miss, you just hang on to them so the official doesn't see you. If you miss, yell 'Look out!' to the quarterback. That was the famous 'lookout' block.

My first year, I weighed in at 220. My second year, I ended up at 275. I was the biggest guy on the Browns for three years. I could eat like a horse, and I was the first guy on the Browns to lift weights. Paul Brown didn't believe in it. No coaches wanted you to lift weights. That was '58, '59, '60, and no one lifted. I went to a boxing gym with Jimmy Bivins, a former boxing champion out of Cleveland, and I trained there. I gained fifty pounds in four months.

At Ohio State, I'd lose twenty pounds during a practice. I would sweat fiercely. I'd cramp up, because they wouldn't let you have water, but they gave you salt tablets. After practice, I'd be deathly sick, and they'd inject me with fluids. It was a horrible problem.

When I get to the Browns, it's the same thing. No water again. You got in the huddle, and they passed around a towel. Everybody was sweating, and wiping the sweat off their heads with the towel, and I'd be sucking on it. They called it 'the healing towel.' All of my career was miserable because I was always in cramps.

After that first year, I knew I had to get bigger. Paul said, 'Do everything in your power to come back at 250.'

SO I WENT AROUND THE STATE OF OHIO entering eating contests. I got free meals, all I wanted to eat. I'd eat to win. I never lost. There was a restaurant in Cleveland called The Bluegrass, and they had all you can eat for $10. One time, I went in there with Gary Collins. They offered me $50 to leave. I said, 'No, I'm hungry.' Gary didn't really care to eat much, but he'd watch and cheer me on. Gary got a cup of coffee and said to the waitress, 'Feed my man. He's hungry.'

They wrote down everything I ate and had it hanging on the wall there. I had five bags of clams and five shrimp cocktails. I had a gallon of milk, a bottle of wine, and I-don't-know-how-many Cokes. That was to start. Then I had twenty-four lobster tails and six chickens with all the trimmings.

After an hour and a half, they said, 'Dick, you have to go,' and Gary is still going, 'Feed my man. He's hungry. Feed my man.'

I said, 'Wait, we can't leave yet.'

He said, 'Why?'

I said, 'We haven't had dessert.'

They said, 'We're going to call the police. This is robbery.'

After college, I worked part-time with a construction company in

Wooster to get into shape for the Browns. They were having me dig six-by-six holes when I wasn't busy doing other jobs. So I'm working my butt off, staying hard, eating like heck. I was fired up, eating and digging. I'm about 220. I said, 'I've gotta weigh 250.'

I go to camp for the weigh-in. I finish the mental test, then I get in line with my T-shirt and shorts on. The scales go a little over 250. Paul says, 'Boy, you don't look that big. Get back up on that scale.'

He starts patting me. He finds the twenty-five pound iron jockstrap my friends at the construction company made for me.

'Anybody who would go to those extremes,' he says, 'I'm gonna keep around.'

That's when he encouraged me to keep weightlifting. When I got up to about 275, he said, 'That's enough. If you're going to stay in front of Jim Brown and Bobby Mitchell, you have to be able to run.'

I THINK PAUL LIKED MY ATTITUDE. I was taught to hustle, which was my second nature. Blanton Collier emphasized hustle all the time. He called it, 'Don't let *George* do it.' Blanton said, 'You've got Jim Brown or you've got Marion Motley or you got Otto Graham. They can win the game alone.' That would be how George would do it, he said. 'But *you* make the big play. Don't wait for George. *You* do it.'

My attitude was always, 'I'm gonna make the big block someplace. I'll hustle downfield. I'll be the one to spring the back loose.' So if you get one block, get up and try to get another one.

I can't be more sincere when I say this: Unless you played offensive tackle, you can't understand it, but the headslap used by defensive linemen was the most vicious thing ever done in football. Some defenders taped their hands, and I don't know if they really did it, but some of us thought they put hard things inside the tape. It cracked, it felt like metal. Your helmet stung, and your head was ringing all the time. I had a stiff neck from the first quarter on.

You couldn't defend against it because you had to have your hands holding onto your chest. So you just stuck your head out and held onto your pads. You were at the mercy of that vicious headslap. I always welcomed inside help from our backs on pass plays, because it meant you could play one side of the defensive man or the other, but other than that, you were at this guy's mercy, taking blows, and just hanging on.

From the headslaps, I've developed three herniated disks. The neck burns aren't as bad as they once were. Every once in a while I'll get a little catch, but for the most part, I feel normal. I'd wear a neck collar some of the time to cushion the blows, but no one understands how bad it was. You had to hold your own chest and let them smash you in the helmet.

In high school, I played in a leather helmet with no facemask. I had a few concussions, but I'd come back in and play. One time, I was knocked out, and my teammates had to dress me and take me to the Homecoming dance. They finally called my mom and said, 'You better come and get him.' I didn't come out of it until the next morning. Nobody thought of taking me to the doctor or the hospital.

When I was playing in the College All-Star Game, I got a concussion. It was before my first training camp with the Browns. We were playing the Colts in Chicago. I got hit in the head by a head slap. It put me in the hospital. I woke up, and I didn't want to stay there, so I left. I called training camp in the middle of the night and left a message that I was on my way and I'd be there soon. I got in my car and drove the wrong way, to St. Louis. I didn't know which way I was going. I called again. I said, 'I'm almost in St. Louis. I'm going to change directions and come back.' When I got to the Ohio line, Paul had a highway patrol car waiting for me, and they drove me to Hiram College, and he let me rest for a couple of days until my head was clear.

PLAYING WITH THE BROWNS was miserable sometimes, because I never had equipment that fit right. Your game shoes were the same shoes you wore in practice. If you had a problem with them, you fixed them yourself. The shoulder pads were the same way. There were boxes of pads, but they were not fitted just for you. If they felt good, you put them on. They were always slipping, always breaking. There was always something wrong. So you just went in the pile and got another used one. Everything was used.

Most of my memories of the Browns are of being like a training camp for experimental equipment. Facemasks went from no bars to three. Then there were air pockets in the helmet. As soon as I got hit, I'd lose at least two air pockets immediately. The pockets were these one-by-one squares. They just popped. About the second series of plays, half my helmet was deflated. It was lopsided and started spinning like a top. I'd come to the sidelines, and they'd air me back up, or get me another helmet. Then, a new theory: They filled the pockets up with water, and water would be pouring down all over me. After a few plays, I was holding my helmet so it would stay on my head. All I remember is problems with the helmets, the head slap, the water, thirteen years of my life.

Last year when he came to the Browns' reunion, I asked Doug Atkins how big he was when he played. He said he was 6' 8", 290, and he could high jump close to seven feet. If you tried to cut him, he'd fly right over you. You had to try to stay straight up on him. I asked him who the toughest guy he ever played against was. He said, 'Nobody.' I thought maybe he'd say me, but he said, 'Nobody.' At least that made me feel better than if he'd said somebody else. I was happy.

I ALWAYS WELCOMED HELP from my back, Ernie Green, and we still laugh about that. I'd be going, 'Ernie, I need help. You're going to help me on the inside, right? You be inside, I'm going outside, right? Huh, Ernie?'

One time I was playing across from Andy Robustelli, I didn't hear the count in the huddle and we're coming out to the line. It's a very noisy crowd. I'm going 'Woots, what's the count?' Woots didn't want to yell it out because he had a guy over him, too. 'Woots, what's the count? What's the count?'

And Robustelli says, 'On two, stupid.'

They snapped the ball on two and I was still in my stance, because I didn't believe him.

I said, 'How the heck did you know?'

He said, 'The first twenty plays were on two.'

A lot of guys played with a lot of pain. We didn't have mouthguards and those things. One time someone came to the sidelines and he had a broken nose. Paul said, 'What are you doing here?'

The guy's on the sidelines. He's bleeding. He says, 'My nose, Coach, it's broke.' It's stuck to his cheek.

Paul, 'A broken nose?'

He calls a trainer over and they wrap tape around his head about six or seven times. He went back in and played the rest of the half with his nose taped to his face and helmet.

One time John Morrow had a bone sticking out of his sock, below his knee. We kept saying, 'Get over to the sidelines.'

'Nope,' he said, 'I'm not getting out until we score.'

Paul was not easy to get close to. He was demanding and controlling. Practices were to the minute. Morrie Kono, the equipment man, carried a watch, and he called out every five minutes for us to change positions. Paul always stressed the same things: basics and fundamentals. I liked that. It was just the lack of emotion. Football's a game of emotion. I don't care what you say, but some players probably weren't playing up to their potential because of the cap on someone pushing them. I was better being pushed. I think more players react better to an emotional coach. Paul thought a pro knew how to get himself ready to play.

He always stressed, 'You are what your foundation shows.' He meant you should wear shined shoes. I never had real good shined shoes. Once in a while, my socks were different colors. But he made an impression on me, and I shined my shoes once in a while. Growing up on a farm, I never cared what I looked like. But between Woody Hayes and Paul Brown, they changed my image, even though my wife and kids say I still had a long way to go.

I had to buy a suit when I came to the Browns. I'd never had a suit. All the players went to Richman Brothers. They had a deal where you could get a suit for $50. The first one was at no cost for me. I never questioned it, but I knew Paul had taken care of the suit for me. It was the first suit I ever owned. He was good to me like that.

A lot of people don't understand that Paul was one of the first people to have prayer before and after the game. When I came to the Browns, he had a priest who traveled with the team. Father Connelly was at every game. One time, Paul went to the Catholic church with us, and they had three different collections. Paul gave the first two times, and the third time the basket came around, I heard him whisper to Father Connelly, 'What're they going to do now, *search* us?'

HE LOVED SEEING PLAYERS' WIVES and kids running around. He loved to see the team dressed up in suits and ties. That was his proudest day: to see all of these tough guys dressed up and acting like gentlemen. He liked that image. He established it, and he wanted to continue it forever.

That first year I played tackle, he criticized me a lot, but I knew it was for my own good. One time this guy who played for the Redskins said, in the newspaper before the game, 'I can't wait to get a chance to play over that Schafrath.'

I did some good things in the game, and Paul stopped the film while we were all watching and said, 'Hey, Schafrath, this is the guy who couldn't wait to get a piece of you.' He was always nice to me that way. He always came up with a line someplace to encourage me.

But it wasn't like you had a friendly on-going relationship with Paul. He had you scared to death. It was a fear that he would cut you, or say something negative to you. If he did that, you just took it like a man, because he did it with everybody. Everybody but Jim Brown and Lou Groza. At the time when you were saying, 'I don't know if this guy even likes me,' the human side of Paul would surface, and he'd say something to make you feel like a million bucks. He knew when to do that at the right time. With Woody and Blanton, it was almost daily. With Paul it might take a week or two weeks. He'd be aware that there was a little tension going on, and he'd say something good.

Now, if he didn't like you, that was a different thing. He usually got rid of the players he didn't like. If he was going to cut you, he never told you. You got an envelope. If he was going to cut two guys, he'd put four envelopes out and say, 'Pick up your envelopes,' so nobody knew which two were going to get cut. Everybody went to get their envelopes, and two of them said, 'Goodbye,' and the other ones said, 'See you tomorrow.'

He had feelings but he had a hard time expressing them. He wanted to keep the control, keep his image.

I CAN STILL PICTURE HIM. He's sick. He's got a bad cold. It's in November. It's an icy, sleeting practice. He's sitting on the sidelines in his car with the window up, still giving each play he wants run in practice. The messenger guards run over. He rolls the window down, gives them the play, and rolls the window back up. He wanted to continually have absolute control. Then, he had no one to blame but himself.

On Tuesdays, when we went through the opponent's scouting report, every player in the room had to write out all twenty-two positions, every man's position, how he played, his strengths and his weaknesses. He personally read the scouting report. He said it very slowly, and we had to copy everything down just as he said it. Everybody was sitting in the same room, writing the same words down. I don't know if everybody copied it down. I don't think everybody did, but I didn't want him to catch *me* not writing it.

Paul Brown had advice on what players should say to the press. He said, 'If you're interviewed by a reporter before the game, you can say three things. One—be short. Two—be positive. Three—compliment the other team. After the game, if you win, say nothing. If you lose, say less. You can't get in trouble that way.'

The press more or less reacted like the players. They said basically what

Paul Brown wanted them to say. Paul never had any problems with the press. They traveled with us. They talked to him daily. They wanted to please him. Nobody wanted to be on his bad side.

His pep talk was usually something like, 'Men, I hope you're prepared to play for your financial lives.' That was about it. Meanwhile, he'd be taping the pipes in the dressing room so nobody would hear his first play. Yeah, he was afraid that somehow there might be a wire or something coming through the pipes or the vents, so before every game he would have Morrie Kono tape every pipe hole, every vent in our dressing room, every crack in the walls. He was afraid somebody would get that first play. I don't know why, because the game was pretty predictable: Block, tackle, run, catch.

WE PRACTICED OUT AT LEAGUE PARK. It was kind of a dungeon, old cement locker rooms, a trough all around the bottom about a foot wide for a drain, in case you wanted to wash the place out. One day, it's raining cats and dogs, lightning, thunder. We're sitting there in our meetings, and all of a sudden, the lights go out. Paul Brown says, 'Morrie, fix it. Morrie, fix it.'

Morrie says, 'Okay, Coach.'

He runs out the door. Across the street from League Park are two bars. It's 9:30 in the morning, and a lot of winos are sitting in there.

Morrie says, 'Anybody want to make five bucks?'

Two of them follow him back. He's got a flashlight. We're still sitting there in the dark. Water is running deep in those drains. The whole thing is full, about a foot deep. These two winos step right in the water, take a fuse, put it in the electric box, and everything comes on.

'Great job, Morrie,' Paul says.

These two guys walk out with their five bucks.

For forty years, Morrie and Leo Murphy were the glue that held everything together. Leo Murphy carried this medicine box around. He looked like a quack doctor. If you were sick, he gave you a pill, you were all right. You didn't care what he gave you. Everybody just knew it cured you.

There were lots of Morrie stories. You'd go to Morrie with a broken shoestring and Morrie would ask, 'Is this your right shoe or your left shoe?' And there were some who answered him.

We played the New York Giants. It's a night game and I was in the second bus. We were going to the New York airport and the bus driver gets lost trying to get to LaGuardia. We're driving around, driving around, and Paul said, 'You having a problem, Bussy?'

He said, 'Yes, sir, I don't think I know where I'm at.'

Paul said, 'Well, why don't you pull over? Maybe we can find a cab or somebody to help you.'

No cabs, no anything.

Paul says, 'Do you have a phone on your bus?'

Bus driver says, 'No, sir, I don't.'

Paul's got a couple of guys out trying to wave down cabs, anybody. Paul's sitting there and sitting there.

Finally, he says, 'You know, Bussy,' he says. 'I don't blame you. I blame the damned people who hired you.'

We finally got out of there, but it was about an hour later.

On Saturdays, before game Sundays, we'd go out and stretch, and, one Saturday, there was a bunch of workers around the opponent's ballpark. Paul looks up as were coming out of the dugout into their stadium, and there's about twenty workers leaning on their shovels. It was snowing, and they were supposed to clean off the field before the game.

They're all shouting at us: 'Hey, you guys are gonna lose.'

Paul looked around at them and said, 'Come here, men.' We all surrounded him. He said, 'I want to give you one word of advice: Never listen to a guy who's leaning on a shovel or a broom.'

PAUL DID NOT HAVE A HARD TIME dealing with the black/white issue. He was the first coach to allow players like Bill Willis and Marion Motley to get started in pro football. The black players traveled on one bus and the white players traveled on the other one, but that was the black players' choice, and they felt more comfortable that way. In the early 1960s, the riots started in LA, Chicago, D.C., and even in Cleveland. The race issue became very touchy, but the Browns stayed out of it.

My first three years I was in the Air Force. I came back just for the games. When I got back, the blacks were still riding in the same bus, with the rookies. I rode on the same bus that whole time. I felt like I was a rookie those first three years, and I was comfortable with the blacks. When I came back, the blacks were all in the same bus with the rookies. I always had a good relationship going with the black players by sharing and laughing with them. That's probably why Jimmy Brown and I are close today. We started out close. We trusted each other from the beginning.

Paul allowed blacks to play in 1946, but he didn't encourage or discourage us to do things together. He kind of let it go. It's not that he did anything intentionally. It just wasn't that big a deal to him. Of course, I never knew that there was much of a difference between us. I didn't *understand* the difference. Everybody always played as a team, and, to me, everybody *was* equal. Everybody busted their butts together to make the team what it was. How could we think different of them?

It was evident that at times, the black players stayed by themselves. Maybe that's what they preferred. They seemed comfortable that way. Reflecting upon it now, I know that when there's a problem, families stay together. In a time of crisis, we stay with the people we're comfortable with. I think that's basically what happened.

I was as comfortable on the black bus as I was on the white bus. I didn't have any prejudice, and I didn't hear them talking about it. I was very close with Johnny Wooten. We sat in meetings together and shared a lot of information. We talked about how blacks were treated in their home areas, particularly in the south. I knew they had to eat in different restaurants, stay in different hotels, drink from their own water fountains, and ride in the back of the bus.

Paul tried to make it comfortable, so that we could all stay in the same hotel, travel together, eat together. I wasn't aware of some of the difficulties he went through. I heard it was difficult to find hotels that would accept us all. But I have no idea what he was going through.

I never noticed any problems on our team. We seemed to get through all the problems. Nothing was ever magnified into a black/white problem, and I'm sure there were individuals who harbored that kind of feeling, but it never surfaced.

I noticed that you'd get the Southern white person under pressure, and he'd say something prejudicial in the heat of a game or a practice. But it was calmed down or overlooked very quickly. It was never a problem on the Browns. It would be interesting for me to hear anything contrary to what I'm saying.

I DON'T THINK THERE WAS EVER much animosity between Paul and Jimmy. I think they respected each other. I think the attitude changed with the team that first year when Paul wasn't there. I don't think Jimmy changed. I think he ran just as hard as he always did. I never saw Jimmy and Paul Brown going at each other. I don't believe Paul gave Jimmy the freedom to run outside, like Blanton did. Blanton introduced option blocking, and the backs could run inside or out.

Jimmy was built like a Greek god, 6' 2", 230, a natural, never lifted weights. He had a lot of strength, a lot of speed. He could outrun Bobby Mitchell, and Bobby was a sprinter in college. They were always neck and neck, but Jimmy beat him every time. Whether he was out as a receiver or returning kickoffs or carrying the ball, he was a threat to go all the way every time. Pads never slowed him down. He could run the same forty time in or out of pads.

I remember a lot of little things about Jimmy because I studied him a lot. Before games, he psyched himself up. He told me about picturing himself making great plays. Later on, I asked him about things, and he said they didn't just happen. He said he visualized himself spinning off a block one way or the other, putting down his hand to save himself from going down, using his forearm to stave off tacklers, making great catches. He anticipated those things. The amazing thing about Jimmy is that he never ran out of bounds. Those people on defense focused their whole defensive plan around Jimmy every play. You knew this guy had to be an exceptional runner to average 5.2 yards per carry when the defense was all strategically planned to stop him. Only once did I see him injured. He got knocked a little dingy, then he went back in. Sometimes I'd notice his eyes were swollen shut or his forearms were bruised, but he would go into the training room at 7 a.m., before anyone else, and no one ever saw him getting treated. He didn't want anyone to see any weakness, and they didn't.

WE WERE PLAYING DALLAS in Dallas, and we were behind, I think, by four points. We were on their four-yard line. There were thirty or forty seconds left, and we called Jimmy off the left side. Well, Jim came off the left side, and we were supposed to run it right off me, to my left side or to my right side. But he took off for the outside. He decided, I guess, that he didn't want to hammer it right for the goal line. He didn't see a hole or something. Eight guys hit him before he circled back around and went back to about the 30-yard line. He came back again, and everyone on the team hit him. It was very close, right at the goal line with everyone hitting him, but he went in just as the gun went off. He ran forty seconds for four yards, and everybody on the defense hit him at least once. It was an amazing run.

In the huddle, all the linemen felt very confident with what they could do with Jimmy behind them. You didn't just say it to say it, but I remember saying on short yardage, 'Run it over me.' It made you really want to produce. If you said, 'Run it over me, Jim. We can make it,' you better do it.

I still have a photograph of Lamar Lundy, against the Rams. We had a fourth and one, and I called it in the huddle, 'Go over me.' Lamar stood me up, and I was scrambling and fighting, not a good block at all, but Jimmy went all the way for a touchdown. He just made a great run. He made me look good.

THERE WAS ONLY ONE TIME I questioned Jimmy on a play. We had a screen designed to go to the left. I said, 'Jim, Blanton said I should sprint to the sidelines on this play. You're going to wait. They're going to toss the screen to you, and you'll never catch me. I don't know why I'm sprinting out there.'

He said, 'Just trust me. I'll be there.'

We ran the play against the Giants. I looked back, because I really didn't believe he would be there, and, brother, he was there, and his cleats were like chainsaws coming up the back of my legs. I think he just purposely ran over me. From then on, I never questioned Jim Brown.

I don't think Jimmy and I ever lost contact with each other over the years, and as I said, we were pretty close from the start. We would get together the night before ball games and go over the game plan, just making sure that we went over those fundamentals again. We had a short list of what we called 'attitude plays' that we really believed in. If we were in the huddle, and it was a critical point, I'd say, 'Jimmy, I'll suggest this play to Frank (Ryan), and I know it's going to work.'

Frank was very good about that. Frank and Jimmy did argue on some things. When Frank got to throwing the ball too much, Jimmy would tell him it was time to run the ball. Frank would want to throw it, and Jimmy would say, 'Throw it when I get tired.'

Jimmy would say in the huddle, 'I'm ready to run. I'm ready to run.' The line always got behind him. We liked to run it, too, so we were always favoring Jimmy when those couple of words were exchanged in the huddle, but on the sidelines, there was never much said.

After Jimmy Brown left, we had a new offensive coordinator, Dub Jones, and Dub really balanced the running and the passing more. We did a lot more throwing than when Jimmy was there. It changed the philosophy of 'run first, pass second.' It was now 'run or pass.' It was a little different theory on how you played the game, but it was still a very effective offense.

Mentally, we were all set for Jimmy in 1966 when Paul Brown unexpectedly retired, but Leroy Kelly moved in there and did an excellent job. Leroy and Ernie Green were both excellent runners and receivers. But nobody was Jim Brown.

Kelly was a good, balanced runner. He had a quick start and it was hard to knock him off his feet. He never got tired as the game went along. He was a good muddy-field runner. If there was a slippery field, you just couldn't get him off his feet. He never got hurt and was very reliable.

But pick any name and ask, 'How many years did he play? How many carries? How many yards per carry?' There was no one like Jim Brown.

IT WAS A LOT OF FUN, but you had to play for fun. It wasn't money. My first contract, I made $600 a month. I could've got the same with construction, and I could've got close to that with teaching. Mom said, 'Why don't you try football? It'll look good on your resume,' so I chose football.

You had to work other jobs in the off-season. I carried mail, worked construction, worked in sales, and I was in the Air Force. Most everybody had second jobs. You had to, to survive.

I couldn't make Paul Brown budge when it came to money. He'd say, 'Jim Brown doesn't make that kind of money. Mike McCormack doesn't make that kind of money. Lou Groza doesn't make that kind of money.'

I'd say, 'I know, but rookies are making a lot more money today, Coach. We've got to look at things different.'

'No, no, we can't do that.'

He was tight.

Now, I'm president of the Browns Alumni Association, and it's hard for me to relate to players who make so much money. The average ballplayer is making over a million dollars. We never even talked money when I played. I asked Jim Brown about that. He said, 'Dick, I never thought about money.'

Of course, you wanted to pay your bills and have a little money, but it was no big deal. Maybe it was because of Paul Brown, maybe it was because of Woody Hayes, but, hell, even statistics didn't mean diddly to us. Nobody said anything about it until the day Bobby Mitchell was going for the single-game rushing record. He had 230 yards or something in a game against Washington, and Paul took him out.

A couple of reporters came up behind the bench and said, 'Hey, listen, he's only four yards off the record.'

Paul said, 'The heck with it. I'm not putting him in anyway. We won the game and we're not playing for records.'

It was the same with Jimmy. The only year he didn't have a thousand yards, he had 996, and he was standing on the sidelines out in San Francisco. Nowadays, a runner has to get his hundred yards, receivers have to get so many yards catching. Then, it was just to win and play well as a team.

When Woody Hayes died, his wife, Anne, found checks in his dresser going back probably ten, fifteen years for speaking engagements. He never cashed them. He didn't care about money. Paul Brown was tight with money. Nobody had an agent to argue his case. Everybody negotiated with him alone. I always thought I was worth a lot more. I guess every player did. But he had a fixed price when you came into his office, and he wouldn't budge.

My first year, I got $7,000. My second year, I got $7,000. My third year, I think I went to maybe $10,000. I was trying to get it doubled, because I was a starter and I didn't get a raise the second year.

Every year it was like, 'I'm going to double it this year.' He would always say, 'Next year, Dick, things will look better.'

I was named All-Pro and we won the world championship, but it never got better.

I'd come in with my statistics, and he'd come in with his, and he wouldn't change.

Paul never got emotional. He was never in a hurry except at contract time. It was like it was going to take one minute: 'Sign here.' You'd come back with what you thought you did and how well we did as a team. That would be it. Heck, I was offered more money by colleges to work side jobs in the summer than I made in pro ball.

But after I settled the contract, I didn't think about it any more. I just wanted to have a great year, then come back the next year and do a lot better. It never got a lot better, but it certainly didn't affect the way I played. I always wanted to be the best. The old-timers who started before '61 never played for money. The money started changing in the early '60s because of the AFL. Anybody who came into the game from the mid-'60s on had a chance to start making good money.

I THINK TWO THINGS REALLY HURT PAUL: the Milt Plum trade and getting rid of Bobby Mitchell. A lot of great ballplayers were traded during Paul Brown's reign: Jim Marshall, Dick LeBeau (an All-Pro defensive back with Detroit) came up from Ohio State with me, Len

Dawson, Doug Atkins, Willie Davis. But those two trades—Milt and Bobby—were the ones that really hurt Paul the most.

I thought Milt Plum was the perfect quarterback for him. I always thought Milt Plum was going to be there forever. Paul wanted a guy to throw the short passes. Milt listened to Paul. Mechanically, he was excellent. All the quarterbacks I ever played with wanted to run the offense on their own, but they understood that with Paul, you just couldn't do that. If Otto Graham couldn't do it, nobody was going to do it. When Milt left, it was unbelievable, because you had a guy who didn't make very many mistakes. He was a Paul Brown-type quarterback.

We never had stability at quarterback for very long. Milt Plum, Jim Ninowski, Gary Lane, Lenny Dawson. We had Bill Nelson, Frank Ryan, Mike Phipps—all short time. When Paul had Otto Graham, that's all he ever had. All through the latter part of the '50s and the '60s, it was a problem to keep one certain quarterback.

ART MODELL DIDN'T UNDERSTAND how much of a control type Paul actually was. Paul had to be in charge of everything, even when you had sex with your wife. After Tuesday, the rule was no sex. His rule. I had to write it down. It might've been a joke. I don't know. But I have it right there in my notes. All the players wrote it down every week. The control didn't bother me.

You could tell there was a problem brewing from the start. One time, we had an exhibition game out in LA. We usually played the Rams and then San Francisco, right before the first regular-season game. We played the 49ers and then we were going down to play the Rams the following week. We were in the airport, and everyone was going into the lounge bar because the plane was an hour late. Art was buying everyone beer. The drinks were on him, he said, and Paul Brown came down the hall and saw it and went berserk.

'Out of here! Out of here! My players don't drink in public,' he said.

Art was apologetic: 'No, Coach, this is on me. I asked them,' but they went at it for a while. That was the first time I had seen that problem. My interpretation of it was that it was just something Art did spontaneously because the plane was late. I respected them both.

Paul's philosophy was that no player should ever drink or smoke in public. That's why everyone was a little bit leery of going in the lounge. They were saying, 'Hmm, I wonder what Paul's going to say,' and, boy, when he came and saw, he was mighty upset.

I was shocked when he was fired. I never thought it would happen. I was out of town when he was fired, but I can remember it. It was almost like Kennedy being killed. You just couldn't believe it.

Before Blanton was picked, we heard rumors that Paul didn't want him accepting the head coaching job. I know Blanton was a little slow at accepting that position. He was the most loyal man I ever met, and he respected Paul. We both lived in Aurora and we talked a lot. It bothered him that first year or two how Paul perceived him, or that he had let Paul down somehow. But he made the right decision, and he was a real winner.

Head coaches don't coach and teach anymore. Woody Hayes did. Blanton Collier did. Paul Brown did, too, although he organized and oversaw more than he taught. Woody Hayes would roll up his sleeves, get involved, show you how. If you didn't hit right, he'd show you how. Blanton Collier was the same. They were three great coaches, but they all had very different styles.

IT WAS A DIFFERENT ATTITUDE, having Blanton Collier as coach. The players were allowed more freedom to express themselves. As an offensive unit, we rose to a different level. We might have under Paul if he had kept that same group. We were maturing. If you look even at the Otto Graham days, as they got older, they just got better. We really starting meshing in '63, but we advanced to a different level because of our experience and attitude. We had more freedom with option blocking and Jimmy running all over the place.

Yeah, maybe we had something to prove. You could say that was true. But we had the same talent. The only players who came in were Paul Warfield and Kelly. Kelly was a great special teams player, and Warfield became a starter right away, but the rest of the team basically stayed the same.

We got very emotional with Blanton. I mean, he loved it. We'd be slapping each other and cheering. It was more enthusiastic and emotional. That was basically it. It was an attitude change, because Blanton Collier kept most of the same coaches. Everything stayed the same. I called it a 'maturing attitude,' because whether Paul was there or not, I was just getting better, I thought, and a lot of the players were maturing the same way.

I thought we actually had a better team in '65 than in '64. It was just the frozen field and all that (in the 23-12 loss to Green Bay in the 1965 NFL title game). You can always say 'if, if, if.' It was a great feeling to beat

Baltimore in the 1964 title game. It doesn't happen too many times. Some teams get to do it three, four, five times, but some teams never get to do it at all.

That's what makes it hard to believe that Paul Brown went from '46 to '56, ten straight years, in the championship game. That's why everybody respected him so much. He'd done it, and he'd done it his way.

It was a good group, and it could've gone on for a couple more years, if Jimmy had stayed. I think he retired prematurely, or we probably would've been in a few more championship games. Everyone was shocked when he retired. We found out in training camp. We knew he was making a movie. We thought he was going to be back maybe a day or two late. The rumor was that Art said, 'If you're late, you're going to be fined, or you might not play this year.' We all thought that that was a pretty harsh threat, but I don't know if that was true or not. That was the rumor.

I WAS GOING TO GO INTO TEACHING and coaching after I retired. I never did teach, but I went with (longtime NFL head coach) George Allen for three years, when he was with the Redskins. My last year with the Browns, I wanted to play another year, but Art and I were arguing over a contract salary of $35,000, and we were a couple of thousand short. The actual amount wasn't that big a deal, but it was a matter of principle. I decided to play out my option. I had to take a cut in pay because I wouldn't sign a contract. I played out my option and got $30,000, and I was a free agent after thirteen years. I talked to George Allen, and he offered me $100,000 to come and play and coach. I got there, and I had neck problems so bad I couldn't run. I'd get these burners, and it just killed me. I couldn't play.

George Allen was a mixture of Paul Brown and Woody. Very demanding, but funny as heck, too. Once, before a ball game, he's got on war paint and a feather bonnet, doing a war dance. We'd be at practice, and he'd have fire trucks come out and spray all the players and then bring ice cream. All kinds of crazy stuff. But he was very committed to the game and very fundamental. He was a heck of a defensive coach. Most defensive-minded people are like him. They want to win the game 3-0. They don't want the offense to really do too much.

In 1978, I had three opportunities to coach, but I decided I was going to come back to Ohio. If I would've taken one of those jobs, I was going to call Blanton Collier and refresh everything I knew. That's the winning attitude, that's the winning game plan, and if I was ever coaching, I would take his philosophy and go with it.

After I left Cleveland, I didn't see Paul until he started with the Cincinnati Bengals, six years later. He was always nice to me when I met him afterwards, and when I became a state senator. He donated to my campaign. Paul did everything he could to help me. He encouraged me to stay in Ohio, and he encouraged me to get into football.

He said, 'I think football needs people like you,' and I think I could still be coaching if I had wanted to stay in it. I just didn't want to work twenty-four hours a day coaching.

I helped Bill Belichick in '94 with the Browns. Jimmy Brown and I were helping the offense. We made the playoffs, so we were having some kind of impact on them. All we did was go over the basics, the basics. Sometimes, I think, you can get too fancy. You can go on tendencies and computer printouts of this and that. I'd tell the players, 'It's still man on man. Don't get too fancy.'

I liked working with Kirk Ferentz, the offensive line coach. He had the tendencies of what this guy did and what that guy did from computer printouts, and I told him, 'Kirk, we could really screw up our opponents if we didn't use the printouts and wrote our own game plan.'

He said, 'Sounds great, Dick, but I don't want to get fired.'

AROUND '83, I WAS TOYING with the idea of getting into politics. I had helped Nixon, and I helped Reagan. In '83, Reagan's chief of staff called me from Washington. They wanted me to work with them on the campaign. I became their national chairman of athletes and entertainers. I worked all fifty states that election year. I put together tours in each state. We'd have, like, Mickey Mantle, Roger Maris, Joe Frazier, Woody Hayes, Joe Paterno, Roger Staubach, and we'd get on a bus, go into a little town, jump out, go up and down the streets for an hour, jump back in the bus, and go on to the next town.

After that, I wanted to farm. I had a friend who had 50,000 acres in Wyoming. I was out there on a ranch, making a decision whether I was going to run the ranch or not, and a guy rode up on a horse. He said, 'Is there a guy here by the name of Schafrath?'

I said, 'Yeah.'

He said, 'If you would, get on the horse with me. We have to go make a phone call.' There was no phone on the ranch.

I rode to town with him, two or three miles, to Saratoga, and made the phone call back to the Ohio senate. In the middle of the term, this guy in my district had retired from his senate seat.

The president of the senate said, 'Would you be interested in coming back and being interviewed for the senate seat?'

I said, 'I don't think so,' but after fifteen or twenty minutes, they convinced me to try it.

I drove back Saturday and Sunday, interviewed on Monday, and I was a state senator on Tuesday.

The deal was that if I took it, I had to run when the next term started, and they knew this guy was going to come back for the seat. He had run for governor and lost, but the leadership didn't want him back, I guess. It was one heck of a battle. I won at 3 o'clock in the morning, by a hundred and ten votes. I had been trailing so badly, the only speech I had was a concession speech. Up until a year ago, it was the most expensive primary senate race they had ever had in the state of Ohio. It still is. It cost our side $1.5 million for a $20,000 a year job, and I never spent $10,000 on any campaign since, general or primary.

IT WAS A DIFFERENT GAME being a senator. It was the same in that you're a team player and that's the way you get things done, but you've got to compromise and compromise. You don't have a bill that's clear-cut. You're trying to do something that really helps, but there always has to be some baggage hanging on it.

Once, I had a third-grade kid say in a question and answer thing, 'Senator, is there anything lower than a senator?'

I said, 'I don't know. That's pretty low.'

When I started as a senator, a woman called me. She was over 80. It was 3 o'clock in the morning.

She said, 'Is this Senator Schafrath?'

I said, 'Yes, ma'am, this is Senator Schafrath.'

She said, 'Can you help me?'

I said, 'What's your problem?'

She said, 'I've got water coming through my ceiling.'

I said, 'Did you call a plumber?'

She said, 'Yes, but all I get is an answering machine.'

She said, 'I called the sheriff, but the sheriff said, "Call your senator.'

She told me where she lived, five miles out in the country, so I told my

417

wife, 'Honey, I don't know how to fix anything. You know that. But I've got to go give her moral support.'

I got to her house, and water was coming down through the ceiling, like she said. She just had too much trouble getting up and down steps. She'd come downstairs and hadn't gone back up, and the john was running over. I had a plunger, and I plunged it out. She was a Democrat, and I'm a Republican, but she said, 'I'm going to vote for you from now on.'

I OFTEN THINK OF AN ATHLETE I was roommates with at Ohio State my senior year. His name was Glenn 'Jeep' Davis. He was an Olympic champion who got three gold medals. He won the Sullivan Award. He was the guy to beat Harrison Dillard in the high hurdles after Harrison had won 119 straight events. He won the high school track state championship himself when he was at Barberton, Ohio. He won first place in four events. He was a very determined guy.

Woody Hayes wanted to give him a scholarship, but he wanted to run track and field, so he didn't play football at OSU, or any college, but he was a starting end for the Detroit Lions. He said one thing to me and I'll never forget it: 'What you have, give. What you save, you lose forever.'

Most guys, unless they've tasted victory, don't really give all that they have. They hold back. I try to tell athletes this: Give, give, even if you're going down, even if you can't suck any more air, give 'til you die, because if you save it and give up, you'll never get another chance. You've lost it forever. You can apply that to anything in life. 'Jeep' used that as an example of how he became an Olympic champion, and I think it's true, because every time I look at how we became elevated into winners or how I played my best seasons, it was when I used the 'George theory,' that every play, you've got to feel you're going to be the factor that will win or lose the game. If you let up one time, it could be the time that loses the game.

What my parents, Woody Hayes, and Paul Brown did for me was to help teach, mold, and push an ordinary farm boy to a higher plateau of athletic accomplishment than he ever dreamed possible. But Paul Brown refined me. I became more confident in everything I did. I was constantly trying to improve myself. I developed into a person who felt a lot better about himself. I'd never had that experience in my home life or in college. He really helped me. Whatever I did, he helped me.

When the Browns left town, it was a tragedy, because it took away kids' dreams. Whenever I'd see a little kid, I'd see myself as a kid, and what a dreamer I was, listening to the radio and pretending I was Lou Groza kicking field goals. There's so many kids that dream. Nobody understands how powerful that could be for a kid. Not that they're going to be even a high school or a college player. A very small percentage ever make pro ball. But that dream is better than dreaming about drugs and alcohol or violence. They can visualize themselves being like that hero some day. **"**

# A Question
# *of* Dignity

JOHN WOOTEN was tired. He had flown in from Phoenix after midnight and had just learned that Walter Johnson had died and that Jim Brown was in trouble with the law again. Wooten was speaking softly into a telephone, assuring John Henry Johnson's widow that he had ordered a fruit basket sent to the family of Marion Motley, who had also recently died. His big shoulders slumped under a white golf shirt, as if he'd been forced to wedge himself into the small office in the Baltimore Ravens headquarters. The bone walls and Wooten's gray hair shimmered in fluorescent light.

Wooten, an All-Pro and Pro Bowl guard for the Browns during the 1960s, cradled the telephone and said, "I knew about Paul Brown before I went to Cleveland. If you watched football on television, you knew who the Cleveland Browns were. You knew who Marion Motley and Bill Willis and Horace Gillom were and what they meant, and you knew the history of the Browns. We knew what Paul Brown meant to football and about the tradition of the Browns. All of that was very, very sacred."

Wooten was attending a segregated elementary school in Carlsbad, New Mexico, when Paul Brown began assembling his first professional team. Brown waited until after training camp opened to quietly sign Willis and Motley, a year before Jackie Robinson played in a major league baseball game. In doing so, the coach ignored the unwritten Jim Crow law which professional football had observed since 1933 and which some owners had attempted to codify in the All-American Football Conference's bylaws.

In Wooten's view, Brown didn't mean his hiring of black players as a social statement. "I don't think race was a part of Paul's thought process at all," he says. "I don't think he would've thought of it like Branch Rickey: 'I'm going to go get a black player and give him an opportunity,' even though Paul did that in a way. What happened was Motley and Willis were available, and Paul knew talent."

Brown, for whom Gillom had starred at Massillon High School, had been coaching integrated teams for almost 15 years. As head coach at Ohio State in 1942, when many colleges didn't recruit blacks, he was pictured in the *Columbus Dispatch* wrapping the leg of Willis, who was then not even a full-time starter. "I didn't care about a man's color or ancestry," he said later. "I just wanted to win football games with the best people possible."

Not everyone in America shared that view. The military was not even fully integrated until Cleveland's third season in the AAFC. Other franchises protested when Brown signed Motley and Willis, but according to the Cleveland *Plain Dealer*, the coach "told the objectors that Willis and Motley were going to play and did they want to make something of it?"

Before Motley joined the team, Cleveland played the Brooklyn Dodgers in an unusually vicious exhibition game. "It was a brutal, bitter game. I saw that quickly," Brown said. "Then I caught on. They were after Willis." A newspaper account accused the Dodgers of using "their forearms on [Willis's] chin, their fists and elbows on his face and their knees and feet wherever they had the chance."

Opposing players called Motley and Willis "nigger" and "alligator bait." Referees looked away as tacklers piled on Motley and ground their cleats into his hands. Hoping to avoid racial brawls, Brown asked the men not to retaliate. Tackles Lou Groza and Lou Rymkus volunteered to handle troublemakers. "If Willis and I had been anywhere near being a hothead, it would have been another ten years until back men got accepted into pro ball," Motley said.

According to the fullback, the mistreatment on the field ended when other teams "found out that while they were calling us names, I was running by them and Willis was knocking the shit out of them."

Off the field, matters remained unpleasant. When Cleveland was preparing to play at Miami in 1946, Brown told reporters that because Florida law forbade blacks and whites from competing in sports, Motley and Willis wouldn't make the trip. Hate mail accused Brown of siding with the crackers who made and enforced the law.

Years later, Motley revealed that he had also received a letter that week, one that vowed, "You black son-of-a-bitch, you come down here and run across our goal line, you'll be a dead black son-of-a-bitch." Motley said he took the letter to Brown, who asked what the fullback wanted to do. When Motley said that neither he nor Willis wanted to go, Brown gave them the day off, with pay.

The Browns played in a post-season exhibition game in Houston in 1949. Gillom, Motley, and Willis

had to stay with black families rather than with the team at the plush Shamrock Hotel, which accepted only whites. Before the game, Motley said, a gate attendant tried to stop him from entering Rice Stadium.

Wooten came to Cleveland a decade later, after earning his degree in history, with honors, and making All-American at the University of Colorado. By then, Brown had been lauded by black organizations, praise the coach said he didn't deserve.

"They talk about me as a champion of the race, 'the Branch Rickey of football.' Baloney," he said. "I take colored boys because I think they can win for me. I ask only that they play football the way I want it played."

When Wooten arrived, black veterans such as Jim Brown and Bobby Mitchell advised him to know his assignments and to go quietly about his business. That business was at first so difficult for Wooten, who had done little pass-blocking in college, that he nearly quit. Paul Brown's patience and the expertise of Fritz Heisler—"a great line coach"— saved Wooten's career.

He became the first Brown since Willis in the old one-platoon days to start at offensive guard—a position, like quarterback, linebacker, and center that teams traditionally reserved for whites. Wooten and Gene Hickerson formed one of the league's fine pairs of guards, helping Cleveland backs lead the NFL in average gain per rush in seven of Wooten's nine seasons with the team. "We didn't have the most talented line in football," Jim Brown said, "but what we had was more important: a perfect blend."

Wooten quickly saw that Paul Brown "didn't favor one over the other." To the relief of black players, the coach scheduled no exhibition games in segregated Southern cities.

According to Mitchell, when Cleveland went to Miami in 1961 to play in the Runner-Up Bowl, the manager of the hotel in which the team was supposed to stay informed Brown that he had a strict "no-colored" policy. Brown told the manager that the team was immediately returning to Cleveland.

"The guy had no choice but to let us stay," said Mitchell. "I'm sure Paul had taken flak before, but this was the first time I saw it thrown in his face. He sure passed the test."

The coach would face more tests, among them Jim Brown. Jim Brown frequently said that his well-documented disagreements with Paul Brown had nothing to do with race. He has always acknowledged that Paul Brown opened pro football to black athletes. Jim Brown also claimed that the "citizenship" his coach offered to blacks was not equal.

In an assertion that has also been made by Mitchell, Wooten, and some white players, Jim Brown said that Paul Brown maintained a quota of "from six to eight" black players, a limit he set not because of his own prejudice but because of the widely-held belief that white customers would pay to see only white heroes.

In a 1964 magazine article, Jim Brown recounted Paul Brown's asking him why black payers did not sit with whites during meals. Brown said he told the coach that black players refused to pretend to be chummy with whites "as long as the club assigned hotel rooms in a manner that suggested that blacks had leprosy." Paul Brown claimed that he didn't know that rooms were being assigned on the basis of race—a common practice in the NFL at the time—and promptly corrected the problem.

Jim Brown admitted that whites had forced him into prejudice. He said he was proud that Cleveland "had the best organized blacks in all of sports" and that he counseled black rookies to "always assert your dignity." Paul Brown, on the other hand, blamed the fullback for creating racial divisiveness on the team. Jim Brown replied that the coach "didn't understand the racial aspects of the 1950s and 1960s."

Some white players agree. "Paul always made sure that we ate together and stayed together, but he didn't go all the way," says former captain Dick Schafrath. "It's not that he did anything intentionally. It's just that he didn't say, 'We can overcome all of that and be something special.'"

Other whites remain puzzled that most black players didn't attend the parties the team threw after games. Jim Brown said that since blacks were not welcome at all functions, they would attend none. Besides, adds Wooten, Brown's closest friend on the team, most black players didn't drink.

Even if the most dire assessments of race relations among the Browns are accurate, the squad's problems seem small in contrast to those on such teams as the St. Louis Cardinals, who were allegedly dominated by a cell of white supremacists. Jim Brown, whose home had to be guarded by police after his views on civil rights drew threats, said he encountered no overt racism by a player or a coach in Cleveland and was treated warmly by most fans.

Wooten said that racial trouble didn't surface with the Browns until 1963, the team's first season without Paul Brown. Previously, at least according to Jim Brown, players were so frightened of the coach that they "banded together for protection against him."

"I felt like we did a good job, all of us, black and white, of keeping our ball club beyond the racial lines," says Wooten. "Look at Gene Hickerson.

He's from Mississippi, and we always got along real well."

If Wooten is correct, the team did not reflect the city. In April 1966, the U.S. Civil Rights Commission warned that "racial antagonism" was deeper in Cleveland than in the South. Months later, the city was on the verge of a race war.

What began as a baseball game between teams of whites and blacks ended in six nights of rioting that devastated Hough, a blighted area of grimy apartment buildings, decaying mansions, and trash-covered lots on the East Side. "Tough Hough" was sutured with despair around the tumble-down remnant of League Park, former home of the Indians, in which the Browns practiced.

Molotov cocktails puddled Superior Avenue with jellied fire. Gangs of looters materialized from phosphorescent clouds of acrid smoke to smash windows and rip iron grates from storefronts. Snipers shot at police and firemen. One local activist gleefully declared, "The great American experience. That's what we are, the great American experience."

Someone in a carload of whites shot a 10-year-old black boy in the groin. A stray bullet killed a black woman who had leaned from a window to call her children. During a confrontation at a roadblock, police wounded a young black mother and her two infants. A black man was shotgunned in the Italian enclave of Murray Hill. The police chief carried his personal hunting rifle on patrol. Bayonets fixed, two thousand National Guardsmen finally restored order.

White officials blamed the riot on a cabal of Maoists and black revolutionaries. The National Committee of Negro Churchmen said it was God's judgment on America. To the people of Hough, it was "a question of dignity."

Wooten became active in the community. When the Police Athletic League said it could no longer afford to support as many youth teams as it once had, he sponsored a pee-wee football team, as did white teammates such as Vince Costello.

Wooten also helped Jim Brown to found the Negro Industrial and Economic Union, an organization whose aim, Wooten said, was to "solve our country's number one problem in a democratic and intelligent fashion."

The NIEU, which later became the Black Economic Union, gave money and advice to black entrepreneurs and planned to establish credit unions, scholarships, and job-training centers in an effort to "rebuild the ghetto from within." Said the *Cleveland Press*, "John Wooten has battled enemies named Grier, Huff, Robustelli, Nitschke, Jordan and Jones. Now, he and his associates of

the NIEU are fighting far tougher enemies: ignorance, prejudice, poverty, hatred and violence."

"What we're talking about is a restoration of black dignity," Wooten said.

With the unemployment rate in Cleveland's ghettos five times the city average despite an economic boom, the NIEU's approach seems sensible. Nevertheless, during the summer of 1967, writers found something sinister in both the NIEU and Wooten's connection with Jim Brown.

Wooten and four black teammates—John Brown, Mike Howell, Leroy Kelly, and Sidney Williams—refused to report to camp until their contracts were renegotiated. The players were represented by Carl Stokes, who was in the midst of a campaign to become the first black mayor of a major American city.

Modell fined "the boys" a hundred dollars a day and stressed that "the Browns' record over the years in regard to the treatment of Negro players speaks for itself."

The *New York Times* called Wooten "the ringleader" of the holdout and pointed out that he was a "longtime disciple of Jim Brown." The paper referred to Stokes as "a militant attorney," although many disenchanted whites also supported him. The five holdouts were viewed as harbingers of a revolutionary united racial front in sports and the NIEU as a labor union for blacks only and a means of boycotting white businesses.

Wooten says that the holdout had nothing to do with race. "From a contractual point of view, maybe I was a radical then, but I was coming off two Pro Bowl years, and I thought I deserved more money," he says. "That was the only way I saw I was going to get it."

The players settled. Within a year, only Howell and Kelly were still Browns, Stokes was the mayor, and Cleveland was again in flames.

Wooten would later call the summer of 1968 a "nightmare," but the bad dream actually began in April with the assassination of Martin Luther King, Jr. Riots destroyed cities throughout the country, but Cleveland remained peaceful.

For eight nights, Wooten and other black players walked the streets of Hough with Stokes and community leaders, urging young people to "play it cool." Wooten said, "We told them, 'Do it my way, because we're going to win if you do.' And they stayed calm because it was a message of hope. It's when despair sets in that you have violence."

In late June, the Ashland Country Club hosted the Fourth Annual Ashland Celebrity Golf Tournament. Browns of both races had played in previous events, but that summer, no blacks were invited. White safety Ross Fichtner had passed out the invitations. Furious, Wooten went to the press. "I was just hurt that one of our guys was willing to let some other group push us away from each other," he says.

A newspaper exacerbated matters by quoting Wooten as saying, "We black Browns are after that white Brown's hide"—words he still insists were fabricated. Wooten did, though, in a statement later released to reporters, criticize the Browns for a lack of black coaches and front office staff. He said that a "plantation philosophy" had fragmented the team.

A national magazine said that the incident indicated "the depth to which racial unrest pervades professional football." Modell claimed that to re-establish racial harmony, he was forced to release Wooten and Fichtner. "Before applauding the gesture toward togetherness, it should also be noted that the Browns are giving up a guard who will not be easily replaced," a columnist said.

Four days after Wooten and Fichtner were cut, five men who allegedly belonged to the obscure Black Activists of New Libya opened fire on a tow truck in the Glenville area of Cleveland. Three police officers and three snipers died in the ensuing gun battle, as did a black man who tried to intervene. Thirteen other policemen—"beasts," some residents of Glenville called them—were shot. Over three nights, the ghetto purged its rage with fire and blood. Wooten took to the streets again, at 6' 3", 250 pounds, an imposing figure rapping about peace.

New Orleans had picked up Fichtner, but no team claimed Wooten. Civil rights activist Harry Edwards, a former Black Panther and organizer of the 1968 Olympic protests, claimed that Wooten had been "white-listed" by the NFL. Until he met with Pete Rozelle and convinced the commissioner that he wasn't a wild-eyed militant, Wooten languished on the waiver list.

When he was claimed by the Redskins, both team owner Edward Bennett Williams and head coach Otto Graham—neither of whom was celebrated for his enlightened views on race—praised him. Some in the Washington media, though, reacted as if Huey P. Newton had been named starting quarterback. One columnist called Wooten "a natural leader" but reminded readers that the Browns had jettisoned him "to avoid a race war on the club."

He started one year for the Redskins, retired, and became a player agent. In 1975, the Dallas Cowboys offered Wooten a job. Assuming the team wanted him as an assistant coach—a career he shunned because, he says, he despised players

who "whine and make excuses"—Wooten said no. However, the Cowboys wanted him to work in their front office.

When the Browns played in Dallas in 1962, Wooten had been barred from eating in a restaurant, watching a movie, or sleeping in a hotel with whites. Thirteen years later, he joined the Cowboys as a scout, eventually rising to player personnel director. The boy who had been brought up by a single mother in a two-room house spent 26 years with three teams as one of the NFL's few black executives.

In the late 1980s, Wooten organized a committee of black executives and coaches who wanted to revamp hiring procedures in the NFL, which at the time had never had a black head coach or general manager. "This could be a civil rights movement in football," Wooten said.

Wooten worked the last three years of his career for the Baltimore Ravens, retiring in 2000. Neither he nor Modell held a grudge over the events of three decades earlier. Wooten, in fact, calls Modell "a caring, sharing person" who has been misunderstood and wrongly attacked over his decision to leave Cleveland.

Much of Paul Brown, for whom he expresses "great respect," remains with Wooten. When Tony Banks wore a do-rag into Baltimore's offices, Wooten advised the quarterback that his attire was inappropriate. After Ray Lewis was charged with murder, the Ravens management and the NFL scrambled to defend him; but Wooten, whom a reporter once called a "compulsive truth teller," asked why a supposedly born-again Christian was hanging with thugs in strip joints. Paul Tagliabue claimed that the league has fewer crime problems than society as a whole, and Wooten bemoaned the commissioner's failure to crack down on players who misbehave.

"A lot of these gangsta rap guys are totally demeaning us, and our children are bringing this junk home," he said. "Now I go into the locker room and hear our black players calling each other a 'nigger,' and it hurts my soul. We've had people killed for that word, and now they're using it like it's nothing."

In his cramped office, Wooten was not eager to discuss race. He points out that had his high school not integrated when he was a sopho-more, he could not have played football, because there were not enough black students in Carlsbad to field a team.

For the most part, Wooten, who was named to the Browns' all-time team in 1979, looks happily on his time in Cleveland. He says that he regrets not keeping the disagreement with Fichtner within the team. He regrets holding out as one of a group

instead of as an individual. He regrets speaking for others when he should have spoken only for himself.

"You live and learn," he says. "If you don't make mistakes, then you haven't done too much."

That is one regret John Wooten will never have.

# *John* WOOTEN

“ GROWING UP, I USED TO SAY
we didn't know how poor we were because everyone around us was so poor.
They were hard-working people, pretty much Hispanic. There weren't a lot
of black people in Carlsbad, New Mexico, then. Most of the blacks were
related somehow, and all of the cousins would get together in the yard,
choose up sides, and play whatever sport was in season. I didn't play football with a real football until I was a sophomore at Carlsbad High School.

They voted to integrate the high schools in New Mexico in 1952 or
1953. If the vote had gone the other way, I would have attended a segregated high school, and I would not have played football, because we wouldn't
have had enough players for a team.

I was around 195 pounds in high school. I wasn't a big guy, but I always
thought about going to college. I didn't want to work in the mines or do
the kinds of labor people did out there. My mother and my dad had separated, and she always talked about college. There were six of us, and my first
three sisters did not have the chance to go to school.

My fourth sister was valedictorian of her class, but she was afraid to
leave home. I had a brother who was a much better athlete than I was, but
he dropped out of school. That broke my mom's heart, and pushed me to
do something for her.

I was recruited by UCLA, most of the predominately black schools,
Colorado, and all of the other schools in that area that were integrated
then. I liked the coach at Dartmouth, but when I showed my mom where
Dartmouth was on the map, she said, 'That sure is a long way from home.'

I could tell she didn't want me to go that far away.

Hugh Davidson was the freshman football coach at Colorado. He came into our home, my mom liked him a lot, and I made the right decision. We had good teams at Colorado. We just could never beat Oklahoma. That's when Bud Wilkinson had those great teams. We beat everyone else, but we'd come right down to the wire with Oklahoma and lose 19-17, something like that. They had a two-platoon system, and we only had fifteen players. I played every down of every game as a guard on offense and a tackle on defense.

By my junior year, scouts were coming around. I thought I was going to be drafted by the 49ers, but ended up being drafted by the Browns. They called me early on the day of the draft and said, 'If you sign the contract, we'll draft you. If you don't, we won't.' So I signed. Of course, they don't do anything like that today.

I WENT TO CLEVELAND for three or four days before the College All-Star Game. They didn't have the minicamps then. Everything in Cleveland was total business. Paul told us how we were supposed to dress, how we studied our plays, what he expected of you. He said that we weren't going to be run to death and get beat up on the field, but we were going to practice hard. It was impressive.

We played Baltimore in the College All-Star Game, in '59. They had just won the championship, and they killed us. I don't know if I blocked Art Donovan all night.

Paul said, 'Don't worry. Work hard. We'll get another shot at them, and you'll be prepared.'

We went to LA next. The tradition with the Browns was that the big guys sat up front on the plane, and the coaches sat in the back. I remember sitting there thinking that I would get off the plane and just keep on going, back to New Mexico.

I had come out of the single-wing, where I did nothing but run blocking. Now, I had to pass block. It was very difficult. But I remember clearly, we played the Lions in the Rubber Bowl in Akron, and after the game, he just went over with me the things I did well. I could come off the ball and get a pretty good pop at the line of scrimmage on run blocks, and he liked that. I was a pretty good run blocker, but my pass blocking was not where it should have been.

He said, 'Stick with it. Work hard, do what you do well, and the rest of it will come.' That's how he talked to me. He just let me learn what I had to learn.

With Paul, you didn't have this hazing of rookies. It wasn't going to be in his act. 'We're here to play football and learn football,' he said. 'We're not here to put on a show or be anybody's flunky.' He said that the first day, to the whole group.

When I got to Cleveland, Jim Brown and Bobby Mitchell were there. Willie Davis was there. They told me, 'Make sure you study. Know your plays. Don't make mistakes.' That was their emphasis. 'Be quiet and go about your business,' they said.

MY FIRST YEAR, I THINK I MADE $8,500. The next year, I asked him for $12,000. I don't even know what made me say $12,000. I had no idea what anyone else was making. He finally gave it to me, after a rage you wouldn't believe. It got so bad I just looked out the window. He told me about every bad play I made. He graded you on every play you made and then put it in the *Plain Dealer*. I graded out pretty good, and I was playing on all the special teams. All I knew is I wanted a raise, and if I didn't ask for it, I wasn't going to get it.

He said, 'You know we gave you an opportunity to play.'

I said, 'I know that if I wasn't doing what was expected of me, I wouldn't be out there.'

I wasn't talking loud, because I'm not like that, but I wasn't going to back down. I got myself all prepared for it. I knew it was going to be bad. If I would've walked in and he would've just given me the $12,000, I would have fainted.

He said, 'I'll tell you one thing. I'm going to give you this money, but if you don't perform this year, you're on your way to Minnesota.'

That's when Minnesota was first coming into the league.

I said, 'I agree with you. If I don't perform, I don't deserve to be here.'

Generally, though, he didn't show much emotion. He wanted to show that he was always under control. I think he planned just about everything he did. I doubt very seriously if there was a time that he didn't know exactly where he was going.

He'd cut your heart right out. He'd say, 'I'll make this very clear to you: You don't understand what we're trying to do. It's not your fault.' In other words, you don't have the capability of understanding. Or, 'You're just here for a cup of coffee. We're not going to worry about you.'

One year, he drafted Rich Kreitling, a receiver, and Rich Kreitling made the mistake of trying to explain why he dropped a ball. Everybody was there, offense and defense.

He said, 'It was too low.'

Paul said, 'Show me exactly where it hit you.'

So Rich points, and Paul turns to Milt and says, 'Milt, you're going to have to throw that ball higher. That ball had to have been at least a quarter to a half centimeter below Rich's hands. Do you think Rick Kreitling can move his hands up and down to catch a ball? It has to be right there.'

The room got real quiet. Rich just went back to his seat with this little grin on his face. Nobody said anything, because you could be next. If he questioned you, you said, 'I just messed up,' and kept on walking. Don't say anything else, because he's going to rip you.

Friday at four o'clock, we'd have 'crystallization.' That's where we'd go over how we were going to block that week. He'd always start, 'Here we are...' This day, though, he didn't even get the 'Here' out, and Jim Brown was in the door. He looked at Jim and said, 'Jim, sooner or later, you're going to learn, there's only one "Brown" who runs this team, and his first name is "Paul."'

They got along about like cats and dogs, even though they had respect for each other. They were probably too much alike in their personalities. Jim and Blanton were like father and son. Jim and Blanton had unbelievable rapport. They liked each other tremendously.

When Marion Motley died, the paper quoted Mike Brown as saying that his father said Marion was the best running back he ever had. I don't know where they got that information, because I heard Paul say too many times that Jim Brown was the best running back he ever had. Mike called me to let me know that was a misquote and to let Jim know that was a misquote. His dad stated clearly that Jim Brown was the best, and there was no question.

Jim didn't think the system was right for him. If you look back at our offense, you didn't see Jim catching passes, you didn't see Jim out wide on the sweeps and the flips. Blanton ran the same offense, but under Blanton, you saw all of that. We had the sweeps and tosses and quick screens. Those plays would get Jim out in the flat with a linebacker and a safety. He was going to run over one of them and make the other one miss him. He was coming out of the backfield and catching the ball more. And this was stuff that was in our playbook the whole time.

Paul had the players to dominate. Look back to when he really did dominate. He did it because his offense was so wide open. The plays were already there, the 'Toss Eight', the 'Nine', and those plays. We just didn't run them. We did some of it with Bobby Mitchell, but I don't think Paul appreciated Mitchell's greatness until he traded him. You think about what would have happened if they hadn't have traded him. You gave away a guy with outstanding quickness. If Paul would've been just a little bit more of a hands-on person at times, I think Mitchell could've broken a lot of records. Bobby could do all kinds of things. That's all Mitchell needed, and I think he got that after he went to Washington. He was getting some of it in Cleveland, but with Jim there, you weren't going to get too much from the fans. He needed a little bit more from the coach.

You couldn't defy Paul. That was a good way to get yourself shipped out to Green Bay. He got rid of Willie Davis, Jim Marshall, Bill Quinlan, Henry Jordan, and all of those guys were good players. During a game, you might be able to say something about this play or that play, but otherwise, you couldn't say, 'Why are we doing this?' You didn't have any voice.

I never crossed him. I never had any problem with him. I just went about doing what we had to do. I think he felt that I was doing my job. I worked hard. I practiced hard. We argued over contracts, but, generally, I went on his numbers. He did the grades; you took his numbers.

A lot of the feeling against Paul Brown at that time was because we didn't win as many games as we probably should have won. There was no question that teams had started to stereotype us a little bit, and that he had become a little conservative in his play-calling.

THE EXPECTATIONS IN CLEVELAND were very high. I came in in '59, and we had been close, but we had never been in the championship game. Two years in a row, we had the lead over the Giants in the game that would have put us in the championship, and both times, we lost. One year, we had Philadelphia beaten, and there were a couple of officials' calls, and they beat us and went on to win the championship.

We just couldn't quite get back up to that championship level. Players wanted to win. We had an outstanding running back and a good enough overall team to win, but we just didn't quite do it. Any time you think you should win, and you don't win, somebody is going to get upset.

Of course, in '63, really at the end of the '62 season, Art fires Paul and hires Blanton. In my opinion, the players didn't cause Paul Brown to get fired. The real thing was, we went 7-6 in 1962. It wasn't so much that we lost some games and didn't make the playoffs; it was *how* we lost them. As opposed to really going after teams, we played right in here close to the vest. I think that's what created the grumbling among the players.

Paul could never get comfortable with a quarterback. He knew that position so well. We had Milt Plum and Jim Ninowski, and he didn't like either of those two guys. And when you come from Otto Graham, you can understand why it was so hard for him to like anyone else.

A lot of the problem he had with Milt Plum was about control. Paul liked to be in control, and that was a part of the conflict with Art. I don't think Art wanted to run the team. He knew that Paul Brown knew his football. But Art wanted to be involved. Paul was used to running things, because the other owners of the Browns had allowed him to do that. I don't think Art wanted to run the team. Art just wanted to be involved. Paul was not used to having to answer to anyone.

YOU COULD SEE VERY CLEARLY that there was tension between the two. You could see it on the practice field, in the locker room, wherever. Most times, the owner shows up, and there is some cordiality. Whenever Art showed up, it was never, 'How you doing? We're doing this or that.' You never saw any of that. Paul thought he didn't have to do that.

You have to understand: he had successful ball clubs and great players. You're talking about Dante Lavelli, Mac Speedie, Otto Graham, Don Colo, Horace Gillom, Lou Groza, Bill Willis, and Marion Motley. Paul developed the system that allowed them to become great players. That system made me a much better ballplayer.

It was an easy pick for Art to hire Blanton. Blanton was a great coach. He could teach anything: kicking, punting, running, jumping, offense, defense. He was a smart man, and his passion for the game bubbled over. I'd go down to the offices in the off-season and sit there and talk to him all day. He loved to talk about football. In '63, we won our first six games and then lost a couple at the end, and the Bears won the championship. In '64, we won the whole thing, and beat a team, in Baltimore, that we should never have beaten.

God, I think back to '64. I don't know if I thought we had a chance or not. We used to stay at the Pick-Carter Hotel in town the night before the games. It's not even there anymore. We'd have the pregame meal, and there was a little drugstore that sold sundaes and Cokes. We'd go in there and play the juke box. We're sitting there, and about eight or ten guys out of the Colt Corral, the fan club, came in. They were wearing their blue and white caps, and one of them had a trumpet. He blew 'Taps.' They were as close to Jim as I am to you. I was sitting a little bit away from him. He never said a word. He didn't even look at them. They left, screaming and hollering. We were walking to the car, and all of sudden Jim said, 'We're going to kick the shit out of them.' Just like that. 'We're going to kick the shit out of them.' He had a great day. He gained over 120 yards rushing.

We weren't supposed to be able to do anything against Baltimore. They had the war horses: Marchetti, Bill Pellington, Bobby Boyd. Offensively, they had John Unitas, Ray Berry, Lenny Moore, Jim Parker and John Mackey. And it ends up 27-0.

JIM BROWN AND LEROY KELLY were different runners, but both of them were easy to block for. The reason I say that is you knew just what you had to get done to help them. We used to call it 'do-dad.' Today, they call it slip wedge or combo blocking. It's another thing Blanton never got credit for. We went to it in '63, because Dallas had that flex defense where the linemen were a little bit back off the line. We went down there, and Jim gained about 237 yards. He had two big long runs of 70 yards plus. We'd go straight at the defensive linemen, and if the lineman went *this* way, you slipped off and blocked *that* way, and someone else picked him up. They hadn't seen that kind of combination blocking before.

Jerry Tubbs played linebacker for them then. By rights, that stacked defense should have protected the linebackers. Every time Tubbs stepped, no matter which way he went, there was a lineman right up in his face. He was cursing and hollering. He couldn't understand how we kept getting clean shots at him. Both of Jim's long runs came right between the guard and the tackle, which you weren't supposed to be able to do. But once Jim slipped through there, if you pinned the middle linebacker, Jim was gone.

Jim was as fast as their safeties. They were screaming and hollering at each other: 'What the hell you doing? You're not getting over here fast enough!' They got so frustrated that on one extra point, Tubbs, who was a judo guy, came down and chopped the center, John Morrow, on the back of the neck and knocked him out. We were cursing, 'You killed Morrow!'

Jerry was the linebacker coach when I got down to Dallas in '75 (as a scout), and we laughed about that for days. He said he was so mad that he really didn't realize what he had done.

I think Paul treated everyone fairly. He treated them a whole lot alike; he didn't favor one over the other. The only guy I think he favored was Mike McCormack. He loved McCormack. Mike was a strong captain, a good leader, and a solid blocker, and Paul treated him like a son.

I don't think race was a part of Paul's thought process at all. I think he saw players as players. I don't think he thought of it like Branch Rickey: 'I'm going to go get a black player and give him the opportunity to play,' even though Paul did that, in a way. What happened was Motley and Bill Willis were available, and Paul knew talent. Yes, we're talking about 1946, but think about who we're talking about. We're talking about Marion Motley and Bill Willis. We're talking about one of the quickest nose tackles that the world has ever seen. We're talking about a big, fast guy who could run over trucks and play linebacker on short yardage. These were Ohio kids. They weren't from Los Angeles or South Carolina. Motley was from Canton. Paul Brown coached against him in high school. Willis was from Columbus and went to Ohio State. Paul saw two Ohio kids who were outstanding football players. He didn't see it like Branch Rickey did.

Paul said, 'These are fine football players and good people who have never been in trouble before, and they're right here in our own backyard. I'm not going to let these guys get away and go play someplace else.' His talent evaluation wouldn't let him do that.

WE WENT IN TO PLAY DALLAS when they first came into the league, and we couldn't just stay at any hotel in Dallas, so we stayed at Love Field, at the Ramada Inn, considerably away from downtown. You couldn't go to the movies, because the movies were segregated. There were thirty-two or thirty-three players, and eight or nine of us black guys. We ate dinner, as always, and then Paul said, 'We're not going to the movies tonight. We're going to stay in our rooms and watch TV. We're not going downtown.' He wouldn't say why, but when Dallas opened up its hotels, we started to stay downtown.

We never played preseason games in the South. Most other teams did, but he wouldn't play there. Teams could play exhibition games wherever they wanted. If you go back and look at the preseason schedules from that time, you'll see that eighty or eighty-five percent of the teams played exhibition games in the Carolinas, Tennessee, Alabama. Cleveland never did. Cleveland played in Akron, Pittsburgh, Detroit, and at home.

Other teams would go into those Southern cites, and the black players would stay in black homes. I know that he purposely did not schedule games in the South. He did not want his team separated. He knew that would cause problems for us, and we appreciated that. We talked about it among ourselves.

I'll give you an example. Remember the Runner-Up Bowl they played down in Florida, between the second-place teams? We played there at least twice. The black players from the teams we played stayed over in Miami, and the white players stayed in Miami Beach. All of the Browns stayed in the same hotel in Kennelworth.

We knew all of this because we would go over to the Jack of Hearts, in Miami, which was a black club. Miami Beach was fully segregated at this time, to the point that when we came across the Biscayne Bridge, guards would stop you and just about make you sign your life away. They'd want to know where you were going. You'd tell them, 'To my hotel.' They'd want to know the name of the hotel and your room number. Blacks were not ordinarily allowed to come over that bridge after dark. You had no reason to come over that bridge. Your work was over, right? You were finished cleaning up.

NO, THERE WAS NO RACIAL DIVISION on the Browns. Any time you get so many guys coming together from so many different cultures, you're going to have different ideas and philosophies, but I felt like we did a good job, all of us, black and white, of keeping our ball club beyond the racial lines. Look at Gene Hickerson. He's from Mississippi, and we always got along well together. The whole team went out together to play basketball. First of all, we had great respect for each other. We worked together. We were around each other in the locker room. We stayed in the same hotels even before home games. And a lot of teams weren't doing that then. You'd go to the hotel on Saturdays and sit around and talk about what your college team had done, make little bets on them, that sort of thing.

As far as the black guys not going to the team parties, most of us weren't drinkers. When we played road games, the wives would all watch the games together, black and white, and then all come out to the airport. They'd meet the plane, and then we would all go where they had been for the afternoon.

When we held out the year before, in 1967, that had nothing to do with race. We were just trying to get some more money. All five guys were starters: me, Leroy Kelly, Sidney Williams, Mike Howell, and John Brown.

None of us were making any money. I was making twenty-five or thirty. There was no question who ran the media back in those days. The owners did, and anything they wanted done, they got done. There was no complete disclosure about contracts that you have now.

Maybe I was a contractual rebel then, but I was coming off two Pro Bowl years, and I thought I deserved more money. You look back now and see you should've fought your own battle, but you live and learn. If you don't make any mistakes, then you haven't done too much.

I don't think that just because you own the team, you should have all of it. I'm for distribution of the wealth. The team is the product. Therefore, the team should have some part of the wealth. Certainly, if you put down your hard cash to buy it, you should profit from it. By the same token, there's fair distribution. The collective bargaining and the things that were going on back in those days were just not right. It's obvious that there's a lot of money to be made now, and if it wasn't for the people who came before, that money wouldn't be there. Many of the players today don't have any idea what went on before them.

RACE RELATIONS ON OUR BALL CLUB were good. We held our relationships in high esteem. That's why the situation with Ross Fichtner was so mind-boggling. It came out of the blue.

The Ashland Country Club held this event in '68. Ross took the position that the year before, several guys had charged things at the pro shop and didn't pay for them. He never said who they were. My opinion was, 'Why don't you check it out, find out who's doing it, and get on those guys?' Then he makes the statement that they weren't going to invite any colored guys. That was his statement. He was in charge of the tournament.

I felt that his position should have been, 'I'm not going to let you do that to my teammates. All of us who want to come and play can come and play, or none of us will come and play.' That's the position I would've taken, and I think that's the right position to take.

As I look back at it, the mistake I made was that I should've said to Ross, 'I'll let the players know, and if they don't want to play, fine.' I should not have allowed myself to get isolated to the point that, quote, *I'm* speaking for the group, or, *I* am the group. We were Browns players, and I should have kept it that way, instead of making it appear as it were a personal thing.

I allowed it to get personal by calling the papers. That was my mistake.

I was angry because Ross had done something that violated a trust within our own group. I had never thought that Ross was a racist. There might have been several guys in our locker room that I did have some suspicions about, but Ross wasn't one of them.

Then Art, for whatever reason, felt like he should get rid of us both. He responded by waiving us. We were waived, and we weren't picked up. I went up to New York to meet with Pete Rozelle about whether or not I was going to be picked up. He said there were teams that were concerned about whether I was becoming a militant, because, remember, I was involved in the Black Economic Union with Jim. The commissioner said that many of them felt that this was going to be the organization that was going to come in and try to disrupt the league and create strikes and pull all the black players together.

I said, 'No, sir. We're totally concerned with our own communities, with building new economic enterprises. We're not creating strikes against the NFL. We're talking about pooling our resources and working to help our community.'

WE TALKED FOR ABOUT TWO and a half hours, and I went on to the Redskins. Vince Lombardi was the coach my last year. He was somewhat like Paul, very driven, but more personable. He liked to get down and coach with you. He wanted to go on the sled drills. He'd be on the blocking sled, yelling, 'Drive! Drive!' One day, I hit a machine and broke it, and he went wild over that. He was hootin' and hollerin': 'That's it! That's the way you do it! That's what I want!'

If I did talk to Ross after that, I don't remember it. Somewhere along the line, I ran into one of his sons, who was in coaching. I was just hurt that one of our own guys was willing to let some other group push us away from each other. As a matter of fact, I had won the tournament the year before. I guess I should've quit golf after that. Golf cost me a good job.

In 1969, I felt like I had had enough. I sort of have a clock in my mind for what I want to do at certain times in my life. I felt that ten years was enough to play. I was that way when I went to college. I told myself, 'In four years, I want to have my degree.' There were no redshirts then, and I'm glad, because I wouldn't have done that. I wanted to play pro ball for ten or eleven years, work until I was 62, then go home and enjoy my life. I was still playing pretty well when I retired, but my mind wasn't into it anymore. I simply did not want to go back out there.

I knew I never wanted to be a coach. As much as I love the game, I knew I didn't have the patience for coaching. By the same token, I never thought I'd be here, either. While I was playing, I wondered where I would be later. I'd listen to players whine and make excuses for missing plays, and that grated on me, even as a player. As a coach, I would have really been upset. I never thought about the front office. Not many former players worked in front offices at that time. I'm just a guy who loved the game. I think that's why I got into the agency.

Pat Summerall and Buddy Young had put together a group out of Boston and New York, and they wanted to be involved with player representation. They were financial planners. Buddy called me and asked me if I would be interested. I worked with them from about '70 to '75, and then out of the blue, (Dallas Cowboy general manager) Tex Schramm called me one night and said, 'This is Tex Schramm. How you doing?' I didn't know Tex except through the players I represented. I had Drew Pearson and Billy Joe Dupree and a couple of other Cowboys.

I thought, *Oh, my, what has happened down there now?*

He said, 'Coach Landry and I have been talking. We'd like to talk to you about coming and being a Cowboy.'

I told him I wasn't interested in coaching, but he said he wasn't talking about coaching. So I went down and talked to him, and that's how I got into personnel work. I stayed sixteen years with them. I went in as a college scout, but from day one, Gil Brandt and Tex wanted me to do contracts and deal with players. The organization made the players feel that they were at a higher level. You'd watch them take the field, and they came on with a certain aura about them. They thought that if the game was close, they were going to win it. That's how we felt in Cleveland.

WHEN THE LEAGUE WENT TO THE 'HOGS'—the big 300-pounders—Coach Landry didn't want to go that way. He didn't like those kind of linemen and all the pushing and shoving. He wanted to stay with the smaller, quicker, 265-, 270-pound linemen. All of a sudden, the defensive linemen were stronger because they were bigger, and the offensive linemen couldn't handle them. He would not make the change, and it caught up with him.

The great players he had along the way—the Dorsetts and the Randy Whites—were going downhill at the same time. Tex couldn't bring himself to fire Coach Landry. Jerry Jones could do it because he came from the outside, like when Art fired Paul. When Jerry came in, I took over pro personnel. I made the trades. I made the deals. And we had some pretty good deals back then.

I did that for two years, and I really appreciated the opportunity because he allowed me to do what I really thought I should do. Look at the Herschel Walker trade to the Vikings. No one ever dreamed what we would get from those draft choices. That's what really brought the Cowboys back. Emmitt Smith was a product of that trade, Russell Maryland was a product of that trade, Darren Woodson, Dixon Edwards. We got about nine guys from that trade, and because of it, we could do a lot of other things.

We thought we had done a pretty good job in Dallas, but Jerry wanted to go in a different direction. Jerry Jones fired me on Mother's Day weekend of 1991. The first thing I did was call Art and tell him what had happened. I kept in touch with Art over the years. Art was a guy I always liked personally. I know how honest he is. I know how hard he works.

I CAME HERE IN JANUARY OF 1998. I'm happy where I am. I'm getting ready to retire. This is going to be my last year. I'm 63, and I've had a good life. I'd just like to see us get into the playoffs before I go, for Art's sake. He deserves it. And I think it's going to happen.

Because of the money and the salary cap, scouting and personnel have become very important. A lot of money is spent on the draft, and even more money is spent on free agency. You realize that a mistake can cost a team ten or twelve million dollars. That's what happened to us here. We had five or six guys we were paying big money to who weren't doing anything. Some of them aren't even on the roster, but yet we were still paying them. You have the reporters questioning everything you do, and they end by beating up Art.

I was at the University of Oklahoma when I heard that Art was moving the team. We were playing a Monday night game in Dallas, and I was getting ready to fly back when I heard on a sports talk show that the Browns were leaving Cleveland. I never dreamed that there wouldn't be a Cleveland Browns. The New York Giants, Pittsburgh, Green Bay, the Cleveland Browns. I just couldn't believe it. I was hurt.

I know Art well enough to know why he did it and I know, in my heart, that it wasn't easy for him make the decision to move. I know he had great turmoil in his mind about leaving Cleveland. I don't buy the idea that he was just greedy. That's not even close to what Art Modell is. Art Modell is probably one of the finest owners in football, and I know all of them pretty good. There's probably none as fine as he is in terms of how much he cares about the league, how much he cares about his players. It hurts to see him beat up the way he's been beat up, and I think it hurts him.

Guys like Brian Billick and Bill Walsh still use things that Paul Brown taught. I read Bill Walsh's book, and it was all familiar, because I grew up under that system: the detail, the structure, the organization. Of course, Paul Brown called all the plays my first couple of years, and I was involved in that as one of the messenger guards.

I looked at Paul Brown the way I would look at a general or a commander. I believed in his concepts. At times, I thought, he was a little close to the vest. The difference between him and Coach Landry, who I was also close to, is that in a close game, Paul would play it close to the vest offensively, and Coach Landry would come at you with everything. Paul would pound it in there. He would go back to hard, basic football. Landry would come at you with a trick play or deception, something to break what you think he's going to do. They were both very conservative people, but Coach Landry would take it upstairs on you when it came to play calling.

I had great respect for Paul Brown. He wasn't really personable, but he was what I think coaches need to be in terms of structure and organization and pushing players to be better and showing them what they need to do. I know how good a coach he was. I know what he did for football. I played for two great coaches, because Blanton was also great. He doesn't get the credit, because he followed Paul, but Blanton believed in many of the same things Paul did.

All of us who played there loved it. You'd come up out of the tunnel, and that cold wind would be coming off that lake. You've got your sleeves rolled up. You had that crowd, and all of a sudden, you're not cold anymore. I've been in a lot of stadiums, but the roar of that crowd in Cleveland was just a different roar, man, a different roar. They call it the Dawg Pound now, but the working people always sat there. Back in the old days, they got in for a dollar. We always went down to that end to warm up. They were screaming and hollering and loving you: 'Go get 'em! Go get 'em! We know you can beat 'em!' There's nothing like that. **"**

# Higher Power

THE REVELATION came strangely to Ross Fichtner. One weekend five years after his career as an NFL defensive back had ended, Fichtner and his wife saw the film *Jesus Christ Superstar*. Afterward, Fichtner says, he felt exultant. God seemed more real.

A week later—on Good Friday—the couple saw *The Exorcist*. Fichtner left the theater troubled. His language became unusually profane. A strange weight seemed to crush the breath from him.

"There was something in there that wasn't me," he says.

The Fichtners didn't regularly attend church, but because his wife had been reared Catholic, he went with her to Easter mass. They arrived late, and Fichtner could see neither the priest nor the altar, but he could see on a wall directly before him a crucifix.

"Lord," he prayed, "I don't know what this is that's in me, but please take it away."

As a scrawny daydreamer growing up in southwestern Pennsylvania, Fichtner envisioned himself a star. Sent each summer to a YMCA camp, he idolized the counselors, many of whom played high school or college football. One evening, Fichtner sat watching them play a pickup game. A halfback from Notre Dame burst through the line and sped toward him. Fichtner leaped up and crashed into the runner. The hit felled the Notre Dame back and left the eight-year-old boy unconscious.

"I was just out, and from that time, the guys loved me," says Fichtner, who still doesn't know what caused him to tackle the runner.

In bed in his grandmother's house, he dreamed of becoming captain of the McKeesport High team. He listed his future occupation as "professional football player" on a survey he filled out in the seventh grade. But he received the last uniform handed out to the freshman team; it was so big he could barely run in it. As a 109-pound sophomore halfback, he seldom played.

Nevertheless, Fichtner accepted as gospel the rules set forth by his coach. He didn't smoke. He didn't drink. He didn't date. Summers, while others loafed, he and a few friends worked out daily at the high

school field. As his coach said he must if he ever hoped to play quarterback, Fichtner slept with a football.

"All the great musicians or artists, when they were in high school, sacrificed their dating life and whatever to practice," he says. "I learned the work habits, the things you have to do to be successful."

Success eluded him. As a junior, he was cut from the varsity. Relegated to the JV team, he slouched home and told his mother he was quitting.

"You have a practice this afternoon. Get ready and go back to practice," she ordered.

The telephone rang. The varsity was loading the bus for camp, an assistant coach said. One seat was available. Did Fichtner want to come?

Evenings at camp, coaches arranged contests among players. Teammates bullied "Ross the midget," fourth-team halfback and fifth-team quarterback, into wagering a quarter on who could throw a football farthest. The boy's shoulder ached so much that he could hardly lift his arm. Frustrated to tears, Fichtner stood at the fifty yard line, gritted his teeth, and threw. He was as amazed as anyone when the ball landed in the end zone and he won the bet.

Several weeks later, Fichtner came off the bench and completed five straight passes. He had realized the first of his "progression of dreams"—the series of ever grander visions he had of himself while he played.

As a senior, he was McKeesport's captain and the most valuable player in the Western Pennsylvania High School All-Star Game. Lightly recruited at first because he was so small, he became a sprint champion and was deluged with scholarship offers.

At Purdue University, Fichtner started three years as an option quarterback and defensive back. He was the Boilermakers' MVP as a senior, but that season also threatened his career. In a victory over Notre Dame, Fichtner tried to run over a linebacker sixty pounds heavier than he. The collision snapped Fichtner's scapula. Doctor's said he was unlikely to play again.

He spent ten days in a cast from his waist to his chin and a month in grueling rehabilitation. Fichtner came back to intercept three passes in a game, returning one for a long touchdown, and attract the attention of Paul Brown.

"I could have gone all through my senior year and had a fairly good season and not been drafted," Fichtner says. "The injury turned out to be in my favor. It was the way I came back that gave me value in their eyes, rather than my ability on the field."

Fichtner was hunting in the remote mountains of Pennsylvania when he heard over a tiny transistor radio that he'd been drafted by the Browns. He ran through the forest, shouting. Teams in the American and Canadian leagues had also drafted him. Fichtner signed with Cleveland for $4,500 less than the Buffalo Bills offered, because, he says, "I wanted to play for Paul Brown. My high school coach worshipped Paul Brown."

Fichtner seemed fated to be cut from the Browns. He missed two weeks of training camp while playing for the College All-Star Team. Shifted among several positions in the defensive backfield, he was uncertain of his assignments and uncomfortable with the footwork.

"He was so eager to make the team that he looked a bit awkward," defensive backfield coach Howard Brinker said. "His feet would get all tangled, and he even fell down a couple of times."

The last player kept in 1960, Fichtner played only one down at cornerback that season, while starter Bernie Parrish had a strap repaired on his shoulder pads. The Browns drafted several defensive backs in 1961, but Fichtner clung to his spot by playing well in an exhibition game after Parrish was hurt. Still, he played during the regular season mostly by sneaking onto special teams when regulars were winded.

His contributions had been scant, but Fichtner complained to the staff that he'd been given no opportunity to compete for a starting position. Brown promised him a chance at the strong safety spot, but military service again kept Fichtner out of camp for two weeks. When he arrived, he learned that Cleveland had acquired veteran defensive back Tom Franckhouser from the Cowboys. Fichtner thought he was about to be traded. Only hours after his army discharge, he picked off two passes in a preseason game and won the starting job.

His parents divorced, Fichtner had been brought up without a father. Therefore, he says, he sought to please Brown. He led the team with seven interceptions in 1962, and Brown uncharacteristically admitted that keeping him on the bench had been a mistake.

Fichtner missed six games of 1964 with a concussion, but held Baltimore's Hall of Fame tight end John Mackey to one reception for two yards in the Browns' NFL title game victory that season. In 1966, Fichtner moved to free safety, a position better suited to his stature and daring. Cleveland topped the league with thirty interceptions, and Fichtner tied Mike Howell for the team lead with eight, three in one game. Teammates and coaches voted him the Browns' defensive MVP, and

Fichtner made second-team All-Pro. *Sports Illustrated* pictured him on its cover, and in a story entitled "Pro Football's Best Deep Defenders," said, "Settled in at free safety this season with carte blanche to wheel and steal, he suddenly has become a defensive star."

Fichtner prospered in ways even he had never imagined. Blond, blue-eyed and wholesome-looking, he married a former Miss Ohio. He zipped around town in a red sports car. He owned a promotional agency for athletes and part of a thriving radio station.

He was also literally a hero. Fichtner was driving home one January day when he saw a Volkswagen microbus smash through a guardrail, plummet twenty feet down an embankment, plunge into the Cuyahoga River, flip, and begin to sink. Fichtner bolted from his car, flung off his jacket, and raced to the microbus.

He stepped onto the frozen river. The ice broke. He fell in. Immersed to his waist, he felt under the stained water.

"All I could think of was someone was going to die, and I couldn't help them," he said.

Fichtner grabbed a woman's dress but couldn't pull her from the Volkswagen. A man's leg bobbed to the surface. Fichtner wrestled him free, dragged him to shore, heard him groan, thought, 'Thank God he's alive.'

He waded back into the river, worked the woman out of the microbus, and carried her to the bank.

"It was like a nightmare coming true," he said.

That statement also describes the end of Fichtner's football career.

For two years, he organized a celebrity golf tournament as publicity for the radio station. He invited numerous teammates to the Ashland Country Club for golf, cocktails, and a dinner-dance. When the country club wanted to continue with a scaled down version of the tournament, including only eighteen Browns, Fichtner says he had no hand in compiling the guest list. He simply gave out the invitations, none of which went to a black player.

Just before training camp in 1968, as Fichtner and Cleveland's management discussed renegotiating his contract and his becoming captain, the story erupted in the press. Offensive guard John Wooten, who said he was a spokesman for other black players, called the slight intentional and Fichtner and the other Browns who participated in the tournament bigots.

Fichtner said he was innocent and dismayed. Wooten said Fichtner should have stood by his teammates, regardless of their color. Fichtner said

that no black players had been invited because they hadn't socialized at past tournaments. Wooten said Fichtner was lying. Fichtner speculated that Wooten was using the tournament to foment racial turmoil.

Wooten would not let the matter drop. Players took sides. The press accused Fichtner of bringing to the surface seething racial tensions on the team.

In the charged atmosphere of the time—only months after riots swept America following the murder of Martin Luther King, Jr.—every word was loaded with emotion and consequence.

Modell's solution was Solomonic. In what one writer called "a sour and unfortunate finale for two players who performed long and well for the Browns," both players were released. Fichtner heard the news over television.

He said he was prepared to play for another team, but after he and Wooten were both claimed off waivers by San Francisco—and inexplicably dropped—no one called. Just as Fichtner became certain that he'd been blackballed, John Mecom, the mercurial owner of the New Orleans Saints, signed him.

His stay in Louisiana turned out to be "a year in hell." Fichtner was embarrassed when Southern rednecks greeted him as a kindred spirit. When Wooten wasn't immediately picked up by another team, Fichtner became the target of threats by the NAACP to boycott New Orleans's games.

"I went from first string with a contending team, the Browns, to the taxi squad of an expansion team that's struggling to win games," Fichtner said. "I also lost a good business (the promotional agency) in Cleveland and, in some places, my good name."

The sole highlight of the year for Fichtner was working as an extra on the film *Pro*, which starred Charlton Heston as an aging NFL quarterback. Fichtner was released before the next season, out of football at age twenty-nine.

"For the next four or five years, my life was absolutely in chaos," he says.

Scorned as a racist, he couldn't find a coaching job—the career he had planned to follow. He says some teammates forsook him, and some friends took perverse satisfaction in his downfall. He divorced. He traveled the highways of New York and Pennsylvania, making sales calls in an unprofitable territory.

His turmoil finally ended after that epiphanic Easter mass in 1974. Leaving the church, he felt as if he could breathe again, Fichtner says.

Several weeks later, on a whim, he called his former roommate in Cleveland, Gary Collins, who was coaching with the Washington Ambassadors of the World Football League. Fichtner asked if Collins knew of any WFL team that needed a coach. Collins answered that the Ambassadors's defensive backfield coach had just resigned. Head coach Jack Pardee immediately hired Fichtner.

He spent nine seasons as an assistant for four different franchises in the WFL and NFL. He began attending team chapel services—where Fichtner had a second revelation.

"I believed that Jesus Christ was God's provision for sin. But I had never heard, and my wife had never heard, that we had to receive him as our personal savior and Lord and confess with our mouths," he says. "At that point, I confessed my sin. I said, 'Lord, I'm a sinner. I can't do it on my own. I do believe that you are my only provision. Please come in and change my heart, change my life.'"

Between coaching stints in Chicago and Green Bay, Fichtner spent two years as a kind of roving apostle for the Fellowship of Christian Athletes, and after leaving football for good in 1985, joined the Coaches Ministry of Athletes in Action.

Just back from eighteen months conducting coaches seminars in Europe, Fichtner was ruddy, balding, and as spare as a marathoner as he played golf on a course owned by an old McKeesport buddy. He played frenetically, bustling across fairways, while dispensing ceaseless advice on club selection, approach angles, putting lines, and swing dynamics. His few errant shots disgusted him.

In the noisy clubhouse, Fichtner sipped iced tea, and, pale eyes narrowing, puffed at a long dark cigar that kept going out almost as soon as he lit it.

Numerous concussions have left him epileptic, Fichtner says. One collision dislodged his right eyeball from its socket. He was unconscious on the field for half an hour. Teammates thought he had died. He takes Milontin to stave off recurrence of the grand mal seizure he had twenty-five years ago.

Fichtner is thoughtful, if hard put to slow the ideas that course through his mind. He has more than a hint of the mystic about him, finding spiritual lessons in almost every occurrence.

Fichtner says the tenets he uses in his own teachings to coaches and athletes mix Jesus Christ and Paul Brown.

"What I do today is so much in line with what Paul Brown demanded," he says. "He didn't come out and say, 'I'm trying to build character,' but he did come out and say, 'I won't put up with anything but character.'"

Fichtner remarried before he began coaching. He had fathered four children from his first marriage, but a vasectomy seemed to preclude children with his second wife. Even after the vasectomy was reversed and the Fichtners had been to physicians and fertility clinics, the couple was barren. Where science failed, God triumphed, Fichtner says. The couple prayed and conceived "a miracle child."

Fichtner says that every obstacle he has faced has been "a tune-up for the Christian life"—even the ugly incident that ended his career. God sent him that trial, he says, so that Fichtner might gain knowledge of human nature, to save him from further injuries, and to teach him to forgive.

He has never spoken to Wooten about their rift but says he is sorry that it happened. Scripture tells him that he must bear no grudge.

"In the greatest sermon ever preached, the Sermon on the Mount, Christ said, 'Everyone who is angry with his brother has committed murder,'" Fichtner says.

For Ross Fichtner, what had once seemed to be a lifetime of coincidence—-fortuitous and disastrous—has become clear evidence of divine intervention.

"My whole life, God has just stepped in and put me where he wanted me to be," he says.

# Ross FICHTNER

" I ALWAYS LOVED FOOTBALL.
I pictured myself being on the high school team, and I always pictured
myself being the captain and the most valuable player. I never pictured
myself just making the team. Even my sophomore year, when I was hardly
playing, I would lie in bed and throw the ball up and catch it and picture
myself being a great player. I pictured myself going to a major college and
being the captain, playing in the College All-Star Game and being most
valuable player, then I played professional ball. I had those kinds of dreams.

The best day I ever had as a pro, I told Gary Collins, my roommate, I
said, 'You know, I'm waking up every night having the same dream. I'm
intercepting a bunch of passes.'

I intercepted three passes that week. I even saw the routes. It was almost
scary. I could have had another one, but when I saw the route, I hesitated a
little bit. I said, 'No, this can't be what I saw,' but it was. I just couldn't
believe it. I should have had dreams like that all the time.

In high school, I was sort of small, and my freshman year I didn't get a
uniform. But I kept hanging around. Finally, I got a uniform, and it was so
big that I had to take a couple of steps just to get it moving. The last game
of the freshman season, I started as a running back.

The high school coach came over to see the freshman team, and he
said, 'No girls. Girls and sports don't go together. You don't drink. You
don't smoke. In the summer, you go out and run track. You work out all
summer. You go to bed early.'

I said, 'I'm gonna do that.'

I was so small it looked like a joke to most people. My freshman year, I was 5' 3 $\frac{1}{2}$" and 109 pounds. My senior year, I was only 5' 10", 154 pounds. My growth spurt came after football my freshman year of college. I grew two and a half inches and put on 25 pounds between football season and spring practice.

As a high school sophomore, I was fourth or fifth team. My coach said, 'If you want to be a quarterback, you're going to have to sleep with a football.'

I told him I didn't have one. He gave me a new football, and I slept with it—literally.

I said, 'Well, maybe some day I'll get a scholarship.'

I didn't have the physical size, and people had grown past me all of a sudden, but I never thought I *couldn't* play.

So I didn't date, I didn't drink. I kept all the rules. But I was taking a lot of ribbing: 'He doesn't date. He doesn't drink. He doesn't go to dances. What a sucker.'

When the games were over, I went home and went to bed. Other guys were going to dances or drinking beer. When I came back from college, some of them complained that the coach didn't get them a college scholarship. I'd say, 'Hey, wait a minute. I never saw *you* out there when we were working out in the summer. When you came riding by yelling, "Sucker," on the way to the swimming pool, *we* couldn't get anybody out there to throw balls to.'

THE FIRST TIME I GOT RECRUITED, I was asked to go to the Pitt-Penn State game. Pitt invited me. They asked me to go with a bunch of guys from Western Pennsylvania. We went up to Penn State on a train with the alumni. When we came back, the coaches talked to each of us. They came to me and said, 'Gee, Ross, we didn't realize you were this small. If something happens, we may have a scholarship later on, but right now, if you have a chance to go someplace else and get a scholarship, take it. Chances are, you won't be coming to Pitt.'

I said, 'Hey, coach, thank you very much.'

At the state semifinal track meet, I ran the first leg of the mile relay. There were a lot of coaches up there watching guys run. I beat the guys who came in first and second in the quarter mile by a big margin. The coaches were out of the stands. They were all over me: 'Boy, we didn't know you could run like that. Hey, we might be able to do something.'

Next, I was captain and most valuable player of the JC All-Star Game in Forbes Field. Pitt and Penn State really started. Joe Paterno had me fly up to Penn State, and I played golf with Joe. I really wanted to play at Penn State, but one of my high school coaches had played for Purdue and now he was returning there as a freshman coach. So I ended up going there.

I played quarterback in college for three years after Lenny Dawson. Freshmen weren't eligible then. That was Lenny's senior season, but I moved in as a sophomore and after the first three games of my sophomore year, I started the rest of the time.

I'm the Rodney Dangerfield of Purdue quarterbacks. I get no respect. We didn't throw the ball much when I was there. When they were trying to recruit Jim Everett at Purdue in 1981, someone came up with the idea for quarterback day. They were going to bring all the quarterbacks back and introduce them at halftime and give them a plaque. As they introduced the guys, they'd tell their stats. Lenny Dawson threw for so many thousand yards and led the Big 10 in this and that. They had Mike Phipps and Bob Greise, Mark Herrmann, Scott Campbell.

I'm the fourth guy out, following Lenny Dawson. They're going on about Lenny: 'Led the Big 10 in passing three years, number one draft pick of the Pittsburgh Steelers, Hall of Famer, threw for 39,000 yards.' He went out to get his plaque.

Then, 'Quarterback the next three years was Ross Fichtner. When Ross was here, third and 25 wasn't necessarily a passing situation.'

Everybody laughed.

In the games I started, we probably had the best won-loss record of all those guys, but one year, I think, I threw only fifty-nine passes all season. We were a wing-T offense. We were just a bunch of no-name guys who pounded teams out. We were fifth in the nation on defense. It wasn't necessarily that I *couldn't* throw. I played at Purdue when we took advantage of other things. We played during the era when *no one* threw much.

I FOUND OUT I HAD BEEN DRAFTED by Cleveland when I was deer hunting. I had a little portable radio, and I tuned it in about 4 o'clock in the afternoon. The sports came on and it said, 'The Cleveland Browns took Jim Houston, Prentice Gautt, and Ross Fichtner.'

Man, I jumped up and was running through the woods, screaming and yelling. I was drafted by the Browns, the perennial champions. It was really something to be drafted by them.

Finally, Eddie Ulinksi, one of the Browns' coaches, came down and we had breakfast. He offered me $8,500. I told him, 'I don't think I can sign that today.'

Oh, he was all worried. He said, 'We have to go and call Paul.' Paul had told him to sign me. I was in my coach's office, and he went and called Paul Brown. He put my coach, on with Paul. Then he put me on.

Paul Brown said, 'What would you sign for?'

I said, 'Well, Coach, if you give me $10,000 and a thousand in advance, that would be fine.'

He said, 'Congratulations, you're now among the upper ten percent of the income earners in the country. We'll be in touch with you. Don't mention that you've signed. We're going to release it.' It was a done deal.

I went to the Blue-Gray Game, got MVP and captain there. After the game, Buffalo offered me $15,500 for three years. I told them, 'Sorry, guys, I already signed at $10,000 with Cleveland.'

PAUL BROWN DIDN'T LIKE MENTAL MISTAKES. If you couldn't pass the IQ test he gave every year, you didn't get a uniform. We had a guy who came to the Browns from Youngstown to try out for quarterback. We did those tests. There were twenty minutes to do sixty questions. When we were done, he asked me, 'How many did you get done?'

I said, 'Fifty or fifty-one.'

I said, 'How many did you do?'

He said, 'Five.'

I said, 'Five!'

I never saw him again. He just disappeared.

A lot of times, we had guys who could lift a house or run like the wind, but if they didn't do well on the mental part, Paul didn't want them. In the long run, he thought, they would hurt you. They would make the key mistake.

The other thing Paul wanted was people with character. I always heard him say, 'You can't win without class people,' because when the going gets rough, they're not going to go south on you. With those kinds of people, you have a chance to turn things around.

The first time I met him, I was pretty much in awe of the man. I had heard a lot of stories about him. My high school coach had been a father figure for me, and Paul Brown had been *his* idol. So I had an automatic respect for Paul through the eyes of the man *I* respected.

My first year, I played all the positions in the defensive backfield. In fact, I was the third quarterback, the fifth running back, second flanker, third split end, and backup for all of the defensive backfield positions. That first four or five years, I usually played when a guy got hurt. It was kind of tough for me, because when you're playing regular, you're studying for one spot. I had to make sure that in case someone got hurt and I got out there, I knew what my responsibilities were.

My first five years, I was on special teams—except for the kickoff team. When you're not starting, you're automatically on special teams. The veterans would say, 'Go down on the kickoff for me.' And I did. I would ask *them* if I could run down on kickoffs for them. One year, I led the team in tackles on kickoffs.

They didn't always grade the special teams, and one day Ulinski said, 'Hey, you're getting me in trouble here. Paul Brown asked me what was going on. He noticed you weren't on the kickoff team. Then he noticed you weren't even on the *backup* kickoff team...'

I just wanted to contribute. Forget about the other stuff. Carry out the details of the assignment. If you're supposed to get your left hand up here, get it up here. If you have to fill a gap or a hole, you make sure you get in there and fill it. If the ball's gone, just try to make a play.


I DIDN'T START MY FIRST YEAR, and when it came time to sign a contract, Paul Brown said, 'You made a contribution on special teams, but it's not enough to get a raise.'

I said, 'Fine. I'll sign the same contract.'

They had drafted me to take Warren Lahr's place. He'd played ten years and was All-Pro, and he was only making $10,500. I was making $500 less than what he was.

A few years ago, I was at a golf tournament in Milwaukee, and (former Los Angeles receiver and New Orleans head coach) Tom Fears and (former Giant and Packer kicker) Don Chandler and (former Packer receiver) Carroll Dale, who played in the '60 College All-Star game with me, were there. I said, 'In the middle of our careers, if your owner came up to you and said, "You're making $16,000. Next year, I'm going to pay you a million, but I want to see some production." Could you have played any harder?'

I couldn't have played any harder for a million than I did for $16,000. I was giving it everything I had. There wasn't anything left. I didn't have $984,000 more effort left in there. And they all felt the same way.

In those days, you didn't go into the whirlpool, because you didn't want to turn to mush; you didn't lift weights, because you didn't want to get muscle-bound; you didn't have off-season programs. The shoes we played in had soles a half-inch thick because they screwed the spikes into them. Now, they have these shoes that are so light, and every player gets forty-five pair of them. They gave us one pair for practice and one pair for games, and we had to buy everything else. Our uniforms were heavy and bulky. That's why I didn't wear hip-pads, I didn't wear thigh boards, I didn't wear kneepads. I wore helmet and shoulder pads. I taped two pieces of sponge rubber on my hips and stripped the rubber off the thick thigh boards and just put the hard part, about a sixteenth of an inch thick, in my pants. Today, you have all of these space-age materials that are built for strength and speed.

Back then, you could get injured and if it was in the knee, you were out for the season. Once they opened it up, it took forever for the stitches to heal. Today, they go in with the scope, and you can have a little fray in there, and be back playing in a couple of weeks.

Today, they do things to enhance every bit of a guy's ability. Back when we played, you just played on natural talent. The way you improved wasn't necessarily through strength or speed; it was through technique and knowledge of the game.

FOOTBALL IS NINETY PERCENT above the shoulders. Part of that ninety percent is knowing your assignment—what to do. The other part is the psychological part. If this happened one time, it happened twenty times. I had friends on other teams. After the game, I'd go over and say hello. They had played hard that day, but we ended up coming back and beating them. And every time, the conversation would go like this: I'd come up and say, 'Hey, good game.' They'd say, 'You lucky son-of-a-gun. We should've kicked your butts today. We had you guys.' And they'd always end it in this way: 'I'm glad it wasn't me who made the mistake that beat us.'

I knew that when it came down to crunch time, they're thinking, 'I hope it's not me who makes the mistake that beats us.'

In the meantime, *we're* all thinking, 'Who's going to make the play that wins it for us? Someone's going to make an interception or pick up a fumble or we're going to make a stand or Jim Brown is going to make a play or Gary Collins is going to make a catch or Paul Warfield is going to break one. Somehow, we're going to do it. We know we're going to win it. We just don't know how yet.'

Paul never gave us pep talks. He never gave us the rah-rah stuff. It was very cut and dried. You knew what you had to do. There were no gray areas. And then he had his 'Wednesday Rule.' We had Mondays and Tuesdays off, then the Wednesday Rule, which was, 'Have all the sex you want Sunday night through Tuesday night, then give me the rest of the week.' I wasn't worried about that. I was single when I played for him, and I couldn't make out in a female penitentiary with a handful of pardons.

ONE OF THE CONFLICTS THAT HAPPENED, in '61, was when Art Modell bought the team, and we had a new owner. Now, nothing changed in the football part of it. Paul Brown is still running it, but Art Modell is now on the scene. Art wanted to be one of the guys. When we traveled, they didn't have the bus that comes out on the tarmac and takes you right off the plane. You had to go through a gate and walk through the airport to the bus. On the way back, the bus dropped us at the airport and we walked through the airport to our gate and boarded our private plane. We'd get on the DC-7B and fly the old prop plane back to Cleveland. Art would get there, and he opened up the bar and gave everybody free beer. So, for half an hour, forty-five minutes, sometimes an hour, when the plane has been ready to go for fifteen or twenty minutes, the guys are sitting down there at the bar, having some beers, and Art Modell is picking up the tab. That really alienated Paul Brown.

In the meantime, Art's becoming buddies with the players. He's talking in their ear. He's coming out to practice. He wants to be a good guy. Paul Brown is just the opposite. He's still the hold-your-nose-to-the-grindstone, no-b.s. guy. He knew what was going on, but you keep the thing quiet, it was fine. He knew he couldn't control guys all the time. If he tried to do that, he wouldn't have a team. He knew that after practice, the guys were going to go down to the local tavern and drink four or five beers and come back for dinner. Everybody's been eating for fifteen minutes and this same group of guys comes in at the same time with these great appetites. He knew.

After the games, when Art was buying rounds, the guys thought Art was a pretty good guy. I had no complaints about Art Modell. He wasn't trying to second-guess anybody. He wasn't soliciting anything that I was aware of. He wasn't trying to turn the hearts of the players from Paul to him. That may have been what happened, but I wasn't aware of him being subversive, and if you would ever have asked me who I would've picked between Paul Brown and Art Modell, as an owner or a coach, there would never have been any question. It was nice of Art Modell to buy me some beers, but he never even negotiated my contract. I was still dealing with Paul Brown. Art was just an owner.

I was shocked when Paul Brown was fired. I know that a lot of the older guys were complaining because they said he didn't have the fire to win. I was still in that process of trying to be accepted and trying to please my boss with what I was doing. All my energy was going toward doing my job. I didn't have the division of concentration that is one of the biggest thieves of talent.

I'm thankful I was one of the few guys who when all this stuff broke about Paul Brown being fired, said nothing negative. I just said, 'I thought he was a great coach, and it was an honor for me to play for him.'

HERE'S WHAT HAPPENED. Art Modell hired Blanton Collier, we went in that next year, and it was like Blanton's mouth was moving but Paul was talking. Paul Brown's influence never left the Browns for all the years I was there. Blanton was more of a technician. He wanted to talk about technique, whereas Paul Brown wouldn't come over and talk to you about footwork or little things like that. Blanton was more approachable. We didn't have to write in our notebooks, 'Quarterbacks, feet parallel, knees flexed, pressure on.' But there really wasn't one major thing that changed. It was just a different guy up there talking.

A lot of people don't put all the parts into the formula when they're talking about the championship year. Number one, we won the largest championship check that was ever paid out, $8,052.82. That was in a year when I was making $14,500. I made over half a year's salary in that one day. Today, you have to win three games to win the Super Bowl, and your entire payout might be $90,000. Ninety thousand might not even be a game salary for some of these guys. We had something to shoot for, not just a ring. They're playing for the ring today. Their share of the Super Bowl is so small it's peanuts. If they were playing for a half million dollars now, there might be a little more team spirit. When we were there, we needed each other. Today, they don't need each other. To make $90,000? Their agents are going to make more than that in a month.

I was playing against John Mackey in that championship game in '64. He was a tough opponent. I had a good game against them that day in man-to-man coverage. But so many of my teammates were having a great game that I was outstandingly inconspicuous. They were averaging thirty-five points a game and a lot of yards, and we held them to zero.

The best thing I remember about the game is that we had a blitz on. They ran a screen pass. I think it was where Galen Fiss hit Lenny Moore and just upended him. It was incomplete, and one of the Colts guards was out in front of it. I was coming from the other direction. Mackey had released to take me downfield, and I saw the screen. I broke off and started running toward it. The guards didn't know the play was over. They're coming downfield, looking for guys to hit, and the guard was right in front of Baltimore's bench. He was trying to put a tracker on me. I was weaving as I was coming in. I knew that the play was already dead. I was trying to make the guard think I was trying to avoid him, but I was going to deck him. All of a sudden, I just turned right in his face and hit him under the chin with my helmet and dumped him on his backside. Don Shula was standing no more than five or six feet from me. When he saw me dump the guard on the ground, his chin went right down to his chest. There must have been five or six players standing there, and they all just turned around and walked back to the bench. It was like, 'This's the ultimate insult. A little defensive back just dropped one of our linemen.'

Of course, I had the advantage, because the guard didn't know the play was over. He thought I would try to avoid him, and he was going to put a forearm on me. All of this happened at the last second. The hit was a great feeling, but the greatest feeling was when I saw those guys turn around like they couldn't believe what was going on. From a game standpoint, it was the probably most important game we ever won.

MY MOM IS 92 YEARS OLD. She's a football person. She's been a football person her whole life. One year, right after the Steelers had won their last Super Bowl game, I'm coaching in Green Bay. Chuck Noll starts out 1-4. I talked to my mom after one of our games. She said, 'I think the Steelers need to get a new coach.'

I said, 'Mom, let me tell you something: If everything was absolutely even, you'd win the Super Bowl once every twenty-eight years, you'd lose it once every twenty-eight years, and you'd come in twenty-seventh, twenty-sixth, twenty-fifth, etc. once every twenty-eight years. If you have really good talent, you have a chance to repeat, so the cycle will take fifty-six years to complete itself. The next time anyone in Pittsburgh has a right to complain is 112 years from now. You have just won four. A lot of teams haven't won one yet. So for the next century, people in Pittsburgh should keep their mouths zipped.'

AFTER WE WON THE CHAMPIONSHIP, I became a partner in a radio station in Ashland, Ohio. That first year, I put on a golf tournament as a promotion for the station. We got the country club, and we invited local businessmen and players and coaches and their wives. We'd tee off at seven in the morning, and the wives had bridge tournaments, a luncheon, the pool. In the evening, there was a cocktail hour and a dinner and dance.

All the coaches came. John Havlicek came up from Columbus. Guys came from the Detroit Lions, the Washington Redskins, all over. There'd be forty or forty-five foursomes. The local businesses would provide some sponsorship, and I'd pay everyone $25 or $40, if they were coming in from a long way off, just for gas. We were just covering expenses.

Everyone in Ashland thought it was great. We did it for two years, and at the end of the second year, it had become a strain for us. It was so big and we had to spend so much time on it that it really became a hassle. Finally, the country club came to me and said they wanted to make it a stag day, no wives, no dinner, no dance. They wanted a shotgun start, eighteen guys, the kind of guys who like to sit around and drink and play cards, the guys who are going to socialize. Twenty or more were not invited, including Dich Schafrath, Bernie Parrish, Havlicek, the four black players, and the coaching staff.

I still passed out the invitations, but when I did, I told everybody, 'Hey, I didn't plan this. It's not my station's tournament any more.' And I explained to them all of the things that had happened.

I don't know if I told John Wooten personally that he wasn't invited, but I told Leroy Kelly and Sidney Williams, and Jim Shorter. I told them what had happened. I told them I was sorry, but there were a lot of other guys who weren't invited anymore, either.

Had I known what the results were going to be, I would have passed on the whole deal, because I got paid nothing, and I ended up getting fired out of the league and losing my job over it.

The day after the tournament, I get this phone call from a reporter: 'A person saying he is John Wooten is accusing you of bigotry.' The reporter wanted to know what I had to say.

I told him, 'I can't believe John said that. John should know I'm not a bigot.'

Maybe I could have avoided the things that transpired from that point on if I would've had the foresight or if John maybe would've had a better understanding of what had gone on. I don't know what John's motivation was. Obviously, it affected both of our careers, because we were done.

I had already signed a contract, and I had been told by Blanton Collier that I was going to be the team captain that next year. Galen Fiss had just retired, and Paul Wiggin had left. They wanted me to come up the next week to renegotiate the contract I had just signed, and they were going to give me a two-year contract. That would have been the first time I had two years on a contract.

I WAS ABSOLUTELY STUNNED when this thing broke. I could see that there were some racial problems on other teams, but I didn't think we had problems on our team. Black players had their social lives, of course, and they were not intertwined much with the white guys. We played basketball together and things like that, but we didn't party together. We weren't together socially. We always had a party after the games, and everybody was invited, but not everybody came. That was strictly a social thing. It was not a team event where if someone didn't come, they were turning their backs on their teammates.

But when we were together on the football field, there was never any kind of a problem. I felt that I could go up to John Wooten any time and just talk to him. We played basketball together in the off-season for all of those years. I never had the feeling that he disliked me, nor that he thought that I was antiblack.

The national press got it, and when Huntley-Brinkley ran it and every place else started to run it, my life was absolutely in chaos. The phone kept ringing; everybody wanted all the controversial stuff. And all of a sudden, the team that was talking about renegotiating my contract went south.

The only statement I ever made about it I made after the team called me and told me what to say. I kept quiet, other than saying, 'Hey, this stuff isn't true. You can ask anybody else. It's not true.'

But none of the stuff on my behalf was ever printed. Finally, we ended up getting fired, both of us, and, I would say, blackballed out of the league.

Once the national news media picked it up, I knew what the consequences were going to be. I knew this was going to be a really tough thing for the Browns to smooth over. In retrospect, if they would've come back and made some kind of statement about unity, it may have been healing and helped to restore friendships. If that had been their goal, we might have survived this thing. But, obviously, the thing that had to happen is that we were both going to go.

I went up the next day and apologized for the problem I had caused the team. They knew that the accusation that I was a bigot was untrue. They basically said, 'Thank you very much.' They said they appreciated my being there, and they told me they were going to work the thing out.

The biggest shock I got was that when we were both cut no one in the league wanted us, even though we were both coming off All-Pro seasons. The Browns didn't bother to contact me and say, 'You're going to hear this, and we're really sorry it had to happen.' I heard it on local television. I never heard from the Browns, and that was probably the most disappointing thing. If they would've called me and told me, things would've been much different for me.

I ENDED UP GETTING PICKED UP by the Saints. I went down to New Orleans and had just a pretty miserable year, overall. I had a contract for the year, but the general manager told me they were going to pay me but not play me. Evidently, there was a lot of pressure put on by outside agencies. We were going to be picketed and so forth.

The thing that was very disappointing to me was that when I was in New Orleans, I really got a chance to see bigotry. You go from growing up in McKeesport, Pennsylvania, and playing with blacks all your life, to all of sudden hearing people who *really* were bigoted. New Orleans, man, everybody wanted to meet me, because I was the guy who hated blacks: 'Man, you're my hero.'

It was degrading and untrue. I had black teammates there, too, and I hated going around trying to explain, 'Hey, all this stuff you're hearing about me is not true.'

Erich Barnes, who I played with in college, and other guys came up and said, 'Hey, we knew this stuff is not true.' But none of that was printed. I felt completely set up.

Art Modell was the president of the National Football League owners. Obviously, he could say, 'Okay, we don't pick either of these two guys up. So, anybody in the future who has a problem between a white player and a black player, they're both out of the league. Anyone on other teams that are having problems, you better keep your nose clean, because this is what's going to happen to you.'

From my eyes, that's what it looked like. Even Tom Place, who was the golf writer for the *Plain Dealer*, was at the tournament. He knew what happened, and never wrote an article. There was never a comment from anyone at the country club. Who did this? Who was in charge of this? No one. There was no defense for me, and after, I'm out of the league.

WELL, I GOT TO BE ON THE SAINTS ROSTER that year. I played in a couple of games. I never started. I was on the inactive list for a couple of games. They gave me a salary. Tom Fears, the head coach, apologized to me. He said, 'I'm really sorry about what happened this year. If you can get another team to pick you up, I'll be glad to recommend you.'

The thing that hurt was that I could have gone directly into coaching. I had an opportunity to go right back to Purdue, but I had to turn them down. Every time I read my name it said 'Ross Fichtner, comma, accused of bigotry and fired from the Browns, comma, just went into a burning building and saved someone's life.' I could do some kind of heroic deed, but I still had that tag.

I had to wait five or six years for all that stuff to go by, because I was afraid that I'd be coaching, and what happens if we play a white player who really deserves the job? Is it going to be bigotry all the time? For the record, it's pretty tough to play and coach in the National Football League if you're a bigot. I think most of the players I coached, and that includes black players, know that I was pulling for them.

I'm not mad at John Wooten. I'm not mad at Art Modell. I forgave them a long time ago. I'd be a wretched person if I would still be upset about what happened. I hope John is successful. I know he's been working in the National Football League for a long time (as a scout for Dallas and Baltimore), and that's great.

It was an unfortunate thing. I'm sorry that it happened. My life would have been a lot different if it hadn't, but my life may not have been as good. There were things that I was being taught. That adversity came at a time that maybe kept me from being hurt. I had some bad head injuries. I might not have been able to take two more shots on the head without being permanently damaged.

I learned a lot about people. I learned that, sometimes, when you put your trust in people, you're going to be disappointed. I learned who the guys were who stayed right behind me. There were a lot of people rejoicing when I went through my problems: 'Now, how's it feel to have to go out and work like a regular person?' I couldn't believe how many people came up with that attitude and made those statements—people who were my friends, who liked to get tickets to the ball games, who liked to be hanging around.

Other guys came up and said, 'I didn't know you hated black guys like that.' As a lesson on human nature, it was invaluable. It taught me that I have to be very careful of what I say and how I say it. Everybody's capable of saying something that's a little bit off. A lot of people have made a thoughtless little remark that is really blown out of whack and ruined a guy's life.

I RETIRED RIGHT BEFORE THE 1969 SEASON, before training camp. I didn't have a team to go to. I knew I wasn't welcome back in New Orleans. I was in working that day in Buffalo, as a sales rep. There was a high school track close to my hotel.

I was thinking, 'I've got to start seeing if I can find a place to play. I've got to keep in shape.' On my way to the track, I hear Don Meredith and Don Perkins announce their retirement from the Dallas Cowboys. We had all played together in the College All-Star Game. 'In every player's career there is a perfect time to retire,' Perkins said. 'Unfortunately, most of them miss the opportunity.'

I went to the track and started to warm up. I was just going to do a mile, before I did some sprinting. I was by myself. I ran around the track, one of those cinder tracks, and the second time around, I saw my footprints. The third time around, I saw the first two sets of prints, and on the fourth time around, I said to myself, 'You're just going around in circles.' I was hearing Don Perkins' voice.

I stopped in the middle of the lap, walked to my car, went back to the hotel, changed clothes, called my wife, and said, 'That's it. I'm retiring.'

It was the thing I had to do. I believe it was supposed to have happened. I've always had peace about it, although I would liked to have gone out a different way. Most guys don't go out the way they want to go out. Gary Collins was my roommate, a great roommate, a great player. He's still upset with Modell and Nick Skorich, because he thought he could play another year. He refused to come to our reunions for years. He said he wouldn't give Modell the satisfaction. I said, 'Don't do it for Modell. Do it for *me*. You don't even have to see him, then you have the rest of the time with your teammates.'

That was a stressful time. I know the blacks were having a rough time at that point in history. I know now how people who are accused falsely can feel and how the press can just absolutely turn things the way they want to.

WHEN I RETIRED, I was not on top of my game. A lot of it was because of all of the concussions I had. My career probably went four or five years longer than it should have. I had one of the original brain scans. They had a special helmet and mouth guards made for me so that I could play.

At that time, I didn't know that I would end up with epilepsy from the head injuries. They said to me, 'Fifteen years from now, you might have some problems.' They never told me what it would be, though. Fourteen and a half years later, I had a grand mal seizure. I had no idea what it was. I know it's from the concussions.

I had the brain scan right after the '64 season. I missed six games of our championship season. I came back for the last game and a half of the season and the championship game. I missed the whole middle of the season because of a concussion.

I got hit in the right temple. I got hit so hard that my left eye was knocked off its axis. It was focused down. Knocking Frank Clark out of bounds, I got a knee to the head. We were in a man coverage, and he went back on a tight end reverse. I'm the only guy there. I'm dodging my own guys to get to him. When he got back around the line of scrimmage in front of their bench, I tackled him and got knocked unconscious. The game was stopped for thirty minutes. I was in convulsions. They had to make sure I didn't swallow my tongue. Jim Houston thought I died on the field. I didn't wake up for forty-five minutes, in the locker room. I was in the hospital for ten days to get the swelling down so that my eye could come back. When I run, this eye still bounces.

Of course, I had some bad injuries when I was a kid. My sophomore year of high school, I got hit in a JV game on Saturday afternoon and woke up in class on Monday. All of a sudden, I was back in the world, dressed for school.

In college, I got dinged at Wisconsin. I had no idea how we got there, where we stayed, nothing. But we used to tackle with the head. Put your nose in the propeller. That's how I tackled. So I take my Dilantin. It's been twenty-three years this month since I had my one and only seizure.

After I remarried in 1974, I decided I was going to go into coaching. Someone had mentioned to me that my old roommate, Gary Collins, was coaching with the Washington Ambassadors in the World League. I got his number from information, and called. We were talking, and I said, 'You don't happen to need a coach, do you?'

He said, 'Are you kidding me? Jack (Pardee, the head coach of the Ambassadors, who would soon fold and become the Blazers) isn't here, but we're going to camp in two weeks. Our secondary coach just quit yesterday. Jack's going crazy wondering who we're going to hire.'

I said, 'Tell him I'm interested.'

I went home. I kept calling Jack. I finally got him, and he said, 'Can you come down tomorrow?'

The next morning, I saw Gary before I saw Jack. I said, 'Boy, I'm glad for the chance to interview.'

He said, 'What do you mean interview? You got the job.'

I said, 'How do you know I got the job?'

He said, 'Who else is he going to hire? Everybody else is working this time of the year.'

Jack came in. He said, 'Can you stay two more days?'

I said, 'I didn't bring extra clothes.'

He said, 'We'll buy them for you.'

They had two more days of meetings, then ten days off, then camp. The players knew the defense as well as I did.

COACHING THE FLORIDA BLAZERS WAS CRAZY. After the third game, we stopped getting paid. We didn't get a regular paycheck the rest of the year. There were a lot of teams that weren't getting paid. A team would come down, and we had to give them part of the gate. You didn't know if you were going to play. You didn't know if the league was going to fold.

My wife and I were just married. She would cry, because she would go to the bank and they wouldn't cash our checks until they cleared. We even had a *league* check bounce. It had the commissioner's signature on it and it was stamped 'insufficient funds.'

From a staff standpoint, though, it makes you pretty close. That's how Jack Pardee got in the NFL. He kept a team together after the third week of the season and went to the playoffs, because he kept saying, 'If we get to the World Bowl, it's going to be $10,000 to the winner and $5,000 to the loser.'

It's the only time I ever played where the starting quarterback, the head coach, and the equipment manager made the same amount of money. We had forty-five guys, and whatever amount of money we got each week, we divided it by forty-five. We all made the same amount of money. We might get a check one week for $232.27, and the next time, we might get $400.

Every day, the guys would go in the locker room and Jack would say, 'Look, I respect anyone who has to go home and take care of their family. That's fine. We start practice in five minutes. The guys who are left are going to play this week.'

Finally, we got to the championship game. We're playing Birmingham, in Birmingham. We lost by six points. The running back broke into the end zone for an apparent score. He was five or six yards in, and when he went down and hit the ground, the ball came loose and bounced out of the end zone. They give the ball to Birmingham on the 20, going the other way.

We end up coming in second. Birmingham was having financial problems, too, and the creditors came in and put a lien on the championship funds. By the time they paid, we each got a championship check for $320.

I WAS FORTUNATE TO HAVE PLAYED and coached in the NFL. I played eight seasons with the Browns and one with the Saints. I coached nine seasons with the Bears, Packers, and Vikings. During this time, I had the opportunity to observe the best situations and the worst. They were in such contrast they made permanent impressions in my mind.

The qualities of character are vital. Duke Weigle, my high school coach, stressed character, and so did Paul Brown. It is the basis of my present occupation, which is teaching coaches how to build these qualities into the lives of their athletes.

Athletes are very insecure. The reason they are so insecure is that their value is on their performance, and their performance can be replaced. They can get hurt. They can get beat out. A coach who builds character gives a player something he can take with him. You base his life on a more permanent value system instead of the temporal one of being cut or being hurt.

I say this because what I do today is so much in line with what Paul Brown demanded. He said, 'I won't put up with anything but character.'

I was at an NFL Alumni golf outing in Milwaukee just last week, and you hear people talking about Vince Lombardi all the time. You always have this picture of Lombardi taking this ragtag bunch of rummy-dummies and with discipline and sheer leadership, putting together a team that wins championships. I want to say, 'You guys are all nuts.' The Packers came out and knocked you off the ball, and it wasn't Lombardi knocking us off the ball. He had great talent. No one could ever say they weren't good football players, that Lombardi just came in there and made them great players.

Of all the guys who were assistant coaches under Lombardi, not one of them has ever had a winning season. But look at all the guys who came up under Paul Brown's system and continued on to have great coaching careers—Weeb Ewbank, Sid Gillman, Don Shula, Chuck Noll. There's a sign of how good a coach he was.

In '83, Green Bay played the Browns in Milwaukee County Stadium. I walk out on the field before the game, and I see Gib Shanley, the announcer. We're having a great conversation. Art Modell's over on the sideline. He comes over and gives me a big hug. He's asking me about coaching. He says something like, 'How's everything in your life going.'

I said, 'Really good, Art. I'm out of the golf tournament business.'

He looked at me. He couldn't figure out where I was coming from. Gib's laughing like mad. The conversation went on a little bit, and Modell gave me a little hug and walked away.

Gib said, 'You know, he doesn't even remember what he did to you. You're still one of his boys.'

I said, 'Gib, let me tell you something: I forgave him a long time ago. I'm not bitter. He might have saved my life.'

I REALLY FEEL THAT THE WAY MY CAREER WENT—coaching and playing—that God allowed me to be a lot of the places and to go through a lot of the things I've been through for what I'm doing right now. I've had the negative; I've had the positive. That was my training. Football was not the critical part of my life. It was the part where I learned the things that I'm teaching people now.

My last year of coaching, '84, with Minnesota, I hosted the team Bible study at our house. One of the things we talked about was drug testing, which was legal, by NFL rules. To a man, they were against it. They thought taking a whiz in a jar was an infringement on their privacy.

Finally, I couldn't listen anymore. I said, 'Guys, I don't know what's happened in the last eighteen years since I played. But I'll just tell you one thing—if they had asked me to whiz in a jar every day for the privilege of playing in the National Football League, I would do it. I'd do it because I want my teammates to know I'm not stealing from them. We're out there trying to win a championship, and if you do stuff like that, you're stealing from me. Everybody talks about their rights. You don't have any rights in the National Football League. You have responsibilities.'

In 1991 I joined Athletes in Action, which is a ministry of Campus Crusade, we went out for a month conference at Colorado State University. When we got back, I had just gotten home when I heard that Paul had died. I told my wife, 'I'm going to try to go to the funeral.'

I drove down to Massillon. I got in late that evening, got a chance to talk with Pete and Mike, his sons. There were very few guys left there. They asked me if I wanted to come to the funeral and I said I was hoping to. The little Massillon church was small and the funeral was by invitation only. On the left side of the church, as you're facing the front, were all the owners and league officials. On the right were the family and players. I was sitting next to Lou Groza and his wife, Jackie. Otto Graham was right in front of me, with Marion Motley, Jim Houston, and Dante Lavelli and his wife.

Because of the crowd—people lined the streets for three or four blocks—we had to be there forty-five minutes early. I sat there and remembered when I was in seventh grade, sending away for autographs. I'd send those little bubble gum cards. I remembered I had autographed pictures of Lou Groza and I had one of Otto Graham, Marion Motley, and Dante Lavelli. That would have been around 1951, and here I was in 1991, forty years later, with them, at Paul's funeral.

If someone would have come up to me in 1951 and said, 'Forty years from now, Paul Brown is going to die, and you're going to be sitting in this funeral home next to Lou Groza and Dante Lavelli and Marion Motley and Otto Graham, and you're going to feel like you deserve to be there, that would've blown my mind.

I'M GLAD I PLAYED WHEN I PLAYED. You didn't become zillionaires. There was character to it. The thing I cherish most about playing with the Browns is the memories of my teammates. Playing with the Cleveland Browns during the 1960s was the highlight of my life, and my teammates are very dear to me. I look forward to each time we have a reunion. We only see each other once or twice a year, and when I see the guys, my heart jumps. Maybe we're a little more out of shape. We're balder, grayer. Our families are grown. All the money we made, which was not much, believe me, has been spent. The cars we bought have long since rotted away in some junk yard.

What are the 1964 Browns? The 1964 Browns are the people and the memories that go along with them. You can read about them or see some films, but that isn't it. It isn't that the 1964 Browns won the biggest championship check that was ever paid to that point. It's that everything comes down to the people, and to the memories. What we went through together remains the same. The memories are the best parts. **"**

# January 9, 1963

IT WAS THE DAY the Terminal Tower hopped off its foundation and danced a polka in Public Square, the day Lake Erie dried up and blew away, the day the Cuyahoga River flowed pink champagne.

It was the day that shocked the National Football League, the day that would eventually reshape three cities.

It was the day that gave Art Modell control of football's most storied franchise, humiliated Paul Brown, elevated Blanton Collier to a position he probably never dreamed he would hold, and made Jim Houston into an All-Pro.

It was January 9, 1963, the day Modell, president of the Cleveland Browns, called head coach Paul Brown into his office and fired him.

A *Cleveland Press* columnist called the decision "the most daringly dramatic in the history of any sport."

After less than two years in football, Modell had dismissed the mastermind who practically created the modern professional game, the absolute ruler who won 10 league championships in 17 seasons. Firing Brown, as one writer put it, was "tantamount to impeaching the president of this country."

According to Brown, Modell told him that afternoon, "Every time I come to the stadium, I feel that I am invading your domain, and from now on, there can only be one dominant image." But on January 9, 1963, Modell said only that he had spent three weeks pondering the move, which he had made "in the best interests of the Browns."

The *Los Angeles Times* wrote of January 9, 1963, "Paul Brown, the unfrocked genius of pro football, has left the game at the end of a toe and there isn't a wet eye in the house"— which wasn't exactly true. When reporters called his home for comment, Brown was unavailable. Between sobs, his wife, Katie, said he "knew it was coming."

When he finally spoke up, Brown said that losing his job had never entered his mind, but even Houston, who spent the 1962 season flying in from the service on weekends to play games and visit his dying father, realized that "Paul and Art were at odds."

Brown and Modell seemed at first to be the perfect combination of technical expert and pitchman. "The biggest asset I'm buying is the coaching genius of Paul Brown," Modell said when he purchased the club, in 1961. He immediately gave Brown a raise and an eight-year contract extension, a deal that made the coach wealthy but stripped him of security.

Modell apparently thought that the money bought privileges no previous owner had dared to assume. He seized Brown's spacious office, hung around practice, schmoozed with players. After Modell listened in on one pregame talk, Brown told him, "This is private between myself and my players. You don't belong here." The coach saw no reason to waste time on an inexperienced ad hustler 20 years his junior. "I resented his lack of background in the football world and did not respect his knowledge," Brown said.

However, the glittering record that Brown had always brandished like a saber when anyone questioned him had begun to tarnish. He finished third in the Eastern Conference in 1961 and 1962 and had not won a league championship in seven years.

Brown claimed that Modell's lust for power had turned the franchise into a nest of schemers in which discipline and loyalty vanished. He said, "Player was set against player, the loyalty of my coaching staff was questioned and attempts made to find out which were 'Paul Brown men.'" Modell—along with many fans and reporters—seems to have become convinced that Brown's lack of emotion and conservative tactics were hamstringing the team.

Late in 1962, the Browns trailed Washington by 10 points near halftime. The ball in Cleveland territory, Brown ordered a series of runs. As the clock turned, according to a Pittsburgh sports editor who was on the sideline, Modell paced behind the bench, grumbling, "That's no way to play winning football! Go for the scoring bomb! Throw the long pass!" A photograph taken that season shows Brown in the locker room after a game, stroking his chin as he eyes a semicircle of reporters. In the background, hands shoved into trouser pockets, Modell regards the coach with equal suspicion.

By the time that photo was shot, January 9, 1963 had become a *fait accompli*.

Without bothering to tell Modell, Brown had traded halfback Bobby Mitchell and a number one draft choice to the Redskins for the right to select Ernie Davis, an All-American running back from Syracuse. The deal left Modell, who had gone deeply in debt to buy the team, in an impossible bargaining position. Forced to outbid the AFL and CFL,

the owner gave Davis the richest rookie contract in history. "Paul had no idea where I was coming from on this, and he didn't care," Modell said.

*Sports Illustrated* predicted that the trade could turn out to be one of Brown's sharper, but Davis died of leukemia without ever playing for Cleveland, while Mitchell made All-Pro in 1962. Reportedly, Modell also caught wind that Brown was thinking about swapping Jim Brown, whom the owner considered untouchable, for Johnny Unitas.

En route to San Francisco for the last game of 1962, the Browns were fogged in at the Sacramento airport. Modell invited players to join him in a lounge, where he set up rounds of drinks. Some who were there say Modell was just trying to be one of the boys; others say he was probing for information to use against the coach. Whichever, an enraged Brown scolded the owner for violating the team's most rigorously enforced rule, against drinking in public.

Modell claimed later that he had fired Brown to prevent a mutiny; players such as Jim Brown and defensive back Bernie Parrish confirmed that assertion. Now, finding someone who will call the palace coup anything more than carping and finger-pointing by also-rans is difficult. Some, including Brown's son Mike, who briefly worked for the team, claim that a disinformation campaign planned by Modell and carried out by his toadies created the perception of an imminent rebellion.

Jim Houston remembers no insurrection. As a defensive player, Houston had little direct contact with Brown. He did, though, notice that the coach changed over the 1961 and 1962 seasons. "In those couple years, he was getting older, or something was going on. The assistants didn't talk to him. I don't know if they were afraid of him or what," he says. "In '62, it was really bad. That's when Jim Brown came out against Paul Brown and all that stuff. That was unfortunate; it really was."

The day the team left for its ill-fated trip to San Francisco, a blizzard nearly paralyzed Cleveland. Still, Brown held practice. In belt-deep snow, the coach led calisthenics while the squad wondered what he expected to accomplish. "It just wasn't rational, didn't make sense," Houston says.

Nevertheless, Houston calls Brown "the greatest coach in existence, ever," as well he might, given the pedigree they share. Houston and Brown attended the same junior high school in Massillon. Houston's older brother Lin played for Brown in high school, college, and the pros, and Houston began visiting the Cleveland locker room when he was a boy. He was a captain, most valuable player, and a two-time All-American end at

Ohio State, where Brown had won a national title as head coach. But where Lin Houston remained friendly with Brown throughout the coach's life, Jim Houston found him austere and distant. He says, "There was no way of having any kind of developed relationship with the guy. You could never say, 'I really like you, Coach.' He had his reputation. He was the top guy."

Houston was on duty in New Jersey when he read that Brown had been fired. "I really wasn't surprised, because of the mannerisms and the way that he acted the last couple of games he was there," Houston says. "Unfortunately, in the last year with Paul Brown, what really sticks in my mind is that stuff."

Even as Brown considered suing Modell, the owner said that he anticipated "a continuing good relationship" with the former coach and hoped to consult him about a successor. As it turned out, the new head man himself—54-year-old backfield coach Blanton Collier— said that he had taken the job with Brown's blessing. Brown and Collier had known each other since World War II, when Collier, a seaman second class and former high school coach, began skipping mess to watch Brown's Great Lakes Naval Station team practice. The first assistant Brown hired in Cleveland, Collier became so close with the head coach that his daughters called Brown "Uncle Paul."

Brown once said that he would rather lose his right arm than Collier, and when the scholarly, unassuming assistant resigned in 1954 to become head coach at the University of Kentucky, Cleveland's record began to slide. "What happened to Brown as a coaching genius?" a former player asked in 1962. "First, Collier left to take the coaching job at Kentucky, and then [quarterback Otto] Graham retired."

When Kentucky fired Collier, Brown created a position for him. However, some former players say that amid the tension of that final season, Brown had begun to resent Collier and might even have suspected his old friend of wanting his job.

Supposedly, after January 9, 1963, Collier refused to speak to Modell for a week. He said he had agreed to become head coach only after Brown insisted that he do so for his family. "I accept this job with all the humbleness and humility that results from replacing not only one of the greatest coaches of all time but also the man who gave me my start in professional football," Collier said. Brown later claimed that Collier had never asked him about the job, and as Brown sold his home in Shaker Heights and moved across the continent, the friendship ended.

Before his first training camp as head coach, Collier said that he didn't want to be "another Paul Brown," but players say little about the team changed except that the head coach was much more easygoing.

Collier did change Houston's position. An undersized defensive end at 6' 3", 240 pounds, Houston became one of the NFL's first big, fast, agile outside linebackers. Houston made All-Pro twice, played in four Pro Bowls, and was named to Browns' all-time team in 1979.

Cleveland went from 7-6-1 in Brown's last season to 10-4 in Collier's first. The Browns won the NFL title in 1964, culminating what Modell called "a vindication year" for himself as well as for Collier. A photo taken that season shows Modell during a practice, listening in on the huddle as Collier calls a play. The team played in three of the next five league championship games.

Meanwhile, Brown's attorney had convinced him that a lawsuit brought by a man being paid $82,500 a year to do little work would achieve nothing, and the deposed coach entered what he called "the darkest period of my life." He compared himself—tellingly—with Napoleon on Elba and said, "I had everything a man could want: leisure, enough money, a wonderful family. Yet with all that, I was eating my heart out." He did not attend a Cleveland game until he was inducted into the Hall of Fame in 1967, on the day Philadelphia beat the Browns in Canton.

Rumors had Brown about to coach several teams or to start his own franchise in various cities. For five years, he did neither, instead traveling with Katie. He was moved to return to football when the plane on which the couple was flying home from the Orient caught fire during takeoff. Sure they were about to die, the Browns said good-bye. The pilot managed to land the plane. Brown knew he had to leave "the equivalent of retirement."

Modell claimed that his influence with the NFL and willingness to move his team into the AFC Central Division with the Bengals made him "the key to Cincinnati getting the franchise and Paul Brown returning to football." Brown disagreed. He noted that when Modell was first asked to join the AFC, the owner replied that doing so would "emasculate" the NFL. "But, then, they put up $3 million to each team that moved with us," Brown said, "and, well, did you ever see a barracuda?"

The merger of the NFL and AFL complete, Brown, Collier, Houston, and Modell reunited in the fourth game of the1970 preseason. Collier said it was the most important day of his life, but the Cincinnati Bengals opened their new stadium with a 31-24 win.  Caressing the game ball,

Brown said, "A football team may have been born tonight." Modell downplayed the loss with strained jocularity, but Houston, now a team captain, said, "We're disappointed we didn't win it for Art. We knew how much he wanted to win."

Brown created a fuss by failing to shake hands with Collier that day, lamely explaining that according to AFL custom, the coach left the field with his team after games. The Browns and Bengals met again six weeks later in Cleveland. Forty-five minutes before kickoff, Brown strode from a dugout toward the visitors' bench. From midfield, Collier called to him several times. Brown didn't respond until he reached the 50 yard line. He pivoted, smiled, held out a hand, and apologized for the to-do he had caused. Few fans saw the handshake, though, and when Brown immediately trotted from the field after a 30-27 loss, boos and catcalls rolled down from Cleveland Stadium like unhappy memories swirling through a bad dream. Brown tipped his hat to the crowd.

He told reporters he was proud of both teams. He said, "When I walked out on that field, I looked at those suits, and they looked very familiar to me. I knew where they originated, and I had my heart there."

Later that season, the Bengals beat Cleveland, 14-10. "Yes, this is my best victory," Brown told the press. "This is the one that makes coming back worthwhile."

Modell had not realized just how much he had helped Brown. The man who had stripped him of everything—including, in a way, his very name—paid the bills while Brown picked the brains of general managers, kept an eye on new franchises, made mental notes about potential staff members, and pored over playbooks given to him by friends such as Vince Lombardi. "I had a kernel of a plan and a long time to think about it," he said.

By creating the Bengals, Brown didn't just restore his reputation. He also made a half-million dollars selling to a four-man partnership the 5.6 percent of the Cleveland franchise that he still owned and had steadfastly refused to allow Modell to buy.

Modell also miscalculated Brown's desire for vengeance. Almost as soon as he was fired, Brown began working on a memoir. Published in 1979, four years after Brown retired from coaching, *PB: The Paul Brown Story* blames Jim Brown's defiance on self-loathing and damns Collier by extremely faint praise. Brown saves his special venom for Modell. Among other accusations, the book claims that at the heart of their quarrel was Modell's asking Brown to play Ernie Davis, whose cancer was briefly in

remission, in an exhibition game so that the owner could advertise the event and recoup some of his investment in the dying fullback.

Modell hotly denied that allegation as well as others in the book, which he called "libelous and trash." Some writers and people involved in the incidents described in *PB* defended the owner. A *Plain Dealer* review charged that the book demonstrated that Brown "saw what he wanted, thought what he wanted and to hell with the truth."

Brown said that he had not meant to attack anyone. He said that any bitterness had dissipated in the face of the far greater tragedy of Katie's death. In the last three words of PB, he calls himself "a happy man." After commissioner Pete Rozelle fined him $10,000 for criticizing a fellow owner, Brown said, "I've sent him his check. However, I stand by the book as written."

At Brown's funeral in 1991, Modell heaped praise on him and said that they had become friendlier over the years—a perception Brown did not share, according to Mike Brown, who says his father never did get over being fired.

Sitting in the living room of his condominium in a bedroom community on the outskirts of Cleveland, Jim Houston says he took no side in the struggle between Brown and

Modell. He says that he liked the owner and respected the coach.

Houston was wearing baggy denim shorts and a wrinkled gray sweatshirt. A wide reddish scar coiled around his right knee. His mussed hair and quick grin made him look like Joe Don Baker in *Walking Tall*. A book, *Massillon Memories*, and a stack of old Massillon football programs sat on a coffee table. His Browns jersey hung in a frame.

About to remarry following a divorce six years earlier, Houston had been helping his fiancée unpack boxes and arrange furniture. Houston was cheerful. At times, he seemed bemused by the realization that a kid who had been cut from his junior high team could play fifteen years in the NFL. An insurance salesman since college, he planned for life after football, trading notoriety for business contacts that led to investments in everything from car washes to a golf course. Despite the divorce and some unpleasantness with a former business partner, he lives comfortably, unbothered by the aggravation that can come with fame.

Other than when Cleveland played Cincinnati, Houston never saw Brown after the coach was fired. "But the only time I saw him when he was here was in practice," he says. "I never saw him at any of our events. I never saw him at a banquet or

anything like that. In a three-year period, you'd think you'd run across your head coach giving a speech someplace, but I never did."

According to Houston, Collier was much easier to play for, but that ease might have cost the team more championships. "Maybe we should have had a little more discipline," he says. When Collier's increasing deafness caused him to retire, Modell replaced him with Skorich, who was under orders to institute a regime of Brown-like severity.

Houston was there on December 20, 1970, when the Browns beat Denver in Collier's last game and carried him from the field. That afternoon, Cleveland could have won the Central Division; however, Cincinnati also defeated the Boston Patriots on December 20, 1970.

Paul Brown called the victory "a dream come true." The Bengals, who had lost six of their first seven games, finished 8-6, edging the Browns for the division title. Brown was named the NFL's best coach, an honor he found particularly satisfying. "I always get a chuckle out of the fact that Modell fired me for the same record I had in Cincinnati and was coach of the year," he said.

For Paul Brown, the journey that had begun on January 9, 1963, was over.

# *Jim* HOUSTON

““    MY BROTHER, LIN, WAS UNDER CONTRACT
with the Browns while he was in the service, in the Philippine Islands.
So as a kid, I went to the games with him. While I was watching the games,
I thought about what it would take for me to do what my brother did.
Would I ever reach that pinnacle?

When I got to the seventh grade, I tried out for football and got cut.
How could a *Houston* get cut from a football team? God almighty, I was
embarrassed. But I was just too small. I started the first grade when I was
five years old. I hadn't developed.

The coach, Roger Price, said, 'Come back when you're really ready.'

It was almost impossible to go home and tell what happened. But the
strength of my family turned me around. It was kind of a reverse psychological thing. My mom just said, 'You got cut? Don't worry about that. Try
again next year.'

No ranting and raving. No problem. Try next year. If you make it
then, fine. If not, there's the year after that. If you don't make it then,
maybe it's time to start thinking about doing something else. That became
my *modus operandi*.

In Massillon, if you had any athletic ability at all, it was simply understood that you were going to be a football player. Paul Brown was responsible for that, but when I was a kid, I had no idea about him. It just wasn't
in my nine-year-old thought process.

My family moved here from southern Illinois because dad found a job
at Republic Steel, right at the height of the Depression. They moved here

in '36, and I was born in '37. Lin was in high school when they moved. He didn't know anything about football. He played in the first football game he ever saw. He was a big farmboy, six foot, about 195 pounds.

Our motivation was simply that mom and dad said, 'We want you to get out of having to go to the mill every day. And since there's no way we can afford to pay for college, you have to earn your own way. The easiest way for you to do that is to play football and earn a scholarship.'

So I went out again in eighth grade, and I had a little bit more success, but not much. I hadn't grown very much. I got run over. I didn't like getting hit, either. It hurt. Finally, by the ninth grade, I weighed 130 pounds , playing against guys who played 170 pounds, 190 pounds.

As a sophomore, I only went to school for a short period of time, because I had my knee operated on. I repeated the sophomore year, so basically, I was red-shirted. And it allowed me to mature. As a senior, I was 6' 2", 205 pounds, and now I was a little bit ahead of everybody else. At that weight, I was a big end.

I had started to get the mailings from college coaches as a junior, then I made All-Ohio and All-American as a senior. I had two brothers who graduated from Purdue, Jack and Walt. Purdue tried to recruit me. So did Blanton Collier, who was at the University of Kentucky then. Blanton was very poor at recruiting, but I remember the breakfast they served there—chicken and peas, mashed potatoes and gravy.

Woody came up, and he talked to my mom and dad about education and staying in Ohio.

'Well,' my mom said after talking to Woody, 'you might as well go to Ohio State.'


YOU HAVE A LOT OF ANXIETY when you step up to a place like Ohio State. One thing that helped me at Ohio State happened in the high school all-star game. There was something wrong with the suspension of my helmet, and in practice the day before the game I hit my head on the ground and got knocked dizzy. At the game, on the kickoff, I hit the ball carrier and, because of the helmet, was knocked out. I woke up just before the half and played the entire second half. Can you imagine that today?

So as a freshman nobody was allowed to hit me, and that was the doctor's orders. You couldn't play as a freshman in those days, anyway. Woody could've left me on the sidelines and forgot about me, but I was a pretty good kid and I could run. I knew the plays, and I had a good background. Woody knew that two of my brothers played at Purdue, and Lin was with the Browns. Woody assigned Ernie Godfrey the responsibility of taking me through a half-line scrimmage.

All they did for most of the practice was show a half-line picture: end, tackle, guard, center, and backs. It was nearly full go, but they wouldn't hit me really hard. It gave me recognition: I learned to pick up a trap immediately. I could stick that guard and be ready to take on the back. I could take the doubleteams or take the kid trying to hook me.

When I reported to spring practice the following year—this is now 1957—I was a year or two ahead of my peers, and at least as good as the seniors. As soon as that quarterback took the snap, ninety-nine percent of the time I knew where the ball was going.

As a sophomore, I played 73 percent of the 600 minutes. As a junior, I played 92.7 percent, and as a senior, I played 93 percent. Everybody asks what the coach was like on the sidelines in that crucial moment. How would I know? I wasn't there. I was on the *field*.

I had a heart rate of 50, so I was in absolutely top condition. I could run all day, and I did. My first 60-minute game was the 1958 Rose Bowl. It was 85 degrees; on the floor it was probably 100 degrees, and we beat Oregon, 10-7, on a field goal.

I caught two passes early in the Rose Bowl, and, basically, that's how we scored. The long one, I was able to get just a little down-and-out flair and Frank Kremblas hit me with the ball. I should have scored, but I fell down. I just cut too hard on the turf. Then I dropped one in the end zone in the second half. Frank threw it behind me, and low. It's the most difficult catch, but I'm supposed to catch it, anyway. But I didn't catch it, and that's the one I catch hell about from all my friends: '*You* dropped the pass in the end zone in the Rose Bowl...?'

I NEVER HAD A PROBLEM WITH WOODY. You knew what kind of guy he was. His assistants was where the strength was, and the best assistant was Bo Schembechler, who was kind of the offensive coordinator. Bo was just as smart as Woody was.

My senior year, I was the only captain. We had Bob White, a great fullback. He was a braggadocio type of guy, if I can use that word. But he was a great fullback, and he was a great because he had good people blocking ahead of him: Dick Schafrath, Jim Marshall, Aurealius Thomas, Bill Jobco, Danny Fronk, Danny James, Leo Brown, Don Clark.

Ohio State had always had dual captains, but Bob wasn't popular. He was always patting himself on the back. We both made All-American as juniors, and the team voted whether we wanted to have one captain or two captains, and the team said, 'We only want one captain.' So they voted one captain, and I had been the only single captain at Ohio State since '52.

We went 4-5, and Woody took his wrath for that 1959 season out on me. It was our last game against Michigan, and we got whipped in the first half. Just before the half, Michigan ran the belly series (a series of option plays, all of which begin with either a fake or a handoff to the fullback). We're five yards from the end zone, and I stuffed the fullback. I didn't have any chance to say, 'Well, he might not have the ball.' I stuffed him right there, got up, and made the tackle on the guy who had the ball, the trailer back, just as he crossed the end zone.

WE WENT IN AT HALF TIME, and Woody started on me, chewing me up one side and down the other.

I'm thinking, 'I gave you all that time, and there is nobody more dedicated than me to Woody Hayes and Ohio State University. I was two times All-American, totally dedicated, and here I am getting my butt chewed. He's swearing, all the coaches are looking. Why would he pick that one place to do all that?

Three or four months later, on the banquet circuit, I asked him about it, and he said, 'Jim, it had nothing to do with you.'

I said, 'Well, it sure sounded like it.'

What he was trying to do was to get everybody *else* to get in gear. I'm the captain, so he chews *my* butt. The rest of the team thinks, if he's going to chew me like that, what's gonna happen to *them*? So we went right out and scored. We beat the hell out of Michigan in the second half but still lost. I had a good game, but what a day he gave me there.

'Geez,' he says. 'That had nothing to do with *you*.'

You remember the strong moments with Woody—jumping on his watch or tearing his hat apart. Have you ever tried to tear a hat apart? I don't care how strong you are, you cannot pull a hat apart. Yet he'd go 'rip,' and pull it apart. The equipment manager caught Woody cutting the strings in the hat. The watches were all six dollars. Everything he did was planned.

In college, I was never hurt. Not once, other than my shin, which was always bleeding, and I had bruises, but no joint injuries at all. I think it was simply because I played most of the time, and my body never cooled down.

You'd go to the sideline and sit and cool down and then rip something.

My senior year in college, I was invited to the Browns/49ers game, as guest of the 49ers, and they told me, 'Jim, we're going to take you first.'

I said, 'They're going to take me first. Great.'

So I almost packed my bags to go to San Francisco, but that day, Cleveland lost to the 49ers, 21-20. That gave Cleveland the pick before the 49ers, and Paul picked me first.

All I had received from Cleveland was a card that said, 'If you are interested in professional football, fill out this card, and send it back.' No one had ever talked to me. That's all it was in those days.

I'm guessing Paul probably took me so high because of his relationship with Lin and the family. I was a good athlete and maybe should have been taken high, but nobody else was interested in me, other than San Francisco.

I said, 'Fifth player taken in the draft. Wow! Man!'

From the experience I had in the stands looking down on the field when I was nine years old, watching my brother, I always had pro football in the back of my head: 'Will I ever be one of those who will even get close to making it?' And now I had.

I WAS THINKING it would be a lot of money. It ended up to be a $10,000 contract and a $1,000 signing bonus. And I had to argue to get the signing bonus up to $1,000. Teachers were making $3,500 a year in those days. And I was poor. I had nothing. Zero. I had a child, and I had a one-bedroom apartment. The living room was down at one end of the hall, and the kitchen was at the other end of the hall.

Dick Gallagher came down to sign me. He started off with a $600 or $700 signing bonus and a $7,000 contract.

I said, 'Dick, I've got to have more than that. Gosh, I got a kid here.'

Dick said, 'Well, I need to talk to Paul. I can't just give you a $1,000 signing bonus. I have to talk to Paul first.'

He went into my bedroom and apparently made a call, but it had nothing to do with what he had to give me. So I got a $1,000 signing bonus and $10,000 contract.

I didn't deal with Paul Brown. I didn't even know who Paul Brown was. Obviously, I knew the name. My brother didn't say very much about Paul or about playing in Cleveland. He liked the idea that I was going to follow his footsteps, but he never said much. None of my brothers ever said a word to me about football. It was humdrum stuff to them.

In the College All-Star Game, I played defensive end against Johnny Unitas, and I went right around the tackle. I was 6' 3", weighed 235 and I got some leverage on him, and I had a dead bead on Unitas. John was just getting ready to throw, and I left my feet. Man, I thought I was going to kill him. I went right over him. I had him dead to the world, and he just ducks, raises up, and hits a guy for a touchdown in the end zone.

I thought, 'What do I have to do?'

After the All-Star Game, I come into Cleveland late. I parked my car on the street at East 66th and Lexington, where League Park is. That was not the best area. 'All-World' is coming into town, right? I'm going to be the savior of the Browns.

Nobody says anything to me. First thing somebody did say was, 'Where's your car?'

'It's out on the street,' I said.

'Go get it,' they said.

I had to bring my car into the compound inside the fence to keep it from being stolen.

THE FACILITIES WERE TERRIBLE. We had a couple of sinks, a mirror, a urinal, and a drinking fountain—right in a row. Why in the hell would they put a drinking fountain right next to a urinal? We'd be trying to get a drink of water, and somebody would be using the urinal, and you'd get splashed.

Bob Gain was the team prankster. He indoctrinated the rookies. I was a rookie, and while taking a shower, he came up, and I got this hot stuff all over my leg.

'*What?*' I say. 'What is he *doing*?'

That's how he indoctrinated the rookies.

He never had his clothes washed. He could take off his practice pants and stand them in the corner. He stunk the whole place up.

My first year, they wanted to see whether or not I could run an offensive pattern.

'Hell, yes,' I said. 'I can.'

'Run an offensive pattern,' they said.

I went down and across, as a tight end.

'Uh, that's enough,' they said. 'He's on defense.'

Running just one pattern didn't show them anything. I knew I could pop as well as any of them, including the guards and tackles, but one route, and you're on defense? Did I miss something here? He drafted me for defense, and I guess he had to back that up with something.

In 1962, Paul Brown allowed me to play as a second lieutenant in the service. I played while I was on active duty. I was in New Jersey and flew in on Fridays. I'd practice on Saturday, play on Sunday, leave Sunday night, and fly back for active duty. I even missed training camp that year.

I was a defensive player, so I didn't have to worry about a gameplan, unless there was a special defense, where the weak side was offset, or there were a couple of extra linebackers on the end. All they had to do was let me know about it. In '62, I was a down defensive end in a 4-3. I didn't need time to prepare for the game. You're the tackle; I got to get by you.

My buddy Galen Fiss was the left outside linebacker when I started as a defensive end my rookie year. We had a game called 'Blue.' It allowed me to start my rush outside on the tackle; he would move to take me on. Then I would take the inside—usually free. I wanted to run it all the time, so Galen started calling me 'Blue.' It became my nickname, and he *still* calls me that when we greet each other some 34 years later.

MY FIRST YEAR OR SECOND YEAR, we played San Francisco out there. San Francisco ran a certain play in a certain formation, and that was key for us on the defensive line to widen out a little bit, another position, if you could.

I was playing against Bob St. Clair. He was 6' 9", weighed 275 pounds. He looked down at me. I looked at him in the chest. But I was quick enough that I could cause trouble. If it was straight back and bull, he'd block me, but if I could get a run on him, I could hurt him a little bit. But not much.

Anyway, Paul sent this other guy in. He said, 'Jim, watch this formation. They're going to run a sweep to your side.'

I was on the open side of the field, and damn if St. Clair doesn't hook me anyway. He actually just reached out and grabbed my foot.

We stopped the play because Bob and I were piled up there, and so the back had to go out wider. The corner came up and got the play. I came off the field, and Paul didn't say a damn word to me. His eyes just went right through me. He had told me, 'Don't let that happen,' and I let it happen. I felt like crawling under this table. He might as well have shot me, because he just looked at me, and he had this unbelieveable power and aloofness.

I say to Paul, 'He grabbed my foot.'

He says, 'You're not allowed to let him grab your foot.'

That's the way he worked. He was cutting. It was always like 'Hey, you dummy, why'd you do that?'

He was very quick and very discerning. You'd get run over on a double-team, and he'd say, 'Well, why were you *in* that position?'

I DON'T EVER REMEMBER PAUL LAUGHING. I'm even having trouble remembering him *smiling*. I don't know whether he had any teeth or not. Can you believe that? *Geez*. I've got a picture here, and you can see the expression on his face: 'This is a serious business, boy.' That's the way he looked all the time. There was no way of having any kind of developed relationship with the guy. You could never say, 'I really like you, Coach.'

Paul never said anything before a game. It would be, 'Let's go get 'em,' or whatever. He made the assistants do the jobs they were supposed to do. That's what made him a great coach. Not a good coach, a *great* coach. He knew how to select his coaches. He knew personnel, or at least the coaches that he hired knew personnel.

Paul didn't have much direct involvement with the defense. Paul was the offensive coach. We saw him at the beginning of every practice, but the assistant coaches were the ones who carried out everything. He was the guy, and the defensive guys didn't really come too close to him. We had to walk around him.

My first coach when I was a defensive end, in '60, '61, '62, was Dick Evans. Big, tall, 6' 4" guy. He always talked to me about how you rush, how you do this, where you hit them, how you get in there. I didn't think he knew much about football.

Now, I played with my right hand down all my career. I was really oriented to the left side from college. Suddenly, I'm putting my left hand down and it just seemed backwards to me. The irony was that I hurt my right hand and had to start with my left hand down the next game. All of a sudden, everything's coming from the other way. It's upside down. I had to play everything coming from my left side, and they put me in there and left me in there.

If you're doing something for your entire career since high school, you have to stay in that stance in order to feel comfortable getting off the ball. You're going to hit a truck that's trying to run over you. Big tackles are going to beat you up. I can't get off the ball. I'd get run over by the truck, and I said, 'Dick, I cannot do that. I just can't do that.'

He was bitching and moaning, so I tried to play like that a couple times for him, but I ended up playing the way I wanted to play. I said, 'Dick , I'm sorry, I can't do that. I mean I just can't do it.'

It was like trying to write with my left hand. I couldn't do anything, but he insisted on it, and that was dumb coaching, I thought. I thought it wasn't utilizing what talent he had, and, actually, it diminished the talent because of the way he was approaching me.

I spent three years at defensive end and Blanton Collier moved me to linebacker. I was as fast or faster than the linebackers, reasonably smart, and Galen helped me learn how to play. Left outside linebacker is different than defensive end, and he helped me get the proper drops. Then he became the right linebacker, Vince Costello was in the middle, and we won the NFL Championship.

I had to learn the theory of how the defensive backs are supported by the linebackers, as far as passing coverage is concerned, how it was important for us to get in the holes, get in the drops, to thwart the pass. A great flanker, for example, would come down and do a hook-in, and if a strong linebacker wasn't there, it would be easy for them to hit that pattern all day. Especially if you had an older cornerback like we had in Erich Barnes.

I was 6' 3" and weighed 255 with my equipment on. I could handle the tight ends; they couldn't handle me. They tried to trick me or run me on deep stuff down the field, but I got some good rushes and was able to play pretty well.

I DIDN'T HAVE A MULTIPLE-YEAR CONTRACT ever, only one year at a time—all thirteen years. I never had contract problems, and I was getting close to the top, as far as I was concerned. I talked to some of the guys in all the Pro Bowls. I was making $30-, $40-, $50,000, and making another $30-, $40-, $50,000 on top of that in the insurance business.

I didn't have any harsh feelings about money. The money? Well, what's the fifth player picked in the draft make today? Boy, I could have been there, quote, unquote. Who cares. If the dog hadn't stopped to pee, he would've caught the rabbit, and all that kind of stuff.

One of the saddest experiences I had in Cleveland was in 1962. We played San Francisco our last game, and we had snow up to our butts. I couldn't understand why we would have practice. The snow was literally knee-high. Paul had practice, and he led calisthenics. There was no way to do anything. He'll get us all sick. It just wasn't rational. Then we had to take a train from Cleveland to Chicago to fly to San Francisco. That's how bad the weather was.

My experience with him was limited because I was defense, but my attitude was he was still the greatest coach in existence. Ever! But in those couple years, he was getting older, or something was going on. The assistants didn't talk to him. I don't know whether they were afraid of him or what. Everybody kind of thought Paul lost it in that year or two, '61, '62.

It was really bad in '62. That's when Jim Brown came out against Paul Brown, which was unfortunate. I thought maybe Art was reacting to Jim Brown's unhappiness. I can't imagine that Art Modell would have tried to use Jim Brown to get rid of a coach. Of course, Paul and Art Modell were at odds then. I was in the army, and I would experience these kicking-game-in-the-snow types of things. On Sunday, I would leave, and they had a newspaper strike at that time. So, hell, I didn't know anything, and I'm in New Jersey. I'm not in Ohio. In Ohio, you're still gonna get the news on the radio or television.

I wasn't around long enough at that time to really evaluate what was going on between Paul and Art. Plus, my dad died in '62. I was going from the game to the hospital to the airport to the army, back to Saturday workout, dinner with a couple guys, and then the Sunday game.

Dad lived six months after he was diagnosed with leukemia, and they could cure it now. He had the acute type. With blood transfusions, he'd've probably lived another ten years. So, unfortunately, in the last year with Paul Brown, what really sticks in my head is that.

I was in New Jersey when I found out Paul Brown was fired. Nobody called me. I picked it up in the Philly paper. I really wasn't surprised, because of the way he acted in the last couple games. And then there were the problems that Jim had with him, whatever that was: wasn't calling his number enough or calling it too much. There was a power struggle, and Blanton was there, too, and maybe Paul thought that Blanton was after his job. Maybe it was a setup, too. Maybe Paul did this to get out. Who knows?

There was no problem whatsoever making the transition between Paul Brown and Blanton. Blanton had been there many years. As a matter of fact, we felt a little bit more relaxed because of this image we had of Paul and his aloofness.

With Paul, he had meetings, and you better be there, and be attentive, or you could get your butt in a real big sling real quick. Maybe that was the key to his success: 'This is my game, guys. This is the way I'm running my game and too bad. If you don't follow it, you're in deep doo-doo.'

In '63 we came back with Blanton, and you know what he changed? Nothing that I am aware of. He kept the system because it was basically Blanton's system—Paul's and Blanton's, Blanton's and Paul's, however you want to look at it. Blanton was the detail guy, always was.

As far as I know, Blanton was probably more responsible for Paul's success—I won't say than Paul himself—but he contributed a great deal to Paul's success.

Blanton talked detail to everybody. Blanton was a quite a learned coach, but he also had this strange laugh and way of talking: 'L-l-l-l e-e t-t-t ge-e-e-e-t out th-h-h-er-r-r-e and d-o-o-o-o it, b-o-o-o-ys.'

He knew his football, and he communicated with us. It wasn't the nonrational Paul Brown that came at the end of Paul's career in Cleveland.

BLANTON DID CHANGE THE ATMOSPHERE. No question about it, because we hadn't done anything for a long time. In '60, '61, '62, we were competitive, but we didn't get into the playoffs, I don't think. Well, in '60, we were in the Toilet Bowl, the runner-up game, but by '62 we were anything but a no-show.

In '64, everything fit together. That year the relationships between everybody was good. Black guys had no problems with the white guys, white guys had no problems with the black guys, nobody was irritated because they weren't playing, and we all made the effort. It was the second year of Blanton as the head guy, and I think it was more our own attitudes.

We knew we had the horse (Jim Brown). Frank Ryan could throw the ball. Gary Collins had a great year that year. The only question was, could we be as strong defensively? That was the rubber band that didn't break, and it was my second year at linebacker, and, man, I was having a good time. We had to beat New York on the last day of the season to win. But we rolled them. It was 50-something to 20 (52-20). We ate up the Giants.

Before we played in the '64 championship, we had two weeks. My neighbor had a party, and he assigned one of the girls to make sure that I had Manhattans. I liked Manhattans, and she just kept handing them to me, and I got smashed. I think I had eighteen of those things. I got drunk. This was a week before the game. I was so sick, I couldn't practice the next day. It was that bad. It took Mike Lucci and another guy as big as he was to take me home. I was a 240-pound rag.

The next day, Blanton Collier talked about how we were going to attack Baltimore's outside linebackers. He's making this point to the tight end, and he used me. I was still drunk and had to hold my head away from him so he wouldn't smell my breath. I didn't smell like a distillery; I *was* a distillery. I had to suck my breath in and hold it. That's the last Manhattan I ever had.

IN '64, WE WENT INTO THAT CHAMPIONSHIP game as an 18-point underdog. You know how I felt about that? There's no guy going to beat me. *Nobody.* First of all, I know they can't; secondly, I'm not going to let them; thirdly, we have our share of All-Americans and All-Pros, so don't tell me I'm playing for an 18-point underdog.

People said, 'Well, the great Unitas and Lenny Moore, and John Mackey and all these guys.'

We thought, 'They're going to have to *prove* their greatness.'

When it was zero-zero at the half, we knew we could win. There had been a battle back and forth, and Gary had the advantage on (Colt defensive back Bobby) Boyd, 6' 4" to 5' 11" or 5'10". That's a distinct advantage. I don't care if Boyd's All-World. He's not as tall; he can't jump as high.

In '64, we had the attitude that we were pretty good. We were proud of that. It wasn't arrogance. We were just proud of the fact that we could deliver. Even though we were still all Paul Brown's players, Blanton was taking us to a new level, and I give Blanton all the credit for putting everybody on the same page.

Dick Modzelewski came from New York that year, and part of it was Dick's maturity. The defensive lineman worked well together. And our deep secondary was good. Bernie Parrish was the left corner. Walter Beech was the right corner. Ross Fichtner and Larry Benz were the safeties.

The strong safeties were funny: 'Hey, Jim, Jim, don't let the tight end inside.'

I'd say, 'Wait a minute. I've got Gale Sayers running wide, and you want me to hit your tight end? You got to be kidding me. He's twice as fast as I am, and I got to run down the field with *him*?'

We also had a good offensive line, and Gary Collins and Paul Warfield were great. I played against Paul when he was down at Miami. Our only defense was double Warfield. The line charge was called, and then I said, 'Double Warfield.' Regular, ram, whatever we wanted to run, and double Warfield. He could go anyplace—flanker, weak side end, tight end, but you still had him doubled. Roll a zone into him on the strong side, a zone on the weak side, too. It didn't do us any good. They blocked a punt on us, and they beat us (21-14 in the 1972 AFC playoffs). Otherwise we'd've stopped them at fourteen games (in a row).

I HAD A GOOD DEAL WITH ART. His wife and I used to play gin while we were waiting on the airplane. I was in my thirteenth year, in '72 , and I had a chance to buy 100 acres in Bath, Ohio, big mansion of a house, 10,000 square feet. I had the money lined up for the mortgage, but I needed 'x' amount in order to consummate the deal. I mentioned this to Art, and he says, 'We'll go to my bank and get it.'

That was it. We did the deal. *Boom*. Anything I ever needed, from my own contract standpoint, advance money, or anything like that, it was done. It was always done. I got along with him and had a good time with him. I understand why he went through the things he went through with Cleveland. He left because it was the only way he was going to get $75 million to buy his partner out. The game is all about money, anyway.

I didn't try to come back the fourteenth year. I decided thirteen is enough. The system slows down; that's all there is to it. I made the Pro Bowl in '70 and '71, but I knew it was time to go.

I played until '72, and we won one championship, and we lost to Green Bay in the championship game in '65. We had a reasonable amount of success every year. We didn't always make the big show, but we always were in the playoffs, and I grew as a player and I thought I knew my stuff.

You know when it's time to get out. You don't run quite as fast. You're 35 years old. And you have the competition coming in. You're at another stage, and you need to move on. There are exceptions, but fifteen years is max. You get tired of going to camp, tired of being away from your family.

Getting out wasn't bad, and it helped me do a little more insurance business. It's not that I didn't miss it. I entertained my clients at games subsequent to that, but then the salaries started going crazy. These guys started making the money. Offensive lineman making $4 million a year guaranteed. *Guaranteed*. It's not logical; it doesn't make sense.

But then when you start looking at the math, at the television income, the stadiums, parking, concessions, clothing. How much money do the owners make? Twenty million dollars? That's not a bad deal, right? If they make twenty million.

Our company bought eight season tickets to Browns Stadium. Eight club seats cost us $22,600. That's the seat license for eight seats. The loges are $60,000 for the worst one. The best one is over $100,000. But you use it year round. I'd use it as a business office downtown, but five grand a month doesn't make sense.

I'M IN PRETTY GOOD SHAPE. I weigh 270, but that's still too heavy. I need to get to 250, and I'm working on it. I went down to a national championship celebration we had for the '57 team at Ohio State. We went on the field, and I thought, 'God, I feel strong.' You know, you run and do everything else, and I still can, but I looked to my right, I looked to my left, and I said, 'No way, Jose.' Guys with bellies and no hair, white hair like mine.

With injuries, I was lucky. I got knocked out a few times. I had the knee operation. I didn't have any serious injuries other than I ruptured my anterior quad, and had to have it operated on. One of my injuries, I hit the back head-on, *bam!* I had the proper angle and I would have crucified the guy, except at the same time, Paul Wiggin hit him in the back. I caught 450 pounds straight on, and, man, I jammed the vertebrae in the back of my neck.

People still remember us. It's almost like you never quit playing. They all remember you. I have people coming up to me and saying, 'I remember you.' The *New York Times* came out to see me. The guy said, 'You intercepted Tarkenton for a touchdown (79 yards in 1967), but, boy, you looked really slow in the last 20 yards.'

'Yeah,' I said. 'Rigormortis had set in.'

I used to scout for the Browns and anyplace I went, they'd have Browns Boosters. They still do, every place. It has to be because of Paul Brown. From '46 to '49, what did they lose, three or four games? Then they go on to the National Football League, and they win it in 1950. That's why all these people throughout the country are followers of the Browns. I don't think any other team in the country has that same kind of loyalty, except maybe Green Bay, because of the Lombardi years.

There wasn't any television in that time. Was it the radio in '46, '47, '48? The Browns had the radio exposure all through the South. Was it the radio and the interest because they were winning so much that all these radio stations picked them up, and, so, down through the South, you had all this interest? You have people every place, boosters every place.

I never saw Paul Brown after he left, but the only time I saw him when he was here was at practice. I never saw him in any of our events. I never saw him at any banquet, anything like that. We didn't do all that well, but in '60, '61 and '62, in a three-year period of time, you'd think you might run across your head coach giving a speech someplace. But I never did. There was nothing emotional there, ever. He wouldn't let that happen. We respected the guy, though. We always did.

It was great that he went down to Cincinnati and established them. They were in the Super Bowl, and the Browns haven't been in the Super Bowl yet. So his abilities obviously were still there. That's what makes me think he might have planned everything. I can't imagine him planning to get fired, but who knows?

I have no complaints, none at all. I had a great career. It was many years ago, but it's tough to leave it alone with the adulation people have for the former players here. I was born in Massillon, played at Ohio State, played for the Browns, and went into business here. It's a perfect scenario. I feel very fortunate. The football success I had in Columbus and Cleveland I'd put up against anybody else.

I could've torn up a knee and still been in the mill. I look back on it, and I had the unbelievable luck of making the team at Lorin Andrews Junior High and Massillon and getting involved with Woody, and then I had the unbelievable luck of being drafted by the Browns. I had the great privilege of playing with two great coaches, Woody Hayes and Paul Brown. What are the chances of that? Less than one in a million. **" "**

# Little Red Corvette

PAUL BROWN had been denounced for years as predictable, but during the 1962 NFL draft, he surprised followers of the Cleveland Browns. For the first time in seventeen years, Brown made a wide receiver—Gary Collins, of Maryland—his number one selection.

His critics called Brown foolish to ignore the quarterback he claimed to need or the fullback he could pair in the backfield with Jim Brown. He had wasted the fourth overall pick on someone who would be lucky to touch the ball twice a game, they said.

The roots of Brown's unusual decision went back to 1956, the year Dante Lavelli, the best receiver in the team's history, retired. Lavelli's was the last in a series of departures that helped end Brown's long dominance of professional football.

Mac Speedie, Lavelli's mate at

end, stormed off to Canada in a salary row. Knees ruined, fullback Marion Motley quit, tried to come back, was traded off. Dub Jones, a halfback equally adept at running with the ball or catching it, followed quarterback Otto Graham into retirement.

Without the three-receiver attack that had turned the NFL into his fiefdom, Brown was vexed. He drafted Jim Brown only because the quarterbacks he wanted had already been taken. He grudgingly settled on Milt Plum as his quarterback. However, the coach could find only one end, Ray Renfro, nearly as proficient as Lavelli or Speedie.

Brown resorted to off-tackle runs, short passes, and an occasional long throw to Renfro. Criticism of its stodgy offense growing more shrill, Cleveland descended through the Eastern Conference.

Brown was about to solve his problems—dramatically—and Collins was an important part of the solution. Collins, a consensus All-American, had set nearly every Atlantic Coast Conference receiving mark although he was often covered by two or three defenders. At 6-4, 215, he was three inches taller and thirty pounds heavier than the swift but brittle Renfro. In his junior and senior seasons, Collins had played virtually every down—on offense and defense. He also appealed to Brown's

frugality. An excellent punter, Collins could do two jobs while drawing one pay check.

As writers and fans carped, Brown said, "This will help Milt Plum and take some of the heat off Ray Renfro."

If he seemed smug, Brown had reason to be. Even before the draft, he had clandestinely worked out an extraordinary trade with the Washington Redskins. With the first pick, Washington would take Ernie Davis, the superb fullback from Syracuse, then send him to Cleveland for halfback Bobby Mitchell and one of Brown's two first-round choices that year.

The deal almost fell through when the Redskins demanded Collins, and Brown insisted they take Leroy Jackson. Washington agreed, and Brown had pulled off his shrewdest trade. He now owned the rookie crop's best runner and its best receiver. As bonuses, he swapped away a halfback who wanted to play flanker and saved a roster spot by releasing punter Sam Baker.

"You just took the best all-around player on the list," San Francisco coach Red Hickey told Brown. "He does a lot of things and all of them well."

Brown's sly bit of horse-trading backfired. Davis never played again. He died of leukemia the following year. In keeping with Brown's policy of using rookies only in emergencies, Collins punted but otherwise languished on the sidelines. He caught only 11 passes, and Cleveland finished 7-6-1. Team owner Art Modell said that his coach hadn't even bothered to tell him about such a significant trade and used the slight as one justification for firing Brown shortly after the season ended.

Blanton Collier replaced Brown and immediately made Collins the starting flanker. The young receiver blossomed. In 1963, he tied for the NFL receiving title and set a team record with 13 touchdown catches. The Browns improved to 10-4. The Cleveland Touchdown Club named Collins the team's most valuable player.

"Collins is a power type of receiver," Collier said of his prodigy. "He doesn't get knocked out of position. He also has the good hands you need. Gary is fast for a big man. He can go deep and grab the football."

The Browns acquired fleet receiver Paul Warfield to complement Collins, in 1964, and Cleveland's offense became as versatile and productive as it had been in Brown's heyday. On its way to the conference title, the team averaged nearly 30 points a game. Collins set a Cleveland mark with at least one touchdown catch in seven straight games.

The 1964 NFL championship game made Collins a national celebrity. He caught three touchdown passes in the second half of Cleveland's 27-0 defeat of the Baltimore Colts. Collins's record-breaking performance established him as one of the league's outstanding players under pressure.

"He's an artist, 'Mr. Clutch,'" said Cleveland linebacker Jim Houston. "He says, 'Throw it to me; I'll get it,' and he does."

That game foretold years of achievement. Collins broke Renfro's team record for receptions and Lavelli's for touchdown catches. He caught two more touchdowns in championship games, setting an NFL career standard. He led the Browns in receiving four times and was the league's top punter in 1965. He was twice All-Pro. He scored on approximately every fifth catch throughout his career, earning the nickname "AW," for "All the Way."

"We had Gary Collins, and damn right we threw the ball to him," says Dub Jones, Cleveland's offensive coordinator at the time. "He's the one who showed me how important hands were. I never had realized that, even though Lavelli had the same kind of hands."

In 1965, cornerback Herb Adderly of Green Bay vowed not to give up a touchdown pass that season. He made good on the promise until the title game. Collins caught a 17-yarder that day and two more scores on Adderly the following season, also the only touchdown receptions Adderly surrendered in 1966. Adderly, a future Hall of Famer, proclaimed, "Collins is the toughest receiver I've faced."

Although he said he was "scared stiff" the first time he replaced Renfro, Collins's play demanded abundant toughness. He took up sports to avoid the dangerous Pennsylvania coal mines in which his father worked, but he earned a living in a no less hazardous place—the middle of the defense, where linebackers and strong safeties prowl like brute creatures. Tutored by Collier and Renfro, he learned the sideline and corner patterns; however, his size and courage suited Collins for the post pattern, a route that is run on dangerous ground.

"You do it. You don't think about it," he said. "Especially in football you don't think about it. Like, people say afterward, 'Boy, did that hurt? How does that feel?' You don't have time to think. You're trying to fulfill your duty that you're getting paid for."

The job exacted a fearsome price. In Collins's rookie year, a Steeler linebacker knocked him unconscious. He awoke two days later in a hospital bed. His ribs often broken, he concentrated on running without grimacing or favoring a side: to reveal

an injury was to make it a target. He once needed seven stitches in a hand at halftime but still caught six balls in the second half. After severely separating a shoulder in the third game of 1968, he bet a friend he would be back  before the end of the season, even though doctors told him it was impossible. He had pins inserted into the shoulder, played in the last game, then against Dallas in the playoffs, caught two passes in the first quarter, drew double coverage the rest of the day, and threw a key block on Leroy Kelly's game-winning touchdown run.

Collins said a receiver had to be crazy to run patterns over the middle. He said if he wasn't hurt on Sunday, he must be doing something wrong. He called himself "the lunch pail guy who showed up every week and did all the crappy jobs."

"He's a proven clutch player, a proven winner, and he's one of the best money players I've ever seen," Collier said.

The money poured in. *Sport* magazine awarded Collins a sleek red, three-speed Corvette Sting Ray as the outstanding player in the 1964 title game. He won a Ford sedan as the league's punting champion the following season. He lived with his wife and two sons in a century-old, 12-room home. The family raised Appaloosas on Frosty Farms, 70 idyllic wooded acres around a wandering stream. Good looking and witty, Collins endorsed products and hosted a radio show. He palled around with actors. He was a partner in an investment firm, a ski resort, and a bowling and billiards center and was involved in a $20 million hotel project in Cleveland.

Collins had come far from the coal fields only to find discontent. He was unsatisfied by his possessions and unhappy in his marriage, which had taken place when his girlfriend became pregnant while both were in high school. He was, Collins says now, "famous and rich and not enjoying shit, the typical movie case."

The unhappiness soon extended onto the football field. Paul Brown had developed the post pattern for Lavelli, and Collins, in his size, his tenacity, his lack of sprinter's speed, his all-around athletic ability, brought to mind an earlier type of receiver. Nonetheless, as he overpowered cornerbacks a half-foot shorter, Collins revolutionized NFL passing offenses. A league obsessed with speed began searching for receivers who could catch passes in crowds and withstand punishment. Every team wanted "a Gary Collins type."

Collins spawned not only imitators, but also a new breed of defensive back and a new kind of defense. Teams drafted more physical cornerbacks—some nearly as big as linebackers—placed them close to the line of scrimmage, and told them to jam receivers there. Collins knew that the "bump and run" didn't bode well for him. He warned that the defense would hamper passing and bore fans. That the league would ultimately eliminate the bump and run didn't help Collins as the 1970s began.

Maladies ranging from pleurisy to cracked ribs slowed Collins in 1970. "Except for getting pregnant, I had just about everything this past season," he said. He caught fewer than half as many passes as he had the year before and scored only four touchdowns. The Browns dropped to 7-7. Fans who had so lately cheered him now called Collins too old and too slow. He countered that he wasn't old; people had just heard his name for so long they *thought* he was old. Besides, he said, he'd never been very fast.

"I play a position where you're either good or bad," Collins said. "At least they're talking about me. I'm not just some obscure guy. If they want to blame our season on me, that's okay, but when a team loses seven games, I should think it's more than one guy."

A year later, Nick Skorich succeeded Collier. With the Browns mired in a losing streak, Skorich pulled Collins from the lineup and inserted younger, faster Frank Pitts. Collins read in the paper that he'd been benched.

He at first seemed to accept his

demotion as inevitable: "It's a mark of a pro to take the bad when it comes. There was a time when I first stepped in, too, and Ray Renfro was in the same position that I'm in now."

Soon, his anger—at Skorich and at Modell, whom Collins believes dictated the move—welled up.

"It was tougher than the injuries, tougher than sitting behind Ray Renfro as a rookie," he said.

Skorich said Collins could come back in 1972 as a spot receiver and to punt, a chore the player said gave him ulcers. Spurned, he said shortly before training camp began, "I won't be back, definitely. I just feel I couldn't take it any more. A player should get out before he's kicked out."

Life after football would be as difficult. When Collins retired, the radio station that carried his sports show dropped it, curtailing the career he'd planned to follow. A hurricane flooded his new horse farm, in Pennsylvania. He spent a brief and bizarre interlude as a player/coach in the misbegotten World Football League. A sporting goods store failed. He divorced. Bad business decisions and worse luck culminated in bankruptcy. A return to broadcasting lasted only two years.

Eventually, Collins remarried and joined a financial planning and investment firm, retiring in 1996

to help out in his son's landscaping business.

"After my career, my life has been rather boring," he says, "just the normal, shitty, no-life nothing. My wife and I have a great relationship, but just common. Nothing competitive, and sometimes you miss that."

Collins's reputation has long been for truculence. The press called him "cocky," "ill-tempered," and "sensitive"; players said he was "moody," "strange," "a loner," and "immature."

"I played mad back then," Collins said. "Every day I fought with someone in our secondary. I was in a bad marriage for twenty years. What do you expect?"

His play might've been out of an older generation, but Collins's temperament anticipated a new one. He was brash enough to predict to a television reporter that Cleveland would easily defeat heavily favored Baltimore for the championship and impulsive enough to run from punt formation twice in the same game.

His college coach said Collins was the greatest athlete he'd ever coached but wouldn't recommend him to professional teams. Otto Graham, who coached Collins in the College All-Star Game, warned Brown that the receiver was nonchalant and defiant. After dealing with Collins in the All-American Bowl, Woody Hayes promised, "If Collins makes it in pro ball, I'll eat my hat."

One wonders how Collins might've fared over time with the prickly Brown. Handling such a high-strung player required a coach as patient as the grandfatherly Collier, whom Collins called "the only man I've ever been able to play for."

"I had my run-ins with Nugent. I didn't really care for my high school coach, either," Collins says. "Paul Brown was okay. I was young; I didn't understand. Blanton Collier, I loved. I performed for him.

"The basic difference between Paul Brown and Blanton Collier was that Blanton had a little more rapport with the ballplayers," he says. "The ballplayers liked Paul Brown, but with Blanton, you loved the guy because he had a direct interest in whatever you were doing and was very helpful in all phases of your game. Blanton got along with everyone."

Munching cold cut sandwiches in the tidy kitchen of his comfortable split-entry home near Harrisburg, Collins was amiable. He talked as if he were catching up an old chum on matters of mutual interest. Known during his career as an apathetic practicer and enthusiastic carouser, he now works out several days a week at a nearby college and neither smokes nor drinks. Sandy-haired and mustachioed, he looked fit, if, with

his thick weight-lifter's shoulders and arms, more like an outside linebacker than a wide receiver. He is bright and passionate and acidly ironic.

Collins says that although he's a grandfather, he's "still fiery." The marital turmoil, the outbursts at teammates, the indiscreet comments to the press are long in the past. Still, there is a smoldering intensity about him, restless energy barely contained. He fidgeted, gestured, crumpled his face. He expelled sentences in hot rushes.

Collins says he should've swallowed his pride and played in 1972. He says he should've practiced harder. He says he should've taken better care of himself.

He probably also regrets saying at the peak of his fame, "I'm the greedy type. I want those first downs and touchdowns. Third and six is my play. I'm not going to try to catch a lot of other, less important passes just to look good in numbers. I'm not interested in statistics. I like money."

The statement wasn't braggadocio. Not among the top one hundred NFL players in career receptions, Collins is twenty-first in career touchdown catches. Now, however, the lack of those "less important" statistics could keep him out of the Hall of Fame.

He rightly points out that he had to share the ball with Brown, Kelly, and Warfield and that he also had to punt. He remains the second-leading receiver in Cleveland history. He played on six playoff teams and in four championship games. The Hall of Fame Selection Committee named him to its All-NFL team of the 1960s.

Jim Brown called him the most underrated receiver in history. "I remember Gary Collins and feel remiss, realize he was much greater than I knew at the time," Brown said.

Likely, though, Collins represents an era that is bygone enough to be overlooked but not to be romanticized; thus, if he is ever inducted into the Hall of Fame, he'll have to wait—something he has never been good at.

"I don't have a lot of resentment about that," he says of not being in the Hall of Fame. "I think I'm deserving, maybe."

Collins is just as ambivalent about the Cleveland Browns. He says he misses the camaraderie and the crowds. During the 1994 season, the Browns honored the team that defeated Baltimore for the NFL title. At halftime of the game that day, Collins lined up with his teammates, caught a post pattern from Frank Ryan, and leaped into the stands. He says, however, that ill feelings over his release and his uninterest in pro football keep him from caring much about his former team.

Collins is torn even about his signature play—the post route, on which he caught his first and last ("my Ted Williams ending") touchdowns as a Brown He resents the pattern as a typecast actor resents the role with which he is forever linked. Collins maintains that the post wasn't his most effective pattern, but he knows people remember him for it and says, "It's nice to be remembered for something."

He says that playing for the Browns was simply a job, yet a part of Collins seems to yearn for the emotion he claims not to feel. Cynicism mars the shimmering surface of his memories. He recalls his youth as if talking about it will help him, finally, to affix some lesson to all of the celebrity—and all of the loss.

Sometimes, he thinks about the red Sting Ray he received as the best player in one of the great upsets in the history of the NFL, the shiny sports car that he predicted would be his, the lustrous embodiment of his boast that his team would surely win and win big.

"I kept it two years, traded it in on a car, and got rid of it," he says, shaking his head. "What an idiot. That car now would be worth a hundred grand. Let's get away from this subject before I get sick."

# *Gary* COLLINS

"    I GREW UP IN A LITTLE COAL-MINING TOWN in the start of the anthracite region. When I was a kid in the 1940s and 1950s, there was about 4,000 people in Williamstown, Pennsylvania, and their life was churches, bars, working in the mines, and Friday night football. I went out for football as a freshman, and I was the only guy in the history of the school who played all three major sports and started as a freshman.

I was a little shit, like 5' 6" and 128 pounds. My junior year, I came back for two-a-days, and I was 6' 3", 188 pounds, and I could run. The starting running back broke his leg the second day of practice, and the coach said, 'Who knows the plays?'

I said, 'I do.'

Two weeks later, we opened up, and I scored five touchdowns. I punted, kicked off, kicked field goals. I was kicking the ball out of the end zone. I did it all. I just left the group my junior year. I got better at everything, because I got bigger and faster and stronger. My senior year, I was 6' 3" and 195 pounds, and in 1957, a kid who could run and jump and dunk was unusual. In those days, a guy that tall was usually a dodo. But I could do what a guy 5' 8" could do.

By the fourth game of my junior year, there were scouts there every week. But there was no one to tell me how to understand it all, because no one had ever done it. No one else went away with a scholarship. One or two guys went to something like a state teacher's college. No one else had a scout from Ohio State sitting in the stands.

A lot of pro baseball scouts came around, and I was ready to sign because of the money, but my advisor in high school, a young assistant football coach, said, 'The hell with the money. Go to school. '

That's when I turned to looking at colleges. I never really applied myself as much as I should have, but I was a 'B' student, 'A' student. I narrowed it down to Penn State and Maryland. I never even visited places like Southern Cal. It was too far. I didn't think I was good enough for Notre Dame. I was going to go to Penn State, but I got a girl in trouble, married her, and I didn't think Penn State would want me. So I went to Maryland.

Two days after I'm at Maryland, (Penn State coach) Rip Engle comes to my house and says to my dad, 'Where is he?'

Dad told him the story, and he broke out his blue chip list. I was the third guy he wanted in the nation. I probably never would have played at Penn State, though. They didn't throw the ball. I probably would have ended up as a free safety.

MY FIRST YEAR AT MARYLAND, at the end of spring practice, there were  six and a half teams. The half team was a Red Cross team (of injured players), which I was on. I went back my sophomore year, and worked my way from the sixth team to getting the game ball in the opener against West Virginia.

We threw the ball a little more than most teams. Tom Nugent, the head coach, brought the original I-formation, which he had at Florida State, to Maryland. He kept the I, but he had two wideouts: Tommy Brown, who played with the Packers, and myself. So we had two athletes out there, and Dick Shiner and Richie Novak were the quarterbacks. We were a little more sophisticated than the average cat. Most teams rolled right and rolled left and just dumped it, like Penn State still does.

Then, if you caught passes, they triple-teamed you. I think it was my senior season, we opened up with SMU, at SMU. First play, I come out, line up, and there's a linebacker, a cornerback, and a safety. I said, 'What the hell's this?'

When I take off, all three of them run with me. I'm out on the right side. Our little running back gains 108 yards going to the left. I think that's the only time he ever went over a hundred yards. When he ran to the left, it was ten against eight. That's all I did the whole game—just run.

My junior and senior year, I was on the field 59 out of 60 minutes. I played on every special team, punted, and played offense and defense. The only time Maryland ever beat Penn State was my senior year. Maryland was 1 and 39 against Penn State, and I scored two touchdowns against them to beat them. I punted, played defense. I had the flu, a fever about 103, puking; I had a great game.

I loved Maryland. I loved playing college. That's why I played so good. The coaching staff sucked. I mean, no one liked them. They were two-faced assholes. I missed a Sunday night meeting because it was the first time I had seen my wife in six weeks. We had lost the game. Nugent comes in the next day, and my picture was on the back of the schedule, an action shot, and he goes to my teammates, who understood why I wasn't there, and said, 'We got his picture on 100,000 programs, and he doesn't even make the meeting.'

But yet, when we beat the number one team in the nation, which was Syracuse with Ernie Davis, and I was the number one player in the nation, who's standing alongside of me with his arm around me? Tom Nugent.

He called a special meeting one time and brought us all in to tell us we were the first team in the nation to have our names on the back of our jerseys. He had a meeting about it, and we're looking around, going, 'You called us in for *this*?'

I'm an All-American, but every Monday in practice, a sixth-team end could challenge me one-on-one in the pits, with the running back behind him. The end blocks me, and I have to tackle the running back. You got three tries on offense, three on defense. Whoever won got the job. So, a sixth-team guy would say, 'I want to challenge Collins.' Everybody challenged me, because I was skinny. I didn't have the forearm. I couldn't beat anybody, so I'd lose. I'd get demoted. Tuesday, I'm on sixth team, and I'm an All-American. Wednesday, they'd throw the ball, and I'd come right to the top. Saturday, I'd be starting again.

Nugent got pissed off at me one time and in practice put me at fullback against the first-team defense. I ran three plays and got creamed, and now, *I'm* pissed off. Next play, I broke 60 yards against his first-team defense. I threw my helmet off and just walked to the sidelines.

UNTIL MY SENIOR YEAR OF COLLEGE, I didn't think I was good enough to play in the NFL. I thought I would probably teach and coach. Toward the end of my junior year, I started to think that maybe I *could* play in the NFL, but I never thought I'd get drafted. Then I started getting questionnaires from teams, mostly Green Bay, who was horrible then. In

Cleveland, they said, 'If you don't straighten up, you're going to get traded to Green Bay.'

Blanton Collier scouted me at Maryland during spring practice of my senior year. He was still at Kentucky (as head coach), but I guess he just got the job as offensive coordinator with the Browns. He said, 'I like what I see,' because I had a hell of a day in a scrimmage or something.

I said, 'Gee, that guy talks funny,' because Blanton sounded just like a billy goat when he talked.

It didn't really matter who drafted me. I was supposed to go to Dallas, I guess, and somehow, with trades and all that, it ended up Ernie Davis and me in exchange for Bobby Mitchell. I was number one with Boston (of the AFL), and they were there with the money. But you didn't know what to do; the league was only two years old. That's what swayed me. And the money wasn't really extreme at that time.

After me, the stuff between the two leagues became excessive. Around '65, the money really escalated. When they gave Namath almost a half a million, Frank Ryan said, 'Well, I'm quarterback of a championship team. What am I worth?' But in '62, the money wasn't great.

Some people down in Maryland helped me negotiate my first contract. I never had an agent. I would say 99 percent of the guys didn't have an agent. The teams would forbid it. Nobody trusted the agents. Jim Brown didn't have an agent. I don't think Paul Warfield had one.

I PLAYED IN THE EAST-WEST GAME, the Senior Bowl, what they called the Buffalo All-American Game, the Chicago All-Star Game. I didn't want to play in the all-star games. I had enough all-star games. I had signed a pro contract. I had it up to here with all-star games.

Woody Hayes coached us in the All-American Game, in Buffalo, New York. It was East against West. They only had it like five years. That was the last game Ernie Davis ever played in. I'll tell you who Woody Hayes said wouldn't make pro ball because we drank beer and stayed out: Me, Lance Alworth, Bill Miller, the receiver from Miami, Roman Gabriel, Merlin Olsen, Bill Saul. He told me I couldn't catch.

He said, 'You catch like this. You have to catch like *this*.'

I said, 'I catch like this.'

Woody coached, so I sat on the bench, got $500, never played a down. Didn't get in the game. Me, Bill Saul, Bill Miller, we never played a down, which was fine with me.

After the game, Woody says, 'You can keep the uniform.'

I said, 'I don't want the fucking thing' and threw it in the garbage can, right past Woody. I was that kind of guy. Paul Warfield told me that for years after that All-America Game, Woody told people in his practice, 'I don't want you to be like that prima donna receiver the Browns have.' Guys from Ohio State would come in and said Woody Hayes always talked about this asshole receiver that he had in an all-star game.

The Browns used to invite coaches out to Hiram to watch workouts. About four years later, they're there on the 50-yard line, and we're in seven-on-seven (passing) drills. I run a deep out where they're at. Woody's right there. The ball is thrown down, and I drop my one knee and stick my hand back, and the ball just stops, *splat*, right in my hand, then I slid out of bounds. I turned around and said, 'I never could catch.'

TWO WEEKS AFTER THE BUFFALO GAME, we came into the Cleveland camp. We had three days of camp with the rookies, and then I drove out to Chicago for the College All-Star Game with Mike Lucci, the linebacker, and it was party time. Otto Graham was the head coach, and my position coach was Dante Lavelli. We stayed out after curfew, and they caught us every night, but we didn't care. We said, 'Hey, we're having a good time this week. Screw it.' I played one play.

Otto Graham said, 'You have a bad attitude.'

I said, 'No, I don't have a bad attitude. I don't want to play this shit anymore. I should be back in Cleveland. I'm not going to play here. Send me home, send me away, I don't care. I'm gonna drink some beer.'

Lucci said the same thing. Mike was a fiery guy. So me and Looch were labeled bad attitudes. Otto Graham called up from the Chicago All-Star Game and told Paul Brown I had a bad attitude.

He said, 'Hey, you made a bad choice. He'll never play.'

That's the first thing PB told me when I walked into camp: 'I hear you have a bad attitude.'

I said, 'What do you mean?'

He said, 'You don't practice. You're out after curfew.'

I said, 'I want to play here. I don't want to play college ball anymore.'

He said, 'We'll find out this week.'

Even though I had a two-year, no-cut deal, I was scared.

Lo and behold, the first day back in camp, they have punt team practice.

He says, 'Bring our first draft choice out, since he's going to punt Saturday night up in Detroit.'

It's my first kick in front of the team. You know those hills over there in Hiram? I shanked it down over the hill. I hear the guys going, 'Aww, we spent money for *that* shit?'

I got pissed off, and the next one just went flying. I got motivated by comments.

I always ask people, 'You remember John Havlicek?'

They go, 'Yeah.'

I go, 'What is the first athletic team he was cut from?'

They go, 'Oh, he just played for the Celtics.'

I go, 'Oh, really?'

He was like the seventh draft choice of the Cleveland Browns. I guess he was an All-State quarterback. Good guy, Hondo. He could catch, too. He would have been a good safety man, like Paul Krause (formerly of the Minnesota Vikings). But there were just too many good people. He ended up playing seventeen seasons with the Celtics. They called us 'The Blades.' He was 6' 5" and 205, and I was 6' 4", 210. We looked like two brothers. I was 86 and he was 85. You couldn't tell us apart.

WE WERE BOTH AFRAID OF BOB GAIN, the defensive tackle. When he walked by our dorm room, we'd close the door. He was a grumpy son of a bitch. Bob Gain went back to another era, when guys didn't train at all. He'd put on a pair of practice pants, and he'd wear them all through the year and never get them washed. They were so salty and smelly, we burned one pair. All you had to do was go like this with a cigarette lighter and *poof*.

Ray Renfro was there ten years when I came up. He taught me the ropes. He was from Texas, and everybody was 'old podnuh.' Paul Brown didn't like him because he said Ray didn't make the big catches in the big games. He says, 'You drop 'em.'

In front of everybody: 'You drop 'em.'

Ray told me when he left Texas, he left in August. That was in '51, I guess. People said, 'Boy, wear something warm. It's cold up there in Cleveland.' He put on his wool suit. He weighed 180 pounds. They didn't have air conditioning in the bus. By the time he got to Cleveland, he weighed 165 pounds and the goddamn wool suit was soaked.

PB never got on me because I never played. I punted. I was on all the special teams. I started when Ray was down with injuries. I really should have started because Ray physically couldn't go. He had psoriasis all over his body all year. He had bad knees. The games I started, I got the game ball, but PB wouldn't start a rookie unless he absolutely had to. Jim Brown was the only one.

I never really saw a relationship between PB and Jim at all. You know, at 22, you walk around with a hard-on, and you don't know what you're doing, but I never saw a relationship. I don't think PB had many with anybody. He had business relationships: 'You're there. I'm paying you to do a job.' That was Paul.

I got along fine with him. But I didn't like his dominance of people. He was a control freak. Then, they used to give you the game plan in two sheets. Paul would actually say, 'For you rookies, when you go away, we want you to fold your game plan like this.' And he'd demonstrate, put the creases on the ends. 'And then like this.' He folded it again. 'And put it in the inside left pocket of your jacket and pat it so you know it's there.' And he'd pat his chest. 'This is the way we do it.'

Jim Ninowski, the quarterback, told me this. On Tuesdays, you'd have the day off, but Paul would have the quarterbacks up at Shaker Heights at a restaurant. There'd be Paul, six coaches, Ninowski and Frank Ryan. Paul did all the ordering. The waitress would come in, and Paul would say, 'We'll have eight cheeseburgers, and I'll have the special,' which might have been a great steak.

After about three meetings, Ninowski said, 'I don't want a cheeseburger.'

The coaches would be sitting there like this: 'Yeah, we'll eat the cheeseburger.'

PAUL WOULD RIDICULE THE COACHES in front of people: 'We can't have that! We can't have that!' If Uli (assistant coach Ed Ulinski) or someone would screwed up the film, oh, he'd be all over them.

He always thought people were spying on him. Down in League Park, a guy was fixing a telephone pole during practice. Paul had the cops remove him. He thought he was a spy.

We're playing an away game. We win the coin toss and he's going, 'OK men. Everybody in,' waving us toward the locker room. And he said, 'We're going to return the opening kickoff...' and he makes this signal with his hand meaning 'up the middle.' He thought people were listening to him.

I went, 'What the hell? You hear the fans? There's 80,000 fans out there.'
'Return it...' and he's signalling with his hands.

He was like a schoolmarm. Night before a home game, you ate your
evening meal, and he'd stand up and say, 'The movie tonight is *007*,' and
you'd all go and you'd see the movie. Eddie Ulinski would be there like this,
'Collins, Ryan....' Crossing your name off as you went into the movie.

He was like the guy in *Stalag 17*. He was the mastermind. Nobody ever
could fight him, nobody. They'd be gone. 'So be it'—those were his famous
words. He'd take complete control, and a lot of guys liked to live under that
regimentation. I was young, and I went with the tide.

Here's a great one: He had these little skinny arms, about like my finger, and he always wore a tee-shirt. First meeting, he'd get up in front of the
team, at Hiram, and he would pull on his sleeves, like he needed more
room for his arms, or he would grab at the air like he caught a fly, to show
his quickness.

I had no problem with him, personally, except he said to me that I
caused interceptions. There was a lot of resentment toward PB from the
older ballplayers, which, again, gets back to the Gestapo thing. People started
changing in the '60s. Even though they were older ballplayers, they looked
around and saw freedom. The change in the society itself hit. Guys started
to think, 'We shouldn't be treated like that.'

Paul Brown never changed: 'Goddamn, we've gotta do this, and we've
got to do that.' It's like practicing in League Park. League Park was rat-
infested, one shitter. It was awful. I had better facilities in my high school.
Hell, Babe Ruth played there. Staying in League Park was just Paul. He ain't
changing his habits, and he didn't. What he had done worked for him, so
he was reluctant to change, and that's why he was ousted. I wasn't surprised
when Modell let Paul Brown go, because you could see it coming.

I guess he didn't deserve what he got, but anybody that got dismantled
by Modell never got a worthy bon voyage, not Jim Brown, Ryan, me; the
list is endless.

BLANTON WAS SUCH A COMPLETE CHANGE. There was total
freedom—guys smoking in the locker room and all that shit. You didn't
have a Gestapo agent in charge, and guys loved it. In '63, we won the first
six games and we said, 'How many games is this team going to win?' We
were 6 and 0, all because of Blanton, and everybody loved him. Then, the
Giants came in, beat us 33-6, and woke us up to reality.

PB would handle you by getting in your pocket book. He would say, 'You will not get your check this week,' or something like that. He would embarrass you. Blanton wouldn't do that. If he had something to say to you, it was after the films. Blanton's style was much more homey.

Blanton knew talent, and he knew the finer little things that people wouldn't notice. One of the positions he knew best was defensive tackle. He knew that pretty damn well, and he really knew quarterbacks and punting. He was about the only guy who ever helped me in punting.

I look at the Browns this way: From '57 to '62, they realized, like in the Second World War, 'We aren't going to win with strategic bombing. We have to have something else.' They could drop all the bombs they wanted in Germany. That wasn't going to beat them. They had Jim Brown, the greatest player of his time, and they didn't do shit. They had to have more ways to attack. They got me, changed a little bit, and then they got Warfield, and what happened? We won a championship.

Our offense didn't change much with Blanton. I think our passing game got a little better, but the running game was the same, basically: the guards pulling, and the lead back; the other team had to stop the sweep. And, I think, Blanton put more emphasis into the tight end catching the ball.

When he got the job, Blanton called me at Maryland and said, 'You're my starting flanker, and don't let me down.' That was it. I had the job when I walked into camp. The starting quarterback when I came up was Jim Ninowski. Frank Ryan and I had some good games when we played in '62, and in '63, Ryan started. Frank made the decisions. I had a real good year. I should've made the Pro Bowl, but they took Frank Gifford instead that year. The next year, we got Warfield, and then we really had the balance.

Blanton's style worked better for me. Again, I was always labeled 'lackadaisical, don't give a shit,' which in athletic terms means I'm lazy and don't care, so that means they've got to get on me to motivate me. Well, that just drove me deeper. Blanton saw this, I guess. He did the complete opposite. He never said diddly-shit to me. On big games he'd come up and say, 'I need a good one out of you.'

'Okay, George, you got it.'

IN 1963, WHEN YOU CAME in second place in the NFL, you played in what was called the Runner-Up Bowl, in Miami. That year, it was us and the Green Bay Packers. The Packers came in second in their division, and we came in second in ours, so we met in Miami. We go down there, and

Blanton Collier still had the old Paul Brown rules. We see the Packers in their hotel. They're in shorts and sandals. We're walking around with suits and ties, because that was the Browns' trademark. If you saw a Browns' player in the lobby, he had a suit and tie on. Some of us younger guys went up to Paul Wiggin, who was the captain, and said, 'Hey, Paul, this is bullshit. We go to practice, we come back, we've got these ties on in the bus and all this shit. Can't we look like the Packers?'

Paul said, 'I'll bring it up with Blanton in the meeting.'

Blanton goes through the meeting that day and said, 'Is there anything else?'

Wiggin stands up and says, 'George, do we have to wear the ties after practice?'

So Blanton says, 'No-oh tie-eyes. It's su-uh-dden de-eh-ath.'

Of course, Blanton was just about deaf. He couldn't hear Wiggin. I was going nuts. Me and Monte Clark fell off the chairs. I was down on the floor. Blanton didn't know what the hell was going on.

If I got a bad punt off, Blanton would go like this, with his toe pointed, and say, 'Keep your foot down, keep it down.' Now, on blitz coverage, you have a post or a corner call (as an automatic checkoff route). One time, we had the post on the checkoff against the blitz, and I wanted to change it to what we call a shake or a fly-pattern.

I come out after the first checkoff and I yelled, 'George, we can't run the post!' I'd get pissed. That's how I played football. I said, 'George, goddammit, we can't run the post! We should be running the fly!'

He said, 'Just keep it down, just keep it down,' and started pointing his toe.

I said, 'I'm not talking about punting!'

Boy, he couldn't hear, and he would *not* get a hearing aid.

ONE TIME, I WAS PUNTING FROM THE END ZONE. We needed a first down, like 20 yards, but I thought sure as hell with the wind blowing in my face, they wouldn't rush me, and they didn't. I didn't tell anybody. I just took off. I got knocked out of bounds right by Blanton, first down on the 50.

Blanton's going, 'Don't do that to me! You're giving me a heart attack!'

But he was smiling. I did that five times. I was five for five. I never told anybody I was going to do it, and every time, Blanton's going, 'You're giving me a heart attack! Don't do this to me! You're killing me!'

Who's to say if we wouldn't have won it in '64 if Paul was still the coach? There were some great moments, but I didn't think that was a great team. Our defense wasn't that good. They made big plays in big games but it wasn't that good. Actually, we should have won more championships. I don't know what happened. I thought that '66 was the best team of all. Leroy led the league in rushing, Ryan was tremendous, I had a great year, Warfield had a great year, our defense was superb, and we didn't go shittin' nowhere. What were we, 11-3 (9-5)? We lost to Dallas in the playoffs. I thought the '66 team was by far the best team I played on. I don't know what happened. This was the team after Jim left, and, obviously, I'm not taking anything away from Jim Brown, because he was the best. You can talk about Barry Sanders and Walter Payton and all these great runners, but Jim Brown was the best. I've always said that. This was Leroy's first year as a starter. No one knew how good he'd be. So we were blessed.

In '64, the game we should have won to get into the playoffs—against St. Louis—we tied. I made a 29-yard reception to put us on the one, and Jim took it in, and we tied 33-33 (this was actually the first St. Louis game of the season; needing a win to clinch the Eastern Division title, the Browns lost to the Cards, 28-19, in the next-to-last game of the season). Then we had to win to get in. We go up to New York, and ran off 55 straight points. Kicked their ass (52-20). That's when Blanton really got loose—in the plane coming back. Everybody was tanked. There were 25,000 people at the airport. It was unbelievable.

I CALLED THE CHAMPIONSHIP WIN in '64, but that's the way I was. Baltimore was a three-touchdown favorite. It was on Wednesday in the old League Park locker room. Kenny Coleman put a mike in my face and said, 'We're getting comments from ballplayers about how we're going to do Sunday.'

I said. 'What do you want me to say, we're gonna lose? We're gonna win. What the hell.' They edited out 'hell,' but it comes out, 'Collins says we're going to win Sunday.' That's the way I felt.

When I said, 'We're going to beat the shit out of the Colts,' I was just being honest. As a competitor, if you don't feel like that, you might as well not even show up: 'I don't come here to lose, my friend. Come in to my house on Sunday and expect to get your ass whipped.'

It's hard to remember a lot of it, but it was exciting. Things just fell into place and snowballed. Everything worked out perfect. The big key in that game was the wind. Every time they'd punt, it was against the wind. We always had field position in the second half, and we were throwing with the wind.

The first pass I caught for a touchdown, I almost dropped it. The goal post was right there and made me take my eye off of it. If you ever watched it, I have it and almost lose it and catch it again. The last one was just a juggling great catch. The second one I knew I had. That was easy. But the first one I almost missed. Frank drilled it like 18, 20 yards but that damn pole. I said, 'It's gonna hit the goddamn pole.' The pole was up on the goal line then. It was a hazard. I hit it many times.

WHAT'S SO UNFORTUNATE—fortunate, but unfortunate—for a guy like me is that that's the only game people remember. That's fine, because a lot of people aren't remembered for anything, but I had far, far greater years after that. Sixty-five, '66 and '69, I had great years, All-Pro years. But it's nice to be remembered for something. Just like Kirk Gibson's remembered for that hobbling home run.

That game was worth some money to me. I made $8,000, plus the Corvette (from *Sport* magazine for being MVP), plus another four. I did an ad for Manhattan shirts, which was $10,000. Then, that was a lot of money for some quick endorsements. Now it would be worth $10 million, at least. Yessir, I had me more Manhattan shirts than I knew what the hell to do with. I got shirts for months. I just gave them to people.

Then I signed a thing with cigars. Christ, I got cigars every two weeks in the locker room. I didn't smoke them. I'd say, 'Cigars are in,' and the guys would be coming over. It was for Cheroots. They just took a picture. Now, you couldn't do that—endorse smoking. You couldn't endorse smoking then, either, but they didn't say you 'smoked' them. They said you 'enjoyed' them.

I drove free cars all the time. In August of 1965 I got a memo, and it said, 'To all punters,' and I got the one for the Browns. It was from The Ford Motor Company: 'The player in the National Football League who leads the league in punting will receive a Ford LTD as a prize.'

That Ford LTD then was a nice vehicle. I'm looking at it in training camp, saying, 'I'm going to win that son of a bitch.' And it ended up I did. I ended up with four guys in it, backed up in a snow drift, and wrenched the doors off.

There were some good guys in Cleveland over the years. My friends up there were Schaf (tackle Dick Schafrath), Ross, Vince, Mo, and although I didn't know him that long, Ray Renfro. You don't make a lot of friends because there's cliques. Still is, I'm sure. Even in a family everybody doesn't get along.

Then, blacks stayed their way, and we stayed ours. In my first year, rookies, coaches, and blacks rode the first bus. I was raised where there wasn't that type of thing. I'm thinking, 'What's the deal here? Why aren't there blacks on the other bus? This isn't right.'

As a rookie, we went down to Dallas, and you'd have to stay at the Ramada Inn at the airport. You got spoiled for three games, four games, five games in the exhibition season, staying at these top hotels in California and Detroit. Then, in Dallas, blacks weren't allowed downtown in the hotels. Jim Brown goes out, gains 237 yards, and says, 'Stick it up your ass.'

I was a white man, and I didn't agree with that racist shit. I think sports did a lot to change it, although I watch today, and on the sidelines, on the bench, college and pro, it's always the blacks together, and the whites together. It's still the same today.

We invited every black guy to our parties. Ernie Green would come, Leroy would show, and Erich Barnes. In fact, Erich and I would go up to Murray Hill and have lunch. Murray Hill in Cleveland, the only outside people allowed up there were the mailmen. No blacks. Erich Barnes and I would go up there and have lunch. Erich and I were good friends. He came to our team parties. The black players were always welcome, but they never came.

SCHAF AND I HAD SOME GOOD TIMES. We used to go through Shaker Heights late to practice, and if he didn't have any room in the street, he'd go over the lawns. We had practice meetings at nine, and Schaf is picking me up at 25 to nine. The drive was 45 minutes. He had a little red Comet. It's snowing; my side of the windshield is covered; his is almost covered. He gets out and goes like this across the windshield with his arm, because the wipers don't work. He says, 'There's traffic. No problem.' *Boom*, through the grass, laughing like hell. Then he got a Volkswagen. The back seat looked like a general store. He had bricks, tennis rackets, jock straps. Somehow, we got into it, and he's passing semis. Here's the truck wheel right here beside my ear.

The best he ever did, he got home about 4 o'clock in the morning. He ran in, took his shoes off, ran back out, locked the door, grabbed the news-

517

paper, then pounded on the door and said he locked himself out. His wife bought it. Then, he had someone call from Shaker Medical that he was in the hospital. One time he hid his car and poured oil all over himself. He came home about 3 o'clock: 'Car broke down, Bonnie.'

Bonnie was his first wife. The second one, Judy, looked like one of those little yodelers from Switzerland. Cute as a button. She was like the tool lady, from *Tool Time*. You needed something fixed, she'd break out the toolbox. He bought her a tool belt for Christmas one year.

You'd say, 'Yeah, my septic tank's blocked up and the motor's shot on the garbage disposal under the sink.'

'No problem.' She'd come over and fix it.

Until the jets came in, we flew those straight props, and every time we got in the airplane, I'd look at Schaf and go, 'Schaf, they don't sound good,' because he was afraid to fly. I'd go, 'Oh, those engines don't sound good.'

He'd be getting up, going, 'Ahhh. Ahhh.'

He was like Jackie Jensen, the baseball player (whose fear of flying forced him out of the major leagues). Jackie Jensen married that famous Olympic diver, Zoe Olson. Who was Jackie Jensen's wife is about as good as you get on trivia. Of course, who caught the first touchdown on *Monday Night Football* isn't bad either. I scored the first touchdown on *Monday Night Football*.

I get asked that at least twenty times a year, 'Do you know who scored the first touchdown on *Monday Night Football*?'

And I go like this: 'Uh, uh, uh...'

THE ONLY THING I REGRET IN MY CAREER is I was a poor practice man. In today's world, I'd get fired. I didn't leave it on the field. I saved it for showtime. When there's 80,000 people out there, I want to show these folks that even if I have a broken rib, they are going to get their goddamn money's worth. I got a lot of flack from that, because you're supposed to set the example of good habits, but I said, 'I'll show you good habits Sunday at 1 p.m., OK?'

A lot of times, I wouldn't even practice the whole week. I'd go out there Sunday, and they'd say, 'He's smoother than silk.' That's just the way I worked. I was a gamer. I was one of those guys who got excited on Sundays, but you never knew I was excited. You'd think I was bored when I was playing. I would just look like I didn't give a shit. Like, getting in the end zone— there ain't no big celebration. I used to tell people: ' This is no big shittin' deal for me. I'm going to be back.' Like scoring a first-quarter touchdown and celebrating—I watch that, and I say, 'What's the big deal here? There's sixty minutes to go.'

I was labeled a bad actor when I really wasn't. All my emotions were projected for Sunday. Study Jim Brown. His habits in practice were like mine. I worked on conditioning. In the morning practices during two-a-days, we only ran the ball. We always threw in the afternoon, because the crowds came then. When we were running the ball, I knew that all the receivers had to do was get downfield. With the great runners we had—Jim and Leroy— all we had to do was just get in the way. On a running play, if Jim was running the sweep to the left, and I was flanked to the right, I would sprint over there, then jog back, so I got my conditioning in that way. People didn't even notice that. I was accused of being a loafer, lackadaisical, didn't give a shit, and that wasn't true. You don't play for ten years and do what I did because you didn't give a shit.

I ran a lot of routes over the middle because Ryan had a very difficult time on out patterns. Any right-handed quarterback does. A right-handed quarterback can't throw outside right, and a left-handed quarterback can't throw outside left. If you remember the Raiders—Snake Stabler and Fred Biletnikoff—their big hookup was an out pattern to the right.

The weakest throw for Ryan was a deep out, which at the end of my career became my best pattern because people played me to make all in moves. But the quarterbacks couldn't throw it. Frank could throw it far, but he didn't have quick feet. That was his biggest problem. He wasn't what you call a great athlete, not that he was a bad player, because he wasn't. Frank could zip it. He could drill a post and a slant and a cross, but the outs and the touch, Ninowski had that. Nino had the touch.

ALL OF THEM HAD THE STIGMA of the legend in front of them— Otto Graham. How many guys for the Browns had to deal with: 'Oh, that guy reminds me so much of Gary Collins'? Take the kid from Colorado, Dave Logan. He was a white guy, 6' 3", 195, 200. I think he was a little faster than me. I was a little bigger. They always compared him to me. Chip Myers down in Cincinnati. All these white guys with mediocre speed who could catch: 'Another Gary Collins'—Cosell would say it every Monday night. The Browns even drafted a guy, Paul Staroba, because he was a Collins look-alike. He never did shit. You get labeled: 'You'll never be like Collins'; 'You'll never be like Warfield.' It's sad guys have to live up to that.

Two years ago, when they had Meet the Browns out at the Hiram, I was there with Dub Jones. We were signing autographs, and I said to Dubber, 'Dub, why in the hell did you call me all the time on third down and going in for touchdowns?'

He said, 'I ain't stupid. You throw it to the guy who can catch it.'

It's that simple: Throw it to the guy who can catch it. A sportswriter told me I had eight legitimate drops in my career. Eight, and being called upon over a thousand times and caught 300. Eight drops and three of them were in a sleet and ice storm, with a broken rib, so he said I really had five.

The ability to catch came from baseball. You need hand placement. And if your hands aren't quick, the defensive back is going to knock the ball out, so just let it come in to your chest. Now, sometimes you have to reach and grab it some way, but only the great ones can pluck it. I didn't have big hands, but I had great eyes, which is an overlooked thing in sports. There were times when I broke early on out patterns, and I looked back and could see the rotation of the ball. I didn't see it clearly, but I could see rotation right here in front of my eyes, which told me it was a bad pass instantly, quicker than a guy that didn't have that. That made the great catches routine.

I THINK IT WAS 1965, a bad day in November. I got a guy beat, Frank throws the ball, and it got hung up in the air. The safety's coming over. I see he's going to intercept it, and I reached back to bat it down, which was difficult. This guy's face mask and the face mask of the guy behind me collided, and my hand was in there. When I came down, this finger went there, this one was like this, and this one was ripped. I mean you saw the tendon. I got a picture in my scrapbook. I'm on my knees; (team physician) Ippolito is pulling all that shit back. This is like three minutes to go before half time, and when we go in, he stitches it up. I think it was seven stitches. I went out and caught six balls, one for a score, punted, and ran from punt formation from the end zone on fourth down, and really won the game with that play.

They'd say 'You're not a 4.4 guy.' They'd always bring that crap up on me. I never had great speed, but I had good speed. I could run.

'Those 4.4 guys wish they could catch like me,' I'd say. The idea was to catch the ball. As a rookie, I was told: 'Catch it,' and that's what I did, no matter what. I knew I was gonna get hit. Everybody knew I was catching it. 'Yeah, but you can't run 4.4,' the reporters said.

'So?' I said. 'Advance the sticks.'
That's what I did.

EVENTUALLY, MODELL FORCED BLANTON'S HAND and brought in Nick Skorich (in 1971). Modell did the same thing as he did with PB: He wanted a change; 'Gotta get sterner.' So he took the opposite approach. When Modell hired Blanton, he wanted a guy that players could communicate with. Then, he wanted somebody who was sterner. So he brought in Skorich and everybody thought, 'Hey, Nick's a great guy.'

As an assistant, he was full of life. Everybody loved him. Overnight, he became a prick. He got like Mussolini. He became just the opposite of what he was. We couldn't believe it. He took a championship team and in one year put it in the commode.

He'd embarrass you in the meetings. He'd fine you for anything: 'Hickerson, cutting gas. That's $50, Gene.' The guys wouldn't play for him. He smoked, and he was so short that his shirt pocket was down around my knees. If you asked him for a cigarette, you had to reach down to get it. We used to call him 'the Exxon gas pump.'

When they had that big trade, with Warfield to Miami for the rights to Mike Phipps (in 1971), I was shoveling shit in my stalls. It's nine in the morning. My wife says, 'Phone call. It's Chuck Heaton.'

I get on the phone, and he says, 'Did you hear about the trade?'

I'm coming off a great season, in '69, but I was 29, going to be 30 soon. I said to Chuck, 'Where'd I go?'

He said, 'No, we traded Warfield.'

I said, 'Who did?'

He said, 'We traded him to Miami for the rights to Mike Phipps.'

I said, 'That's the end of us.'

To call Skorich a 'son of a gun' is mild. He wanted to lay the hard rules down and guys wouldn't take it. He took a team that had won a title in '69, and by '72, they were dismantled.

I found out I was benched by reading it in the newspapers that morning. I come in and I said to Skorich, as any man would do, 'Where do we go from here?'

'If you don't like it, we'll get rid of you this afternoon.'

No discussion; no mercy.

This was the seventh game in '71. So that's when we incorporated something that no team had ever done. I would go in for the fullback, go in motion, and run pass patterns. They got a guy named Frank Pitts to replace me. The next year, he dropped more balls in two or three games than I did in my entire career. He dropped four or five in one game. But the game he took over for me, against Kansas City, he caught one right by our bench between his helmet and his shoulder pad.

I said, 'Jesus, I'll never get back in there.'

THE YEAR AFTER THEY BENCHED ME, I went back for the mile run in May. I think I came in third. I was ready to play.

I said to Skorich, 'I want a shot at tight end when I come back in '72.'

He said, 'No, you'll be a backup or we'll get rid of you.'

I said, 'Fuck you.'

On the way home, I said, 'I ain't going back there.' I never went back.

I knew the game, and I lined up tight enough (as a flanker) that I knew the position. I may have not been a great blocking tight end, but I could have done it. They never gave me the opportunity. And I was stubborn. I just said, 'Screw it,' and retired, which was dumb.

The first pass I ever caught and the last pass I ever caught was on a post for a touchdown. The first was a post in a doubleheader exhibition game, and the last was my last game, against the 'Skins, for a touchdown, in Washington. I had a Ted Williams ending.

I went down to the 'Skins in June or early July. George Allen wanted me to back up Roy Jefferson and Charley Taylor. That's the year they went for the Super Bowl. Boy, I was excited, but the Browns wouldn't release me. I was on what they called the retirement reserve. Later on that year, when I was coaching at Lebanon Valley (a Division III college near his home), Weeb Ewbank called me and wanted me to go with the Jets, but I wasn't going with a non-contender.

I guess stubbornness made me quit. I should have gone back in '72. I probably would have backed up, but I still was able to play. Three years later, in '74, I went out and played in the World Football League. I could still punt. I just called a friend at the University of Maryland and said, 'How can I reach somebody with the Washington Ambassadors? I'd like to coach.'

Washington coach Jack Pardee talked me into being a player/coach. So I come back, and I was in great condition, didn't miss a beat. First scrimmage we had, I think I caught six balls, against good personnel from an opposing team. Then they stopped paying us. Washington never played a game. They became the Florida Blazers. A guy that owned the Holiday Inn bought the franchise. About the fourth game, they stopped the paychecks. We're going out and winning, but we're playing without money. We got nothing! We got zero! No paychecks.

The last two weeks of the season, there was no soap or towels in the locker room. The idea was to stay with Pardee and, hopefully, we'd get to the NFL. There were eight coaches in Orlando; he took two. He took Ross Fichtner, because Ross did all his work as a defensive coordinator, and he took the line coach. That was it. The rest of us, we didn't even get money to get out of Florida.

For a while, I really didn't do shit, then I opened up a sporting goods store. Eventually, I got divorced. When that went down the tubes, I got taken over the coals by my wife. In '79 I started in the insurance and financial claim business. I did that until about two years ago. Now, I help my son out with his business. He does lawn care and landscaping, which is hard work. It's a hell of a business, though.

I GOT VERY BITTER TOWARDS FOOTBALL in the '70s and '80s. The way the Browns let me go, berated by newspapers after I'd given the best years of my life. I got bitter, which was wrong, and all I did was look at that championship mug and championship ashtray, and there's Modell hugging me. When I see players today, and they win a game, being embraced by the crowds, I think, 'Five years from now, I don't care how much money you make, your ass is gone.'

I see guys I played with at the same time in college—Roman Gabriel, Merlin Olsen—all these guys have made the College Hall of Fame, and me and Stan Jones (a Maryland lineman who played for the Bears) haven't made it.

Stan was almost the lineman of the year in 1951, with those great Maryland teams. Why isn't he in? I don't have the stats, but, geez, I was a two-time All-American, All-Conference for three years, set ACC records before they really started throwing the ball. I set the records with a minimal number of catches because I got triple-teamed, and I played both ways. Statistics aren't always the whole story.

As far as the Pro Hall of Fame, Swanny (Pittsburgh Steeler receiver Lynn Swann), who I have nothing against, keeps getting mentioned. A guy sent me this. Swanny had 336 and I had 331 catches career. He has 51 touchdowns; I have 70. His average per catch was 16.3. Mine was 16. He was MVP of the Super Bowl. I was the MVP of the then-Super Bowl. I punted for five years, led the league, with one of the highest averages ever. Next to Sammy Baugh's 52.9, my 46.7, I think it was, was like the third highest of all time (16th). Every third catch was a touchdown or a first down. I was in four championships.

TO ME, 400 RECEPTIONS IS THE NUMBER, and the year I got hurt, I had eleven catches in one and a half games. On the eleventh, I tore out my shoulder and missed the rest of 1968. I was on my way to a 60-, 70-catch year—with the Browns, which would have been phenomenal. You'd have 45 catches then, and it'd be great. That year would have taken me over that 400 barrier, and that's what people look at thirty years down the road.

They say, 'Well, you couldn't play in today's world.' Maybe not, but I see (Denver receiver) Ed McCafferty playing. I think we were a lot alike. Maybe I was a little bit more physical. And they feed him the ball. I mean, hey, they pump you the ball, and you're going to have the numbers. I knew I was going to get called on five to seven times a game. You figure, you'll get fifty percent. I'll catch three of the six they call. You weren't called much more than that. Three times fourteen gave me 42 catches.

I think a couple times I caught six or eight. In a game against the Bears I think I caught eight for 150 yards or something. And then the championship game I had only five catches, for 130 yards. Let's say you average 65 plays on offense. You got Jim getting his 25-35, you had the other back getting ten, you had Warfield, me, the tight-end. After Jim, you had four people splitting the remaining plays. How many are you going to get?

Ozzie Newsome was catching one-yard passes. I would've caught 90 balls a game, too, if they had thrown me one-yard passes. They threw the ball all the time then. And that's what gets you into the Hall of Fame, sad to say. These guys that vote don't even remember you playing. They're ten years younger than you, and they don't even know who in the hell you are. They think, 'He only caught 300 passes? Well, shit, he couldn't have been that good.'

But like the guy said, 'If you're looking for sympathy, it's in the dictionary between shit and syphilis.' If you're going by numbers, I'll never make the Hall of Fame. If you're going by wining and moving the chains—I'm the guy. When the heat's on, throw me the goddamn ball.

I don't have the stats, but I never played on a losing team. The worst we were was 7-7. I played with great runners, and it was a whole different world then. I got a questionnaire once. There were questions on there like 'What do you think of the NFL?'

My answer? 'I don't.' Of course, I'm an ass, but that was a good answer.

'Name me the three best linebackers.'

Well, everybody goes, 'Dick Butkus, Ray Nitschke, Sam Huff.' I played against Huff three years. He was overrated, couldn't cover the pass.

I said, 'Tommy Nobis, Chuck Howley, and Dave Robinson.'

I played against Dave Robinson in college, too. He was an end at Penn State. He knocked the shit out of me when we played the Packers. He got you. He was very underrated. When you're part of a surrounding cast that's as good as Green Bay, you get lost in the shuffle. I'm an example of that. Warfield, Kelly, Brown—you got lost. Tommy Nobis never played on a winning team, so nobody ever gave him his due.

Somebody said, 'Who was your toughest defensive back? Was it Herb Adderley?'

'No.'

'Pat Fisher (of the Cardinals)?'

'No. It was Jimmie Johnson, Rafer Johnson's brother. He played for the Niners. He was 6' 2", 212, could run, very underrated. He was great.'

The first time I played against Bubba Smith (of the Colts), he got down, and his *shadow* covered me. I knew I was in trouble. He was huge. He was 6' 7" and played at about 275.

Doug Atkins was big like that. The story I like about him is he was traded to the Saints. He's practicing, and this rookie lineman comes out, hits him, and just fell down.

'I admire your courage,' Doug said to him, 'but you made a poor selection.'

Doug dwarfed me. He played at 6' 8", about 270. He wears like a 16 ring. Everything about him is big. A monstrous man, and mean and ugly. His hand was so monstrous that shaking hands with him would be like putting a baby's hand in yours.

I DON'T 'RESENT' WHAT HAPPENED. I don't know what the word would be, not 'hurt,' not 'pissed,' but you don't go out of your way to do anything. That's the thing. You don't go out of your way. That's the way I feel. Especially if it pertains to the league and the teams. Fans ask you or individually, OK, I'll do that, but to go back to pump up the Browns, they don't need me. I don't cheer for the Browns. Sorry. My son does;

does that count? I don't know what it is. It's like, 'I was there for a visit. I'm gone. See ya.'

Art Modell underpaid me for years, but I have nothing against him, either. I signed a two-year deal, then one for '64 and one for '65. In '65, I made All-Pro, and we got in the championship and lost. I think I caught fifty balls, which was high, for thirteen or fourteen scores and led the league in punting—in Cleveland, my friend, in Cleveland, in the muck and the wind. After that, I go in, and they want to give me a ham sandwich. So, you were grossly underpaid, but you can't dwell on this kind of stuff for a lifetime. I don't resent it anymore, because I really don't give a shit. I'm 58 years old, I'm a grandfather, remarried, got a wonderful wife for eighteen years. I'm still fiery, but I've mellowed.

WHAT THE FAN HAS TO UNDERSTAND is that the ten years I was there was like going to grade school and high school. You graduate. My high school class reunion was last night, forty years, and I didn't even go. I don't know anybody. It's the same thing with Cleveland. You were there, then you're gone. The fans who lived in Cleveland for fifty years have more part of it than me. I'm just on a lease. The people of the city are the true people of the Browns, not the Gary Collinses, not even the Jim Browns. You can't expect that guy who comes in for ten years to have the same feeling of someone who lives in Parma for forty-four years. That's the way I look at it.

I liked David, Modell's son. We went back in '94, when they honored the 30th year of our championship team. I got with Schaf, and we were talking with David in his office. I said, 'What would you sign me for, all things being equal?'

He said, 'Well, I'd probably give you around three million. I'd probably give you a 2.2 million one-year deal and with that, $500,000 up front.'

So I called him back the next night. I said, 'You told me you could get me some tickets for the Sixers and the Cavs. I need five tickets for my son, his three buddies, and myself. If you can, let me know, and I'll pay you for them.'

His secretary called me back and said there's five tickets down at will call. We go to the game, and they're the best seats in the house, $50 seats, and there's a note: 'You paid for these a long time ago.'

None of us got paid very well. I'd imagine all of us were underpaid. No one was in a position to argue. If you did, you were considered a malcontent, like Bernie Parrish. Bernie was just honest, that's all. He just said it like it was, but if you voiced your opinion in the '60s, you were called a rebel.

Of course, they don't care now; they make so much money it doesn't matter. Money is the overriding factor of anything that happens in the organization. It's 'Screw you. I'll go make my nine million.' I mean, what's Jerry Rice make, two million a game? I'm not disputing the fact that he's good, but is even he worth that?

I'm not even going to discuss what we made. It's embarrassing. I think the highest Jim Brown ever made was $65,000. Give me a break! Just the revenue from doubleheader exhibition games we played in, alone, should've meant something. My first exhibition game, up in Detroit in 1962, I got $39 net.

When I signed, the average guy on the street was making $3,027. My base was twenty grand. I was making seven times more than the guy on the street. That doesn't hold true today. Now, they're making fifty times more. What does the average guy make, twenty-seven? Fifty times doesn't even put you near what players are making today.

I WENT BACK IN '94. My nickname was 'A.W.,' because Ralph Smith used to call me 'All the Way.' Anyway, this is Cleveland, '94:
'Oh, hey, hey, A.W., how you doing? You're looking good.'
'You're looking bad.'
'Where do you live?'
'I live in Hershey.'
'What do you do?'
'I'm retired.'
'What did you do?'
'I did this.'
'You still married?'
'No, yes, whatever.'
'Uh huh. Yeah, uh, well...'
'Remember when...'
That's the first thing you say to someone: 'You look good.' It's like if you don't have a gut out to here, you're okay. I work harder at keeping myself fit than I did when I played. People have to go, 'Collins gotta weigh 900 pounds.' I don't smoke, don't drink, take drugs, and I work out. If that's taking care of your body, then I'm the guy.

The money's gone, the fame's gone, a lot of the friendships are gone. Time and geography ruined that. But guys like Dick Modzelewski and Ross and Schaf, guys like that, you talk to them for five minutes, and it's like you never left, because I haven't changed, and they haven't changed.

My son gets that Browns paper, and they always list in there the guys that died. That's not comforting, all these guys you played with are starting to kick the bucket. My old compadre, Ray Renfro, died. I talked to his wife, and she said he just got sick and died. What a good guy.

Now, Lavelli looks great, but don't get near him. The son of a bitch will knock you out saying hello. He hits you. He hit me in my bad shoulder in '94. He goes, 'Hey, how's it goin'?' And he lets it fly.

I said, 'Dante, I'm going to knock you out! You gave me a headache!' I was going to plow into him. He knocked the shit out of me.

My son Gary said, 'That guy's crazy.'

I said, 'I know.' Yeah, he's nuts.


I SAID I DIDN'T MISS THE GAME after I got out, but I did. Sunday, when you get fired up, I liked that. I didn't miss the practices and flying and that crap, but the Sunday when you were called upon to do a job in front of a lot of folks, yeah, I missed that. That fired me up. I still get that feeling sometimes in my body, but you can't do anything about it.

I'd go back when Jim Houston ran the alumni chapter. I was at the Holiday Inn out by the airport. They had a luncheon. I stood up, and I spoke from the heart, about drinking and smoking, and all that stuff I used to do and I don't do anymore, and about my bad marriage. Ernie Kellerman (former Browns defensive back) was there, and he had a question. He stood up and says, 'A.W., I ask you a question?'

I said, 'Sure, Ern.'

He said, 'Excuse me, ladies in the audience, but why were you such a prick in practice?'

I said, 'Well, I was unhappy, and I took it out on you and a lot of other defensive backs, and I apologize.' Things wouldn't go right on a pass play in practice, I'd turn around and kick or start a fight or something. I said, 'Because I was unhappy,' and Ernie appreciated it. I got a standing ovation because people like to hear honesty. And that's me. That's the way I felt, just like when they asked me if we were going to beat the Colts.

Forty years ago, I was a freshman at Maryland. I graduated in '58, got married for the first time in '58, and went to Maryland in '58. Forty years ago. It goes so fast. When you're young, you think, 'The money and fame ain't ever going to end. I'm never going to get gray hair and a gut. No, ain't nothing going to happen to me.' You try to avoid it forever, and yet there it is. **,,**

# Fathers *and* Sons

MIKE BROWN resembles his late father enough to make someone meeting him for the first time look twice. He has the same hawklike features as Paul Brown: the long curving nose, the prominent cheekbones, the crown of thin, receding hair. At first, the two men's eyes also seem to be the same large chips of luminous blue-gray quartz; however, the differences between son and father begin in the eyes.

Paul Brown's eyes flashed as if they had been connected to an electrical outlet. He fixed them on wrongdoers in what those who played for him call "The Look": the smoldering glare that required no words.

His son's eyes are less flinty and less direct. Softer, drooping slightly at the corners, Mike Brown's eyes are unstill, a restlessness caused by shyness rather than by dishonesty.

Brown is fleshier than his father, what Paul Brown would have been had he allowed himself to weigh something more than the 160 pounds he carried for thirty years.

Brown also lacks his father's stamped-from-tin neatness. Paul Brown's hat was set T-square level across his high, broad forehead. His tie dropped like a plumbline from collar button to belt buckle. As Mike Brown talked in his office at the Cincinnati Bengals' training center, his white, short-sleeved shirt bunched over the waist of his form-less khaki trousers, and his too-short tie hung crookedly.

Brown gestured over his desk at a visitor sitting in a chair. "I would start the day sitting where you're sitting," he said. "He would be where I'm sitting. And we would talk about things, whatever they were."

The chair in which Brown himself was sitting represents the complex relationships among four generations of his family. He helped convince his father to occupy it after Paul Brown had spent five years in exile from the career his own father virtually forbade him to pursue. Mike Brown inherited the chair only because Paul Brown refused to allow his son to follow in his footsteps.

At 65, the owner, president, and general manager of the team he and his father founded, Mike Brown will probably see the chair passed on to

his own child, one many will view as an unlikely successor. Father and son both became enthralled with football while very young. To Paul Brown, the game combined the competitiveness he learned from his mother with the discipline and order his father demanded.

"Do you want to call it miniature war or chess in shoulder pads?" he once asked. "Whatever. Football is absorbing, exciting, intriguing. It's a man's life."

Mike Brown grew up watching film with his father, idolizing Tommy James, playing hearts with Bill Willis and Marion Motley. Inspired by a comic book hero, he once leaped from a garage roof and broke his leg. Paul Brown left off preparing for an important game and rushed to the hospital. "I'll bet you're glad it wasn't Horace (Gillom, Massillon star and future Cleveland Brown)," his son said.

Both men played quarterback. Always undersized, Paul Brown failed to make the freshman team at Ohio State, and at Miami University, was known more for his intelligence and leadership than for his athletic ability. As a Dartmouth senior, Mike Brown was among the nation's top scorers. But when the Chicago Cardinals expressed interest in drafting his son, Paul Brown stepped in, telling the team, "I won't take him if you won't."

True to his word, Paul Brown

wouldn't allow his son to try out for his team. "I don't think my father ever saw me play football, either in high school or college, because my schedule conflicted with his," Brown says. "My mother was always there, or there a lot of the times, I should say, but my father never was."

When Paul Brown decided to make a career of coaching, his father objected. Lester Brown had the ageless blue-collar dream of seeing his son become a lawyer, and Paul Brown began coaching with the tacit understanding that the job would finance law school. He did take some law classes at night when he began coaching at Massillon, but he soon stopped. Lester Brown didn't forgive his son until Paul Brown became head coach at Ohio State University.

Paul Brown took the job just before his father died and just after his youngest son, Pete, was born. Paul Brown once described coaching as "a privileged profession and rendered service to young men." Nevertheless, he insisted that his son become a lawyer.

While attending Harvard Law School, Mike Brown held what he calls "really the happiest job I ever had"—coaching freshman football. After graduating, though, he was "redirected" by his father, working briefly in a Cleveland law firm before becoming business manager of his father's team.

"He felt coaching was a tough life, and I can understand why he felt that way," Brown says. "He thought I should do something that would lift me beyond that, as, probably, he imagined he should have. It might have been dreaming on his part for both of us. Fathers do that."

On the wall behind his desk, Mike Brown has hung a team photograph of his father's undefeated 1948 AAFC championship team. Brown was twelve when the picture was taken. He still speaks of the Browns as "we" and says that the city of Cleveland "always brings back memories—happy memories."

For the Brown family, however, Cleveland was the scene of calamity as well as of joy. Soon after Mike Brown went to work for his father, Art Modell bought the team. Selling his shares in the club made Paul Brown wealthy but drew him into a struggle for control with the new owner, whose own father died mysteriously when Modell was 14.

"Art was continually striving for a larger role, and my father was probably hesitant about that, and then there became a conflict over it," Mike Brown says.

A service commitment forced Mike Brown to leave his position in 1961, further isolating Paul Brown.

Modell resolved the conflict—for the time being, at least—by firing the coach early in 1962. "He called me on the phone and made the comment that Art had taken his team away from him," Mike Brown says. "I remember that's how he put it. For him, it was heartbreaking. It was something he never anticipated could be done, and it shook him to his core. His voice in that conversation quavered, which was not like him—ever."

"Outside of my family, what else except football have I known in my life?" Paul Brown asked. Six years remaining on his contract, Paul Brown retreated to La Jolla, California. He golfed, swam, and cared for his increasingly infirm wife, Katie, a diabetic. When Cleveland won the 1964 NFL title, Paul Brown and his three sons were watching the game on television at the home of his eldest boy, Robin.

"What weighs heavily on the father weighs heavily on the sons," Paul Brown said afterward. "The boys don't say anything about it, but I know it's always on their minds." Certainly, "it"—his family's separation from football—was on the mind of Mike Brown, who had returned to practicing law.

As part of its merger with the American Football League, the NFL granted Cincinnati a franchise in 1967, and Paul Brown's return to the game dominated headlines. As one reporter put it, Paul Brown became "part-owner, coach, general manager, and the absolute boss of the Bengals."

"Football is my life. I had a strong desire to live again," Paul Brown said. Actually, it was Mike Brown who handled the grueling research and negotiations for the fifteen-man group that purchased the club. Along with his mother and brothers, Brown also convinced his father to return to football thirty-eight years after Paul Brown took his first coaching job.

Years later, Nancy Brown, Mike Brown's wife, said, "Paul didn't do it all. Mike was at the helm. Of course, Mike would never tell you that, because he thinks it would diminish his father's reputation."

Mike Brown was named assistant general manager and legal counsel. Pete Brown became director of player personnel. Robin Brown, who ran a dairy in Arkansas, scouted. "Mikey-Boy," as he is known in the family, negotiated contracts, dealt with the media, took flack for unpopular decisions, watched games from the assistant coaches' box.

He describes working with his father as "wonderful": "The two of us could talk about the business in a fashion that was, for me, special. I've never had that kind of relationship with anyone else, because we were in it up to our necks. We didn't have to talk in anything but shorthand, because we understood each other."

Brown said his family's venture

in Cincinnati was "risky." The gamble was not just financial. Paul Brown's reputation was also at stake. A Hall of Fame coach who had always been obsessed with winning would lead a collection of rookies and castoffs guaranteed to lose.

Things began badly. Nattily attired as ever, Paul Brown, 59 years old, was bowled over on the sidelines as the Bengals lost their first exhibition game by twenty-one points. When he learned that Cincinnati's regular-season opener would be televised, Paul Brown called NBC's president to warn that his team might be so bad that broadcasting the game could disgrace both the network and the league.

The "Baby Bengals" lost eleven games during only the second losing season in Paul Brown's career. Father and sons, though, soon fashioned the most successful expansion team in the era before free agency. In 1969, the Bengals won only four games but improved so much that Paul Brown became the first man to be named coach of the year in two different leagues.

In 1970, the first season of interleague play in the NFL, Cincinnati swept its last seven games to win the Central Division title by one game over the Browns. When the Bengals beat Cleveland that year, Paul Brown doffed his plaid hat, waved it over his head, and raced from the field as the crowd roared. "Wise old Paul Brown" was again coach of the year. *Sports Illustrated* wrote that the Bengals had "one recognizable marvel: Head Coach Paul Brown. Like Vince Lombardi, Brown is worth points when the oddsmakers figure the line."

He went 48-36 during his last six years as a coach. In 1973, the Bengals won another division title and in 1975, Paul Brown's last year on the sidelines, finished eleven and three. After a three-point loss to the Raiders in the playoffs, he said, "I was proud of my team."

He retired on New Year's Day 1976, but Cincinnati remained Paul Brown's team for the next fifteen years. Robin Brown died of cancer in 1978, but the two younger sons remained at their father's side. "Pete and myself have some say, but my father makes the final decision. What he decides is it," Mike Brown said.

The Bengals went to two Super Bowls and became a model for operating frugally but sanely in a league gone money-mad. At Cincinnati's second Super Bowl, in 1989, Paul Brown, nearing 80, said that he wanted to work for another twenty-five years. He seemed capable of doing just that.

Most days, he came to the office by 8:30 and spent six or seven hours viewing film, preparing for the draft, or advising his coaches. His secretary still answered the phone: "Coach Brown's office." He even looked like a man twenty years younger. Late in 1990, blood clots in his leg caused Paul Brown to finally miss a Bengal game. Throughout the next year, his health failed.

"He was clear-minded right to the very end," says Mike Brown. "He knew on Sunday that he was going. He told me he was dying and that he had a couple of family matters that he wanted me to be sure to look after."

Paul Brown attended to one concern himself. He gave his son a check for his birthday, on August 10, five days away. He died at home the next morning, of complications caused by pneumonia.

"Our relationship changed over time, but we pretty much saw things eye to eye. I was truly blessed, and I knew it, but I didn't fully realize it until it was over," Mike Brown says.

"I've never seen a son love his father more than Mike loved Paul," Nancy Brown said.

Mike Brown assumed his father's duties with the Bengals—and his role as family patriarch. "Now, I have to be right," he said. "Before, I always had somewhere to turn."

According to many in Cincinnati, he has almost never been right. In Paul Brown's last season as general manager, the team won the division title; in Mike Brown's first season, it

finished last. The Bengals have had no winning season since Paul Brown died, losing 107 games in the 1990s.

Inevitably, the decline has invited comparisons between father and son. Fans have called for Brown to step aside, claiming that he simply doesn't know enough about football, an accusation to which he is particularly sensitive. Paul Brown loathed "non-football people" who meddled in the game. He had placed in his Bengal contract a clause stating that "no one who had never put on a headgear would ever be in a position to take my job."

"People say, 'Oh, he's a good businessman, but he's a lousy football guy.' Oddly, I think of it in reverse," Mike Brown says.

Paul Brown was nothing if not a football guy, but for years in Cleveland, he listened to complaints that his idea of the game was hopelessly outdated. Some allege that Mike Brown's only goal is to make money, that the NFL salary cap and a lucrative stadium deal have killed any incentive to win championships.

Brown scoffs at the charge, but it differs only in degree from the bizarre theory set forth by some in Cleveland that Paul Brown tried to finish second every year. Thus, that line of thinking went, he could attract large crowds to title races without carrying a hefty payroll.

Father and son have both been

criticized by their own players, and both seem to have dealt summarily with dissidents. In 1962, quarterback Milt Plum's public complaints about Paul Brown quickly landed him in Detroit.

Thirty-six years later, Bengal punter Lee Johnson, a fourteen-year veteran, railed against the team's front office. He was released the next day. Although Mike Brown said Johnson was not let go because of his comments, the Bengals recently added a loyalty clause to rookies' contracts, threatening them with loss of signing bonuses if they criticized management.

Some detractors say that Brown is still too much influenced by his father's Victorian point of view. "Any time you listen to those two boys (Mike and Pete Brown) talking, you know it's really the father talking," says Walt Michaels, a former Cleveland Brown captain and New York Jet head coach.

But Mike Brown is as different from the young Paul Brown as today's NFL is from the old AAFC. Brown has neither his father's faintly patrician air nor his keen awareness of his image. In public, Paul Brown was as severe as a vicar, but Mike Brown has a natural kindness that he tends to hide behind a veil of formality and circumspection.

Where people respected the father without liking him, they like the son without respecting him.

Brown seems, if anything, like a harried but kindly high school principal. He is self-deprecating and subtly amusing, delivering dry punch lines in a monotone, his head cocked. He is reminiscent of the Paul Brown who carried candy to pass out to children, the man of whom a reporter said in 1974, "The years have added a warmth to Brown. Gone is the bureaucrat in the brown suit and hat."

Still, son remains unlike father in at least two significant ways. Brown says his father "became more forgiving" as he aged, but Paul Brown could have lived indefinitely without ever proposing, as his son has, that the time might have come to end the feud with Art Modell.

Five years after Modell jilted Cleveland—in part, he claimed, to secure his stepson's future—Mike Brown said, "What has Modell done to us that we have to complain about, anyway? He's the guy responsible for sending my dad to Cincinnati. Maybe we should be thankful for that."

According to Nancy Brown, Paul Brown would also have reacted much differently than her husband to the attacks of fans and the media: "Paul would have been tougher than Mike is being. Maybe we wouldn't be in Cincinnati."

Brown seems to have no great

affection for the job he never sought. In fact, he still wishes he had become a coach. "The fun is in coaching," he said. "This job is all about money, and that's no fun."

Brown went so far has to hire as the Bengals' coach David Shula, the son of one of Paul Brown's former players. Shula "sort of lived the life I wished I had led," Brown said. "He's my Walter Mitty."

Of course, Shula's disastrous tenure in Cincinnati and subsequent firing are testament to Paul Brown's wisdom in choosing a career for his son.

Mike Brown isn't about to abandon what he refers to as his "charge."

"His father entrusted the Bengals to him, gave him the torch," said former Cincinnati guard Dave Lapham. "Mike wants to be sure that he carries it through to the end."

Brown sounds exactly like his father when he professes his love for football and responds to detractors by saying, "My faith in what we do has not been shaken." He also frequently declares confidence in the people around him, as well he might. Brown has made certain that his father's business will remain in the family.

His son, Paul H. Brown (named for his maternal grandfather, Paul Houston) grew up shagging kicks and taping ankles at Bengal practices. He decided as a boy that "it would be

neat to be a scout" and after working for several years as one, is now a vice president of the organization.

Brown's daughter, Katie Blackburn, namesake of his mother, who died in 1969, says she "never thought about not liking football." The former tomboy who played pick-up games with neighborhood boys has worked for the team as everything from ticket seller to chief legal counsel.

Pete Brown is next in line for the general manager's chair, but Blackburn, another vice president, could become the first woman to operate an NFL franchise.

"It's very special to me," she said of that possibility, "because they are my grandfather's team and my father's. I would love to be able to follow in their footsteps."

"We're all football. There's not a whole lot else that we do, really," said Paul H. Brown, sounding eerily like his grandfather.

And so the Bengals remain a tribute—animate and inanimate—to Paul Brown. When Bruce Coslet replaced Shula as head coach seven games into the 1996 season and met with the team for the first time, he carried with him a sort of mystical document—a copy of the speech Paul Brown delivered to every one of his teams on the first day of pre-season camp, a parchment complete with the old coach's marginal notes.

"These guys aren't all like my father," Brown said of the coaching staff, "but there's a little bit of him inside all of us."

When Coslet quit, Mike Brown replacedf him with another former player who had first ben drafted by Paul Brown—Dick LeBeau.

Rather than sell the rights for millions to a corporation, Brown named the team's new stadium for his father. "We stood for a principle by having the stadium reflect his name and the tradition it represents," Brown said.

In a day of dizzying irony, Paul Brown Stadium opened with the Cleveland Browns easily defeating the Bengals.

Mike Brown keeps on a bookcase along one wall of his spare, antiseptic office a meticulously bound and arranged collection of programs from every game his father coached in Cleveland. Next to the programs sit a pair of binoculars and a book that he used to identify birds that light in the Spinney Field training complex.

As Brown spoke, a summer thunderstorm raged. Water sluiced off the room of the office, cascading in front of two barn swallows sitting on cables that form a railing around the balcony from which Brown watches practice. He seemed familiar with the birds, a family of which had constructed a nest under the balcony.

His voice soft, Brown said, "See out there, that little bird—this one here—how long his feathers are in the back? That's a mommy or a daddy."

He indicated the smaller of the swallows. "This is his first flying day," Brown said. "He thinks the world's a pretty rough place. He's saying, 'Is this all there is?'"

Mike Brown's father was also an amateur ornithologist, of sorts. Banished to California, he delighted in the humming birds that darted around his house and closely watched a nest of meadow lark eggs.

Incongruously, Paul Brown also confessed admiration for a pair of blacksnakes that dwelled in his backyard in Cincinnati, a regard borne of the snakes' mastery of their domain, he said.

"You have to know where he came from and how he was brought up, to understand his life," Mike Brown says. "His life was developed in the tough days of the 1920s and before. His father was a railroad dispatcher. His father was a very precise man, which went along with the job. He believed in doing things right and traditional values."

# *Mike* BROWN

" MY EARLIEST MEMORY OF MY FA-
THER is when I was three years old. My mother was putting me to bed,
and he was going off to coach a game at Massillon High School. Then,
Massillon was a great example of a Midwestern steel town. It had a main
street. It was dominated by the churches. It was a blue-collar town. My
dad's father worked for the Wheeling and Lake Erie Railroad. He was a
dispatcher. My mother's father worked for a foundry in town. He had a
place with an orchard on it and chickens and geese, so I have very fond
memories of all of that.

Massillon was my father's hometown, and when he sat down with my
brother and me to tell us what he wanted done for his funeral—he knew he
was failing—he was insistent that he be buried in Massillon, that he be
buried out of my mother's church, and he directed us that the service should
be short.

The stadium there (Paul Brown Tiger Stadium) is a wonderful thing.
Keep in mind that it was built in the 1930s, and even today, it is probably
the best high school stadium in Ohio, maybe even in the country. It was a
project so far ahead of its time that it is quite remarkable. One of dad's
stories was that when he went back many years later, after he retired as a
coach here (in Cincinnati), they were giving him great credit, and one of
the things they credited him for was having the foresight to retain the land
where they built the new high school, which is adjoining the stadium. He
laughed at that, because as he put it, all he really wanted was lots of practice
fields and a stadium network with parking and a field for the band.

The whole town would turn out for Massillon games. The town itself wasn't much larger than 25,000, and the stadium would have twenty-some thousand at the games. Everything stopped for the games. That was the Depression era, and the games were a focus of the community. That's the way people lived back then, and I think that tradition has carried on, and you still see it there.

Becoming involved in sports just seemed to come natural to all of us (Mike and his brothers, Pete and Robin). I was always around the football team. Even as a kid, my heroes were his football players. There's a story that one time I jumped off the garage roof and broke my leg. It really wasn't as dramatic as it sounded because the garage was built into a hillside. I must've jumped off something two feet high, at most. But when my dad was called at practice, he came over to the hospital, and I thought I was saying something funny when I said, 'I bet you're glad it wasn't Horace.' Horace Gillom (future Cleveland Brown punter) was his star player.

I went to Shaker Heights High School, in the Cleveland suburbs. I don't think my father ever saw me play football, either in high school or college, because my schedule conflicted with his. He never coached me about things, never, although he gave my high school coach parts of the Cleveland Browns' playbook, so my high school playbook was based on the Browns' playbook. The numbering system was the same, with some of the basic plays. It was what the Browns were doing, in simpler fashion.

I think my father was like a lot of fathers. He wanted me not to fall into the pitfalls he did. He wanted me to become a lawyer; eventually, I did. It was not anything that really delighted me, and I gravitated back to football. He had his master's degree from Ohio State, and after that, he was studying to become a lawyer. When he was at Massillon High School, he went to night school in Canton. All of that went by the wayside, though, when he went down to Ohio State as the head coach.

I WAS ALWAYS HANGING AROUND. I remember being on the sidelines and watching the team practice, at Massillon and at Ohio State, certainly with the Browns. He allowed me to sit in on meetings he had with the coaches. It was something I got involved with at a very early stage of my life, and I just thought of it as normal. I guess it wasn't usual but I didn't know that. I thought it was what everybody did.

When I was in law school, I helped coach the freshman team and on game days I was involved in the press box, calling plays with the varsity team, and that was the happiest job I ever had. I really enjoyed that. I would have liked to have been a coach but I was, ah, 'redirected.' He didn't want me to be a coach.

He thought coaching was a tough life, and I can understand why he felt that way. He thought I should do something that would lift me beyond that, as, probably, he imagined he should have. It might have been just dreaming on his part, for both of us. Fathers do that. Anyway, there came a point, in the 1960s, when we got the Cincinnati Bengals franchise up and running, then I left the practice of law behind. I only practiced law for five years. I came down here and got involved in getting the franchise.

My father was formed by the values that existed in small-town America early in this century, good values: hard work, honesty, straightforwardness. He was not deceptive in any way. That wasn't good form. My father was intense, focused, demanding, very quick-minded. He could condense thoughts and ideas into a concise statement. He had a way of simplifying things, and that made it easier for people around him. When he coached we had a schedule that didn't vary. It helped make things run smoother. He lived his life that way, too. Everything had its time and place. He led a structured existence.

HE HAD A TREMENDOUS SENSE OF HUMOR. The guys who knew him understood that, but his public persona at that stage of his life was shaped more by the New York media. Believe it or not, that's where all of that 'cold genius of the lakefront' stuff came from. He was forceful, and if the team didn't perform at the standard he thought it should be performing, he could be kind of rough with them, momentarily. It was different times. Different rules applied to coaching. The players were going to do it the right way, or someone else was going to do it, and everyone understood that pretty well, so they toed the line. There was both a carrot and a stick, but in the old days there was more stick.

His ability to handle people and situations evolved over time. He wasn't the same at all stages of his life. He changed. I wouldn't say he stopped being demanding, but he was less forceful. When he was younger, he could be, I'd have to say, harsh on occasion with his guys on the Browns. Later, there was less of that. He became more forgiving. He knew the Bengals, an expansion franchise, weren't going to be a championship team. He treated them differently than when he had a bunch of guys who could be, if they only would.

One time here, a player got on the plane late, and my father walked back to confront him. As he walked down the aisle, he looked at the player and said, 'You're drunk.' He smelled alcohol. He said, 'You're no longer on this team. Get off of my plane.' The other guys sat there and their eyes grew large. They got a pretty strong message.

Today, it would've been six months of arbitration. It's harder to respond quickly and firmly to personnel issues now, because you don't have as much control over the players. These days, there are thirty teams and there aren't just thirty-three players per team. There are literally squads today of fifty-three plus others. If you tell players good-bye, they just pack up and go somewhere else. Back in those days, if they hit the street, they could not go someplace else. That's why Lombardi and my father and other coaches of that era were a little more on the stick side. You had guys who were more fearful of what might happen. The pendulum has swung too far, and I trace it back to the union. It's just harder to step in than it used to be or than it should be.

MY FATHER WAS FIRM WITH US and we knew the rules. It was actually the case that if he told me to do something, I would find myself out of my chair en route to do it even before I could consciously think of what the instruction was. So he had us pretty well under control. He was not harsh, just demanding. There was never any question that when he said something, that was the rule, and we had better well take care of it yesterday.

He was the best extemporaneous speaker I've ever heard. He could stand up and say things concisely. With his team, he was always preaching, but it wasn't oppressive. It would be short little statements or discussions, but he would be trying to make a point about how they could get along in this world a little better, if they only would.

Always, in his heart, he had real feeling for his players. He took those Massillon kids and he worked hard to get them in college. He drove them to colleges all over. He thought that was important and he was successful at it. During World War II, in Columbus, he occasionally got calls about some of his Massillon players who were in the war, who'd been killed, and things like that were hard for him.

Even in pro football he wanted his guys to be working in the off-season to improve themselves, either going back to school to graduate, or holding down a job. Some of that was the economics of the time, but he believed pro football was just a stepping stone to their future lives, and he didn't want them to waste opportunities. He wanted them to progress. He felt that way even here. We're the one football team in the NFL that seems to believe that the off-season for players oughtn't to be just workouts. It ought to be employment or education. I guess I was brought up that way so I still feel that way. I feel that it's better for them to have a job or get their degree than to just be around here doing the things they need to do for football.

WHEN HE WENT TO CLEVELAND, he set a standard. He was way ahead of his competitors. I like the statement that Paul Tagliabue shared with me when Pete Rozelle was on his deathbed. Paul Tagliabue had occasion to ask Pete Rozelle who was the most productive owner in the NFL, and Pete Rozelle said, well, it was probably a tie between George Halas and Art Rooney, because when they got together, things could get done, but they rarely seemed to get together. But he said that the man who was probably the most important was my father, because he made the game better for both the players and the fans.

My father changed the way teams had gone about their business. He made it a more serious undertaking. He did all kinds of things that hadn't been done before, and he instituted them as a routine. He was also good at selecting players. When my dad went to the Cleveland Browns, he had come out of college football and the service, coaching at the Great Lakes Naval Station, and he really did know where there were a lot of players. He knew where to go after them, and we got guys who hadn't been quite as well known as others, such as Marion Motley and Mac Speedie and Dante Lavelli and Lou Groza. Even Otto Graham was not considered such a hotshot as my dad considered him. Of course, these guys all went on to become great, great players. So you put those two things together, and we were just a better-formed football team than the teams we played.

I keep this picture behind me of the 1948 Cleveland Browns. They were undefeated. I was 12 years old, so they were big heroes to me. They always will be. My favorite memories of guys who were nice to me were of Marion Motley and Bill Willis and Horace Gillom. I guess the other guys would go out and about after meetings in the evenings, but these guys were restricted about where they could go. I went up there, and they would allow me to play Hearts with them. They were just toying with me, but I thought I was part of the gang. I really enjoyed that.

They were called 'colored' players then. There hadn't been 'colored' players in pro football for some years. There had been a few in the past, but there had never been very many. When my dad came to the Browns, he worked the guys there in a practice, and he knew he had better players at Ohio State and at Massillon High School and at Great Lakes. Motley had played against Massillon for Canton and played for my dad at Great Lakes. Bill Willis had played for my dad at Ohio State. He called those two and asked them to come—Horace came in the next year—and they came.

He did it because he knew they were better. He had black players on his football teams before that, and they were no different to him. It didn't bother him much that someone else didn't think that was the way to do things. And that was before Jackie Robinson went into baseball. He literally set the path for them. There were problems that sound strange to our ear today, but that was the way the country was back then. The Browns were the pioneers for black athletes in football.

THE RELATIONSHIP BETWEEN MY FATHER and Jim Brown was an interesting one. Both recognized each other's abilities. There was always a respect between the two of them, and even though that was the case, my father was probably bothered some by the fact that Jim was not as responsive to his instructions as other players had been. He wasn't able to discipline Jim as well as he could other players because by that time, Art Modell was on the scene, and my father felt that, suddenly, in some way, his power had been affected. And Jim, for his part, came into pro football just at the time that the civil rights movement was starting, and he had thoughts about his role in that movement. Those thoughts began to grow, and there was the element that Jim was difficult to control sometimes, off the field. Some of the things that Jim did bothered my father.

But there was never a doubt in my father's mind about Jim's role as a football player. He used him effectively. Jim set a lot of records in pro football at that time. He still holds the record for average per attempt, which, in my mind, is the record that really singles out Jim Brown as the greatest runner ever. My father always thought he was that. Of course, what really mattered and what was most important was how Jim played and the team performed with him. My father always had great respect for Jim as a player.

We won throughout the years of the All-American Football Conference—1946-1949—and we won our first year in the NFL—1950. Then, off and on for a period of years there, we either won or Detroit beat us. There were other good teams, but we were always the one team that went back to the NFL title game year after year. He expected to win, and anything less than that was considered a failure.

Of course, he had great players. I don't want to underestimate the fact that we had Otto Graham, who was truly a great, great player. To win in this league, you have to have a quarterback who is a dominating player, and he was. It was never easy, though. The Browns always felt the breath of the opposition on their backs, and they fought hard to stay ahead.

I DIDN'T 'TRY OUT' WITH THE BROWNS. I had good thoughts about my own ability, but my father knew better. In those days, they had thirty rounds in the draft. There were only twelve teams, so the number of players picked was about the same. At the very end of the draft, the Cardinals came over and said they were considering drafting me, but they didn't want to do it unless he said it was okay, and he said to them, 'I'll make you a deal. If you don't pick him, I won't.' And, of course, he was right. I always thought I could throw the ball accurately, more accurately than some of the guys he had playing for him, but that was just my thought.

Modell came around 1960. I was in law school or just out of law school. I remember being in a hotel room with my dad. We were playing the Philadelphia Eagles, and the discussion was about selling the team to Modell. My dad had his disappointments in this area. He was not a businessman in the sense that you see so much of these days. He was a coach, first and foremost. When he first went to Cleveland, Arthur McBride, the team's first owner, promised that if he ever moved the team, he would first tell my dad. But he didn't. He sold the team, and my dad found out about it when he was on a fishing trip with one of Arthur McBride's partners.

My father always had an ownership interest in the team—a significant ownership—but he was never a majority owner. Yet whoever owned it, prior to Modell, had totally delegated the operation of the team to my father, and he grew to understand that as his prerogative. Before, whoever owned the team had other businesses or focus, so it worked as a good arrangement for both sides. But when Art came, he came without any of that. His focus was the football team. It quickly became apparent, I think to both, that it was not a good situation. Art was continually striving for a larger role, and my father was probably hesitant about that, and then there became conflict over it. I think my father wanted it to remain the way it had been, and Art wanted to take over much of that authority for himself. He couldn't as long as my father was there.

The complaint that the game had passed him may have developed in Cleveland at the time. That was the kind of talk that was put out to discredit him. It didn't turn out to be so. A lot of things that he was doing we're still doing. Maybe they've been refined some, but he's the one who set the pattern initially.

WHAT HAPPENED IN CLEVELAND WAS, simply, at the end, we didn't have a gifted quarterback. We were working around that as best we could, and that's hard to do. You work with what you have. They began to say that 'Brown hadn't kept pace with the game.' It was one of the story lines put out to undercut my father.

He called me on the phone at my office and said that Art had taken his team away from him. I remember that's how he put it. For him, it was heartbreaking. It was something he never anticipated could be done, and it shook him to his core. His voice in that conversation quavered, which was not like him, ever.

Then, he was embarrassed by it all. I remember one story he told: He was at a luncheon downtown. In the Union Commerce Building. There used to be a club on the top floor where the business people went. He happened to be there with someone, and some guys were talking to him. One of them made the comment that he didn't need have any concern, because he would still be paid what was then a large amount of money. And to my father, the money was the least of it. His way of living and what he did was gone, taken from him, and it really undercut his life.

He felt he had to leave Cleveland, because he was just unable to stay there. Yet that was where his heart was. In many ways, the two cities most important to him were Massillon, as a young man, and Cleveland. It was hard for him to leave, but he just couldn't hold his head up there, so he left and went out to San Diego.

It was a difficult thing, and he had a hard time contending with it. He went out to San Diego, and he played golf, and he did the things I guess you would do if you retired. But he was too young to retire, and he was not happy with his life there because it was, in his mind, purposeless. But he had no alternative. It was a predicament.

He never really forgave Modell. In his mind, he had a contract, and he thought that people should fulfill contracts. In fact, it never even occurred to him that they couldn't. He felt that Modell had undercut him in his relationships with the players, that he did it to further his own ambitions. It was always a sore spot with my father. He eventually sold his shares of the Browns to other people in Cleveland. They had to be sold when we came down here. By league rules, he couldn't own stock in more than one team. He had a friend up there in the brokerage business, and the friend had people who were willing to buy the shares. I don't think my father would ever have thought about selling them to Modell.

HIS FOCUS CHANGED. He was no longer responsible for the football team. My mother's health had started to fail. She eventually went blind from diabetes, and he cared for her remarkably as she went through all of this. They traveled, and they had adventures in their travels. The one I was always told about was when they went over to the Orient, and they were taking off from Hong Kong and an engine caught fire. They eventually landed with the engine on fire. He thought they weren't going to make that one, and they were lucky that they did. I guess, maybe, that was a message to him that life is short; make sure to do some of the things that ought to be done.

The opportunity came for him to come back into football, and he did. I was involved in this thing from the beginning, and I don't say that to toot my own horn. In fact, I was pushing him to get involved. He was reluctant. My mother played a big role in that. She only had a couple of years to live at the time. She encouraged him, and, finally, he agreed to come down. It was a big step, a very risky step. Who was to say that we could even get the franchise? Who was to say that it could work? If, today, you were to imagine a situation with someone in his position trying to get into the NFL and what the odds were, you would say, 'Well, the odds are certainly not very good.' He understood that, so, at times, he held back. But, eventually, he made the commitment, and it all worked out.

He came to Cincinnati because he wanted to be involved with football. That's what he knew; that's what he enjoyed; it was the life he liked. That's what he craved. He didn't come back for the money. If anything, he thought that he had jeopardized his reputation as a coach (Brown had been inducted into the Hall of Fame in 1967) because he was coming to an expansion team. In those days, they didn't give you the best players. You had to work a while to get off the ground. He knew that if he came back into NFL football, he wasn't going to have the team that he had had, and he wasn't going to have the winning record that he had posted. It was going to be different in that sense.

We got off the ground in record time for that period. He had an excellent coaching staff. He was always very good at selecting coaches. He delegated more down here than he had in Cleveland, but it was his stage of life. He was always happy to be back in football. He left a big part of his heart in Cleveland. That's something that was always in his mind.

HE WAS OFFERED OTHER JOBS when he was out of football, but they were always short of what he wanted. He was offered the job to coach other pro teams, but not in any role that he felt gave him control, or the kind of control that he would be comfortable with. He never accepted any of them until he could come down here and fashion the whole thing. He wanted to run the team. That's what he did in Cleveland. He ran the business, he ran the team, he was responsible for it all.

At the end of the year, he reported to the owner about what had happened and if the team made money, which it generally did, he was pleased, but money wasn't really important to him. He wanted to make money so that there weren't problems, but it wasn't on his radar screen in the sense that your usual businessman would be aware of where they were that month or that week or that period, and how things were compared to last year. He never even thought much about it until he got through the year. Then he'd look back and see where it was and quickly put it out of mind and go on to the next season. He was always focused on the 'product,' if you will—although that's a word he would never have used—all aspects pertaining to football: the team, the coaches, the halftime entertainment. That's where his mind was.

I think in Art's mind he helped my father get this franchise, and he very well could have. I think Art felt that the way it ended up in Cleveland could have been better handled, and he wanted to make amends.

There were tremendous changes in the NFL during those five years my father was out of football, and he was never comfortable with the fact that there was a players union, which, as you may know, began in Cleveland with his players. He had a remarkably low opinion of agents. He felt they were totally unnecessary and did nothing in any useful fashion for the players or for football in general. Those things were bothersome to him, and when he came back into football, there was more of that than before.

In 1987, during the strike, I remember working out problems with the guys who came in, the rookies, and the pickets. He was unhappy with the fact that this is where the game had come. He didn't think it was necessary, and I think he was basically right. Back when he coached in Cleveland, the players got paid based on what they had done the previous year. They got, probably, as much as the team could afford to pay and remain a viable economic entity. There were never great problems. He was never against the players getting what he thought the structure could bear. Some of the demands the union has made have impacted the public and the relationships in the game in a very unfortunate way, and I don't think he felt they were good or necessary.

When the players union formed, it came to his notice in a strange way. In Cleveland, he rode downtown on the rapid transit from his home, and then he walked down from the Terminal Tower to the stadium office. One day, he was on the rapid transit, and there was a piece of paper on the seat next to him—just by coincidence—and it happened to be a communication between some of his players. One was quarterback George Ratterman. It had to do with the formation of a 'players association,' they called it. They were reluctant to term it a 'union,' even in their own minds, at that stage. They felt that a union was something for factory workers, but not for them. They were beyond that, much as teachers felt then.

This communication had to do with what their initial demands were. Their initial concerns were about pensions and health care, which was what this communication was about. It's so odd, because that is a frequent initial step with this kind of thing. We see it today with our coaches, who've got what they call an 'association.'

Anyway, it stunned him that the players were doing this kind of thing. He just didn't feel it was necessary, that the problems could be solved without that sort of confrontation and distraction and all the other problems that would develop. He was right about the fact that problems would develop with it, which is the case. Once you have the union, you can't react as well as you could before. Your hands are tied. You have to get approval from the union, which is frequently not forthcoming. It just makes you less nimble. That's a fact, and he understood that intuitively.

I THINK THAT PEOPLE WHO WORKED FOR HIM admired him early on, maybe, for different reasons than at the end of his career. At the end, he was somewhat of a larger-than-life figure in coaching, but early on, he was hard charging and very involved. When he was in Cleveland, his closest friends were his coaches. That was his principle social group, so there must've been something about their relationship that was good.

He was someone who set clear guidelines. He never kept his coaches late. He didn't believe in that. He thought that if you couldn't figure it out during normal working hours, then maybe there was something wrong with you. Today, coaches stay until the middle of the night two, three days a week. There was none of that when he was here. He gave Bill Walsh clear jurisdiction over the passing game, and Bill Johnson did the running game. Defensively, it was very much the same way. They closed up shop about 5:30, 6 o'clock, and everybody went home. That was it. Now, when they went home, I'm sure they did some things, but there was none of this midnight oil stuff.

My dad had friends who were lifelong friends, and he didn't lose many as the years rolled on. He even brought George Bird, the band director at Massillon and in Cleveland, to this operation. George had been our next-door neighbor in Massillon. He brought George from Massillon to Cleveland. George put on a great band show in Massillon. It's a tradition there, even today. In Cleveland, they had the marching majorettes and they had their own band, à la the Washington Redskins, and, I would argue, a step ahead of them. I think George was living down here when the Bengals franchise was being formed. He had different roles as the years went on. We no longer had a marching band; he went out and got the bands for halftime. But we had a band that played music. We didn't have canned music, as you do today.

ONE OF THE STORIES THAT ALWAYS AMUSED me about George was that he thought the national anthem should be sung in an upbeat tempo and it should be done in a certain fashion. As years went on, people began to experiment with the national anthem. They would have their ways of presenting it, and they would tell George they wanted to do this or that, but we always played the music the same way, so they had to catch up to it.

Oh, yeah, my father wanted to beat the Browns badly. They were our main rival, when he coached here, and even afterwards. He didn't have to say much about it; everyone understood. The same was true of Cleveland. Modell didn't want to lose to us, either. The players on their side understood, too. The games were all-out games. It was a good rivalry, for that reason (the enmity between Brown and Modell), as well as some others, but maybe for that reason more than any other.

When my father decided to step down as coach, he knew that at the age he was then—67—not many were still coaching. He felt, if anything, he had probably pushed it longer than he should have. He knew, too, that more and more, he was delegating responsibility, and he had very good coaches to turn to. Bill Walsh was one, Bill Johnson, and others. And he had seen other coaches hang on too long. He used the term 'front it,' and he didn't want to be known as someone who merely fronted the operation.

I think he timed his retirement well. He did an odd thing: He announced his retirement on New Year's Day, because he felt that's when it would get the least publicity. Of course, that's what happened. He made sure to announce it at the very last moment so that it couldn't be made much of.

He had tremendous regard for Bill Walsh and Bill Johnson, both. So, choosing a successor was not an easy decision. They were both very, very fine coaches. The expectation was that if Bill Johnson took over, Bill Walsh would stay, and they could work together, that Bill Johnson would be a good guy to manage the overall thing. If you knew Bill Johnson, you'd know what I'm talking about. He was a man's man and is a man's man now. That seemed like the best way to put it together.

The problem—and my father realized it was a risk—was that Bill Walsh might not accept that, and he didn't. Eventually, he left. It would have been better for the team had he stayed. I think Bill Walsh aspired to go further as a coach, and when he wasn't promoted here, he was upset, and he reacted to that. In my mind, any disagreement between him and my father wasn't much more than that.


MY FATHER UNDERSTOOD that coaches had to be let go, but he was reluctant to do that. I think it was a difficult assignment for him when he did make a change with a coach. We were down in the office downstairs, before this building addition was added on, and he called Bill Johnson in. I think Bill knew why he was being called in. Bill actually resigned. My dad didn't say anything, but I think Bill knew, and that's why he did what he did. That was a sad moment. It was like a funeral or something of that nature for him, a very depressing kind of experience.

He understood what went on when you did something like that and how it impacted somebody. After all, this is what these guys aspired to all their lives, and then you take it away from them. That is a very unhappy moment.

He didn't hire Forrest Gregg because Gregg had been let go in Cleveland. He hired him because he thought he was a strong personality, and we needed that. We had fallen on hard times, and Forrest really fit our team perfectly when he came. He was demanding, the players respected him, and that shaped our guys up.

After my father retired from coaching, he was general manager and the principle officer. They would call it a CEO, I guess. He remained involved and active in the decisions that were made. He delighted in being on the NFL competition committee, which got him at the table with people he liked and respected: Jim Finks, Don Shula, Tex Schramm and others. In those days, the principle, driving committee through the league was the competition committee. It was more focused on football, which was good. Today, so often we go to meetings and scarcely talk about football. We merely talk about business aspects of the game.

He enjoyed being involved with the draft. He sat in with the coaches every Monday and reviewed the films. That kept him up to date with what was going on. He was active in the business until his health failed, and that wasn't until close to the end of his time.

Two days before he died, we were at his house. We were watching the Detroit Lions play the Bengals in a preseason game. He said, 'What the heck did they put him in there for?' Even then, literally a couple of days before he died, when he was flat on his back, hardly able to breathe, and in and out of consciousness.

I HAD A VERY WONDERFUL RELATIONSHIP with him, working with him on a daily basis, as I did. I talked with him every day. The two of us could talk about the business in a fashion that was, for me, special. I've never had that kind of relationship with anyone else. We didn't have to talk in anything but shorthand because we understood each other. Occasionally, I'd say things that would aggravate him. I suppose he'd say a few things that would aggravate me, maybe purposefully at times, I don't know.

It was a wonderful relationship. When it stopped, a big piece of my day, every day, went with it. I'd talk to him on the phone when he was out in California in the wintertime. Each day, at about 10:15, I'd call him on the phone. It was 7:15 their time. We'd talk about whatever happened the day before. It wasn't so much to get instruction. We just continued to have this relationship and talk over things together. It was an enjoyable thing for me. I missed him a lot. I was lucky to have him.

We've honored him, we've named the stadium for him. But I'm not sure he would've liked the honor. I've wondered about that a lot. We think it's fitting down here because he played a big role with the Bengals. He's the one who is responsible for the team being here, more than anyone else. He got it up and running. He stood for a lot of things that I think pro football at its best should want. I think it's good that we honor people who contributed to the game, in this way, instead of taking a dollar more from some big soda pop company. He would not have been particularly pleased with the fact that around the league now, you see stadiums named for sponsors.

My father was competitive at everything he did, no matter if he was playing golf or gin rummy. He talked about his mother and how competitive she was. He probably had her competitiveness. That's probably where it sprung from. I don't know. I just know what his nature was as I saw him, and he liked competition. It was serious fun. It made life lively and interesting. He always strove to win, and he always competed hard, even when it was social. I don't mean that he was unsociable as he did that, but he had every intention of winning.

THERE WOULD BE THINGS about the National Football League today that he would not want. He wouldn't want the confrontation we have between the players and management. He wouldn't want quite as much of what he'd call the 'marketing' and ballyhoo that goes with the game today, because he would probably take his football in a purer form.

His legacy to me is about everything I have: the way I think, the very job I hold. He formed my life and my way of thinking more than anything else, by far. Now, my son, my daughter, and my son-in-law work here. That's a nice thing. I regret that others don't have that opportunity. I think that our society might have been better—and small-town America might have been better—when people tended to stay in family groups. Today, everyone grows up and goes hither and yon and I guess we communicate by e-mail. I don't think it's as good a situation as what we had.

I would say his legacy to the NFL is a style of coaching that is efficient and demanding, and a high standard about the game and what it should be. After all, people in Cleveland, to this day, think the NFL is a pretty good thing, don't they? And a lot of the reason why they feel that way is that they feel the old Cleveland Browns represented something they admired. He was responsible for instilling that standard in those teams, of both play and behavior. People think that there was something good about that. 🗩🗩

# $I\ n\ d\ e\ x$